Y0-BAY-602

E 276 .C5 1991

Claghorn, Charles Eugene
 1911-

Women patriots of the
 American Revolution

DATE DUE

NOV 18 02
7/7/05

WITHDRAWN FROM THE EVAN'S
LIBRARY AT FMCC

Lydia Darrah

Women Patriots
of the
American Revolution:
a biographical dictionary

by
CHARLES E. CLAGHORN

The Scarecrow Press, Inc.
Metuchen, N.J., & London
1991

Frontispiece illustration reprinted courtesy of the artist, Hilde Strait Cardwell. Her work has been shown in national shows of the American Pen Women, at the Lever House in New York City, and at the Hudson River Museum in Yonkers, NY, among other exhibitions.

British Library Cataloguing-in-Publication data available

Library of Congress Cataloging-in-Publication Data

Claghorn, Charles Eugene, 1911-
    Women patriots of the American Revolution : a biographical dictionary / Charles E. Claghorn.
       p.   cm.
    Includes bibliographical references.
    ISBN 0-8108-2421-3 (alk. paper)
    1. United States--History--Revolution, 1775-1783--Women--Dictionaries. 2. United States--History--Revolution, 1775-1783--Biography--Dictionaries. I. Title.
E276.C5   1991
973.3'15042--dc20   91-15495

Copyright © 1991 by Charles E. Claghorn
Manufactured in the United States of America

Printed on acid-free paper

To

My Dear Wife

For Her Loving Support

Julia Rush

CONTENTS

Acknowledgments	vii
Introductions	ix
Abbreviations and Sources	xv
PART I: BACKGROUND	1
PART II: SELECTED BIOGRAPHIES	9
PART III: COMPLETE LISTING	215

"Molly Pitcher"

ACKNOWLEDGMENTS

The author wishes to thank Col. and Mrs. Richard Irvin, Jr., for lending their copies of the DAR Patriot Index, and Lorraine Black and Lory Baker, Reference Librarians of the Cocoa Beach Public Library, for obtaining books and microfilm on interlibrary loan.

Gratitude is also extended to the illustrator, Hilde Strait, for her renderings of these patriotic women.

Cornelia Beekman

INTRODUCTIONS

Most Americans are familiar with two women of the American Revolution: Molly Pitcher and Betsy Ross. But what a surprise to learn that there were over five thousand women heroines! Charles E. Claghorn has done all American women a great service in bringing to their attention the contributions of the founding of our great nation by pioneer women of the eighteenth century.

The 250,000 members of the National Society Daughters of the American Revolution should clap their hands with delight! Here is a book that deserves an honored place in the national library in Constitution Hall, and certainly should be included in every state library of the D.A.R.

The author has displayed a deep respect for, and understanding of, the role of women during the Revolutionary period. We owe him a debt of gratitude.

> Dr. Elaine Fairbanks Stone
> Organizing Regent of the Rufus
> Fairbanks Chapter of the
> National Society Daughters
> of the American Revolution

* * *

Historical facts and stories pertaining to women whose patriotism and hardships endured during the American Revolution are invaluable for historical and genealogical research. We are indebted to Charles E. Claghorn for this tremendous work.

> Esther Whitten Koski
> Historian National, 1986-89
> Women Descendants Ancient
> and Honorable Artillery
> Company

* * *

Before television, radio, automobiles, and telephones, even before suffragettes, the women of America played a significant role

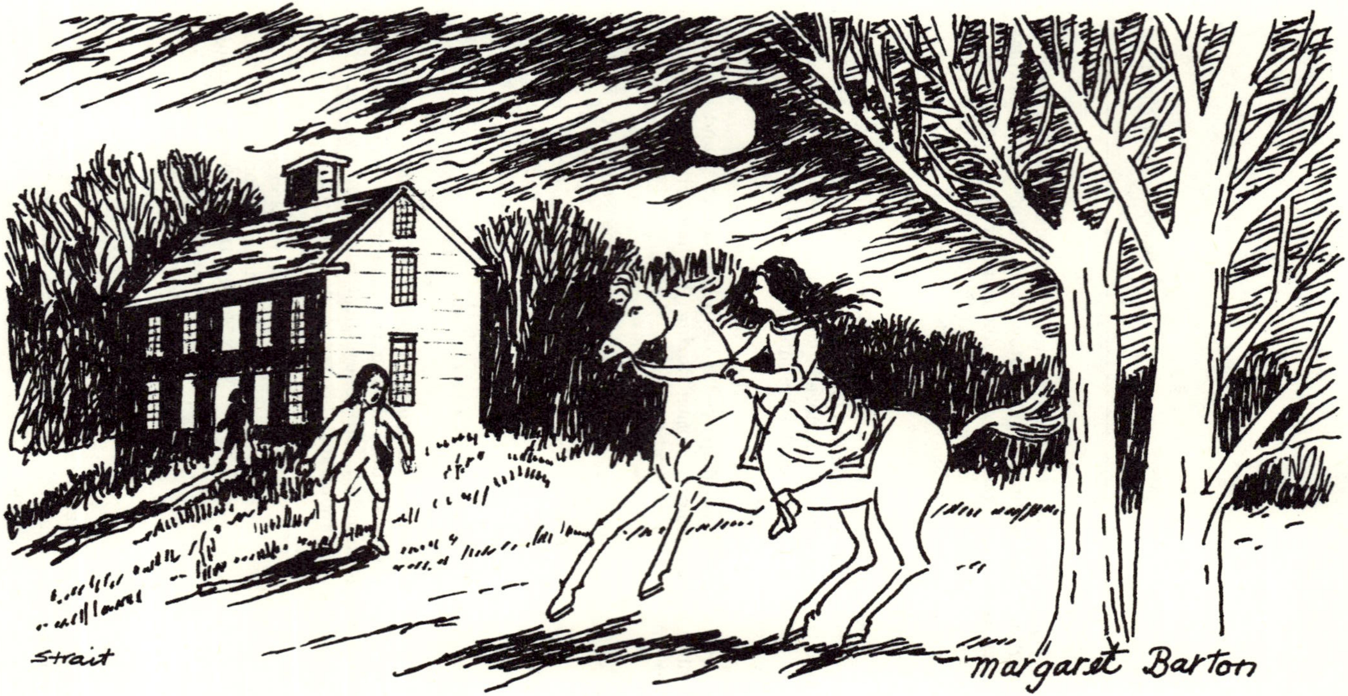
Strait
Margaret Barton

INTRODUCTIONS

in the founding of the United States. Few people realize how valuable many of these women were in the fight for independence of our great country.

These were the days when dipping your own candles, carding and spinning wool, then weaving cloth to make your clothes was a daily chore. The days when hoeing the garden and tending the cattle became additional burdens because sons and husbands had shouldered guns to fight the oppressive regime that threatened their liberty.

The author of Women Patriots of the American Revolution, Charles E. Claghorn, has done a tremendous job of compiling over five thousand women who either served actively in the revolution or, by refusing to help the British, surreptitiously aided the revolutionaries through a wide variety of ways, thus earning the title of Patriot.

The Women Patriots of the American Revolution is destined to become an important addition to historical and genealogical libraries throughout America.

Cynthia Scott Drolshagen
Florida State Regent, DAR,
1988-90

* * *

It is indeed a pleasure to commend the most recent publication of Charles E. Claghorn dealing with events and people involved in the Revolutionary War.

All too often we overlook the important role of women in most wars since the dawn of history, and especially in those prior to the twentieth century.

Herein is the first and only comprehensive book covering in detail the patriotic acts of six hundred women during our Revolutionary War. The last section contains a listing of more than five thousand women who contributed in some manner to the winning of the Revolution. It will indeed serve as a valuable reference and is enlightening evidence of the patriotic acts and spirit with which they served. It may also serve as a valuable reference in tracing ancestry to someone who served in the great Revolution which changed the course of Western civilization forevermore.

Colonel Richard Irvin, Jr.
President, 1989-90
Florida Society, Sons of the
American Revolution

Rebecca Motte

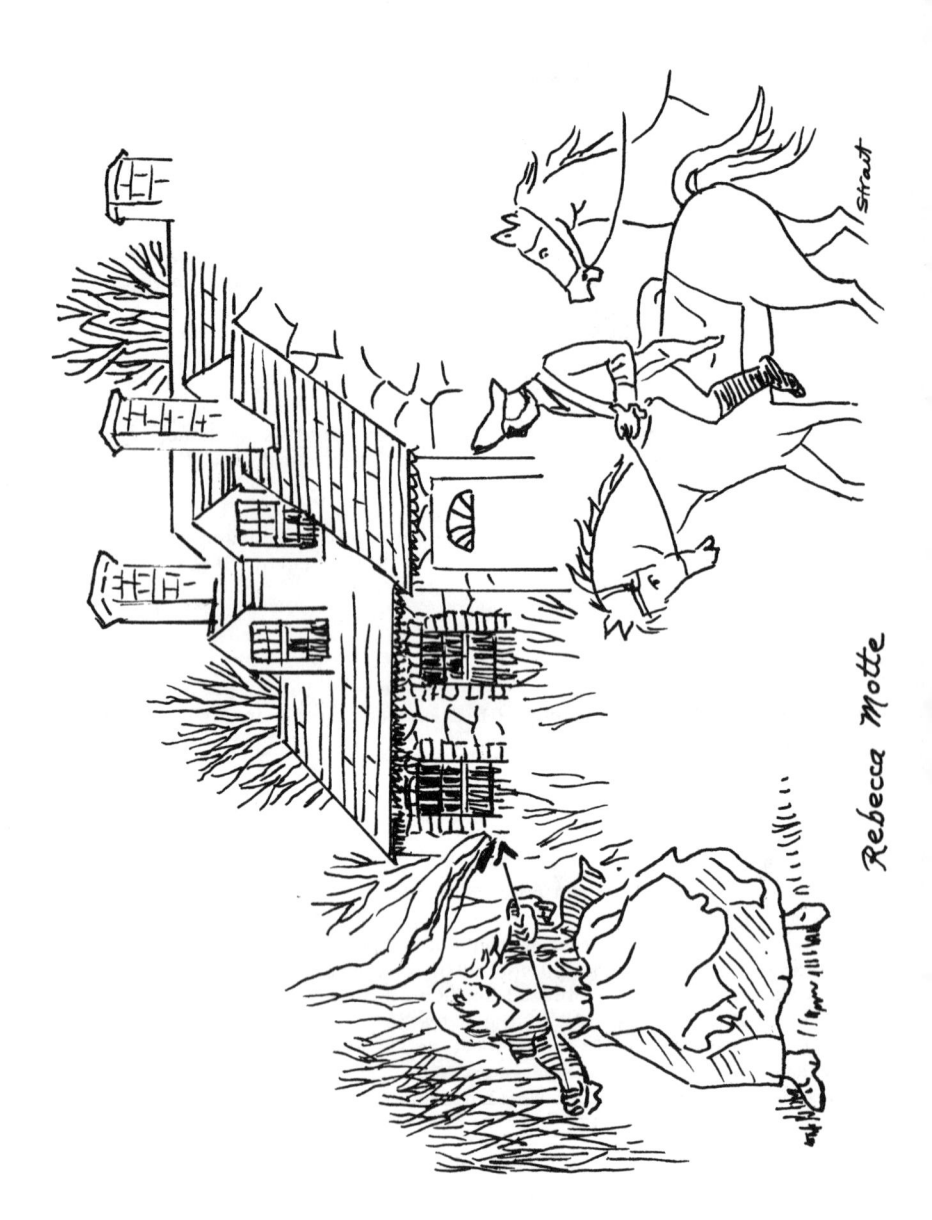

INTRODUCTIONS xiii

* * *

It is a distinct honor to introduce this volume on Women Patriots of the American Revolution. Author Charles E. Claghorn has done splendid research to bring together in one volume, the comprehensive biographies of 600 women who served in the patriot cause during the American Revolution.

The eight years of conflict to win American Independence seems distant and remote. However, this volume shows the human element in its fullness as the wives, daughters, and friends of the American military helped in so many ways in the winning of the war.

Mr. Claghorn is adept at bringing together unique presentations of little-known facts about the American Revolution. It is a great service to historical archives. The National Society of the Sons of the American Revolution is proud to endorse this book by Compatriot Claghorn. It's what we are all about: the development of historical facts about our War for Independence and the era of the late eighteenth century. This book will grace the shelves of many historical libraries. It is interesting and unique. It is commended to all true students of American History.

                         James R. Westlake
                         President General, 1989-90
                         National Society of the Sons
                            of the American Revolution

ABBREVIATIONS AND SOURCES

AA	Accounts Audited of Revolutionary Claims Against South Carolina (Historical Commission of South Carolina)
AM	Ahlin, John Howard. Maine Rubicon (Calais, ME: Calais Advertiser Press, 1966)
BA	Butterfield, L. H., editor. The Adams Papers (Cambridge: Belknap Press of Harvard University, 1961)
BI	Baker, William S. Itinerary of General Washington (Philadelphia: J. B. Lippincott, 1892)
BJ	Beck, Henry C. The Jersey Midlands (New Brunswick, NJ: Rutgers University Press, 1939, 1984)
BOW	Massachusetts: Board of War, 1776-1784 (Index photocopied)
BW	Blumenthal, Walter Hart. Women Camp Followers of the American Revolution (Philadelphia: G. S. MacManus, 1952)
CA	Cook, Jacob E. Alexander Hamilton (New York: Charles Scribner, 1982)
CAR	Connecticut Archives: Revolutionary War (microfilm)
CD	Clement, J. Noble Deeds of American Women (1854; repr. Williamstown, MA: Corner House Publishing, 1975)
CDB	Claims for Damages by the British and Americans in New Jersey, 1776-1782 (microfilm)
CG	Crofut, Florence S. M. Guide to the History and Historic Sites of Connecticut (New Haven: Yale University Press, 1937)
CH	Collins, Lewis. History of Kentucky (1847; repr. Lexington: Henry Clay Press, 1968)
CN	Claghorn, Charles E. Naval Officers of the American Revolution (Metuchen, NJ: Scarecrow Press, 1988)

CP	Clyne, Patricia Edwards. Patriots in Petticoats (New York: Dodd, Mead, 1976)
CS	Commager, Henry S., editor. The Spirit of Seventy-six (New York: Harper and Row, 1958)
DAR	DAR Patriot Index (Washington, 1966, 1980, 1982, 1986)
DB	Dictionary of American Biography (New York: Scribner's, 1928-81)
DC	DeBruin, Ruth Mary, editor. History of Chapter Names of the New Jersey State Society of the Daughters of the American Revolution (printed privately, 1985)
DD	Dwyer, William M. The Day Is Ours (New York: Viking, 1983)
DH	Draper, Mrs. Bell. Honor Roll of Massachusetts Patriots Heretofore Unknown (Boston: Merrill and DAR, 1899)
DM	DePauw, Linda Grant. Founding Mothers: Women of the Revolutionary Era (Boston: Houghton Mifflin, 1975)
DR	DePauw, Linda Grant, and Conover Hunt. Remember the Ladies (New York: Viking Press, 1976)
DT	DePauw, Linda Grant. Four Traditions: Women of New York During the American Revolution (Albany: New York State, 1974)
DW	DePauw, Linda Grant. Fortunes of War: New Jersey Women and the American Revolution (Trenton: New Jersey Historical Commission, 1975)
EP	Egle, William Henry. Pennsylvania Women in the American Revolution (1898; repr. Cottonport, LA: Polyanthus, 1972)
ES	Evans, Elizabeth. Weathering the Storm: Women of the American Revolution (New York: Scribner's, 1975)
ESC	Ervin, Sarah S. South Carolinians in the Revolution (Baltimore: Genealogical Publishing, 1976)
EW	Ellet, Elizabeth F. The Women of the American Revolution (1850; repr. New York: Haskell House, 1969)
FG	Fehrenbach, T. R. Greatness to Spare (Princeton, NJ: Van Nostrand, 1968)
FH	Flick, Alexander C. History of the State of New York, vol. 4 (New York: Columbia University Press, 1933)

ABBREVIATIONS AND SOURCES   xvii

FP   Order of the Founders and Patriots of America Register
      (1926, 1940, 1960, and 1980)

FS   Ferris, Robert G. Signers of the Declaration (Washington:
      Department of the Interior, 1973)

FW   Fitzpatrick, John C., editor. The Writings of George
      Washington (Washington: GPO, 1937)

GA   Gifford, Edward S., Jr. The American Revolution in
      the Delaware Valley (Philadelphia: Pennsylvania Society
      of the Sons of the Revolution, 1976)

GP   Green, Henry, and Mary Green. The Pioneer Mothers
      of America (New York: G. P. Putnam's Sons, 1912)

HC   Hart, Albert B. Commonwealth History of Massachusetts,
      vol. 2 (New York State History Company, 1929)

HD   Hanaford, Phoebe A. Daughters of America; or, Women
      of the Century (Augusta, ME: True, n.d.)

HP   Haldimand Papers (21,843 MSS), British Museum, London
      (microfilm A-765); compiled by Chris McHenry, 1981: "Rebel
      Prisoners at Quebec, 1778-1783"

HS   Harkness, David J. Southern Heroines of the American
      Revolution (Knoxville, TN, 1973)

IM   An Inventory of Maryland State Papers, 1775-1789, vol. 1
      (Annapolis: Archives Division, Hall of Records Commission,
      1977)

KC   Kelley and Feinstine. Courage and Candlelight: The
      Feminine Spirit of '76 (Harrisburg, PA: Stackpole, 1974)

LP   Lopez and Herbert. The Private Franklin (New York:
      W. W. Norton, 1975)

LV   Lebsock, Suzanne. Virginia Women, 1600-1975: A Share
      of Honor (Richmond: Virginia State Library, 1937)

MP   Military Papers, Revolutionary War, vol. 16 (Rhode Island)

MR   McHenry, Chris. Rebel Prisoners at Quebec, 1778-1783
      (Lawrence, IN, 1981)

NL   Norton, Mary Beth. Liberty's Daughters (Boston: Little,
      Brown, 1980)

NW   Nordham, George W. George Washington's Women (Philadelphia:
      Dorrance, 1977)

RA	Revolutionary Army Account Books, North Carolina (on microfilm)
RN	Robinson, Victor, MD. White Caps: The Story of Nursing (Philadelphia, 1944)
RP	Records of Pennsylvania's Revolutionary Governments, 1775-1790 (microfilm; Harrisburg: Pennsylvania Historical and Museum Commission)
RW	Reddy, Anne W. West Virginia Revolutionary Ancestors (Baltimore: General Publishing, 1979)
SC	South Carolina Historical and Genealogical Magazine (April 1933)
SI	Stub Entries to Indents (Claims for Provisions Supplied to the Armies) (Historical Commission of South Carolina)
SP	Smith, Samuel S. A Molly Pitcher Chronology (Monmouth Beach, NJ, 1972)
ST	Sachachner, Nathan. Thomas Jefferson (Cranbury, NJ: Thomas Yoseloff, 1951)
SW	Somerville, Mollie. Women of the American Revolution (Washington, 1974)
VR	Virginia Revolutionary War Public Service Claims (microfilm)
WA	Wilson, Caroline Price. Annals of Georgia (Georgia Genealogical Reprints, 1969)
WJ	Wilbur, Marguerite Eyer. Thomas Jefferson (New York: Liveright, 1962)
WT	Whitton, Mary Ormsbee. These Were the Women (New York: Heritage House, n.d.)

PART I: BACKGROUND

This is the first and only comprehensive biographical dictionary of the heroines and patriotic women of the Revolutionary War, compiled from many sources. While books have been published with biographies of from ten to thirty women, this book contains in Part II short biographies of six hundred women who performed patriotic acts during the war. After a lapse of over two hundred years, these women deserve national recognition for their heroism and dedication to the cause of American independence. In Part III, the more than five thousand women who performed some type of patriotic service are listed with brief comments about the manner in which they participated.

There was strong opposition in America to the Townshend Tea Act. In 1767 Benjamin Franklin formed a militia called the Association. A group called the Sons of Liberty was formed in Boston, New York, Philadelphia, and other cities and towns. The Daughters of Liberty was formed in Boston in 1768. In that year the people of Newburyport opposed the British tax on the importation of tea and manufactured goods. Phebe Parsons, the wife of the Rev. Jonathan Parsons, and the ladies of Newburyport, presented the Rev. Parsons, minister of the Presbyterian congregation, with 270 skeins of good yarn for the poor. Mrs. Parsons died on December 26, 1770, in her fifty-fifth year (information from Marianne Ventura, Newburyport, MA).

In 1769 the ladies of Virginia opposed the importation tax on tea, including Christina Blair Burwell, the daughter of John Blair, president of the Virginia Council. She married Col. Armistead Burwell. Later her father was a signer of the Constitution of the United States. Also active in the ladies' association was Anna Harrison Randolph of Richmond, the daughter of Col. Benjamin Harrison of Berkeley. She married Col. William Randolph of "Wilton," Henrico County. After his death Anna was active in the ladies' association (Virginia Gazette, July 27, 1769).

By January 31, 1770, some three hundred mistresses of families in Easton-Ipswich, Massachusetts, bound themselves to abstain totally from tea, except during sickness. In Boston, 126 young ladies signed the agreement. The Daughters of Liberty in Connecticut passed a resolution against the drinking of tea, according to the Connecticut Courant of February 22, 1774, but the names of the ladies attending were not included in the newspaper articles.

On August 20, 1774, John Adams and the other delegates from Massachusetts spent the night at the home of Catherine Van Velech Stoutenberg in New York City. She was the wife of Col. Tobias Stoutenberg. While there, the delegates saw the statue of King George III, of solid lead and gilded with gold, on Bowling Green.

On October 18, 1774, the ladies of Easton, Massachusetts, refused to buy British manufactured goods, including tea.

> We hear from Easton, that on the 18th of October last, 53 of the amiable Daughters of Liberty met at the Reverend Mr. Campbell's, and presented Mrs. Campbell with 280 skeines of cotton, linen, worsted, woolen, and tow yarn, some stockings, and pieces of cloth, etc. Then they walked in orderly procession to the meeting-house, where a sermon was preached by their reverend pastor, suitable to the occasion; and after divine service they returned to the house of their reverend pastor, in the same orderly manner, where they pleasantly regaled themselves with cake, cheese, and wine. Then each one of them seasonably returned to their respective families. The whole was conducted with the greatest decency and good order, and every countenance indicated noble spirit for liberty, and the promotion of our own manufacturers. [Boston Supplement 4, Virginia Gazette, February 24, 1775, submitted by Frances Pollard, Richmond, VA]

On October 24, 1774, a group of ladies of Edentown (now Edenton, North Carolina), met at the home of Elizabeth King and drew up a document supporting the Resolutions of the First Provincial Congress of North Carolina, which prohibited the importation of British manufactured goods, including tea. Forty-four ladies signed the document (Elizabeth Roberts signed in three places and Elizabeth Vail signed twice). The ladies who signed were:

Anne Anderson (later Mrs. John Mount)
Penelope Pagett Barker (Mrs. Thomas Barker)
Elizabeth Beasley
Sarah Beasley
Ruth Benbury
Lydia Bennett
Jean Gamble Blair (Mrs. John Blair)
Mary Blount

Rebecca Bondfield
Lydia Bonner (later Mrs. Joseph Blount)
Mary Bonner (later Mrs. John Harvey)
Margaret Cathcart
Abigail Charlton
Grace Clayton
Elizabeth Creacy
Mary Creacy
Elizabeth Cricket

I: BACKGROUND

Teresa Cunningham
Penelope Dawson
Elizabeth Green
Anne Hall (later Mrs. James Blount)
Frances Hicks Hall (Mrs. Durham Hall)
Sarah Haskins
Anne Horniblow
Anne Houghton
Sarah Howcutt
Sarah Howe
Mary Hunter (later Mrs. Joseph Bryan)
Mary Jones
Mary Littdie
Sarah Blount Littlejohn
Sarah Matthews (later Mrs. Thomas Pagett)
Elizabeth P. Ormond
Elizabeth Patterson
M. Payne
Margaret Pearson
Mary Ramsay
Elizabeth Roberts
Elizabeth Vail
Susanna Vail (Mrs. Edward Vail)
Sarah Valentine
Marion Wells
Jane Wellwood
Mary Woolard

On Courthouse Square in Edenton a large bronze teapot has been mounted atop a Revolutionary War cannon.

On October 14, 1774, the Continental Congress adopted a series of resolutions, including the right of the American people to "life, liberty and property." They formed what was called the Association and asked every male adult (Indians and the insane excepted) to sign or officially reject what was called the Association Test. This agreement was sent to every county, city, or town in all the original thirteen colonies.

Hannah Phillips Cushing, of Boston, was the wife of William Cushing. Mrs. Cushing was a true patriot and opposed the Tea Act of 1773. After the First Continental Congress of 1774 recommended that, barring a few articles, the colonies should buy nothing from the British, Mrs. Cushing wrote, "I hope there are none of us but would sooner wrap ourselves in sheep and goat skins than buy English goods of people who have insulted us in such a scandalous manner."

Mrs. Cushing died in 1834.

Mrs. Allen Mather lived in Fairhaven, Connecticut. "Yesterday the ladies belonging to the Fairhaven Parish in this Town met at the home of the Rev. Allen Mather and presented Mrs. Mather with One Hundred and Nine Skeines of well spun linen. And after having drank tea, as usual on such occasions, they unanimously came to their resolution (as recommended in the third Article of the Association of the Continental Congress), They would drink no more of that pernicious Weed, 'till the late oppressive Acts of the British Parliament are repealed" (Connecticut Courant, March 6, 1775, submitted by Carolyn M. Picciano, Hartford, CT).

In June 1776 Eliza Bend, the wife of Grove Bend of New York City, made flags for the regiments of the New York line.

After he signed the Declaration of Independence, Oliver Wolcott left Philadelphia on October 1, 1776, and passed through New York, where the Sons of Liberty had torn down the lead statue of King George III in Bowling Green. They gave the statue to Wolcott, who carried the statue in his cart to his home in Litchfield, Connecticut. His wife, Laura Collins Wolcott, and Ruth Welch Marvin, and their children, molded the lead statue into 42,088 bullets, according to the official count.

In 1777 Betsy Ross of Philadelphia made flags for the Pennsylvania navy.

In 1777 Elizabeth Gates, the wife of Gen. Gates of Berkeley County, Virginia (now West Virginia) and New York City, spent several months making bandages for the American army and opened her home as a hospital for wounded soldiers.

Grace Starr Meigs, the wife of Col. Return Jonathan Meigs of Middletown, Connecticut, in 1778 formed a committee of women to make clothing for the soldiers.

Molly Gutridge, a leader of the Daughters of Liberty, printed a broadside in Boston in 1779.

Susannah Smith Elliott of Charles Town (Charleston, South Carolina) embroidered two standards for the 2nd South Carolina Regiment of Infantry commanded by Col. Moultrie. Mrs. Elliott presented these flags to the regiment at the fort on Sullivans Island on June 28, 1776.

Deborah Putnam, the wife of Gen. Israel Putnam of Brooklyn, Connecticut, was with him in the 1775/76 campaign in New York state. With her daughters, she spun flax for shirts for the Continental Army. In 1780 in Philadelphia a group of women met in the home of Esther De Berdt Reed and formed a ladies' organization called the Association devoted to spinning, sewing, and knitting clothes for the soldiers. This organization spread to six states. Upon the death of Mrs. Reed in September 1780, the organization was taken over by Sarah Franklin Bache, the natural duaghter of Benjamin Franklin.

In 1781 Derby, Connecticut, voted to divide the inhabitants into forty-one classes to procure clothing for the American soldiers, and the town became a manufacturing shop with twelve apartments under Deacon Eliphalet Hotchkiss.

The foregoing remarks are examples of the dedication of the women to support the cause of independence in the only way they could, since they were tied down with their children and housework. Some of these women had two or three children, but many of them had from seven to fifteen children.

I: BACKGROUND

Other women had their homes taken or burned by the British. Elizabeth Lewis was the wife of Francis Lewis of Whitestone, Long Island, New York, who signed the Declaration of Independence. In September 1776 her home was burned by the British, and she was imprisoned by the enemy. Shortly after her release in 1779, Mrs. Lewis died.

In 1779 the British burned Fairfield, Connecticut. Eunice Burr, the wife of Thaddeus Burr, a member of the Council of Safety, tried to stop the enemy from burning her home, to no avail, as the pillage and burning continued. The local chapter of the Daughters of the American Revolution is named in her honor. When the British captured Charleston, South Carolina on May 12, 1780, the enemy demanded that Elizabeth Heyward, the wife of Thomas Heyward, Jr., a signer of the Declaration of Independence, light up her windows to celebrate the British victory. When she refused to do so a second time, they occupied her home and shipped her to Philadelphia, where she died in 1781.

Other women acted as nurses and cared for the wounded soldiers. Faith Huntington of Lebanon, Connecticut, daughter of Governor John Trumbull, married Col. Jedediah Huntington, who later became a general. She was a camp follower and was with him at Cambridge, Massachusetts, in 1775. After the Battle of Bunker Hill some 450 Americans were killed, wounded, or captured. The wounded were taken to the halls of Harvard College, where Mrs. Huntington nursed the soldiers and tried to alleviate their suffering. The strain was too much for her, and her nerves were shattered. Mrs. Huntington died in her home on November 24, 1775.

On the morning of September 6, 1781, a British force under Benedict Arnold attacked Fort Griswold at Groton, Connecticut. After the American Col. William Ledyard surrendered, he was bayoneted to death and eighty-five American soldiers were slaughtered. Some sixty men were wounded. Among the first women to nurse the American soldiers were Anna Warner Bailey of Groton and Fanny Ledyard Peters of Southhold, Long Island, New York, who was visiting her uncle. The Groton chapter of the Daughters of the American Revolution is named after Anna Bailey and the Mystic, Connecticut, chapter of the DAR after Fanny Ledyard.

Letters of marque and reprisal were authorized by the Continental Congress. Continental bonds were issued to sea captains to command armed vessels to capture and destroy British shipping. These bonds were signed by three men of substance and witnessed by two individuals. Some forty women witnessed these bonds. This was an act of patriotism--if the enemy had won the war, the property of these individuals would have been seized by the British and the Tories. The champion woman witness was Sarah Hodge of Newburyport, Massachusetts, who witnessed twenty-three such bonds.

WOMEN PATRIOTS

It is with regret that we cannot include the biography of Elizabeth Strong Hale of Coventry, Connecticut, the mother of Nathan Hale, in this book, since she died in 1767. Elizabeth Strong married Richard Hale, and they had twelve children. Six of her nine sons served in the American Revolution. Nathan Hale was hanged as a spy by the British on September 22, 1776.

Many women acted as "Paul Reveres" and carried messages to the Americans that the British were coming, or took messages that additional troops were needed at a certain location where a battle was expected. These women were:

Agnes Hobson Bacon (GA)
Margaret Catherine Moore Barry (SC)
Margaret Galbraith Barton (WV)
Katherine Montgomery Bledsoe (VA)
Susanna Bolling Bolling (VA)
Lydia Barrington Darragh (PA)
Ann Simpson Davis (PA)
Mary Ramage Dillard (SC)
Betsy Dowdy (NC)
Phebe Reynolds Drake (NY)
Sarah Bradlee Fulton (MA)
Emily Geiger (SC)
Deborah Champion Gilbert (CT)
Anne Kennedy Hamilton (SC)
Altje Schenck Harris (NJ)
Anne Myers Howard (PA)
Mary Lafoone Keith (SC)
Agnes Dickinson Lee (CT)
Mrs. Richard B. Lloyd (NY)
Sybil Ludington (NY)
Sarah Wayne Gardiner McCalla (SC)
Behethland Foote Moore (SC)
Charlotte Reeves Robertson (TN)
Catherine Van Winkle Shepherd (NJ)
Laodice Langston Springfield (SC)
Elizabeth Page Stark (NH)
Jane Black Thomas (SC)
Nancy Kingfisher Ward (TN)

Women who were scouts, soldiers, or spies were:

Ann Hennis Bailey (WV, scout and spy)
Martha McFarland Bell (NC, spy)
Margaret Cochran Corbin (PA, cannoneer)
Deborah Sampson Gannett (NY, soldier)
Anna Maria Lane (VA, wounded in battle)
Mary Hays McCauley (NJ-PA, cannoneer)
Grace Waring Martin (SC, waylaid a British courier)
Rachel Clay Martin (SC, waylaid a British courier)
Sarah Matthews (NY, sentinel)
Mom Rinker (PA, spy)
Mary Ritchie (SC, soldier)
Sarah Hartwell Shattuck (MA, waylaid a British courier)
Eliza Veach (SC, soldier/washerwoman)
Jimmie Waglun (NJ, scout)
Prudence Cummings Wright (MA, waylaid a British courier)

During the war, Gen. Washington had his headquarters at or visited the homes or taverns of the following women:

I: BACKGROUND

Mrs. Joseph Appleby (NY)
Mrs. Charles W. Apthrop (NY)
Catherine Beekman Arden (NY)
Elizabeth Tuttle Arnold (NJ)
Elizabeth Putney Baldwin (NJ)
Mary Hoops Barclay (PA)
Anne Marie Dandridge Bassett (VA)
Margaret Eaton Berrien (NJ)
Hannah Mandeville Birdsall (NY)
Anna De Wint Blauvelt (NY)
Sarah Brown Bowen (RI)
Mary Hite Bowman (VA)
Gertie Wycoff Brinckerhoff (NY)
Jennetjie Van Voorhies Brinckerhoff (NY)
Theodosia Bartow Burr (NJ)
Elizabeth Oswald Chew (PA)
Mrs. Cogswell (CT)
Esther Schuyler Colfax (NJ)
Dorothy Whitney Coolidge (MA)
Annatie Koeme Couenhoven (NJ)
Esther Bowes Cox (NJ)
Elizabeth Saltonstall Deane (CT)
Agnes Tyler Delavan (NY)
Antje Kermer De Wint (NY)
Hester Schuyler Dey (NJ)
Mary Morris Dickinson (PA)
Maritje Dey Doremus (NJ)
Mrs. Dorrance (CT)
Keziah Dunham (NJ)
Sibbil Dwight (MA)
Mrs. Thomas Ellison (NY)
Mrs. George Emlen (PA)
Rebecca Wilson Fell (PA)
Susanna Marschalk Fell (NJ)
Ann Trip Ferris (NY)
Theodosia Johnes Ford (NJ)
Phebe Cole Godwin (NJ)
Catherine Littlefield Greene (RI, NJ)
Ann Wiley Hammond (NY)
Hannah Stewart Harris (PA)
Tryntje Debois Hasbrouck (NY)
Martha Smith Hay (NY)
Deborah Hewes (PA)

Mrs. Henry Hill (PA)
Mary Harvey Holcombe (NJ)
Mrs. Andrew Hopper (NJ)
Hannah Holstein Hughes (PA)
Margaret Guild Hunt (NJ)
Elizabeth Wilson Keith (PA)
Sibbil Dwight Kent (MA)
Lucy Flucker Knox (MA)
Countess de la Luzerne (PA)
Mary Diggs Lee (MD)
Mary Cushing Lincoln (MA)
Mrs. James Logan (PA)
Elizabeth Blauvelt Mabie (NY)
Mrs. Joseph Malin (PA)
Anne Lord McCurdy (CT)
Mrs. John McIlvain (PA)
Joanne Beekman Mehelm (NJ)
Ann Fisher Miller (NY)
Sarah Sherrell Morehouse (CT)
Mrs. Morgan (CT)
Mrs. James Morris (PA)
Mary Philipse Morris (NY)
Mary White Morris (PA)
Hannah Gerbert Pennypacker (PA)
Mrs. Potter (RI)
Mrs. Isaac Potts (PA)
Elizabeth Willing Powell (PA)
Deborah Lothrop Putnam (CT)
Rachel James Ring (PA)
Lucretia Harris Shaw (CT)
Mrs. Samuel Sheldon (CT)
Margaret Frances Shippen (PA)
Widow Sidman (NY)
Marretje Van Dusen Sloat (NY)
Mary Predmore Stites (NJ)
Widow Strong (CT)
Mary Meyers Suffern (NY)
Mrs. Thomas Tompkins (NY)
Mrs. Tracy (CT)
Joanna Livingston Van Courtlandt (NY)
Helena Clark Vandenberg (NY)
Martha Lott Van Doren (NJ)
Sarah Middah Van Veghten (NJ)
Mary Maddox Wallace (NJ)
Catherine Magdelin Roth Wampole (PA)
Abigail Chester Webb (CT)
Rosanna Margaretta Wentz (PA)

Mrs. Thomas Wetheral (NJ)
Laura Collins Wolcott (CT)

Mrs. Reuben Wright (NY)
Elizabeth Taliaferro Wythe (VA)

After the war ended, Washington visited:

Jame Campbell (NY)
Sarah Bradlee Fulton (MA)

Polly Masters Penn (PA; his
   residence in 1790)
Margaret Todd Whetten (NY)

    Many American women suffered the death or imprisonment of their husbands or sons during the war. In consideration of the suffering endured by these patriotic women, it was decided to include them in these volumes. Not all of the names of such women are included here as that would be an impossible task. But the author has included as many as he could locate as a representative sampling to honor those women who suffered emotionally for a belief in the independence of the colonies.

    There are many women who collected funds, made shirts, knitted stockings, nursed the wounded, or carried messages to army camps warning the Americans of impending British or Tory attacks. Also included are women who housed Gen. Washington, John Adams, Thomas Jefferson, and the various generals, or whose homes were pillaged or burned by the enemy for their patriotic acts and beliefs.

PART II: SELECTED BIOGRAPHIES

ABBOTT, ALICE FULLER   PA
of Wilkes Barre. The daughter of Stephen Fuller, Sr., of Andover, Massachusetts, she was born in 1740. On November 4, 1762, she married John Abbott of Hampton, Windham County, Connecticut, and they had nine children. They came to Wilkes Barre in 1772 and resided in the fort there until about 1774 when they built their farmhouse in what is now Plains Township. John Abbott took part in the Battle of Wyoming as a private in the 6th Wilkes Barre Company of the 24th Regiment, Connecticut Militia, commanded by Capt. Regin Geer.
    During the massacre, Abbott fled the battle in the general rout while the Americans surrendered the fort to the enemy. Abbott took his family down the river to Sunbury and left them there. He then joined the detachment of militia under the command of Lt. Col. Zebulon Butler and marched to Wilkes Barre on August 4, 1778.
    Abbott found his house and barn burned, his cattle taken away, and his fields ravaged. Then on August 18, Abbott was shot and killed by Indians. Alice Abbott and her nine children walked about three hundred miles back to Hampton, penniless, and stayed with relatives and friends. After the war ended Mrs. Abbott returned to Wilkes Barre and married Stephen Gardiner. She died in June 1816. Her daughter Lydia Abbott married Artemas Swetland, son of Hannah Tiffany Swetland. (Submitted by James R. Hopkins, Mount Vernon, OH)

ADAMS, ABIGAL SMITH   MA
daughter of Elizabeth Quincy and the Rev. William Smith, she was born on November 11, 1744, in Weymouth. On October 25, 1764, Abigail Smith married John Adams. In 1774 John Adams was a delegate to the First Continental Congress held in Philadelphia, and served in the second congress from 1775 to 1777. In November 1775 Mrs. Adams wrote to her husband that she expected the Americans would declare their independence from Great Britain, one of the first women to do so. While living in Braintree, Massachusetts, she wrote to her husband on March 31, 1776: "And by the way in the new Code of Laws which I suppose it will be necessary for you to make I desire you would Remember the Ladies, and be more generous and favourable to them than your ancestors.

Do not put such unlimited power into the hands of the Husbands."
Thus, Abigail Adams was not only a patriot advocating independence, she was also a strong supporter of women's rights. From 1778 to 1788 John Adams served on diplomatic missions to France, England, and the Netherlands. In 1789 he was elected vice president and served as president of the United States from 1797 to 1801. Their son, John Quincy Adams, served as president of the United States from 1825 to 1829 and as a member of Congress from 1832 to 1848. Abigail Adams died on October 28, 1818. (DB; DR)

ADAMS, ELIZABETH WELLS   MA
of Boston. She was born in 1735, the fifth daughter of Francis Wells. On December 6, 1764, she became the second wife of Samuel Adams (1722-1803). His first wife, Elizabeth Checkly Adams, died in 1757. They had five children, but only a son and a daughter survived to maturity. After the Battle of Bunker Hill in 1775, Mrs. Adams and her daughter were forced to flee Boston to her father's home in Cambridge.

Samuel Adams was a signer of the Declaration of Independence. Adams succeeded as governor of Massachusetts on the death of John Hancock in 1793 and was reelected in 1795. The Adamses were impoverished by the Revolution, but on the death in 1788 of Dr. Samuel Adams, Jr., the son by his first wife, they received six thousand dollars representing a claim of his son. Mrs. Adams died in 1803. (GP)

ALEXANDER, AGNES BREWSTER   VA
of Augusta County. She was born on April 25, 1763. Agnes and her sisters Elinor Brewster Dunn and Jennet Brewster Irvin spun, knitted, wove, sewed, and cooked to supply what comforts they could to help the Revolutionary War soldiers. A Dutch oven, preserved by a descendant, was in constant use for six weeks as they melted down their household articles of pewter and molded them into bullets. Agnes in 1785 married William Alexander, and they lived in Fayette county, Virginia. They had five sons and two daughters. Agnes died on August 25, 1830, in Monroe County, Indiana. (Ann S. Alexander, Revolution Service of the Brewster Sisters; submitted by Beverly A. Hendricks, Glendale, CA). The three sisters are buried on the campus of the University of Indiana in Bloomington.

ALLAN, MARY PATTON   ME
of Machias. She was born on February 3, 1746, the daughter of Mark Patton. On October 10, 1767, she married John Allan (1746-1805), one of nine children, born in Edinburgh Castle. The Allans had moved to Cumberland, Nova Scotia, in 1749 when John was only two years old. Mary and John Allan had six sons and three daughters. John served in the Nova Scotia Provincial Assembly from 1770 until 1776.

After learning of the battles of Lexington and Bunker Hill in

II: SELECTED BIOGRAPHIES

1775, John dedicated himself to the American cause of liberty. Allan traveled and secured for the Americans the cooperation of the Micmac Indian tribe. He then left Cumberland on August 3, 1776, by boat for the United States to offer his services in the patriotic cause. He entered Machias Bay on the thirteenth, where he spent some time, arriving in Boston on November 7.

Meanwhile an American, Col. Jonathan Eddy, with twenty-eight men, sailed from Machias in an attempt to capture Fort Cumberland in Nova Scotia. The attack on November 17, 1776, resulted in a disaster for the Americans, and John Allan was charged by the council in Halifax with inciting a rebellion, and they placed a bounty on his head.

Many of the residents had emigrated to Nova Scotia from New England, and then returned to the States. The soldiers from Fort Cumberland burned the homes of the Americans who had fled. One of the first homes destroyed was the Allans'. Mrs. Allan and her five children were without food except for some potatoes baked by the fire, which she found when she crawled up to the smoking ruins. Mrs. Allan and the children were rescued by her father, Mark Patton, and taken to his home, but the British soldiers arrived and took Mrs. Allan prisoner. The children were left with her father. Mrs. Allan was taken to Halifax and before the governor, who demanded to be told the whereabouts of her husband, or else he would imprison her.

Mrs. Allan gave the British authorities no information for some time, then told them that her husband had "escaped to a free country." She was held in prison for six or eight months.

On November 29 Allan left Boston for Philadelphia on horseback. He crossed the Delaware River at Fishkill and met with Gen. Gates who took him to the headquarters of Gen. Washington, where Allan dined on December 22. He left Philadelphia on December 25 and arrived in Baltimore on December 30, 1776. He was received by Congress on January 4, 1777, and was appointed superintendent of eastern Indian affairs and a colonel of infantry, serving from 1777 to 1783. Allan left Baltimore on January 17 and arrived in Boston on February 3. En route he learned of Col. Eddy's disastrous repulse at Fort Cumberland and the imprisonment of his wife.

After her release, Mrs. Allan and her children joined her husband in Machias. In 1780, while dealing with the Indians, Allan was forced to leave his two eldest sons with them as hostages until negotiations were completed. The boys remained with the Indians for one year. John Allan died on February 7, 1805, on Allan's Island in Passamoquoddy Bay.

Mrs. Allan's son William had eleven children, her son Mark had thirteen children, and her son John had thirteen children. The others had from five to eight children each. Her granddaughter, Charlotte Allan, married James Miller and had sixteen children. Her other grandchildren had from three to nine children each. She thus left many descendants. Mary Patton Allan died on June 8, 1819. She is listed as a patriot in the DAR Patriot

Index. (George H. Allan, Memoir of Colonel John Allan [Albany: Joel Munsell, 1867]; submitted by Dee C. Brown, Jr., Readfield, ME)

ALLEN, ELIZABETH PARSONS   MA
of Northampton. Betty was born in 1733, the daughter of Mindwell Edwards and Noah Parsons. In 1753 she married Joseph Allen and they had twelve children--eight boys and four girls. Six of her sons fought in the American Revolution: two were majors, two were chaplains, one a lieutenant, and one marched to the aid of Bennington. Church records show that Betty Allen assisted at the birth of three thousand infants. The Northampton chapter of the Daughters of the American Revolution is named in her honor. (GP)

ALLEN, MARY BAKER   CT
of Cornwall. The daughter of Remember Baker of Roxbury (Woodbury), she was married to Joseph Allen by the Rev. Anthony Stoddard on March 11, 1736. Their first child was Ethan Allen, born in Litchfield on January 10, 1737, O.S., or January 21, 1738, N.S., followed by Herman, Lydia, Heber, Ira, Levi, Lucy, and Zimri born on December 10, 1748. In 1739 the Allens moved to Cornwall, where they were harassed by Indians for the next few years. Mary's husband died on April 14, 1755, leaving her to raise and support eight children. (Information from the Sheldon Museum, Middlebury, VT)
      Ethan Allen, while residing in the New Hampshire Grants (now Vermont), commanded the Green Mountain Boys, 1770-1775. He assisted in the capture of Fort Ticonderoga in 1775, but during the expedition against Canada in December 1775, Allen was captured by the British and imprisoned until 1778.
      Mary Baker Allen suffered during the imprisonment of her son. A local Vermont chapter of the Daughters of the American Revolution is named in her honor. (Information from Dorothy Durhan, Shoreham, VT; DAR)

AMBLER, REBECCA BURWELL   VA
was active in the ladies relief association for the soldiers. Mrs. Ambler and her daughters Betsy Ambler Brent and Polly Ambler Marshall in 1776 knitted stockings for the American soldiers. (NL)

ANDERSON, REBECCA   SC
of Charleston. She apparently was the wife of William Anderson (1706-1783). After the fall of Charleston in May 1780, the British commandant, Lt. Col. Balfour, required all the women who were heads of households to take an oath of fidelity to the Crown or be banished from the city. Mrs. Anderson refused to do so and was banished, along with 120 other women and 264 children. (SC) Mrs. Anderson provided funds for the army during the Revolutionary War. (AA, 2:72)

II: SELECTED BIOGRAPHIES 13

ANDERSON, SARAH CARNEY   SC
of the 96th District. The daughter of Mary and John Carney,
she was born about 1732. In Overwharten Parish, Stafford County,
Virginia, on November 28, 1752, she married John Anderson (1724-
1781), and they had eight sons and three daughters. Five of her
sons--Scarlet, Joshua, Bailey, William and John Jr.--fought in the
Revolutionary War from the 96th District.
    Sarah's husband, while serving in Roebuck's regiment, was
wounded during the Battle of Camden, South Carolina, on August
16, 1780, and died of his wounds on October 8, 1781. Her sons
Scarlet and Joshua also served in Roebuck's regiment and died
of war injuries in 1783. (Submitted by Marylou Evans Peacock,
San Francisco, CA) Mrs. Anderson supplied provisions to the
army during the Revolutionary War. (SI, B:89)

APPLEBY, AELTJE CONKLIN   NY
of Ardsley. After he left the home of Joanna Livingston Van Courtlandt in Peekskill, Washington's army marched from Valentine's
Hill, Dunwoodie, to an area "near Dobbs Ferry." At that time,
town lines were not drawn, and Ardsley was part of Dobbs Ferry.
The general arrived at the Appleby house on July 5, 1781. While
here, Washington wrote to Brig. Gen. James Clinton and ordered
all Continental troops from the northward to West Point. (FW)
    Aeltje Conklin, the daughter of Deliverance Conklin, was
the second wife of Joseph Appleby. By his first wife, Rachel Van
Wert, he had three sons and two daughters. Rachel died on September 30, 1771. On October 30, 1773, Joseph married Aeltje Conklin, and they had two sons and two daughters. Their son Thomas
married Harriet Tompkins. Joseph Appleby was a second lieutenant
of the Tarrytown militia from October 19, 1775, to October 23,
1776. The Ardsley High School now stands on the Appleby farmland.
    Gen. Washington left the Appleby house on July 7, 1781,
and took his headquarters to the home of Mr. and Mrs. Thomas
Tompkins in Phillipsburg (now Hartsdale). Thomas Tompkins was
the uncle of Joseph Appleby. (Some information received from
Sr. Mary Agnes Parrell, Mercy College, Dobbs Ferry, NY)

APTHROP, MARY McEVERS   NY
of New York City. She was born on July 10, 1734, the daughter
of Catherine Van Horne and John McEvers. In February 1755 she
married Charles Ward Apthrop, the son of the Boston merchant
Charles Apthrop. Mary and her husband had ten children. They
lived on 9th Avenue (now Columbus Avenue) between 90th and
91st streets. Mrs. Apthrop died in April 1792 and her husband
in 1797 (Ruth Lawrence, Colonial Families of America, 1933, 13:
35,39)
    On September 13, 1776, Gen. Washington was at the Apthrop
house near the Hudson River when four ships of war--two with
forty guns and two with twenty-eight guns--sailed up the East
River. The next day, when Gen. Washington heard gunfire, he

rode to the spot and found American troops retreating. Washington tried to rally his men, to no avail. The men left the general there within eighty yards of the enemy, according to a letter of Gen. Greene dated September 17, 1776. Gen. Washington barely escaped capture as he rode away. Then on September 18, 1776, the Apthrop house was requisitioned by General Sir Henry Clinton as his headquarters. (FW)

ARDEN, CATHERINE BEEKMAN   NY
of Haverstraw. Catherine was the wife of Pvt. Jacob Arden. Gen. Washington left the home of Mrs. Prevost (later Mrs. Aaron Burr) in Paramus, New Jersey, on July 14, 1778, and had breakfast at the home of Mrs. Arden on July 15. The general then established his headquarters in the William Smith house in Haverstraw occupied by Mrs. Hay. (FW)

ARMSTRONG, REBECCA LYON   PA
of Carlisle. The daughter of William Lyon of Enniskillen, county Fermanagh, Ireland, she was born on May 2, 1719. About 1739 she married John Armstrong, and they settled in the Kittatinny Valley. John Armstrong was a lieutenant colonel of the colonial troops and defeated the Indians in September 1756 at the battle of Kittanning on the Allegheny. On February 29, 1776, he was promoted to brigadier general by the Continental Congress and given command of the forces in South Carolina. On June 5, 1777, he became a brigadier general of the State of Pennsylvania and took part in the battles of Brandywine and Germantown. Gen. Armstrong died at Carlisle on March 9, 1795.

During the Revolutionary War, Gen. and Mrs. Armstrong lived in Carlisle, and she organized a group of women making clothing for the American soldiers. This was the first such organization in Pennsylvania. She died at Carlisle on November 17, 1797. (EP)

ARNETT, HANNAH WHITE   NJ
of Elizabeth. She was born on January 15, 1733. After her marriage to Isaac Arnett, the couple lived in Elizabethtown (now Elizabeth), New Jersey. In June 1776 the fleet of Adm. Lord Howe sailed into New York Harbor, and on July 2, 1776, his brother, Gen. Sir William Howe, landed 10,000 men on Staten Island. In August, Gen. Clinton arrived with a large British army and the Battle of Long Island took place August 27 to 29, with the Americans' retreating to New York. The Battle of White Plains took place on October 28, 1776, and on November 16 Gen. Howe took Fort Washington in New York and then Fort Lee in New Jersey.

After their victories, the British on November 30, 1776, issued a proclamation promising a pardon to all who would sign a declaration of allegiance to Great Britain within sixty days. Many Americans felt their cause was hopeless at this point, and a group of men met at the house of Mr. and Mrs. Arnett to discuss their fate. While the men sat in one room discussing the matter, Mrs.

II: SELECTED BIOGRAPHIES

Arnett sat in another room, listening to the conversation. Finally she could restrain herself no longer and burst into the room where the men were seated. She called them cowards and told them, "God is on our side and every volley of our muskets is an echo of His voice."
 Mrs. Arnett urged the men to continue the struggle, and at the conclusion of the meeting each man pledged his support to the cause for independence from Great Britain. Mrs. Arnett died on January 10, 1824. Her story appeared in the New York Observer in 1876. A bronze tablet marks the grave of Mrs. Arnett in the First Presbyterian Churchyard on Broad Street, Elizabeth, New Jersey.

ARNOLD, ELIZABETH TUTTLE   NJ
of Morristown. She was the wife of Col. Jacob Arnold (1749-1827). Gen. Washington established his headquarters here on January 6, 1777. Mrs. Washington arrived in Morristown on March 27. Gen. Washington was in Morristown until May 28, 1777. On April 25, two thousand British troops under Governor Tryon of New York landed at Compo Beach near Fairfield, Connecticut. The next day at Danbury, Connecticut, they burned the public stores and some homes. At Ridgefield they were met by generals Silliman, Arnold, and Wooster. Gen. David Wooster was wounded and died on May 2. (BI)

ARNOLD, HANNAH WATERMAN   CT
of Norwich. Her first husband was named King. After his death she married Benedict Arnold. Their son, Benedict, was born on June 14, 1741. His mother was very strict and endeavored to instill in him religious thought, but he rebelled and ran away at age fourteen to join the colonial troops during the French and Indian War. Her son was brought home at her insistence, but ran away again. In 1775 he raised a company of volunteers to fight for the patriotic cause. Since there was a scarcity of gunpowder and cannons, he proposed to capture Fort Ticonderoga, New York, where he knew he could obtain munitions. Arnold was made a colonel of militia and with troops under Ethan Allen of Vermont, they took the fort on May 10, 1775, and captured the munitions.
 Arnold led an attack on Quebec and reached the Saint Lawrence River on November 8, 1775. Meanwhile Gen. Richard Montgomery captured Montreal and joined forces with Arnold. They attacked the fort at Quebec on December 31, 1775, in a blinding snowstorm. Gen. Montgomery was killed, and Arnold was wounded. Arnold blockaded Quebec, but when British reinforcements arrived in the spring of 1776, Arnold was forced to retreat. Arnold became a brigadier general.
 On February 19, 1777, the Continental Congress promoted five brigadier generals (all of whom were junior to Arnold in rank) to major generals and bypassed Arnold. This embittered him. Later Arnold was promoted to major general, but ranked below the five promoted earlier. Arnold was still bitter.

As we all know, Arnold became a traitor. His mother, Hannah Arnold, was a patriot, and suffered greatly for the actions of her son. (DB)

ATLEE, SARAH RICHARDSON   PA
of Philadelphia. The daughter of Alice and Isaac Richardson, she was born on September 7, 1742, in Salisbury Township, Lancaster County. On April 19, 1762, she married Capt. Samuel John Atlee, who had served in the Colonial Wars. Later he served in the Revolution.
   Mrs. Atlee contributed funds for the American soldiers and provided meals for them whenever possible. Her husband died in Philadelphia on November 25, 1786, and Mrs. Atlee went to live with her daughter Alice Amelia Boude, the wife of Capt. Thomas Boude. She died in Columbia, Pennsylvania, on December 27, 1823. (EP)

ATWATER, MARY SALTONSTALL   CT
of New London and Groton. On June 18, 1778, Benjamin Pratt of Saybrook, Connecticut, obtained a letter of marque and reprisal to command the Connecticut sloop Princess Mary with seven guns and twenty-six men. Witnesses to the bond were Gurdon Saltonstall and Mary Saltonstall. She also witnessed bonds on September 22, 1778, to Thomas Chester, Jr., of Groton and on December 2, 1779, to Edward Latham of Groton. Mary Saltonstall was the daughter of Rebeckah and Gurdon Saltonstall. She was born on March 28, 1744. She was the younger sister of Ann Saltonstall. She also witnessed bonds on March 28, 1780, for Ludowick Champlin of New London; on March 7, 1781, for Michael Mellay of New London; and on May 6, 1782, for Daniel Tappan of Newburyport, Massachusetts. (CN) She became the third wife of Jeremiah Atwater. (DAR)

AVERIT (or EVERITT), HANNAH   CT
of Winchester. She was born in 1714. After the death of her husband, Capt. Josiah Averit of Bethlehem, Pennsylvania, in 1765, she walked to Winchester with her seven children to claim some undivided land which her husband had purchased. Mrs. Averit was a true patriot during the war, and was the only woman to take the oath of fidelity to the State of Connecticut under the Articles of Confederation. She died in 1803. (CG)

B

BACHE, SARAH FRANKLIN   PA
the illegitimate daughter of Deborah Reed and Benjamin Franklin was born on September 11, 1743, in Philadelphia. On October 29, 1767, Sarah married Richard Bache, a native of Settle, Yorkshire, England. In December 1776, fearing an attack by the British on Philadelphia, they moved to Goshen Township in Chester County, Pennsylvania. In 1777 they moved to Manheim Township in

II: SELECTED BIOGRAPHIES   17

Lancaster County, where they remained until June 1778 when the British left Philadelphia for New York City.
Benjamin Franklin wrote to his daughter on June 3, 1779, "If you happen again to see General Washington, assure him of my very great and sincere regards, and tell him, that all the old Generals here [in France] amuse themselves in studying the accounts of his operations, and approve highly of his conduct."
Upon the death of Esther Reed in 1780, Mrs. Bache and four other women took over the leadership of the Association, a group of women devoted to spinning, sewing, and knitting clothing for the American soldiers. Upon the suggestion of George Washington, they purchased material with their own money and made shirts for the soldiers. From his headquarters at New Windsor, New York, on January 15, 1781, Washington wrote to Mrs. Bache:

> Dear Madam: I should have done myself the pleasure to acknowledge the receipt of the Letter you did me the favor to write on the 26th of Decr. at the moment of its receipt; had not some affairs of a very unusual nature, which are too recent and notorious to require explanation, engaged my whole attention. I pray you now to be persuaded, that a sense of the Patriotic Exertions of yourself and the Ladies who have furnished so handsome and useful a gratuity for the Army, at so critical and severe a season, will not easily be effaced, and that the value of the donation will be greatly enhanced by a consideration of the hands by which it was made and presented.
> Amidst the distress and sufferings of the Army, whatever sources they have arisen, it must be a consolation to our Virtuous Country Women that they have never been accused of with holding their most zealous efforts to support the cause we are engaged in, and encourage those who are defending them in the field. The Army do not want gratitude, nor do they Misplace it in this instance....
> Mrs. Washington requests me to present her Compliments to Mr. Bache and yourself, with which you will be pleased to accept of mine and believe me to be....

On February 13, 1781, Washington wrote letters of thanks to Anne Francis, Henrietta Hillegas, Mary Clarkson, Sarah Bache, and Susan Blair.
In 1794 Mrs. Bache moved to a farm on the Delaware River about seventeen miles above Philadelphia. In 1808 she was stricken with cancer, and moved back to Philadelphia, where she died on October 5, 1808. She was survived by three sons and three daughters. (DR; FW)

BACON, AGNES HOBSON   GA
lived near Augusta, which had been captured by Lt. Col. Archibald Campbell and the British forces on January 29, 1779. Gen. John Ashe and the Americans attempted to retake Augusta on March 3,

1779, but were unsuccessful and lost 350 men at Briar Creek. The
British held Augusta for two years. In 1781 Gen. Stephen Heard
decided to retake Augusta, but needed reinforcements. Agnes
Hobson volunteered to ride to North Carolina to take a message
to Gen. Nathaniel Greene. Gen. Heard gave Agnes his Arabian
horse, who was called Silver Heels.
It took Agnes three days to make the trip, stopping off at
farmhouses to rest at night. Finally she arrived at Gen. Greene's
camp and delivered the important message. Greene immediately
dispatched troops under Gen. Light-Horse Harry Lee. The Americans recaptured Augusta, with many thanks to Agnes Hobson for
her daring ride. (HS) She married William Bacon. (DAR)

BAILEY, ANN HENNIS   WV
of Point Pleasant. Ann Hennis was born in Liverpool, England,
in 1747 and came to Covington, Virginia, in 1761. She married
Richard Trotter, and they had a son William, born in 1767. Her
husband was killed in battle with the Indians at Point Pleasant
on October 10, 1774. At this point she donned male clothing and
became a scout and messenger for the Americans among the Kanawha
Indians and along the frontier against the British. She met and
married another scout, John Bailey. Ann was known as the White
Squaw of the Kanawha. She died in Gallia County, Ohio, on November 22, 1825.
    In Point Pleasant her grave is marked in Tv-Endie-Wei Park
at the point where the Kanawha and Ohio rivers meet. On Kanawha
Boulevard in Charleston, West Virginia, a large boulder is marked
to commemorate her journey to carry powder to Fort Lee in 1791.
In Falling Springs, West Virginia, near Covington, Virginia, is
Ann Bailey's Cave, and on Route 22 about eight miles north of
Covington is a marker for "Mad Anne's Ridge" where she once
lived. Her maiden name is also given as Anne Dennis. (CP)

BAILEY, ANNA WARNER   CT
of Groton, was born in 1758/59. She lived with her uncle, Edward
Mills, who was killed at the Battle of Groton Heights on September
6, 1781, when over eighty American soldiers were murdered by
the British under Gen. Benedict Arnold. She was the first person
to enter Fort Griswold after the massacre. After the battle she
assisted Dr. Downer in nursing the wounded American soldiers.
Later she married Capt. Elijah Bailey.
    During the War of 1812 when Commo. Stephen Decatur was
blockaded in Groton Harbor by the British, she donated her red
flannel petticoat for wadding for the guns. Over the years, "Mother"
Bailey received visits from presidents James Monroe, Andrew Jackson,
and Martin Van Buren. The Marquis de Lafayette also honored her
with a visit. She died on January 10, 1851. The local chapter of
the Daughters of the American Revolution is named after her. (For
more details about Fort Griswold, see Fanny Ledyard Peters, below;
some information on Connecticut women received from Elizabeth
Anne Reiter, Groton, and Margaret Brughers, New London, CT)

II: SELECTED BIOGRAPHIES   19

BALDWIN, ELIZABETH PITNEY   NJ
of Darlington. Elizabeth was born in 1760 and married Caleb Baldwin, Jr. Gen. Washington had his headquarters at the home of Mrs. Hopper in Ramapo on September 18, 1780, and then spent that night in the home of Mrs. Baldwin. Her second husband was William Thorne. Elizabeth died in 1850. (FW; DAR)

BALFOUR, ELIZABETH TODD DAYTON   NC
of Salisbury. She became the second wife of Col. Andrew Balfour (1735-1783) in Newport, Rhode Island, in 1774/75. Later the Balfours moved to Salisbury. While on leave at his home on March 11, 1783, Col. Balfour was murdered by a band of British and Tories under the notorious Col. Lanning. (Caruthers, Revolutionary Incidents) They had one son, Andrew.
    In 1789 President George Washington gave her, in her son's name, the position of postmaster at Salisbury, which she held for twenty-five years. She was probably the first postmistress in the United States. (Submitted by Margaret L. Miezejewski, Okeechobee, FL) Mrs. Balfour supplied provisions for the Revolutionary Army. (RA, 4:61, fol. 3)

BARCLAY, MARY HOOPS   PA
of Morrisville, Bucks County. She was the wife of Thomas Barclay (1728-1793). Their house was about half a mile from the Delaware River opposite Trenton. Gen. Washington made his headquarters there on December 7, 1776, and the next morning crossed the Delaware, then returned. His headquarters were at the Barclay home until December 14. Mr. Barclay was an Irishman by birth, and one of the original members of the Friendly Sons of Saint Patrick and its president from June 17, 1779, until June 17, 1781. Later it was called the Hibernian Society. In November 1791 the property known as the "Summer Seat" was purchased by Robert Morris, financier of the Revolution. (BI)

BARKER, PENELOPE PAGETT   NC
of Edenton. Previously she was married first to John Hodgson and and then to James Craven, and after their respective deaths she married Thomas Barker, an attorney. On October 24, 1774, in the home of Elizabeth King, the women of Edenton drew up a document supporting the Resolutions of the First Provincial Congress of North Carolina, which prohibited the importing of British manufactured goods, including tea. Forty-eight women, led by Penelope Barker, signed this resolution. This was a patriotic act.
    During the Revolutionary War the British marched into Edenton and attempted to steal Mrs. Barker's carriage horses from the stable. She took her husband's sword from the wall, went outside, and cut the reins held by the soldiers. An officer in charge, admiring her courage, let her lead her horses back into the stable. Mrs. Barker's home on South Broad Street in Edenton is open to the public. On Courthouse Square, a large bronze teapot has been mounted atop a Revolutionary War cannon. (CP; DR)

BARNETT, ANN SPRATT   NC
of Mecklenburg County. She was the daughter of Thomas Spratt.
Ann married John Barnett (1717-1804). Their daughter, Mary,
married Capt. James Jack, the bearer of the Mecklenburg Declaration of Independence to the Continental Congress. After the British
captured Charleston, South Carolina, on May 12, 1780, men, women,
and children fled the city into the countryside of South Carolina
and into North Carolina. Mrs. Barnett established a camp at Clem's
Branch, making clothing and preparing food for the hundreds of
refugees, including many soldiers, who came there.
    The British and Tories attacked the home of Gen. Thomas
Sumter, the "Game Cock of the Carolinas," in an attempt to capture
the general, but he escaped. His wife, Mary Canty Sumter, an
invalid, was left behind. Gen. Sumter returned for his wife and
their son, and the three fled with their housekeeper, Nancy Davis,
for North Carolina. Ann Barnett took in the party, including Mrs.
Sumter on a featherbed atop a horse led by the housekeeper. The
Sumters stayed a month with the Barnetts.
    After the Battle of Waxhaws, the wounded were brought to
the Barnett's house, fed, and cared for by Mrs. Barnett and her
daughter, afterward Mrs. George W. Smart. One of the soldiers
who stopped by was Andrew Jackson. (GP, vol. 2)

BARRY, MARGARET CATHERINE MOORE   SC
of Walnut Grove. She was born in 1752 in North Carolina, the
first of ten children of Mary and Charles Moore. At the age of
fifteen she married Capt. Andrew Barry, an elder in the Nazareth
Presbyterian Church. "Kate" and Andrew settled across the Tyger
River about two miles from Walnut Grove in Spartanburg County.
They had five sons and six daughters. During the Revolutionary
War, Kate acted as a volunteer scout and guide for the patriots
of the South Carolina Piedmont area.
    After Gen. Gates's defeat by the British at Camden and Bu-
ford's loss at Waxhaws, Gen. Greene called upon Gen. Daniel Morgan to gather the defeated patriots together. As a scout for Gen.
Morgan, Kate Barry rounded up the men and sent them to Gen.
Morgan, who won the Battle of Cowpens on January 17, 1781.
    Before the battle, Kate Barry warned her neighbors of the
impending attack by riding through the countryside. She was
called the Heroine of the Battle of Cowpens. Kate died on September 29, 1823, and was buried in Walnut Grove. Kate is listed as
a patriot in the DAR Patriot Index and there is a Kate Barry Chapter of the Daughters of the American Revolution in South Carolina.
(HS; Mary Montgomery Miller, "Kate Barry," DAR Magazine, November 1984; submitted by Joy Alexander Ansley, Oklahoma City, OK;
DAR)

BARTLETT, MARY BARTLETT   NH
of Kingston. The daughter of Joseph Bartlett of Newton, New
Hampshire, she was born in 1729, one of ten children. In January
1754 she married her cousin, Dr. Josiah Bartlett, and they had

II: SELECTED BIOGRAPHIES

twelve children, of whom eight reached maturity. Three of her sons became physicians. In 1774 Dr. Bartlett was elected a member of the Continental Congress and was a signer of the Declaration of Independence. As a result, Governor Wentworth revoked Bartlett's commission as a colonel of militia, and the Tories set fire to the Bartlett homestead, which burned to the ground.

Mrs. Bartlett and her children lived on their little farm while Dr. Bartlett rebuilt a mansion on the grounds of his burned home. In July 1789 Mrs. Bartlett died in Kingston, while her husband was chief justice of New Hampshire. From 1790 to 1793 he served as president of New Hampshire, and then as governor. (GP)

BARTON, MARGARET GALBRAITH   WV
near Wadestown. She was born on January 24, 1752, near Winchester, Virginia, and married Roger Barton (1747-1822). In 1772 they settled on the Middle Ford of Dunkard Creek in the Monongalia Valley. In August 1772 the noted Tory, Simon Girty, visited Fort Pitt (Pittsburgh) under a pretext of raising men to fight the Indians, but on August 25 it was learned that Girty had spoken at Cheat River to a group of Tories to raise an army against the American rebels. Meanwhile the American Col. Zackquill Morgan and his men had gone to Fort Statler on Dunkard Creek, about twelve miles from the Barton's home. When Margaret Barton learned about a possible Tory attack in 1777, she got on her horse and rode at night to warn the Americans. The exact date and destination of her ride are unknown, but a government citation signed by Gen. T. C. Ainsworth, after mentioning Roger's services in the Revolution, adds: "Margaret Galbraith, wife of Roger Barton, also rendered an act of special service in the war by going at night with some danger to herself to warn a body of patriots of the approach of a number of Tories who were serving the British by betraying the whereabouts of their neighbors and others in the patriotic cause. They were thus able to disappoint the plans."

After the Revolution the family moved to Tennessee. (Information furnished by Annie Barton McFall Armstrong of Columbia, TN, a descendant, to Dr. Earl Core, Mason-Dixiland Panorama, January 4, 1976) The Bartons had two sons. Their son Hugh and Mary Shirley Barton were the parents of twelve children. Margaret Barton died on June 24, 1828. (Submitted by Sue Malone Vardaman, Birmingham, AL)

BASSETT, ANNE MARIE DANDRIDGE   VA
of Eltham, near Buffins Ferry. She was the sister of Martha Washington and the wife of Col. Burwell Bassett (1734-1793). John Parke Custis, the only son of Mrs. Washington, was seized with an attack of typhus and taken to Eltham. Washington was there on November 5, 1781, and was present at the death of his stepson. Washington had planned to journey to Philadelphia after the battle of Yorktown, but instead stayed at the home of Mrs. Bassett until November 9 and then returned to Mount Vernon. (BI; FW)

BEAM, MRS. WILLIAM   TN
was captured by the Cherokee Indians and was saved by Princess
Nanye'hi (see Nancy Ward), high priestess of the Cherokees, according to a plaque erected by the Tennessee and Polk County
American Revolution Bicentennial Commission in 1976.

BECKEL, LIESEL   PA
of Bethlehem was a Moravian sister. In the autumn of 1777, under
her careful nursing, the Marquis de Lafayette recovered from the
wound he received at the Battle of Brandywine. (BI)

BEDFORD, MERCY RAYMOND   NC
of Rutherford County. She was born on June 3, 1740, in Middleboro, Massachusetts, the daughter of Christianna MacHaan (or
McKahan) and Peter Raymond. About 1755 she married Jonas Bedford, Sr., of Elizabethtown (now Elizabeth), New Jersey. Sometime
later the family moved to North Carolina.
    Mercy was a patriot, but her husband was loyal to the Crown
and served with the British at Bedford Hill and King's Mountain
and in Charleston, South Carolina. After Whig partisans raided
her farm in Rutherford County, Mercy and her children were forced
to flee to Charleston. When the British evacuated Charleston on
December 14, 1782, Jonas went with them to England and Mercy
returned to her farm with the children in an attempt to recover
the Bedford property.
    During 1783/84 Mercy and her son Raymond Bishop furnished
supplies for the American Patriots. (Accounts of U.S. with North
Carolina, War of the Revolution, A:245, no. 370847) On December
29, 1785, the General Assembly of North Carolina restored the
Bedford lands to Mercy Bedford and her heirs. (State Records of
North Carolina, 24:761-62) Jonas returned from England in 1786/87,
but the lands were not restored to him. He is listed as an elderly
man, not the head of household, in the home of his son-in-law,
David Lyles, in the census of 1820.
    While her husband was a Loyalist, Mercy and her son furnished supplies for the American army and for her patriotism her
lands were restored to her. (Submitted by Carolyn M. Backstrom,
Gautier, MS)

BEEKMAN, CORNELIA VAN CORTLANDT   NY
of Van Cortlandtville (Peekskill). She was the daughter of Joanna
Livingston and Lieutenant Governor Pierre Van Cortlandt, who
served from 1777 to 1795. The Van Cortlandt mansion was called
the Upper Manor House. The original Manor House near the Croton
River was in an area in Westchester County ravaged by the British
and Tories, so Van Cortlandt built his mansion in a more secure
area. Cornelia married Gerard Beekman in 1769 when she was
only sixteen.
    Gen. Washington left White Plains on the morning of November
10, 1776, arrived in Peekskill at sunset, and established his headquarters at the Van Cortlandt house. Cornelia was hostess for her

father. The next day Gen. Washington, together with generals Heath, Lord Stirling (William Alexander), James and George Clinton, and Mifflin inspected the fortifications at Fort Montgomery. On November 12, Washington and his staff left Peekskill and crossed the Hudson River at Verplanck's Point headed for the "Jersies."
After he left his headquarters at West Point, Gen. Washington spent the night of November 29, 1779, in Peekskill. On his trip from Providence, Rhode Island, to Philadelphia, Gen. Washington again had his headquarters at the Van Cortlandt Manor House from June 25 to July 2, 1781, inspecting defenses and reviewing his troops. On June 29 Claude Blanchard, commissary general of the French army in America wrote in his Journal:

> On the road, I met General Washington, who was going to review a part of his troops. He recognized me, stopped and invited me to dine with him at three o'clock. I repaired thither; there were twenty-five covers used by some officers of the army and a lady to whom the house belonged, in which the General lodged. One of the aides-de-camp did the honors. The table was served in the American style and pretty abundantly; vegetables, roast beef, lamb, chicken, salad dressed with nothing but vinegar, green peas, puddings and some pie, a kind of tart, greatly used in England and among the Americans, all this being put upon the table at the same time. They gave us on the same plate beef, green peas, lamb, etc.

On July 2 Washington left the Manor House with his troops for Valentine's Hill (now in Yonkers). From August 31 to October 24, 1782, Washington was at Verplanck's Point, where he met with the Comte de Rochambeau, and the two men reviewed the troops. During this time Gen. Washington made several visits to the Beekman's house to spend the night. "Mrs. Beekman allowed no hands but her own to make his bed and arrange his room, which, for fear of surprise, was a secluded one." (Mrs. Pierre E. Van Cortlandt in Scharf, History of Westchester County, 2:431)
    A tablet was erected on the Van Cortlandt House on January 19, 1904, by the Daughters of the American Revolution, and the Washington Room in the house was furnished by the Van Cortlandt Chapter, Daughters of the American Revolution, on June 25, 1932. (Evening Star, Peekskill, February 21, 1947, and February 21, 1952; Barbara Zimmer, Field Library, Peekskill, NY)
    Cornelia was born in 1752. After the war, the Beekmans moved to Tarrytown, where Cornelia died in 1847.

BELL, MARTHA McFARLAND   NC
of Randleman, Randolph County. She was born on September 9, 1735, in Orange County. In 1759 she became the second wife of Col. John McGee, a widower with two children. Martha and John had a farm and a gristmill on Muddy Creek, near the junction of Deep River, about two miles from Randleman. The mill was

demolished in 1967 to build the Randleman dam and reservoir. John
and Martha had three sons and two daughters. He died in 1773,
leaving Martha the richest widow in that frontier region. On May 6,
1779, Mattie McGee married William Bell, who then operated the
mill. Mattie served as a nurse and midwife for the countryside.

After the Battle of Guilford Courthouse on March 15, 1781,
Lord Cornwallis spent two days at Bell's Mill. She extracted a
promise from him that he would not harm her home while a guest
there. After Lord Cornwallis left Bell's Mill, Gen. Harry Lee arrived, and Martha acted as his guide, as she was well acquainted
with the countryside. As a nurse and a spy, she was able to
penetrate enemy lines and report on troop movements to Gen. Lee.

Martha Bell was a founder of the Old Methodist Church. Two
of her sons were ministers: John a Methodist and William a Presbyterian. She died on September 9, 1820. Martha and her husband
were buried in the Bell-Welborn graveyard near New Market School
in Randolph County. Martha supplied provisions during the war.
(RA, 4:90, fol. 5)

The Alexander Martin Chapter of the Daughters of the American Revolution placed a marker at the site of the Battle of Guilford
Courthouse in 1929 which reads: "Loyal Whig, Enthusiastic Patriot,
Revolutionary Heroine." (William S. Powell, Dictionary of North
Carolina; submitted by Mildred G. Bryan, Hattieville, AR)

BEND, ELIZABETH   NY
was the wife of Grove Bend. In June 1776 she made flags for
the regiments of the New York Line. (FH)

BENEZET, JOYCE MARRIOTT   PA
of Philadelphia. The daughter of Mary and Samuel Marriott of
Burlington, New Jersey, in 1736 she married Anthony Benezet of
Wilmington, Delaware. In 1742 they moved to Philadelphia. In
1755 he established a girls' school there. In 1766 they moved to
Burlington, New Jersey, but returned to Philadelphia in 1768, where
they resided at 918 Locust Street. From 1781 until his death in
1784, Mr. Benezet taught at a Negro school in Philadelphia.

Mrs. Benezet was active in the ladies' assocation and collected
money to aid the American soldiers. (Pennsylvania Gazette, June
12, 1780)

BENJAMIN, SARAH MARY MATTHEWS   NY
of Port Jervis. She was born in 1756 in Blooming Grove, Orange
County, New York. About 1763 the family moved to land on the
Bushkill River between Pike and Monroe counties, near Port Jervis.
Sarah married William Read (Reid), who died during an early Revolutionary War battle. In January 1780 she married Aaron Osborn
who served under Capt. Gregg at West Point. Sarah was a camp
follower and washed clothes for the soldiers. She was with the
soldiers at Kingsbridge and wore her husband's coat and carried
his gun while her husband was loading cannons.

When Washington moved his army to Philadelphia in August

II: SELECTED BIOGRAPHIES

1781, Sarah went along and baked bread for the soldiers. Then the army marched to Baltimore, and some boarded vessels and sailed down the Chesapeake Bay to the James River. Then they marched to Williamsburg, and Sarah went along. She cooked meals for the soldiers and did their wash.

Sarah was there when the British soldiers surrendered their arms at Yorktown. The British musicians played a melancholy tune with their instruments draped with black ribbons, according to her report.

After the battle Sarah and Aaron Osborn went with the commissary wagons to Pompton Lakes, New Jersey, for the winter of 1781/82. In the spring of 1782 they went to West Point and then to New Windsor where the men of the Continental Army were discharged in June 1783. Sarah had a son and a daughter, but then her husband deserted her.

In April 1787 at White Lake, New York, Sarah married John Benjamin, and they had one son and two daughters. Sarah died on April 26, 1858, aged 101 years and 5 months. (LV; DAR Magazine, November 1984)

BERRIEN, MARGARET EATON   NJ
of Rocky Hill, Somerset County. She lost property to the British army. (CDB, p. 162) Margaret was the widow of Judge John Berrien. Her home was near Princeton, and Gen. Washington had his headquarters there from August 25 to November 9, 1783. Washington attended the annual commencement exercises of the College of New Jersey (now Princeton University) on September 24, 1783. (BI) Mrs. Berrien died in 1819 at age ninety-five.

BIDDLE, MARY RICHARDSON   PA
of Philadelphia. She was the wife of Col. Clement Biddle and was a camp follower. She was a good friend of Mrs. Greene, Mrs. Knox, and Mrs. Washington. While Gen. Washington was encamped near the Brandywine River in the summer of 1777, some foragers stole food from the camp during the night. When this was discovered the next morning, Gen. Washington ordered some officers and men to pursue the thieves. Realizing that the troops would be hungry upon their return, Mrs. Biddle sent her servant to buy provisions. Upon the return of the servant, Mrs. Biddle cooked a large meal for the troops. (CD)

BIDDLE, MARY SCULL   PA
of Philadelphia. She married William Biddle of an old aristocratic family. Their son, Nicholas Biddle, was born in Philadelphia on September 10, 1750. At the age of thirteen he went to sea. In 1772 he decided to join the Royal Navy, and went to London where he became a midshipman on the sloop of war Portland, commanded by Capt. Sterling, who later became an admiral. In 1773 Biddle left the Royal Navy and joined the polar expedition of the Royal Geographical Society. On this expedition he became friends with young Horatio Nelson, who later became England's greatest naval hero.

Upon his return to America, Biddle was given command of the galley Franklin, outfitted by the Pennsylvania Committee of Safety on August 1, 1775. On December 22, 1775, he was commissioned a captain by the Continental Congress and given command of the fourteen-gun brig Andrea Doria with a crew of 130 men. He was ordered to join the squadron of Commo. Esek Hopkins, who commanded eight vessels. Hopkins's flagship was the Alfred.

The squadron sailed from the Delaware Bay on February 17, 1776, with orders to attack enemy vessels off the coast of Virginia and the Carolinas. But Commo. Hopkins changed his mind and decided to attack Fort Nassau on New Providence Island in the Bahamas because of the cannons and the gunpowder stored at the fort. Maj. Samuel Nicholas (or Nichols), with 220 marines, and Lt. Thomas Weaver with 50 men staged a surprise attack on forts Montague and Nassau and were successful in seizing seventy-one cannons, fifteen brass mortars, and twenty-four barrels of gunpowder.

Capt. Nicholas Biddle continued to cruise on the Andrea Doria and captured several British vessels carrying arms and gunpowder, which became of great value to the Americans. Biddle also captured two armed vessels transporting four hundred Scottish Highlanders bound for Boston for the British army. On February 1, 1777, Biddle sailed from Philadelphia to Charleston, South Carolina, in command of the thirty-two-gun ship Randolph. He then cruised the West Indies and captured HMS True Britain with twenty guns, together with three merchant vessels, and took them into the Charleston Harbor. Biddle became engaged to a Charleston lady, but never had the opportunity to marry. He sailed out of Charleston Harbor on the Randolph accompanied by four smaller vessels. On March 7, 1776, they encountered the sixty-four-gun British frigate Yarmouth. A cannonball struck the powder magazine of the Randolph and exploded. Biddle was killed instantly. Of the 315 men on the Randolph, only 4 seamen were saved.

Mary Biddle suffered the supreme sacrifice by losing her son. (CN)

BIRDSALL, HANNAH MANDEVILLE   NY
of Peekskill. She was born on November 7, 1737, the daughter of Cornelius Mandeville. On December 20, 1757, Hannah married Daniel Birdsall, a merchant who had a store on the riverfront at Travis Landing, later called Birdsall's Landing. During the Revolutionary War, Mr. Birdsall was chairman of the Peekskill Committee of Safety. They had one son and four daughters. The Birdsall House was on North Street (now Main Street).

During the Revolutionary War the Birdsalls kept what was known as open house for officers and prominent citizens, whom they entertained. After he left his headquarters at the home of Hester Schuyler Dey in Preakness (Paterson, New Jersey), on July 29, 1780, Gen. Washington established his headquarters in the Birdsall house from August 1 to 5. On August 1, Washington wrote to the Marquis de Lafayette:

II: SELECTED BIOGRAPHIES

"We are thus far, my dear Marquis, on our way to New York. Tomorrow the whole army was to have taken up its line of march, and would have moved with all the rapidity in our power to see this object, but we not a few hours since received advice from the Sound, dated yesterday, that the fleet of transports [of the enemy] had put back, and were steering Westward." (BI)

Benedict Arnold met with Gen. Washington at the Birdsall house on August 3. Since Gen. Arnold had been wounded in battle, Gen. Washington gave Arnold command of West Point.

After Gen. Washington crossed the Hudson at King's Ferry on August 18, 1780, he met with Gen. Arnold, and the two men spent the night in Peekskill. Arnold then returned to the Robinson house, which the Americans had confiscated since Robinson was a noted Tory. On September 23 Major André was captured at Tarrytown and taken to Tappan. Washington returned to the Robinson house on September 25, 1780, after he learned of Gen. Arnold's treason.

General Washington visited the Birdsalls again in 1783 after the war had ended. Hannah Birdsall died on April 4, 1813. The Birdsall house was torn down in 1853.

The Friendly Town Association on December 19, 1931, erected a bronze tablet on the Meyer Building on Main Street in Peekskill marking the site of the Birdsall house where Washington stayed. (Evening Star, Peekskill, February 21, 1951; Barbara Zimmer, Field Library, Peekskill, NY)

BISHOP, RACHEL RUGGLES   VT
of Monkton. The daughter of Rachel Tolles and Joseph Ruggles, she was born on July 7, 1732, in New Haven, Connecticut. On January 1, 1751, she married John Bishop in New Haven. They had five sons and five daughters. About 1752 they moved to New Milford, Connecticut, and sometime after 1765 to Monkton.

John was a soldier in the Revolutionary War, and in 1778 the British and Indians attacked their farm. Their house was burned, and John and his sons John Jr. and Timothy were captured by the enemy. While the family was being attacked, Rachel repelled the Indians from burning her hay and wheat stacks by having a kettle of hot water handy, which she tossed at the Indians, who then fled.

Rachel's third son, Elijah, feigned a limp and was not taken prisoner. He was only fifteen years old and had managed to hide a rifle. After the British and Indians left, Rachel and Elijah built a crude shelter around a stump. They pounded the grain from the unburned stacks on the top of the stump. Elijah shot game with his rifle and the bullets he had hidden to provide food throughout the winter. There was also a horse the Indians did not see and had failed to take away. In the spring Rachel loaded the horse with the small children and proceeded to the nearest settlement, Castleton, which was about sixty miles away. (The American Historical Society 15 (1924):33; History of Monkton, Vermont, 1734-61; Bishop Family in America, 1965)

Elijah enlisted at sixteen and served throughout the war.

John Bishop and his sons John Jr. and Timothy were finally exchanged at Skeensboro (now Whitehall), New York. In 1786 Elijah married Tabitha Holcombe and they had three sons and two daughters. After his wife's death, Elijah in 1818 married Hannah Bugg. (Submitted by Barbara J. Blaylock-Marek, Eagan, MN)

BLAIR, SUSAN SHIPPEN   PA
of Philadelphia. She was the wife of the Rev. Samuel Blair of Germantown, a chaplain in the Continental Army. Mrs. Blair was a member of the ladies' association for the relief of the American soldiers, founded by Sarah De Berdt Reed. Upon the death of Mrs. Reed in September 1780, Mrs. Blair and Mrs. Bache, together with three other women, took over the management of the association. With their own money they purchased material and made shirts for the American soldiers. (Pennsylvania Gazette, June 12, 1780)

From his headquarters at New Windsor, New York, on December 22, 1780, Gen. Washington wrote to Mrs. Blair:

> Madam: I had the pleasure, a few days ago, of receiving your favor of the 8th: inst. I am to thank you, in behalf of the Army, for the trouble you have taken in prosecuting the very benevolent business begun by the late worthy and amiable Mrs. Reed. You will be good enough to deliver the shirts which are made to Colo. Miles Dy, Qr.M. Genl. in Philada. who will have my particular orders to forwd. them on to the Penna. line at Mors. Town and to this place. I have a sum of money which was sent to me by the Ladies of Trenton, and which I shall take the liberty of forwarding to you by the first safe opportunity, with a request to dispose of it in the same manner of the donation of the Ladies of Pennsylvania. My Compliments to Mr. Blair, whose indisposition I hope will be but of short continuance. (FW)

The ladies of Philadelphia made about two thousand shirts. (FW)

BLAUVELT, ANNA MARIA DE WINT   NY
of Tappan. The daughter of Antje Kermer and John De Wint, one of eight children, Anna Maria married Maj. Fredericus Blauvelt, and they had one daughter, Elizabeth. The Blauvelts lived with her parents, Mr. and Mrs. John De Wint. Elizabeth married Cornelius Mabie, the son of Casparus Mabie, and they had six children.

Gen. Washington had his headquarters at the De Wint house from August 9 to August 23, 1780. While here, on August 11, Washington wrote to Gen. Benedict Arnold: "We shall have occasion to throw up some small works at Dobbs Ferry, to secure the intended communication at that place."

Meanwhile, Gen. Arnold was plotting with Maj. John André, adjutant general to the British general, Sir Henry Clinton, to turn

II: SELECTED BIOGRAPHIES   29

West Point over to the British. On September 23, 1780, Maj. André was captured at Tarrytown, and taken to Tappan on the twenty-eighth, where he was held in the Casparus Mabie house, later called the "Old Stone Tavern" (after 1800) and now called the "'76 Stone House."

Gen. Washington arrived at the De Wint house on September 28 and ordered a court-martial of Maj. André, who was hanged on October 2, 1780. Washington had his headquarters there from September 28 to October 7, 1780. On September 30, while at the Mabie Stone House, Washington signed Maj. André's death warrant. The house is still standing and open to the public.

Gen. Washington again had his headquarters at the De Wint house from May 4 to May 8, 1783. After the general left Princeton, New Jersey, he made his fourth visit to the De Wint house in Tappan, from November 10 to November 13, 1783.

While Gen. Washington referred to his headquarters as the De Wint house, all local historians write that the actual hostess was Anna Maria De Wint Blauvelt. (Wilfred Blanch Tallman, How Things Began in Rockland County, 1977; A Chronicle of Major André at Tappan, Tappentown Historical Society, 1980; submitted by Sally Dewey, Tappan, NY) In 1966 the De Wint house was designated a National Historic Landmark.

BLEDSOE, KATHERINE MONTGOMERY   NC, KY, TN
was the daughter of Margaret and Robert Montgomery of Virginia. Katherine Montgomery on one occasion carried messages to Gen. Washington, riding horseback through the woods. Her descendants have a letter from Washington thanking her for her services. Katherine married Maj. Isaac Bledsoe (ca. 1735-1793) of North Carolina, and they were pioneer settlers of Kentucky and Tennessee. A chapter of the Daughters of the American Revolution in Washington, D.C., is named the Katherine Montgomery Chapter. (GP)

BLEWER, MRS. JOSEPH   PA
of Philadelphia. Her husband was a captain in the Philadelphia militia. Lt. Col. George Baylor was sent from camp to escort Martha Washington to Gen. Washington's headquarters at Cambridge, Massachusetts, and Capt. Blewer sent Washington's request to the Continental Congress and a letter to President Joseph Reed of Pennsylvania on November 28, 1775. Mrs. Washington arrived at Cambridge on December 11. With her were Mrs. Horatio Gates, Mr. and Mrs. John Park Custis, and Mr. and Mrs. Warren Lewis. (FW)

Mrs. Blewer was an active member of the ladies' association for the benefit and welfare of the American soldiers. (Pennsylvania Gazette, June 12, 1780)

BLOOMFIELD, MARY McILVAINE   NJ
of Burlington. The daughter of Dr. William McIlvaine, on December 17, 1778, she married Joseph Bloomfield of Woodbridge, New Jersey. He served as a major and judge advocate in the northern Continental Army. Mrs. Bloomfield was active in the ladies' relief

association for the welfare of the American soldiers. (New Jersey Gazette, July 4, 1780) She died in 1818.

BOLLING, MARY MARSHALL   VA
of Petersburg. She was born in 1737/38, and was married to Robert Bolling. When the British attacked Virginia in 1780, they occupied her home and placed her under arrest. Her horses were taken and her tobacco crop was burned, but they spared her slaves. She died on February 24, 1814. (LV; DAR)

BOLLING, SUSANNA   VA
of Hopewell, formerly City Point. She was born on December 5, 1764, the daughter of Susanna Bolling and Alexander Bolling, who were first cousins. They lived at "Mitchells," Prince George County, and had twelve children.

    One night in 1781, Lord Cornwallis took over the Bolling house to quarter his officers, and the sixteen-year-old Susanna came face to face with British soldiers. After Susanna heard the officers discussing a plan to attack the troops of the Marquis de Lafayette, she escaped from the house through a tunnel which had been designed for use in case of Indian raids. The tunnel led to the Appomattox River. At this point the Bollings had a small boat, and Susanna rowed across the river to a farmhouse. She awakened the farmer and borrowed a horse from him. From there she rode to Half Way House, the headquarters of Lafayette. Susanna was taken to Lafayette himself, and told him about the plans of Lord Cornwallis. Lafayette was thus prepared to evade the British troops and to warn Gen. Washington of the enemy's plans, which resulted in the defeat of Cornwallis at Yorktown. (Information from Frances Pollard, Pattie J. Scott, and Ted Polk, all of Richmond, VA)

BOONE, REBECCA BRYAN   KY
of Boonesborough. She was born on January 9, 1739. In 1756 she married Daniel Boone (1734-1820), who was born near Reading, Pennsylvania, and later settled in North Carolina. In March 1775 Daniel Boone led a party of settlers to Kentucky. From March 22 to April 14, Boone and his party constructed a fort, afterward called Boonesborough. In June his wife and daughters joined him, and in September Mrs. Denton, Mrs. Ray, Mrs. McGary, and Mrs. Hogan, with their husbands and children, settled at Harrodsburg. Early in the spring of 1776 Elizabeth Calloway, her husband Col. Richard Calloway, and her children settled in Boonesborough. While Rebecca's daughter, also named Rebecca, and Elizabeth's daughters, Betsey and Frances, were playing outside the fort, they were carried away by Indians. The men heard the girls screaming, followed the Indians, and finally rescued the girls.

    On April 15, 1776, the Indians attacked the fort, and again on July 4, but were repulsed. On February 7, 1778, while on a trip to Blue Licks to make salt for the garrison, Boone and twenty-seven of his men were captured by Indians and taken to Chillicothe

II: SELECTED BIOGRAPHIES

(now in Ohio), where he remained a prisoner until June 16, 1778, when Boone escaped. Meanwhile Rebecca Boone, fearing that her husband had been killed, returned to North Carolina with the children. The British and Indians attacked the fort on August 8, 1778, and after several days they retreated.

That fall Boone went back to North Carolina for his family, and in the summer of 1780 they all returned to live at Boonesborough. But in October, Daniel and his brother, Squire Boone, returned to Blue Licks for salt and were attacked by Indians. Daniel escaped, but he saw the Indians shoot and scalp his brother before his very eyes.

At the disastrous Battle of Blue Licks on August 19, 1782, sixty Americans were killed and seven taken prisoner by the Indians. Boone witnessed the death of his youngest son, but Boone himself managed to escape again. He had nine lives!

Boone had gone to Kentucky in March 1775 as an agent for Col. Richard Henderson and had purchased land from the Indians for Henderson. But then the State of Virginia repudiated all his land titles, so in the spring of 1780 Boone returned eastward and collected twenty thousand dollars for new land warrants, but on his way back to Boone's Station he was robbed of the entire amount. Although later Boone acquired many tracts of land, his claims were ruled invalid, and in 1785 Boone lost all his holdings.

Boone left Kentucky in 1785 and settled in Point Pleasant, now in West Virginia. He was appointed lieutenant colonel of Kanawha County in 1789. Boone then moved to Missouri about 1798, but again had his new holdings of land voided by the land commissioners.

Rebecca Boone died on March 18, 1813. She suffered through his capture by Indians and the loss of all his property in Kentucky and Missouri. But finally, in February 1814, after many delays, Congress confirmed Boone's land titles. Boone died on September 26, 1820, at the home of his son, Nathan. Mrs. Boone was named as a patriot in the DAR Patriot Index. (CH; DAR; DB)

Rebecca's son James (b. 1757) was killed by Indians in Kentucky in 1776. Her son Israel (b. 1759) was killed at the Battle of Blue Licks in 1782. Her daughter Susannah (1760-1800) married William Hays, Sr. Jemima (1762-1834) married Flanders Calloway at Boonesborough. Livinia (1766-1802) married Joseph Scholl. Rebecca (1768-1805) married Philip Goe in 1788. Daniel Morgan Boone (1769-1839) married Sarah Griffin Lewis. Jesse Bryan Boone (1733-1820) married Chloe Van Bibber in 1790. William (b. 1775) died young. Nathan (1781-1856) married Oliver Van Bibber in 1799. (Submitted by Katherine Blaylock, Winston-Salem, NC)

BOONE, SARAH DAY   KY
of Boone's Station. She was born in 1734 and in 1748 married Samuel Boone, brother of the famous frontiersman, Daniel Boone. A well-educated Quaker, she taught her brother-in-law, Daniel Boone, how to read. They lived on the Congree River, Camden District, South Carolina, but in 1779 they moved to Kentucky and settled at Boone's Station in Fayette County. She had four sons

and five daughters. Her son Thomas was killed in August 1782
at the Battle of Blue Licks in Kentucky.
   Sarah's daughter Mary married Leonard K. Bradley, who
was captured on May 12, 1780, when the British took Charleston,
South Carolina. He disregarded his parole by reentering the service and fighting until the end of the war. Sarah Boone died in
1819 at the home of her daughter and son-in-law, Mr. and Mrs.
Leonard K. Bradley in Missouri. (Submitted by Katherine D. Blaylock, Winston-Salem, NC) Mrs. Boone is listed as a patriot in
the DAR Patriot Index. (DAR)

BOONE, SARAH MORGAN   KY
of Boonesborough. The daughter of Edward Morgan, she was born
in 1701. On October 4, 1720, she married Squire Boone (1696-
1765) in the Gwynedd Meeting House, Berks County, Pennsylvania.
About 1750 they moved to North Carolina. She had seven sons
and five daughters. One of their sons was Col. Daniel Boone, the
famous frontiersman. On July 11, 1754, Squire Boone was licensed
to operate a public house on his plantation.
   In January 1778 Daniel Boone and some men from the forts
around traveled to the Blue Licks at the Licking River to make
salt for the forts. Daniel and some other men were captured by
Indians. Later he escaped and warned the settlers of an impending Indian attack.
   Sarah's youngest daughter, Hannah (1746-1808), married
John Stewart in 1765. He was killed by Indians in Kentucky in
1770. Her daughter Mary (1736-1819) married William Bryan, who
was wounded by Indians and died about a week later, on May 30,
1780. Her son Edward (1740-1780) was killed by Indians at Blue
Licks on October 6, 1780. Her eldest daughter Sarah (1734-1815)
married John Wilcoxsen, who was killed by Indians in 1782 close to
Bryan's Station, Kentucky. Sarah Boone died in 1777 and was
buried in Jappa Cemetery, Mocksville, North Carolina. (Submitted
by Katherine Blaylock, Winston-Salem, NC)

BORDEN, ELIZABETH ROGERS   NJ
of Bordentown. She married Joseph Borden, who, with his father,
Joseph, founded the village of Bordentown in 1750. Elizabeth and
Joseph Borden had two daughters and one son. Her husband was
a member of the New Jersey Committee of Correspondence in 1774
and a member of the Council of War in 1775. He served as a colonel
in the Revolutionary War.
   During the war, Lord Cornwallis occupied the Borden home.
When he was about to leave, he told Mrs. Borden that if her husband and son would leave the American army and join the British
army, he would spare her home. But Mrs. Borden, a true patriot,
replied, "The application of a torch to my dwelling I should regard
as the signal of your departure." So Maj. Garden, who was in
attendance there, ordered her home to be burned. (CD)
   Mrs. Borden was a member of the ladies' relief association
for the welfare of the American soldiers. (New Jersey Gazette,

II: SELECTED BIOGRAPHIES

July 4, 1780). She was born in 1725 and died in 1807. (DAR)

BOUDINOT, CATHERINE SMITH   NJ
of Essex County. Her husband, Elisha Boudinot (1749-1819), was the younger brother of Elias Boudinot (1740-1821), who was the commissary-general of prisoners, a member of the Continental Congress (1777-1784) and the president of the Congress in 1782. In a letter to George Washington dated October 16, 1778, Lord Stirling (General William Alexander of the Continental Army), mentioned "a Grand Wedding of Miss Smith to Mr. Elisha Boudinot" at Elizabethtown (now Elizabeth), New Jersey. (FW)
    Mrs. Boudinot was active in the ladies' assocation for the benefit and welfare of the American soldiers. (New Jersey Gazette, July 4, 1780)

BOWEN, LILY McILHANEY   VA
of Augusta County. She was born in 1705 in Ireland, and about 1733 she married John Bowen, who was born in Pentoc, Wales. They had twelve children. Lily had five sons and one daughter-in-law who served in the Revolutionary War. (See Margaret Louisa Bowen, below)
    Lily McIlhaney Bowen is listed in the DAR Patriotic Index as having performed a public service during the Revolutionary War. Lily died in Washington County, Virginia, on April 1, 1780. Lily's son Lt. Hugh Rees Bowen was at the Battle of Point Pleasant with Capt. William Russell's company and was in command of volunteers from Washington County, Virginia, when he was killed at the Battle of King's Mountain on October 7, 1780. (Submitted by Frankie McNeil Stevens and her sister, Arraga McNeil Young, Wytheville, VA)

BOWEN, MARGARET LOUISA SMITH   VA
of Maiden Spring, Tazewell County. The daughter of Col. John Smith of Augusta County, Virginia, she was born about 1741. About 1756 she married Lt. Hugh Rees Bowen, the son of Lily McIlhaney and John Bowen in what is now Botetourt County, Virginia. She had eight children. About 1772 the Bowens settled on the Clinch River at Maiden Spring. To protect his family from attacks from Indians, Mr. Bowen built a strong stockade around his house. From this beginning, a larger and stronger fort was later erected near his home, which became the historical Maiden Spring Fort, into which surrounding neighbors gathered for safety from the frequent attacks by the Indians.

    About 1776 Rees Bowen and his neighbors went to intercept the Ohio Indians who were on the warpath and coming up Big Sandy toward Fort Maiden Spring. No men were left at the fort. Louise Smith Bowen, who was diminutive in physical stature but possessed a keen and resourceful brain and courage developed in the hardships of pioneer

life after the men had departed, went alone along the
foothills of Short Mountain to drive home the cows. While
passing over some marshy ground, she discovered fresh
moccasined footprints of Indians. She did not scream
or faint as many women reared in idleness, luxury, and
ease, would have done, but she continued on her way
and brought the cows to the milk gap. She informed
the women of the fort that they must all dress in men's
clothing and take their turn in marching around outside
of the palisade all night to deter the Indians from their
contemplated attack.

To her surprise, not one consented to thus expose
herself. The only one she had authority over was a large
negro woman whom she dressed in Mr. Bowen's clothes,
while she put on her son's clothes. She shouldered the
only gun left in the fort and had the negro shoulder a
large stick which looked like a gun. Armed with these
implements of war, they marched around the palisade all
night.

The military march terrorized the Indians and thus
prevented what would have been a massacre of all the
women and children in Maiden Spring Fort, for on the
day following the military display of Mrs. Bowen and her
colored lieutenant, remains of the campfire of the Indians
were found on the side of Short Mountain overlooking
the Fort. (Submitted by Frankie McNeil Stevens and Ar-
raga McNeil Young, Wytheville, VA)

Mrs. Bowen's husband, Lt. Hugh Rees Bowen, was killed
at the Battle of King's Mountain on October 7, 1780, and she had
several small children to raise. Mrs. Bowen died at Maiden Spring
on February 16, 1834. The Bowen farm remained in the family
into the twentieth century. (Detailed information is included in
John N. Harmon, Annals of Tazewell County, Virginia; and William
Pendleton, History of Tazewell County)

BOWEN, SARAH BROWN   RI
of Providence. Sarah was the wife of Col. Jabez Bowen. On his
trip from New Windsor, New York, to Providence, Gen. Washington
stopped at Fishkill, New York, Norwich, Connecticut, Newport and
Little Rest, Rhode Island, then had his headquarters in the home
of Mrs. Bowen from March 13 to March 15, 1781. On the evening
of March 14, Gen. Washington attended a military ball in Providence.
(BI)

BOWERS, MRS. DANIEL   MD
of New Germantown, Baltimore County. She made a cloth of buffalo
hair which her husband, Daniel Bowers, sent to Gen. Washington.
On May 28, 1779, Gen. Washington replied: "Your letter of the
26th of last month, accompanied by a piece of Cloth made of Buf-
faloes hair, and manufactured in your own family came safe to my

II: SELECTED BIOGRAPHIES

hands. For the flattering Sentiments contained in the letter, and for the novelty of the Cloth which you have been so obliging as to present me with the first fruits of, I thank you. I am highly sensible of these proofs of your approbation of my conduct, and thank you kindly for your good wishes." (FW)

BOWMAN, MARY HITE   VA
of Winchester. Mary was the daughter of Anna Maria DuBois and Capt. Joist Hite, who purchased a tract of some 4,000 acres in 1731 from John and Isaac Van Meter, which soon became Frederick County. In 1732 the Hites moved to his lands with sixteen other families and became the first settlers of the Shenandoah Valley. The Hites settled on the Opequon Creek, about five miles south of the present city of Winchester. Among their children were John, Jacob, Isaac Sr., and Mary.

In 1736 Thomas, Lord Fairfax, made his first trip to Virginia to determine the boundaries of lands granted to his ancestor, Lord Colepeper, by King Charles II. Lord Fairfax decided that the settlers in the Shenandoah Valley were within his grant and forced them to pay ground rent. But Hite refused to do so, and sued Lord Fairfax. The case was in the courts for fifty years and finally decided in favor of the Hite heirs in 1786. The new Lord Fairfax, George William, was represented by John Marshall (later chief justice) and the Hites by Edmund Randolph (attorney general under President Washington).

Anna Hite died in 1738, and in 1741 Joist Hite married Maria Magdelina Relict, the widow of Christian Neuschwanger (now Niswander).

At age sixteen, George Washington was hired by Lord Fairfax in 1748 to survey his lordship's lands, which Washington determined to be about five million acres. Washington kept a diary of his trip and recorded on Monday, April 11, 1748: "We Travell'd from Coddys down to Frederick Town [now Winchester] where we Reached about 12 o Clock. We dined in Town and then went to Capt. Hites and Lodged."

On October 23, 1750, Washington surveyed a tract of land (now Berryville) in Frederick County for Isaac Pennington which Pennington sold in 1754 to Gabriel Jones and John Hite, who built a home there. From 1756 to 1759 Washington, while in charge of frontier defenses, had his headquarters in Winchester. Joist Hite died in 1760. Washington often visited the Hites, and after he spent a night in John Hite's house, he wrote in a letter of June 1767 to Capt. John Posey stating that as he entered the bedroom he found livestock in his bed!

Jacob Hite's second wife was Mrs. Francis Madison Beale, an aunt of James Madison. Maj. Isaac Hite, Jr., married Nelly Conway Madison, a sister of James Madison. His sister, Sarah Hite, married Jonathan Clark, a brother of George Rogers Clark.

Mary Hite married George Bowman, whose brother, Abraham Bowman, married Sarah Henry, the sister of Patrick Henry. So Washington was well acquainted with the Bowman and Hite families

and visited them many times. (Washington Irving, Life of George Washington)
   Mary and George Bowman lived in Fort Bowman on Cedar Creek between Strasburg and Middletown in Frederick County. It was named Fort Bowman since many of the fortress-like houses were built to repel Indian attacks, which were an ever-present threat. Later it was called Harmony Hall, by which name it is known today. (Submitted by Geraldine Sanders Smith, Saint Louis, MO; and Rebecca A. Ebert, Handley Library, Winchester, VA)

BRADLEE, ANN DUNLAP   MA
of Boston. She was the wife of Nathaniel Bradlee (1746-1813). Ann Bradlee and her sister-in-law, Sarah Bradlee Fulton, put makeup on their husbands' faces so they could pretend to be Mohawk Indians before they dumped tea into Boston Harbor on December 16, 1773. (For details, see Sarah Fulton, below; GP)

BRATTON, MARTHA ROBINSON   SC
of Yorkville. She was born in Rowan County, North Carolina in 1750 and married Col. William Bratton, who resided in the York District of South Carolina. Before the fall of Charleston in May 1780, Governor Rutledge sent a supply of ammunition to all the American regiments, and Col. Bratton had his ammunition hidden on his property and he told his wife where he had hidden it. When the Loyalists learned of this, British troops were sent to the Bratton's property to seize the ammunition. When Mrs. Bratton learned the British troops were approaching her property, she laid a trail of powder to the spot where the ammunition lay, and then set fire to the trail, and it exploded.
   After the fall of Charleston to the British on May 12, 1780, British troops under Capt. Huck invaded the area of the York District and stopped at the home of Mrs. Bratton. They forced her to prepare dinner for the British officers, then they retired to another house to spend the night. Fortunately Col. Bratton arrived home with seventy-five men, and she warned him of the presence of British troops nearby. After the Americans defeated the British, Mrs. Bratton opened her house to care for the wounded, a patriotic act. She died in her residence about two miles from Yorkville in January 1816. (HS)

BRAXTON, ELIZABETH CORBIN   VA
of Elsing Green. She was the daughter of Richard Corbin, colonial receiver general. In May 1761 she became the second wife of Carter Braxton and bore him sixteen children. His first wife, Judith Robinson Braxton, whom he had married in 1755, died in childbirth in 1757, leaving him with two children, so the second Mrs. Braxton had eighteen children to raise.
   Mr. Braxton was a signer of the Declaration of Independence. They lived at Chericoke, a couple of miles northwest of Elsing Green. Braxton was a merchant, and he lost a fortune when his ships and cargo were seized by the British. When the British army

II: SELECTED BIOGRAPHIES

invaded Virginia in 1781, they burned the Braxton homestead, and he lost all his papers and furnishings. Meanwhile he had mortgaged his lands to pay for the captured ships and cargo, so the Braxtons lost their entire fortune.

Mrs. Braxton and her ten surviving children suffered for their patriotic views. (FG)

BRINCKERHOFF, GEERTIE WYCOFF   NY
of Fishkill. She was the wife of Col. Derick Brinckerhoff (1720-1789). Gen. Washington had his headquarters there on October 1, 1778. On this date, Washington wrote to Maj. Gen. John Sullivan: "I rec'd. yours of the 29th at this place to which I have removed for convenience of gaining intelligence of the Motions of the Enemy, who are out in considerable force on this side of Kingsbridge, and in Bergen County in Jersey. They seem to be foraging, in which they are busily employed." (DAR; FW)

On his return trip from Newport, Rhode Island, Gen. Washington was entertained at the home of the Brinckerhoffs on March 20, 1781. (FW)

BRINCKERHOFF, JANNETJIE VAN VOORHIES   NY
of Fishkill. She was the wife of Col. John Brinckerhoff (1701-1785), who was the uncle of Col. Derick Brinckerhoff. Gen. Washington spent October 1 to October 10, 1778, and had his headquarters at various times, between the two Brinckerhoffs. On October 8, 1778, Washington visited the army hospital in the Robinson house just below West Point and spoke to the soldiers in the various wards. Dr. Thatcher in his Military Journal wrote about Washington:

> The personal appearance of our Commander in Chief, is that of the perfect gentleman and accomplished warrior. He is remarkably tall, full six feet, erect and well proportioned.... The serenity of his countenance, and majestic gracefulness of his deportment, impart a strong impression of that dignity and grandeur, which are his peculiar characteristics, and no one can stand in his presence without feeling the ascendency of his mind, and associating with his countenance the idea of wisdom, philanthropy, magnanimity, and patriotism. There is a fine symmetry in the features of his face indicative of a benign and dignified spirit.... His uniform dress is a blue coat, with two brilliant epaulettes, buff colored under clothes, and a three cornered hat with a black cockade. He is constantly equipped with an elegant small sword, boots and spurs, in readiness to mount his noble charger. (BI)

BRINK, HUSELTY (URSULA)   WV
of Hampshire County. She married Huybert Brink, the son of Annetje Kuykendahl and Roelof Brink, who was born in Kingston, New York. They had six children. Huybert died in April 1778. On February 10, 1781, Huselty donated 433 pounds of flour, and

on January 5, 1782, she gave 250 pounds of beef and a fifth of a quarter for the army. (RW; submitted by Betty E. Johnson Jones Robinson, San Jose, CA)

BROADHEAD, ELIZABETH DEPUI   PA
of Reading. The daughter of Nicholas Depui, she was born in 1740. Elizabeth was married in 1776 to Lt. Col. David Broadhead of the 2nd Battalion of the Pennsylvania Regiment. On March 12, 1777, he was commissioned as a colonel of the 8th Regiment, Pennsylvania Line, and in January 1781 he was assigned to the 1st Regiment. On September 30, 1783, he was promoted to brigadier general.
    During the Revolutionary War, Mrs. Broadhead took care of wounded American soldiers who had returned home. With other women in Reading, she made clothing for the soldiers. Mrs. Broadhead died in Philadelphia in 1799. Later Gen. Broadhead married Rebecca, the widow of Gen. Thomas Mifflin. Broadhead died at Milford, Pennsylvania, in 1809. (EP)

BROOKS, SARAH BOONE   KY
of Bryan's Station. She was born in 1763 and married Thomas Brooks. When the Tories and Indians attacked on August 15, 1782, she was one of the women who went for water. Sarah is listed as a patriot in the DAR Patriot Index. Sarah later married David Montgomery. Her name is inscribed on the monument erected in 1896 by the Lexington, Kentucky, DAR.

BROWNLEA, ELIZABETH   PA
was captured with her daughter, Jane, aged one year and two months, at Mount Pleasant in July 1782 and taken to Montreal." On December 24, 1782, she was reported as "distressed sickly." (MR)

BRYAN, MARY BOONE   KY
of Bryan's Station. The daughter of Sarah Morgan and Squire Boone, Sr., she was born on November 3, 1736, in Berks County, Pennsylvania. She was the sister of the famous frontiersman, Daniel Boone. In 1755 she married William Bryan, son of Martha Strode and Morgan Bryan, of Rowan County, North Carolina.
    Mr. Bryan served as a private in the Revolutionary War and rose to the rank of captain. While on a hunting trip to get food for the fort, he was wounded by Indians, but returned to the stockade. The Americans won the battle with the Indians, but William Bryan died of his wounds about a week later, on May 30, 1780.
    Mrs. Bryan helped to defend Bryan's Station when the Tories and Indians attacked on August 15, 1782. Jemima Johnson, Polly Craig, and Mary Bryan led a group of women to the spring to get water for the fort when it was surrounded by Indians under the leadership of Capt. William Campbell and the renegade Simon Girty. By helping to defend the fort, she helped to halt the invasion of Kentucky by the British.

II: SELECTED BIOGRAPHIES

Mrs. Bryan had five sons and five daughters. Besides losing her husband, she also lost three sons--John, William Jr., and Abner --in Indian attacks. William Bryan, Jr., went to Blue Licks with a party of men to get salt. The fort could not keep the meat fresh without salt; the defense of the fort was crucial to the war effort. William Bryan, Jr., was killed at Blue Licks on March 9, 1780. Mary Bryan died on July 6, 1819, and is buried in Kentucky. She is recognized as a patriot in the DAR Patriot Index. (Submitted by Katherine D. Blaylock, Winston-Salem, NC) (DAR)

BULL, MARY PHILLIPS   PA
of Philadelphia. The daughter of James Phillips, she was born on August 3, 1731, in Chester County, Pennsylvania. On August 13, 1752, she married John Bull, and they had seven children. Bull was appointed a captain in the provincial service in 1758. In 1775 he was appointed a colonel in the 1st Pennsylvania Battalion and was a member of the Pennsylvania Constitutional Convention of July 15, 1776. In December 1777 he commanded the 2nd Brigade of the Pennsylvania militia and served in Philadelphia in 1778/79.

In 1777 Lord Howe seized their farm and told Mary, "Madam, if you will send or write to your husband and prevail upon him to join us, I will take you to England, present you to the king and queen. You shall have a pension and live in style." To which Mrs. Bull replied, "General, my husband would despise me, and I should despise myself if I did so." The Hessian troops gathered all the wheat they could and then burned the fields. Mrs. Bull also had to put out a fire in her cellar. Later the Bulls moved to Northumberland, Pennsylvania, where Mrs. Bull died on February 23, 1811. (EP)

BURD, SARAH SHIPPEN   PA
of Tinian, on the Susquehanna River, six miles below Harris Ferry. The daughter of Sarah Plumley and Edward Shippen, she was born on February 22, 1730/31 in Philadelphia. After she married James Burd in 1751, they settled in Shippensburg, Pennsylvania, later moving to their farm at Tinian. He served as an officer during the Colonial Wars and was promoted to colonel in 1757. He served as a colonel in Lancaster in 1775. He retired at age fifty-one to work on his farm.

The Burds lived on a large plantation with slaves who aided Mrs. Burd in making clothes for the soldiers. She also took care of the wounded men on their return home. Mrs. Burd died at Tinian on September 17, 1784, and was buried in Middletown in the Presbyterian cemetery there. (EP)

BURGIN, ELIZABETH   NY
operated an escape line for American prisoners of war from 1776 to 1779. (FH)

BURKE, MARY FREEMAN   NC
of Hillsborough. In 1770 she married Thomas Burke, an attorney. They lived on his estate, "Tyaquin." They had one daughter.

Mary's husband was a member of the North Carolina Congress,
1773-1776 and the Continental Congress, 1776-1781, when he was
elected governor of North Carolina in 1781. Burke was able to
rally the people, enlist soldiers, and obtain provisions for the army.
The Tories raided Hillsborough on September 12, 1781, and captured
Governor Burke. He was taken to Wilmington, North Carolina,
then to Sullivans Island, Charleston, South Carolina. Burke was
paroled to James Island, South Carolina, and managed to escape in
1782. This is another example of the suffering endured by the
patriotic American women. (DB)

BURNET, MARY CAMP   NJ
of Newark. The daughter of Nathaniel Camp, in 1754 she married
Dr. William Burnet of Elizabethtown (now Elizabeth), New Jersey.
They had eleven children. Her husband was chairman of the Committee of Safety of Essex County. On June 17, 1776, George Washington wrote to the committee:

> The absolute necessity of preventing all correspondence
> between the Inhabitants of this County and our Enemies,
> obliges me to every degree of intelligence, that lead to
> the Channel of such Intercourse. Doctor William Burnet
> of New Ark can inform you of certain Insinuations and
> charges against part of the Army under my Command,
> as if they were liable to bribery and Corruption, in permitting persons to go from Staten Island to the Men of
> War at or near Sandy Hook, and as the Person from whom
> he has received Intelligence, resides at New Ark, within
> the district of your Committee, I must request it, as a
> Matter of great importance, that your Committee will as
> soon as possible call on David Ogden, Esqur., to declare
> who the person was, who informed him, that he had engaged the guard of the Rifle men at Staten Island, to
> carry him on Board the Men of War; with all the circumstances within his knowledge; and also that you do call
> on the person whom he points out, to be his Informant,
> to declare every Circumstance within his knowledge, relative to the Matter.

Mary's husband was a delegate to the Continental Congress,
1776/77, and again in 1780. Mrs. Burnet was active in the ladies'
relief association for the welfare of the American soldiers while
they lived in Hunterdon County during the Revolution (New Jersey
Gazette, July 4, 1780) before returning to Newark. (FW; a photocopy of the newspaper of this date was supplied by Richard W.
Reeves, Trenton, NJ)

BURR, EUNICE DENNIE   CT
of Fairfield, was born in 1730. Eunice married Thaddeus Burr, a
member of the Constitutional Convention and of the Council of Safety. In 1779 Gen. Tryon and his troops burned Fairfield and her

II: SELECTED BIOGRAPHIES

home on the south side of the Old Post Road. She tried to stop him, but to no avail, and the pillage and burning continued. She died in 1805. The Fairfield chapter of the Daughters of the American Revolution is named in her honor. (CG; CAR 15:254)

BURR, THEODOSIA BARTOW   NJ

of Paramus. The daughter of Ann Stilwell and Theodosius Bartow, she was born in 1746. Theodosia married Frederick Prevost, the son of Maj. Gen. Augustine Prevost of the British army. But Mrs. Prevost was a rebel and was helpful in supplying information to the American forces during the British occupation of New Jersey. She had one son, Bartow Prevost.

After Gen. Washington had breakfast with the Dunhams in Piscataway, New Jersey on July 10, 1778, the general and his staff stopped by Passaic Falls for a picnic luncheon, then proceeded to Paramus and had his headquarters at the Hermitage, the home of Mrs. Prevost, until July 15. James McHenry, secretary to Gen. Washington, wrote in his diary: "We talked and walked and laughed and danced and gallanted the leisure hours of four days and nights" (George Washington in the American Revolution by James T. Flexner, p. 318). Washington then stayed at the home of William Smith, which was occupied by Col. and Mrs. Ann Hawks Hay, who was a sister of Mr. Smith.

Mrs. Prevost's husband died in 1782 and in July of that year in the old Paramus Church near Saddle River, Theodosia married Aaron Burr, who was ten years younger than she. They had a daughter, Theodosia Burr, born in Albany, New York, in 1783.

Burr killed Alexander Hamilton in a pistol duel in Weehawken, New Jersey, on July 11, 1804. Their daughter, Theodosia, married Joseph Alston in 1802. She died in 1813; meanwhile her mother had died also.

In July 1833, at age 77, Burr married Eliza Jumel, the wealthy widow of Stephen Jumel. In 1836 Eliza Burr charged her husband with adultery and sued for divorce. She was granted her divorce on September 14, 1836, the very day that Burr died at his home in Port Richmond, Staten Island, New York, at the age of eighty. (DR; FW)

BUSH, RUTH LYON   NY

of Port Chester (previously Sawpit). She was the daughter of Hannah and John Lyon, Sr., and a sister of Capt. Roger Lyon. Ruth married Abraham Bush (born 1720), and they lived in a house on King Street in Sawpit. According to tradition, her home was the headquarters of Gen. Israel Putnam on several occasions during the Revolutionary War. (Griffin, Westchester County and Its People, 1946).

The Bush homestead is located in John Lyon Park in Port Chester. The Ruth Lyon Chapter of the Daughters of the American Revolution is named in her honor and now maintains the house. (Submitted by George M. Norton, Cocoa Beach, FL)

BYERLY, BEATRICE GULDEN   PA
of the Bush Creek area, Westmoreland County. She was born about
1727/28 in the canton of Berne. Switzerland, and married Andrew
Byerly about 1747/48. He was a baker in Gen. Braddock's army.
They had five sons and one daughter who survived. On July 22,
1760, they were living in Fort Pitt, according to the census taken
there on that date. Later they established Byerly's Station on
the Bush Creek watershed. In August 1763, while her husband
was away, Mrs. Byerly was warned by a friendly Indian of an
impending Indian attack. So she fled with her children to Fort
Ligonier. The Battle of Bushy Run was fought near Byerly's Station.

During the British-inspired Indian raids in the Revolutionary
War, Mrs. Byerly and her younger children took refuge in Fort
Walthour. While there she nursed and cared for the wounded American soldiers. Mrs. Byerly married an Englishman named Benjamin
Lord, who died in 1793. She died sometime after 1801.

In 1918 the schoolchildren of Westmoreland County donated
their pennies to purchase six and a half acres of establish the
Bushy Run Battlefield Memorial Association, which later was expanded
to 162 acres of state park. In 1963 the battlefield was transferred
to the Pennsylvania Historical and Museum Commission. Driveways
and paths wind through the battlefield. In 1939 the Beatrice Gulden
Byerly Memory Lane was dedicated. (Submitted by Ruth Watson
Spaw, Uniontown, PA)

C

CADWALADER, ELIZABETH   NJ
of Trenton. She was the daughter of Hannah Lambert and Dr.
Thomas Cadwalader, who settled in Trenton. In 1746 Dr. Cadwalader was elected the first chief burgess of Trenton. Elizabeth was
the sister of Martha, the first wife of Brig. Gen. Philemon Dickinson, and the sister of Rebecca, the second wife of Gen. Dickinson,
and Margaret, the wife of Brig. Gen. Samuel Meredith of Philadelphia.
Elizabeth Cadwalader never married.

She was an active member of the ladies' relief association
for the welfare of the American soldiers. (New Jersey Gazette,
July 4, 1780)

CALDWELL, HANNAH OGDEN   NJ
of Elizabeth. On March 14, 1763, she married the Rev. James
Caldwell, pastor of the First Presbyterian Church of Elizabethtown
(now Elizabeth). He served as chaplain of Dayton's New Jersey
brigade and converted his church into a hospital for American soldiers where Mrs. Caldwell helped care for the sick and wounded.
On January 25, 1780, his church was burned to the ground by
Tories. The family moved to Connecticut Farms at Union, but
during Knyphausen's attack, Mrs. Caldwell was killed by a stray
bullet on June 7, 1780. There is a Hannah Caldwell Chapter of
the Daughters of the American Revolution in Davenport, Iowa. (DAR)

II: SELECTED BIOGRAPHIES

CALDWELL, RACHEL CRAIGHEAD   NC
of Guilford. The daughter of the Rev. Alexander Craighead, she was born in 1738. Rachel married the Rev. David Caldwell, a Presbyterian clergyman in Trenton, New Jersey, in 1766. He became a missionary in North Carolina and head of a classical school in Guilford. Mrs. Caldwell was a staunch patriot, and on numerous occasions her home was ransacked by Tories. A courier bearing dispatches from Gen. Washington to Gen. Nathaniel Greene stopped at her home. When the Tories attacked her home, Mrs. Caldwell led him to a back door where he escaped. After the Battle of Guilford Courthouse on March 15, 1781, her home was destroyed. Mrs. Caldwell assisted her husband in the care of the wounded soldiers. She died in 1835 in her eighty-seventh year. (CD; EW)

CALLOWAY, ELIZABETH HOY   KY
of Boonesborough. She was the second wife of Col. Richard Calloway (1722-1780). In 1776 Col. Calloway brought his wife and two daughters to Boonesborough. In July 1776 three young ladies (Elizabeth's daughters Betsey and Frances, and a daughter of Daniel Boone) were playing near the fort when they were captured by Indians. The screams of the girls were heard by the men in the fort, and Col. Daniel Boone and a party of eight men left the fort in pursuit of the Indians. They followed the trail of the Indians all night, and came upon them the next day. The Indians were taken by surprise and were routed immediately, and the girls were rescued. Two Indians were killed, but the Americans suffered no injuries. Col. Calloway was killed on March 8, 1780. (CH; DAR)

   Joice Craig Falconer, who was present when Col. Calloway was killed, many years later said in an interview: "Calloway was the worst barbecued man I ever saw. The Indians cut his bones up. They stripped him stark naked and rolled him in a mudhole. There was not a bone as big as your hand." (Bettye Lee Mastin, Lexington 1779, Lexington-Fayette County Historic Commission)

CALMES, LUCY NEVILLE   VA
of Frederick County. She was born on January 18, 1732, in Prince William County. In May 1754 Lucy married William Waller Calmes (1727-1773) of Stafford County, Virginia. She was a descendant of John Neville (1612-1664), who was a passenger on the Ark and Dove, landing on Saint Clement's Isle, Maryland, on March 25, 1634. Lucy had six sons and two daughters.

   During the war, the Widow Calmes furnished beef for the Revolutionary Army. (Frederick County Court, Virginia, August 7, 1782, p. 37) Four of her sons fought with the Virginia militia. One became a colonel, one a major, and two were lieutenants. Her eldest son, Marquis Calmes, and her youngest son, Henry Waller Calmes, served as generals from Kentucky in the War of 1812.

   In 1784 Lucy married William Helm. She died in Frederick County, Virginia, on May 20, 1789. (Submitted by Frances W. Hayes, Princeton, KY)

CAMP, LYDIA   NJ
of Morristown. She was the wife of Caleb Camp, a member of the
New Jersey legislature from Essex County. (FW) Lydia was an
active member of the ladies' association for the welfare of the American soldiers. (New Jersey Gazette, July 4, 1780)

CAMPBELL (CAMPBLE), ELIZABETH   SC
of Charleston. After the fall of the city to the enemy on May 12,
1780, the British commandant, Lt. Col. Balfour, required all women
who were heads of households to take an oath of fidelity to the
Crown, and Mrs. Campbell refused to do so. She was banished
from the city along with 120 other women and 264 children. (SC)
During the Revolutionary War she supplied provisions for the army
(SI, Y-Z:13).

CAMPBELL, JANE CANNON   NY
of Cherry Valley. She was the wife of Col. Samuel Campbell of
the New York militia. Mrs. Campbell was seized by the Seneca
Indians and kept a prisoner for over a year. Then she was taken
by the British, through an exchange, and carried to Fort Niagara
and imprisoned for two more years before she was released. This
is an example of the suffering endured by the American pioneers.
Before the close of the Revolution in 1782, she was living in Otsego
County, New York, and was visited by Gen. Washington and Governor Clinton. (FH)

CAMPBELL, LADY SARAH IZARD   SC
of Charleston. The daughter of Alice DeLancey and Ralph Izard
(1741-1804) of "The Elms," a plantation near Charleston, they were
the wealthiest family in South Carolina. Her father was a delegate
to the Continental Congress in 1782/83. While captain of the British
ship Nightingale, Lord William Campbell, the fourth son of the fourth
Duke of Argyll, visited Charleston and met Sarah Izard. They
were married on April 7, 1763.
    Lord Campbell served as governor of Nova Scotia from 1766
to 1773, when he became governor of South Carolina. Lady Campbell and her family were patriots. After the Revolutionary War
started, Governor Lord Campbell dissolved the assembly and in
1778 he fled to the British ship Tamar. When the British attacked
Charleston, Lord Campbell was wounded in battle, returned to
England, and died on his arrival in Southampton on September
5, 1778.
    Lady Campbell remained a staunch patriot, and supplied provisions for the troops in South Carolina during the Revolutionary
War. (SI, B:152)

CARTER, MRS. EDWARD   VA
of Charlottesville. On June 3, 1781, Lt. Col. Sir Banastre Tarleton
set out to capture Thomas Jefferson, so Jefferson sent his family to
Mrs. Carter's home for safety. Later Jefferson joined his family at
the Carter's house, and then sent his family to his second residence
at Poplar Forest. (ST)

II: SELECTED BIOGRAPHIES

CARTER, HANNAH BENEDICT   CT
of New Canaan, was born in 1733, the daughter of Thomas Benedict of Norwalk, Connecticut. She married Capt. John Carter. During the Revolutionary War she opened her home, "Clapboard Hills" in Norwalk (now Carter Street, New Canaan), to military officers to hold meetings and plan strategy. She died in 1780. The New Canaan chapter of the Daughters of the American Revolution is named in her honor. (CG)

CASEY, JANE MONTGOMERY   KY
of Logan's Station. The daughter of Jane Patterson and William Montgomery, Sr., she was in her father's cabin when the Indians attacked one day in March 1780. When her father left the cabin, he was shot and killed by the Indians. Jane secured a rifle and was ready to defend herself. The Indians did not enter her cabin, but attacked three cabins nearby where her brothers and sisters resided. After her brother John was also killed, Jane and her sister, Mrs. Joseph Russell, and Mrs. Russell's children were captured by the Indians.
　　　　Jane's brother-in-law, Col. Benjamin Logan, rescued Jane and the others from the Indians. (See Jane Patterson Montgomery, below) After the war Jane married Sgt. William Casey (1761-1820) of Virginia. (CH; DAR)

CAVE, ELIZABETH CRAIG   KY
of Bryan's Station. She was born about 1752 and married Richard Cave (1750-1816). On August 15, 1782, the Tories and Indians attacked Bryan's Station. (For details of how the women got water for the stockade, see Polly Hawkins Craig, below) She died in 1827 and is listed as a patriot in the DAR Patriot Index. The names of Elizabeth and her daughters Hannah and Polly Cave are inscribed on the limestone monument erected in 1896 by the Lexington Chapter of the Daughters of the American Revolution. (DAR)

CHAMIER, MRS. ACHSAH   NY
was a rebel and wanted to leave New York and live with relatives in Maryland. Gen. Washington gave her permission in his letter of May 21, 1779, to Col. Israel Sheve: "I have duly received your favour of yesterdays date. The inclosed letter to Mr. Daniel De Hart contains permission for Mrs. Chamier and her daughter, a chariot, two horses, a servant and baggage to pass to Maryland. You will therefore suffer her on her coming from New York to proceed on her journey." (FW)

CHAPMAN, MERCY BEAUMONT   PA
of Washington Crossing. She was the wife of Dr. John Chapman (1740-1800), and they lived at Brownsburg, between New Hope and Yardley, now known as Washington Crossing. Gen. Washington stayed at the home of Mr. and Mrs. William Keith from December 14 to 25, 1776, and Col. Alexander Hamilton had his headquarters at the home of Dr. and Mrs. Chapman. On December 25, 1776, Gen. Washington and his army crossed the Delaware River

about nine miles north of Trenton, New Jersey, to attack the
British and Hessian mercenaries. (Alfred G. Petrie, Lambertville,
New Jersey, 1949)

CHAPMAN, SARAH KETCHUM   CT
of Fairfield. The daughter of Sarah Wakelee and Nathaniel Ketchum,
she was born in 1723 in Norwalk, Connecticut. On September 22,
1742, she married Phineas Chapman who served as a captain during
the Revolutionary War. During the Battle of Fairfield on July 8,
1779, the British and Hessian troops burned the town. As Capt.
and Mrs. Chapman were removing their prized possessions, Capt.
Chapman and their son Daniel were taken prisoners. They were
taken first to Ridgefield, Connecticut, and then to New York City,
where they were jailed in the notorious Sugar House, where the
British abuses and cruelty to the American prisoners were legendary.
Cold and starving, Daniel Chapman died in his father's arms in
the Sugar House in 1780.
    While her husband was in prison and two other sons were
soldiers in the war, Mrs. Chapman remained at home with her four
youngest children. Her husband was freed in September 1781 in
ill health and died in 1782. Sarah died at Fairfield on November
21, 1811. (Submitted by Edward L. Woodyard, Armonk, NY)

CHEW, ELIZABETH OSWALD   PA
of Philadelphia. She was the second wife of Benjamin Chew (1722-
1810). Gen. Washington lived in the Chew house at 110 South 3rd
Street from November 26, 1781, to March 22, 1782. Mrs. Washington was with the general. On the twenty-seventh Charles Wilson
Peale exhibited at his house, southwest corner of 3rd and Lombard
Streets, a number of transparent scenes which he painted himself
to celebrate the arrival of the commander-in-chief of the Continental
Army. (BI)
    Judge Chew was chief justice of the Pennsylvania supreme
court from 1774 to 1776 and president of the high court of appeals
from 1791 to 1808.

CHILES, ELIZABETH FAULKNER   VA
of King and Queen County. She was born about 1756, the daughter
of Frances Johnson and Benjamin Faulkner. About 1772 she married
Walter Chiles when she was only sixteen and he was seventy-three
years old. They both were killed in 1779, apparently by the British.
Their two young sons, Benjamin and William, were placed under
the guardianship of Elizabeth Chiles's brother, Lt. Johnson Faulkner
of the Virginia Line. (Submitted by Edward L. Woodyard, Armonk,
NY)

CHINN, SARAH BRYAN   KY
of Bryan's Station. She was the daughter of Mary Boone and Capt.
William Bryan (1733-1780). Her mother was a sister of Daniel Boone.
Her father was wounded in a battle with the Indians, and died
on May 30, 1780. When the Tories and Indians attacked the fort

II: SELECTED BIOGRAPHIES

on August 15, 1782, Mrs. Bryan, together with her daughter Sarah and several other women, left the fort for the spring to get water and returned safely.

In 1784 Sarah married Col. John Chinn, and they left a number of descendants. The Wentzville, Missouri, Chapter of the Daughters of the American Revolution is named in her honor. (DAR; GP)

CILLEY, ELIZABETH   NH
of Nottingham. She was the wife of Capt. Joseph Cilley, agent of the proprietor of the New Hampshire grant of Nottingham. Mrs. Cilley was the mother of Gen. Joseph Cilley and Col. Cutting Cilley of the American Revolution and the grandmother of Jonathan Cilley and Benjamin Butler who also served during the war.

In 1774 Elizabeth Cilley refused to drink British imported tea because of the infamous tea tax, and said: "I am not going to the East Indies for any part of my breakfast."

When she was ninety-eight years old she rode on horseback to Pawtuckaway Mountain and designed a floral pattern for a quilt for her granddaughter. She was famous for her quilt designs. She died at age ninety-nine. The local chapter of the Daughters of the American Revolution is named in her honor. (Elizabeth Knowles Folsom, New Hampshire DAR Historian, 1924-1931; DAR)

CLAGHORN, THANKFUL DEXTER   MA
of New Bedford was born in 1738 in Falmouth. On November 11, 1756, she married William Claghorn, a sea captain, of Edgartown, Martha's Vineyard, Massachusetts. Later they moved to New Bedford. On September 6, 1778, the British attacked New Bedford and her house on the east side of South Water Street was burned to the ground, along with nine other homes in town. On February 12, 1782, Capt. Claghorn took command of the privateer ship <u>Virginia</u> with ten guns and twenty-five men complying with the Resolves of the Continental Congress. They had two daughters and one son. She died in 1795. The burning of their homes is an example of the anguish suffered by patriotic Americans. (CN)

CLARK, ELIZABETH ZANE   WV
of an area near Wheeling. She was born about 1764 in Berkeley County, Virginia, and later lived on a farm near Fort Henry. Elizabeth was the younger sister of Col. Ebenezer Zane, who later founded Zanesville, Ohio. While a teenager she attended private school in Philadelphia. When she returned home for a visit on September 17, 1782, she learned that the Indians were attacking Fort Henry. The garrison of forty men had been reduced to twelve, and they were badly in need of ammunition stored in the home of Col. Zane who lived nearby. Betty Zane was in the fort and volunteered to run for the ammunition.

When she left the fort the Indians called, "A squaw," and did not fire upon her. When whe arrived at the house she poured the gunpowder into a tablecloth that she carried back to the fort, which was saved. Elizabeth Zane was married twice, first to Henry McLaughlin, who died early, then to Capt. John Clark. They resided in Saint Clairsville, Ohio, where she died about 1829.

At the entrance to the Walnut Grove Cemetery in Martins Ferry, Ohio, there is a monument of her likeness which was erected to her memory. She is known as the Heroine of Fort Henry. There is also a marker to her memory at 12th and Chapline Streets in Wheeling, West Virginia. (CP; EW; HS; EP)

CLARK, HANNAH ARRINGTON GA
of Wilkes County. She was born in 1737 in North Carolina and married Col. Elijah Clark (1733-1799), and they moved to Wilkes County. They had several children. Once when Elijah was stationed at a fort guarding the frontier, the British and Tories ransacked and burned their home. Another time Hannah accompanied her husband on a campaign, and her horse was shot from under her. Hannah died on August 26, 1827, and was buried at Woodburn next to her husband. Hannah is listed as a patriot in the <u>DAR Patriot Index</u>. The Hannah Clark Chapter of the Daughters of the American Revolution in Quitman, Georgia, is named in her honor. (GP, DAR)

CLARK, SARAH HATFIELD NJ
of Elizabeth. About 1749 she married Abraham Clark, and they had ten children. Later he was a signer of the Declaration of Independence. Two of their sons served as officers in the army, and were captured by the British and held in the prison ship <u>Jersey</u> in New York Harbor. Disease, especially smallpox, was rampant on this prison ship. It is estimated that some eight thousand American soldiers and seamen died on this vessel. Her son Thomas, a captain of artillery, was placed in a dark hole in the forecastle of the ship and was often denied food and water.

When the news of the horrible treatment of their sons reached the Clarks, both remained steadfast in their patriotic beliefs. After Gen. Washington learned of the treatment of the Clark sons, he protested to the British Gen. Howe, and the harsh treatment ceased. (FG)

CLARKSON, MARY BONDE PA
of Philadelphia. She was the wife of Matthew Clarkson, later the mayor of Philadelphia. Mrs. Clarkson was a member of the ladies' association for the relief of the American soldiers, founded by Sarah De Berdt Reed. Upon the death of Mrs. Reed in September 1780, Mrs. Clarkson and Mrs. Bache, together with three other women, took over the management of the association. With their own money, they purchased material and made shirts for the American soldiers. (FW)

CLAY, ANN LEGARDIRE GA
of Savannah. On January 2, 1763, she married Joseph Clay, a merchant. In 1775 he was a member of the Committee of Safety

II: SELECTED BIOGRAPHIES

and in 1776 was appointed paymaster of the Continental Army for the Southern Department. He was a member of the Continental Congress from 1778 to 1780.

After the Battle of Cowpens in South Carolina on January 17, 1781, which ended in an American victory, Mrs. Clay attended to the wounded American soldiers. In the Colonial Park Cemetery at Abercorn Street and Oglethorpe Avenue in Savannah is a marker on the graves of Ann and Joseph Clay. (CP)

CLEMENT, SUSANNAH HILL   VA
of Pittsylvania County. She was born in 1700, the daughter of Col. Isaac Hill of King and Queen County. Susannah married Capt. Benjamin Clement (ca. 1700-1780). During the Revolutionary War, Susannah assisted her husband and his partner, Col. Charles Lynch, in the manufacture of gunpowder at their factory in Pittsylvania. The gunpowder was used by the patriotic Americans in their war against the British. She died about 1785. (History of Pittsylvania County, Virginia; submitted by John W. Dobbins, Iva, SC)

CLINGAN, JANE ROAN   PA
of Donegal, Lancaster County. The daughter of Anne Cochran and John Roan, she was born on May 3, 1753, in Derry Township, Lancaster County. She was a staunch Whig, a rebel, and would marry only a patriotic American soldier. On June 11, 1778, she married William Clingan, Jr., who had served in the battles of Trenton, Princeton, Brandywine, and Germantown. They had seven children who reached maturity.

The notice of her wedding appeared in the Pennsylvania Packet in June 1778 and included the following statement: "After the marriage was ended, a motion was made, and heartily agreed to by all present, that the young unmarried should form themselves into an association by the name of the 'Whig Association of the Unmarried Ladies of America,' in which they should pledge their honor that they would never give their hand in marriage to any gentleman until he had first proved himself a patriot."

Mrs. Clingan and her husband moved to Buffalo Valley after the Revolutionary War, where she died on May 7, 1838. (EP)

CLOKE, ELIZABETH COOK   DE
of Smyrna. She was the daughter of Capt. John Cook (1730-1789), who served as a supply purchaser for the army, justice of the Delaware supreme court, and speaker of the Legislative Council. Elizabeth married Ebenezer Cloke (ca. 1740-1781), who was captain of a privateer during the Revolutionary War. Capt. Cloke was captured by the British and confined on a prison ship where he died of typhus. During the war, Elizabeth molded bullets for the soldiers. The Smyrna Chapter of the Daughters of the American Revolution is named in her honor. (DAR; GP)

CLYMER, ELIZABETH MEREDITH   PA
of Chester County. The daughter of Reese Meredith, she married

George Clymer in 1765, of the firm of Meredith and Clymer. In
1775 he was a member of the Pennsylvania Council of Safety. He
was a signer of the Declaration of Independence.
After the Battle of Brandywine (a British victory), the enemy
terrorized Mrs. Clymer, ransacked her home, and destroyed her
furniture and liquor. This is an example of the suffering endured
by many valiant women. (DB)

COATES, LYDIA SAUNDERS   PA
of Philadelphia. In 1775 she married Samuel Coates, a merchant.
Lydia was active in the ladies' association for the welfare of the
American soldiers. (Pennsylvania Gazette, June 12, 1780)

COCHRAN, GERTRUDE SCHUYLER   NY
of Albany. She was the sister of Maj. Gen. Philip John Schuyler.
Gertrude married Dr. John Cochran (1730-1807) who was chief
physician and surgeon-general of the Continental Army. While
the American army was in New Jersey, Dr. Cochran was quartered
in the home of Dr. Jabez Campbell in Morristown. Mrs. Cochran
entertained the officers (including Lt. Col. Alexander Hamilton)
who were stationed at Fort Mansion. While on a visit to her aunt
Gertrude, Elizabeth Schuyler, the daughter of Gen. Philip Schuyler,
met Alexander Hamilton in the winter of 1779, and a stormy romance
began between Betsey, as she was called, and Hamilton, who was
serving on Gen. Washington's staff. In 1780 she married Alexander
Hamilton.
In 1804 Hamilton defeated Aaron Burr in the election for
governor of New York, which incensed Burr, who sought revenge.
Burr challenged Hamilton to a duel, and at Weehawken, New Jersey,
on July 11, 1804, Hamilton was mortally wounded by Burr and died
the next day. (DB; DAR Magazine, July 1976)

COCKRILL, ANN ROBERTSON   TN
of forts Watagua and Nashborough (now Nashville). The ninth
child of Mary Gower and John Randolph Robertson, she was born
on February 10, 1757, in Wake County, North Carolina. In 1771
the family migrated to Fort Watagua, Rowan County, North Carolina
(now Tennessee). At age fourteen Ann became the second wife
of Isaac Johnston, who had two grown sons. Isaac and Ann had
three daughters. In 1778/79 Isaac was killed by a falling tree.
In 1779 the Cherokees, British, and Tories attacked Fort
Watagua while the men were absent hunting. Ann Johnston led
the women to defend the fort, and they suffered wounds while
hanging over the walls to fire on their attackers. It being wash
day at the fort, Ann ordered the women to pour caldrons of boiling
water on the Indians. After the attackers retreated, her brother
Capt. James Robertson and the other men found many dead and
wounded Indians around the fort, and Ann was credited with saving
the settlement.
On December 22, 1779, the widow Ann and her three daughters
set forth from Fort Watagua (now Elizabethtown) and migrated to

II: SELECTED BIOGRAPHIES

Fort Nashborough (now Nashville) in the company of 125 settlers. The trip took four months, and many stragglers died of the cold or starvation or were killed by the Indians. On April 24, 1780, they arrived on the Cumberland River bluffs and enjoyed some safety in the developing Fort Nashborough. In the fall of 1780, Ann married John Cockrill. In 1781 the Indians attacked the fort, which was defended by Ann and her sister-in-law Charlotte Robinson. Fourteen-year-old Rachel Donelson (later Mrs. Andrew Jackson) was also in the fort.

For her heroism, in 1784 Ann Cockrill was the sole female grantee of 640 acres of land in her own right. In 1935 the Nashborough Chapter of the Daughters of the American Revolution placed a bronze marker on the granite tablet covering her grave:

> Ann Robertson Johnston Cockrill
> 1757-1821
> Intrepid Pioneer, Heroine of
> the Battle of the Bluffs, 1781
> Recipient of Land Grant

(Submitted by Helen Haywood Hahn and William Thomas Haywood, Columbia, TN; DAR)

COGSWELL, MARY BACKUS   CT
of Uniontown. On his return trip from Wethersfield, Connecticut, on May 24, 1781, Gen. Washington had breakfast with Capt. and Mrs. Samuel Cogswell. He then retired to Sheldon's Tavern, where he spent that night on his return trip to Fishkill, New York. (FW)

COLFAX, ESTHER SCHUYLER   NJ
of Pompton Falls (now Pompton Lakes). She was the sole child of Casparus Schuyler, who was a grandson of Arent Schuyler and a second cousin of Maj. Gen. Philip Schuyler. Their house is situated between the Ramapo River and the western side of a bend in the Paterson and Hamburg Turnpike, at no. 2342. Gen. Washington had his headquarters in the Schuyler house from July 11 to July 14, 1777.

Hester, as she was called, entertained Gen. Washington and eight of his officers at the Schuyler house. Present was Lt. William Colfax of New London, Connecticut, commander of Washington's Life Guards. Later Lt. Colfax often called on Hester Schuyler. He served at Bunker Hill in 1775, was at the surrender of Lord Cornwallis at Yorktown in 1781, and was promoted to captain in 1783. Hester and William were married on August 27, 1783, by the Rev. Benjamin Vanderlinder.

General Washington attended the christening of their first child, George Washington Colfax, in November 1784, and as godfather, presented Hester with a baby cap crocheted by Martha Washington. Hester and William had six children, and the marriage lasted fifty-five years. William Colfax retired as a general after the War of 1812. Hester Colfax died in October 1839. Their grandson, Schuyler Colfax, served as vice president during the term of President U. S. Grant.

The Schuyler-Colfax house is now the private residence and office of Dr. Jane Colfax. (Information from John Donovan, director of the Emmanuel Einstein Free Public Library, Pompton Lakes, NJ)

The Pompton Lakes, Passaic County, New Jersey, chapter of the Daughters of the American Revolution is named in her honor.

COLOMBE, MARGARET MOORE RANSTEID, DE LA
was the wife of Philippe Louis de la Colombe, who held the rank of captain in the Continental Army. He served as an aide to Lafayette and de Kalb. Capt. Colombe was taken prisoner at Savannah, Georgia, in December 1778. After the war ended in 1783, Colombe returned to France and was imprisoned with Lafayette by Austria in 1792. Later he returned to America to live and left descendants in this country. (DAR; FW; see the interesting story about the Marquise de Lafayette, below)

CONE, KEZIAH BARBER   GA
of Statesboro. She married William Cone, Sr. (1745-1815), who was born in the Pee Dee River area of South Carolina. He served as captain of the Richmond County, Georgia, militia and was present in the battle of Augusta in 1779 (Knight, Roster, p. 46); which the British held until 1781. Their son Aaron was a courier in the Revolutionary War at age seventeen and was captured by the British on the Oconee River.

The Tories used Bullock County as a retreat, coming up from Florida through the Okefenokee Swamp. Capt. Cone gathered together a party of men in 1781, and they drove the Tories back into Florida, but Capt. Cone, William Williams, and one or two other men were captured by the British, who held Saint Augustine from 1762 until 1783, when the Treaty of Paris was signed and the British ceded Florida back to Spain. Capt. Cone and the other men were imprisoned in the Saint Augustine stockade until 1783, when they managed to escape. Fortunately they were able to secure horses from the camp and rode to the river at "Old Cow Ford" near Jacksonville. With their horses they swam the river, which at that point was nearly a mile wide.

For his work in driving the Tories out of Bullock County, the "House of Assembly recommended by the Board to make a compliment of 200 acres of confiscated land late of William Powell on S. Side of Great Ogeechee to Captain Cone for use of himself and men and 25 pounds Sterling." (Chandler, Revolutionary Records of Georgia, 2:767)

Mrs. Cone suffered through the capture and imprisonment of her son Aaron and of her husband, who died in Effingham County in 1815. (Submitted by George M. Norton of Cocoa Beach, FL)

On March 15, 1930, the Briar Creek Chapter of the Daughters of the American Revolution unveiled a marker at the grave of Capt. William Cone, Revolutionary hero, in the Cone Cemetery at Ivanhoe.

II: SELECTED BIOGRAPHIES

CONWAY, ELIZABETH BRIDGEWATER   KY
of Ruddle's Station, Bourbon County. She was born in 1735. About 1752 she married John Conway, Sr., a schoolteacher, and they had nine children--five daughters and four sons. They lived in Spotsylania County, Greenbrier County, and Montgomery County, Virginia. Their sons--Samuel, John Jr., Jesse, and Joseph--served in the Revolutionary War, or were captured. Their son John Jr. served in the Western Country (now Kentucky) in 1777 and later induced the family to move westward. They settled at Ruddle's Station (also called Hinkson's Station) on the east bank of the South Licking River on the buffalo trace which flowed into the Blue Lickings, where there was an army fort nearby. Mrs. Conway furnished clothing and food for the soldiers at the fort.

On June 19, 1780, Joseph Conway, aged sixteen, was shot and scalped by Indians and left for dead. But at the point of death, Joseph was taken to the fort and an application of wads and cobwebs was made into a poultice to stanch the blood, and Joseph's life was saved.

On June 22, 1780, Capt. Henry Bird with British troops and Indians attacked the fort, and the Americans were forced to surrender. Mrs. Conway, her husband, their sons John Jr. and Joseph, and daughters Elizabeth, Nancy, and Sarah were captured and forced to march, with other American prisoners, to Detroit, where they were imprisoned by Lord Henry Hamilton. Five-year-old Sarah was separated from her parents and adopted by an Indian couple as their own child. The Conways were imprisoned for four years until June 1, 1784, when they were released. There was no transportation, and they had to walk home to Kentucky. The Conways finally arrived home in August 1784.

In 1789 Joseph Conway finally located his sister Sarah and paid the Indians for her release, nine years after her capture. During the Revolutionary War, Joseph Conway was scalped three times, tomahawked three times, shot three times, and left for dead three times, and lived to the age of seventy. (Ripley's "Believe It or Not") Conway served with the rank of captain during the War of 1812.

Elizabeth's husband died in 1801 in Campbell County, Kentucky, and Elizabeth died on July 30, 1809, in Millersburg, Kentucky. She was accredited by the Daughters of the American Revolution as a Patriot, Defender of the Fort, and as a Prisoner of War for four years. (Virginia Walton Brooks, in Ansearchin' News, 10 [November 3, 1963], submitted by Lt. Col. Clifford H. Pohl, president, Cincinnati Chapter of the Sons of the American Revolution)

CONYNGHAM, ANN HOCKLEY   PA
of Philadelphia. In 1773 she married Gustavus Conyngham, a sea captain. On July 16, 1777, he sailed as captain of the Continental cutter Revenge and cruised the North and Irish seas and the Atlantic Ocean. Conyngham took many prize vessels. In 1778 he captured prizes around the Azores and Canary Islands, then sailed for the West Indies. He returned to Philadelphia in February 1779,

having taken a record of sixty prize vessels. The Revenge was
outfitted as a privateer, and on April 27, 1779, Conyngham was
taken by the British vessel Galatea.

Conyngham was imprisoned in the "condemned dungeon" of
the vessel, then sent to England in chains in July 1779 and confined
in Pendennis Castle, Falmouth, and later in the Mill Prison near
Plymouth. At first he was put in irons and lodged at night in
the "black hole" and half starved to death. Twice Conyngham
tried to escape. On his third attempt, on November 3, 1779, he
escaped with other Americans by digging a tunnel out of the prison.
Conyngham and the men escaped to Holland and were received by
Commo. John Paul Jones aboard the Alliance.

Conyngham was a passenger on the Experiment, bound for
America, but on March 17, 1780, his vessel was captured by the
British once again. Conyngham was sent to the Mill Prison again,
where he spent a year in confinement. This is an example of the
suffering endured by the American patriots and their patriotic
wives. Capt. and Mrs. Conyngham are buried in Saint Peter's
churchyard in Philadelphia. (CN; DB)

COOKE, MRS. SAMUEL   CT
of Watertown. John Adams lodged here while attending the Massachusetts Council. Abigail Adams was with her husband in the
Cooke's home from August 22 to 24, 1775, according to a letter
she wrote to Mercy Otis Warren on August 27, 1775. (BA)

COOKE, SARAH SIMPSON   PA
of Northumberland. The daughter of Rebecca and Samuel Simpson,
she was born on May 7, 1742, in Paxtang Township, Lancaster
County. In 1762 she married William Cooke, and in 1767 they moved
to Fort Augusta, later called Sunbury, and then in 1775 to Northumberland. They had two sons and five daughters who reached
maturity and were married. Her husband was appointed colonel
of the 12th Regiment of the Pennsylvania Line, which suffered
severe losses in the battles of Brandywine and Germantown. As
a result, Col. Cooke was relieved of his command.

Mrs. Cooke turned her home into a hospital for the wounded
soldiers in 1778, and widows and children were also cared for.
Mrs. Cooke died at Northumberland in 1822. (EP)

COOLIDGE, DOROTHY WHITNEY   MA
of Watertown. On September 19, 1751, Dorothy Whitney married
Nathaniel Coolidge, who operated a tavern there from 1764 until
his death in 1770. They had three sons and three daughters.
Her son Daniel had nine children, and her grandson Daniel Jr.
had nine children. Her grandson Nathaniel had one son and thirteen daughters!

The Coolidge Tavern, located on Galen Street in Watertown,
was torn down in 1918. After her husband's death, Mrs. Coolidge
continued to operate the tavern, in which hung a portrait of King
George III. On the day of the Battle of Lexington in April 1775,

II: SELECTED BIOGRAPHIES

Dorothy fed the volunteer soldiers her celebrated hot golden Johnny cakes and rum. Mrs. Coolidge took down the portrait of King George III and later placed one of Gen. Washington on the wall.

On his way to Cambridge in 1775, Gen. Washington was received by a welcoming committee in Watertown on July 2, where he spent the night in Mrs. Coolidge's tavern.

After he became president, Gen. Washington spent the night of November 5, 1789, in her tavern. (<u>Bicentennial Tour of Historic Watertown</u>; submitted by Cynthia A. Fordham, Watertown Free Public Library)

COOPER, POLLY   NY
of Oneida. She was an Oneida Indian woman who served as George Washington's cook and housekeeper during the Revolutionary War. Polly refused any remuneration for her services. Although she served Washington for seven years, she insisted that it was her patriotic duty. Later Congress authorized funds to buy Polly a shawl in recognition of her services. (CP)

CORBIN, HANNAH LEE   VA
of Westmoreland County. The daughter of Hannah Ludwell and Thomas Lee, she was the sister of Arthur, Francis Lightfoot, Richard Henry, and Alice Lee Shippen. At thirty-two she was a widow and lived with a man without benefit of marriage, since she would have lost her late husband's estate if she remarried. With her live-in lover she had two children.

In 1776 the constitution of the State of New Jersey confirmed the right of property owners to vote, which included widows and spinsters who owned property. In 1807 New Jersey disfranchised women.

Common law in the colonial period allowed unmarried women who owned large tracts of property to vote, but very few did so. In fact, very few women knew of this right. In 1778 Mrs. Corbin asked her brother Richard to give widows the right to vote, complaining that she was a victim of taxation without representation. After her plea, Richard wrote that he favored giving the vote to widows and spinsters who obtained property, but he did nothing about it. He failed to tell her it was her right to vote.

Hannah Corbin was courageous in her attempt to have a Virginia law passed granting the right of widows and spinsters to vote. (DR; LV) During the Revolutionary War, Hannah supplied provisions for the army. (VR, Court Book, p. 2)

CORBIN, MARGARET COCHRAN ("Captain Molly")   PA
the daughter of Robert Corbin, she was born on November 12, 1751, in Franklin County. When she was only five years old, her father was killed by Indians and her mother was carried away. She was raised by an uncle. In 1772 Margaret married William Corbin, and in 1776 he served as a matross in the 1st Company of the Pennsylvania Artillery. Margaret accompanied her husband into battle, and while tending a cannon at Fort Washington in New

York, he was killed on November 16, 1776. Margaret then fired the cannon herself, but was wounded. The Americans surrendered to the British at Fort Washington, but Margaret Corbin was allowed to leave. She became known as "Captain Molly."

Mrs. Corbin traveled to Philadelphia, but her injuries were so severe that she became completely incapacitated. On July 6, 1779, the Continental Congress voted her a disability pension for life at one-half the monthly pay of a soldier. She was the first woman of the American Revolution to receive a pension. She lived in Highland Falls, New York, and died there on January 16, 1800. Through the efforts of the New York State and the National Society of the Daughters of the American Revolution, her skeleton was disinterred and taken to the Military Academy cemetery at West Point for reburial.

Mrs. Corbin's heroism at Fort Washington is marked by a bronze plaque on a granite stone at West Point. Other bronze markers commemorating her are at Fort Tryon Park in New York City and at the Holy Rood Church at West 179th Street and Fort Washington Avenue. (CP; DB; DR; EP)

CORNELL, HANNAH FINCH   NY
of Delhi. She was the wife of William Cornell and they lived on a farm nearby. Her husband and three neighbors were captured by Indians, but they made their escape. After this harrowing experience, Hannah and William fled to the fort in Schoharie, and he helped defend the fort during a long but unsuccessful siege by the Indians and Tories. It is said that he also defended Middle Fort, north of the Old Stone Fort, which is still standing.

Their daughter Rebecca Cornell was born in the Old Stone Fort, Schoharie, on June 7, 1778. The Battle at Fort Schoharie occurred in September 1780 and an Elizabeth Snyder was also a patriot there. The Cornells had ten children.

In 1801 Rebecca Cornell married Horace Townsend, and they had eleven children. Later in life Rebecca went to live with a daughter, Lavine Townsend Barnes, and was buried in the New York Bay Cemetery, Jersey City, New Jersey.

Since Rebecca Cornell was a true daughter of the American Revolution, the Rahway, Union County, New Jersey, Chapter of the Daughters of the American Revolution is named in her honor. (DC)

COUENHOVEN, ANNATIE KOEME   NY
of Tarrytown. Annatie Koeme (or Roeme) married Edward Couenhoven. Lieutenant Governor Pierre Van Courtlandt lodged at the home of the Couenhovens, where he met George Washington and his aides on November 19, 1783. That night, the lieutenant governor of New York dined with Gen. Lewis Morris and spent the night of November 20 at the home of Mr. and Mrs. Frederick Van Courtlandt in Yonkers. (BI; some information from Florence S. Kane, Tarrytown, NY)

II: SELECTED BIOGRAPHIES

COX, ESTHER BOWES   NJ
of Bloomsbury. She was the daughter of Francis Bowes, part owner of the Black Creek Forge at Bordentown. On November 16, 1760, Esther married John Cox of Philadelphia, and they had six daughters. Mr. Cox owned the Batsto Iron Furnace at Little Egg Harbor, New Jersey. In 1775 he was a member of the General Committee of Correspondence and the Council of Safety. He was elected a lieutenant of the 2nd Battalion of the Philadelphia Associators. In March 1778 he was appointed assistant quartermaster-general and was on intimate terms with Generals Henry Knox and Nathaniel Greene.

     Owing to ill health, early in 1780 Mr. Cox purchased a mansion on the Delaware River at Bloomsbury, just below Trenton, where Mr. and Mrs. Cox entertained Generals Washington, Knox, Greene, the Count de Rochambeau, and the Marquis de Lafayette in August 1783. Their house is now called the Trent House. Mrs. Cox was active in the ladies' relief association for the welfare of the American soldiers. (New Jersey Gazette, July 4, 1780; some information from Richard W. Reeves, Trenton, NJ)

CRAFTS, NABBY   MA
of Manchester. Her father was a colonel in the Revolutionary Army. In 1781, when blankets, stockings, and shirts were needed, ten-year-old Nabby helped her mother make shirts, and when the supply of needles was exhausted, she rode to Boston to obtain more. Nabby had to be ferried over rivers and streams to get to the town occupied by the British, but she obtained the needles and returned home safely. (HC)

CRAIG, ELIZABETH JOHNSON   KY
of Bryan's Station. She was born about 1738 and married Tolliver Craig II (1738-1819). On August 15, 1782, the Indians attacked Bryan's Station. (For details of how the women obtained drinking water, see Jemima Johnson and Mary Craig, below) Elizabeth Craig is listed as a patriot in the DAR Patriot Index. The names of Elizabeth and her daughters Polly and Nancy Craig are inscribed on the memorial erected in 1896 by the Lexington Daughters of the American Revolution. (DAR)

CRAIG, MARY (POLLY) HAWKINS   KY
of Lexington. The daughter of Mary Long and John Hawkins of King William County, Virginia, she was born in 1716. Polly married Taliaferro (Tolliver) Craig, Sr. (1704-1795), in Virginia. They had six sons and four daughters who reached maturity. Their son John married Sally Page and founded Craig's Station in Kentucky in December 1779.

     In December 1781 the Craigs left Virginia and settled at Gilbert's Creek Station with the Falconers. Polly and Tolliver Craig brought along their three sons--Lewis, Elijah, and Joseph--and all three were Baptist ministers who were imprisoned in Virginia for preaching. Lewis Craig's congregation--pastor, officers, and members--all voted to go to Kentucky. "There were 180 of us.... We were sometimes in a string of three miles," according to Mrs. John Arnold. (G. W. Rank, The Traveling Church, Louisville, 1891; and Frank M. Masters, A History of the Baptists in Kentucky, Louisville, 1953)

When the Shawnee and the Wyandots, inspired by the Tories, attacked on August 15, 1782, the Craigs and the others were at Bryan's Station in Fayette County, about five miles from Lexington. The stockade was desperately in need of water to sustain a long siege, and so Jemima Johnson and Polly Craig led the other women to the spring. Normally the Indians did not disturb women when they were ready to assault a stockade, since all the men were needed for the assault. Thus the women were able to return with the water, a courageous act.

Polly Hawkins Craig died in 1804. She is listed in the DAR Patriot Index. There is a Polly Hawkins Craig chapter of the Daughters of the American Revolution in Lexington. (Submitted by Sue M. Bogardus, Warsaw, KY) The names of Polly Craig and her daughter Sally Craig are inscribed on the limestone monument erected in 1896 by the Lexington Chapter of the Daughters of the American Revolution (Virginia Webb Howard, Bryan's Station, Heroes and Heroines, 1932; submitted by Linda Reed, Plainview, TX)

CRAIG, SALLY PAGE   KY
of Lexington. She was born in 1738 and married John Craig (1732-1814), who established Craig's Station near David's Fork in eastern Fayette County, Kentucky, on Christmas Eve 1779. In the family of settlers were the Falconers, Hamptons, Johnsons, and Singletons. On March 10, 1781, the Craigs learned of an impending Indian attack, so the families fled the station, which was burned to the ground, and was thereafter called "Burnt Station."

In 1782 John and Jeremiah Craig, sons of Polly Craig, were in charge of Bryan's Station when the Tories and Indians under Capt. William Caldwell and Simon Girty, attacked on August 15, 1782. Jemima Johnson led Sally Craig and the other women to the spring for water for the fort despite the presence of Indians. The Americans held the fort, and the Indians retreated. (Submitted by Dr. and Mrs. Carl Bogardus, Sr., Warsaw, KY) Sally Page died in 1835. She is listed as a patriot in the DAR Patriot Index. The names of Sally and her daughters Polly and Frankey Craig are inscribed on the limestone monument erected by the Lexington Chapter of the Daughters of the American Revolution in 1896. (DAR)

CULBERTSON, MARTHA THOMAS   SC
of Spartanburg. The daughter of Jane Black and Col. John Thomas, she was the wife of Josiah Culbertson (1742-1839). Col. Thomas had ammunition stored in his house, and when the Tories attacked, only Martha, her husband Josiah, Mrs. Thomas, her children, and one other man were in the house, which they defended against the attack. Martha and Jane loaded the muskets for the two men,

II: SELECTED BIOGRAPHIES

who fired on the Tories. Finally the Tories gave up their attack and retreated, and the ammunition was saved. (EW; HS)

CUSTIS, ELEANOR CALVERT   VA
married John Parke Custis, Gen. Washington's stepson, who served as the general's aide-de-camp without rank or pay at the siege of Yorktown. John died there from typhus. On November 6, 1781, Gen. Washington wrote to the president of Congress: "But an event which I met with at this place, very distressing to Mrs. Washington, will retard my arrival at Philadelphia a few days longer than I expected, which I hope Congress will have the goodness to excuse as I am not conscious that any important public duty will be neglected by it." Washington wrote this letter while at the home of Col. and Mrs. Burwell Bassett. Anne Maria Dandridge Bassett was related to Mrs. Washington. (FW)

Eleanor Custis's son, George Washington Parke Custis (1781-1857), was a playwright who also produced several plays. His most successful was Pocahontas; or, The Settlers of Virginia, which was produced in Philadelphia in 1830. His daughter, Mary Ann Randolph Custis, in 1831 married Robert E. Lee, who became the great Confederate general. (DAR; DB; FW)

CUTLER, ELIZABETH ROCKWOOD   MA
of Holliston. The daughter of Elizabeth Perry and Timothy Rockwood, she was born on December 23, 1753, in Holliston. In 1770 she married Simeon Cutler (1749-1798), who opened an inn on the family farm. After the alarm at Lexington, Simeon joined the militia and left his wife at home with three small children. Since by law, the innkeepers had to entertain soldiers and travelers connected with the army, and receive payment in Continental currency, most of the inns in the vicinity were forced to close, since the money soon became worthless.

Elizabeth decided to keep the Cutler Inn open so that the officers traveling through would have a place where their horses could be stabled. It was not kept open as a profitable undertaking; rather, she felt it was her patriotic duty.

Elizabeth helped her neighbors in time of need. Her husband rose in the ranks and was promoted to colonel at the close of the war. At Elizabeth's birth the Indians had just recently left the neighborhood, and she lived to see a railroad built through the town and five generations sit at her dining room table. She had four sons and two daughters, and at the time of her death on May 1, 1849, at the age of ninety-five she left behind seventy-four living descendants. (History of the Holliston Branch of the Cutler Family, 1897; submitted by Winifred Ager, Melbourne Beach, FL)

D

DAGGETT, POLLY   MA
of Eastville (previously Homes Hole), Martha's Vineyard. With two

other schoolgirls, she destroyed the flagpole in front of the inn of
Joseph Claghorn so that it would not fall into the hands of the
British. The girls feared that the British might use it as a mast
for one of their vessels. (William C. Claghorn, The Claghorn Family, Philadelphia, 1912).

DANIELSON, SARAH WILLIAMS   CT
of Pomfret. The sister of William Williams of Lebanon, Connecticut,
a signer of the Declaration of Independence, she was born in 1737.
She was married in 1758 to Col. William Danielson of Killingly, Connecticut, and was a camp follower. Mrs. Danielson shared his
sorrows and gave him support and comfort. She died in 1809.
The local chapter of the Daughters of the American Revolution
is named in her honor. (CG)

DANNELL, RACHEL   NC
of Wolkes County. She married John Dannell, and they had four
sons. Her husband was killed on August 6, 1780, at the second
Battle of Hanging Rock in Camden, South Carolina. Rachel supplied two cows for the army. (North Carolina Archives; submitted
by Dorothy Beveridge Joyce, Clemson, SC)

DARRAGH, LYDIA BARRINGTON   PA
of Philadelphia. The daughter of John Barrington of Dublin, Ireland, she was born about 1728. She was married to William Darragh
there on November 2, 1753. They came to America in 1775 and
settled in Philadelphia, where Lydia was a midwife and made grave
clothes.
    On the banks of the Brandywine Creek in Pennsylvania on
September 11, 1777, some 13,000 men under Gen. Washington were
defeated by 18,000 soldiers under Lord Howe. Gen. Washington
and his men retreated and encamped at Whitemarsh, Pennsylvania.
In panic, on September 19, the Continental Congress fled to Lancaster and then to York on September 30. Gen. Howe and his
army occupied Philadelphia on September 26, 1777.
    At this time Lydia Darragh was living at 177 South 2nd Street,
almost directly across the street from Gen. Howe's headquarters.
On occasions, British staff meetings were held in the home of Mr.
and Mrs. Darragh, since they were Quakers. Such a meeting was
held in her home on the evening of December 2, 1777, and when
the British officers arrived at eight o'clock, the Darraghs and
their children were told to go to bed. They did so, but Lydia
was curious, and leaving her room, she listened by the door to
their conversation.
    Lydia heard Whitemarsh mentioned. She opened her needle
book, took out a piece of paper, and jotted down some notes:
Gen. Howe was leaving on December 3 with 5,000 men for Whitemarsh, thirteen pieces of cannon, baggage wagons, and eleven
boats on wagon wheels. After the British officers left her house,
Lydia told her husband that she had to buy flour at Pearson's
Mill. She walked three miles to a small post at the Rising Sun,

II: SELECTED BIOGRAPHIES   61

where she met Elias Boudinot, who was director of intelligence in
Washington's army. Lydia gave Boudinot the scrap of paper on
which she had written her notes. This fact is verified in the published Journal of Elias Boudinot. He did not know her name, but
immediately rode to post headquarters to give the alarm.

Lydia continued on her journey to Whitemarsh, where she
encountered Lt. Col. Thomas Craig of the American Light Horse
Cavalry, whom she knew. She also gave him the warning message,
and then returned to pick up her bag of flour and journey home-
ward.

The Americans were ready when the British troops arrived.
Their cannons were mounted and the troops under arms, so the
British retreated to the safety of Philadelphia. On December 17,
1777, Gen. Washington and his army encamped at Valley Forge
for the winter. Lydia Darragh died in Philadelphia on December
28, 1789. (CD)

DAVENPORT, MEHITABLE COGGESHALL   CT
of Stamford. On December 17, 1781, Ebenezer Jones obtained a
letter of marque and reprisal to command three Connecticut boats--
the Rattlesnake, the Viper, and the Saratoga--each with one gun
and ten men. Deborah Davenport and Mehitable Coggeshall signed
as witnesses to the bond. (CN) On November 6, 1790, Mehitable
married James Davenport. (Information from Robert J. Belletzkie,
Stamford, CT)

DAVIDSON, CATHARINE MARTIN   PA
of Northumberland. The daughter of Robert Martin, she was born
there on May 16, 1768. After the Tory and Indian massacre in
the Wyoming Valley on July 3, 1778, the Americans fled to Fort
Augusta (now Sunbury) near the home of Robert Martin. His ten-
year-old daughter Catharine nursed and cared for the sick and
wounded. Catharine married Dr. James Davidson on March 31,
1785.

After the Revolutionary War, they moved to a farm on Pine
Creek near the Jersey shore. They had five sons and three daugh-
ters. Mrs. Davidson died about 1816 and is buried in the Pine
Creek Cemetery. (EP)

DAVIS, ANN SIMPSON   PA
of Bucks County. The daughter of Nancy Hines and William Simpson, she was born on December 29, 1764, in Buckingham Township.
During 1780, at the age of fifteen, Ann was handpicked by Gen.
Washington to carry messages to his generals while the army was
in eastern Pennsylvania. Ann was an accomplished horsewoman
well-known to her Tory neighbors, so she was able to slip unnoticed
through areas occupied by the British army. She carried secret
orders in sacks of grain to various mills around Philadelphia and
Bucks County, and sometimes carried messages in bullet cartridges
or in her clothing. Ann was never caught, but on occasions when
she was searched she had to swallow the messages. Later she

received a letter of commendation for her services from Gen. Washington.

On June 26, 1783, Ann married John Davis who had served as an ensign in William Hart's company of the Bucks County Battalion of the Flying Camp. He was born on September 6, 1760, in Solebury Township, Bucks County, the son of Sarah Burkley and William Davis. Ann and John had six sons and three daughters. After the war they moved to Brookville, Maryland, and then in 1816 to Perry Township, Franklin County, Ohio. Ann Davis died on January 6, 1851, in Dublin, Ohio. She is listed as a patriot in the DAR Patriot Index. (Dublin [Ohio] History and Culture, Spring 1988; submitted by Lucile Wulfmeyer, Clearwater, KS)

DAVIS, MARGARET DOZIER   KY
of Spencer County. She was the wife of James Davis, and they resided at Kincheloe's Station on Simpson's Creek. In August 1782, after the Battle of Blue Licks, a report was received that Indians were in the area of the settlement, which consisted of six or seven families. Col. John Floyd ordered the militia to scour the area. While the militia was gone, in the dead of the night, while everybody was asleep, the Indians attacked the cabins of the station and broke open the door, commencing a massacre of men, women, and children.

Mrs. Davis, whose husband was killed, managed to escape and fled into the woods with another woman (apparently her daughter, as her descendants survived). Fortunately they met a lad named Ash who conducted them to Cox's Station. (See also Delilah Tyler Polk, below). Margaret Dozier is listed as a patriot in the DAR Patriot Index. (CH; DAR)

DEANE, ELIZABETH SALTONSTALL   CT
of Wethersfield. Elizabeth was a granddaughter of Governor Saltonstall of Connecticut. She lived in Norwich, Connecticut, prior to her marriage to Silas Deane, after the death of his first wife in 1767. Deane was a delegate to the First Continental Congress in Philadelphia in 1774 and to the Second Congress in 1775.

On his way northward to take command of the Continental Army in Cambridge, Massachusetts, Gen. Washington spent the night of June 29/30, 1775, in the Deane's home. It is next to the Webb House, where Washington stayed in 1781. (BI; FW)

DELAVAN, AGNES TYLER   NY
of Crompound. She was the wife of Capt. Samuel Delavan. On his trip from Haverstraw, New York, to White Plains, New York, Gen. Washington had breakfast at the home of Mrs. Delavan on July 18, 1778, but apparently his officers did some damage, since the Delavans billed Washington Ł1.12.6 for "damage done in the barn." (FW; DAR)

DE VANE, ANN ROBINSON   NC
of New Hanover. She married John De Vane, Sr., about 1752/53,

II: SELECTED BIOGRAPHIES 63

the son of Princess Margaret Conde and Thomas De Vane. They had five sons and four daughters. In 1775/76 he served as a major in the New Hanover militia. Her sons John Jr. and James served in the militia in 1775/76. Then John Jr. served as a lieutenant in Captain Ellis's company from 1777 to 1780 at Fort Johnson, North Carolina.

In July 1780 Lt. De Vane was captured by the British and confined on a vessel in Wilmington, North Carolina, harbor. De Vane contracted smallpox and was put ashore unattended to prevent the spread of the disease on board ship. No one would come near him, but he called out his father's name and finally received help. By 1781 he had fully recovered and became captain of the New Hanover County Cavalry Company.

Ann's daughter Margaret married William Rufus King and their son William Rufus De Vane King served as a United States senator from Alabama, 1820-1844, United States minister to France, 1844-1847, and in 1852 was chosen as vice president of the United States on the ticket with Franklin Pierce. King resigned due to illness and died in 1853. (Submitted by Aida Register, Dunedin, FL) There is a John De Vane Chapter of the Sons of the American Revolution in Plant City, Florida.

DE VOE, ELIZABETH PARCELLS   NJ
of Hackensack. She married Abraham De Voe in 1758. In 1776 there were British troops stationed near Hackensack. About midnight one night they heard a noise outside and looked out the windows. There was a company of enemy soldiers and Tories surrounding the house and stationed at every window except one in a closet that was hidden by high shrubbery. Mrs. De Voe urged her husband to flee, but he protested. Finally he agreed, and slipped out of the window unnoticed by the soldiers and escaped.

The British soldiers pounded on the front door, and Mrs. De Voe let them in. They scoured the house, but couldn't find Mr. De Voe. After realizing that he had escaped, the men took all the food they could find and other valuable items. The next day Mrs. De Voe walked to the enemy camp and complained to the commanding officer that her house had been plundered. The officer demanded to know if her husband had been there, and she admitted he had. The officer admired her bravery and honesty, and ordered two soldiers to guard her house during the period of their encampment. She died in 1818. The local chapter of the Daughters of the American Revolution is named in her honor. (Information from Mrs. Robert C. Lake, Harrington Park, NJ; DAR)

DE WINT, ANTJE KERMER   NY
of Tappan. She married John De Wint, and they had eight children. Washington had his headquarters at the De Wint house twice in 1780 and twice in 1783. Historians agree that their daughter, Anna Marie De Wint Blauvelt, was the actual hostess at the time. (<u>See</u> Mrs. Blauvelt, above)

DEY, HESTER SCHUYLER   NJ
of Paterson. The granddaughter of Arnet Schuyler, she married
Theunis Dey, a colonel in the New Jersey militia. They had seven
sons and three daughters. On July 1, 1780, Gen. Washington
established his headquarters in Pracaness (Preakness). On July 29,
1780, the general left their home. Mrs. Dey was an active member
of the ladies' association for the welfare of the soldiers. (New
Jersey Gazette, July 4, 1780)
    General Washington also had his headquarters there from
October 8 to November 27, 1780. On October 13, Washington wrote
to Col. Brodhead, commander at Fort Pitt: "The want of provisions
is a clog to our operations in every quarter. We have several
times, in the course of this campaign, been without either Bread
or Meat and have never had more than four or five days before-
hand."
    Note that the other Hester Schuyler married William Colfax,
and that Maritje Dey married Peter Doremus, so that Gen. Washington was well acquainted with the Dey and Schuyler families.
    The Dey mansion is located at 199 Totowa Road, Paterson,
adjoining the entrance of the Passaic County Golf Course, and
is maintained as a museum by the Passaic County Park Commission.
(Information from John Donovan, Director, Emanuel Einstein Free
Public Library, Pompton Lakes, NJ)

DICK, MARY ROY   VA
of Fredericksburg. She was the wife of Maj. Charles Dick. The
State Manufactory of Arms at Fredericksburg was established in
1776 by the Virginia Convention. Five men were named as commissioners to superintend the work, and the two men who took the
most active role in the factory were Fielding Lewis and Charles
Dick.
    Mrs. Dick assisted her husband and the other Fredericksburg
women in making cartridges for the American soldiers while the
men were making guns. Maj. Charles Dick on January 4, 1781,
reported to the governor of Virginia that the men and women at
the gunnery had made 100 guns and 20,000 cartridges with bullets.
(Calendar of State Papers, 1:416; from Barbara P. Willis, Fredericksburg, VA)

DICK, SARAH SINNICKSON   NJ
of Salem. She married Dr. Samuel Dick who served in the Colonial
Wars. He was commissioned as a colonel by the Provincial Congress
of New Jersey in 1776. Mrs. Dick was an active member of the
ladies' relief association for the welfare of the American soldiers.
(New Jersey Gazette, July 4, 1780; information from Linda L.
Willis, Salem, NJ)

DICKINSON, MARY MORRIS   PA
of Philadelphia. She was the wife of John Dickinson (1732-1808),
who was a member of the Continental Congress from 1774 to 1776
and in 1780 was elected president of the Supreme Executive Council

II: SELECTED BIOGRAPHIES

of Delaware and Pennsylvania. The Chevalier de la Luzerne, the French ambassador, resided at the Dickinson house on Chestnut Street and on July 15, 1782, gave a party to celebrate the birth of the dauphin. Gen. Washington, the Comte de Rochambeau, and other notables attended the party. (BI) Mary Morris married John Dickinson on July 19, 1770.

DICKINSON, REBECCA CADWALADER   NJ
of Trenton. She was the daughter of Hannah Lambert and Dr. Thomas Cadwalader of Philadelphia who settled in Trenton. Rebecca was the sister of Martha, the first wife of Brig. Gen. Philemon Dickinson. Later he was promoted to major general. Rebecca became the second wife of Gen. Dickinson. They had one son and one daughter. John Adams was in Trenton on September 20, 1777, and wrote in his diary: "Walked with Mr. Duane to General Dickinson's house, and took a Look at his Farm and Gardens, and his Greenhouse, which is a Scene of Desolation. The floor of the Greenhouse is dug up by the Hessians, in Search for Money. The Orange, Lemon and Lime Trees are all dead, with the Leaves on. There is a spacious Ball Room, above stairs a drawing Room and a whispering Room. In another Apartment, a huge Crash of Glass Bottles, which the Hessians had broke I suppose--These are thy Triumphs, mighty Britain."
General Dickinson was a U. S. senator from New Jersey, 1790-1793. Rebecca Dickinson was an active member of the ladies' relief association for the welfare of the American soldiers. (New Jersey Gazette, July 4, 1780) She died on August 5, 1791. (BA)

DILLARD, MARY RAMAGE   SC
of Laurens County. The daughter of Elizabeth Roberts and Joseph Ramage, she was born in 1754, and had seven brothers. Mary married James Dillard (formerly d'Illard) who served as a scout for George Greene in 1777. One day Mary was outside her house and saw British troops in the distance, coming down the road. She ran and told her husband of the approaching danger, and James asked her to spy for him as he was badly in need of information. Then James hid. As the troops marched by, Mary was in her garden counting the number of soldiers. After they passed by, Mary gave the number of the enemy troops to James.
The following act of courage and patriotism by Mary Dillard was recorded by Capt. Samuel Hammond (later a colonel), who served under Col. Clarke of the Volunteers: They received an intelligence report that a body of Tory militia under the command of Col. Ferguson was about to attack. Col. Ferguson with a group of Tories arrived at the Dillard home and requested supper. In going back and forth to the kitchen, which was in a separate building, Mrs. Dillard heard some of their conversation. The Tories planned to surprise Col. Clarke and his men, who were encamped for the night at Green Spring. After she served the food, Mrs. Dillard left the house and rode to Green Spring to warn the Americans of the impending attack. About half an hour before daybreak

she arrived at the American camp and delivered her message to Col. Clarke. The Americans were prepared when the Tories arrived, and a fifteen to twenty minute battle ensued with the Tories forced to retreat. When Mrs. Dillard returned home she found her house in ashes. Mary Ramage Dillard is listed as a patriot in the <u>DAR Patriot Index</u>. She died in 1789. (Prepared by Margaret Ray Holt and submitted by Annie Miller Ray Haney, Sr., of Pontotoc, MS) (CD)

DODGE, NANCY HUNTER   PA

The daughter of Mary and Joseph Hunter of Carlisle, Pennsylvania. The family moved westward during the Revolutionary War when Joseph joined the expedition of Col. George Rogers Clark. Nancy had two married sisters and three brothers who went along with their parents. Her brother James was killed while serving in the army, and his wife, son, and youngest daughter were killed by Indians.

When the Indians attacked the Hunter's fort, the men were low on ammunition, which was hidden in a cache some distance away. Since the men could not be spared, Nancy volunteered to obtain it, which she did on horseback. She returned safely but with two arrows which had pierced her clothing.

Later, while at Fort Jefferson, Indiana, Nancy married Israel Dodge, and they had a son and a daughter. Her son, Henry, became governor of Wisconsin and a United States senator. The Cape Girardeau, Missouri, Chapter of the Daughters of the American Revolution is named in her honor. (GP)

DOREMUS, MARITJE DEY   NJ

Cornelius Doremus built a house on the south side of Montville just west of Towaco, Pequannock Township (now part of Montville Township), on the road from Morristown, New Jersey (now Route 202), to Pompton and the Ramapos. On February 15, 1774, Cornelius J. Doremus and Pieter (Peter) Doremus were elected elders of the Reformed Dutch Church at Persepeney (now Montville). Later Henry Doremus, the son of Cornelius, built a house across the street on the north side. Of the two houses, this is the only one still standing. The Doremus house is a story-and-a-half stone house with two main rooms on the ground floor, and two rooms in the half-story above. The two ground floor rooms have separate entrances, which would indicate that the house was occupied by two families.

Gen. Washington spent the night of June 24/25, 1780, in the home of Mr. and Mrs. Peter Doremus in Pequannock Township, according to the Washington papers. (FW) In 1771 Maritje Dey, the daughter of Sarah Toers, and Dirck Dey, married Peter C. Doremus. Gen. Washington was friends of the Dey and Schuyler families, since he stopped at the Schuyler-Colfax house in 1777 and the Dey house in 1780.

In 1780 the home of Henry Doremus was occupied by his brother, Capt. Thomas Doremus. According to the descendants of Thomas Doremus, Gen. Washington spent the night there and

II: SELECTED BIOGRAPHIES

was present at the time of the birth of Simon H. Van Ness, the son of Susan Doremus and Henry Van Ness, and a grandson of Thomas Doremus, on June 25, 1780. Gen. Washington held the baby in his arms when the boy was only a few hours old, according to family tradition. (Alex D. Fowler, Splinters from the Past: Discovering History in Old Houses, Morris County Historical Society, 1984; information from Susan Gulick, Joint Free Public Library, Morristown, NJ)

Perhaps the two families lived in the same house, with separate entrances. Later Maritje Dey Doremus married John DeHart.

DORRANCE (or DORRENCE), MRS.   CT
of Lebanon. On his return trip from Newport, Rhode Island, to Fishkill, New York, Gen. Washington was entertained at the home of the Dorrances on March 16, 1781. While there he wrote to the Comte de Rochambeau that in a letter from the Marquis de Lafayette, he found that the latter "was embarked and had determined to fall as low down the Chesapeak as Annapolis as the passage is more certain from thence than from the Elk River." (FW)

DOUGHERTY, ELIZABETH   KY
After Canadian and Indian forces under Col. Bird captured Ruddell's and Martin's stations on June 22, 1780, Elizabeth and her husband, John Dougherty, and her son Jesse were captured and taken to Niagara and then to Montreal, where they arrived on October 4, 1782. Later they were taken to Quebec. They were released in 1783. (HP)

DOWDY, BETSY   NC
of Currituck County, was born in 1759. After she learned in December 1775 that the British planned to attack the small garrison at Great Bridge, Virginia, under the command of Col. Robert Howe, she rode fifty miles to Perquimans to the headquarters of Gen. William Skinner to warn him of the impending attack. After her warning, the general was prepared for the British, and won the Battle of Great Bridge, forcing Lord Dunmore to evacuate Norfolk, Virginia. (HS)

DOWNS, JANE DOUGLAS   SC
married Col. William Downs (1728-1802), and during the Revolutionary War she accompanied him on all his excursions. Jane donated her fortune of sixty thousand dollars to the patriotic cause. A chapter of the Daughters of the American Revolution in Dallas, Texas, is named in her honor. (DAR; GP)

DRAKE, PHOEBE REYNOLDS   NY
of Monroe. She was born in 1771, the daughter of Henry Reynolds. In 1782 Tories under Benjamin Kelly raided the Reynolds farmhouse and hanged Reynolds, but Phoebe cut the rope and released her father. The Tories then stuffed Reynolds into a chest, and pillaged and set fire to his house. After they left, Phoebe put out

the fire and rescued her father, who survived. Phoebe then rode to the nearest farmhouse to warn the neighbors. Word spread from farm to farm, and the Americans were ready for the Tories.

Later Phoebe Reynolds married Jeremiah Drake and lived in Neversink, Sullivan County, New York. A white marble slab marks her grave in the Pound Cemetery on Myers Road in Neversink off Route 55. (CP)

DRAPER, MARY ALDIS   MA
of Dedham. She was born in 1719. Her first husband was Abel Allen, and after his death she married Capt. Thomas Draper. In 1775 after the Battle of Bunker Hill, there was a call by Gen. Washington upon the inhabitants to supply lead and pewter to make ammunition for the army. Mrs. Draper, who had a large supply of pewter in her home, donated it to the rebel cause, a truly patriotic act. She died in 1810. (DAR; HC) She also baked bread for the soldiers. (DAR Magazine, July 1976)

DRINKER, ANN SWENT   PA
of Philadelphia, was the wife of Henry Drinker. Ann kept a diary during the occupation of Philadelphia by the British troops. Mrs. Drinker was a true patriot, and recorded on October 6, 1777, that a British officer asked her to take in a wounded British captain, but she refused. She told him that two of the Presbyterian Meetinghouses had been made into hospitals for the wounded soldiers. (CS)

DU BOIS, AMEY GREENMAN   NJ
of Salem County. Her husband was on the roll of minutemen formed at Pittsgrove, New Jersey, in 1775 under Capt. Jacob du Bois, Sr. He served for eight years, attaining the rank of captain. Her brother, the Rev. Nehemiah Greenman, pastor of the Pittsgrove Presbyterian Church and schoolmaster, was forced to flee into the "wilderness" of Egg Harbor on March 17, 1778, when a British regiment some fifteen hundred strong marched into Salem County. Presbyterian ministers, foremost in the cause of American independence, could expect no favors from the enemy.

While her brother was in hiding, Amey du Bois taught in the local school and performed a public service during the Revolutionary War. (Submitted by Mary Coates Martin, Norfolk, VA)

DUETT, MARY   KY
After Tory, Canadian, and Indian forces under Col. Bird captured Ruddell's and Martin's stations on June 22, 1780, Mary and her husband, Henry Duett, were captured and taken to Niagara. Later they were taken to Montreal, arriving there on October 4, 1782, and were then taken to Quebec. They were released in 1783. (HP)

DUNHAM, KEZIAH FITZ RANDOLPH   NJ
of Piscataway, was the wife of Jonathan Dunham, Sr., also known as John. On his trip from New Brunswick to Paramus, New

II: SELECTED BIOGRAPHIES   69

Jersey, Gen. Washington had breakfast at the Dunhams' on
July 10, 1778. He then stayed at the home of Mrs. Prevost
(later Mrs. Aaron Burr) in Paramus. (FW)
  At this time, Eunice Dunn and her husband, Jonathan
Dunham III, were also living in Piscataway. (Some information
submitted by Mary H. Newling, John F. Kennedy Memorial
Library, Piscataway, NJ)

DUNN, ELINOR BREWSTER   VA
of Augusta County. She was born on January 25, 1754. Elinor
and her sisters Agnes Brewster Alexander and Jennet Brewster
Irvin spun, knitted, wove, sewed, cooked, and made bullets for
the Revolutionary War soldiers. Later she married Samuel Dunn
(1750-1802). Elinor died on November 3, 1841. The three sisters
are buried on the campus of the University of Indiana at Bloomington. (Ann S. Alexander, Revolution Service of the Brewster Sisters; submitted by Beverly A. Henricks, Glendale, CA)

DWIGHT, SIBBIL (SIBYL)   MA
of Warren. She married Col. Simeon Dwight, Sr., who was born
on February 18, 1719/20, the son of Sydney Dwight. Col. Dwight
built a tavern in 1746 located on what is now the corner of Burbank
and Main streets in Western (now Warren).
  On his journey from New York to Cambridge, Massachusetts,
in 1775, Gen. Washington spent the night of June 29, at the home
of Mr. and Mrs. Silas Deane in Wethersfield, Connecticut. Then
on the morning of June 30, he proceeded northward and took the
road from West Brimfield to Warren. Upon his arrival in Warren,
Gen. Washington was offered a drink of water by a Mr. Keyes,
while Washington was standing under an elm tree on Mr. Keyes's
property. Later a bronze tablet was placed on the tree which
reads, "Beneath this elm, General Washington sought refreshment
and rest. 1775." Washington then proceeded onto West Brookfield
and then to Watertown.
  Gen. Howe and his British troops evacuated Boston in March
1776, and early in April Gen. Washington and his troops commenced
their march to New York City. On his trip southward, Gen. Washington and his officers spent the night of April 8, 1776, in Dwight's
Tavern.
  Simeon Dwight, Jr., sold the hotel, now a house, in 1815
to John A. Burbank, whose son Allen sold the house in 1895 to
Frank Keith. (Information from a 1924 Springfield, Massachusetts,
newspaper, supplied by Sylvia G. Buck, Warren Public Library).
In 1981 the house was carefully dismantled and taken to Guilford,
Connecticut, where it was restored, and now serves as a private
residence.

E

EASTMAN, MARY BUTLER   NH
of Gilmanton. She married Ebenezer Eastman, who was born on
April 24, 1746, in Kingston, New Hampshire. He was a lieutenant
in the Revolutionary War and commanded a company in Gen. John
Stark's brigade at the Battle of Bunker Hill on June 17, 1775.
The next Sunday at church, Mrs. Eastman was told by neighbors
of hearing cannon fire and that the battle was still raging on the
heights of Charlestown (Boston).
  Mrs. Eastman became alarmed, and with no friend to accompany
her, the young woman rode on horseback with her infant child
through the forest wilderness, guided only by blazed trees, to
her father's house in Brentwood. Here she left her baby with
the child's grandparents. She then rode to Charlestown, a distance of some ninety miles, where she found her husband safe.
  Benjamin F. Taylor wrote a poem, "Mary Butler's Ride."
(Guy S. Rix, History and Genealogy of the Eastman Family in America,
1901)
  The Laconia, New Hampshire, Chapter of the Daughters of
the American Revolution is named the Mary Butler Chapter in her
honor. (Submitted by Hazel Oliver, Cocoa Beach, FL; DAR)

EDDY, OLIVE MORSE   ME
of Cumberland County, Nova Scotia. She was the wife of William
Eddy, son of Jonathan Eddy, who led the attack on Fort Cumberland, Nova Scotia, on November 16, 1776, when the Americans
were repulsed.
  Olive was taken prisoner by the British. Finally Olive was
released on September 27, 1777, and the family migrated to Maine.
She had three children. (DAR Magazine, February 1983)

EDGAR, RACHEL   IL
Her husband was in the British navy. Mrs. Edgar convinced her
husband and three British soldiers to desert. Rachel and her
husband fled to the settlement of Kaskaskia, now in Illinois. (DAR
Magazine, July 1921)

ELLERY, ABIGAIL CAREY   RI
of Newport. The daughter of Elizabeth Wanton and Nathaniel Carey,
in 1767 she became the second wife of William Ellery, whose first
wife had died in 1764. She was the grandmother of Richard H.
Dana, the author and poet. Abigail and her husband had eight
children, but only two lived to maturity. Mr. Ellery was outspoken
as a proponent of liberty and was a signer of the Declaration of
Independence. As a result, their home was burned by the Tories.
After the war Mr. Ellery became chief justice of Rhode Island.
Abigail died in 1793. (GP)

ELLIOTT, SUSANNAH SMITH   SC
of Charleston. She was the wife of Col. Barnard Elliott. In June

II: SELECTED BIOGRAPHIES

1776 she embroidered two standards for the 2nd South Carolina Regiment of infantry commanded by Col. Moultrie. Mrs. Elliott presented these flags to the regiment at the fort on Sullivans Island on June 28, 1776. (CD)

ELLISON, ELIZABETH POTTS   SC
of Winnsboro, Fairfield County. She came with her parents from Belfast, Ireland, on the scow Betty Gregg in 1767/68. On November 6, 1772, in Charleston she married Robert Ellison (1742-1806). They had six sons and three daughters. Her husband organized a company of volunteers as a captain under Lt. Col. John Winn. In 1775 they were marched to the Congaree River and joined the regiment of Col. William Richardson, in pursuit of a body of Tories called Scofilites, and captured a number of them. The campaign lasted through the winter of 1775/76 in up-county South Carolina and was called the Snow Campaign since the snowfall was heavy. In June 1776 a British expedition attempted to capture the fort on Sullivans Island where Robert was stationed. The fort was under the command of Col. William Moultrie (later a general) and is named in his honor.

Major Ellison participated in Gen. Lincoln's attack on Augusta, Georgia, which was held by the British in 1779. At Stono, Ellison had his horse killed under him. In the retreat of the Americans from Augusta to Charleston under Moultrie, Ellison was taken prisoner and carried to Charleston, then to Johns Island, then to Dry Tortugas, where he was imprisoned for two years and cruelly treated.

Elizabeth was left alone and unprotected with five children. She was molested during the depredations by the Tories and had her hair torn out by the roots and bore the marks the rest of her life. She fled with her children to Charleston, and while she was gone her home was burned by the Tories. (Charles Ellison Erath, Descendents of John and Robert Ellison, 1972)

Elizabeth died on January 15, 1793. Later Robert married Jane (Jennie) Seawright. (Submitted by Kathryn G. Crawford, El Paso, TX; Mrs. W. J. Dalrymple, Vicksburg, MS) During the Revolutionary War she supplied provisions for the army in South Carolina. (SI, U-W:67)

ELLISON, MARGARET GARRABRANT   NY
of New Windsor. In 1723 she was married by the Rev. Mr. Bull, Dutch minister in New York, to Thomas Ellison (1701-1784), the son of Eleanor and John Ellison. Margaret had eleven children, seven of them surviving to maturity: four daughters and three sons. About 1724 Thomas erected a house, Dutch-cottage style, which became the headquarters of Gen. Washington during the Revolutionary War. He also built a warehouse and dock. Soon Thomas was the principal merchant and banker of that area. In 1754 he erected a stone building, near Vail's Gate, known as the Ellison House, and also a flour mill. The stone mansion, still standing, was the headquarters of Gen. Henry Knox during the war. Thomas Ellison served as a colonel in the Ulster County militia

prior to the Revolution. (Ruttenger, History of New Windsor)

Gen. Washington had his headquarters in the Ellison cottage from June 21 to July 21, 1779. On June 23, Gen. Washington wrote to the president of Congress: "Two days since I removed my quarters to this place where I am more contiguous to the forts and best situated to attend to the different parts of the army. By my last advices the enemy at Kings Ferry were embarking their baggage and some heavy cannon and preparing for a movement either up or down the river." (FW)

On June 22, Washington visited West Point, which was only six miles above Ellison's cottage, and again on June 24 to inspect the fortifications being constructed. From his orderly book of July 4: "This day being the anniversary of our glorious independence, will be commemorized by the firing of thirteen cannon from West Point at 1 o'clock P.M. The Commander-in-Chief thinks proper to grant a general pardon to all prisoners in this army, under sentence of death. They are to be released from confinement accordingly."

Gen. Washington was also here from December 6, 1780, to March 2, 1781, and from March 20 to May 18, 1781. Mrs. Ellison died in 1783. (Some information from Donald C. Gordon, Town Historian, New Windsor, NY)

EMERSON, NAOMI BLAISDELL   ME
of Nova Scotia. She migrated from New England to Nova Scotia in 1776 with her parents, Anna and Moses Blaisdell. She was the wife of Samuel Emerson, and they had five children. The Blaisdells and the Emersons were American patriots, and in 1783 they were forced to flee from Nova Scotia to Maine where the Emersons settled in Hampden. (DAR Magazine, February 1983)

EMLEN, MRS. GEORGE   PA
of Whitemarsh. Gen. Washington had his headquarters at the home of Mr. and Mrs. George Emlen from November 3, 1777, until December 11. A part of the left wing of the army encamped at the rear of the house. Later Mr. Emlen complained to Gen. Washington about the damage to his farm, and Washington replied on December 13, 1778, that Emlen must file his claim with the quartermaster's department. (FW)

EMMONS, LUCRETIA   NJ
of Monmouth County. She was a black woman, aged twenty, and a servant in the home of Capt. Joshua Huddy. When about sixty Tories stormed Huddy's house, Lucretia loaded the muskets so Huddy could keep firing at the enemy as he ran from room to room and window to window. In desperation at their failure to capture Huddy, the Tories set fire to his house. Soon afterward a party of men arrived to save Capt. Huddy and Lucretia Emmons. Later Capt. Huddy was captured while manning a blockhouse in Toms River, New Jersey, without the assistance of Emmons. The Huddy house is located on the Colts Neck-Freehold Road (NJ Route 34). (CP)

II: SELECTED BIOGRAPHIES

ERSKINE, ELIZABETH   NJ
of Bergen County. She married Robert Erskine, a civil engineer in England, and they came to Bergen County where he became a captain in the militia in 1775. Gen. Washington made Erskine geographer and surveyer-general of the Continental Army, and he was commissioned on July 27, 1777. He became ill while on a surveying job and died on October 2, 1780.
    Mrs. Erskine was active in the ladies' relief association for the welfare of the American soldiers. (New Jersey Gazette, July 4, 1780)

ESPY, JEAN   PA
of Northumberland County. She was the wife of George Espy, and they had six sons and three daughters who survived to maturity. Her husband died before the war. Jean and her son Josiah lived near McClure's Fort, which was commanded by Maj. Van Campen. On one occasion Jean and her son fled to the fort for protection from the Indians. While there, Jean molded bullets for the soldiers during an Indian attack and later baked corn dodgers for the men.
    Six of her sons served in the Revolutionary War, together with her three sons-in-law, various grandsons, and one great-grandson, who at age sixteen spent the winter at Valley Forge, Pennsylvania. Jean Espy died in 1781 in Carlisle, Pennsylvania. The Fort Madison, Iowa, Chapter of the Daughters of the American Revolution is named in her honor. (GP)

F

FALCONER, JOICE CRAIG   KY
of Lexington. The daughter of Polly Hawkins and Tolliver Craig II, she was the sister of John Craig who founded Craig's Station near David's Fork in eastern Fayette County. She married John Falconer (Faulkner) in Spotsylvania County, Virginia, and about September 1779 they left for western Virginia, now Kentucky. Three generations of the families started construction on the station on Christmas Eve 1779. There was prejudice against the Scotch-Irish, and so on April 2, 1780, the Falconers moved to Francis McConnell's Station about one mile from Fort Lexington. (There is a Kentucky Historical Highway marker at 1213 Old Frankfort Pike near the site.)
    Later in 1780 they were living at Gilbert's Creek Station with Joice's relatives, the Hamptons and the Johnsons. In March 1781 when it was reported that the Indians were approaching, the Falconers crossed the river into now what is Garrard County. In December 1781, along came the Craigs--her parents, Polly and Taliaferro Craig, Sr., and their three sons--Lewis, Elijah and Joseph --all three of whom were Baptist preachers.
    In her old age, in an interview with the Rev. John D. Shane, Joice said: "The first buffaloes I ever saw, there were pretty near perhaps a thousand in number, and the woods roared with their tramping, almost as bad as thunder ... I've seen a hundred turkeys

roosting within sight of our station. Their craws would be full of mistletoe and they were so fat that when they fell, the fat would on their backs split open."

Joice Falconer was living in 1792, apparently in the house of her son, Lewis Falconer, which still stands at 3564 Clays Mill Pike, Lexington, Kentucky. (Bettye Lee Mastin, Lexington 1779, Fayette County Historical Commission)

FANNING, ANNE BREWSTER   CT
of Jewett City. She was born in Griswold, Connecticut, in 1753, and in 1774 she married Charles Fanning of Groton, Connecticut. They lived in Jewett City. He served in the Revolutionary War for the duration--seven years and eight months--one of the few men who did so, and was retired as a captain. Fanning was an original member of the Society of the Cincinnati, founded by Washington's officers in 1783. Mrs. Fanning died in 1813. In recognition of the suffering and patriotism of Mrs. Fanning, the Jewett City Chapter of the Daughters of the American Revolution is named in her honor. (CG; DAR)

FARRAND, RHODA SMITH   NJ, VT
of Morristown, New Jersey. She was born in 1747, and at age fifteen she married Bethul Farrand who was a lieutenant in the militia. They lived on a farm at Pine Brook, Morris County. Rhoda had eleven children. When Lt. Farrand was stationed in Morristown in 1778, the men were dying of scurvy. Rhoda visited her husband, and met Gen. Washington, who told her that he thought cabbage would counteract the scurvy. So Rhoda went around the countryside collecting cabbage for Washington's army. Then with her daughters Hannah and Bet, the women knitted socks for the American soldiers. She also persuaded her neighbors on Whippany Road to knit socks.

After the death of her husband, Rhoda was taken to Vermont by her youngest brother, Jacob Smith. For many years she resided with her daughter Hannah, the wife of Capt. Newton Hayward. Rhoda died at Bridport, Vermont, on June 30, 1839, at age ninety-two. At her death, her descendants numbered more than 150. On June 30, 1916, the Rhoda Farrand Chapter of Addison, Vermont, Daughters of the American Revolution placed a marker on her grave. (DAR; submitted by Nancy Polk Woolford, Jacksonville, FL)

FARROW, ROSANNA WATERS   SC
of Musgrove's Mill. The daughter of Sarah Bordroyne and Philemon Waters, she was born about 1734 in Prince William County, Virginia. She married John Farrow, and they had five sons and three daughters. They moved to the 96th District (Spartanburg County) on the banks of the Enoree River, about five miles above Musgrove's Mill. Unfortunately Mr. Farrow was stricken with smallpox and died in 1776, leaving Rosanna with eight children to raise.

Rosanna's five sons served in the Revolutionary War. The oldest, Thomas, although not yet twenty-one years of age, was

II: SELECTED BIOGRAPHIES   75

placed in charge of a cavalry company. Rosanna was left at home
with her four daughters, unprotected, surrounded by treacherous
Tory neighbors. Mrs. Farrow and her girls were forced to hide
in the woods and swamps from the Tory marauders--often without
food.
    In the summer of 1780 Mrs. Farrow was informed that three
of her sons had been captured in a skirmish and were confined
in the 96th District jail. She was told that the British Col. Cruger
intended to shoot his American prisoners before he left the district.
At Musgrove's Mill the American colonel had captured some Redcoats,
and Mrs. Farrow was told that an exchange of prisoners was possible
--two Redcoats for each American soldier.
    Rosanna seized a rifle and informed her daughters of her
mission to rescue her sons. She went to the stable, saddled an
unbroken black colt, and with a prayer she galloped away. Rosanna
rode through the dark woods inhabited by Indians and some hunters.
    Mrs. Farrow rode to the camp of the American Col. Williams
located at the Fair Forest stream, near the present site of Spartanburg, South Carolina. She told him her story, and Col. Williams
readily granted her request since he needed more men. Col. Williams released six British soldiers and a guard. Before daybreak
of the second night they reached the British camp, and Mrs. Farrow requested the prisoner exchange of Col. Cruger, to which
the colonel replied, "Well, you are just in time, for I ordered these
rebellious youngsters of yours to be shot at sunrise." And Rosanna
replied, "I have given you two for one, Colonel Cruger, but I
understand I consider it the best trade I ever made, for rest assured hereafter the Farrow boys will whip you four to one."
    The boys were exchanged, and her son Samuel lived to rep-
resent the Pinckney District in Congress. He also served as lieutenant governor of South Carolina. (John Belton O'Neall, Biographical Sketches of the Bench and Bar of South Carolina, 1859; Ruth
Petty, Rosanna Farrow, Spartanburg County Revolutionary Heroine)
    Rosanna Waters Farrow is listed as head of household in the
census of 1790 in the old 96th District. The Rosanna Waters Chapter
of the Daughters of the American Revolution in Clarksdale, Mississip-
pi, is named in her honor. (A complete article on Rosanna Waters
Farrow is in the American Monthly Magazine, 19, July-December
1901; submitted by Sarah H. Delgado, Oxnard, CA, and Mary Jo
Roberts, Columbia, MS)

FELL, REBECCA WILSON   PA
of Doylestown. The daughter of Rebecca Canby and Samuel Wilson,
she married Jonathan Fell in 1767. They had a daughter, Ann,
born in 1768 and a son, Jonathan, born in 1771.
    On his way from Valley Forge into New Jersey, on June 20,
1778, Gen. Washington pitched his tent on the property of Mrs.
Fell. (BI) The general then crossed the Delaware River and spent
the night of June 21 at the home of Susanna Fell in Coryells Ferry,
New Jersey. (FW; information from Terry A. McNealy, Spruance
Library, Doylestown, PA)

FELL, SUSANNA MARSCHALK   NJ
of Coryells Ferry. She was first married to a Mr. McIntosh, and then to John Fell, a merchant. In 1776 he was a member of the New Jersey Provincial Congress, but on April 22, 1777, his home was raided by Loyalists and he was taken a prisoner. Mr. Fell was kept in jail in New York City until he was released on May 11, 1778.

General Washington had his headquarters in their home on June 21, 1778. While there he wrote to the president of Congress: "This will be delivered to you by Major Wemp [Major Myndent of Schenectady, New York] who has the care of some Warriors from the Seneca Nation. The inclosed copy of a Letter from our Commissioners will shew, that they come to obtain the release of Astiarix, another Warrior, who has been taken on the Frontiers of Virginia."

Mr. Fell then served in the Continental Congress from November 1778 until November 1780. Mrs. Fell was active in the ladies' association for the welfare of the American soldiers. (New Jersey Gazette, July 4, 1780; DAR; FW)

FERGUSON, ELIZABETH GREENE   PA
of Philadelphia. The daughter of Ann Diggs and Dr. Thomas Greene, she was born on February 3, 1737. She became engaged to William Franklin, the son of Benjamin Franklin in 1754, but he quarreled with her, and in 1762 he married a Miss Elizabeth Downes in London. Miss Greene was heartbroken and turned to writing poetry. On April 21, 1772, she married Henry Hugh Ferguson, a Scot, who became British commissary of prisoners in Philadelphia in September 1777. She was a patriotic American and a friend of Gen. Washington. Mrs. Ferguson devoted much of her time to caring for the American prisoners and gave freely to charity. She assisted the American prisoners taken at the Battle of Germantown.

She was empowered by Governor Johnstone to offer a bribe to Joseph Reed, president of the Pennsylvania council, to make peace in 1778. President Reed scorned the bribe. Historians believe that Mrs. Ferguson was a patriot and desired peace, but was misled by her husband and by Governor Johnstone. After the war Mrs. Ferguson's property was confiscated, but she was allowed to keep her home in Graeme Park because she had nursed the American prisoners of war. She died on February 23, 1801. (DB)

FERRIS, ANN TRIP   NY
of Pawling. Gen. Washington had had headquarters at the home of Pvt. Reed and Ann Ferris from September 22 to 25, 1778. On September 23, Washington wrote to his brother John Augustine Washington, "Your letter of the 30th Ulto. came to my hands a few days ago, and gave me the pleasure of hearing that you are all well, and an opportunity of congratulating you on the birth of a grandchild, tho you do not say whether it be male or female." (FW; DAR)

II: SELECTED BIOGRAPHIES

FEW, MARY WHEELER   NC
of Hillsborough. She married William Few of Baltimore, and in 1758 they moved to North Carolina. The Few family members were active in the "Regulators" who defied British rule. Two thousand Regulators were defeated by the British on May 16, 1771, at the Battle of the Alamance River. James Few, a brother, was hanged following the battle, and the British took the cattle and horses and burned the Few family home. Mr. and Mrs. Few were true patriots. Their son William was a signer of the Constitution of the United States. (DB)

FITCH, ELIZABETH MARY MIX   CT
of New Haven. She was the second wife of Jonathan Fitch (1727-1793), who was a colonel in the army. On June 2, 1780, Israel Bishop obtained a letter of marque and reprisal to command the Connecticut brig *Sally* with six guns and a crew of twelve men. Witnesses to the bond were Jonathan Fitch and Elizabeth M. Fitch. She also witnessed bonds for Ebenezer Peck on May 13, 1782; for Daniel Jones on June 1, 1782; and for David Phipps on September 17, 1782. (CN; DAR)

FITHIAN, ELIZABETH BEATTY   NJ
of Bridgeton. She resided in New York, and on October 25, 1775, she married the Rev. Philip Vickers Fithian in Princeton, New Jersey. In 1776 he enlisted as a chaplain in the army. Mrs. Fithian spun wool and linen for the American soldiers. In October 1776 the Rev. Fithian became ill and died. Mrs. Fithian moved to Cumberland County, New Jersey, and in 1780 was active in the ladies' relief association for the welfare of American soldiers. (*New Jersey Gazette*, July 4, 1780)

FITZHUGH, ANNE FRISBY   MD
the daughter of Peregrine Frisby of Cecil County, Maryland, she was born in 1727. Her first husband was John Rousby. After his death she married Col. William Fitzhugh in 1759. They lived on a plantation at the mouth of the Patuxent River. At the beginning of the Revolutionary War, Col. Fitzhugh was nearly blind and a supporter of the patriotic cause. As a result, he was a marked man to the British and the Tories. Her sons Peregrine and William served in the Continental Army. One day while her husband was away, the enemy attacked. Mrs. Fitzhugh gathered her sons' hunting rifles and ammunition and with her slaves fired upon the Tories. When the firing started, the enemy fled the area.

The next time they learned that the British were approaching, Col. and Mrs. Fitzhugh left their home. When they later returned, they found it burned to the ground, so they moved some distance away for the duration of the war. In the fall of 1782 the British came to take Col. Fitzhugh to New York as a prisoner. Mrs. Fitzhugh insisted that she go along since he was blind and she had to care for him. The British released him on parole in her custody.

Anne Fitzhugh died in 1793 and was buried at Rousby Hall in Maryland in a grave beside her husband. The Bay City, Michigan, Chapter of the Daughters of the American Revolution is named in her honor. (GP)

FLOYD, HANNAH JONES   NY
of Mastic, Long Island. She married William Floyd of Brookhaven, Long Island, a wealthy landowner who was an officer in the Suffolk County militia and later rose to be a major general. Floyd served as a delegate to the Continental Congress from 1774 to 1777 and was a signer of the Declaration of Independence.

On August 27, 1776, the British Gen. Sir William Howe landed his troops on Long Island. Washington's army was driven westward to Harlem Heights, then beyond New York City and forced to retreat across the Hudson River into New Jersey. As the British troops neared her house, Mrs. Floyd was warned to leave. She fled across Long Island Sound with her son and two daughters, ferried by a local fisherman, and found haven with friends in Middletown, Connecticut, where she remained until her death on May 16, 1781.

Meanwhile the Floyd homestead was looted. Everything of value was taken, including the farm animals and equipment. The place was a shambles. In 1784 William Floyd married Joanna Strong. (FG) Some books give the first Mrs. Floyd's name as Isabella, but the marriage certificate reads Hannah. (GP)

FLOYD, JANE BUCHANAN   KY
was the wife of Col. John Floyd of Virginia. They came to Boonesborough, Kentucky, early in 1775. Col. Floyd accompanied Daniel Boone in pursuit of Indians who had captured Boone's daughter in July 1776, and they rescued the girl. Later Col. and Mrs. Floyd settled in Beargrass, Kentucky. He was killed by Indians on April 13, 1783. Later, in 1785, Col. William Christian moved from Virginia to Kentucky and settled on the land of Jane Floyd. On April 18, 1786, he led a party of men against Indian raiders, but Col. Christian was killed in battle. (CH)

FORD, THEODOSIA JOHNES   NJ
of Morristown. Gen. Washington's Guard was stationed in her home during the winter of 1777. She was the widow of Jacob Ford, Jr. On his way from Pompton to West Point and back, Gen. Washington was to spend a night or so here, but stayed much longer. He was supposed to arrive on December 1, 1779, according to a letter from Gen. Washington to Maj. Gen. Nathaniel Greene. In a letter dated January 22, 1780, Gen. Washington complained: "I have been at my prest. quarters since the 1st of Decr. and have not a Kitchen to Cook a Dinner in ... Eighteen belonging to my family and all of Mrs. Fords are crowded together in her Kitchen and scarce one of them able to speak for the colds they have caught." (FW)

So while Mrs. Ford did the best she could, with all her children Gen. Washington and his party suffered great inconvenience. Gen. Washington left Mrs. Ford's house on June 23, 1780.

II: SELECTED BIOGRAPHIES   79

On December 27, 1779, Gen. Washington attended the celebration of the festival of Saint John the Evangelist given by the American Union Lodge of Ancient Free and Accepted Masons. (BI)

FORMAN, ANN MARSH   NJ
of Monmouth County. On February 28, 1767, she married David Forman, an attorney, and they had eleven children. In 1776 he was appointed a colonel of a New Jersey regiment and in 1777 was promoted to brigadier general of the New Jersey militia, but he resigned his commission in November 1777. Forman then devoted himself to suppressing the Loyalists in New Jersey and was called the Devil David by the Loyalists.

Mrs. Forman was active in the ladies' relief association for the welfare of the American soldiers. (New Jersey Gazette, July 4, 1780)

FORNEY, MARIA BERGNER   NC
of Tryon County. She was born in 1724 in Switzerland, and in 1752 in Pennsylvania she married Jacob Forney (1721-1806), who was born in Alsace, where his family had fled for safety. The couple met while on board a ship to America. About 1754 they migrated to North Carolina. Their sons Peter, Jacob Jr., and Abram served in the Revolutionary War.

During the war Gen. Cornwallis took possession of the Forney homestead, consigning Maria and Jacob to the cellar. When Lord Cornwallis and his troops left for Wilmington, North Carolina, after the Battle of Guilford Courthouse on March 15, 1781, the family discovered that all their provisions had been confiscated--all stored food and livestock, as well as their buried gold and silver.

Although Maria was a true patriot, she restrained her husband from killing Lord Cornwallis. (Hunter, Sketches of Western North Carolina; Sherrill, Annals of North Carolina History; Wheeler, Sketchbook of North Carolina History)

Maria died in Lincoln County, North Carolina, in 1808. (Submitted by Mary Louise Hinton Vance, Miloki, MS)

FRANCIS, ANNE WILLING   PA
of Philadelphia. She was the wife of Trench Francis the Younger. Mrs. Francis was a member of the ladies' association for the relief of the American soldiers, founded by Esther De Berdt Reed. Upon the death of Mrs. Reed in September 1780, Mrs. Francis and Mrs. Bache, together with three other women, took over the management of the association. With their own money, they purchased material and made shirts for the American soldiers. (NL)

From New Windsor, New York, on February 13, 1781, Gen. Washington wrote a letter addressed to Anne Francis, Henrietta Hillegas, Mary Clarkson, Sarah Bache, and Susan Blair.

> Ladies: The benevolent office, which added lustre to the qualities that ornamented your deceased friend [Esther Reed] could not have descended to more zealous or more deserving successors.

The contributions of the association you represent have exceeded what could have been expected, and the spirit that animated the members of it, intitles them to an equal place with any who have preceded them in the walk of female patriotism. It embellishes the American character with a new trait; by proving that the love of country is blended with those softer domestic virtues, which have always been allowed to be more peculiarly your own.

You have not acquired admiration in your country only; it is paid you abroad; and you will learn with pleasure by a part of your own sex, where female accomplishments have attained their highest perfection, and who from the commencement have been the patronesses of American liberty. (FW)

FRAZER, MARY WORALL TAYLOR   PA
of Thornbury Township, Chester County. The daughter of John Taylor, she was born in 1745. Her grandfather, Dr. John Taylor, built a forge in 1742 on the Chester Creek (now Glen Mills), which became so successful that the British Parliament in 1750 passed an act forbidding the erection of iron works in the American Colonies. In 1766 Mary married Persifor Frazer, and they had ten children.

Capt. Frazer commanded a battalion of Pennsylvania troops and in May 1776 served under Col. Anthony Wayne on Long Island. On September 4, 1776, Frazer was promoted to major while at Fort Ticonderoga. On March 12, 1777, Gen. Wayne appointed Frazer lieutenant colonel of the 5th Batallion of the Pennsylvania Line. While Lord Howe's army was at Kennett Square, Pennsylvania, Gen. Washington's army was at Chadd's Ford on the Brandywine Creek. Washington stripped his army for action and sent three wagonloads of officers' baggage on August 29, 1777, to Mrs. Frazer's home for storage. The Battle of Brandywine took place on September 11, with a loss to the Americans, and Col. Frazer was captured by the British on September 13, 1777.

At this time the British troops arrived at the house of Mrs. Frazer, including fifty horsemen commanded by Capt. de West. A British officer entered her house and demanded, "Where are the damned rebels?" Meanwhile the soldiers ransacked the house and drank liquor they had found.

As Capt. de West entered the house, a drunken soldier was about to hit Mary, so the captain made the soldiers leave. He said he was told that the house was full of ammunition and arms, but he found nothing because the ammunition had already been removed. Capt. de West suggested that her husband join the British army, to which Mary replied, "You do not know Colonel Frazer, or you would not suggest such a thing; nor would he listen to me were I to propose it; but if he did listen, and was persuaded to change sides, I would never consent to have anything to do with him."

The men discovered the baggage containing clothes but not

II: SELECTED BIOGRAPHIES   81

arms or ammunition. They raided the barn and took fifty bushels
of wheat and also the horses.
    In October 1777 Mrs. Frazer went to Philadelphia to see her
husband, with the permission of Gen. Washington. With her she
took food for the imprisoned soldiers, and in Philadelphia she received help from Mrs. Jenkins who had been providing food for
the American prisoners.
    During the winter of 1777/78 Mrs. Frazer collected food and
clothing for the soldiers at Valley Forge. She took over 300 pairs
of stockings plus large quantities of blankets and clothing for the
soldiers.
    While in Philadelphia on October 11, 1777, Mrs. Frazer drove
to Whitemarsh and visited Gen. Washington and his guest, the Marquis de Lafayette. On Saint Patrick's Day 1778, while the British
guards were drunk, Col. Frazer escaped his imprisonment. On
May 25, 1782, he was made a brigadier general of the Pennsylvania
militia.
    In 1824 Mrs. Frazer was in Philadelphia again, and Lafayette
called on her. Mrs. Frazer died in 1830, leaving no fewer than
fifty grandchildren. She was buried in the Middletown Presbyterian Church next to her husband. (There is a ten-page article
about Mary Frazer in the DAR Magazine, August-September 1979;
submitted by Jean B. Shaw, Beesley Point, NJ; DAR; FW)

FRENCH, RACHEL DREW   NY
of Echo Lake. She was married to Robert French, who was a
scout for Gen. Washington. One day the British stopped at her
home and asked for her husband. She told them he had gone to
the mill, when actually he was hiding in the barn. The soldiers
asked for cider. Mrs. French told them it was in the cellar and
they could help themselves. They left their arms in her kitchen
and proceeded to the cellar. Then Rachel bolted the door and
called for her husband, who took the British soldiers as prisoners.
(FH; information from Susan Gulick, Morristown, NJ)

FROST, ANNA FUNCH   MA
of Tewksbury. The daughter of Elizabeth Davis and Jacob Funch,
she was born on August 16, 1728, in Billerica, Massachusetts.
On January 1, 1749, she married Edmund Frost of Tewksbury.
Her son Jacob, born on July 9, 1753, was wounded at the Battle
of Bunker Hill on June 17, 1775, and was captured. Jacob was
imprisoned in Boston until the following spring, and then taken to
Halifax, where he was imprisoned until his escape. The bullet
he had received in his hip "was not extracted until he was over
80 years old." (Daniel Shed Genealogy, 1327-1920) His imprisonment shows the suffering endured by the patriotic American women.
    After his escape, Jacob Frost married Lydia Shed, the daugh-
ter of Lydia Kittredge and Lt. Jonathan Shed, on October 2, 1777.
They had twelve children. (Submitted by Rebecca Shedd Thomas,
Luray, VA)

FULTON, SARAH BRADLEE   MA
of Medford. She was born on December 24, 1740, in Dorchester
(now part of Boston). In 1762 Sarah married John Fulton, and
they moved to Medford. Sarah and her husband often visited her
brother, Nathaniel Bradlee, in Boston. While on a visit to her
brother's house on December 16, 1773, Bradlee and Fulton joined
a group of activists dressed as Mohawk Indians, boarded the tea
ships in Boston Harbor, and dumped 342 casks of the tea into the
water. This became known as the Boston Tea Party.

Mrs. Bradlee and Mrs. Fulton helped their husbands arrange
their disguises in advance, and upon their return washed the men's
faces to remove the red stains. Sarah Fulton became known as
the Mother of the Boston Tea Party.

After the Battle of Bunker Hill on June 17, 1775, Sarah was
on hand with a basketful of lint and bandages. Other women came
to help, and since few surgeons were available, Sarah was placed
in charge of care for the wounded soldiers.

About March 1776 Maj. John Brooks of Medford had a message
for Gen. Washington and called upon the Fultons. Sarah agreed
to carry the message through enemy lines--which she did--and
returned home safely. Later Washington visited the Fultons to
thank Sarah and partook in a bowl of punch, served by Sarah
with a brand new ladle. A number of years later the Marquis de
Lafayette visited the Fultons and was served from the same punch-
bowl, which is now in the possession of the Medford Historical
Society.

Sarah Fulton died in 1835 and was buried in the Salem Street
Cemetery in Medford. Her grave is memorialized with a tablet which
reads: "Sarah Bradlee Fulton, 1740-1835. A Heroine of the Revolution. Erected by the Sarah Bradlee Fulton Chapter D.A.R. 1900."
(GP, vol. 2)

G

GAGE, JENNET PIKE   NJ
of Woodbridge. The daughter of Mary Harriot and James Pike,
she was born in 1748. Jennet was the sister of Zebulon Pike.
She married Philip Gage, a Tory, and they lived at Strawberry
Hill. In 1779 Gage's property was confiscated, but since Jennet
was a patriot, she was allowed to purchase the property. Her
husband died in 1780. Jennet Gage, who was a Methodist, died
in Woodbridge in 1821. (DW)

GALLOWAY, MRS.   NJ
of Southfield. After he left Suffern's Tavern on July 20, 1777,
Gen. Washington established his headquarters in the log cabin of
Mrs. Galloway, some eleven miles in the Ramapo Pass. He was
there for three nights, then on July 23 rode to Mahwah to the
home of Maria LaRue Hopper. (<u>Ramsay Journal</u>, chap. 3, July
1957)

II: SELECTED BIOGRAPHIES

GANNETT, DEBORAH SAMPSON   MA, NY
of Middleborough, New York. Deborah Sampson was born on December 17, 1760, in Plympton, near Plymouth, Massachusetts, the daughter of Deborah Bradford and Jonathan Sampson, Jr. Later she moved to Middleborough. On May 20, 1782, Deborah, who was five feet seven inches tall, donned male clothing and enlisted in the 4th Massachusetts Regiment of Capt. George Webb's company, for a term of three years. She used the assumed name of Robert Shurtliff. Deborah was the first woman to enlist as a soldier in the American army. She was mustered into service on May 23, 1782, at Worcester, Massachusetts, where she had traveled from Middleborough.

At the Battle of Tarrytown, Deborah suffered a bullet wound in her left thigh just below the groin, but did not report this to the army doctor. She treated herself, fearing her sex would be discovered. Later, while she was with the army in Philadelphia, she came down with a fever and was sent to a hospital. There Dr. Barnabas Binney discovered that she was a woman and decided to keep it a secret for the time being, though he did put through her papers for a medical discharge. Pvt. Robert Shurtliff was honorably discharged on October 23, 1783 at West Point, New York, by Gen. Henry Knox.

After her military discharge, Deborah Sampson went to live with an aunt and uncle, Mr. and Mrs. Zebulon Waters. In 1785 Deborah married Benjamin Gannett of Sharon. They had one son and two daughters.

On January 11, 1792, Deborah Gannett applied for a pension, which was endorsed by her neighbor, Paul Revere, in a letter to Congressman William Eustis of Massachusetts. The Massachusetts Assembly passed a resolution granting her Ŀ34 bearing interest from the date of her discharge from the Continental Army. This resolution was approved by John Hancock, president of the assembly.

During 1802 Mrs. Gannett went on a lecture tour, speaking in Boston, Providence, Worcester, Massachusetts, and in Lislie, New York. Her son, Earl Bradford Gannett, married Mary Clark. Her daughter Patience married Seth Gay, and Polly married Judson Gilbert. Later Mrs. Gannett received a federal pension retroactive to January 1, 1803, amounting to $4 a month, but even then she was almost penniless. In 1806, when she was ill, she wrote to her good friend and neighbor, Paul Revere, asking for a loan of $10.

Deborah Gannett died on April 29, 1827, and in December 1837 a bill was proposed that her husband, Benjamin Gannett, receive an annual pension of $80. But Benjamin Gannett died on January 9, 1838, and so a lump sum of $466.66 was granted to her three children.

The Deborah Sampson house is at 46 Elm Street, Plympton, Massachusetts. Adjacent to the Soldier's Memorial there is a monument to her on Main Street. There is also a monument on her grave in the Rock Ridge Cemetery in Sharon, Massachusetts. (CP; DB; EW)

GATES, MARY VALENCE   WV, NY

On October 20, 1754, in Halifax, Nova Scotia, she married Capt. Horatio Gates of the British army. In August 1772 Gates, his wife, and son moved to Berkeley County, Virginia (now West Virginia). He renounced his British commission and in 1775 was made a brigadier general in the Continental Army. Gen. Gates in 1776 was stationed at Fort Ticonderoga until December when he was sent to Philadelphia. In August 1777 he was given command of the Northern Army in New York state. Gen. Gates won the Battle of Saratoga in 1777, defeating the British forces under Gen. Burgoyne. Mrs. Gates spent months making bandages for the American army and opened her home at Rosehill, New York, as a hospital for the wounded soldiers. After Gen. Kosciusko was wounded, he lay for six months in her home as she nursed him back to health.

    Her maiden name has also been given as Elizabeth Phillips, but Gen. Gates called her Mary. In 1780 she returned to her Virginia home. In 1790 Gen. and Mrs. Gates freed their slaves and returned to New York, where he died in 1806. Their only son had died at the Battle of Camden in August 1780. (DB; FH; GP)

GATLIFF, CHRISTINA McGUIRE   KY

of Martin's Station. She married Capt. Charles Gatliff (1745-1838) of Virginia, the son of Martha and James Gatliff. When the Canadians and Indians under Col. Bird attacked Martin's Station on June 24, 1780, Capt. Gatliff was on an expedition. Mrs. Gatliff and her five children were taken captive. They were marched to Niagara with other civilians. The trip took twenty-six days, and one of her children died en route. The men were allowed one cup of flour a day and the women and children only one-half a cup. They were released in 1783 and walked back to Virginia. Mrs. Gatliff had no knowledge of the whereabouts of her husband.

    Meanwhile Capt. Gatliff was a spy among the Indians. In 1786 he was appointed a spy and pilot by Col. Logan. He also served as a spy and pilot against hostile Indians gathered on the banks of the Miami in Harmer's company and was appointed to command the pioneers. In 1793, after Kentucky became a state, Capt. Gatliff learned the whereabouts of his family in Virginia. He joined them, after thirteen years, and brought them back to Kentucky. Kentucky Historical Marker 919 entitled "Pioneer Hero-Heroine" tells of Charles and Christina Gatliff and was placed on Kentucky Highway 92, Williamsburg, near the burial plot of the Gatliffs. (The <u>Whitley [Kentucky] Republican</u>, July 9, 1987, reported this marker stolen; submitted by Freda Ball Bates, Coarsegold, CA; HP)

GAYLORD, KATHERINE COLE   CT

of Bristol (formerly New Cambridge). She was born in 1745 and subsequently married Lt. Aaron Gaylord (1745-1778), who fought at Bunker Hill in 1775. Katherine had one son and two daughters. Early in 1776 they migrated to the Connecticut settlement in the Wyoming Valley of Pennsylvania, and settled at Forty Fort. On

II: SELECTED BIOGRAPHIES

July 3, 1778, Col. William Butler, in command of some four hundred British regulars and some six hundred Indians, camped about twenty miles from the fort and sent an emissary to demand its surrender.
 Aaron went out to fight that day, and Katherine never heard from him again. With two horses and all the provisions one horse could carry, she left the fort with her three children. For weeks they traveled through the wilderness, meeting some friendly Indians who fed them. Finally they reached the home of her father, James Cole. After her son and daughters were married, Katherine went to live with her daughter and son-in-law, Lorena and Lynde Phelps of Burlington, Connecticut, where she died at age ninety-five. On her grave is a monument which reads: "Katherine Cole Gaylord, wife of Lieutenant Aaron Gaylord. 1745-1840. In memory of her sufferings and heroism at the massacre of Wyoming, 1778, this stone is erected by her descendants and the members of the Katherine Gaylord Chapter of the Daughters of the American Revolution, July 3, 1895." (DAR)

GEIGER, EMILY   SC
resided on the Broad River, where Gen. Nathaniel Greene and his army were encamped in May 1782. He needed a volunteer to carry a message to Gen. Thomas Sumter who was camped on the Wateree River about a hundred miles away. Gen. Greene could not spare one of his own men, so he asked for a volunteer from among the local farmers.
 A young girl, Emily Geiger, stepped forward and volunteered to carry Greene's message to Sumter. Greene gave Emily the message, but also had her memorize it. Emily took off on horseback, but she was stopped by Tory scouts on the second day of her journey. They took her to a Tory farmhouse and had a woman examine her. Meanwhile Emily tore the paper into bits and swallowed them, so the Tory woman found nothing and Emily was released. Emily continued on her journey and delivered the message to Gen. Sumter. Later Sumter and Greene joined forces and the British army under Lord Rawdon retreated to Orangeburg.
 In 1900 the South Carolina Daughters of the American Revolution erected a tablet to the memory of Emily Geiger in the State House in Columbia. (EW; HS) There is an Emily Geiger Chapter of the Daughters of the American Revolution in Honea Path, South Carolina. (DAR)

GIBBONS, MARGERY HANNUM   PA
of Chester County. She was the wife of Joseph Gibbons, Jr. (1738-1798). After the Battle of Brandywine her brother Col. John Hannam (1740-1799) was captured by the British along with Col. Persifor Frazer. The two men were taken to Philadelphia and imprisoned.
 Mrs. Frazer and Mrs. Gibbons, with the permission of Gen. Washington, went to Philadelphia to visit their husbands. The women took along food for the imprisoned soldiers, and while in Philadelphia contacted Mrs. Jenkins, who ran the Conestoga Wagon Tavern. Mrs. Jenkins had managed somehow to find ways to get

money and food to the prisoners. After the two women arrived in Philadelphia on October 10, 1777, they found Col. Frazer and other prisoners in the State House (now Independence Hall).
On Saint Patrick's Day 1778, the prison guards were drunk and Col. Frazer, Col. Hannum and a Maj. Harper escaped. (DAR Magazine, August-September 1979)

GIBBONS, SARAH   GA
from near Savannah. On September 13/14, 1779, Gen. Pulaski spent the night at her home and while there on his way to Ogeeche's ferry, he wrote to Gen. Lincoln. (The original letter is in the Archives and Museum of the Polish Roman Catholic Union in Chicago) She also provided provisions and forage for public use. (WA, p. 125)

GIBSON, ANNE WEST   PA
of Cumberland County. The daughter of Francis West, Jr., she was born on March 4, 1750, near Sligo, Ireland. The family emigrated to Philadelphia where Anne was educated. Anne married George Gibson in 1772, and they moved to a farm on Shearman's Creek in Western Pennsylvania where they operated a granary mill. They had four sons. During the Revolutionary War, George Gibson was commissioned a colonel in the 1st Virginia Regiment (that part of Pennsylvania was claimed by Virginia). He served for the duration of the war.
After the Indian massacre on July 3, 1778, Mrs. Gibson cared for the refugees from the West Branch. During the Revolution, Mrs. Gibson supplied the American army with flour (which was never paid for) from Gibson's mill. Mrs. Gibson had not expected payment anyway--she considered it her patriotic duty. (EP) Mrs. Gibson died on February 9, 1809, on her farm.

GILBERT, DEBORAH CHAMPION CT
of New London. The daughter of Col. Henry Champion, she served as a courier for her father. Deborah rode over one hundred miles from her home through enemy territory to deliver dispatches and the army payroll to Gen. Washington in Cambridge, Massachusetts, in 1775. Deborah married Samuel Gilbert (1734-1818) and was his second wife. (DAR Magazine, July 1976) There is a Deborah Champion Chapter of the Daughters of the American Revolution in Adams, New York. (GP)

GILLETT, ELIZA   CT
of West Hartford. Her husband, Jonathan Gillett, was captured by Hessians in the Battle of Long Island, New York, on August 27, 1776. They disarmed him and took all he had: watch, buckles, money, and some clothing, and bruised him with the butts of their muskets, knocking him down and beating upon him. Gillett was put in a prison ship in New York Harbor, and almost starved to death. Then he was put in a prison in New York City, and later in a house. He wrote to his wife on December 2, 1776, describing his horrible experiences.

II: SELECTED BIOGRAPHIES

Gillett reported that captured American soldiers were crowded into churches and guarded night and day, wore tattered garments and rags, and were beset with vermin. He reported that he had no money to send to his wife to care for her and their children. This is an example of the suffering of the women patriots. (CS)

GILLON, MARY CRIPPS   SC
was a widow when she married Alexander Gillon on July 6, 1766. He established a mercantile business with her son, John Splatt Cripps, which proved to be very successful. Her husband was made commodore of the South Carolina navy. He went to Europe in 1778 to secure financial and military aid for the Americans. He leased the frigate Indien built in Amsterdam and renamed it the South Carolina. Gillon put to sea in August 1781 and captured the sixteen-gun privateer Liverpool. On May 7, 1782, he assisted the Spanish in capturing New Providence (Nassau, Bahamas). (CN)
    Mary Gillon died in 1787, and Alexander Gillon in 1789 married Ann Purcell. They had three children. During the Revolutionary War, Mary Gillon supplied provisions for the South Carolina troops. (SI, B:150) Alexander Gillon was in Europe when the British captured Charleston on May 12, 1780. The British commandant, Lt. Col. Balfour, demanded that all women who were heads of households sign an oath of fidelity to the Crown or to be banished from the city. Mrs. Gillon refused to sign the oath and was banished from Charleston. (SC)

GILMAN, REBECCA IVES   NH
of Exeter. On September 29, 1779, William Friend of Newburyport, Massachusetts, obtained a letter of marque and reprisal to command the New Hampshire ship Postillion mounting eight carriage guns and navigated by twenty men. The bond was issued to "John Jay, President, and the other members of the Congress of the United States of America" and was signed by Friend, Michael Hodge, and Joseph Gilman of Exeter. Witnesses to the bond were Rebecca Gilman and Anne Sewall. Rebecca Gilman was born in 1745. She was the wife of Joseph Gilman, chairman of the Committee of Safety. Samuel Adams spent the night in their home in 1776. In 1788 the Gilmans moved to Ohio. Mrs. Gilman died in 1823. (CN; from Nancy C. Merrill, Exeter, NH)

GLIDDEN, ALICE MILLS   NH
of Northfield. While her husband, 2nd Lt. Charles Glidden, was in the army, she cut firewood for the family, felling trees herself, and used a yoke of steers to haul the logs, with only her children to help. She used her husband's old flintlock gun to hunt game for the family table. (Submitted by Dorothy Wilcox, Durham, NH)

GODDARD, MARY KATHERINE   CT
was born in 1738, the daughter of Sarah Updike and Dr. Goddard of Groton. After her father's death she moved to Providence, Rhode Island, with her mother in 1762, and then to Philadelphia in 1768 to join her brother William in the printing business. She

assisted her brother in publishing the Pennsylvania Chronicle.
Then they moved to Baltimore and published the Maryland Journal.

In January 1777 the Continental Congress ordered an authentic copy of the Declaration of Independence with the names of the members on the Continental Congress inscribed on the document. The printing order was given to Mary Katherine Goddard of Baltimore. It was dated January 18, 1777, a broadside, signed a "True Copy" by John Hancock, president, and one copy of this broadside was sent to each of the thirteen United States. (IM, 3490, January 18, 1777)

Mary Katherine Goddard also served as postmaster of Baltimore. In 1781 she published An Almanac and Ephemeris, which included the schedule of court sessions in Maryland, Virginia, and Pennsylvania, which was a patriotic service. Mary Goddard was also a bookseller in Market Square, Baltimore. She died in 1816. (DR) There is a Mary Katherine Goddard Chapter of the Daughters of the American Revolution in Omaha, Nebraska.

GODWIN, PHEBE COLE   NJ
of Totowa. The widow of Abraham Godwin, she ran a tavern in Totowa, where Gen. Washington held courts-martial.

> GENERAL ORDERS, Head Quarters, Totowa, Thursday, November 9, 1780. Parole Lancaster. Countersigned Watchword Wolfe. For the Day Tomorrow: Brigadier General Wayne, Lieutenant Colonel Commdt. Sherman, Lieutenant Colonel Fernald, Major Tudor, Brigade Major Smith.
>
> The General court martial whereof Colonel Bailey is president, to assemble tomorrow morning, 9 o'clock at the Widow Godwin's for the trial of such persons as shall come before them. All persons concerned to attend.
>
> Major Oliver, Inspector to the 1st Massachusetts Brigade, having obtained a leave of absence, Captain Sewall of the 12th Massachusetts regiment is appointed to do that duty in his Absence. Geo. Washington (FW)

GORHAM, REBECCA CALL   MA
of Boston. The daughter of Caleb Call, she married Nathaniel Gorham in 1763. On June 17, 1775, Gen. Gage ordered his artillery on Copps Hill to shell Charlestown (now Boston). British marines from the ship Somerset came ashore and burned all the houses and buildings which were missed by cannon fire. The townspeople lost all their possessions as Charlestown was reduced to ashes. The Gorhams were left homeless and moved to Lunenberg in Worcester County where they found refuge. In 1775 Gorham was appointed a delegate to the Continental Congress in Philadelphia, and served again in 1782/83, and in 1786, when he became president of the Continental Congress. He was a signer of the U.S. Constitution.

Mrs. Gorham deserves recognition for the struggles she survived in the destruction of her home in 1775. (HC; some information on Boston women supplied by Richard B. Trask)

II: SELECTED BIOGRAPHIES

GRAAF, MRS. JACOB   **PA**
of Philadelphia. On May 23, 1776, Thomas Jefferson took lodgings at the Graaf's house at 230 High Street, on the southwest corner. (Later it was renumbered 700 Market Street.) It was built by a young bricklayer of German parentage. Jefferson wrote the Declaration of Independence in the second floor parlor. He showed his original draft to John Adams and to Benjamin Franklin, then drove north on the Bristol road and showed it to the aged philosopher, Edward Duffield. (ST; WT)

GRANT, ELIZABETH BOONE   **KY**
of Bryan's Station. The daughter of Sarah Morgan and Squire Boone, she was born on February 5, 1732, in Berks County, Pennsylvania. She was the sister of the famous frontiersman Daniel Boone. In 1750 the family moved to North Carolina. Elizabeth Boone married William Grant (1726-1804). They had six sons and five daughters. In 1779 they moved to Kentucky and lived in Boonesborough for a time, then moved to Bryan's Station.

    Elizabeth helped to defend the forts when the men were away. In 1782 Bryan's Station was besieged by Indians under the leadership of Capt. William Caldwell and the renegade Simon Girty. The defense of the fort helped to halt the invasion of Kentucky by the British.

    Elizabeth's sons Samuel and Moses were killed by Indians in 1789. Her sons John and William III married the sisters Mary (Polly) and Salley Moseby, and her daughter Elizabeth married John Moseby. Elizabeth Boone Grant died on February 2, 1814. She is listed as a patriot in the <u>DAR Patriot Index</u>. (Submitted by Katherine Blaylock, Winston-Salem, NC)

GRAVES, ANN DAVENPORT   **VA**
of Spotsylvania. She was born about 1696 and married Thomas Graves. They had eight sons and six daughters. In 1780/81, at the age of eighty-five, she was supplying provisions for the soldiers during the Revolutionary War, as recorded in the Virginia State Archives. Ann died sometime after 1782. She is listed as a patriot in the <u>DAR Patriot Index</u>. (Submitted by Ophelia Wade, Bragg City, MO; VR, Court Book, p. 4)

GREEN, ALICE KOLLACK   **PA**
of Philadelphia. The daughter of Lt. Jacob Kollack, in June 1763 in Christ Church she married John Green, a sea captain. On October 10, 1776, he received a commission in the Pennsylvania State Navy, in 1778 he was commissioned a captain in the Continental Navy, and in 1779 in the Pennsylvania Navy again as captain of the ship <u>Nesbitt</u>. Capt. Green was captured by the British and imprisoned in the Mill Prison near Plymouth, England.

    Alice Green turned all her jewelry and other belongings into gold, which she sent to her husband. How the gold arrived in England is unknown, but apparently John bought his freedom, since later in 1779 he was in France without a parole. Capt. Green alleviated the suffering of his crew by giving them gold. Upon his return to America, Green commanded the twenty-gun ship Duc du Lausan carrying gold to pay the troops in America. In 1783, upon a voyage from Cuba north together with Capt. John Barry of the Alliance, the men encountered a British fleet. The last naval shots of the American Revolution ensued between Fort Lauderdale and Cape Canaveral, Florida, and the Americans escaped a superior fleet. Capt. Green became a charter member of the Society of the Cincinnati. Mr. and Mrs. Green had one son and three daughters who survived infancy.

On February 22, 1784, Capt. Green, as commander of the Empress of China, sailed to the Orient and carried the American flag to Chinese waters for the first time. Mrs. Green died in 1832 in Bristol, Pennsylvania. (GP)

GREENE, CATHARINE RAY   RI
of Warwick. In 1754 Benjamin Franklin met Catharine Ray when he was forty-eight years old and she was in her early twenties. Catharine was enchanted with Franklin. Later they corresponded for some time, but then Franklin told her to find a husband and have babies. So she married William Greene, and they had six children.

In June 1775 when the British occupied Boston, thousands of Americans fled to the countryside. Mrs. Greene opened her home to refugees who were friends of hers, and took in Jane Franklin Mecom, a sister of Benjamin Franklin. When Jane arrived at the Greenes', there were already dozens of relatives and friends there, and more were expected.

Franklin left Philadelphia for Cambridge, Massachusetts, and then went to Warwick, where he spent the night with the Greenes. Franklin brought his sister Jane and ten-year-old Ray Greene back to Philadelphia to enroll the boy in school there. William Greene served as governor of Rhode Island from 1778 to 1786. (LP)

GREENE, CATHERINE LITTLEFIELD   RI, NJ
of Coventry. The daughter of John Littlefield, she was born in 1753 in New Shoreham, Block Island. On July 20, 1774, she married Nathaniel Greene, who was appointed a brigadier general by the Rhode Island Assembly in May 1775 and the Continental Army in June 1775.

The Greenes built a large house in Coventry. During the early hostilities between the Americans and the British in 1775, Mrs. Greene turned her house into a hospital to inoculate American soldiers against smallpox. Mrs. Greene was also a camp follower and was with her husband at Valley Forge during the harsh winter of 1777/78 to give him encouragement, and she was with him during the campaigns in New Jersey in 1779.

While stationed in New Jersey, Gen. Greene had his headquarters in the home of Mrs. Van Veghten, located between Bound Brook and Somerville. On March 19, Gen. Greene wrote to Col. Wadsworth: "We had a little dance at my quarters a few evenings past. His Excellency [General Washington] and Mrs. Greene danced upwards of three hours without once sitting down." (BI)

II: SELECTED BIOGRAPHIES

Gen. Greene commanded the southern campaign from October 1780 until December 1782, when the British evacuated Charleston, South Carolina. In 1785 the State of Georgia presented the Greenes with the plantation of Mulberry Grove, near Savannah, Georgia, the confiscated property of Loyalist John Graham. Here Gen. and Mrs. Greene resided until his death in 1786. Some years later she moved to Cumberland Island. The Coventry, Rhode Island, chapter of the Daughters of the American Revolution is named in her honor.

GRIFFING, SARAH STILWELL   NJ
of Egg Harbor. She was the daughter of Nicholas Stilwell, who bought a plantation at Beesley's Point in 1748. Sarah and her sister Rebecca were American patriots. Their brother Capt. Nicholas Stilwell, Jr., served in the war.

Sarah married Capt. Moses Griffing. Toward the end of the war he was captured by the British and confined in the prison ship Jersey in New York Harbor. Here the sick and wounded were huddled together in the scandalous vessel. Smallpox was rampant, together with dysentery and other diseases, and the men were half starved.

When Sarah learned that her husband was on the ill-fated ship Jersey, she vowed to visit him and ask for his release. She rode over a hundred miles through woods and plains to Gen. Washington's camp where the general arranged for a flag of truce to escort her to Gen. Clinton's headquarters in New York. The British general listened to her pleas, and finally agreed to release her husband. She was born in 1753 and died in 1804.

The local chapter of the Daughters of the American Revolution in the Ocean City area, Cape May County, is named the Sarah Stilwell Chapter. (DC)

GUTRIDGE, MOLLY   MA
of Marblehead. She was a member of the Daughters of Liberty, a patriotic organization in favor of independence. In 1779 she published a broadside entitled "A New Torch on the Times," which displayed a picture of a woman holding a musket. (DR)

GWINNETT, ANN BOURNE   GA
of Saint Catherines Island, near Savannah. Ann Bourne lived in Wolverhampton, Staffordshire, England, and on April 19, 1757, she married Button Gwinnett, a merchant. They came to Georgia in September 1765. Later Gwinnett purchased thirty-six acres on Saint Catherines Island. Gwinnett was a delegate to the Continental Congress and a signer of the Declaration of Independence. In 1777 Gwinnett and Gen. Laughlin McIntosh had an argument over the command of troops and decided to settle the matter with a pistol duel. Both men were wounded in the duel on May 15, 1777, and Gwinnett died on May 19, 1777, from the wounds. He was the first signer to die, and his autograph is very valuable.

The British attacked Savannah in December 1778 and took

the city. They seized Saint Catherines Island and the home of the Widow Gwinnett. What happened to her is unknown. (FG)

When Savannah fell, Dorthea (Dorothy) Camber Walton, whose husband was also a signer of the Declaration of Independence from Georgia, was captured by the enemy. She was taken to the West Indies, imprisoned, and later released and returned to Savannah. It is likely that Ann Gwinnett was also captured and taken to the West Indies. The Georgia State Archivist, however, could not furnish any information on Ann Gwinnett.

The Savannah Public Library had no information on her nor did the British Library in London, but they suggested the Public Records Office, Chancery Lane, London. N. Evans, of the Search Department, replied as follows:

>We hold the will of Ann Gwinnett, reference PROB 11/1129, folios RH 295-LH 296. The will is dated 24 August 1770, when she describes herself as formerly of Wolverhampton, Staffordshire but late of the province of Georgia in South Carolina. It was proved on 4 May 1785. Unfortunately no indication is given either of the actual date or of the place of decease. But as the original index describes the residence as "Parts beyond the Seas" it seems very probable that she died in the West Indies....
>
>This will is the only document relating to either of these ladies which we can immediately trace. It is just possible that a systematic search into Colonial Office records relating to Georgia and to the several West Indian islands might produce references but these records are very voluminous and are unindexed for the period in question. We could supply the names of record agents able to search on your behalf if you wish but you will appreciate that a search would be protracted and could well prove fruitless.

Apparently Ann Gwinnett did not die in Savannah, but somewhere else in the Americas, probably in the West Indies or in another state in the United States.

The will of Ann Gwinnett contains some interesting information. It is dated August 24, 1770, and mentions a deed made by her father, Aron Bourne, disposing of his effects to her mother, Sarah Bourne, for her lifetime "if she does not let David Towes sit in the seat in the church, if he does she forfeits every claim" to his estate. Eventually the estate would go to his nearest relative.

There is a codicil to the will dated "Charles Town, October 20, 1780," whereby Ann Gwinnett left to her daughter Elizabeth, the wife of Peter Bolin, all of her "Effects Real and personal."

The will of Ann Gwinnett was probated in London on May 4, 1785, but it mentions that Elizabeth Gwinnett Bolin died "without taking upon her the Debtors of Administ." and so the goods of Elizabeth Bolin were granted to her husband, Peter Bolin.

II: SELECTED BIOGRAPHIES   93

  The British captured Charles Town (now Charleston, South
Carolina) on May 12, 1780. Ann Gwinnett was either captured by
the British in Georgia and taken to Charles Town sometime before
November 1780, or she moved there voluntarily.
  In those days it took a sailing vessel about thirty days to
sail to England from New York, and about forty days or so from
Charleston. Ann Gwinnett probably died some time between January
and March 1785, since the will was probated early in May.

H

HALE, ABIGAIL GROUT   NH
of Rindge. The tenth of thirteen children of Johannah Boynton
and John Grout of Lunenburg, Massachusetts, she was born on
March 23, 1746. Abigail was the sister of Maj. Hilkiah Grout, whose
wife, Submit, with her three children, were captured by Indians.
Later Submit Grout was ransomed with her two younger children,
but the eldest son was adopted by the Cattaraugus. He became
a chief and took the name of Peter Westfall.
  Abigail Grout on January 28, 1766, married Nathan Hale, the
son of Elizabeth Wheeler and Moses Hale of Rindge, and they had
seven children. Col. Nathan Hale had four brothers who served
in the Revolutionary War. Nathan Hale was a captain of a company
of Rindge volunteers who marched in 1775 for the alarm at Lexington and later fought at Bunker Hill. Col. Hale was captured during
the Battle of Long Island. The shadow of disloyalty was cast against
him by Ethan Allen, probably because of jealousy by junior officers.
Col. Hale appealed to Gen. Washington, but on September 23, 1780,
he died as a captive within enemy lines before he had an opportunity
to vindicate his honor.
  Abigail inherited the property of Col. Nathan Hale and thus
became a taxpayer. She was a strong believer that taxation without representation was tyranny, and since she was not permitted
to vote, she refused to pay her taxes. Abigail Hale was arrested
and spent a month in jail in Rindge. She had strong opinions
on women's rights and can be considered an original advocate of
women's suffrage in America.
  On October 30, 1796, Abigail married Samuel Parker of Rindge,
but later she divorced him. She died in 1838 at the home of her
son, the Honorable Harry Hale, esquire, of Chelsea, Vermont.
(From Wilma Hale Jewell, DAR Chapter Registrar, Jeffrey, NH)

HALL, MARY OSBORNE   GA
of Sunbury. After his wife, Abigail, died in 1753, Dr. Lyman
Hall married Mary Osborne, and about 1757 they moved to Dorchester, South Carolina, and then to Sunbury. He also cultivated
a rice plantation near Midway, Georgia. Dr. Hall was a delegate
to the Continental Congress. After the British conquered Savannah
and other parts of Georgia in December 1778, the Halls were forced
to flee their home.
  Since Dr. Hall was a signer of the Declaration of Independence,

their home in Sunbury was confiscated. He served as governor of
Georgia in 1782. Their only son predeceased Dr. Hall. (GP)

HALL, PERSIS TOWER LINCOLN MA
of Cohasset. She was born on August 1, 1759, at Hingham, Massachusetts, the daughter of Bethia Nichols and Daniel Tower. On
November 23, 1775, Persis married Allen Lincoln, and she lived
on Elm Street, Cohasset. Shortly after their marriage, Allen went
to sea and was captured by the British. He was confined in Princetown Prison, on Dartmoor in Devon, England, where he apparently
died, as he never returned. When the British occupied Boston
in 1776, Persis, who knew how to sail a boat, crossed the Boston
Bay to Gloucester several times to obtain provisions for Cohasset,
as the port of Boston was blockaded by the British vessels of war.

  On May 21, 1786, Persis Lincoln married Capt. Lt. James Hall
(1750-1819), and they left a number of descendants. She died at
Boston on September 29, 1828. (E. Victor Bigelow, Narrative History of Cohasset, Boston, 1808; submitted with dates by Margaret C.
Wenham, Hoquiam, WA)

HAMILTON, ANNE KENNEDY SC
of Pendleton. She was born in 1760. Anne Kennedy lived sixty
miles from Cowpens in Spartanburg County, where Gen. Daniel
Morgan and the American army was encamped. When she learned
that British forces under Col. Tarleton had camped near her home
in June 1781, she rode the distance to warn the Americans of an
apparent attack. Gen. Morgan prepared his defenses, and when
the British arrived the Americans were ready. In the Battle of
Cowpens which ensued, the British lost 230 men killed and the
Americans captured about 600 British soldiers. The Americans
suffered a loss of 72 men.

  Later Anne Kennedy married Thomas Hamilton, who served
as a private during the Revolutionary War. Anne Hamilton died
in 1836. (DAR; EW; HS)

HAMMOND, ANN WILEY NY
of Dobbs Ferry. "Nancy" was the wife of Lt. Col. James Hammond
(or Hamman) of the Westchester County militia. On his trip from
Providence, Rhode Island, in March 1781 to Williamsburg, Virginia,
in September 1781, Gen. Washington stayed in Dobbs Ferry at the
Applebys', the Tompkins', and then at the Hammonds' from July 10,
1781 for several weeks. He did leave there to have dinner with
Gen. and Mrs. Benjamin Lincoln in Phillipsburg, New Jersey, on
July 14. (BW)

HAMPTON, MARY (POLLY) FALCONER KY
of Craig's Station. The daughter of Joice Craig and John Falconer
(Faulkner), she was born in 1749. Polly married Andrew Hampton
(1731-1808). He raised a crop of corn at Harrodsburg in the spring
of 1779, then on Christmas Eve 1779, they settled at her uncle
Craig's place. The Indians attacked Craig's Station in 1780 and

II: SELECTED BIOGRAPHIES

burned it to the ground, and the Hamptons and the others moved to Bryan's Station and later to Gilbert Creek. Andrew Hampton served with Gen. George Rogers Clark. (Submitted by Sue M. Bogardus, Warsaw, KY)

HANCOCK, DOROTHY QUINCY   MA
of Boston. On August 28, 1775, in Fairfield, Connecticut, she married John Hancock of Braintree, Massachusetts. He was president of the Massachusetts Provincial Congress and a delegate to the Second Continental Congress. The Hancocks maintained a home in Boston, which was seized by the enemy and occupied by the British Gen. Thomas Gage until October 1775 when he was recalled to London. Her home continued to be occupied by the British until Gen. Washington forced the enemy to evacuate Boston in March 1776. John Hancock was elected president of the Continental Congress and signed the Declaration of Independence in 1776. Mrs. Hancock suffered the loss of her home for a period of one year. (DB; HC) There is a Dorothy Quincy Hancock Chapter of the Daughters of the American Revolution in Greenfield, Massachusetts.

HAND, CATHARINE EWING   PA
of Lancaster. The daughter of Sarah Yeates and John Ewing, she was born on March 25, 1751, in Philadelphia. After her father's death in 1759 her family moved to Lancaster. On March 13, 1775, Catharine married Dr. Edward Hand, and in that year he was commissioned a lieutenant colonel in Col. William Thompson's battalion of riflemen. He took part in the battles of Long Island, White Plains, Trenton, and Princeton. In 1777 he was promoted to brigadier general in command of Fort Pitt, and in 1778 was in command in Albany, New York. He was present at the siege of Yorktown, Virginia, in 1781. He was commissioned a major general of the Pennsylvania Line in 1783. He was an original member of the Society of the Cincinnati founded in 1783.
    Mrs. Hand was a camp follower and ministered to the wounded, sick, and dying soldiers. Mrs. Hand and her husband are buried in St. James's churchyard cemetery in Lancaster. (EP)

HARDING, AMY GARDNER   PA
of Wyoming Valley. She was born on February 17, 1726, in Connecticut and married Stephen Harding (1723-1789). They settled in the west part of Salem, Connecticut. He served in the Colonial Wars. Stephen and Amy were among the original settlers of the Wyoming Valley, and on May 19, 1762, he was a member of the Directory Commission and had one right in the Susquehanna Purchase. The Hardings survived the first Indian massacre on October 15, 1763. When Fort Dundee was captured in 1769 by the Penamite Indians, Stephen Harding was taken prisoner and carried to Easton, Pennsylvania.
    During the Revolutionary War, Stephen served as captain of the 7th Company, 24th Connecticut (Westmoreland) Regiment in command of Fort Jenkins. At that time western Pennsylvania was a part of Connecticut.

On July 3, 1778, the British-inspired massacre in the Wyoming Valley took place. Capt. Stephen Harding was forced to surrender Fort Jenkins. Two of the Harding boys--Benjamin and Stuckley-- were killed, and David Harding, a boy of eleven years, was captured and forced to turn a grindstone all day for the Indians to sharpen their knives and tomahawks. Forty Fort, a short distance away, fell the next day: 340 people were massacred, leaving 150 widows and 600 children fatherless.

The Dial Rock Chapter of the Daughters of the American Revolution, West Pittston, Pennsylvania, erected a monument to the persons who lost their lives in the massacre. Amy Harding died in 1795 and is listed as a patriot in the DAR Patriot Index. (Submitted by Adena Charlton, Aurora, IN)

Captain Stephen Harding had a brother, Abraham Harding (1746-1836/37), who served as a captain during the Revolutionary War. He was a direct ancestor of President Warren G. Harding. (FP1)

HARRIS, ALTJE SCHENCK   NJ
of Somerset County. When her servant told her the British were coming, Mrs. Harris climbed a tree and, from her vantage point, heard the British officers discussing their plans. After the men left, she drove her harmless-looking milk wagon through the lines and revealed the enemy's plans to Washington's staff. (BJ)

HARRIS, HANNAH STEWART   PA
of Newton. She was born in 1741. Hannah was the wife of John Harris, a prominent merchant in Newton. In 1757 they bought a house on the west side of the Common at the southwest corner of Swamp Road. John Harris died on August 13, 1773, aged fifty-six, so it was the Widow Harris who entertained George Washington in her home from December 27 to 29, 1776. Lord Stirling stayed at the public house of Amos Strickland, Sr., now called Brick Hotel.

Hessian troops who were captured after Washington's crossing of the Delaware on December 25 were brought to Newtown. A report was circulated among the Hessians that the Americans killed and ate their prisoners. On December 28 Gen. Washington invited several Hessian officers to dine with him to dispel the rumors. Lt. Widerhold, a Hessian officer, recorded in his diary on that night his meeting with Washington.

While at the home of the Widow Harris, Gen. Washington wrote to Congress telling them of his plan to cross the Delaware River a second time. The captured Hessian officers were detained in Newtown until December 30, 1776, and twenty of them were released on their own parole of honor.

At some point Gen. Israel Putnam stayed at the home of the Widow Harris, since he cut a glass window with a diamond ring with his signature. It is a matter of record that Dr. Benjamin Rush visited Washington at the Harris house before the Battle of Trenton.

Mrs. Harris died in 1805. She is listed as a patriot in the

II: SELECTED BIOGRAPHIES

DAR Patriot Index. In 1863 Alexander German tore down the Harris home and built a new one on the same foundation. (DVA Newtown Supplement, December 11, 1969; submitted by Frances T. Cronin, Newtown Library Company, Newtown, PA [this library was founded in 1760 and incorporated in 1789])

HARRISON, ELIZABETH BASSETT   VA
of Petersburg. About 1746 she married Benjamin Harrison, who owned a shipyard on the James River. He was a signer of the Declaration of Independence. Much of the cargo shipped on Harrison's vessels was lost to the British, and his shipyard was burned and destroyed during the Revolutionary War.

Their son, Gen. William Henry Harrison, became president of the United States. Their great-grandson, Benjamin Harrison, also became president of the United States. (DB)

HARRISON, MARY GRAY   VA
of Prince Edward County. She married William Harrison, who died before the Revolutionary War. Mary provided patriotic services during the war, according to the records of the Daughters of the American Revolution. (Submitted by Mrs. W. O. Pearson, Mission, TX; VR, 5:90)

HART, DEBORAH SCUDDER   NJ
of Hopewell. The daughter of Hannah Reeder and Richard Scudder of Ewing, New Jersey, about 1740 she married John Hart and bore him thirteen children. He was a signer of the Declaration of Independence. When the British were advancing to the Trenton area in the winter of 1776/77, John Hart rode back to save his wife and children. When he arrived at their homestead, his wife was dying. Hart would not leave his wife's bedside. When the Hessian cavalry arrived, they stole his livestock and burned his gristmills.

Mrs. Hart, as she lay dying, pleaded with her husband to flee into the woods, and he finally did. The Hessians chased after him, and the Tories were after him also. He managed to hide in a patriotic American's farmhouse, but couldn't spend more than one night in any one place, fearing for the safety of his friends. He had to hide for a month in the Sourland Mountains while being hunted by the enemy. Meanwhile Mrs. Hart died.

This is another example of the patriotic Americans, and even their wives, who also suffered during these trying times. (FG)

HART, NANCY MORGAN   GA
of Elbert County. She was the daughter of Rebecca Alexander and Thomas Morgan who moved from Pennsylvania to North Carolina in the mid-eighteenth century. Anne Morgan was called Nancy. She married Benjamin Hart of Orange County, North Carolina. They moved to Edgefield, South Carolina, then about 1771 to a log cabin on the Wahatache Creek. Capt. Hart served under Col. Elijah Clarke of the Continental Army.

One day in 1779 several British soldiers and Tories headed by Col. John Dooley arrived at the Hart's cabin and demanded dinner. Nancy sent her thirteen-year-old daughter, Sukey, supposedly out to the spring for water, but instructed the girl to blow a prearranged signal on a conch-shell horn. The men in the cabin had stacked their rifles in a corner and were relaxing by the fire when Nancy seized two of the rifles before the Tories realized what had happened. Holding a rifle, she demanded they remain in a corner of the room. One Tory misjudged her and approached. She fired her rifle and killed him. Just then her husband arrived with their sons and neighbors to help. The men then hanged the remaining Tories on a tree nearby.

In 1825 the Marquis de Lafayette visited the Hart homestead while on a tour of the United States, but apparently Nancy had moved away to Henderson County, Kentucky, to live with her second son, John Hart. She was buried in the Hart family plot there in 1830.

There is a Nancy Hart Chapter of the Georgia Daughters of the American Revolution which presented a five-acre plot to the State of Georgia in the Nancy Hart Forest Park. Her cabin has been reconstructed on the plot using some of the original chimney stones. Highway 17 in parts of Georgia is named the Nancy Hart Highway, and there is a Hart County. Near the city of Hartwell the U.S. government erected a monument "to commemorate the Heroism of Nancy Hart." (CP; EW; HS)

HART, PENELOPE ANDERSON   NJ
of Pennington, Mercer County. The daughter of Thomas Anderson, she married Ralph Hart in 1770. He was a first cousin of John Hart, a signer of the Declaration of Independence. During the Revolutionary War the British troops searched vainly through New Jersey for John Hart, since he was a marked man.

When John Hart was hiding in a rock house in the Sourland Mountains, Penelope Hart took food to him daily. In order to prevent being discovered, she changed her disguises constantly and took a different route to the mountain hideout. Penelope never walked on public roads, or stayed in the same house twice in succession, to avoid being caught by the British or the Tories, who never found John Hart's hideout.

The Pennington Chapter of the Daughters of the American Revolution is named in her honor. (DC; information on Penelope Hart is also included in Alice B. Lewis, Hopewell Valley Heritage, 1973; Audrey H. Sperling, Trenton, NJ; DAR)

HART, RUTH COLE   CT
of Meriden. She was born on October 29, 1742, the daughter of Mary Newell and Matthew Cole. In 1763 Ruth married Selah Hart. In 1776 her husband was commissioned a captain in the Continental Army and later a colonel. On August 27, 1776, when the Americans retreated from New York, Col. Hart was captured and confined on Long Island for several months. He was exchanged in

II: SELECTED BIOGRAPHIES

1777. Hart was appointed brigadier general of the 6th Brigade of the Connecticut militia in May 1779. Ruth died on January 15, 1844, aged 101 years. The Daughters of the American Revolution chapter in Meriden is named in her honor. (GP)

HARTZOG, CATHERINE MAGDALINE SNELL   SC
of Cow Creek, Orangeburg District. The daughter of Margaretta Utsey and Hans Adam Snell (Schnell), Sr., she was born about 1757. Her father was a member of the South Carolina Provincial Congress in 1775. She was the second wife of George Hartzog (b. 1736), who was killed by Tories in 1782 at Rush's Mill, Denmark, South Carolina.
 In 1782 Catherine Hartzog provided beef and sheep for the American soldiers and was reimbursed on November 24, 1784. (AA, no. 3405) Mrs. Hartzog died in 1787. (Submitted by Gladys M. Smith, Augusta, GA)

HASBROUCK, TRYNTJE DEBOIS   NY
of Newburgh. She was the widow of Col. Jonathan Hasbrouck (1722-1780). Gen. Washington established his headquarters there on April 1, 1782. On April 10, 1782, Gen. Washington wrote to the secretary of war:
 "I have devoted almost my whole time and attention since leaving Philadelphia to reviewing and examining into the particular state of the Troops which compose the Army, under my immediate command. It gave me equal surprise and concern to find that several Corps had not been able to get the new Cloathing compleated, so as to be delivered to the Soldiers, and that the men were actually in the most naked and distressed situation that can be conceived. Under these circumstances, I could not hesitate, to Order the Uniform Coats and Breeches in the hands of the State Clothier of Massachusetts to be immediately issued and to press the completion of the Cloathing by every possible means." In his letter Washington mentions the need for hats and shoes.
 Mrs. Washington left Newburgh on July 10, 1782, for Mount Vernon. Gen. Washington left Newburgh and arrived in Philadelphia on July 14, 1782. He returned to Newburgh on July 27, 1782. (FW)
 Washington occupied Mrs. Hasbrouck's house from March 31 to June 24, 1782; from July 27 to August 30, 1782; and from October 22, 1782, to August 18, 1783. While there on March 30, 1783, Washington received the news of the signing of the Peace of Paris on January 20, 1783. On April 18, 1783, Washington announced the cessation of hostilities. (BI)

HATFIELD, HANNAH DE MONEY   NJ
Her husband, Moses Hatfield (1750-1809), was a major in Drake's New York militia and was taken prisoner at Montresors Island in September 1777. Gen. Washington granted Mrs. Hatfield a pass through enemy lines into New York City in an endeavor to secure his release. Maj. Hatfield was exchanged in 1778 and served as a colonel in the New York militia in 1780/81. (FW; DAR)

HAY, MARTHA SMITH NY

of Haverstraw. Martha Smith married Col. Ann Hawkes Hay of the New York militia. She was the sister of William Smith, who lived in Haverstraw (now West Haverstraw). The Honorable William Smith, the "historian," maintained this house as his summer seat. Since Smith refused to take the oath of allegiance to the new United States, he was put on parole and was required to live at Livingston Manor. Col. and Mrs. Hay had their home burned to the ground by the British, and so were permitted to live in the Smith House. (Rockland County Bicentennial Publication 5)

After Gen. Washington had bid adieu to the lady of the Hermitage (Mrs. Prevost, later Mrs. Aaron Burr), he proceeded to Haverstraw and stayed in the home of Mrs. Hay from July 15 to July 19, 1778. On July 15, Gen. Washington wrote to the Comte d'Estaing: "I take the liberty in behalf of the United States to present you with a small quantity of live stock, which I flatter myself, after a long sea voyage, will not be unacceptable." (FW)

HEMPHILL, MARY ANN MACKEY NC

of Old Fort. In 1773 she married Thomas Hemphill (ca. 1750-1826), a captain of the Rowan County militia. They built their home on Crooked Creek at Davidson's Fort (now Old Fort). The British Col. Patrick Ferguson seized Mary's sheep, and after an argument with the colonel, he agreed that she could keep half of her sheep, and that she could select the ones she wanted. She selected the old bellwether, leader of the flock for years, and as she expected, he led the whole flock back to her farm, outwitting the distinguished colonel. Mary Ann had five sons and eight daughters. She and her husband are buried in the Siloam Presbyterian Church graveyard, McDowell County, North Carolina. (Submitted by Joseph M. Duncan, Dunwoody, GA)

HENDEE, HANNAH HUNTER VT

of Royalton, Windsor County. She was born in 1753 and was married to Robert Hendee (or Handy). A Lt. Horton came down from Canada in command of seven white men and about two hundred Indians, led by the Caughnawaga tribe. They raided and burned Royalton on October 16, 1780. Robert Hendee decided to warn the men at nearby Bethel Fort and directed Hannah to take their two children to a neighbor's house as quickly as possible. But on her way Mrs. Hendee encountered a scouting party of Indians who grabbed her seven-year-old son, Michael, from her and rode away. Mrs. Hendee with her daughter, Lucretia, were unable to keep up with the fast-riding Indians, but she was determined to rescue her son. She rode along the bank of the White River until she spotted the Tory and Indian encampment on the opposite bank. Mrs. Hendee and her daughter were carried across the river by an Indian. She pleaded with Lt. Horton to release her son, but he had difficulty convincing the Indians to do so. Meanwhile the Indians brought in nine more boys who had been kidnapped. Finally Lt. Horton and the Indians agreed to release the

II: SELECTED BIOGRAPHIES

boys, and Hannah Hendee took them home. Later she married Gideon Mosher (or Moshier).

There is a marker on Route 14 in Royalton Village which mentions Mrs. Hendee, and in South Royalton, Vermont, is a memorial arch with her name spelled "Handy." (CD; CP)

HEPBURN, CRECY COVENHOVEN   PA
of the West Branch Valley. Crecy was born on January 19, 1759, in Monmouth County, New Jersey, and later the family moved to the West Branch settlement. In 1777 she married William Hepburn. He was a captain of a company of men stationed at Fort Muncy in 1778. During the Indian and Tory raids on the West Branch settlement in that year, Mrs. Hepburn cared for the sick and wounded. She died on April 8, 1800. (EP)

HEWES, DEBORAH   PA
of Philadelphia and Valley Forge. In December 1777 Mrs. Hewes returned to her home in Valley Forge from her townhouse in Philadelphia. When Gen. Washington requested her home as his headquarters in January 1778, she readily agreed, but asked for time to move her personal possessions into a neighbor's house. Meanwhile Gen. Washington pitched his marquee (a large tent) under a gum tree in her yard. (GA)

General Washington used her house as his headquarters again in June 1778. (FW)

HEYWARD, ELIZABETH MATHEWES   SC
of Charleston. The daughter of John Mathewes, and the sister of Governor John Mathewes, she was married on April 20, 1773, to Thomas Heyward, Jr., the son of Col. Daniel Heyward. (He used the "Junior" because there was another relative named Thomas Heyward.) He was a member of the South Carolina Congress, which met on January 11, 1775. Heyward was a delegate to the Second Continental Congress in 1776 and was a signer of the Declaration of Independence.

When the British took Charleston on May 12, 1780, the enemy demanded that Elizabeth light up her windows to display the British victory, but she refused to do so. After she was ordered again, and refused again, the Tories attacked her house with stones and mud. Mrs. Heyward's sister died during the riot. The British occupied her home, and shipped Mrs. Heyward to Philadelphia, where she died in 1781. Her husband died in 1809. She is remembered for her heroic act in defying British orders. (CD; DB) During the Revolutionary War she also supplied provisions for the troops. (SI, O-Q:288) Her husband and two other signers of the Declaration of Independence from South Carolina, Arthur Middleton and Edward Rutledge, were captured by the British on May 12, 1780, when the enemy took Charleston. The three men were taken to Saint Augustine, Florida, where they were held in the State House until 1781. (Information from Luis R. Arana, Historian, Saint Augustine, FL)

HILL, ANN MEREDITH   PA
of Germantown (now in Philadelphia). The daughter of Reese Meredith, she is also referred to as Anne. Ann was the sister of Brig. Gen. Samuel Meredith, and of Elizabeth Meredith, who married George Clymer, a signer of the Declaration of Independence. In 1770 she married Henry Hill in Christ Church, Philadelphia. There were no surviving children. In 1771 Henry Hill acquired Roxborough Plantation (now called Carlton), located on Indian Queen Lane, a large tract of land which at that time was bordered by School House Lane in the north, Township Line Road (now Wissahickon Avenue) on the east, and on the west by the Schuykill River. Mr. Hill was an original member of the First City Troop and commanded a battalion of Associates in 1776. The house is now a private residence.

Gen. Washington established his headquarters there on August 4, 1777, and wrote in his general orders: "In the present marching state of the army, every incumbrance proves greatly prejudicial to the service; the multitude of women in particular, especially those who are pregnant, or have children, are a clog upon every movement. The Commander in Chief therefore earnestly recommends it to the officers commanding brigades and troops, to use every reasonable method in their power to rid of all such as are not absolutely necessary." (FW)

Washington remained there until August 8, and with the Marquis de Lafayette reviewed the troops. (BI)

After the Battle of Brandywine, the army encamped here again in September for two days. Mrs. Hill predeceased her husband, who died in 1798. (Information from William Handley, Free Library of Philadelphia)

HILL, HANNAH GORTON   RI
of Warwick. She was born on September 16, 1770, the daughter of Submit Briggs and Lt. William Gorton of the Rhode Island militia. In the summer of 1779, as a girl of eight years, she carried water to the soldiers, fed them, changed their bandages, and washed their hands and faces. (Submitted by the Rev. Garford F. Williams, Nicholson, PA) Hannah married Jonathan Hill of the Rhode Island militia, who advanced from ensign to lieutenant to captain.

HILLEGAS, HENRIETTA BOUDE   PA
of Philadelphia. The daughter of Deborah and Samuel Boude, on May 10, 1753, she married Michael Hillegas, a merchant. They had ten children. Hillegas was made the Continental treasurer in 1776 and served as the first treasurer of the United States from September 6, 1777, to September 11, 1789.

Mrs. Hillegas was active in the ladies' relief association for the welfare of the American soldiers. (Pennsylvania Gazette, June 12, 1780)

HINMAN, JOANNA HURD   PA
of Wyoming Valley. The daughter of Esther Curtiss and surgeon

Zadoc Hurd of New Milford, Connecticut, she was married on July 16, 1757, to Ens. Titus Hinman of Southbury, Connecticut. They were part of the Susquehanna Company that settled in the Wyoming Valley of then Westmoreland, Connecticut, now western Pennsylvania.

Titus Hinman was killed by Indians during a massacre in the Wyoming Valley on July 3, 1778. Joanna and her four children escaped up the Susquehanna River and then walked many miles back to Connecticut to be with relatives and friends. (Submitted by Lola Kimmel, Federal Way, WA)

HODGE, SARAH   MA
of Newburyport. On February 12, 1780, Isaac Pearson obtained a letter of marque and reprisal to command the New Hampshire ship Uriah mounting six carriage guns and navigated by twenty men. The bond was issued to Samuel Huntington and other members of Congress. Witnesses to the bond were Sarah Hodge and Michael Hodge.

Sarah Hodge was also a witness to all of the following bonds: May 27, 1780, for Keyran Walsh; August 1, 1780, to George Thompson; August 10, 1780, to Jonathan Jewell; January 17, 1781, to William Knapp; February 27, 1781, to Jeremiah Pearson, Jr.; March 27, 1781, to John Coombs; May 30, 1781, to Samuel Coffin; August 14, 1781, to Nathaniel Arnold; August 14, 1781, to Joseph Seveir; September 1, 1781, to Joseph Wells; September 1, 1781, to Seth Thomas; December 22, 1781, to John Lee; February 11, 1782, to Jonathan Jewett; February 16, 1782, to Wingate Newman; May 11, 1782, to Offin Boardman, Jr.; May 23, 1782, to William Russell; June 5, 1782, to Paul Stevens; June 18, 1782, to James Sellars; June 21, 1782, to John Harmon of York, Maine; July 10, 1782, to William Noyes; July 16, 1782, to Joseph Atkins; August 24, 1782, to Zebulon Roe; August 24, 1782, to Enoch Pike; November 23, 1782, to Thomas Tracy; December 2, 1782, to Samuel Coffin. (CN)

HOLCOMB, LUCY LITTLEBURY   SC
of Cowpens. She was born about 1742 and married William Holcomb of Prince Edward County, Virginia. They had six sons and one daughter. William was a soldier in the Revolutionary War and was killed by a Tory scout during the fighting in the Spartanburg area. On January 17, 1780, the Battle of Cowpens was fought on the Holcomb farm. Lucy furnished a horse for the American soldiers, which was later lost, and on January 29, 1791, she was reimbursed by the State of South Carolina. (Submitted by H. E. Wilson, Jr., Long Beach, MS; SI, X, Pt. 1:159)

HOLCOMBE, MARY HARVEY   NJ
of Lambertville. She was the first wife of Richard Holcombe (1752-1835), son of Elizabeth Woolrich and John Holcombe of Abington, Pennsylvania. They had one daughter.

Gen. Washington had his headquarters at the Holcombe house at Coryell's Ferry (now Lambertville) from July 28 to August 1, 1776, and referred to it as the "Oakham" house. On July 30

Washington wrote to Gen. Gates: "General Howe's in a manner abandoning General Burgoyne is so unaccountable a matter, that, till I am fully assured it is so, I cannot help casting my Eyes continually behind me."

Gen. Washington stayed at the Holcombe house again on June 21 and 22, 1778. While there he wrote to Congress on June 22: "I have the honor to inform you that I am now in Jersey, and that the troops are passing the river at Coryel's and are mostly over.... As soon as we have cleaned the arms and can get matters in train we propose moving toward Princeton, in order to avail ourselves of any favorable occasions that may present themselves of attacking or annoying the enemy."

Ann Atkinson Emley, known as the Widow Emley, became the second wife of Richard Holcombe. They had a son, John, and a daughter. The Holcombe house is still standing on North Main Street and is privately owned. (James P. Snell, History of Hunterdon and Somerset Counties, N.J., Philadelphia, 1881; submitted by Thomas B. Wilson, Free Public Library, Lambertville, NJ)

HONEYMAN, MARY HENRY   NJ
of Griggstown. She was the first wife of John Honeyman (1729-1822), who served in the British army under George Washington during the French and Indian Wars. When the Revolutionary War broke out, Honeyman joined the British army as a butcher in charge of provisions, which caused great antagonism among Mary's neighbors, but only Mary and Gen. Washington knew that he was a spy for the Americans. Often Honeyman would leave the British camp in search of cattle and would be captured by the Americans. Then he would relate valuable information to Gen. Washington.

In December 1776 Honeyman gave Washington information which led to the general's successful attack on Trenton, New Jersey. When the American patriots stormed her house, Mary read them the following letter:

> New Jersey, Nov., A.D., 1776. To the good people of New Jersey and all others whom it may concern. It is hereby ordered that the wife and children of John Honeyman of Griggstown the notorious Tory, now within the British lines and probably acting the part of a spy, shall be and hereby are protected from all harm and annoyance from every quarter, until further orders. But this furnishes no protection to Honeyman himself.
> Geo. Washington, Com. in Chief

The mob dispersed, but the neighbors continued to snub Mary Honeyman. It was not until after the war that Gen. Washington himself revealed the fact that Honeyman was an American spy. John and Mary Honeyman are buried in Lamington, New Jersey. (GP)

HOOKER, SARAH WHITMAN   CT
of West Hartford, was born there in 1747. She married Thomas

II: SELECTED BIOGRAPHIES

Hart Hooker of Farmington, Connecticut, who died shortly after his enlistment at the beginning of the Revolution. Mrs. Hooker was a true patriot, and after the Americans captured Fort Ticonderoga, she volunteered to quarter three captured British officers in her home. Her second husband was Seth Collins. Mrs. Hooker died in 1837 at the age of ninety. The local chapter of the Daughters of the American Revolution is named after her, and placed a marker on the grave of Mrs. Hooker (1906) and a marker on her home on Four Mile Road (1928). (CG; DAR) In 1778 she supplied a blanket for the army. (CAR, 12:213)

HOOPER, ANNE CLARK   NC
of Wilmington. The daughter of Thomas Clark, she was married in 1767 to William Hooper, an attorney. While Mrs. Hooper's relatives were Loyalists, she was a true patriot. Mr. Hooper served in the Continental Congress from 1774 to 1777, and while there moved his family to "Finian" on Masonboro Sound, Cape Fear. He was a signer of the Declaration of Independence. When the British invaded North Carolina in 1780, Hooper sent his family back to Wilmington, deciding they were safer there than on the cape, where British vessels fired upon their house. Hooper himself fled to Edenton, North Carolina, where he was housed and fed by his patriot friends. Mrs. Iredell cared for him when he came down with malaria.
    Mrs. Hooper suffered for many months while her husband was in hiding, and when the war ended they found that their home had been destroyed by the enemy. (FG) In 1782 the family moved to Hillsborough, where Mr. Hooper died in 1790. (DB)

HOOPS, MRS. ROBERT   NJ
of Sussex County. Her husband was Maj. Robert Hoops, brigade major to Gen. Dickinson. When Gen. Washington was at Morrisville, Pennsylvania, on December 8, 1776, he sent a message to Gen. Charles Lee by way of Maj. Hoops.
    Mrs. Hoops was an active member of the ladies' association for the benefit and welfare of the American soldiers. (New Jersey Gazette, July 4, 1780)

HOPKINSON, ANN BORDEN   DE, NJ
of Bordentown. The daughter of Col. Joseph Borden, the founder of Bordentown, she was married on September 1, 1768, to Francis Hopkinson, an attorney and musician. He was a signer of the Declaration of Independence. In 1772 Hopkinson was collector of customs in New Castle, Delaware, but early in 1774 moved back to Bordentown and became a successful attorney there. During the occupation of Philadelphia by the British in the winter of 1777/78, the enemy plundered his home in Bordentown. Their son Joseph wrote "Hail, Columbia." Mrs. Hopkinson, a true patriot, suffered during the Revolutionary War in the loss of her home. (DB)

HOPPER, MRS. ANDREW   NJ
of Ramapo. Gen. Washington had his headquarters in her home

from July 23 to July 25, 1777, and again from June 26 to June 30, 1780, according to the Washington papers. (FW) The general was also in Mahwah-Ramapaugh from September 6 to September 18, 1780. At a council of war held on September 6, it was decided that it was not advisable to make any attempt against New York City at that time, unless and until there should be naval support, which would cooperate with the army on land. (BI)

HORNBLOWER, ELIZABETH KINGSLAND   NJ
of Belleville and Trenton. The daughter of Margaritta Coerten and Col. William Kingsland, she was born in 1734. She became the bride of Josiah Hornblower in 1755, and they had eight sons and four daughters. He operated a coal mine for Col. John Schuyler on the Passaic River. He was elected to the New Jersey legislature, 1779-1780, and lived in Trenton.

Mrs. Hornblower was active in the ladies' relief association for the welfare of the American soldiers. (New Jersey Gazette, July 4, 1780) She died in 1808.

HOTCHKISS, TAMAR RICHARDSON   CT
of Waterbury. The daughter of Nathaniel Richardson of Break Neck (now Middlebury), she was born in September 1758. During the Revolutionary War, Tamar and her mother prepared meals for the soldiers passing by their home to and from Boston and Fishkill. Later she told how her arms were burned from the heat of the brick oven and how she had to climb over sleeping men to get to her bedroom. On December 31, 1778, she married Stephen Hotchkiss. Tamar died on March 29, 1853, aged ninety-four and a half years. (EW)

HOWARD, ANNE MYERS   PA
of Philadelphia. When Anne Myers heard that John Robinson of Shermans Valley, Pennsylvania, was collecting a force of Loyalists to seize all civil officers he could and to join the British in Philadelphia, Anne notified Maj. John Jameson of the 2nd Continental Dragoons, who had been wounded near Valley Forge, Pennsylvania, in January 1778. In February 1778 Jameson gave this information to Gen. Washington, who notified the Board of War on February 26, 1778. (FW) Anne Myers became the fourth wife of Thomas Howard (1742-1837). (DAR)

HOWELL, KEZIAH BURR   NJ
of Bridgeton. The daughter of Joseph Burr of Burlington County, in November 1779 she married brigade Maj. Richard Howell, who on April 7, 1779, had been commissioned secretly in intelligence work by Gen. Washington. They had nine children. Since Howell was spying among the Loyalists to obtain information, he was arrested as a Tory and brought before Judge David Brearly and accused of treason. Only after Howell showed the judge his secret orders from Washington was he discharged. Mrs. Howell, a true patriot, suffered during this period. Their great-granddaughter,

II: SELECTED BIOGRAPHIES

Varina Howell, married Jefferson Davis, president of the Confederate States of America. (DB)

HUDDY, MARY   NJ
was the wife of Capt. Joshua Huddy of the New Jersey State Artillery. He was captured by Loyalist refugees on March 24, 1782, at Toms River, New Jersey. Huddy was carried to New York City and kept in irons until April 8. He was then put on board a sloop and taken to Sandy Hook, New Jersey, and confined on a prison ship there. On April 12, 1782, Capt. Huddy was hanged on orders of Capt. Richard Lippincott, who accused him of killing the Tory refugee Philip White. Philip White was in fact killed by Loyalists on March 30, while Huddy was still in irons in New York.

While at Elizabethtown (Elizabeth), New Jersey, Gen. Washington learned what had happened to Huddy and wrote to the general and field officers of the army asking that retaliatory measures should be taken. The British ordered a court-martial for Capt. Lippincott, which convened on May 3, but apparently Lippincott was acquitted. (FW) This is another example of the suffering of the patriotic American women during these difficult times.

HUGER, MARY ESTHER KINLOCH   SC
of Charleston. She was the second wife of Maj. Benjamin Huger (1746-1779), and they lived on the coast near Charleston. In 1777 Gen. Lafayette and Baron de Kalb came to America on the *Victoire* and landed in South Carolina on the property of Maj. Huger. The two men spent the night there with Maj. and Mrs. Huger. The next day Maj. Huger provided horses for Lafayette and de Kalb to proceed northward to confer with Gen. Washington.

During the French Revolution, Lafayette was placed in charge of the National Guard and while in Belgium, Lafayette was charged with high treason by Robespierre. Lafayette fled to Austria, where he was imprisoned by the emperor, who considered Lafayette a rebel and a menace to royalty. Lafayette spent five years in prison, and a son of Maj. Huger went to Austria to help him escape, but the attempt failed. (*DAR Magazine*, January 1984, in an article by the Marquis and Marquise de Chambrun)

Mary Huger supplied provisions for the army in South Carolina during the Revolutionary War. (SI, B:11)

HUGHES, HANNAH HOLSTEIN   PA
of Gulf Mills. She was the wife of Lt. Col. Isaac Hughes of the Pennsylvania militia. Gen. Washington had his headquarters there from December 13 to 19, 1777, on which date the army reached Valley Forge, where they encamped for the winter. (BI)

HUMASTON, ABI BLACKESLEE   CT
of Thomaston (formerly Plymouth). She was born there in 1759. Her husband, Jesse Humaston, served in the Continental Army in 1775. During the war she was warned of a raid by the Tories, and so chopped up some flannel and turnips and made fake sausages

which were eaten by the enemy. Mrs. Humaston also wrote poetry
which was published. The Thomaston and Plymouth chapter of
the Daughters of the American Revolution is named in her honor.
She died in 1847. (CG)

HUMPHREY, PHOEBE   CT
of Collinsville. She was born in Canton, Connecticut, in 1763.
During the Revolutionary War, in 1779, she was baking bread in
her home when she was attacked by a Hessian soldier, whom she
put to flight with her bread shovel. Phoebe Humphrey died
in 1848. The Collinsville chapter of the Daughters of the American
Revolution is named in her honor, and erected a tablet to her memory in the Canton Street Cemetery on November 16, 1930. (CG)

HUMPHREYS, SARAH RIGGS   CT
of Derby. She was born in 1711 and married John Bowers. After
he died she married the Rev. Daniel Humphreys in 1739. Four
of her sons served in the Revolutionary War, including Gen. David
Humphreys. The local chapter of the Daughters of the American
Revolution is named in her honor. She died in 1787.

HUNT, MARGARET GUILD   NJ
of Hopewell. She was the daughter of the Rev. John Guild, minister of the First Presbyterian Church of Hopewell at Pennington.
On September 18, 1771, Margaret married John Price Hunt, a breeder
of famous horses. They had four sons and four daughters. In
April 1776 Hunt advertised his brown horse Whirligig to stud at
his stables. Whirligig's bloodline was through Slamerkin, bred
in the Bouwerie stables of James DeLancy. Slamerkin was a great
early racehorse, and his descendant Nashua was a leading money
winner in 1956.
    The Hunts occupied the house of his late brother-in-law,
Jonathan Stout, at the time of Gen. Washington's visit there, and
Washington gave it the name the Hunt House. On June 24, 1778,
Gen. Washington held a council of war at the Hunt House to discuss plans for the Battle of Monmouth. Present were generals
Duportial, Greene, Knox, Lafayette, Lee, Patterson, Poor, Steuben,
Stirling, Wayne and Woodford, plus Colonel Scammell, Washington's
adjutant. (BJ; FW; some information from Richard W. Reeves,
Trenton Public Library, NJ)

HUNT, MARY DAGWORTHY   NJ
of Trenton. Mary Dagworthy was active in the ladies' association
for the welfare of the American soldiers and was elected secretary
of the association. (New Jersey Gazette, July 4, 1780) On July
17, 1780, she wrote to Gen. Washington: "By order of Mrs. Dickinson and the other ladies of the committee, I have transmitted
to your Excellency by Colonel Thompson, Fifteen thousand four
hundred and eighty dollars, being the subscriptions receiv'd at
this place to be disposed of in such manner as your Excellency
thinks proper, for the benefit of the Continental soldiers."

II: SELECTED BIOGRAPHIES

On August 6, 1780, Gen. Washington wrote to Miss Dagworthy: "Some time since I was honored with your letter of the 17th of July, with a sum of money the result of your subscriptions at that time. So much patriotism, while it is pleasing and fresh proof of the spirit of the ladies of New Jersey, entitles them to every applause. The army feel most sensibly both the design and the benefaction."

On December 29, 1780, Miss Dagworthy wrote to Gen. Washington that 380 pairs of stockings were on their way to the general, but they arrived too late. (FW) Later she married Abraham Hunt. (DAR)

HUNTINGDON, SELINA SHIRLEY, COUNTESS OF   SC
was born on August 24, 1707, the daughter of Washington Shirley, second earl Ferrers. On June 3, 1728, she married Theophilus Hastings, ninth earl of Huntingdon and they lived at Dunnington Park in Leicestershire, England. Lady Huntingdon introduced the "New Light" of Methodism to her friends when she became intimate with John and Charles Wesley, founders of the church. Her husband died on October 13, 1746.

When George Whitfield returned from America in 1748, she opened her house in Park Lane, London, for him to preach there. Whitfield died in 1770 and left his possessions, which included large tracts of land in America, to the countess, who sent missionaries to America and also hired workers to farm her large plantations. Selina supported the rebel cause and supplied provisions for the American troops. (SI, B:11) She died in London on June 17, 1791.

HUNTINGTON, ELIZABETH TRACY BACKUS   CT
of Norwich was the first wife of Col. Jabez Huntington. On his trip from Cambridge, Massachusetts, to New York City in 1776, Gen. Washington spent the night of April 7 at Dwight's Tavern in Warren, Massachusetts, then proceeded to Norwich, where he spent the night at the home of Col. and Mrs. Jabez Huntington. This is confirmed in a letter of Col. Jedediah Huntington, his son, to Governor Trumbull, his father-in-law: "The General will take Bed at Col. Jz Hungtington ... the General intends for New London Tomorrow ... 3 o'clo. 8th April 1776, Colo. Jed. Huntington."

On that date Gen. Washington met and conferred with Governor Trumbull in Norwich, as confirmed in Washington's letter of thanks to the governor dated April 22, 1776. The second wife of Jabez Huntington was Hannah Williams. (DAR; CG)

HUNTINGTON, FAITH TRUMBULL   CT
of Lebanon. The daughter of Faith Robinson and Governor Jonathan Trumbull, she was born in 1743. She married Col. Jedediah Huntington, and later he became a general. Mrs. Huntington visited her husband at his camp in Roxbury, Massachusetts, and then accompanied him to Cambridge. After the Battle of Bunker Hill, on June 17, 1775, some 450 Americans were killed, wounded, or captured.

The wounded were taken to the Halls of Harvard, where Mrs. Huntington nursed the soldiers and tried to alleviate their suffering. The strain was too much for her, and her nerves were shattered. She died in her home on November 24, 1775.

HUNTINGTON, HANNAH WILLIAMS   CT
of Norwich. Born on July 23, 1726, Hannah was the daughter of the Rev. Ebenezer Williams of Pomfret, Connecticut. She was married on July 10, 1746, to Col. Jabez Huntington (later a Major General). She was his second wife. His first wife, Elizabeth Tracy Backus Huntington, died in 1745. One of Elizabeth's sons was Brig. Gen. Jedediah Huntington.

On his trip from Cambridge, Massachusetts, to New York City in 1776, Gen. Washington spent the night of April 7 in Dwight's Tavern in Warren, Massachusetts, then proceeded to Norwich, where he spent the night of April 8 at the home of Col. and Mrs. Jabez Huntington. This is confirmed in a letter of Jedediah Huntington to Governor Jonathan Trumbull, his father-in-law: "The General will take Bed at Col. Jz Huntington ... the General intends for New London Tomorrow ... 3 o'clo. 8th April 1776, Colo. Jed. Huntington."

On that date Gen. Washington met and conferred with Governor Trumbull in Norwich, as confirmed in Washington's letter of thanks to the governor dated April 22, 1776. (BI) Hannah died on March 25, 1807. (Some information from Camp S. Huntington, Bartlesville, OK)

HUTCHINSON, LYDIA BIDDLE   PA
of Philadelphia. She was the wife of Dr. James Hutchinson who was surgeon general of Pennsylvania from 1778 to 1784. Mrs. Hutchinson was a member of the ladies' relief association for the welfare of American soldiers. (Pennsylvania Gazette, June 12, 1780)

HYLTON, MRS. DANIEL   VA
of Westham. When the British under Benedict Arnold with fifteen hundred men attacked Richmond on January 5, 1781, Thomas Jefferson sent his family to Pine Creek, which was his father's first home. Jefferson spent the night with Mr. and Mrs. Hylton. Arnold's forces burned many buildings in Richmond, destroying factories and public records. They also seized five to six tons of gunpowder and threw muskets, uniforms, tools, and wagons into the river before leaving Richmond on January 8. (ST)

I

IREDELL, HANNAH JOHNSTON   NC
of Edenton. She was the sister of Samuel Johnston, an attorney there. On July 18, 1773, she married James Iredell, an attorney. In 1768 he was appointed comptroller of customs in Edenton and held that office until 1774, when he became collector of the port,

II: SELECTED BIOGRAPHIES

which office he held until 1776. He served as state attorney general from 1779 to 1781.

When the British invaded North Carolina in 1781, William Hooper, a signer of the Declaration of Independence, fled to Edenton, where he depended on friends for food and shelter. Hooper became violently ill with malaria, and Mrs. Iredell cared for him and nursed him back to health. Mrs. Iredell was a kind and helpful patriotic woman. (FG)

IRVIN, JENNET BREWSTER   VA
of Augusta County. She was born on April 11, 1761. Jennet (Jane) and her sisters Alice Brewster Alexander and Elinor Brewster Dunn, spun, knitted, wove, sewed, cooked meals, and made bullets for the Revolutionary War soldiers. Later she married Samuel Irvin (1760-1837) of South Carolina. She died on July 17, 1839. The three sisters are buried on the campus of the University of Indiana at Bloomington. (Submitted by Beverly A. Hendricks, Glendale, CA)

IRVINE, ANNE CALLENDER   PA
of Carlisle. The daughter of Mary Scull and Robert Callender, she was born on February 18, 1758. About 1775 Anne married Dr. William Irvine and they lived on his farm near Carlisle where there was a flour mill. In January 1776 Dr. Irvine was colonel of the 6th Battalion of the 7th Pennsylvania Regiment of the Continental Line. While on the expedition to Canada, Dr. Irvine was captured by the enemy. He was not exchanged until May 6, 1778. Irvine again became colonel of the 7th Pennsylvania Regiment. Mary Hays (later McCauley), known as Molly Pitcher, was a maid in the home of Dr. and Mrs. Irvine. Molly was with her husband, Pvt. Hays, and Dr. Irvine at the Battle of Monmouth, New Jersey, on June 28, 1778. (See Mary Hays McCauley, below)

During Dr. Irvine's absence, Mrs. Irvine ran the flour mill to supply the American army. Flax was supplied to make clothing and the ladies also knitted stockings for the soldiers.

In 1779 Col. Irvine was commissioned a brigadier general and was in command at Fort Pitt from 1781 to October 1783. He was an original member of the Society of the Cincinnati formed in 1783 by the officers of the Continental Army. After the war the Irvines moved to Philadelphia, where Mrs. Irvine died on October 15, 1823. (DAR; DB; EP)

IRVINE, SARAH HAINES   PA
of Carlisle. The daughter of Catharine and William Harris, she was born on March 20, 1741, in Lancaster County. In 1760 she married James Irvine, who served as an officer during the Revolutionary War. He was a brother of Gen. William Irvine.

During the war, Mrs. Irvine and her neighbors spun and made clothing for the American soldiers and fed the men at Valley Forge. She died in Carlisle on March 5, 1837. (EP)

ISRAEL, HANNAH ERWIN DE
of Wilmington. She married Israel Israel, a farmer who resided
on the banks of the Delaware River. He had been captured by
the British and was a prisoner on HMS Roebuck. He was a true
patriot and remarked that he would sooner drive his cattle to Gen.
Washington than receive British gold for them. The British soldiers
drove his cattle down the Delaware, but Mrs. Israel intervened,
and despite musket shots from the British, she drove the cattle
back to the barn. (CD)

J

JACKSON, ELIZABETH HUTCHINSON SC
of the Waxhaws District, New Lancaster. She was born in Ireland
and came to America with her Irish husband, Andrew Jackson, who
died in 1767. After the British captured Charleston, South Carolina,
on May 12, 1780, many of the Continental seamen and soldiers were
confined on prison ships in the Charleston harbor. In 1781 Mrs.
Jackson traveled from Waxhaws to Charleston to bring clothing and
food to the American prisoners on board the prison ships. En
route home, Mrs. Jackson suffered from yellow fever, contracted
from the prisoners, and died in a tent. She was buried along
the road in an unmarked grave. Her son, Andrew Jackson, born
after his father's death, became a famous general and president
of the United States. (HS)

JACKSON, RACHEL DONELSON VA, TN
the daughter of Col. John Donelson, she was born in 1767. On
December 23, 1779, some 125 men, women, and children left Fort
Watauga and took a trip down the Watauga, Holston, Tennessee,
Ohio, and Cumberland rivers to settle at Fort Nashborough (now
Nashville) on the Cumberland River bluffs. The captain of the
Adventure and leader of the flotilla was Rachel's father. The trip
took four months, and the passengers faced frozen and swollen
rivers, Indian attacks, rapids, treacherous shoals, starvation,
and abandonment before reaching Fort Nashborough on April 24,
1780. Many of the settlers died or were killed by Indians during
the trip. (Submitted by William Thomas Haywood)

The thirteen-year-old Rachel endured these trials. In 1781
the Indians attacked the fort, and the fourteen-year-old Rachel
assisted Charlotte Robertson and Ann Cockrill in defending it.
Later Rachel married a man named Robards. After her father's
death, her mother ran a boardinghouse in Nashville. One of her
boarders was Andrew Jackson, who fell in love with Rachel. She
applied for a divorce from Robards, but married Andrew Jackson
in 1791 before her divorce was final.

When Jackson ran for president of the United States in 1828,
his wife was called a bigamist, and the scandal caused Andrew
and Rachel much distress. She died in 1828, before he entered
the White House on March 4, 1829. The Jacksons had no children,

II: SELECTED BIOGRAPHIES

but they raised her nephew, Andrew Jackson Donelson (1799-1871),
as their son. He served as Jackson's secretary (1824-1836) and as
minister to Prussia (1846-1849). (DB)

JEFFERSON, MARTHA WAYLES   VA
of Monticello. She was born in 1747 and was first married to a
Mr. Skelton. In 1770 she was a wealthy widow aged twenty-three
when she first met Thomas Jefferson. They were married in 1772
and had six children, but only two daughters lived to maturity.
Jefferson is credited with having written the Declaration of
Independence.

Together with Martha Washington, Mrs. Jefferson raised thousands of dollars for the American soldiers by organizing collections through churches.

Governor Thomas Jefferson left office and retired to Monticello
in 1781. Lt. Col. Banastre Tarleton with 180 dragoons and 70
mounted infantrymen was sent by Lord Cornwallis to Charlottesville
to capture Jefferson and other members of the state assembly on
June 3, 1781. Jefferson was warned while at Monticello and sent
his family to stay at Blenheim, the home of Col. and Mrs. Edward
Carter. Later they were joined by Jefferson, who then sent his
family to his second residence at Poplar Forest.

Meanwhile Lord Cornwallis seized Jefferson's house at Elk
Hill on the James River and remained there for ten days. The
British army destroyed the corn and tobacco crops and burned
Jefferson's barns and fences. They also stole his cattle, horses,
hogs, and sheep. In 1781 the British plundered Jefferson's plantations at Cumberland and Shadwell. (LV; ST)

Mrs. Jefferson died on September 6, 1782.

JENKINS, BETHIA HARRIS   PA
of Philadelphia. She was born on September 14, 1752, and married
John Jenkins, Jr. (1751-1827), of Connecticut, who was a lieutenant
in the army. During the British occupation of Philadelphia in 1777/78,
Mrs. Jenkins operated the Conestoga Wagon Tavern and found means
to take money and food to the American prisoners of war. During
this period she assisted Mary Frazer and Margery Gibbons. Mrs.
Jenkins died on August 12, 1842. (DAR Magazine, August-September
1979)

JOHNSON, ANN ROBERTSON   TN
of Cumberland County. She was the sister of James Robertson,
the first schoolteacher in Tennessee. Mrs. Johnson lived in the
Watauga Settlement in Virginia, then later in Tennessee. During
an Indian raid in July 1776 at Fort Caswell, she had the women
pour kettles of hot water on the Indians climbing the sides of the
stockade. Her husband, Isaac Johnson, was killed by the Indians
at Johnson's Fort, leaving her with three young daughters. In
December 1779 she was at Fort Nashborough, where she loaded
muskets and fired at the Indians who were attacking the fort. (EW;
HS)

JOHNSON, ELIZABETH CRAIG   KY
of Bryan's Station. She was born about 1766 in Spotsylvania County, the daughter of Sallie Page and John Craig. When the Tories and Indians attacked on August 15, 1782, Elizabeth Craig was one of the girls who went for water to the spring (see Jemima Johnson, below, and Polly Craig, above). In 1784 Elizabeth married Cave Johnson (1760-1850), who was an ensign in the army. He was the brother of Capt. Robert Johnson who married Jemima Suggett. Elizabeth had three sons and five daughters. The name of Betsy Craig is inscribed on the monument erected in 1896 by the Lexington Chapter of the Daughters of the American Revolution. (Virginia Webb Howard, Bryan's Station Heroes and Heroines, 1932; submitted by Linda Reed, Plainview, TX)

JOHNSON, JANE FALCONER   KY
of Craig's Station. The daughter of Joice Craig and John Falconer (Faulkner), she married Andrew Johnson (1750-1826), and together with the Falconers, Hamptons, and Singletons, settled at John Craig's Station in Kentucky on Christmas Eve 1779. In 1780 Craig's Station was burned to the ground by Indians and thereafter called Burnt Station, and the family moved to Bryan's Station. Andrew was captured by the Indians at Blue Licks along with Daniel Boone, and they were both adopted by the Indians. Later Andrew escaped with a scouting party and scalped some Indians in retaliation for his capture.

On August 15, 1782, the Tories and Indians attacked Bryan's Station. Water was desperately needed by the colonists for a long siege, and so Jemima Johnson led Jane and the other women to the spring to get water--a very brave act--and they were not molested by the Indians. (CH)

JOHNSON, JEMIMA SUGGETT   KY
of Lexington. She was born on June 29, 1753, and married Capt. Robert Johnson (1745-1815). They had eleven children. During a Tory and Indian attack on Bryan's Station, Kentucky, near the present site of Lexington, on August 15, 1782, the wounded soldiers were asking for water. Mrs. Johnson, together with Mary Boone Bryan, Polly Hawkins Craig, and several other women went with buckets to obtain water from the spring outside the stockade, despite the presence of Indians. Danger was lurking everywhere, but the women accomplished their mission.

It is a matter of record that her son James a boy of eight years, was lifted to a cabin roof ignited by a flaming arrow, and was given a piggin of water by his mother to put out the fire.

Her husband, Robert, was promoted to colonel and founded Fredericksburg on the Ohio River, since 1831 called Warsaw, Kentucky. In 1896 a limestone memorial enclosing the famous spring was erected by the Lexington Daughters of the American Revolution. Mrs. Johnson is recognized as a patriot in the DAR Patriot Index. Their daughter saved the life of her infant son (see Elizabeth Johnson Payne, below). (Submitted by Sue M. Bogardus, Warsaw, KY;

II: SELECTED BIOGRAPHIES

CD; EW; HS; Virginia Webb Hammond, Bryan's Station Heroes and Heroines, 1932; submitted by Linda Reed, Plainview, TX)

JOHNSTON, ALICE ERWIN   PA
of Philadelphia. The daughter of James Erwin, she was born about 1754 in Chester County. On December 15, 1775, she married Francis Johnston, an attorney. In January 1776 he was appointed a lieutenant colonel for the 4th Pennsylvania Battalion and commissioned a colonel of the 5th Regiment, Pennsylvania Line in September 1776. He was active in the battles of Brandywine, Germantown, Monmouth, and Stony Point. He served until 1781.

During the winter of 1777, Alice gathered and sent supplies to the army at Valley Forge. (EP)

JOHNSTON, HEPSIBATH TYLER   VT
was born on December 5, 1754, and became the fourth wife of James Bell. After his death she married Col. Robert Johnston (1739-1824), who served as a scout. Mrs. Johnston is credited with patriotic service in the DAR Patriot Index. She died on July 8, 1866, in her 112th year. (Submitted by Barbara B. Marden, Rochester, NH)

JONES, SARAH DAVIS   GA
of Savannah. The daughter of John Davis, she married Dr. Noble Wymberley Jones, and they had six children. In 1775 he was a member of the Council of Safety, but the family fled Savannah in 1778 when it fell to the British. They went to Charleston, but when the British captured Charleston on May 12, 1780, Jones was captured and imprisoned by the British in an old Spanish fort in Saint Augustine, Florida, along with Thomas Heyward, Jr., Arthur Middleton, and Edward Rutledge, South Carolina signers of the Declaration of Independence. Jones was exchanged in 1781 and represented Georgia in the Continental Congress in 1781/82. He died in 1805. (DB)

JOYNER, ELIZABETH NORTON   GA
of Savannah. She married John Joyner and was the sister of Pvt. William Norton who was captured by the British when they took Savannah on December 29, 1778. Hearing that her brother was ill, she rode on horseback to the enemy camp and obtained a pass to see the company commander. Mrs. Joyner asked for the release of her brother. The commander agreed, since the man was ill, and gave her another horse on which they placed her brother. She wore a cap with a white feather in it to show that she was on the American side. Every British officer pulled off his cap as she passed, and the ranks opened for her to pass through them.

After her husband's death, she married the Rev. William Graham. Mrs. Graham died in 1832, aged eighty-three, and was buried in the Robertville churchyard. (Submitted by George M. Norton of Cocoa Beach, FL)

K

KEITH, ELIZABETH WILSON   PA
near Newtown. She married William Keith (1714-1781). Gen. Washington had his headquarters there from December 14 to 25, 1776. While there Washington wrote to the Council of Safety of Pennsylvania about the British capture of Gen. Charles Lee. On December 25, 1776, Washington and his men crossed the Delaware River about nine miles north of Trenton, New Jersey. (BI)

KEITH, MARY LAFOONE   SC
of Pickens. The daughter of William Lafoone, she was the wife of Cornelius Keith (1743-1820), who was a corporal during the war. While her husband was away, Mary rode many miles to warn the Americans whenever the enemy was approaching the area. Once while she was gone the Indians burned her log cabin, but her faithful slaves saved her children and carried them to a cave where they hid until the Indians left. The cave, known as the "Mary Lafoone Cave" is near the Miracle Hill School. (Echoes, Easley, SC, 1980; submitted by Beth H. Heiss, Warner Robins, GA)

KELLEY, HANNAH BARTLETT   MA
of Amesbury. The daughter of Mary Ordway and John Bartlett of Newbury, she was born on November 16, 1704. Hannah was a cousin of Josiah Bartlett of Kingston, New Hampshire, a signer of the Declaration of Independence and the first governor of New Hampshire. On December 16, 1725, Hannah married Capt. Richard Kelley (1704-1774) in Newbury.

On December 28, 1780, the town of Amesbury called twenty-one men to serve for three years during the war and asked citizens to provide funds to support the militia. The widow Hannah Kelley provided Ŀ128. She died in Amesbury on April 6, 1789. (Joseph Merrill, History of Amesbury and Merrimac, Massachusetts, 1978; submitted by Frederick J. Nicholson, New York, NY)

KENT, SIBBIL DWIGHT   MA
of Warren. After he left Dorothy Coolidge's Tavern in Watertown, Massachusetts, on the morning of July 3, 1775, Gen. Washington proceeded to Cambridge, Massachusetts, where on July 3, 1775, the general took command of the Continental Army. He established his headquarters in the home of Col. Vassal, a Tory, whose house was confiscated and sequestered by the United States. Mrs. Washington was with her husband in the Vassal House. Gen. Washington were here for nine months. After the British evacuated Boston and sailed for Halifax, Nova Scotia, on March 17, 1776, Washington remained in Cambridge until April, when he led the main part of his army toward New York, anticipating the strategy of Gen. Howe to secure New York City as his base of operations. In 1792 Andrew Craigie purchased the Vassal house, and it is known today as the Craigie House. Later the Craigie house was occupied by Henry Wadsworth Longfellow.

II: SELECTED BIOGRAPHIES 117

Sibbil was the daughter of Col. Simeon Dwight. She was born in 1744. In 1774 she became the third wife of her second cousin, Maj. Elishu Kent. On his trip to New York from Cambridge, Massachusetts, Gen. Washington was entertained for dinner by Mrs. Kent on April 8, 1776. He then stayed in Dwight's Tavern, owned by her father. Mrs. Kent died in 1822. The Suffield, Connecticut, chapter of the Daughters of the American Revolution is named in her honor. This chapter restored the old cemetery in Suffield and marked the graves of Revolutionary soldiers. (BI)

KENTON, MARTHA DOWDEN   KY
of Washington. She was the first wife of Capt. Simon Kenton (1755-1836), the pioneer settler in Kentucky. In 1775 he erected a log cabin upon the spot where Washington now stands, and raised a crop of corn there. In the fall of 1775 they moved to Boonesborough. In the fall of 1778 he was captured by Indians. They beat him, then placed him on the ground with his legs apart and lashed each foot to stakes driven into the earth. Then they placed a pole across his breast and tied his hands to the pole, then another thong was tied around his neck to a stake in the ground. In the morning they took him to the Indian village where he was to be burned at the stake. But Kenton was saved by the Tory Simon Girty and later by Mingo, the Indian chief. Kenton was taken to Detroit and imprisoned.

Finally in the summer of 1779 Kenton managed to escape with the help of Mrs. Harvey, the wife of an Indian trader. Later Kenton became a general, and moved to Urbana, Ohio in 1802. Kenton County, Kentucky, was named in his honor. (CH)

KING, ELIZABETH   NC
of Edenton. On October 24, 1774, in the home of Elizabeth King, the women of Edentown (now Edenton), drew up a document supporting the Resolutions of the First Provincial Congress of North Carolina, which prohibited the importation of British manufactured goods, including tea. Forty-eight women signed this resolution.

On Courthouse Square in Edenton a large bronze teapot has been mounted atop a Revolutionary War Cannon. (CP; DR)

Mrs. King supplied provisions for the Revolutionary Army during the war. (RA, X:30, fol. 5)

KIRBY, RUTH MARVIN   CT
of Litchfield was born on December 20, 1763, the daughter of Ruth Welch and Reynold Marvin, an attorney. After the lead statue of King George III was brought to Litchfield, Connecticut, by Oliver Wolcott, Ruth and her mother molded 11,592 bullets from the statue. (CG) (See also Laura Collins Wolcott, below) Ruth married Ephriam Kirby. She died on October 17, 1817. (DAR)

KIRKPATRICK, LYDIA LEWIS   NJ
of Kerr's Corner. She was born in 1742 and married Captain John Kirkpatrick (1739-1822). They lived in Somerset County, New

Jersey, then moved to Frelinghuysen Township in Warren County
and settled near where the Ebenezer Church and the schoolhouse
now stand. Her husband was Capt. of the 2nd Sussex County
Militia. Lydia's granddaughter, Catherine Read, was born in 1818,
the tenth child of Lydia's son John Jr. Catherine in 1906 made
the sworn statement "that my grandmother, Lydia Lewis Kirkpatrick,
wife of Captain John Kirkpatrick of the Second Sussex County,
N.J., Militia, who resided near Kerr's Corner, N.J., told me herself that at different times she gave cattle to be killed, and food
to the Revolutionary soldiers. She also made salves for them,
tore up her linen sheets to make bandages with which to bind their
bleeding feet, and aided them in many other ways."

    Lydia Kirkpatrick died in 1832. She is listed as a patriot
in the DAR Patriot Index. (William C. Armstrong, Captain John
Kirkpatrick, 1927; submitted by Esther Dillon Marsh, Millard, OH)

KNIGHT, MARY WORRELL   PA
from near Valley Forge. She was born in 1759 and was the sister
of Gen. Isaac Worrell. Mary was a widow during the winter of
1777 when she brought food to the soldiers suffering at Valley
Forge. The British had a ransom on the head of Gen. Worrell,
and her house was ransacked several times. Mary died of cholera
in July 1849 in Rahway, New Jersey. (CD; GP)

KNOX, LUCY FLUCKER   MA
of Boston. She was the daughter of Thomas Flucker, secretary
of the Province of Massachusetts. In 1775 she married Maj. Henry
Knox of Boston, and quickly supported the rebel cause in defiance
of the Loyalist wishes of her father. When the British occupied
Boston, the couple fled the city.

    Henry Knox served as a colonel in the Continental Army
and brought captured cannons and rifles from Ticonderoga to use
in the siege of Boston. While in New York, Mrs. Knox lived on a
farm with her children a short distance from his headquarters at
Verplanck's Point. Lucy was a camp follower, and was near her
husband whenever possible. She spent the winter with him at
Valley Forge (1777/78) and gave him comfort, support, and encouragement. On other occasions she danced with Gen. Washington as Martha Washington sat and watched.

    On February 18, 1779, a celebration in honor of the French
alliance was held in Pluckemin, New Jersey. The artillery corps
provided the entertainment with a discharge of thirteen cannon
at four o'clock in the afternoon, followed by a supper at which
many toasts were drunk. Next came a fireworks display, and then
the ball opened by Gen. Washington and Mrs. Knox in the Academy.
Col. Knox wrote to his brother that there were about seventy ladies
present, and three or four hundred gentlemen, and that they danced
all night.

    Knox was promoted to major general in the Continental Army
in November 1781 and was a founder of the Society of the Cincinnati
in 1783, an organization consisting of officers of the Continental

II: SELECTED BIOGRAPHIES

Army and Navy. This organization is still in existence today, being composed of the descendants of the Continental officers. (DB; BW; FW)

L

LAFAYETTE, ADRIENNE DE NOAILLES, MARQUISE DE   PA
the daughter of the Duke d'Ayen, on April 11, 1774, at age fourteen, she married in Paris the Marquis de Lafayette, who was only sixteen. Then at age nineteen, Lafayette was given the rank of lieutenant general by Silas Deane, the acting American envoy in Paris. He came to America in 1777 with Baron de Kalb on the ship Victoire, and the trip took fifty-four days to cross the Atlantic from Spain. Gen. Washington reduced his rank to major general in the Continental Army. After returning to Paris in 1779, Lafayette convinced the king to send a fleet of ships and some six thousand men to help the American rebels. The Marquise de Lafayette and his wife arrived in Philadelphia in April 1780, and Lafayette was given command of an army in Virginia.

Mrs. Lafayette was a member of the ladies' association for the welfare of the American soldiers and was a substantial contributor to the cause. (Pennsylvania Gazette, June 12, 1780)

Lafayette had Cornwallis and the British army trapped at Yorktown in July 1781, along with the French fleet. When additional Continental Army troops arrived, Lord Cornwallis surrendered on October 19, 1781.

After the American Revolution, Lafayette and Adrienne returned to Paris. They had one son and two daughters. During the French Revolution, Lafayette was in command of a French army in Belgium until Robespierre accused him of high treason, and he fled to Austria, where he was imprisoned at Omultz by the emperor, who accused Lafayette of rebel thoughts and deeds. Lafayette was put in chains in a dungeon, and was imprisoned for five years.

Meanwhile Adrienne was arrested in Paris and imprisoned. On June 2, 1794, her mother and her sister Louise were beheaded. The sudden downfall of Robespierre resulted in her release from prison.

Adrienne went to Austria with her two daughters and was permitted to remain in prison with her husband. Soon her daughters caught an infection in the dungeon, and Adrienne became ill with blood poisoning. Sick as she was, however, she remained in prison with her husband and her daughters. Only after Napoleon's victories was Lafayette released.

Adrienne died on December 24, 1807, as a result of the blood poisoning she contracted in prison. Lafayette lived another twenty-seven years and made his final visit to America in 1824/25. He died on May 20, 1834. Adrienne and Lafayette are buried in the little cemetery of Picpus, and the flag of the United States flies over their graves. (DAR Magazine, January 1984; article by the Marquis and Marquise de Chambrun)

LA LUZERNE, COUNTESS DE   PA
of Philadelphia and Paris. Her husband was Anne Cesar, Chevalier de la Luzerne, minister of France to the United Colonies. The Chevalier de la Luzerne and his wife came to America on the Sensible, along with John Adams, returning from his first mission to Paris, landing at Boston on August 2, 1779. Later, on September 30, 1779, the chevalier visited Gen. Washington at West Point.

On May 11, 1780, Gen. Washington wrote to the chevalier: "You will participate in the joy I feel at the arrival of the Marquis de La Fayette. No event could have given me sweeter pleasure on a personal account, and motives of public utility conspire to make it agreeable. He will shortly have the honor to wait upon your Excellency and impart matters of the greatest moment to these states." (FW)

The Countess de la Luzerne entertained Lafayette. She was a member of the ladies' association for the welfare of the soldiers and was a substantial contributor to the cause. (Pennsylvania Gazette, June 12, 1780).

The Chevalier and Countess de la Luzerne lived on the north side of Chestnut Street between 6th and 7th avenues. They gave a great dinner for Gen. Washington and his generals on September 14, 1781, and another party on July 15, 1782, while living in the Dickinson house. (BI)

LANE, ANNA MARIA   VA
of Richmond. She was born about 1735, probably in New Hampshire, and was a camp follower. Her husband, John Lane, fought in the battles of Trenton, Princeton, White Plains, and Germantown, where she suffered a severe wound and was hospitalized in Philadelphia (it was reported that she had donned an army uniform). After the British captured Savannah on December 29, 1778, John Lane was captured. After his exchange, he served as a major in the Virginia Cavalry Regiment under Col. John Nelson.

Mrs. Lane worked as a nurse in the soldiers' barracks in Richmond. In 1807 Governor William H. Cabell requested financial remuneration for Mrs. Lane's military service from the Virginia legislature, and she was granted a pension of a hundred dollars a year. (CP)

LATHAM, EUNICE FORSYTHE   CT
of Groton. She was the wife of Capt. William Latham (1741-1792), who was stationed at Fort Griswold in Groton. The fort was commanded by Col. William Ledyard. On September 6, 1781, British forces under Benedict Arnold attacked the fort. Eunice and her children fled the fort, but her young son William remained with his father. So did Lambo, the captain's body servant.

The British soldiers massacred the American defenders. Lambo tried to protect his master, but was killed, and Capt. Latham was badly wounded by a broadsword. Eunice's son William was taken prisoner. She went to the headquarters of Benedict Arnold and demanded the return of her son, who was in the room. Arnold

II: SELECTED BIOGRAPHIES 121

told her to take her son, but not to raise him as a rebel. "I shall take him and teach him to despise the name of a traitor," Eunice replied, and took her son away. (GP)

LEDYARD, ANNE WILLIAMS   CT
of Groton. In January 1761 she married Capt. William Ledyard and they had nine children. He defended Fort Griswold in Groton when the forces under Benedict Arnold attacked on September 6, 1781, with eight hundred men. Ledyard was forced to surrender and then was murdered by the British. Mrs. Ledyard suffered in this horrendous tragedy. (DB) Mrs. Ledyard also suffered property loss in the raid. (CAR, 27:333a)

LEE, AGNES DICKINSON   CT
of Guilford. She was born in 1745, the daughter of Azariah Dickinson of Haddam, Connecticut. On November 7, 1764, Agnes married Samuel Lee, Jr., of Guilford, and they lived in a house now standing at the corner of State and North streets, known in the early days as Crooked Lane. Agnes had three daughters, and Samuel's brother Levi lived with them. Samuel Lee became a lieutenant in the Coast Guard, and Agnes and her husband were staunch patriots. They melted lead into bullets which they stored in their home, along with gunpowder, and maintained a small arsenal. Later Samuel was promoted to captain.

One evening when Samuel was away, Tories burst through their front door and searched for contraband. Agnes's brother-in-law, Levi, appeared with two muskets and handed one to Agnes, who cried out, "Shoot, Levi, I can load as fast as you can fire!" History records that the Tories fled in terror as Levi fired his musket.

The Lees had a cannon in their backyard to warn the countryside of an impending enemy attack. One day in 1781 when the British did attack, Capt. Lee fired his cannon from the shore. The signal was heard by Agnes, who immediately fired her cannon to warn her friends far into the hills of North Guilford, and the British were repulsed. Agnes died in 1830.

The local chapter of the Daughters of the American Revolution--comprising Guilford, Madison, and Clinton--is named in her honor. (Submitted by Ada F. Trecartin, Branford, CT)

LEE, ANNE GASKINS   VA
of Arlington. The daughter of Col. Thomas Gaskins, she was married first to Thomas Pinckard and then in 1769 became the second wife of Richard Henry Lee, a signer of the Declaration of Independence. His first wife, Anne Aylett Lee, died in December 1768, leaving him with four small children. They lived at "Chantilly," her frame house on the Potomac River. On June 7, 1776, Lee proposed in the Continental Congress his dramatic resolution declaring independence of the United States.

After his return home in June 1776, a British vessel landed nearby, and a detachment of marines broke down Lee's front door and demanded his surrender. Fortunately he was not there, but was visiting neighbors, and the frustrated marines left the house. Mrs. Lee went through many trying times. (FG)

Later the Lees lived on the family estate, Stratford Hall Plantation, Westmoreland County, Virginia, which was the birthplace of Richard Henry Lee and Francis Lightfoot Lee. It is open to the public and located on State Route 214, six miles northwest of Montross, Virginia.

LEE, MARY DIGGS   MD
of Annapolis. On October 27, 1771, she married Thomas Sim Lee. In November 1779 the legislature chose him to be governor of Maryland. Mrs. Lee mobilized the women of Maryland on behalf of the ladies' relief association for the welfare of the American soldiers. She wrote to friends in every county of Maryland to serve as local treasurers of the association. (NL; DB)

Mrs. Lee received the following letter of appreciation from Gen. Washington:

> Headquarters near Passaic Falls, New Jersey, October 11, 1780. Madam: I am honored with your letter of the 29th of Septr. and cannot forbear taking the earliest moment to express the high sense I entertain of the patriotic exertions of the Ladies of Maryland in favor of the Army.
>
> In answer to your inquiry respecting the disposal of the Gratuity, I must take the liberty to observe; that it appears to me, the Money which has been, or may be collected, cannot be expended in so eligible and beneficial in manner, as in the purchase of Shirts and Socks for the use of the troops in the Southern Army.
>
> The polite offer you are pleased to make of your further assistance in the execution of this liberal design, and the generous disposition of the Ladies, insure me of its success, and cannot fail to entitle both yourself and them, to the warmest gratitude of those who are the objects of it. (FW)

Gen. Washington visited Governor and Mrs. Lee from November 21 to 23, 1781, on his return trip north after the Battle of Yorktown, Virginia. The general's arrival in Annapolis was announced by the discharge of cannons, he was greeted by the people, and all business ceased. (BI)

LEWIS, BETTY WASHINGTON   VA
of Fredericksburg. The daughter of Mary Ball and Augustine Washington, she was born on June 23, 1733, at Bridges Creek, Virginia. She was the sister of Gen. George Washington. Betty married Col. Fielding Lewis, and they had eleven children, but five died in infancy. Five sons and one daughter survived. The State Manufactory of Arms at Fredericksburg was established in 1776 by the Virginia Convention. Five men were named as commissioners

II: SELECTED BIOGRAPHIES

to superintend the work, but the two men who took the most active role in the factory were Fielding Lewis and Charles Dick.
    Betty Lewis was an active patriot and knitted many dozen pairs of socks for the soldiers and provided provisions for the army. Many Fredericksburg women were employed in the factory making cartridges for the American soldiers, while the men were making muskets. Maj. Charles Dick on January 4, 1781, reported to the governor of Virginia that the men and women at the gunnery made 100 rifles and 20,000 cartridges with bullets. (Calendar of State Papers, 1:416)
    Betty Lewis died on March 7, 1797. (GP) (Information from Barbara P. Willis, Fredericksburg, VA)

LEWIS, ELIZABETH ANNESLEY   NY
of New York City. On June 15, 1745, she married Francis Lewis of Whitestone, Long Island, New York, who signed the Declaration of Independence in 1776. Three of their seven children survived infancy. Mrs. Lewis was a staunch rebel and was captured by the British. In September 1776 her home in Whitestone was burned, and she was imprisoned by the enemy in New York City. There was no bed in her cell. Food and other supplies were brought to her by a faithful black servant. Shortly after her release in 1779 she died. Her husband died on December 31, 1802. (FH)

LINCOLN, MARY CUSHING   MA, NJ
of Hingham. She was the wife of Gen. Benjamin Lincoln, who was stationed in New Jersey in July 1781. While Washington had his headquarters in Dobbs Ferry, New York, in the home of the Hammonds, he visited Phillipsburg, New Jersey, to review the troops. Gen. and Mrs. Lincoln entertained Gen. Washington and the Comte de Rochambeau for dinner on July 14, 1781. (BW)

LINDSAY, ANN KENNEDY   KY
was born in 1735 and married John Wilson. After his death she married William Poague (1735-1778), then Capt. Joseph Lindsay. He was killed by Indians at Blue Licks, Kentucky on June 24, 1780. Her fourth husband was James McGinty. Ann died on November 11, 1815. She is listed as a patriot in the DAR Patriot Index. (Bettye Lee Mastin, Lexington 1779, Lexington-Fayette County Historic Commission)

LIVINGSTON, CHRISTINA TEN BROECK   NY
of Brooklyn Heights. The daughter of Col. Dirck Ten Broeck, of Albany, New York, on April 14, 1740, she married Philip Livingston, who later was a signer of the Declaration of Independence. After the British invaded Long Island on August 27, 1776, and marched toward New York City, the Livingstons fled to Kingston, New York. The enemy plundered and confiscated the Livingston property in New York City, and their mansion on Duke Street became a barracks for British troops. Their estate on Brooklyn Heights was turned into a Royal Navy hospital. Then the British attacked

Kingston and burned the town, so the Livingstons had to flee again. This is an example of the suffering endured by the patriotic American women. (FG)

LIVINGSTON, SUSANNA FRENCH   NJ
of Elizabeth. About 1745 she married William Livingston, a lawyer. They had one son and three daughters. Their daughter Sarah married John Jay, and Susanna married John Cleves Symmes. Mr. and Mrs. Livingston built "Liberty Hall" on his estate near Elizabethtown in 1772. He was elected to the Continental Congress in 1775 and 1776, and served as the first governor of New Jersey from 1776 to 1790.

On May 10, 1780, Gen. Washington wrote to Brig. Gen. Jedidiah Huntington: "Mrs. Livingston would not choose a guard as she looks upon one rather as an inducement to the Enemy to come up to the House."

Mrs. Livingston was a brave American patriot. She was active in the ladies' relief association for the welfare of the American soldiers. (New Jersey Gazette, July 4, 1780)

LLOYD, MRS. RICHARD B.   NY
the wife of Richard Bennett Lloyd, she carried messages to and from Gen. Washington. Washington mentions this fact in his letter dated March 12, 1782, at Philadelphia to James McHenry of Fayetteville, Maryland. McHenry was appointed secretary to George Washington in 1778 and subsequently served on Lafayette's staff and continued in service until 1781.

In his letter of June 5, 1782, dated at Newburgh, New York, to Gouverneur Morris, who designed our decimal coinage system, Gen. Washington wrote:

> If Mr. Morris shou'd have postponed his report, respecting the business entrusted to him by Mrs. Lloyd, till information could be had from hence, of the conveyance of her packet to Mr. White; the General prays him to present his compliments with it, and assure her, that the packet went by returning Flag in less than 24 hours after it came into his hands.
>
> The General entreats Mr. Morris to add further, that nothing will give him more pleasure than to be honored with the commands of that Lady, whenever she shall find occasion to write to England. Her letters by Post, under cover to the General, will be more certain of a safe passage to New York, than by any other conveyance; and he shall be happy in becoming the means of facilitating her wishes.

Mrs. Lloyd corresponded with friends in England and passed news on to Gen. Washington, since the British occupied New York City and did not leave there until November 25, 1783. Gen. Washington wrote to Mrs. Lloyd on September 4, October 2, November 26,

II: SELECTED BIOGRAPHIES   125

1782, and February 15, February 25, and May 7, 1783. Washington
also wrote to Mr. Lloyd. Apparently Gen. and Mrs. Washington
were on very friendly terms with Mr. and Mrs. Lloyd. (FW)

LOCKE, POLLY   NH
of New Ipswich. She became known as the New Hampshire champion
weaver. Within forty hours from the time she began shearing,
she completed new pantaloons for her sixteen-year-old brother,
so he could leave for military service. (Submitted by Dorothy
Wilcox, Durham, NH)

LOGAN, ANN MONTGOMERY   KY
of Logan's Station. The daughter of Jane Patterson and William
Montgomery, Sr., she married Col. Benjamin Logan (1743-1802),
of Augusta County, Virgnia. In 1775 he traveled to Kentucky
with Daniel Boone, and in 1776 took a farm there. He left his
wife and children at Harrodsburg where he felt his family would
be safe. He built a fort at Logan's Station, and his family joined
him in 1777, together with several other families.
    On May 20, 1777, the Indians attacked the fort, and the
siege lasted over ten days. Ann Logan and the other women molded
bullets, but gunpowder was scarce, and the supply they had was
soon exhausted. Col. Logan left the fort under cover of darkness,
with two companions, and rode through the Cumberland Gap to
Holston where he secured powder and lead. The trip took him ten
days. When Col. Bowman's party from Holston arrived with men
and supplies, the Indians retired.
    The Indians attacked again in March 1780 (see Jane Patterson
Montgomery, below). Logan County was named in honor of Col.
Benjamin Logan, who later became a general. (CH; DAR)

LOGAN, MRS. JAMES   PA
of Nicetown. Their home was called "Stenton." Gen. Washington
had his headquarters there on August 23, 1777. On this date
in his general orders, Washington wrote in part:

> The army is to move precisely at four in the morning,
> if it should not rain. The division commanded by Genl.
> Wayne is to take its proper place in the line, to wit, be-
> tween Lord Stirling's and Genl. Stephen's division and
> it is strongly and earnestly enjoined, upon the commanding
> officers of corps to make all their men who are able to
> bear arms, except the necessary guards, march in the
> ranks; for it is so great a reflection upon all order and
> discipline to see such a number of strollers, for they
> cannot be called guards, with the waggons, that it is
> really shocking.
>   The army is to march in one column thro' the City of
> Philadelphia, going in at and marching down Front street
> to Chestnut street, and up Chestnut street to the Common.
> (FW)

LORING, KEZIAH GOVE   MA
of Lexington. She married Joseph Loring, who was born on December 27, 1747. He was a member of the Lexington Militia, which was under the command of Capt. Phineas Parker. When Paul Revere reached Lexington on his memorable ride, Joseph Loring rode with Revere to Concord where Loring was captured. He managed to escape and joined his company the same day. He took part in the Battle of Lexington on April 19, 1775, and also fought at Bunker Hill.

In 1779 Loring joined the marines and served under Capt. Samuel Tucker, commander of the frigate Boston, which sailed for Charleston, South Carolina, on November 23, 1779. After the British fleet arrived at Charleston in February 1780, Capt. Tucker destroyed the lighthouse and Fort Johnson to prevent them from falling into enemy hands. Joseph Loring was captured by the British and imprisoned. On May 12, 1780, the Americans surrendered Charleston to the British.

Later Loring was released by the British, but was forced to walk to his home in Massachusetts, as the government had made no provision for transporting released prisoners. (FP1)

LOWREY, ANN WEST   PA
of Lancaster. The daughter of Francis West, Jr., of Sligo, Ireland, she was born about 1730. Shortly thereafter the family moved to Carlisle. In 1765 Ann married Hermanus Alrichs and they had four sons and one daughter. Alrichs died in 1772, and the next year she married Alexander Lowrey of Donegal Township, Lancaster County, a widower with five children. He served on the Committee of Correspondence for Lancaster in 1774 and was a member of the Pennsylvania Constitutional Convention of July 15, 1776. He was a colonel of the Lancaster County militia and participated in the Battle of Brandywine.

During the Revolutionary War, Mrs. Lowrey collected clothing for the soldiers and also spun material. Later the family moved back to Donegal township where Mrs. Lowrey died on November 21, 1791. (EP)

LOWREY, ESTHER FLEMING   NJ
of Hunterdon County. She was born in 1738, the daughter of Esther Mounier and Samuel Fleming. When she was young Esther married Col. Thomas Lowrey. Esther was an active member of the ladies' association for the welfare of the American soldiers. (New Jersey Gazette, July 4, 1780)

During the occasion of Gen. Washington's reception in Trenton in April 1789, Esther was one of the matrons assisting in the ceremonies. Mrs. Lowrey died in Milford, New Jersey, in 1814. Chapters of the Daughters of the American Revolution in Flemington, New Jersey, and in Independence, Kansas, are named in her honor. (GP)

LUCK, SARAH   VA
of Pittsylvania County. She was born about 1730 and married

II: SELECTED BIOGRAPHIES

Capt. Francis Luck. Sarah died sometime before March 1821. She performed patriotic service during the Revolutionary War and is listed as a patriot in the DAR Patriot Index. (Submitted by Jessie Mae Harry Rau, Arlington, TX; VR, pp. 25, 56)

LUDINGTON, SYBIL   NY
of Ludington. She was born in 1759/60, the daughter of Abigail Luddington and her mother's cousin, Henry Ludington, who had dropped the second "d" from his name. They resided in Fredericksburg, New York, where her father was a colonel in the New York militia.

In 1777 some two thousand British troops and Tories loyal to Governor William Tryon of New York sailed into Danbury, Connecticut, and burned the town on the night of April 26. An exhausted messenger from Danbury arrived at Col. Ludington's home and informed him that militiamen in his area must be summoned to come to the defense of the city. Sybil, who was only sixteen years old, volunteered to spread the alarm. After mounting her horse, Sybil rode to Carmel and on to Mahopac and Mahopac Falls, knocking on the door of each house. She then rode over Barret Hill to Kent Cliffs, Peekskill, and Farmers Mill, then on home through Stormville.

After the British burned Danbury, they marched to Ridgefield, where they met the American militiamen, who had responded to the call of the female Paul Revere. The British ships met their troops on Long Island Sound and embarked for New York City. As a result of this action, the British reported 27 of their men killed, 15 officers and 104 men wounded, and 29 men missing. The British also reported that among the Americans, Gen. Wooster, 6 other officers and 100 privates were killed, 3 officers and 250 privates wounded, and that they captured 50 privates.

The town of Fredericksburg, New York, changed its name to Ludington. In 1961 a statue was erected to Sybil Ludington beside Gleneida Lake in Carmel, New York. There is a replica of this statue in Memorial Continental Hall of the National Society of the Daughters of the American Revolution at 1776 D Street NW, Washington, DC (CD; DR; EW) The large statue shows Sybil Ludington mounted on a horse, and has the following inscription:

SYBIL LUDINGTON
Revolutionary War Heroine
April 6, 1777
Called out the volunteer militia by riding through the night alone on horseback at the age of 16 alerting the countryside to the burning of Danbury, Connecticut by the British.
Placed by Enoch Crosby Chapter DAR
Presented by Anna Hyatt Huntington
1961

An outdoor sculpture garden on Highway 17 between Pawley's

Island and Myrtle Beach, South Carolina, features the sculptures of Anna Hyatt Huntington.

LUX, MRS. WILLIAM   MD
of Baltimore. Their home was called "Chatsworth." Mr. Lux was a wealthy merchant, shipowner and the Continental marine agent in Baltimore. On February 7, 1777, John Adams, Samuel Adams, Dr. Witherspoon, Lyman Hall, and others dined with Mr. and Mrs. Lux, their son George, and his wife. John Adams wrote in his diary: "The whole Family profess great Zeal in the American cause. Mr. Lux lives like a Prince." (BA)

LYON, MARY WILLSON   NY
of North Castle. The daughter of Susannah Ogden and Samuel Willson (or Wilson), she married Capt. Roger Lyon (1715-1797), who was born in the ancestral Lyon home in Byram, Connecticut. As a young man, he moved to North Castle. Mary Lyon had two daughters and seven sons. All of the sons served in the Revolutionary War. They lived on the Danbury Post Road (now State Route 22).

Gen. Washington left Valentine Hill (now in Yonkers) on the morning of October 22, 1776, and on his way to White Plains he stopped at the Lyon farmhouse for refreshments.

Preserved to this day is an exquisite silver cup monogrammed with the initials of Capt. Roger Lyon and his wife, Mary, from which Washington is reported to have drunk on that occasion. Capt. Lyon, being blind, handed the cup to Washington saying: "General, the ladies say you are a handsome man, but I cannot see." To this Washington replied, "Tell the ladies I am afraid they are as blind as yourself." (Robert Dolton, <u>The History of the County of Westchester</u>, 1881) The Lyon cup used by Washington is now in the possession of the Westchester County Historical Society. Washington then proceeded to White Plains and spent the night in the home of Ann Fisher Miller.

Mrs. Lyon died in North Castle on May 19, 1813, aged eighty-three years. The Lyon house and barn burned down about 1930, but the foundations are still visible at the corner of Chestnut Ridge Road on Route 22 about five miles south of Bedford and four miles northeast of Armonk. (Information from Richard N. Lander, Armonk, NY)

LYTLE, SUSANNAH PERKINS   NC
of Old Fort. In 1772 she married Capt. Thomas Lytle (1750-1835). Her husband in 1776 commanded companies of mounted riflemen against the Cherokee Indians. Later he raised an expedition against Col. Patrick Ferguson. While her husband was gone, the colonel stopped by her home and told her that her husband would come to harm if he persisted in rebellion, but Susannah replied her husband would "never prove a traitor to his country." She died on November 17, 1840, and was buried in the Bethel Presbyterian Church in McDowell County. Her grandson, Thomas Young Lytle,

II: SELECTED BIOGRAPHIES   129

on June 8, 1860, fired the first shot at the Battle of Bethel in
the Civil War. (Submitted by Joseph M. Dunca, Dunwoody, GA)

M
_____

MABIE, ELIZABETH BLAUVELT   NY
of Tappan. The daughter of Anna Maria De Wint and Fredericus
Blauvelt, she married Cornelius Mabie, the son of Casparus Mabie.
After Maj. André, the British spy, was brought to Tappan, he
was confined in the Mabie house. Gen. Washington was in this
house on September 30, 1780, when he signed the death warrant
of Maj. André. (A Chronicle of Major André at Tappan, Tappentown Historical Society, 1980)

MALIN, MRS. JOSEPH   PA
of Chester County. They lived about a half a mile west of the
Warren Tavern. On September 15, 1777, Gen. Washington spent
the night with the Malins after the Battle of Brandywine. On the
sixteenth, Washington learned that the enemy was advancing toward
the Americans. (BI)

MARTIN, GRACE WARING   SC
of the Edgefield District, previously called the 96th District. She
was born about 1764, the daughter of Benjamin Waring of Dorchester,
who later resided in Columbia, South Carolina. At age fourteen
Grace married William M. Martin, who served as a captain of artillery
at the sieges of Savannah and Charleston.
    One evening during the sieges of Augusta and Cambridge in
1780, Grace Martin and her sister-in-law, Rachel Martin, were at
home when they learned that a courier with important messages,
accompanied by two British officers, would pass by their house.
The two women, disguised in their husbands' clothing and armed
with pistols, decided to waylay the courier and his guards. They
hid in the bushes, and when the three men approached, the women
surprised the men and took possession of the papers and paroled
the men. The women made a hasty retreat and contacted an American rebel who took the papers to Gen. Greene.
    Capt. Martin was killed in the siege of Augusta. They had
two sons and one daughter. (DR; EW)

MARTIN, KATHERINE   NJ
of Somerset County. Her husband, Ephriam Martin, was a colonel
of the New Jersey militia. He was in the advance guard in the
Battle of Long Island and was wounded in the breast in August
1776, according to a letter of George Washington to the president
of Congress dated August 26, 1776. Col. Martin died in 1806.
    Mrs. Martin was an active member of the ladies' association
for the relief and welfare of the American soldiers. (New Jersey
Gazette, July 4, 1780)

MARTIN, RACHEL CLAY SC
of the Edgefield District, previously called the 96th District. She was born about 1764, the daughter of Henry Clay, Jr., of Macklenburg County, Virginia. Rachel married Barkley Martin of the 96th District.

Rachel and her sister-in-law, Grace Martin, in 1780 apprehended a courier carrying important messages for the British army. They took the papers at gunpoint and later had a trusted messenger take the papers to Gen. Greene (see details under Grace Martin, above). Rachel and her husband had no children. (DR; EW)

MARVIN, RUTH WELCH CT
of Litchfield. She was the wife of Reynold Marvin, an attorney. After a lead statue of King George III was brought to Litchfield by Oliver Wolcott, Ruth and her daughter, Ruth Marvin Kirby, molded 11,592 bullets from the statue. (CG; see also Laura Collins Wolcott, below) She was born in 1739 and died in 1783. (DAR)

MATTHEWS, SARAH NY
of Orange County. While her husband loaded munitions for the defense of the Hudson River, Mrs. Matthews donned his large overcoat, and with a rifle in her hands she acted as a sentinel. In 1781 she was with him at the Battle of Yorktown, Virginia, and cared for the wounded soldiers after the battle. (FH)

MAXWELL, NANCY ROBBINS WV
of Wheeling. When the British and Indians attacked on September 10, 1782, Nancy's father was killed and scalped. Nancy and her mother fled to Fort Henry and arrived just as the gates were closing. While the Indians were attacking the fort, Nancy made bullets for the men. Nancy lived with Col. Zane's family for several years, and after the war she married William Maxwell of Cincinnati, who established the Sentinel of the North-western Territory in 1793. (MR)

MAYHEW, SARAH VAN METER NJ
of Daretown, Salem County. She married Eleazer Mayhew (1756-1828), who served as a private in Capt. Nieukirk's company, 2nd Regiment, Salem County Militia, from 1776 to 1777. At Cooper's Creek Bridge, Eleazer Mayhew was captured by the British and imprisoned on the notorious prison ship Jersey in New York Harbor. It was reported in the newspapers in 1783 that 11,644 American prisoners suffered death by the inhuman, cruel, savage, and barbarous treatment on board that filthy and malignant British prison ship. Sarah's husband was not freed until the war ended in 1783.

During the war, Mrs. Mayhew made all the cloth needed for her family and traded her surplus at the country store. She served as doctor for her family and assisted neighbors during epidemics of smallpox, dysentery, and other unidentifiable diseases carried by sickly soldiers left quartered with the inhabitants when the armies passed through. Washington's army wintered nearby three

II: SELECTED BIOGRAPHIES

times, each time sending foraging parties into the surrounding countryside for livestock and other supplies. Mrs. Mayhew was a member of the ladies' association and assisted in collecting funds for the welfare of the American soldiers. (New Jersey Gazette, July 4, 1780)

A monument to the "Prison Ship Martyrs" was dedicated at Fort Greene Park, Brooklyn, New York on November 14, 1908, by President William Howard Taft. It contains the bones of over 11,500 men from the thirteen colonies, taken prisoner by the British. It is the tallest Doric column in the world, 148 feet 8 inches high. A gas flame burns perpetually in the lantern on the top. Four bronze eagles are placed at each corner of the 220-foot-square plaza. (Submitted by Mary Coates Martin, Norfolk, VA)

McCALLA, SARAH WAYNE GARDINER   SC
of Kershaw County. (The name is also spelled McCulla.) Her husband, Pvt. Thomas McCalla, was a prisoner of the British in Camden, South Carolina. After visiting him several times, she was determined to secure his release, so she rode to Winnsboro where Lord Cornwallis and his army were camped. After several hours she managed to see the British general, who admired her courage and agreed to release her husband on parole if Gen. Sumter would be personally responsible for the soldier. Mrs. McCalla then rode to Sumter's camp in January 1781, near Cowpens, South Carolina, but was taken by Gen. Morgan's scouts, who thought her to be a Tory spy. They took her to Gen. Morgan's tent. After she showed him the note from Lord Cornwallis to Gen. Sumter, she was released. Sarah told the general what she saw and heard at Cornwallis's camp, which was helpful to the Americans. Later her husband was released. Mrs. McCalla died in 1821. (DAR; EW; HS)

McCAULEY, MARY HAYS ("Molly Pitcher")   NJ, PA
the daughter of John George Ludwig Hass, she was born on October 13, 1754, near Trenton, New Jersey, according to some reports, but this is disputed--some researchers say that she was Irish, not German. On July 24, 1769, she married John Caspar Hays of Carlisle, Pennsylvania, although other researchers report his name as William Hays. During 1776 her husband served in the 1st Pennsylvania Regiment of Artillery, then in 1777 in the 7th Regiment. "Molly" Hays was a maid in the home of Dr. William Irvine of Carlisle, who was colonel of the 7th Pennsylvania Regiment. He took her along on his expeditions. Molly's husband, Pvt. Hays, served in the same regiment. All three were at the Battle of Monmouth on June 28, 1778.

Molly brought water to the wounded soldiers, and made many trips back and forth between the well and the battlefield, thus earning the nickname "Molly Pitcher." Her husband suffered from exhaustion and the heat, and fell beside his cannon. Molly then fired the cannon in his place for the remainder of the battle. Hays's Pennsylvania State Regiment of Artillery on September 3, 1778, became the 4th Continental Artillery Regiment under Col. Thomas Proctor.

Many women accompanied their husbands in camps and in battle, and the term "Molly Pitcher" became used for any soldier's wife who brought pitchers of water.

Molly and her husband had one son, who then had seven children. Her husband died in 1789, and some time later she married George McCauley (or McAuley). On February 21, 1822, the General Assembly of Pennsylvania recognized the Revolutionary War activities of "Molly M'Kolly" and granted her a pension of $40 annually for life. Molly McCauley died on January 22, 1832.

Mrs. McCauley is buried in Carlisle, Pennsylvania. There are two monuments erected in her honor in the Old Graveyard on South Street. On the County Courthouse green in Freehold, New Jersey, there is a monument commemorating the Battle of Monmouth with a bas-relief depicting Mary Hays McCauley firing a cannon. (CP; SP; EP)

McCLELLAN, SARAH LOWRY   KY
of Georgetown. She was the wife of John McClellan, a private in the Virginia militia. In the summer of 1776 several families from Kingston's settlement and from Drennon's Lick built a fort at Royal Spring, where Georgetown now stands, which was called McClellan's Station. Col. John Patterson assisted in building the fort and in defending it until October 1776 when he left for Pittsburgh to obtain gunpowder for the fort. On the way his men were attacked by Indians, and Col. Patterson was severely wounded and remained under a doctor's care for a year, and was thus unable to return to McClellan's Station.

Meanwhile, on December 29, 1776, Indians attacked McClellan's fort, and Sarah's husband was killed on January 1, 1777. (CH; DAR)

McCLENACHAN, MRS. BLAIR   PA
of Philadelphia. Her husband was a merchant, importer, and exporter. He had an interest in privateer vessels with Robert Morris during the Revolutionary War. Morris and McClenachan sent a case of liquor to Gen. Washington, and he responded on June 20, 1780: "Gentn: I am honoured with your favor of the 3d and have received, in good order, the Pipe of Spirits you were pleased to present me with; for both permit me to offer my grateful thanks. and to assure you that the value of the latter was greatly enhanced by the flattering sentiments contained in the former ..." (FW)

Their son John was a privateer captain during the American Revolution. (CN) Mrs. McClenachan was active in the ladies' relief association for the benefit of the American soldiers. (<u>Pennsylvania Gazette</u>, June 20, 1780)

McCORMICK, MARTHA SANDERSON   VA
of Midway. The daughter of Catharine Rose and George Sanderson, she was born in 1747 in Ireland. Later the family emigrated to

II: SELECTED BIOGRAPHIES

America and settled in Cumberland County, Pennsylvania. In 1770 she married Robert McCormick, and they lived in the Juniata Valley. He served with the Associators in the New Jersey campaigns. In 1779 they moved to a farm near Midway, situated on both sides of the Augusta-Rockbridge county line. Mr. McCormick served in the Virginia Line and was at the Battle of Cowpens, South Carolina, on January 17, 1781.

During her husband's absence in the army, Mrs. McCormick supplied large amounts of produce for the Virginia Commissary of Purchases. She died in Augusta County, Virginia, sometime prior to 1808. Her youngest son, Robert McCormick, invented a reaping machine. (EP)

McCULLOCH, MARY MITCHELL   WV
of Fort Henry, Virginia (now Wheeling, West Virginia). She married Maj. Samuel McCulloch, the son of Sarah Inskeep and John McCulloch, Sr., in February 1782 while he was stationed at the fort. When a British-inspired attack was made by Indians on the fort on July 30, 1782, Mary was in the fort awaiting the arrival of her husband.

While bringing relief to the fort, Samuel and his brother John Jr. were ambushed by Indians. John Jr. managed to elude the Indians and escape. Samuel also escaped by leaping his horse over a precipice some two hundred feet over Wheeling Creek and swimming his horse to the farther shore, which is now known as McCulloch's Leap; a monument there commemorates his feat. However, Samuel was caught by the Indians outside the fort. His heart was cut out and eaten by the Indians while still throbbing in order to make the Indians brave like Samuel McCulloch. What happened to Mary McCulloch is unknown. (Submitted by Edward L. Woodyard, Armonk, NY)

McCULLOCH, SARAH INSKEEP   VA, WV
of Albemarle County. The daughter of Mary Miller and James Inskeep, she was born in 1730 in Gloucester County, New Jersey. In 1749 she married John McCulloch, and they had five children. In 1760 they moved from their home in Marlton, New Jersey, to Hardy County, Virginia. Ten years later the family moved to Ohio County, Virginia, just south of the present day Wheeling, West Virginia. Her daughter Elizabeth married the famous frontiersman, Col. Ebenezer Zane (1747-1812).

During the Revolution the McCulloch and Zane families settled in Fort Henry, also called Fort Van Metier, Virginia (now Wheeling, West Virginia), on the western Virginia frontier, where settlers were protected from attacks by Indians allied with the British. While on a visit to Pittsburgh in 1775 to visit his son George, her husband died of cholera. The widow Sarah then returned to Albemarle County, although her sons Samuel and John Jr. were still at the fort. Maj. Samuel McCulloch was a commander and John McCulloch, Jr., served as a scout and spy under Broadhead in 1781 and under Williamson in 1782. John sent his wife, Mary, and their four children to live with their mother in Albemarle County.

Samuel married Mary Mitchell in February 1782, and she was at the fort when the Indians attacked on July 30, 1782.

While bringing relief to the besieged fort, John and Samuel were ambushed by Indians. John managed to escape, but Samuel was killed. Sarah McCulloch died about 1793 in Albemarle County. (Submitted by Edward L. Woodyard, Armonk, NY)

McCURDY, ANNE LORD   CT
of Lyme. She was the wife of John McCurdy (1724-1785). Gen. Washington spent the night at the McCurdys' home on April 10, 1776, on his trip from Cambridge, Massachusetts, to New York City. (BI)

McDONALD, REBECCA   SC
of the Fairfield District. On September 22, 1778, she married Hugh McDonald. In 1780 Hugh was a horseman in Capt. McClure's Dragoons in Col. Sumter's regiment. At the Battle of Camden in August 1780 Hugh and several other horsemen were taken by the British and made prisoners of war. They were put in jail in Camden where they lay ill for about six weeks with smallpox. Then they were taken to Charleston and put on a prison ship. Since the men were stricken with the fever, they were transferred to barracks.

Rebecca visited her husband and nursed him and the others in the barracks. After her husband was returned to the prison ship, she insisted on going along with him. The British sent Mr. and Mrs. McDonald to Jamestown, Virginia, where in August 1781 he was exchanged. They were five hundred miles from home, with no transportation or money, and had to walk the entire distance. They arrived home on May 10, 1782.

After her husband's death in 1828, Rebecca went to live with her daughter, Rebecca Cain, in Russell County, Kentucky, where she died in 1840. (Submitted by Ellen Byrne, Juliaetta, ID)

McDOWELL, ELLEN   NC
of King's Mountain. She was born about 1743 and married William McDowell, who served at the Battle of King's Mountain, North Carolina, on October 7, 1780, when the American colonels Isaac Selby and William Campbell defeated a Tory force led by Col. Patrick Ferguson, who was killed. Some twelve hundred Tories were captured by nine hundred American soldiers, and the Tories surrendered.

William McDowell manufactured gunpowder in a cave near his dwelling, but as he could not burn the charcoal there without detection, Mrs. McDowell burned it in small quantities in her fireplace, and carried it to him. In this way part of the powder used at King's Mountain was produced.

When Mrs. McDowell and her daughter Jane heard the firing, Mrs. McDowell went to the scene of the battle, where she remained for several days, nursing and caring for the wounded soldiers. Later Jane McDowell married Robert Wilson, son of Eleanor and

II: SELECTED BIOGRAPHIES

Robert Wilson of Mecklenburg County, North Carolina. In 1850, at age eighty-seven, Jane Wilson had 140 living descendants. (EW; submitted by Mary Lancaster, Florence, AL)

McDOWELL, MARGARET O'NEAL   NC
of Quaker Meadows, Morgantown. She was born in Ireland about 1723 and migrated first to Pennsylvania, then to Winchester, Virginia. Margaret married Capt. Joseph McDowell (1715-1775), and about 1765 they moved to Quaker Meadows. They had four sons and two daughters. After the death of her husband in 1775, she was mistress of the Quaker Meadows estate. During the Revolutionary War, Mrs. McDowell quartered American soldiers and furnished them with food and supplies. She died sometime before 1790. Mrs. McDowell is recognized as a patriot in the DAR Patriot Index. (Emmett R. White, Revolutionary War Soldiers of Western North Carolina)

McFALL, BARBARA   KY, OH
of Cynthiana. On June 24, 1780, Capt. Henry Bird from Fort Detroit with Tories, British soldiers, and a thousand Indians, attacked and captured the American fort at Martin's and Ruddles' Station. Mrs. McFall and her children were captured, along with many other Americans, and taken to Detroit. She was held in captivity until after the Battle of Fallen Timbers on the Maumee River in northwestern Ohio on August 20, 1794, when Gen. Anthony Wayne defeated a two-thousand-man Indian force.
    Poor Mrs. McFall was held captive for fourteen years. (Alan Eckert, "The Frontiersman"; submitted by Charlotte L. Mallan, Chelan, WA)

McILVAIN, MRS. JOHN   PA
of Ridley (formerly Leiperville, Delaware County). Gen. Washington had his headquarters in the McIlvain's home on September 11, 1777. On this date Gen. Washington wrote to Col. Theodorick Bland: "I earnestly entreat a continuance of your vigilant attention to the movement of the enemy, and the earliest report not only of their movements, but of the numbers and the course they are pursuing. In a particular manner I wish to gain satisfactory information of a body confidently reported to have gone up to a ford seven or eight miles above this. It is said the fact is certain. You will send up an intelligent, sensible officer immediately with a party to find out the truth, what number it consists of, and the road they are on now. Be particular in these matters." (FW) Washington spent the night there after the fateful Battle of Brandywine. (BI)

McINTOSH, SARAH THREADCRAFT   GA
of Savannah. On January 7, 1776, her husband, Laughlin McIntosh, was appointed colonel of a battalion of Georgia troops, and on September 16, 1776, a brigadier general in the Continental Army. Button Gwinnett, a signer of the Declaration of Independence, endeavored

to bring the Continental troops under local control, which ended
in a pistol duel between McIntosh and Gwinnett. Gwinnett was
mortally wounded on May 16, 1777. Gen. McIntosh was acquitted
of killing Gwinnett. In October 1779 McIntosh led the American
troops in the battle for Savannah. Mrs. McIntosh and her five
children suffered during the bombardment, and a British officer
refused to let them leave the city. (Memorial to the Georgia Legislature, June 27, 1783, New York Public Library)

The British captured Savannah, and Gen. McIntosh was taken
prisoner. This is an example of the suffering of the women patriots.
Gen. McIntosh was an original member of the Society of the Cincinnati founded in 1783. (DB)

McKEAN, SARAH ARMITAGE   PA
of Philadelphia. On September 3, 1774, she became the second
wife of Thomas McKean of New Castle, Delaware, an attorney. Shortly
after their marriage, they moved to Philadelphia. They had five
children, four of whom survived. (All six children by his first
wife had died young.) On October 11, 1774, John Adams dined
at the home of the McKeans on Market Street, along with Messrs.
Reed, Rodney, Chase, Johnson, Paca, Dr. Morgan, and Richard
Penn.

In 1776 Mr. McKean was a delegate to the Continental Congress
as a representative from Delaware and was a signer of the Declaration
of Independence. In 1777 he was appointed chief justice of Pennsylvania.

Mrs. McKean was active in the ladies' relief association for
the welfare of the American soldiers. (Pennsylvania Gazette, June
12, 1780)

McKEE, MARTHA HOGE   PA
of Butler. The daughter of Letitia and Robert Hoge, she was
born on December 17, 1759, in the Juniata Valley, Pennsylvania.
In the winter of 1777/78 Martha married Thomas McKee, a rifleman
of the Cumberland County Associators. Later he was first lieutenant
in the 7th Battalion.

During the Revolutionary War Mrs. McKee and her neighbors
spun flax to make material to clothe the American soldiers. She
died on her farm near Butler, Pennsylvania, on July 26, 1836.
(EP)

McKINLY, JANE RICHARDSON   DE
of Wilmington. She was the twelfth child of John and Ann Richardson. She married Dr. John McKinly, a surgeon. In 1775 he was
appointed colonel of a regiment of the New Castle County militia
and later was made a brigadier general. In Feburary 1777 McKinly
was elected president and commander-in-chief of Delaware for a
term of three years.

After the Battle of Brandywine, the British captured Wilmington in September 1777 and took McKinly prisoner. He was taken
to Philadelphia, and then to New York. McKinly was pardoned by

II: SELECTED BIOGRAPHIES   137

Gen. Clinton in August 1778. He returned to Wilmington and resumed his practice of medicine. Mrs. McKinly suffered during her husband's imprisonment. (DB)

MEAD, SYBIL WOOD   CT
of Greenwich. She was the wife of Sylvanus Mead (1739-1780), who was an ensign in Capt. Ebenezer Hill's company, 7th Connecticut Regiment, Continental Line. At the siege of Boston in May 1776, he was promoted to first lieutenant in Bradley's Battalion, Wadsworth's Brigade, Connecticut State Troops, and was later promoted to captain. Early in 1780 Capt. Mead was shot and killed by Cow Boys (FP1).

Mrs. Mead suffered damage to her property during the British and Tory raids on Greenwich in March 1779 and in December 1783. (CAR, 26:19d) She was a Western Lands Grantee.

MEASE, MRS. JOHN   PA
of Philadelphia. Her husband was a man of some wealth. He served in the Continental Army and was with Washington's troops when they crossed the Delaware River on December 25, 1779. Mrs. Mease was a member of the ladies' relief association for the welfare of the American soldiers and with her husband contributed Ł4,000 to the army in 1780. (Pennsylvania Gazette, June 12, 1780)

MECOM, JANE FRANKLIN   MA
of Boston. She was a sister of Benjamin Franklin. At age fifteen, Jane married an illiterate saddler, Edward Mecom, and they had twelve children--eight boys and four girls--but all the children were inflicted with some strange disease, perhaps tuberculosis or syphilis.

In June 1775 Jane and her family fled Boston when the British occupied the city. They stayed with Catharine Ray Greene in Warwick, Rhode Island. Jane's son Josiah was killed at the Battle of Bunker Hill and apparently buried in an unmarked grave, since he was never heard of again.

When Jane Mecom was in her seventies, only one daughter of her twelve children had survived. Her sons Peter and Benjamin died insane. But her brother, Benjamin Franklin, provided her with a home, and she remained cheerful to the end. Jane Mecom died in 1794. (LP)

MEHELM, JOANNA BEEKMAN   NJ
was the wife of Col. John Mehelm (1735-1809), who was commissary general of hides in New Jersey. Gen. Washington stayed at their home in 1777 and mentioned this fact in a letter dated August 15, 1777, to Capt. Ephraim Anderson. (FW; DAR)

MEIGS, GRACE STARR   CT
of Middletown. On December 22, 1774, she became the second wife of Capt. Return Jonathan Meigs who was commissioned as a major after the Battle of Lexington and a colonel in 1777. In 1778,

the ladies of Middletown, including Mrs. Meigs, Mrs. John Sumner, and Mrs. Jonathan Johnson, formed a committee to make clothing for the American soldiers. In 1788 Col. Meigs was a surveyor for the Ohio Company, and in 1801 Indian agent to the Cherokee tribe. Mrs. Meigs died in Tennessee in 1807. (CG)

MERITHEW, PATIENCE BURGESS   MA
of Boston. The daughter of Priscilla Getchell and Benjamin Burgess, she was born on October 4, 1716, in Rochester, Massachusetts. On February 24, 1736/37, she married Roger Merithew who served in the British navy prior to the Revolution and for his services was given land near Yarmouth, Nova Scotia. They moved to Nova Scotia, but in 1775 at the outbreak of the Revolutionary War, they refused to take the oath of allegiance to King George III and returned to the States with their three sons and grandchildren. Two sons, Aaron and Roger Jr., stayed in Frankfort, Maine, while Mr. and Mrs. Merithew, their son William, and the grandchildren traveled on to Boston where Mrs. Merithew remained during the war. Roger made a visit to Yarmouth and was found dead there.

In 1779 her son William served as a seaman on the frigate Providence under Commo. Abraham Whipple and was taken prisoner in May 1780 when Charleston, South Carolina, fell to the British. Later he escaped and returned to Rhode Island and stayed in the navy. He was naval paymaster during the War of 1812. (Submitted by Edward L. Woodyard, Armonk, NY)

MIDDLETON, MARY IZARD   SC
of Charleston. The daughter of Walter Izard, she was married on August 19, 1764, to Arthur Middleton. They had nine children and lived at "Middleton Place." Later he was a signer of the Declaration of Independence.

During the British siege of Charleston in May 1780, Middleton, his wife, and children were captured by the enemy. The British ransacked their mansion, and their paintings were slashed with sabers. Their silver, glassware, china, and furnishings were stolen, and his slaves were carried away. After her release, Mrs. Middleton, with her husband in prison, had no income to support herself and her children, and humiliated herself by applying to the British commissioner in Charleston for the return of her property, which was denied, but she was allowed a small income for support.

Middleton was held by the British in the State House in Saint Augustine, Florida, along with Thomas Heyward, Jr., and Edward Rutledge, two other signers of the Declaration of Independence. They were released in 1781.

MIFFLIN, SARAH MORRIS   PA
of Philadelphia. The daughter of Elizabeth Mifflin and Morris Morris, she was born on April 5, 1747, O.S., in that city. On March 4, 1767, she married Thomas Mifflin. In 1774 he was a delegate to the First Continental Congress, and in 1775 he was aide-de-camp to Gen. Washington. In 1776 he became a brigadier general, and then a major general in 1777.

II: SELECTED BIOGRAPHIES												139

In 1776 Mrs. Mifflin moved to Reading, Pennsylvania, where she remained during the war. During this time she cared for the sick and wounded who were brought to Reading. She also prepared food for the soldiers. In 1783 Gen. Mifflin was elected president of the Continental Congress. Mrs. Mifflin died in Philadelphia on August 1, 1790, and was buried in the Friends Meeting graveyard. (EP)

MILLER, ANN FISHER   NY
of North White Plains. Annetjie, or "Ann" was born in 1727 and married Elijah Miller. They lived at the base of Miller Hill in the North White Plains area. Elijah served as adjutant of a Westchester County regiment under Col. Samuel Drake. Elijah was wounded at Hurlgate and died on August 21, 1776.

Gen. Washington left Valentine Hill October 22, 1776, and spent the night at the home of the Widow Miller. According to her daughter, Zipporah Miller Davis, "George Washington had his headquarters at our house for one day and one night when my mother gave him her own bed, the only time she ever resigned it." (MacDonald Papers)

Washington then moved to the Purdy House, where he had his headquarters during the Battle of White Plains, leaving the Purdy House on October 31. Meanwhile Gen. Charles Lee ordered the Miller family to leave their home and travel northward because of the approaching British troops. After the Battle of White Plains, Gen. Washington returned to the Miller House, where he had his headquarters from November 1 to 10, 1776, while the family was absent. (Some information from Stephen Holden, Jr., White Plains, NY)

Besides entertaining Gen. Washington in her home, Mrs. Miller nursed the sick and wounded soldiers. Two of her sons who served in the war--John and Elijah Jr.--died on December 22, 1776 of typhus. Some reports ignore the possibility of Washington's leaving the Miller House for the Purdy House. Two bronze tablets were placed on her house: "Washington's Headquarters, The Property of the County of Westchester, Dedicated October 27, 1917"; and "General Washington occupied this house as his headquarters from October 23rd to November 10, 1776. This tablet is dedicated to his memory, May 11, 1918 by White Plains Chapter, Daughters of the American Revolution."

Gen. Washington had his headquarters again in White Plains from July 27 to September 16, 1778. Later the organizers of the Methodist faith in White Plains met in Mrs. Miller's home. She died on June 13, 1819, at age ninety-two. (Submitted by Karyn DeLuca, White Plains Public Library, and Susan C. Swanson, Westchester County Historian, White Plains, NY)

MITCHELL, MRS. JOHN   PA
of Philadelphia. Her husband was the deputy quartermaster general. Gen. Washington wrote to Mr. Mitchell on October 17, 1779, asking him to find lodgings for Mrs. Washington in Philadelphia. Mr. Mitchell reponded on October 30, 1779, that he had found lodgings

for Mrs. Washington at the home of Mrs. Roche and that "Mrs. Mitchell will do every thing to render her Accommodations convenient and agreeable, and as it is near to me it will be more Easy and Convenient." (FW)

Mrs. Mitchell was a member of the ladies' relief association for the welfare of the American soldiers. (Pennsylvania Gazette, June 20, 1780)

MONTGOMERY, JANE PATTERSON KY
of Logan's Station. She was the wife of William Montgomery, Sr. (1727-1780). In the fall of 1779 Mr. and Mrs. Montgomery moved from Virginia westward into what is now Kentucky and took refuge in Logan's fort with their five sons and five daughters. William, with his eldest four sons and son-in-law Joseph Russell, built four log cabins on the headwaters of the Greene River, about twelve miles southwest of the fort. They moved into their cabins in the winter of 1779/80. In March 1780, when the Indians attacked, William Montgomery, Sr., was in one cabin with his daughters Jane and Betsey and his youngest son, James. Thomas and Robert were out spying. William Montgomery, Jr., and his wife and son Thomas (by a former wife) were in the second cabin. John and his bride were in the third cabin, and Joseph Russell and his wife with their three children occupied the fourth cabin. Col. Benjamin Logan (1743-1802) and his wife, the former Ann Montgomery, together with Jane Montgomery and her youngest child, Flora, were at the fort.

The Indians surrounded the cabins, and William Montgomery, the eldest, stepped out of his cabin with a Negro boy, and both were immediately shot and killed. Jane, then a young woman, called for her brother Thomas's gun. Her sister Betsey, then about twelve years old, escaped from the cabin and ran to Pettit's Station, a distance of about two and a half miles, to seek help. An Indian chased after her, but she was too fast for him. From Pettit's a messenger carried a warning to Logan's fort. Meanwhile Jane Montgomery had a rifle ready, but for some reason the Indians did not attack her cabin again after they had killed her father. (Later Jane married Col. William Casey of Adair County.)

William Montgomery, Jr., fired upon the Indians, killing one and wounding another. John was in bed and arose when he heard the shots, but he was killed by Indians and his wife was taken prisoner. Joseph Russell escaped from the cabin leaving his wife and three children to the mercy of the attackers. The children were with a mulatto, and all were taken prisoner.

After the messenger reached Logan's fort, Col. Benjamin Logan, husband of Ann, sounded the alarm with his horn, and about nine men immediately responded. Mrs. Russell broke some twigs and left a trail while in the company of the Indians, which was a great help to Col. Logan and his men. They came upon the mulatto, who had been scalped, but she recovered. Col. Logan caught up with the Indians. A daughter of Mrs. Russell, a girl twelve years old, exclaimed, "There's uncle Ben." But sad to

II: SELECTED BIOGRAPHIES

relate, an Indian struck her with his tomahawk and killed her. The Indians fled, and the remainder of the captives were freed. (Details of this story were furnished by Jane Casey, one of the younger captives, to Lewis Collins.)

Mrs. Montgomery lost her husband, son John, and a granddaughter--killed by Indians. Mrs. Montgomery and her daughter and granddaughter were captured, but were rescued by her son-in-law, Col. Benjamin Logan, who later became a general. (CH; DAR)

MONTGOMERY, JANET LIVINGSTON   NY

of Rhinebeck. The daughter of Margaret Beekman and Robert R. Livingston, she was married on July 24, 1773, to Richard Montgomery, and they lived on her estate, "Grassmere," near Rhinebeck. In June 1775 he was appointed a brigadier general by the Continental Congress. Montgomery was second in command to Maj. Gen. Philip Schuyler in the expedition to Montreal, Canada. After Gen. Schuyler became ill, Montgomery took charge. He captured Montreal, and in December 1775 joined the forces of Benedict Arnold in the attack on Quebec.

Gen. Montgomery was killed during the assault on December 31, 1775. Mrs. Montgomery, a true patriot, suffered the loss of her husband. (BD) Janet received letters of sympathy from Abigail Adams, Mercy Otis Warren, and Martha Washington. She died in 1828.

MONTGOMERY, RACHEL RUSH   PA

of Philadelphia. The daughter of Rachel and Thomas Rush, she was born there on May 7, 1741. She was the sister of Dr. Benjamin Rush who signed the Declaration of Independence. About 1761 she became the second wife of Angus Boyce, and they had one son, Malcolm, before Angus died. On July 11, 1770, Rachel married the Rev. Joseph Montgomery of New Castle, Delaware, and they had one child. In 1776 he moved his family to a farm at Paxtang, Lancaster County, Pennsylvania. In 1777 the Rev. Montgomery served as chaplain in the Maryland Line. He served in the Continental Congress, 1778-1783.

Mrs. Montgomery supplied food and clothing to the American soldiers. In 1785 they moved to Harrisburg, where she died on July 28, 1798. (EP)

MOORE, BEHETHLAND FOOTE   SC

of Edgefield was born about 1765. She was loyal to the American cause, and when she learned that the American forces camped on the South Fork River were to be attacked by the British in 1780, "Bess" paddled down the river with her younger brother and warned the Americans of the impending attack. When the British arrived there, the Americans were gone. (DR; EW; HS) She married Capt. William Moore. (DAR)

MOREL, MRS. JOHN GA
of Savannah. On September 15, 1779, French troops under the Comte d'Estaing ransacked her plantation at Beaulieu and carried away nine horses, twenty-three cows, thirty hogs, thirteen sheep, three hens, five wagons and a carriage, crystal goblets, candles, and other items. She submitted a bill for Ł267, but apparently was never paid for her loss. This is an example of the suffering of the women patriots. The original bill is in the Archives Nationales in Paris.

MORGAN, MRS. CT
of Washington. On his trip from New Windsor, New York, to Litchfield, Connecticut, Gen. Washington spent the night of May 18, 1781, in Morgan's Tavern. (FW)

MORGAN, ABIGAIL BAILEY VA
of Shenandoah Valley. She married Capt. Daniel Morgan (1736-1802), who was born in New Jersey. While he was still a youth his family settled in the Shenandoah Valley. He served in the Colonial Wars. In June 1775 he commanded a company of Virginia riflemen and was captured at Quebec on December 31, 1775, and taken prisoner. After his exchange in the autumn of 1776, he commanded a corps of sharpshooters and distinguished himself at the Battle of Saratoga, New York, on October 17, 1777, and won a decisive victory at Cowpens, South Carolina, on January 17, 1780. Morgan County, Kentucky, was named in his honor. (CH; DAR) Abigail died in 1816 at the home of her granddaughter, Matilda O'Bannon, near Russellville, Kentucky.

MORGAN, MARY BAYNTON NJ
of Princeton. The daughter of John Baynton, senior partner in Baynton, Wharton and Morgan in Philadelphia, she was married on October 21, 1763, to George Morgan, the junior partner of the firm. They had eleven children. Mr. Morgan represented his firm in Illinois and served as Indian agent from 1776 to 1779, when he retired to his farm near Princeton. Mrs. Morgan was active in in the ladies' relief association to assist the American soldiers. (New Jersey Gazette, July 4, 1780) In 1796 the family moved to a farm near Washington, Pennsylvania.

MORISON, MRS. THOMAS NH
of Peterborough. When her husband, son, and hired man left on foot to join the army, Mrs. Morison led the family horse, which carried saddlebags stuffed with her freshly baked bread and a goodly supply of pork. (Submitted by Dorothy Wilcox, Durham, NH)

MORRIS, MRS. JAMES PA
of Ambler. Their home was called "Dawsfield." Gen. Washington

II: SELECTED BIOGRAPHIES

had his headquarters there from October 21 to November 2, 1777. On November 2nd he wrote to John Hancock, in part: "I have ordered Cornet Buckmer, with 12 Dragoons, to attend you as an escort and to receive your Commands. For this purpose, you will be pleased to retain them, as long as you may consider their attendance necessary." (FW)

MORRIS, MARGARET   NJ
of Burlington. She was born in 1737, married but was widowed at an early age. Mrs. Morris kept a diary during the Revolutionary War, and under date of June 14, 1777, recorded how she cared for the sick and wounded soldiers and their wives at the governor's house. The victims were ill with the "camp or putrid fever." She was a member of the Society of Friends. Mrs. Morris died in 1816. (CD)

MORRIS, MARY PHILIPSE   NY
of New York City. The daughter of Adolph Philipse of Philipse Manor, Westchester County, New York, she was married to Col. Roger Morris. Their house was located on high and commanding ground at Washington Heights. Gen. Washington visited the Philipses on his trip to Boston in 1756, and he had his headquarters at the Morrises' on September 16, 1776.

While there, Washington wrote to the Continental Congress about the British attack and the American retreat on September 14. (For details, see Mrs. Charles Ward Apthrop, above; FW)

MORRIS, MARY WALTON   PA
of West Chester. On September 24, 1749, she married Lewis Morris and they had ten children. Mr. Morris was a signer of the Declaration of Independence. They owned about a thousand acres of fine woodland. When the British invaded Pennsylvania, the Morrises left their home, "Morrisana," before the British arrived. Their manor house was vandalized, with the furnishings stolen or destroyed. Their fences were burned, and the livestock taken to feed the British army. Many of the trees were cut down. Three of the sons of Mr. and Mrs. Morris served as officers during the Revolutionary War.

Mrs. Morris was a true patriot and suffered during the war along with her husband. (FG)

MORRIS, MARY WHITE   PA
of Philadelphia. The daughter of Esther Hewlings and Col. Thomas White and a sister of William White, the first Protestant Episcopal bishop of the diocese of Pennsylvania, she was born on April 13, 1749, in Philadelphia. On March 2, 1769, she married Robert Morris, a partner in the counting house of Willing and Morris. In June 1775 he became president of the Committee of Safety. He was a delegate to the Second Continental Congress in 1776 and

signed the Declaration of Independence. He was reelected to the Congress in 1777/78. He served as superintendent of finance from February 1781 until November 1784 and has been called the "Financier of the Revolution."

Mrs. Morris was an active patriot and a member of the ladies' association which collected money in Philadelphia to help the American soldiers. (Pennsylvania Gazette, June 12, 1780)

Mr. Morris financed the North American Land Company in 1795, which was a failure and caused his financial ruin. He was thrown into debtor's prison where he remained for over three years. He died in poverty on May 7, 1806, in Philadelphia. Mrs. Morris died there on January 16, 1827. She was buried next to her husband in Christ Church graveyard. (EP)

Upon Washington's arrival in Philadelphia on August 30, 1781, the Morrises held a large dinner party for the general. Among the guests were the Comte de Rochambeau, the Chevalier de Chastellux, and generals Knox and Moultrie. Gen. and Mrs. Washington also dined at the Morris home on Christmas Day 1781. (BI)

MORTON, ANN JUSTIS   PA
of Chester. In 1754 she married John Morton, and they had five daughters and four sons. He served as a delegate to the Continental Congress (1774-1777) and was a signer of the Declaration of Independence. John Morton died in 1777. As the British invaded southeastern Pennsylvania, Mrs. Morton and her surviving five daughters and three sons had to flee their property--another example of the suffering of the patriotic women. (FG)

MORTON, MRS. JOHN   NJ
of Basking Ridge. Her husband had the same name as a signer of the Declaration of Independence. On December 12, 1776, Morton invited Gen. Charles Lee, who was spending the night at Mrs. White's tavern, to have breakfast with him the next morning. But that morning the British cavalry seized Gen. Lee and carried him away. A soldier tried to defend Lee, but was wounded by the sabers of the horsemen. Mr. Morton took the soldier to his home, where Mrs. Morton cared for and nursed the soldier back to health.

This event was witnessed by their daughter, Eliza Susan Morton, who later told the story after she had married Josiah Quincy, later a member of Congress, mayor of Boston, and president of Harvard University. (J. H. Van Horn, Historic Somerset, 1965)

MOSSE, DOROTHY PHOEBE NORTON   SC
of Saint Helenas Island. She was the wife of Dr. George Mosse. They were Episcopalians, but later became Baptists. Dr. Mosse served in the Revolutionary War as a surgeon and was captured at the Battle of Camden, South Carolina, on August 16, 1780, when the forces of Lord Cornwallis defeated the American forces under Gen. Horatio Gates.

II: SELECTED BIOGRAPHIES

Dr. Mosse and the other American soldiers captured were marched to Charleston and placed on the prison ship Forbay in Charleston Harbor with their hands tied. When the ship was full of captives it started down the inland waters. After the vessel was beyond Charleston, the bonds of the men were loosened and they were allowed on deck.

Dr. Mosse was listed as a prisoner on the schooner Pack Horse on May 18, 1781. Eventually he jumped overboard and made his escape, swimming under water as far as he could. He finally reached his home on Saint Helenas Island.

Since Dr. Mosse had several daughters to educate, the family moved to Savannah, Georgia, about 1799, where Dr. Mosse practiced medicine. He became port doctor and was a charter member of the Medical Society. He also helped establish the First Baptist Church of Savannah. (From Edward P. Lawton, A Saga of the South; submitted by George Mosse Norton)

MOTT, MRS. SAMUEL   CT
of Preston. On his trip from his headquarters in New Windsor, New York, to Providence, Rhode Island, after he had dinner with Mr. and Mrs. Tracy in Norwich, Connecticut, Gen. Washington and his staff apparently spent the night of April 5, 1781, in the home of Col. and Mrs. Samuel Mott in Preston. This is evidenced by a billing of $1,104 for his junior officers in that town.

Col. Samuel Mott (1736-1813) had three wives: Abigail Rossiter, Abigail Stanton, and Lydia Tyler. (DAR; CG)

MOTTE, REBECCA BREWTON   SC
of Charleston. The daughter of Robert Brewton, she was born on June 15, 1737, in Charleston. In 1758 she married Col. Jacob Motte, and they had six children, but only three daughters survived to maturity. Her daughter Elizabeth was the first wife of Maj. Thomas Pinckney (1750-1828), and her sister Frances married Charles Pinckney (1731-1782).

After her husband died, Rebecca lived at Fort Motte on the south side of the Congaree River. In 1780 Gen. Light-Horse Harry Lee made the Motte mansion his headquarters and a hospital for the wounded soldiers, and Mrs. Motte cared for the wounded men.

In May 1781 her mansion was occupied by Capt. McPherson and some British troops under Lord Rawdon. The Americans under Francis Marion and Light-Horse Harry Lee decided to storm the Motte mansion and sent a message to Mrs. Motte to set fire to her home so as to force the British outside. Rebecca had some fire arrows which had been given to her by her brother, a sea captain. Reluctantly, but with delight, Rebecca set fire to her own home.

The British, realizing their situation was hopeless, surrendered and helped the Americans put out the fire. Mrs. Motte was a true patriot, willing to destroy her home to help the Americans. She died on January 10, 1815. The Congaree Swamp area was designated as a National Monument in 1976. (EW; GP; HS)

MOULTRIE, HANNAH MOTTE   SC
of Charleston. The daughter of Jacob Motte, treasurer of South Carolina, she married the Honorable Thomas Lynch, and after his death she became the second wife of Maj. Gen. William Moultrie in 1779. In May 1780, after the fall of Charleston, Gen. Moultrie was captured and imprisoned for two years by the British. He later served twice as governor of South Carolina and died in 1805. The Society of the Cincinnati erected a tablet to his memory in Saint Philip's Church in Charleston. (GP, vol. 2)

MURRAY, MARY LINDLEY   NY
of New York City. She married Robert Murray, and they had twelve children. Mrs. Murray was a rebel at heart, although her husband had Loyalist tendencies. On September 15, 1776, the British landed at Kip's Bay with the intention of capturing Manhattan Island. Mrs. Murray invited the British officers to stay and rest in her house, thus giving time for Gen. Israel Putnam and his men secretly to leave Manhattan Island and to join the main Continental Army on Harlem Heights. James Thatcher, a surgeon in the Continental Army, wrote in his Journal on September 20, 1776, that Mrs. Murray, a Quaker and a friend of the American cause, delayed Governor Tryon and the British forces by two hours, thus saving that part of the American army as was reported to him. (Thatcher, Military Journal, Boston: Cattons and Barnard, 1827) She died in 1782. (DAR)

In New York City on the southwest corner of 35th Street and Park Avenue there is a tablet commemorating Mrs. Murray's "signal service in the Revolutionary War"; there is another marker on 37th Street and Park Avenue. (CP; DB; FH)

N

NEIL, ELIZABETH MALLAM   NJ
was the wife of Maj. Daniel Neil, of the New Jersey Artillery, who was killed at Princeton, New Jersey, on January 3, 1777. On February 19, 1777, she wrote to Gen. Washington asking for a widow's pension. On February 28, Washington wrote to the president of Congress asking if any provision was made. On April 27, 1777, Washington wrote to Mrs. Neil acknowledging receipt of a piece of buff cloth and sent her a copy of the resolution of the Continental Congress dated March 14, 1777, stating that it was too early to take any action on widow's pensions, but Gen. Washington sent her fifty dollars. (FW)

NEILSON, CATHERINE VOORHEES   NJ
of New Brunswick. The daughter of Catherine Schuyler and John Voorhees, she was married on December 31, 1768, to John Neilson, a shipping merchant. They had eleven children. In 1775 he was a colonel of a battalion of minutemen of Middlesex County. In 1777 he was made a brigadier general of the militia. When the British

II: SELECTED BIOGRAPHIES 147

occupied New Brunswick, Neilson's house was sequestered by Lord Howe.

Mrs. Neilson was active in the ladies' relief association for the American soldiers. (New Jersey Gazette, July 4, 1780) She died on August 2, 1816. (Information on the Neilsons from O. Griminger of New Brunswick, NJ)

NEILSON, GANNITTE HARRISON   NJ
of New Brunswick. On July 19, 1768, she married James Neilson, an importer. In July 1774 he collected funds for the relief of Boston. Mrs. Neilson was active in the ladies' relief association for the welfare of the American soldiers. (New Jersey Gazette, July 4, 1780)

NEILSON, GRACE CARWILL   NJ
of New Brunswick. She was born in Monmouth, and on March 28, 1743, she married Andrew Neilson of New Brunswick. She was active in the ladies' relief association for the welfare of the American soldiers. (New Jersey Gazette, July 4, 1780)

NELSON, LUCY GRYMES   VA
of Yorktown. The daughter of Mary Randolph and Philip Grymes, she was married on July 29, 1762, to Thomas Nelson and bore him eleven children. Mr. Nelson was a signer of the Declaration of Independence. After being appointed a brigadier general and commander of the Virginia troops in 1778, he raised an army at his personal expense and marched to Philadelphia in 1778, but the troops were disbanded when the Continental Congress could not afford to support them any longer.

In 1781 Nelson was elected governor of Virginia, succeeding Thomas Jefferson, and raised a militia of 3,000 men at his own expense to aid Gen. Washington at Yorktown. He even offered his own mansion as a target for the bullets of his own countrymen. The Nelsons' funds were exhausted, and after the war they lived in poverty. Mrs. Nelson supported her husband, even in the loss of his fortune to pay for the American troops. (DB)

O

OGDEN, MARY GOUVERNEUR   NJ
of Newark. The daughter of Samuel Gouverneur, she was married in 1776 to Uzal Ogden of Newark. He had studied theology and was ordained by the bishop of London in 1773. Ogden served as a missionary in Sussex County between 1773 and 1785, when he became rector of Trinity Church in New York City and then in 1788 rector of Trinity Church in Newark.

Mrs. Ogden was active in the ladies' relief association for the welfare of the American soldiers. (New Jersey Gazette, July 4, 1780) She died in 1814.

O'HARA, MARY CARSON   PA
of Pittsburgh. The daughter of William Carson, proprietor of the
Harp and Crown, she was born in Philadelphia on December 11,
1760. During the Revolutionary War she made clothing and knitted
socks for the American soldiers. Concerned about conditions in
Philadelphia in 1777, her father sent Mary and her sister, Elizabeth
Febiger, to Lancaster, Pennsylvania, where they spent the winter
of 1777/78. About 1782 Mary married Capt. James O'Hara who
supplied provisions for Fort Pitt. She died in Pittsburgh on April
8, 1834. (EP)

ORTH, ROSINA KUCHER   PA
of Lebanon. The daughter of Barbara and Peter Kucher, she was
born there on March 19, 1741. Her parents had emigrated from
the Palatinate (now in Germany). On April 26, 1763, she married
Balzer Orth who served in the Colonial Wars. After the Battle
of Trenton he was in command of a company which guarded Hessian prisoners of war in Lebanon. In 1780 Orth was a major in
the 2nd Battalion under Col. Greenawalt.

During the Revolutionary War Mrs. Orth made clothing for
the American soldiers, along with other women in Lebanon. She
died there on April 3, 1814, and was buried in the Hebron churchyard next to her husband. (EP)

OSGOOD, HANNAH   NH
of Concord. Mother Osgood was a strong American patriot, and
her hospitality drinks were spiked with fervor for freedom. State
and town officials frequented her tavern, and her spunk helped
spark Bunker Hill's immortality in 1775.

Mother Osgood became the only woman in American history
to sign the "Association Test" of rebellion. This was an oath
against use of British goods and in support of the rebellion, and
men who failed to sign were jailed or fled and forfeited their properties. Officials vainly argued that the oath was for males only,
and that women did not count in such things. But Mother Osgood's
patriotism prevailed, and sign she did. The record remains in
Concord for all to witness, to this very day.

As the war for freedom dragged through eight long years,
Mother Osgood and her tavern struck yet another blow for democracy. She induced her patrons to muster spare pewter from their
homes, for melting into bullets in a rear room of her hostelry.
This tavern-tailored ammunition was later needed at Bunker Hill
and other battles, where the men helped serve world notice that
the homespun-clad colonists dared defy and stop the handsomely
groomed and officially equipped elite of the British forces.

Mother Osgood lives in history on yet another score. Her
tavern became beloved for its "Flip": A mug was nearly filled
with malt beer, sweetened with sugar, then a heated iron called
a "loggerhead" was thrust into it, which produced a rapid foam.
Instantly, a quantity of the "ardent" (half a pint of rum for a
quart mug) was dashed in, a little nutmeg grated on the top, and

II: SELECTED BIOGRAPHIES

the whole quaffed off by two or more men, as they could bear it.
(Submitted by Dorothy Wilcox, Durham, NH)

OVERSTREET, SARAH BOOTH   SC
The daughter of Mary and Capt. John Booth, she was born on
December 10, 1756. Her father was killed at the Battle of Hutson's
Ferry, South Carolina, in July 1779. Sarah married James Overstreet, Sr., who was fatally wounded at the Battle of Cowpens,
South Carolina, on January 17, 1780.

Sarah Overstreet performed public service and was named
by the president of the United States for her assistance in the
war effort. Mrs. Overstreet died on December 14, 1818. (Submitted by Dr. Martha Lulle Shaw of Young Harris, GA) Sarah
Booth Overstreet is listed in the DAR Patriot Index.

P

PACA, ANNE HARRISON   MD
of Annapolis. In 1777 she became the second wife of William Paca,
and they had five children. His first wife was Mary Chew, who
died about 1774. He was a signer of the Declaration of Independence.
Mr. and Mrs. Paca spent a fortune of their own money supplying
troops. Anne Paca died in 1780. (FG)

PATERSON, CORNELIA BELL   NJ
of New Brunswick. The daughter of John Bell of Union Farm,
Hunterdon County, she was married on February 9, 1779, to William Paterson, an attorney. They had three children. He served
as attorney general of New Jersey from 1776 to 1783.

Mrs. Paterson was active in the ladies' relief association for
the welfare of the American soldiers. (New Jersey Gazette, July
4, 1780) Mrs. Paterson died in February 1783, four days after
the birth of her third child.

PATTON, MARY   TN
of Elizabethtown. She lived at the Powder Branch in the Watauga
Settlement of Virginia, which later became apart of Tennessee. She
made powder for the overmountain men of East Tennessee at King's
Mountain prior to the rendezvous of the American troops on September 25, 1780, at Sycamore Shoals. Elizabethtown erected a monument to Mary Patton on the Carter County Courthouse lawn. (EW;
HS)

PAYNE, ELIZABETH (BETSY) JOHNSON   KY
of Lexington. The daughter of Jemima Suggert and Robert Johnson, as a young girl she was with her parents on August 15, 1782,
when the Tories and Indians attacked Bryan's Station. Betsy promptly extinguished the flames when a lighted arrow from an Indian bow
fell upon the sugar-trough cradle in which her brother, the infant
Richard M. Johnson (1780-1850), was lying, and thus saved the

boy from certain injury and possible death. Richard afterward became the hero of the Battle of the Thames in 1813 where he killed the Shawnee chieftain, Tecumseh. Later Richard M. Johnson served as vice president of the United States under President Martin Van Buren.
    Betsy Johnson married John Payne of Scott County, Kentucky. (Submitted by Dr. Carl R. Bogardus, Sr., Warsaw, KY)

PELOT, CATHERINE STOLL SCREVEN   SC
was the wife of the Rev. Francis Pelot. During the Revolutionary War, the Widow Pelot provided provisions and forage for Continental use in 1782 and 1783. (SI; DAR Magazine, August/September 1985) Mrs. Pelot died prior to August 1785. (Submitted by Catherine Pelot Curtius, Tulsa, OK)

PENN, POLLY MASTERS   PA
of Philadelphia. The daughter of William Masters, she married Richard Penn, and they lived at 190 High Street (old number). When the British occupied Philadelphia on September 26, 1777, they sequestered her home, and Lord Howe, the British general, resided there. After the Americans regained Philadelphia, her home became the headquarters of Benedict Arnold, who was a loyal American general at that point. It was then occupied by Sieur John Holker, consul general of France. In 1786 it was the home of United States Senator Robert Morris, and in 1790 the home of President George Washington. (DAR Magazine, January 1927)

PENNINGTON, HANNAH BOONE STEWART   KY
of Boonesborough. The daughter of Sarah Morgan and Squire Boone, Sr., she was born on August 24, 1746, in Berks County, Pennsylvania. In 1765 she married John Stewart (1745-1770), and they had four daughters: Sarah (1765-1815), who married the Rev. John Stewart and had ten children; Mary; then Rachel (1768-1853), who married James King, a Revolutionary War soldier; and Elizabeth Ann. Hannah's husband, John Stewart, was Daniel Boone's best friend and was killed by Indians in 1770.
    In 1777 Hannah married Richard Pennington, and they had three sons and one daughter: Joshua, Daniel, John, and Abigail. (Submitted by Katherine Blaylock, Winston-Salem, NC)

PENNYPACKER, HANNAH GERBERT   PA
of Schwenksville. She was the wife of Samuel Pennypacker (1746-1826). Pennypacker was the owner of Paulbig's Mills. Gen. Washington established his headquarters there from September 26 to 29, 1777. Lord Cornwallis took Philadelphia on September 26 and Washington was forced to leave the city. The house was also Washington's headquarters from October 5 to 8, 1777. On this date Washington wrote to Gen. Varnum: "The army here marches this morning from hence to the Baptist Meeting House in Towamencia Township." (BI)

II: SELECTED BIOGRAPHIES

PERCIVAL, MARY FULLER   CT
of Chatham. She was born in 1737 in East Haddam, Connecticut, the daughter of Mary Andrews and Elkanah Fuller. In 1754 she married Capt. Timothy Percival. In 1777 her husband and her son Elkanah were captured and imprisoned on the prison ship Dartmouth. Her husband was later released, but her son died of hunger and thirst. Another son, Jabez, was captured and imprisoned in the Sugar House in New York City from August 1781 to September 1783. During the Revolutionary War Mrs. Percival turned her home into a hospital for sick and wounded soldiers. Mary Percival and her daughter knitted socks for the soldiers and made bread dough to bind their blistered feet.

After the war the Percivals moved to Ohio and then to Boone County, Kentucky. Mrs. Percival died in 1819. She is the patron saint of the Van Buren Chapter of the Daughters of the American Revolution in Arkansas. (GP)

PETERS, FANNY LEDYARD   NY
of Southhold, Long Island. On the morning of September 6, 1781, a British fleet under the command of Benedict Arnold entered the harbor of Groton, Connecticut. The British forces under command of Col. Eyre and Maj. Montgomery landed at Groton, and Arnold proceeded to New London. Fanny's uncle, Col. William Ledyard, commanded Fort Griswold at Groton. After the British stormed the fort, Maj. Montgomery was killed. Col. Ledyard surrendered to the British, but the onslaught continued and Col. Ledyard was bayoneted to death. The British then slaughtered eighty-five American soldiers. Some sixty American wounded were taken to the home of Ens. Ebenezer Avery.

Fanny Ledyard was on a visit to her uncle when the massacre occurred. She was one of the first persons, along with Mrs. Bailey, to volunteer to nurse and assist the wounded soldiers, according to the eyewitness report of Stephen Hempstead (1754-1831).

Fanny Ledyard later became the wife of Richard Peters of Southhold. She died in 1816 aged sixty-two years. In 1895 a bronze tablet was placed over her grave. The Mystic, Connecticut, chapter of the Daughters of the American Revolution was named in her honor. (CG; GP)

PINCKNEY, ELEANOR LAURENS   SC
of Charleston. She was the twelfth child of Henry Laurens and Eleanor Ball Laurens (d. 1770), and the sister of Martha Laurens Ramsay. The Continental Congress sent Laurens as minister to Holland, and he sailed from Philadelphia on August 13, 1780, but three weeks later he was captured by the British and charged with high treason against the Crown. Laurens was imprisoned in the Tower of London from October 6, 1780, until December 31, 1781, when he was exchanged for Lord Cornwallis, who had been captured at the Battle of Yorktown, Virginia.

Eleanor Laurens suffered during the imprisonment of her

father. On April 27, 1788, she married Gen. Charles Pinckney, who was a second cousin of Charles Cotesworth Pinckney and Thomas Pinckney. (CS)

PINCKNEY, ELIZABETH MOTTE   SC
of Charleston. The daughter of Rebecca Brewton and Jacob Motte, she was married on July 22, 1779, to Thomas Pinckney, an attorney. Gen. Prevost in 1779 burned "Auckland," the Pinckney home on the Ashepoo River and carried away all the farm stock, provisions, and servants. This is an example of the suffering of the patriotic women of the Revolutionary War. Mr. Pinckney served as governor of South Carolina, 1787-1789. Mrs. Pinckney died in 1794 while on a visit to England. (DB)

PIPER, EVE LEAR   CT
of New Haven. She married Col. George Piper and gave him Ł325 in gold, her inheritance, to buy clothing and shoes for the soldiers of his company during the Revolutionary War. The Eve Lear chapter of the Daughters of the American Revolution in New Haven is named in her honor. (CG; the DAR Patriot Index includes an Eve Sear who married a George Piper of Pennsylvania who served as a private during the Revolutionary War)

POINDEXTER, ELIZABETH PLEDGE   NC
was the second wife of Capt. Thomas Poindexter (1733-1807). Elizabeth sewed letters of warnings into the petticoats of her daughter, who went through enemy lines to deliver the letters to the proper authorities. She is listed as a patriot in the DAR Patriot Index. Elizabeth died on February 29, 1816. (Submitted by Dorothy Knox Brown, Dallas, TX)

POLK, DELIAH TYLER   KY
of Spencer County. The daughter of Nancy Mangley and Edward Tyler, she was born on February 10, 1755, in Virginia. In November 1774 she married Capt. Charles Polk (1745-1823) of Maryland, a first cousin of Ezekiel Polk, the grandfather of President James K. Polk. They resided at Kincheloe's Station on Simpson Creek in Western Virginia, now Kentucky. They had six sons and six daughters. In 1781 he was a delegate to the Virginia Convention. In August 1782, after the Battle of Blue Licks, a report was received that Indians were in the area of the settlement, which consisted of six or seven families. The militia with Capt. Polk included, was ordered to scour the area. While the militia was away, in the dead of the night, while everybody was asleep, the Indians attacked on August 31, 1782.

    Mrs. Polk escaped into the woods with four of her children, but she was pregnant and had great difficulty running. The Indians captured her and her children, and mounted her and her two younger children on a horse. During the trip she was separated from her two older children, her daughter being left with one of the Shawnees near Piqua. Mrs. Polk and her two younger children

II: SELECTED BIOGRAPHIES

were taken to Detroit, where they arrived on September 25. They were turned over to the British Col. de Peyster, commandant of the fort, and were well treated. On October 27 she bore a son. Finally, on July 1, 1783, her missing children held by the Indians were returned to her while she was still held in Detroit.

Meanwhile her husband was searching for her and the children not knowing they had been taken to Detroit. Capt. Polk joined Gen. George Rogers Clark in a campaign against the Shawnee villages on the Great Miami River, hoping to find his wife and children, but was disappointed. Finally Col. McKee, superintendent of the Indian Department, learned that the prisoners had been taken to Detroit. Upon his return to his headquarters in Louisville, Kentucky, Gen. Clark proposed an exchange of prisoners and sent a letter by express to Col. de Peyster in Detroit. It was not until the spring of 1783 that Col. de Peyster agreed to release some prisoners.

Captain Polk was joined by Jonathan Zane of Wheeling, West Virginia, as his guide and proceeded through the wilderness to Upper Sandusky to the residence of the noted Tory, Simon Girty, who supplied Polk with an Indian guide to take him to Detroit, and Zane returned home. Col. de Peyster released Mrs. Polk and Mrs. White and their children and supplied Polk with a guide to take them as far as Sandusky. Capt. Polk left Detroit on October 25 with Mrs. Polk and Mrs. White and the children, arriving in Louisville on December 24, 1783. Mrs. Polk and her children had been held hostage for thirteen months. (See also Margaret Dozier Davis, above) Mrs. Polk died on June 6, 1797, in Kentucky. (CH; William Polk, Polk Family and Kinsmen) Mrs. Polk is listed as a patriot in the DAR Patriot Index. (Submitted by Maude Goodman, Leesburg, FL, Jane Short Mallinson, Sugar Creek, MO, and Sarah Margaret Jones, Tombstone, AZ)

PORTER, ELIZABETH   KY
After Tory, Canadian, and Indian forces under Colonel Bird captured Ruddell's and Martin's stations on June 22, 1780, Elizabeth and her husband, Samuel Porter, their daughter, and two sons were captured and taken to Niagara. Later they were taken to Montreal and arrived there on October 4, 1782, and were then taken to Quebec. They were released in 1783. (HP)

PORTER, MEHITABLE HINE   CT
of Union City. She was born in 1739 and married Thomas Porter. Her home was used as a tavern during the Revolutionary War and housed many soldiers. When the rooms were filled with soldiers, many of the weary slept on the floor. Mrs. Porter and her attendants cooked meals for the soldiers. She died in 1837. (EW; DAR)

PORTER, MELICENT BALDWIN   NJ
of Monmouth. Melicent (or Meliscent) was born in 1750 in Waterbury, Connecticut, the daughter of Mary Bronson and Lt. Col. Jonathan Baldwin (1722-1802). In 1770 Melicent married Isaac Booth Lewis, and they moved to New Jersey. They had two children.

He died or was killed in 1777. During the Battle of Monmouth on June 28, 1778, Melicent cooked for and fed the soldiers.
Melicent returned to Waterbury, and in December 1778 she became the second wife of Capt. Phineas Porter (1739-1804), who rose to the rank of colonel. After his death, she married Abel Camp. Melicent died in 1824. A DAR chapter in Waterbury is named in her honor. (DAR; GP)

POTTER, DEBORAH REYNOLDS   RI
of Little Rest (now South Kingston). Deborah's first husband was Thomas Potter, Jr., owner of Potter's Tavern. He was the son of Margaret Helms and Ichabod Potter.
On his trip from Fishkill, New York, to Newport, Rhode Island, Gen. Washington was entertained in the home of the Potters on March 7, 1781. (FW) After the British surrendered, Washington visited the Potters again, and their daughter, Susie, sat on Washington's knee. (Holly Higbee, Historic Kingston) At the time Lt. Potter was in the Rhode Island militia, the "Kingston Reds." (Information from Phyllis Silvia, Pawtucket, RI)

POTTER, LYDIA BARNES   PA
was born in Connecticut in July 1757 and met Cpl. Lemuel Potter while he was on a mission gathering provisions and clothing for Washington's army, which was wintering at Valley Forge. They were married early in 1779. An affidavit by a descendant in 1911 described her war service: "She spun and wove the wool and cut and made the garments, learning the tailor's trade that she might more expeditiously supply the soldiers' needs. She worked so unremittingly at her task, standing continuously in a half-bent position over her cutting table, that she was never able to stand upright."
After her husband's death in 1826 she moved to Michigan. Mrs. Potter died on August 28, 1836, and was buried in the Paint Creek Cemetery, near Addison. She is the only known Revolutionary War female patriot buried in Michigan. The General Richardson Chapter of the Daughters of the American Revolution marked her grave in 1911, and in 1975 the chapter placed a new bronze marker on the site. (From an article in the SAR Magazine, Fall 1987)

POTTS, MRS. ISAAC   PA
of Valley Forge. Gen. Washington arrived there on December 19, 1777, and made his headquarters in the Potts' home. On December 31, he wrote to Governor Livingston of New Jersey: "I sincerely feel for the unhappy condition of our poor fellows in the hospitals, and wish my power to relieve them were equal to my inclination. It is too melancholy a truth, that our hospital stores are exceedingly scanty and deficient in every instance ... Our sick naked, and well naked, our unfortunate men in captivity naked!"
Mrs. Washington arrived on February 10, 1778, and Baron von Steuben dined with the Washingtons on February 23. On

II: SELECTED BIOGRAPHIES

Wednesday, April 22, 1778, by order of Congress, Washington observed a day of fasting, atonement, and prayer. On Saturday, May 2, Washington directed that Divine Service be performed every Sunday at eleven o'clock by the chaplains.
On June 18, 1778, the enemy evacuated Philadelphia, and on June 19 Washington left Valley Forge. (BI)

POWELL, ELIZABETH WILLING   PA
of Philadelphia. She was the wife of Samuel Powell, mayor of Philadelphia in 1775 and again in 1789. They lived on the west side of 3rd Street between Walnut and Spruce streets. On January 6, 1779, Mrs. Powell entertained Gen. and Mrs. Washington at a party. Sarah Bache, the daughter of Benjamin Franklin, danced with Gen. Washington. (BI)

POWERS, ANNA KEYES   NH
of Hollis. She was the wife of Capt. Peter Powers, who settled in 1730 in the wilderness of what is now Hollis. Anna had four sons who served in the Revolutionary War. The local chapter of the Daughters of the American Revolution is named in her honor.
(Submitted by Ruby M. Towle, Farmington, NH)

PRATT, ABIGAIL BUTLER   NH
of Nottingham was one of many patriotic women who boycotted English products. In a most dramatic way she once demonstrated her displeasure regarding the sipping of British tea. Once while staying at her tavern, a traveler took a package of tea from his pocket. What happened then is recorded in a simple poem--

>   Then quickly she darted forward,
>   Her plate of meat she let fall,
>   And with one deft stroke of the carver
>   Cut coattails, pocket and all.
>   Threw them into the blazing fireplace
>   Before he had time to think,
>   While she said in a voice triumphant,
>   "That tea you shall never drink."
>   (Submitted by Mrs. Philip Wilcox of Durham, NH)

Abigail Butler was born in 1750 and married Jaspar Pratt of Connecticut, a corporal during the war. She died in 1845. (DAR)

PRATT, ELIZABETH HAGER   MA
of Concord. She was born in 1750 in Boston, and her parents died when she was about nine years old. Betsy was bound out to Samuel Leverett, a blacksmith, and learned the trade. After the Battle of Concord, Betsy took bandages and nursed the wounded soldiers. She noticed that the British left behind six brass cannons, but they had spiked the guns before their retreat. Betsy notified Mr. Leverett and told him they could make the cannons as good as new.

John Pratt and several other minutemen with their horses took the cannons to Mr. Leverett's blacksmith shop. Betsy and her boss repaired the cannons for future use by the militia. During the Revolutionary War, Betsy visited the sick and wounded and nursed them. After the war she married John Pratt.

In 1816 the Pratts left Massachusetts and moved to the Connecticut Reserve in Bradford County in western Pennsylvania, near the New York state line. They had several children and left many descendants. Betsy and her husband are buried in Granville, Pennsylvania. (GP, vol. 2)

PROVOST, MRS. (see BURR, THEODOSIA BARTOW)

PURDY, ABIGAIL SMITH   NY
of White Plains. She was born in Rye, New York, on March 22, 1746, the youngest daughter (and twelfth child) of the Rev. John Smith. Later they lived in White Plains. On October 18, 1762, Abigail married Jacob Purdy, Sr., of White Plains, who served as a lieutenant under Capt. Jonathan Horton, and then as a captain under Col. Thomas Thomas in the Westchester County militia. The Purdys had four sons and six daughters. They moved to Bedford in 1778 and then back to White Plains in 1783. Mrs. Purdy died in Greenburg, Westchester County, New York, on November 12, 1839, aged ninety-three.

Gen. Washington left Valentine Hill on October 22, 1776, and spent the night in the home of the Widow Miller in North White Plains. On October 23 he established his headquarters at the Purdy House. Washington remained there during the Battle of White Plains and left the Purdy House on October 31, 1776, according to research by the Westchester County Historical Society. Others claim that the general was at the home of Mrs. Miller.

Washington's General Orders state: "Headquarters, October 24th, all officers who have assisted in the works [fortifications] to meet at Colonel Putnam's headquarters, just above [my] headquarters at 3 o'clock this afternoon, in order to lay out the number of works." Gen. Putnam's headquarters apparently were in a tent on Purdy Hill just above Washington's headquarters on the "plains."

On October 28 the right wing of the American lines withdrew to North Castle. After the battle, on October 31, Gen. Heath reported: "The British advanced before throwing up work, etc. At night, the Americans evacuated their works on the plains near late Headquarters, setting fires to barns." Gen. Washington then stayed at the home of the Widow Miller from November 1 to November 10, 1776. The general had his headquarters again in the Purdy House from July 27 to September 16, 1778. Lafayette, Governor Clinton, and Gen. Gates were with Gen. Washington for a time in 1778.

The Purdy House was located on what was then called the Dobbs Ferry Road and near a wooden bridge (now the Main Street Bridge). Due to urban renewal, the Purdy House was moved in 1973 to 60 Park Avenue, White Plains, and restored by the Battle

II: SELECTED BIOGRAPHIES

of White Plains Monument Committee. (Information from Stephen Holden, Jr., White Plains NY)

PURVIANCE, MRS. SAMUEL   MD
of Baltimore. Her husband was a member of the Baltimore Committee of Correspondence, which corresponded with the other thirteen colonies. On February 21, 1777, while the Continental Congress met in Baltimore, John Adams dined with the Purviances. Present were Richard Henry Lee and Francis Lightfoot Lee, delegates from Virginia, their ladies, and others. John Adams wrote in his diary: "The Virginia Ladies had ornaments about their Wrists, which I dont remember to have seen before. These Ornaments were like Minature Pictures, bound round the Arms with some Chains." (BA)

PUTNAM, DEBORAH LATHROP   CT
of Brooklyn. The daughter of Debora Crow and Samuel Lathrop, she was born in 1719 in Norwich, Connecticut. After her marriage to the Rev. Ephraim Avery in 1738, they lived in Brooklyn, Connecticut, and then in Pomfret. In 1754 the Rev. Avery died. Her second husband was John Gardiner, the fifth proprietor of Gardiner's Island, New York, and in 1764 he died. Deborah then became the second wife of Israel Putnam in 1767 and lived in Brooklyn, Connecticut. Mrs. Putnam lived in Gen. Putnam's headquarters in 1775/76 and with her stepdaughters spun flax for shirts for the American army. At this time they were visited by Gen. and Mrs. Washington. While her husband was erecting fortifications at West Point, she was with him and died there on October 14, 1777. The Plainfield chapter of the Daughters of the American Revolution is named in her honor. (CG)

PUTNEY, SUSANNAH FRENCH   MA
of Goshen. She married Ebenezer Putney (1739-1802), who served as a lieutenant during the war. Mrs. Putney opened her house for use to inoculate smallpox patients during the war. She inoculated thirty patients, and after sending them home she nursed them until they recovered. On one occasion she nursed a sick soldier, and the sickness proved to be contagious. Two of her own children died in one day from the disease. A chapter of the Daughters of the American Revolution in El Dorado, Kansas, is named in her honor. (DAR; GP)

R

RAMSAY, MARGARET JANE PEALE   MD
After the British occupied Boston, there was a call in Maryland for help. Mrs. Ramsay joined her husband, Capt. Nathaniel Ramsay, on the trip to Boston. She was given a small military chest of supplies and ministered to the wounded soldiers. (<u>DAR Magazine</u>, July 1921)

RAMSAY, MARTHA LAURENS   SC
of Charleston. She was the daughter of Henry Laurens and Eleanor
Bell Laurens (d. 1770) and a sister of Eleanor Laurens Pinckney.
In 1775 Henry Laurens was elected president of the Provincial Congress of South Carolina, succeeding Charles Pinckney, and he
served as president of the Continental Congress, succeeding John
Hancock, from November 1, 1777 to December 9, 1778. The Continental Congress appointed Laurens minister to Holland to negotiate
a $10 million loan. He sailed from Philadelphia on August 13, 1780,
on the brigantine Mercury, but three weeks later was captured
off Newfoundland by the British.

Laurens threw his diplomatic pouch into the water, but it
failed to sink and was retrieved by a British seaman. Laurens
was charged with high treason against the Crown, taken to the
Tower of London, and confined there from October 6, 1780, until
December 31, 1781, when he was exchanged for Lord Cornwallis,
who had been captured at the Battle of Yorktown, Virginia, in
1781.

Martha Laurens suffered during the imprisonment of her father.
On January 23, 1787, she became the third wife of David Ramsay.
She died on June 10, 1811. (CS)

RANDOLPH, MRS. BENJAMIN   PA
of Philadelphia. When Thomas Jefferson attended the Continental
Congress in Philadelphia in 1774/75, he stayed at the Randolph's
home on Market Street. On October 22, 1775, Peyton Randolph
of Virginia, the president of the Continental Congress, dropped
dead at the dinner table, which was a great shock to Thomas Jefferson. (WT)

RANDOLPH, ELIZABETH HARRISON   VA
of Williamsburg. The daughter of Col. Benjamin Harrison, on March
8, 1745/46, she married Peyton Randolph. She was the sister of
the Benjamin Harrison who signed the Declaration of Independence.
Mr. and Mrs. Randolph were dedicated American patriots. Her
husband was president of the Continental Congress in 1774 and
1775. He dropped dead at the dinner table in the home of Mrs.
Benjamin Randolph in Philadelphia on October 22, 1775, in the presence of Thomas Jefferson, who was deeply shocked.

Elizabeth had no children. She inherited his large estate,
(including 105 slaves) as a life tenure, and on her death the estate went to his nephew, Edmund Randolph. (WT; DAR Magazine,
July 1976)

RANDOLPH, ELIZABETH NICHOLAS   VA
of Williamsburg. She was the wife of Edmund Randolph, who was
a delegate to the Continental Congress (1779-1782) and governor of
Virginia (1786-1788). He was the first United States attorney general
(1789-1793) and served as secretary of state (1794-1795).

Mrs. Randolph and her neighbors supplied horses, cattle,
and crops for the American army before the Battle of Yorktown.

II: SELECTED BIOGRAPHIES 159

The French army foraging for supplies also seized many articles
from the plantations and farmers. Mrs. Randolph appealed to Gen.
Washington, and he replied from Yorktown on October 25, 1781:

> I have been favored with your polite Note of yesterday,
> and beg leave to assure you, that your obliging Congratu-
> lations are very acceptable to me. I have also the pleasure
> to inform you, that measures are adopting for making
> an equitable compensation to the Inhabitants for such
> Articles as have been taken for the use of the Allied Army.
> The Governor has engaged to have a valuation made of
> them, Inconsequence of which, the Quarter Master Genl.
> of the American Army, or State Agent, will be accountable
> for whatever has been made use of by our Troops; and
> His Excellency the Count de Rochambeau has been so ob-
> liging as to assure me, that payment will be made for
> that proportion of Forage, etc. which has been furnished
> for the Troops of His Most Christian Majesties. (FW)

RANDOLPH, LUCY BOLLING   VA
of Richmond. The daughter of Robert Bolling of "Bollingbrook,"
she was married to Col. Peter Randolph of "Chatsworth," Henrico
County. After his death she was active in the ladies' association
which opposed the British tax on the importation of tea. (Virginia
Gazette, July 27, 1769) She supplied provisions for the army during the Revolutionary War. (VR Commissioner's, 3:105)

RANSOM, ESTHER LAWRENCE   PA
married Capt. Samuel Ransom (1738-1778). On June 22, 1778,
Gen. Washington from his headquarters at Coryells Ferry, New
Jersey wrote to the Board of War: "From the apprehensions of
the Public, of an Indian war in the western department and the
earnest applications of General McIntosh for Troops, I was induced
the 15th of the month to detach Durkee's and Ransom's companies
for that command." Both Capt. Robert Durkee and Capt. Ransom
were killed in the Wyoming Valley massacre by the Indians on July
3, 1778. (FW; DAR)

READ, GERTRUDE ROSS   DE
of New Castle. The daughter of the Rev. George Ross, rector
of Immanuel Episcopal Church, New Castle, she was married on
June 18, 1752, to Thomas Till. After his death, she married George
Read on January 11, 1763. They had one daughter and four sons.
Her husband was a signer of the Declaration of Independence.
    The British took Wilmington in September 1777 and captured
President John McKinly of Delaware. Mr. Read and his family were
in Philadelphia, and since Read was speaker of the legislative council, he succeeded McKinly as president of Delaware. While crossing
the Delaware River, the family barely escaped capture by the British, and took a circuitous route and safely crossed the Susquehanna
to return home. Read assumed charge of the state in November

1777, and was tireless in raising troops, clothing, and provisions for the militia and Continental Army. This is another example of the suffering and endurance of the patriotic women of the Revolutionary War. (DB)

READ, MARY PEELE   NJ
of Fieldsboro. The widow of Robert Field, early in 1780 she married Thomas Read of New Castle, Delaware, who had recently moved to Fieldsboro. He was a captain in the Continental Navy, being commissioned in June 1776. Shortly after their marriage, on July 22, 1780, he obtained a letter of marque and reprisal to command the privateer Patty out of Philadelphia. Mrs. Read was active in the ladies' relief association for the American soldiers. (New Jersey Gazette, July 4, 1780)

REED, ESTHER DE BERDT   PA
the daughter of Dennis De Berdt, she was born on October 22, 1746, N.S., in London. Sometime later the family came to America, and on May 31, 1770, she married Joseph Reed of Trenton, New Jersey. Her husband was president of the Second Provincial Congress in Philadelphia in 1775, and later served as adjutant general of the Continental Army. They had five children. On October 28, 1775, Mrs. Reed wrote to her brother in England that she expected the American colonies to declare their independence. When the British occupied Philadelphia in September 1777, she lived in Flemington, New Jersey, until January 1778.

Early in 1780 Mrs. Reed founded the Association in Philadelphia, which was the largest wartime women's organization in America. They were devoted to spinning, sewing, and knitting clothing for the American troops. This organization spread to six states. The women in the association canvassed every house in Philadelphia soliciting money for the benefit of the troops. Even the Marquis de Lafayette made a contribution of a hundred guineas in a letter to Mrs. Reed dated June 25, 1780.

Joseph Reed served as president of the Supreme Executive Council of Pennsylvania from December 1778 until 1781, and Mrs. Reed was known as Mrs. President. She died in Philadelphia on September 18, 1780, and Sarah Franklin Bache and four other women took over the leadership of the association. (DR)

On July 4, 1780, Mrs. Reed wrote to Gen. Washington:

> The Subscription set on foot by the Ladies of this City for the use of the Soldiery is so far compleated as to induce me to transmit to your Excelly, an account of the Money I have received, and which, alto it has answered our Expectations, it does not equal our Wishes but I am perswaded will be as proof of our Zeal for the great Cause of America, and of our Esteem and Gratitude for those who so bravely defend it.

She sent $200,580 and ₺625.6.8 in specie.

II: SELECTED BIOGRAPHIES 161

In his reply of July 14, 1780, from Bergen County, New Jersey, Gen. Washington wrote:

> Madam: I have received with much pleasure, but not till last night, the subscriptions already collected for the use of the American Soldiery. This fresh mark of the patriotism of the Ladies entitles them to the highest applause of their Country. It is impossible for the Army, not to feel a superior gratitude, on such an instance of goodness.
> If I am happy in having the concurrence of the Ladies, I would propose the purchasing of course Linen to be made into Shirts, with the whole amount of their subscription. A Shirt extraordinary to the Soldier will be of more service, and do more to preserve his health than any other thing that could be procured him; while it is not intended, nor shall exclude him, from the usual supply which he draws from the public. This appears to me, to be the best mode for its application, and provided it is approved by the Ladies. (FW)

Gen. Washington wrote to Mrs. Reed again on August 10, 1780, from Tappan, New York, to explain his position:

> A few provident Soldiers will, probably, avail themselves of the advantage which may result from the generous bounty of two dollars in Specie, but it is equally probable that it will be the means of bringing punishment on a number of others whose inclination, propensity to drinking overcoming all other considerations too frequently leads them into irregularities and disorders which must be corrected.
> A Shirt would, render the condition of the Soldier in general much more comfortable than it is at prest.

As a result, the ladies' association then made shirts, stockings, and other clothing for the soldiers.

From his headquarters at Orange Town (Tappan, New York) on October 1, 1780, George Washington expressed his regrets to President Joseph Reed of Pennsylvania on "the loss of your amiable lady." (FW)

REID, MARY WOODBURN   NH
of Derry, formerly Londonderry. "Molly" was the wife of Gen. George Reid, and she took charge of their farm during the eight years the general was in the army. Gen. John Stark said, "If there is a woman in New Hampshire fit for governor, 'tis Molly Reid!" (Willey, Book of Nutfield, 1895) Mrs. Reid died on April 7, 1823, at age eight-eight years.

The Molly Reid Chapter of the Daughters of the American Revolution of Derry, New Hampshire, is named in her honor. The chapter was organized in 1894 by Annie Bartlett Shepard, the grandmother of Alan B. Shepard, Jr., America's first astronaut. (Information from Elsie R. Richardson, Derry, NH, and Dorothy Wilcox, Durham, NH)

REILY, ELIZABETH MYER   PA
of Lancaster. The daughter of Isaac Myer, the founder of Myerstown, she was born on April 2, 1755, and educated in Philadelphia. On May 20, 1773, she married John Reily, an attorney. During the winter of 1776/77 he served as first lieutenant in the 12th Regiment of the Pennsylvania Line in the Jersey campaign. Lt. Reily was severely wounded on April 15, 1777, in a skirmish with the British at Bonhampton, New Jersey. After he returned home he recovered, and in July 1778 was transferred to the 3rd Regiment of the Pennsylvania Line and was in the Invalid Corps from August 1780 to December 1784.

    During the war Mrs. Reily made clothing for the American soldiers and forwarded food to the soldiers at Valley Forge. She had a large family. Mrs. Reily died on April 2, 1800, at Myerstown and was buried in the Reformed Church cemetery. (EP)

REINHARDT, BARBARA ELIZABETH WARLICK   NC
of Lincolnton. The daughter of Barbara Schindler and Daniel Warlick, she was born on June 17, 1754, in Lincoln County, North Carolina. In 1769/70 she married Christian Reinhardt (1735-1818). Her father was killed in 1772 during an Indian raid. On May 12, 1780, the British captured Charleston, South Carolina. The British under Maj. Welch moved into North Carolina to enlist the Dutch Loyalists to the Crown to enter the fighting. As a result by June 19, 1780, some thirteen hundred Tories were assembled at Ramsour's Mill. Meanwhile the news reached the American Gen. Griffith Rutherford who ordered Col. Francis Locke of Rowan to disperse the Tories.

    On the night of June 19, 1780, Adam Reep, an American patriot who had learned about the massing of the Tories, arrived at the home of Elizabeth Reinhardt, about one-half mile north of Lincolnton, where the subsequent battle was fought. He came to await the arrival of Locke and to give Locke directions and information about the strength of the Tory forces. Elizabeth secreted Adam Reep in the cellar of her home. Reep, a heavyweight, had difficulty squeezing through the narrow cellar door, but received help from Mrs. Reinhardt. The next morning he managed to squeeze through the door again in time to meet Colonel Locke, who had marched some four hundred men to a point nearby. Reep informed Locke of the Tory position and the lay of the land.

    The suddenness of the American attack surprised the Tories, and the Battle of Ramsour's Mill lasted only two hours. The men wore no uniforms. The patriots had white paper pinned to their hats while the Tories had green twigs on theirs. After the rebels had dispersed the Tories, this victory inspired the American patriots and helped assure their victory at King's Mountain on

II: SELECTED BIOGRAPHIES

October 7, 1780. (Hunter, Sketches of Western North Carolina; Sherrill, Annals of Lincoln County)
  Elizabeth had three sons--Christian, Michael, and John--and several daughters. Her brothers Philip and Capt. Nicholas Warlick were killed at the Battle of Ramsour's Mill. Mrs. Reinhardt died in Lincoln County on June 22, 1806. A monument was placed on the battlefield on June 20, 1934 honoring Nicholas and Philip Warlick and a neighbor, Israel Sain, who was also killed in the battle. Mrs. Reinhardt is listed as a patriot in the DAR Patriot Index. (Submitted by May Horsley Goodman, Memphis, TN, and Barbara J. Colvin, Sperryville, VA)

RICE, ABIGAIL HARTMAN   PA
of Chester Springs. She was born on September 4, 1742, and married Zachariah Rice (1731-1811), who served as a private during the Revolutionary War in the Chester County militia. He worked on the construction of the Yellow Springs Hospital, and after its completion Abigail made many errands of mercy to care for the sick and wounded soldiers there. Their home, now known as Pine Creek Farm, lies east from State Road 113, first right off State Road 401, through the Pennsylvania Turnpike to Pine Creek Road. The original homestead contained 303 acres. In 1955 the DAR placed a marker on their house: "Erected 1767. Home of Zachariah Rice and Wife Abigail Hartman Rice. Zachariah as a soldier helped build the Yellow Springs Hospital where Abigail served as a nurse during the American Revolution. Presented 1955 by the Daughters of the American Revolution, Abigail Hartman Rice Chapter, Washington, D.C."
  In 1789 the Rice farm was seized for a defective title and foreclosed on by the old English mortgage of Samuel Hoare. Following the foreclosure, the house and farm were purchased by John March. This was a disastrous event for Mrs. Rice, and she died on November 6, 1789. Zachariah and his family, including five married children, traveled westward to find cheaper land and settled in Perry County and some of his children in Juniata County, Pennsylvania. Mrs. Rice is listed as a patriot in the DAR Patriot Index. (The Thomas Hench Family in America; submitted by Mary C. Kennedy, Regent, Abigail Hartman Rice Chapter, National Society, Daughters of the American Revolution, Washington, DC)

RICHARDS, HULDA HOPKINS   CT
of Waterbury. The daughter of Capt. Timothy Hopkins, she was married on December 15, 1749, to Abijah Richards. They had four sons and four daughters. Her husband died on October 4, 1773. The Widow Richards furnished clothing for the American soldiers. (EW; information from Patricia L. Joy, Naugatuck, CT)

RICHARDSON, DORCAS NELSON   SC
of the Sumter District. She was born in 1741, the daughter of Capt. John Nelson of Clarendon. In 1761 she married Capt. Richard Richardson (1741-1817), the son of Gen. Richardson. After the fall

of Charleston on May 12, 1780, Capt. Richardson, his brother Edward, and their father were taken prisoners and sent to a military prison on Johns Island, South Carolina. Capt. Richardson nearly died of smallpox. After he recovered, he escaped and hid in the swamps near his house.

British officers under Col. Tarleton occupied her home, but from time to time Mrs. Richardson managed to take food to her husband. When the enemy learned that the captain had escaped, the officers told Dorcas what they would do to her husband when he was captured. She replied, "But capture or conquer my husband before you boast of what you are going to do, and let me tell you that some of you are likely to beg for his mercy before he will ever ask or accept yours."

The British were unable to capture her husband again. Meanwhile Richardson joined the forces of Francis Marion. Dorcas had ten children, and six of them lived to maturity, married, and raised families. Mrs. Richardson died in 1834, aged ninety-three years. (GP)

RICHMAN, REBECCA KEEN NJ
of Salem County. She was born in 1731 and married Michael Richman (ca. 1728-1773). Her son Nehemiah served as a private in Capt. Nieukirk's Company of the 2nd Regiment, Salem County Militia, and was later promoted to sergeant class 2. He was captured by the British and imprisoned in the ship Jersey in New York Harbor. With five to eleven men dying daily, the ship was ridden with dysentery, smallpox, and other diseases. Nehemiah survived but was not released until the war ended in 1783.

During the winter of 1777/78 the British sent some fifteen hundred troops into Salem County foraging for livestock. There were several skirmishes at Quinton and Hancock's Bridge, and many American soldiers were wounded. Rebecca hid some of the wounded men in the attic of her home and nursed them back to health. The old house is still standing, with its blood-stained attic floors, in an area previously called Whig Lane. Mrs. Richman died in 1791. (Submitted by Mary Coates Martin, Norfolk, VA)

RING, RACHEL JAMES PA
of Chadds Ford. The daughter of Samuel James, on December 6, 1758, she married Benjamin Ring, the son of Lydia Vernon and Nathaniel Ring, Jr. They had six sons and three daughters. (History of Chester County, 1881; submitted by Andrea Withers, Chadds Ford, PA)

On September 11, 1777, Gen. Washington had his headquarters at Ring's Tavern. At the Battle of Brandywine, Washington had a guide take him and Lafayette to the scene of the fighting with the British. Gen. Sullivan's line broke, and Washington and Lafayette tried to rally the fleeing army, and Lafayette was shot in the leg. During the defeat, the Americans suffered a thousand casualties and the British half that number. (CS)

II: SELECTED BIOGRAPHIES

RINKER, "MOM"   PA
of Germantown (now a part of Philadelphia). She was a tavern
keeper and an American spy. While knitting upon a high rock in
Fairmont Park in Philadelphia, she placed messages in a ball of
yarn which she dropped to American couriers below. (EW)

RITCHIE, MARY   SC
is listed as a soldier in the Revolutionary War at the Historical
Commission Library. (ESC, v. no. 342) She also supplied provisions for the army during the war. (SI, U-W:51)

ROBERDEAU, MARY BOSTWICK   PA
of Philadelphia. The daughter of the Rev. David Bostwick, a Presbyterian minister in New York, she was married on October 3,
1761, to Daniel Roberdeau. They had nine children. At the outbreak of the Revolution he was a colonel of the 2nd Pennsylvania
Battalion, and on July 4, 1777, was elected brigadier general of
the 53rd Battalion. When the British occupied Philadelphia, the
Continental Congress met in York and Lancaster, Pennsylvania.
Mr. Roberdeau was a delegate to the Continental Congress, and
on September 30, 1777, John Adams spent the night at the Roberdeaus' home. Later Col. Roberdeau became seriously ill, and Mrs.
Roberdeau nursed him. Then she became ill and died.
    On December 2, 1778, Roberdeau married Jane Mulligan of
Philadelphia and established a lead mine in western Pennsylvania
at his own expense to provide bullets for the army, and he built
Fort Roberdeau to protect the mine. (BA; DB)

ROBERTSON, CHARLOTTE REEVES   TN
of Nashville. She was born in North Carolina on January 2, 1751,
and later married Gen. Reeves Robertson. Prior to the Revolution
two of her sons were murdered by Indians, so she trained mastiffs
to attack. When she learned the enemy was about to attack Fort
Nashborough on April 2, 1781, she rode on horseback with her
baby son Felix, with the mastiffs following, to warn the American
army there. Mrs. Robertson encouraged the mastiffs to attack
a party of Indians who were trying to steal the soldiers' horses,
and the Indians fled in panic. Her husband, known as the Father
of Tennessee, was the founder of Nashville. She died in 1843.
(EW; HS)
    Charlotte's efforts are memorialized in a mural on the wall
of the governor's office in Nashville, where she is pictured lying
majestically across the Cumberland Bluffs in determined protection
of the settlement. (Submitted by William Thomas Haywood, Columbia,
TN)

ROGERS, MARY LARABEE   CT
of New London. She married John Rogers who was born there
on July 1, 1748. He was a mariner on the brigantine Rising States
with twenty guns and a hundred men commanded by Capt. James

Thompson. In June 1777 this vessel was captured by the British vessel Terrible, and on June 14, 1777, Rogers was committed to the Fortun Prison at Gosport, near Portsmouth, England. Later he escaped. After he returned to America he served on the privateer Oliver Cromwell, which was commanded by Capt. Timothy Parker. On June 5, 1779, this vessel was captured by the British and the crew was imprisoned. (CN; FP) When the British raided New London, Mary's property was burned (CAR, 1:63j, 95f) She was a Western Lands Grantee.

ROSS, BETSY GRISCOM   PA
the daughter of Rebecca James and Samuel Griscom, she was born on January 1, 1752, in Philadelphia. On November 4, 1773, she eloped with John Ross, the son of the Rev. Aeneas Ross of New Castle, Delaware, to Gloucester, New Jersey, where they were married. He enlisted in the militia, and was killed on January 21, 1776, by an explosion of gunpowder on the wharf where he was working.

The Pennsylvania Navy Board on May 29, 1777, paid her for making ships' flags. Betsy Ross was a seamstress and also ran an upholstery shop. On June 15, 1777, she married Joseph Ashburn, and they had two daughters. On December 7, 1780, he boarded the privateer brigantine Patty as first mate, and in 1781 he commanded the Lion. Ashburn was captured by the British, and on August 31, 1781, he was committed to the Mill Prison near Plymouth, England, where he died in 1782.

A fellow prisoner, John Claypoole, who was released by the British, brought the news of Joseph's death to Betsy Ross Ashburn. They were married on May 8, 1783, and had five daughters. Capt. Claypoole died on August 3, 1817. In 1870 Betsy Ross's grandson told the story that Gen. George Washington and a secret committee visited her upholstery shop and asked her to design a flag for the Continental Army. This story is traditional and has never been proved, but she did make flags for the Pennsylvania Navy in 1777, a patriotic act. Betsy Ross Claypoole died on January 30, 1836. (CN; DB)

RUDDELL, ELIZABETH BOWMAN   KY
of Ruddell's Station. She was the wife of Capt. Isaac Ruddell (1738-1812), who served with Col. George Rogers Clark in the American capture of the British post of Kaskaskia (now in Illinois) on the evening of July 4, 1778. Capt. Ruddell established Ruddell's Station in 1779 on the eastern bank of the south fork of the Licking River.

In 1780 a military force of six hundred Canadians and Indians under the British Col. Bird, accompanied by six cannons, made an incursion into Kentucky (previously part of Virginia). Since the Americans were overwhelmed by such a superior force, Capt. Ruddell surrendered his stockade on June 22, 1780. The British and Indians also took Martin's Station. The men, women, and children from both stations were taken to Niagara and held as prisoners

II: SELECTED BIOGRAPHIES   167

for from three to five years. Capt. Ruddell, his wife Elizabeth, two sons, and three daughters were captured and marched northward. They arrived in Montreal on October 4, 1782, and were then taken to Quebec. The Ruddells were released in 1783. (CH; HP)

RUSH, JULIA STOCKTON   PA
of Philadelphia. The daughter of Richard Stockton of Princeton, New Jersey, on January 11, 1776, she married Dr. Benjamin Rush. In 1776 Dr. Rush was elected a member of the Continental Congress and was a signer of the Declaration of Independence. They had thirteen children, of whom six sons and three daughters reached maturity.

Mrs. Rush was an active member of the ladies' relief association for the welfare of the American soldiers. (Pennsylvania Gazette, June 12, 1780)

RUTGERS, ELIZABETH   NY
of New York City. She owned and operated a brewery on the north side of Maiden Lane. Mrs. Rutgers was a dedicated patriot. In September 1776 when the British occupied New York, Mrs. Rutgers followed the American army across the Hudson River into New Jersey. The British military authorities seized her brewery and ran it for two years. Then they licensed it to Joshua Waddington, a hated Tory, who operated the brewery until March 1783.

In October 1779 the New York legislature enacted the Confiscation Act, which provided for forfeiture and sale of the estates of the Loyalists, and in March 1783 the Trespass Act, which provided redress for any American whose property was occupied by any person other than the legal owner while within British lines, and gave the legal owner the right to sue such occupant for damages. The British evacuated New York City on November 25, 1783, and in 1784 Mrs. Rutgers sued Waddington under the Trespass Act demanding rent payments for her property for the period of the British occupation.

The case was heard on August 7, 1784, before the Mayor's Court in New York City, and Mrs. Rutgers was represented by Egbert Benson, the state attorney general, and Waddington by Alexander Hamilton, who called down upon himself the outrage of the public since Waddington was the most hated Loyalist in the city.

Hamilton took the case to make a point of law. The litigation, called Rutgers v. Waddington, has become entrenched in American constitutional law. Hamilton pointed out that under international law, and customs and usage of nations in warfare, a commanding general can seize property for the use of his army. But was a brewery essential to his men? Hamilton also claimed that under the peace treaty with Britain all claims for damages arising out of the war were renounced, and thus the Trespass Act was null and void, since federal acts took precedence over state laws. The public was enraged, but Alexander Hamilton established a cornerstone of American constitutional law, contending that state and local courts had no jurisdiction to contradict federal laws and treaties.

On August 27, 1784, Mayor James Duane handed down a compromise decision, granting Mrs. Rutgers compensation for only part of the four-year period claimed, avoiding the constitutional arguments presented by Hamilton, but in doing so technically agreeing that Hamilton was right.

Mrs. Rutgers suffered hardships during the Revolutionary War and was a victim of constitutional law. (CA)

RUTLEDGE, HENRIETTA MIDDLETON   SC
of Charleston. On March 1, 1774, she married Edward Rutledge, and they had three children. He was a signer of the Declaration of Independence.

Mr. Rutledge was captured when the British took Charleston on May 12, 1780, and held in the State House in Saint Augustine, Florida, along with Thomas Heyward, Jr., and Arthur Middleton, two other signers of the Declaration of Independence. They were released in 1781. Mrs. Rutledge, a patriotic woman, suffered during his absence and died later. On October 28, 1792, Rutledge married Mary Shubrick Eveleigh, a widow. (FG)

RUTLEDGE, SARAH HEXT   SC
of Charleston. She was the wife of Dr. John Rutledge. Sarah was a widow by age twenty-seven with seven children to raise. Her eldest son, John, married Elizabeth Grimke in 1763 and had ten children. John served as governor of South Carolina from 1779 to 1782. Another son, Edward Rutledge, was a signer of the Declaration of Independence.

When the British occupied Charleston in 1780, Mrs. Rutledge was arrested at her plantation home and confined in Charleston. Her manor house was plundered and sequestered by the British. She was born in 1724 and died in 1792. (DAR)

S

ST. CLAIR, PHOEBE BAYARD   PA
of Westmoreland County. She was the daughter of Balthazar Bayard and a niece of Governor James Bowdoin of Massachusetts. On May 15, 1760, Phoebe married Lt. Arthur St. Clair, who served in the French and Indian War. They had seven children. She received Ŀ14,000 from the Bowdoin estate, and her husband purchased 4,000 acres in the Ligonier Valley in Pennsylvania with the money. At the outbreak of the Revolutionary War, her husband was made a major general.

Gen. and Mrs. St. Clair advanced their own funds to support the army during the war and were never repaid. Gen. St. Clair died in 1818 at Chestnut Ridge, now Greensburg, Pennsylvania. (GP)

II: SELECTED BIOGRAPHIES 169

SALISBURY, ABIGAIL   RI
of Barrington. Abigail was born on May 26, 1738. She married
George Salisbury on March 12, 1761, in Warren. Apparently they
had four sons and one daughter. In 1775 her husband was a sergeant in Capt. Thomas Allen's Company. Later he was a sergeant
of the guard at Rumstick Point and served to the end of the war.
Abigail loved to knit, and during the Revolutionary War she knitted
socks for the entire guard. (Thomas W. Bicknell, A History of
Barrington, 1898) Abigail died on August 30, 1839, aged 101 years
and three months. Abigail and George are buried in Prince's Hill
Cemetery in Barrington. (Submitted by Sally P. Small, Barrington,
RI)

SANDRIDGE, ELIZABETH GRAVES   VA
of Spotsylvania. She was born there on February 14, 1720. Elizabeth married William Sandridge, Jr. (or Sandidge), and she performed a patriotic public service. Elizabeth died on January 6,
1826, in Green County, Kentucky. She is listed as a patriot in
the DAR Patriot Index. (Submitted by Susie Price Steele, Birmingham, AL) Mrs. Sandridge supplied provisions for the army in
Virginia during the Revolutionary War. (VR Court Booklet, p. 16)

SCHREIBER, REBECCA RACHEL   NY
of Tyrone County. She was the wife of Steffan Schreiber. In
1779 the Indians attacked and left the settlement in ruins. All
men, women, and children were murdered except four--Rebecca
and her six-year-old daughter Elizabeth, son Abraham, and infant
daughter Maria. These four were carried off by the attackers.
Rebecca and the children were taken northward. Rebecca tried
to escape with her daughter Maria, but was drowned in a river.
Elizabeth was adopted by an Indian tribe and taken to Canada.
For years Steffan tried to find his wife and children, to no avail.
    Finally in 1783 an English officer seeing a blonde hair child
with the Indians knew she was a captive. So he purchased Elizabeth for thirty gallons of rum. Elizabeth was finally sent to New
York and her father was notified. Steffan recognized his daughter
and embraced her. (DAR Magazine, November 1981)

SCHUYLER, CATHERINE VAN RENSSELAER   NY
of Albany. The daughter of John Van Rensselaer of Claverack,
she was married on September 17, 1755, to Capt. Philip Schuyler.
They had fourteen children. Three sons and five daughters survived infancy. On June 15, 1775, Schuyler was appointed a major
general in the Continental Army. Mrs. Schuyler lived on a farm
near Saratoga, New York, and in 1777 with her own hands she
set fire to the grain fields of their estate in an effort to defeat
Gen. Burgoyne. After the British general surrendered at the
Battle of Saratoga, Mrs. Schuyler graciously had him over for dinner.
    On April 6, 1782, from his headquarters at Newburgh, New
York, Gen. Washington wrote to Catherine Schuyler: "Madam.

I have been honored with your favor of the 2nd Isnt. as it is your wish to retain the old guard in preference to the New one ordered, I will direct Genl. Clinton to suffer them to remain till further orders from me, or till circumstances may render it necessary to recall them. Mrs. Washington joins me in best respects to you, Mrs. [Elizabeth Schuyler] Hamilton." (FW) Mrs. Schuyler died in 1803. Their daughter Elizabeth married Alexander Hamilton.

SCHUYLER, MARGARET   NY
of Albany. She was the daughter of Gen. Philip John Schuyler. In August 1781 a band of Tories, Canadians, and Indians led by John Waltermeyer attacked the Schuyler home with the intention of kidnapping the general. Immediately the general went into the bedroom to obtain his musket. While ascending a staircase, Margaret was met by Waltermeyer who demanded, "Wench! Where is your master?" Margaret, undaunted, exclaimed, "Gone to alarm the town." Meanwhile the Tories were plundering and bagging the silver and other valuables in the house. Waltermeyer feared that Margaret could be right, when Gen. Schuyler called from a window, "Come on, my brave fellows, surround the house and secure the villains who are plundering." Although no men were nearby, Waltermeyer and his men, in great fear, fled the house into the woods. (CD)

SCUDDER, ISABELLA ANDERSON   NJ
of Freehold. The daughter of Kenneth Anderson of Monmouth County, she was married on March 23, 1752, to Dr. Nathaniel Scudder. They had three sons and two daughters. Dr. Scudder practiced in Freehold, Manalapan, and other sections of Monmouth County. In 1776 Dr. Scudder was speaker of the New Jersey legislature and colonel of the First Monmouth County Regiment. During the British occupation of Freehold his property was damaged. He was a delegate to the Continental Congress, 1777-1779.
    Mrs. Scudder was active in the ladies' relief association for the welfare of the American soldiers. (New Jersey Gazette, July 4, 1780) Col. Scudder was killed on October 16, 1781, when some Loyalists from Sandy Hook, New Jersey, landed at Black Point, near Shrewsbury, New Jersey.

SEARLE, ANN SMITH   PA
of Philadelphia. In 1762 Ann, or "Nancy," married James Searle of New York City, a merchant. Shortly afterward they moved to Philadelphia. In 1775 he was a lieutenant colonel in the Pennsylvania militia and was elected to the Continental Congress in 1778.
    Mrs. Searle was active in the ladies' relief association for the welfare of the American soldiers. (Pennsylvania Gazette, June 12, 1780) She died in 1781.

SERGEANT, MARGARET SPENCER   NJ
of Princeton. The daughter of the Rev. Elihu Spencer, a Presbyterian minister in Trenton, she was the wife of Jonathan Dickinson

II: SELECTED BIOGRAPHIES

Sergeant, an attorney serving in the Continental Congress. When the British army was nearing Princeton in December 1776, Mrs. Sergeant, her infant child, and her sister, fled the town and crossed the Delaware River into Pennsylvania. They found haven in Saint Georges, Delaware, where her father had previously served as a pastor. (DD)

SEVIER, CATHERINE SHERRILL   TN
of the Watauga Settlement, Elizabethton. She was born on August 3, 1755. While living at the Fort Lee stockade, she was known as "Bonny Kate." One day in 1779 she was outside the fort when the Indians attacked. She ran to the fort, climbed the walls, and fell into the arms of Capt. John Sevier (1745-1815), known as "Nolichucky Jack." Sevier's first wife, Sarah Hawkins, bore him five sons who served in the War for Independence. After her death, John Sevier married Catherine.

After her marriage, she made clothes for her colonel husband and for his five sons--a patriotic act. They all participated in the Battle of King's Mountain, Tennessee. Later her husband became the first governor of Tennessee. Catherine died on October 2, 1836. There is a Bonny Kate Chapter of the Daughters of the American Revolution in Knoxville, Tennessee. (EW; HS; DAR Magazine, July 1921)

SHARPE, JEMIMA ALEXANDER   NC
of Mecklenburg County. She was the daughter of Margaret McKnith and James Alexander of Cecil County, Maryland. In 1748 Jemima married John Sharpe of Lancaster, Pennsylvania. They emigrated to Mecklenburg County. Jemima had six children. Her husband died in 1759. Jemima, Mrs. Polk, and another woman carried food, clothing, and medicine to the British prison ships in Charleston Harbor in 1781 to comfort the American prisoners there. The Booneville, Missouri, chapter of the Daughters of the American Revolution is named in her honor. (GP)

SHATTUCK, SARAH HARTWELL   MA
of Groton was born on March 19, 1738. She married Job Shattuck. After Col. Prescott's warning of 1775, Mrs. Shattuck together with other women defended the Nashua River Bridge with muskets and pitchforks. They captured Capt. Leonard Whiting, a notorious Tory, who was carrying dispatches to the British in Boston. (For further details, see Mrs. David Wright, below; CD; DAR) She died on May 5, 1798.

SHAW, LUCRETIA HARRIS   CT
of New London. She was born in 1737 and married Nathaniel Shaw, Jr. Gen. Washington was entertained by Mrs. Shaw, and on April 9, 1776, he spent the night in her home. She frequently entertained, and among her distinguished guests were also Gen. Nathaniel Greene, Nathan Hale, and Governor Jonathan Trumbull of Connecticut. During the Revolutionary War her home was used for important conferences and meetings.

Mrs. Shaw turned her home into a hospital for the sick and wounded and nursed the American soldiers. Unfortunately she fell ill of typhus herself and died in 1781. The New London chapter of the Daughters of the American Revolution is named in her honor. (CG)

SHELBY, SUSANNA HART   KY
of Boonesborough. She was the daughter of Sarah Simpson and Capt. Nathaniel Hart of Caswell County, North Carolina. Nathaniel Hart and his brothers David and Thomas (whose daughter married Henry Clay), with Col. Richard Henderson formed Henderson and Company, which purchased a large part of Kentucky from the Indians. They became proprietors of the "Colony of Transylvania in America." But the purchase was rendered null and void by the Virginia legislature. Later they paid the legislature Ł10 thousand for two hundred thousand acres.

The Harts moved to Kentucky in 1779 following Daniel Boone. On August 11, 1782, Capt. Hart was killed and scalped by Indians. In 1784 Susanna married Col. Isaac Shelby (1750-1826), and they had ten children, all of whom reached maturity. The Frankfort, Kentucky, chapter of the Daughters of the American Revolution is named in her honor. (GP)

SHELDON, MRS. SAMUEL   CT
of Litchfield. Gen. Washington on his return trip from Wethersfield, Connecticut, spent the night of May 24, 1781, at the Sheldons' tavern. Before leaving Fishkill, New York, on May 18, Gen. Washington wrote that Maj. Gen. Arthur St. Clair would command the army during Washington's absence at Wethersfield. (FW)

SHELL, ELIZABETH PETRIE   NY
of Herkimer. She was the wife of John Christian Shell and they had six sons. On August 6, 1781, when a band of Tories and Indians under Donald McDonald raided the blockhouse of the Shells, Elizabeth loaded the flintlocks for her husband and her sons. When the enemy put their flintlock muskets through loopholes, she smashed them with an ax. Finally the Tories and the Indians gave up the battle. (CD; FH)

SHEPHERD, CATHERINE VAN WINKLE   NJ
of Jersey City (formerly Hudson City). The daughter of Rachel Camneger and Lt. Jacob Van Winkle, she was born on June 1, 1763.

> From the steeple of the old church at South Bergen, she beheld the British fleet take possession of the city of New York, and not long after, she saw King George's army march past her father's house on its way to Philadelphia. About this time the British took possession of her father's house--converting it into an arsenal, and they made an attempt to hang her father, because he

would not disclose the whereabouts of money which he
was supposed to be possessed of. After swinging him
from a beam in the house, they left him for dead; but,
fortunately, the last spark had not fled, and his life was
saved by being cut down by the daughter who is the
subject of this notice. While the British were operating
in this vicinity, she performed one of those heroic acts
for which the women of those trying times were celebrated,
in carrying a message, under perilous circumstances,
to a section of the American army encamped at Belleville,
informing the commandant of a designed night attack upon
his forces by the British, and thus giving him time to
frustrate the designs. (Obituary, American Standard
[Jersey City], December 16, 1863)

The British occupied New York City on September 15, 1776,
so she was only thirteen years old when she saved the life of her
father and carried messages to the American army. On August
26, 1782, Catherine married George Shepherd who served in the
New Jersey Militia. Mrs. Shepherd died on December 5, 1863,
at the age of 100 years 6 months and 5 days. (Information from
Corrine E. Weis, Midland, TX)

SHERMAN, REBECCA PRESCOTT   CT
of New Milford. The daughter of Rebecca Minot and Benjamin Prescott of Salem, Massachusetts, she was born in 1743. She became
the second wife of Roger Sherman on May 12, 1763. Rebecca had
eight children of her own, and she raised the seven children of
Roger's first wife. During the Revolutionary War, according to
a niece, Rebecca traveled to help Betsy Ross make a flag. Later
she was chosen to make the first flag in the state of Connecticut,
assisted by Mrs. Oliver Wolcott, as officially recorded. Her husband was a signer of the Declaration of Independence. (GP)

SHIPPEN, ALICE LEE   PA
of Philadelphia. The daughter of Hannah Ludwell and Thomas Lee
of Westmoreland County, Virginia, she was the sister of Arthur,
Francis Lightfoot, and Richard Henry Lee. Sometime around 1760
she married Dr. William Shippen, Jr., of Philadelphia. When the
first Continental Congress met in Philadelphia in 1774, John Adams
had breakfast on September 3 with Dr. and Mrs. Shippen. In
his diary on that date John Adams wrote: "Mrs. Shippen is a
religious and a reasoning lady. She said she had often thought
that the people of Boston could not have behaved through their
trials with so much prudence and firmness at the same time, if
they had not been influenced by a superior power."

In 1778 Dr. Shippen was appointed director general of the
Continental Army hospital in New Jersey and of all the hospitals
on the west side of the Hudson River in New York. He was chief
of the medical department of the Continental Army until 1781.

Mrs. Shippen was active in the ladies' relief association for the welfare of the American soldiers. (Pennsylvania Gazette, June 12, 1780; supplied by William Handley, Philadelphia, PA)

SHIPPEN, MARGARET FRANCIS   PA
of Philadelphia. The daughter of Trench Francis, an attorney, she was married on November 29, 1753, to Edward Shippen, an attorney who worked in her father's office. They had nine children. Their daughter Margaret married Benedict Arnold.

On September 28, 1774, Col. George Washington dined at the Shippens' home, and later Washington conferred with John Adams and Col. Lee.

Edward Shippen was a Loyalist, but neutral, and Mrs. Shippen favored Gen. Washington. The Shippens were prominent in the social life of Philadelphia, and continued their friendship with Gen. Washington. (BA; BD)

SIBLEY, ANNA   NH
of Hopkinton. While her husband was serving at Fort William and Mary, she was pregnant with their third child. In spite of this, she managed to hoe three acres of corn on their farm. (Submitted by Dorothy Wilcox, Durham, NH)

SIDMAN, WIDOW   NY
of Ramapough (Ramapo). Samuel Sidman (Sydman) married a daughter of Isaac Van Duzer. He operated a tavern which stood on the Orange Turnpike, just south of Sloatsburg, and owned a large tract of land on the lower part of the Ramapo Pass which was called "Sidman's Clove." Mr. Sidman died early in the Revolutionary War, and the Widow Sidman continued to operate the tavern.

On November 11, 1778, a party of Tory Smith's gang plundered the homes of Ebenezer Erskine and Mrs. Sidman. Gen. Washington stopped at the Widow Sidman's tavern in June 1779 and also at Stephen Sloat's Inn, and a part of Washington's army camped on the Sidman lands. Mention of Sidman's Clove can be found in the Washington papers. (Suffern: Two Hundred Years, 1773-1973, Bicentennial Committee)

SILLIMAN, MARY FISH   CT
of Fairfield. The daughter of the Rev. Joseph Fish, she was born in 1736 in North Stonington, Connecticut. In 1758 she married the Rev. John Nagle, who died in 1767. She then became the second wife of Col. Gold Selleck Silliman in 1775.

During the Revolutionary War she hid the church communion silver in her home to prevent its being taken by the British. Mrs. Silliman died in 1818. The Mary Silliman Chapter of Bridgeport, Connecticut, of the Daughters of the American Revolution is named in her honor. (CG)

SIMMS, SARAH DICKINSON   NC
of Edgecombe County. The daughter of Mary Barnes and John Dickinson, her father, grandfather, and two brothers served in

II: SELECTED BIOGRAPHIES

the Continental Army. Sarah's mother died when Sarah was young. Once Sarah and her lover, Robert Simms, captured five Tories. In retaliation other Tories burned her home. Later Sarah married Robert Simms (1755-1815). The Newman, Georgia, Chapter of the Daughters of the American Revolution is named in her honor. (DAR; GP)

SIMPSON, MARGARET MURRAY   PA
of Bristol. The daughter of Rebecca McLean and James Murray, she was born on February 2, 1756, in Paxtang Township, Lancaster County, Pennsylvania. On May 7, 1776, she married John Simpson, a blacksmith. They had several children. In August 1775 he was commissioned as a second lieutenant in the 4th Battalion of the Lancaster County Associators and served in the 1776 Jersey campaign. In 1777 he was stationed at the Continental smithshop in Bristol.
     During the occupation of Philadelphia by British troops, Mrs. Simpson and her neighbors supplied food and clothing for the American soldiers at Valley Forge. In 1793 the Simpsons moved to Huntington, Pennsylvania, where Mrs. Simpson died on April 27, 1826. (EP)

SIMS, ISABELLA   SC
was the wife of Capt. Charles Sims, and they resided on the Tyger River. Just after the fall of Charleston on May 12, 1780, the forces of Col. John Thomas were surprised by Tory and British soldiers at Fairforest Creek in the Spartanburg District, and an engagement ensued. The Americans lost the battle, and when Mrs. Sims learned of the disaster, she proceeded to the area and for several days nursed the wounded American soldiers. The American troops were imprisoned in the 96th District prison.
     While the captain was away in 1781, her house was plundered by the Tories. When all the men had left except one, she ordered the remaining thief to leave, but he refused. So she broke his arm with a pole and immediately he departed from her house. (CD; EW)
     Later the Sims moved to the York District of South Carolina, and then to Virginia. (EW) She was born in 1750 and died in 1818. (DAR)

SINGLETON, SARAH (SALLY) CRAIG   KY
of Craig's Station. She was born about 1747 and was a sister of John Craig. On November 10, 1765, in Virginia, Sally Craig married Manoah Singleton. Together with the Hamptons and the Johnsons, they settled at Craig's Station, Kentucky, on Christmas Eve. After Craig's Station was burned, they moved to Bryan's Station. On August 15, 1782, the Tories and Indians attacked. The fort was badly in need of water, so Jemima Johnson led Sally and the other women to the spring to obtain water, despite the presence of Indians--a very courageous act. They returned successfully with the much-needed water.

Later the Singletons settled near Keene in Jessamine County. Sally Singleton is listed as a patriot in the DAR Patriot Index. (Submitted by Sue M. Bogardus, Warsaw, KY)

SLOAT, MARRETJE VAN DEUSEN NY
of Suffern. She was the wife of Steven Sloat (or Slot), captain of the Orange County militia. Gen. Washington had his headquarters there on June 6/7, 1779. On this date Washington ordered the Pennsylvania division to take a position nearby and to send three or four hundred men into the pass of the mountain, at the crossroads of Haverstraw and Clove roads, to join Col. William Malcolm. The Virginia division was ordered to Smith's Tavern in Smith's Clove. (FW)

SLOCUMB, MARY HOOKS NC
of Goshen. She was born in Bertie, North Carolina, in 1760. Later the family moved to Duplin County, North Carolina. In 1775 Mary Hooks married Ezekiel Slocumb, the son of John Charles Slocumb of Goshen, and she lived there on the family plantation, which Ezekiel had inherited from his father.

In 1776 the Scotch Highlanders marched through North Carolina to join forces with Sir Henry Clinton at Cape Fear, but they encountered the American forces of colonels Lillington and Caswell at Moore's Creek on February 27, and a bloody battle ensued. Mrs. Slocumb had a dream that her husband was in danger, and so rode on horseback to the battlefield, following the well-marked trail of the troops. Before she located her husband, she gave water to the injured American soldiers and nursed them.

Meanwhile Mary's father married the widow of John Charles Slocumb. In 1781 the British Col. Tarleton occupied the plantation of the Slocumbs while Lt. Slocumb, Mary's husband, was nearby with a small force of men. Mary sent her slave, Big George, to carry a message of the British occupation to her husband and the men. Her husband and the men then attacked the plantation, and in the surprise the British colonel lost half of his men. Lt. Slocumb and his men then disappeared into the woods.

Mrs. Slocumb's son Jesse became a congressman. She died on March 6, 1836. Her name is also spelled Slocum. In the 1940s a monument was erected on the battlefield to her memory. Mrs. Slocumb and her husband are buried in the Moore's Creek Battleground near Wilmington, North Carolina. (EW)

SLOPER, HANNAH NEWELL WOODRUFF CT
of Southington was the wife of Capt. Daniel Sloper, who commanded the company from Southington in the Revolutionary War. Six members of Hannah Sloper's family served in that company, a great sacrifice during time of trial. The local chapter of the Daughters of the American Revolution is named after her. (CG) When the British raided New Haven, her property was destroyed. (CAR, 1:63d, 91g) She was a Western Lands Grantee.

II: SELECTED BIOGRAPHIES

SMART, SUSANNAH BARNETT   NC
of Mecklenburg County. The daughter of Ann Spratt and John Barnett (1717-1804), her mother established a camp at Clems Branch to care for the refugees after the fall of Charleston, South Carolina, on May 12, 1780. After the Battle of Waxhaws, Susannah and her mother fed and cared for the soldiers. Afterward Susannah married George W. Smart. (GP)

SMITH, DEBORAH KNAPP   CT
of Roxbury. She was born on September 2, 1739, and married Amos Smith (1747-1823). Her husband served as a captain during the Revolutionary War, and Deborah guarded the British prisoners her husband had captured. Once Capt. Smith captured a lieutenant of the Continental Army who had deserted to the British, and the prisoner was put in the charge of Deborah. A band of rebels came to the house, incensed that the man had deserted, took the prisoner, and hanged him to a tree. Deborah insisted that the men cut him down and return him to her care. Deborah's courage and firmness impressed the men, so they cut down the prisoner. Later he was court-martialed and hanged by the Americans. A chapter of the Daughters of the American Revolution in Washington, D.C., was named in her honor. (DAR; GP)

SMITH, SARAH   NY
of New York City. She was the widow of John Smith, a cabinet-maker. After the American soldiers were captured at Fort Washington in 1776 they were imprisoned at various locations in New York City. Mrs. Smith visited the various jails and passed out food to the prisoners. One of these prisoners was Robert Keith, a chaplain, who recorded these events later while on board the vessel Confederacy at Martinico on December 19, 1779.

    Chaplain Keith recorded that Mrs. Smith told prisoners that the day might come when they would guard the enemy who were guarding them now. A guard overheard her and locked Mrs. Smith in another room, saying that was the fittest place for a damned rebel. After her release from the jail, she canvassed the houses of her friends seeking money to buy bread for the prisoners, but was arrested again and questioned by the mayor and aldermen. They asked on what authority she acted, and she replied, "By authority of the word of God."

    They turned her over to a British general, and she gave him the same answer. The general banned Mrs. Smith from the city; she was allowed only to take her bed and wearing apparel with her. Mrs. Smith left New York City in 1777 and resided in Clarkstown, near Tappan Bay, where she lived in poverty. (John Jay, "Letter Books," Columbia University Library)

SMITH, SUSANNAH BAYARD   PA
of Philadelphia. The daughter of Col. Peter Bayard of Maryland, she married Jonathan Smith, a merchant. After his marriage he

took Bayard as his middle name. He served as a lieutenant colonel in the militia. On September 30, 1774, John Adams and other delegates to the First Continental Congress dined in the Smiths' home. On this day Adams introduced a series of resolutions in support of Massachusetts's resistance to royal authority. In 1777 Mr. Smith was elected to the Continental Congress. Their son, Samuel Harrison Smith, was the founder of the National Intelligencer in Washington, D.C.

Mrs. Smith was an active member of the ladies' relief association for the welfare of the American soldiers. (Pennsylvania Gazette, June 12, 1780; BA; BD)

SMITH, MRS. WILLIAM   MD
of Baltimore. Her husband became a member of the Continental Congress in February 1777. On February 23, 1777, John Adams dined with the Smiths, along with Elbridge Gerry and some gentlemen from Maryland. John Adams wrote in his diary:

> This Mr. Smith is a grave, solid Gentleman, a Presbyterian by Profession--a very different Man from the most of those We have heretofore had from Maryland.
> The Manners of Maryland are somehat peculiar. They have but few Merchants. They are chiefly Planters and Farmers. The Planters are those who raise Tobacco and the Farmers such as raise Wheat, etc. The Lands are cultivated, and all Sorts of Trades are exercised by Negroes, or by transported Convicts, which has occasioned the Planters and Farmers to assume the Title of Gentlemen, and they hold these Negroes and Convicts, that is all labouring People and Tradesman, in such Contempt, that they think themselves a distinct order of Beings. Hence they never will suffer their Sons to labour or learn any trade, but they bring them up in idleness or what is worse in Horse Racing, Cock fighting, and Card Playing. (BA)

SNYDER, ELIZABETH CATHERINE MANN   NY
of Schoharie. She was born there in 1722 and married Capt. Peter Snyder in 1741. Two of her sons and two sons-in-law served in the Revolutionary War. During the Battle of Fort Schoharie in September 1780, Mrs. Snyder passed to the American soldiers biscuits and rum laced with gunpowder, as the old records state, "to divert them from fear."

Peter Snyder later was presented with a cannonball taken from the rafters of a church there, acknowledging the bravery of his wife. She died in 1790.

The Dunellen, Middlesex County, New Jersey, chapter of the Daughters of the American Revolution is named in her honor. (DAR; DC)

SPRINGFIELD, LAODICES LANGSTON   SC
of the Spartanburg area. "Dicey" was born on May 14, 1766, the

II: SELECTED BIOGRAPHIES

daughter of Sarah Bennett and Solomon Langston in Granville County, North Carolina. Later the family moved to the Laurens District, near the Spartanburg County line. One day in 1781 Dicey Langston learned that a company of Loyalists, called the Bloody Scouts, were about to attack the rebels on the other side of the Tyger River. Dicey walked through the countryside and woods to warn her brother and the other rebels of their imminent danger. The rebel Americans left the area, and when the Loyalists arrived, no one was there.

In 1783 Dicey married Capt. Thomas Springfield (1766-1845) of Greenville, South Carolina, and they had twenty-two children! About 1793 they moved to Greenville. She died there on May 23, 1837, leaving 140 living descendants. (DAR Magazine, July 1976; EW; HS)

STARK, ELIZABETH PAGE   NH
of Manchester. She was born on February 16, 1737, and married Maj. Gen. John Stark (1728-1822), who called her Molly. As a colonel of a New Hampshire regiment, he distinguished himself at the Battle of Bunker Hill in 1775. Elizabeth Stark was in camp with her husband during the evacuation of Boston by the British on March 17, 1776. Gen. Washington ordered Col. Stark to capture a battery at Copp's Hill. Before the battle, Col. Stark instructed Molly to mount her horse and upon his signal to ride into the countryside to spread the alarm, which she did. Her home became a hospital for wounded men and those ill with smallpox. This kindly, modest, patriotic woman from the backwoods is held in affectionate and admiring remembrance by the Daughters of the American Revolution in New Hampshire. She died on June 29, 1814. (DAR Magazine, July 1921) There is a Molly Stark Chapter of the Daughters of the American Revolution in Manchester, New Hampshire. (Submitted by Mrs. Philip Wilcox, Durham, and Ruby M. Towle, Farmington, NH)

STEEL, KATHARINE FISHER   SC
was born in 1725 in Pennsylvania. In 1745 Katharine married Thomas Steel, and they moved to South Carolina. They settled on Fishing Creek about a mile from the Catawba River. Soon John Gaston built a house about a mile away on the opposite side of Fishing Creek. When the Cherokee Indians became troublesome, Mr. Steel turned his home into a blockhouse known as Steel's fort. At the first sign of danger, when men were fighting the Indians, the women and children would assemble in Steel's fort.

Katharine, who was an expert shot, was placed in charge when the men were away, and she became known as "Witty Kate of the Fort." In 1763 her husband went on a trading expedition and was killed by Indians. Kate was left with two sons and three daughters to raise. In 1775 her son John was captain of a company from Chester fighting the Indians and later at the Battle of Fort Moultrie on Sullivans Island. Seven of the Gaston boys fought with him during the siege of Savannah, which the British then occupied, on December 29, 1778. After the fall of Charleston on

May 12, 1780, the American soldiers were discouraged. But Kate's son John rallied the men to action. Katharine called on her youngest son, then seventeen, to join the war against the British--a patriotic action. She died in 1785. (GP)

STEELE, ELIZABETH MAXWELL   NC
was born in 1733 and married Robert Gillespie. After his death, she married William Steele. Elizabeth lived in Salisbury County. During the dark days of the war, Gen. Nathaniel Greene stayed at her home. In despair, he cried out to her, "All is lost, my troops are discouraged. I am without money or friends; unless help comes we are lost."

Mrs. Steele handed the general two bags of money and said, "Take them, general, it is all I have, but my country needs them more than I." The next day the general left in high spirits with the money, and continued his campaign, resulting in the success at the Battle of Guilford Courthouse on March 15, 1781. She died on November 22, 1780. Mrs. Steele is listed as a patriot in the DAR Patriot Index. (DAR Magazine, July 1921)

STEPHENS, MARY BOWMAN   VA
of Frederick County. She was born on November 19, 1735, the daughter of Mary Hite and George Bowman. She was named Anna Maria, but later took the name Mary. The Bowmans often entertained George Washington in their home (see Mary Hite Bowman, above). At age sixteen, in 1752, Mary Bowman married Lawrence Stephens who was thirteen years older than she. This apparently caused a rift in the family. The Bowmans had six sons and two daughters. Unfortunately Lawrence died in 1776.

Mrs. Stephens supplied products for the Continental Army and the militia. This is evidenced by a receipt for seven thousand pounds of hay for which she was paid eighteen pence per hundredweight (5 pounds, 5 shillings), dated January 7, 1782, signed by Richard Eakin, Commissary, Frederick County. (Book 2:208-210)

Mary had four sons, four brothers, two sons-in-law, two brothers-in-law, and five uncles who fought for American independence. Since she furnished supplies for the army during the war, she was named a patriot and listed in the DAR Patriot Index. Mrs. Stephens died in 1820. (Submitted by Geraldine Sanders Smith, Saint Louis, MO)

STILWELL, REBECCA   NJ
of Egg Harbor. She was the daughter of Nicholas Stilwell and the granddaughter of John Stilwell of Town Bank, Cape May, New Jersey. In 1748 Nicholas Stilwell bought a plantation at Beesley's Point. Rebecca and her sister, Sarah Stilwell Grigging, were American patriots, and their brother Capt. Nicholas Stilwell, Jr., served in the Revolutionary War.

The Stilwell home was situated on the southern shore of Egg Harbor Bay. One morning a British sloop appeared there. Since

II: SELECTED BIOGRAPHIES

no men were at home, and the family had a small cannon on the property, Rebecca fired the cannon. The sloop sailed away.

The Stilwell house has been rebuilt and expanded several times, but the kitchen of the original house is still in use. (Submitted by Gladys J. Kuhlmann, Linwood, NJ; DC)

STIRLING, LADY (SARAH LIVINGSTON ALEXANDER)   NJ
of Basking Ridge. The sister of Governor William Livingston of New Jersey, she married William Alexander, Lord Stirling, and was known as Lady Stirling for the rest of her life. On November 7, 1775, William Alexander was made a colonel of the 1st New Jersey Regiment. In January 1776, assisted by forty volunteers, he captured the British transport Blue Mountain Valley at Sandy Hook. On March 1, 1776, he was commissioned a brigadier general in the Continental Army. He held Brooklyn, New York, in August 1776, but was forced to surrender and was captured. After his exchange, he fought at Trenton, New Jersey, and was made a major general in 1777. He served with distinction at the Battle of Monmouth.

Lady Stirling was active in the ladies' association for the relief of the American soldiers, and the New Jersey Gazette of July 4, 1780, included her name as a major contributor.

STITES, MARY PREDMORE   NJ
was the daughter of Ruth Bayles and John Predmore of New Brunswick, New Jersey. Mary married Dr. Hezekiah Stites of Cranbury, New Jersey, who served as president of the Medical Society of New Jersey from 1775 through its dormant years until 1783. They had no children.

Col. Alexander Hamilton had his headquarters at the home of Dr. and Mrs. Stites at 53 South Main Street, Cranbury, on June 25, 1778. On this date he wrote to Lafayette: "We are just informed that General Scott passed by Hooper's Tavern, five miles from Allen Town, this afternoon at 5 o'clock." Gen. Washington had his headquarters here on June 26, 1778. (FW)

Mrs. Stites died on April 14, 1794, and on March 13, 1795, Dr. Stites sold their house to Commo. Thomas Truxton. On June 12, 1976, the Francis Hopkinson Chapter of the Daughters of the American Revolution placed a new marker on the graves of Dr. and Mrs. Stites. (Information from Mary Ellen Malague, Cranbury, NJ)

STOCKTON, ANNIS BOUDINOT   NJ
of Princeton. The daughter of Catherine Williams and Elias Boudinot of Princeton, she married Richard Stockton, an attorney. He was a signer of the Declaration of Independence. In the fall of 1776 the British army invaded New Jersey, and Mrs. Stockton and her children fled to the home of John Covenhoven in Monmouth County, where she was joined by her husband. But after being betrayed by Loyalists, they were taken to Perth Amboy and confined in jail. Meanwhile their estate in Princeton was pillaged. Later Mr. and Mrs. Stockton were taken to New York City and imprisoned

there. Finally released in 1777, Mr. Stockton was in poor health. He died at Princeton on February 28, 1781.

Mrs. Stockton was active in the ladies' relief association for the welfare of the American soldiers. (New Jersey Gazette, July 4, 1780) The Stocktons had two sons and four daughters. Their daughter Julia married Dr. Benjamin Rush.

Mrs. Stockton sent a pastoral to Gen. Washington, and on July 22, 1782, he thanked her for it: "Madam. Your favor of the 17th, conveying to me your Pastoral on the subject of Lord Cornwallis's Capture, has given me great satisfaction. Had you known the pleasure that it would have communicated, I flatter myself your diffidence would not have delayed it till this time. Amidst all the compliments, which have been made on this occasion, be assured Madam, that the agreeable manner, and the very pleasing Sentiments in which yours is conveyed, have affected my Mind with the most lively sensations of Joy and satisfaction." (FW)

STODDARD, EUNICE SANFORD   CT
of Woodbury. About 1767 she married Nathan Stoddard, one of fourteen children of Olive Curtis and Gideon Stoddard. Eunice and Nathan (1742-1777) had seven children. In 1775 Nathan was commissioned an ensign in the 13th Connecticut Regiment. Later, while in the 4th Regiment, stationed at Fort Ticonderoga, he was captured and taken prisoner to Quebec. Nathan managed to escape and returned to Woodbury. He became a captain, and in April and May of 1777 he participated in the engagements near Danbury, Connecticut, and Horse Neck, New York. Later Nathan joined the army of Gen. Washington and was stationed on Mud Island, Pennsylvania, opposite Fort Mifflin on the Delaware River.

On November 15, 1777, the men of the blockhouses on Mud Island were attacked by six British ships of war, with one vessel mounting twenty-four-pounders. The blockhouses were reduced to rubble, and Capt. Stoddard was instantly killed by a cannon shot which severed his head from his body.

Mrs. Stoddard was left with one son, Nathan Ashbel, aged nine, and six young daughters to raise. Nathan Stoddard's uncle, Eliakim Stoddard, was an ancestor of Gen. William Tecumseh Sherman. (Edward Deacon, Some of the Ancestors of Rodman Stoddard, 1894; submitted by Irene Damon MacGregor Bowron of Bradenton, FL)

STOKES, ELIZABETH   VA
of Lunenburg County. She married Young Stokes, and they had four sons and six daughters, but one daughter died young. Her husband died in 1770.

Mrs. Stokes supplied beef and bacon for the Continental Army, which is certified in the Public Service Claims in the files at the Virginia State Library. (Lunenburg County, pages 203 #1, 203 #2, and 275 #12) Elizabeth Stokes died on December 23, 1789. (Submitted by Dr. Dixon A. Barr, Richmond, KY)

II: SELECTED BIOGRAPHIES

STORY, ANN   VT
of Salisbury. She was born in 1725 in Connecticut, and in 1742 she married Amos Story of Norwich, Connecticut. In 1774 she moved to Salisbury, Vermont, with her husband and four children. After they built a log cabin and cleared the land, Amos was killed by a falling tree. During the Revolutionary War her home became a refuge for the Green Mountain Boys, heroes of the capture of the British-held forts at Crown Point and Ticonderoga on Lake Champlain in 1775.

Near her home, Ann found a small cave on the bank of Otter Creek, and she excavated the earth until she made it large enough for herself and her family to protect themselves from the Indians and Tories, since she was known to be an ardent patriot protecting American soldiers. In the summer of 1776 she saw her log cabin burned to the ground. In 1777 she moved to Rutland, Vermont, to a farm near the Pittsfield line.

In 1792 Ann Story married Benjamin Smalley, who died in 1808. Then in 1812 she married Capt. Stephen Goodrich and lived in Middlebury until she died on April 5, 1817. There is an Ann Story Chapter of the Daughters of the American Revolution in Rutland, Vermont. (GP)

STOW, FREELOVE BALDWIN   CT
of Milford. The granddaughter of Col. Samuel Eells of the Colonial Wars, she was born in 1728. Later she married Stephen Stow of Middletown, Connecticut. Mrs. Stow gave her husband and four sons for the Revolutionary War. On January 1, 1777, some two hundred American soldiers suffering from smallpox were cast from a British ship onto the beaches of Milford. They swarmed into the home of Mr. and Mrs. Stow. Nobody would care for them except Stephen and Freelove Stow, who turned their home into a hospital. Her husband died of smallpox in 1777 after caring for the men, and forty-six of the soldiers died also. Mrs. Stow died in 1805.

The Milford chapter of the Daughters of the American Revolution is named in her honor. In 1870 the Connecticut Legislature inscribed a monument praising Mr. Stow for his heroism. (CG)

STRONG, MRS.   CT
of Litchfield. On his return trip from Newport, Rhode Island, to Fishkill, New York, on March 19, 1781, Gen. Washington spent the night at the home of the Widow Strong. (FW)

SUFFERN, MARY MEYERS   NY
of Suffern. She was the wife of John Suffern (1741-1836), who had emigrated from County Antrim, Ireland, and founded New Antrim, New York (which name was changed to Suffern in 1814). Gen. Washington had his headquarters at Suffern's Tavern from July 15 to 20, 1777. On July 15 Washington wrote to Gen. Schuyler: "The evacuation of Ticonderoga and Mount Independence is an Event

of Chagrin and surprise ... The stroke is severe indeed, and has distressed me much."

Lt. Col. Aaron Burr, later vice president of the United States, had his headquarters at Suffern's Tavern in the fall of 1777. In August 1781 the Comte de Rochambeau was quartered in the house. After Mary died, John Suffern married Elizabeth Berthoff Bogart.

The house was taken down in 1856 by George W. Suffern. Later a bronze tablet was put near the place, reading: "Erected in 1773 by John Suffern. Site of Suffern's Tavern, a noted hostelry of the Revolution. Headquarters of General George Washington July 15th to 20th, 1777. Headquarters of Colonel Aaron Burr commanding troops guarding the Ramapo Pass. Erected by the Rockland County Society October 4, 1924."

In 1904 J. Bogart Suffern, a great-grandson of John, gave a quarter-acre of the troop entrenchment area to the Ramapo Valley Chapter of the Daughters of the American Revolution, who continue to maintain this historic lot, which lies to the right side of Route 17 less than a mile south of the Route 59 intersection. (Suffern: Two Hundred Years, 1773-1973, Bicentennial Committee; submitted by Matilda A. Gocek, Suffern Free Library, Suffern, NY)

SUGGETT, JEMIMA SPENCE   KY
of Bryan's Station. She was born in 1715, and some time prior to 1751 "Mimey" became the second wife of Lt. James Suggett (ca. 1712-ca. 1786). They lived in Orange County, Virginia. They had one son, John, and two daughters, Jemima Suggett Johnson and Catherine Suggett Merry. The family left Virginia for Kentucky about 1779. All the family was in the fort when the Tories and Indians attacked on August 15, 1782. Jemima Suggett's daughter, Jemima Johnson, led the women to the spring for the water during the Indian attack. She is listed as a patriot in the DAR Patriot Index. (Virginia Webb Howard, Bryan's Station Heroes and Heroines, 1932)

SULLIVAN, LYDIA WOOSTER   NH
of Durham. In 1765 she married John Sullivan, an attorney, who was elected a delegate to the First Continental Congress in 1774. They had three sons and three daughters. He was made a major general and was taken prisoner at the Battle of Long Island in 1776, but was exchanged after serving as the bearer of Lord Howe's peace proposal. In 1778 he was successful in his expeditions against the Iroquois Indians in New York and in western Pennsylvania.

Gen. and Mrs. Sullivan advanced their personal funds to supply the Continental Army, for which she suffered on many occasions. (GP, vol. 2) Gen. Sullivan was elected president of New Hampshire and served from 1786 to 1789.

SULLIVAN, MARGERY BROWN   NH
of Dover. She was born in 1714 in Cork, Ireland, of English ancestry and came alone to America in 1723 at the age of nine. She married John Sullivan, a schoolteacher, and they had five sons and

II: SELECTED BIOGRAPHIES

one daughter. The sons were Benjamin, born in 1736, an officer in the British navy, who died in service before the Revolution; Daniel (1738-1782), a captain in the Revolutionary War and founder of the town of Sullivan, Maine; John (1740-1795), a major general during the war, a governor of New Hampshire, 1786-1787 and 1789, then United States district judge, 1789-1795; James (1744-1808), attorney general in the district of Maine and governor of Massachusetts, 1707-1708; Eben, born in 1748, a captain during the Revolution. Their daughter Mary was born in 1752.

George Sullivan (1771-1838), son of John, was New Hampshire attorney general, 1815-1835. William Sullivan (1774-1839), son of James, was a lawyer and Massachusetts legislator who wrote The Public Men of the Revolution, published in 1834.

Credit must be given to Margery Sullivan who raised such a distinguished family, with three sons who served as officers during the Revolutionary War. Mrs. Sullivan died in Berwick, Maine, in 1801. The local chapter of the Daughters of the American Revolution is named in her honor. (Elizabeth R. Folsom, New Hampshire DAR Historian, 1924-1931)

SUMTER, MARY CANTY   SC
of Eutaw Springs. Her first husband was William Jameson, and after his death she was married in 1767 to Thomas Sumter. Mrs. Sumter gave encouragement to her husband, Col. Sumter. On the Tyger River in South Carolina on November 20, 1780, he defeated Col. Tarleton in the battle of Blackstocks Hill. After the Revolutionary War he obtained grants for 150,000 acres and founded Statesburg, South Carolina. (EW)

SWAIN, MELISCENT BARRETT   MA
of Concord. The daughter of Meliscent Estabrook and Col. James Barrett, who had served in the French and Indian Wars, she was born in 1759. Joseph Swain (1754-1831) was a blacksmith and son of the Rev. Joseph Swain of Wenham. In 1774 young Joseph, who was in charge of Mrs. Proctor's edge-tool factory in Salem, came to Concord with an anvil and other tools to set up an armory. Joseph showed Milly Barrett how to cut paper to make cartridges and put her in charge of the factory, which employed females only. James Barrett drove the last load of cartridges from her house before the British arrived in April 1775.

After the Revolutionary War, Joseph Swain returned to Concord and married Milly Barrett. Later they moved to Halifax, Vermont. She died in 1838. (GP, vol. 2; information received from Susan Cooney, Salem, MA)

SWETLAND, HANNAH TIFFANY   PA
of the Wyoming Valley. The daughter of Thomas Tiffany, she was born on July 15, 1740, in Lebanon, Connecticut. On April 1, 1762, she married Luke Swetland, and in 1776 they settled on a tract of land near Mehoopany. In 1777 he was a private in Captain Durkee's company at Morristown, New Jersey.

Since the women at home were menaced by Tories and Indians, they had to make their own gunpowder for a cannon they had to defend themselves, and also gunpowder for their muskets. Mr. Egle in his book published in 1898 quotes from an earlier book written by a Mr. Miner: "The women took up their floors, dug out the earth, put in casks, and ran water through it--as ashes are leaded--took the ashes in another cask and made lye, mixed the water from the earth with weak lye, boiled it, set it to cool, and the saltpeter rose to the top. Charcoal and sulphur were then used, and powder produced for the public defence!"

Mrs. Swetland and her neighbors made gunpowder in this fashion. She died on her farm on January 8, 1809. (EP)

SYMMES, SUSAN LIVINGSTON   NJ
of Elizabeth. She was the daughter of Susannah French and William Livingston, who became the first elected governor of New Jersey in 1776. While her father was away from the house in February 1779, he had left in his library a carriage bag filled with his correspondence with George Washington, the Continental Congress, and state officials. Some British officers raided the house. They were on orders to capture Governor Livingston and his papers. The officers asked for Livingston and were told he was not there. One officer demanded his papers, and Susan took him to the library, and asked him not to touch the carriage bag which she said contained her private correspondence. She gave him some worthless papers, and he did not touch the carriage bag.

After the war Susan (or Susannah) married John Cleves Symmes, who later became justice of the Supreme Court of New Jersey. Their daughter, Anna Symmes, married William Henry Harrison, later the ninth president of the United States. (GP)

T

TARRANT, SARAH   MA
of Salem. The British Lt. Col. William Leslie led an attack on Salem on February 26, 1776, to seize provisions, gunpowder, and cannons which the patriots had stored there. He sailed for Marblehead with 240 men, disembarked, then marched to Salem. But the British army was denied passage over a drawbridge by the resolute American patriots. Sarah cried out, "Go home and tell your master he has sent you on a fool's errand and broken the peace of our Sabbath. What, do you think we were born in the woods, to be frightened by owls?"

After a soldier pointed a musket at her, she exclaimed, "Fire if you have the courage, but I doubt it."

Then the British retreated playing an old-fashioned tune, "The World's Turned Upside Down," without either side firing a shot, and marched back to Marblehead. What could have been the first shots of the Revolution did not happen in Salem, but did happen at Lexington and Concord. (William Gavett, "Account of the Affair at North Bridge," Essex Institute, 1859)

II: SELECTED BIOGRAPHIES

THOMAS, JANE BLACK   SC
of Spartanburg. The daughter of Ann and Robert Black, she was
born on July 8, 1723, in Chester County, Pennsylvania. She was
the sister of John Black of Carlisle, Pennsylvania, the first president of Dickinson College. About 1740 Jane married John Thomas,
a native of Wales. In the 1750s they moved to the Chester District
of South Carolina, and then about 1762 to the Spartanburg District.
They settled on the banks of Fairforest Creek. At the outbreak
of the Revolutionary War, Thomas was appointed as colonel of the
Spartanburg regiment.

After the Tories learned that Governor Rutledge had stored
ammunition in the home of Col. Thomas, they sent a large party
under Col. More to obtain the munitions. Col. Thomas and his
men fled with all the ammunition they could carry, and left the
balance in charge of his wife and two young men, one being his
son-in-law, Josiah Culbertson. When the Tories arrived, Jane
Thomas refused to open the front door. So the Tories fired on
the house. Jane and her daughter, Martha Culbertson, loaded
the muskets for the men, who returned the fire. Finally the Tories
gave up and left the premises. The ammunition was saved and was
used in the skirmishes at Rocky Mount and Hanging Rock.

After the fall of Charleston on May 12, 1780, Col. Thomas
and their two sons were captured and imprisoned in the 96th District
prison until almost the end of the war. Once, while visiting the
prison, Mrs. Thomas overheard the conversation of some Tory women.
One said, "Tomorrow night the Loyalists intend to surprise the
rebels at Cedar Spring."

Mrs. Thomas left the prison at once and rode home on horseback. She had to stop for the night on the way since it was a
trip of sixty miles, but Cedar Springs was only a short distance
from her house. After being warned, the soldiers were ready
for the Tories. When the enemy advanced, the rebels opened fire,
and the Tories were defeated.

Col. and Mrs. Thomas had nine children. Four of her sons
served in the rebel army, together with her four sons-in-law. After
the war the Thomas family moved to the Greenville District. Mrs.
Thomas died on April 16, 1811. She is listed as a patriot in the
DAR Patriot Index. (EW; HS; submitted by Mrs. Robert S. Daniel,
Gladewater, TX)

THOMPSON, CATHERINE ROSS   PA
of Carlisle. The daughter of Catharine Van Gezel and the Rev.
George Ross, she was born on January 3, 1739, in New Castle,
Delaware. She was the sister of the George Ross who signed the
Declaration of Independence and the sister of Gertrude Ross who
married George Reed of Delaware, who was also a signer of the
Declaration of Independence. On March 29, 1762, in Lancaster,
she married Capt. William Thompson. Shortly after their marriage,
they moved to a farm near Carlisle and had many children. Her
husband served in the Colonial Wars, and then as colonel of the
1st Pennsylvania Battalion and was with George Washington at Cambridge, Massachusetts, in 1775. In March 1776 he was promoted to

brigadier general and relieved Gen. Charles Lee in command of
the forces in New York. In June 1777 he was captured by the
British at Three Rivers and imprisoned. He was finally exchanged
in October 1780.

During Gen. Thompson's absence, Mrs. Thompson managed
the plantation, and almost all of the crops were sent to Washington's
army. Mrs. Thompson died at the home of her daughter in Chambersburg, Pennsylvania, on March 24, 1808. (EP)

THOMPSON, MARY TORR   NH
of Durham. She was the daughter of Vincent Torr, an immigrant
who settled in Dover, New Hampshire, and later fought in the Revolutionary War. Mary Torr married Judge Ebenezer Thompson (1737-1802), who was one of a company of men who marched to Fort William
and Mary in Portsmouth, New Hampshire, four months before the
Battle of Lexington in 1775 and captured the powder stored there,
the first overt act of the Revolution. Judge Thompson was the
first secretary of state of New Hampshire.

Mary was one of the most active women working for the Continental soldiers. Not only did she spin and weave with her own
hands, but she directed her household in making clothing and organized her neighbors into groups to spin, weave, and sew clothes
for the American soldiers. The ladies made enough clothing to
outfit a company for the army. She was the leader of the whole
community and a tower of strength to all who came under her influence.

Mrs. Thompson left many descendants. Her grandson Benjamin willed his property in Durham to the State of New Hampshire
for the purpose of establishing an agriculture college; the University of New Hampshire is the result of his bequest. Mary and
her husband are buried in the Durham cemetery. The Mary Torr
Chapter of the Daughters of the American Revolution includes Rochester, Farmington, Union, and Milton, New Hampshire. (Per Norma
Studley Currier, past DAR Regent)

TOMPKINS, MRS. THOMAS   NY
of Hartsdale, near Dobbs Ferry, according to the Washington Papers.
She was the wife of Thomas Tompkins, the son of Joseph Tompkins.
Her maiden name is not known, but records show they had six
sons: Elijah, Noah, Thomas, Nathaniel, Gilbert, and Joseph. Noah
married Helena Underhill. Nathaniel Tompkins's first wife was
Susan Underhill, and his second wife was Effie Underhill.

After he left the Appleby house on July 7, 1781, Gen. Washington established his headquarters at the home of Mr. and Mrs.
Thomas Tompkins, the aunt and uncle of Joseph Appleby. While
there Washington wrote a letter to Governor John Hancock of Massachusetts complaining that Hancock had not replied to his letters
dated May 24 and 25, and June 2, 4, 15, and 25, requesting supplies to be furnished by Massachusetts for the Continental Army.
(FW)

Washington left the Tompkins house on July 10, 1781, and

II: SELECTED BIOGRAPHIES

established his headquarters in the home of Ann Wiley Hammond near Dobbs Ferry. (Some information from Sr. Mary Agnes Parrell, Mercy College, Dobbs Ferry, NY)

TOWER, BETHIAH NICHOLS   MA
of Cohasset. She was born on June 12, 1724, in Hingham, Massachusetts and was the wife of Daniel Tower (1720-1800), and they lived on King Street in Cohasset. In April 1778 there was a smallpox epidemic, and a hospital was built on an open pasture southeast of Little Harbor near Mohawk Stream. Mrs. Tower was the keeper of the hospital, which cared for the civilians and soldiers smitten with smallpox. She was a dauntless woman, nicknamed "Resolution Tower." Bethiah was the mother of Persis Tower Lincoln Hall, another Cohasset heroine. Mrs. Tower died on April 25, 1813. (E. Victor Bigelow, <u>Narrative History of Cohasset</u>, Boston, 1808; submitted by Margaret C. Venham, Hoquiam, WA, with birth and death dates)

TOWNSEND, SARAH   NY
of Oyster Bay, Long Island. "Sally" was the daughter of Samuel Townsend of Raynham Hall and the sister of Robert Townsend of New York City. Her brother, a journalist and merchant, was actually a spy for Gen. Washington working under the pseudonym of "Culper Junior." During the Revolutionary War their home was occupied by Col. John Graves Simcoe of the British army. Meanwhile Maj. John André made many visits to Raynham Hall to talk with Col. Simcoe. Maj. André, the British spy, used the pseudonym "John Anderson."

One day Sally spotted a strange man in her kitchen who placed a letter in the cupboard, then quickly left the house. Sally went to the cupboard and looked at the letter. It was addressed to John Anderson, but its contents meant nothing to her, so she replaced the letter. Later Maj. André entered the kitchen, went to the cupboard, and took the letter.

That evening Sally overheard a conversation between Maj. André and Col. Simcoe, and could distinguish the words: "West Point." Sally figured that the British were planning an attack on the unfinished fortress at West Point. Actually Gen. Benedict Arnold was planning to turn West Point over to the British, but Sally did not know that at the time. Anyway, she made a good guess and sent a message to her brother in New York City by a market boat on Long Island Sound, since he dealt in merchandise. After Robert Townsend received Sally's message, he informed Gen. Washington. Maj. André was captured by the Americans in September 1780 and executed later as a spy, but Benedict Arnold escaped to England.

Raynham Hall is located on West Main Street in Oyster Bay, and the famous cupboard is on display there. Sally Townsend is buried on the south side of Fort Hill in Townsend Cemetery, Oyster Bay, New York. (CP)

TRACY, ELIZABETH DORR   CT
of Norwich. The first wife of Dr. Elisha Tracy was the former
Lucy Huntington (1712-1751). They had five daughters. His second wife was the former Elizabeth Dorr, and she bore the doctor
nine more children.
    The <u>Norwich Packet</u> on March 8, 1781, reported: "On Monday
last [March 5] his Excellency General Washington and Major General
[Robert] Howe with their suits [party], passed through this town,
on their way to Newport and were saluted by a discharge of thirteen
cannon."
    Generals Washington and Howe were entertained for lunch
at the Tracys', while the junior officers had their meals at Lothrop's
Tavern, owned by Azariah Lothrop and his second wife, Abigail
Huntington Lothrop. (Some information from Diane Norman, Otis
Library, Norwich, CT, and Camp S. Huntington, Bartlesville, OK;
FW)

TREFETHEN, MADAM   NH
of New Castle. When the officers and crew of the British man-
of-war <u>Scarborough</u> were in town, they apparently left a few men
who fell asleep. Madam Trefethen boarded the vessel, emptied
the water casks, removed the bungs from all the casks, tipped
them over, and sent them smashing to pieces as they rolled down
the bank. (Submitted by Dorothy Wilcox, Durham, NH)

TREUTLEN, ANNE UNSETT   GA
of Saint Matthews Parish. After his first wife, Margueretta, died
in 1777, Governor John Adam Treutlen of Georgia married Anne
Unsett, a widow, about 1779. Shortly after his second marriage,
the Tories burned their home and confiscated their furnishings
and silverware. After this disaster, Governor Treutlen moved
his family to Saint Matthews, South Carolina. Sometime in 1782
the Tories lured Governor Treutlen from his home and killed him.
The second Mrs. Treutlen suffered during these trying times.
    After the Revolutionary War, while a guest in the home of
Col. Rumph, Mary Treutlen, the governor's daughter, recognized
her father's watch on one of the young men present. She told
her brother, who was also a guest, and with the help of his friends,
her brother seized the young man who then confessed and named
the other men who were involved. Later they were all hanged.
While this story is traditional, it seems to be authentic. In 1914
the Daughters of the American Revolution erected a monument to
the memory of Governor Treutlen in Saint Matthews, South Carolina. (<u>DAR Magazine</u>, 1964)

TREUTLEN, MARGUERETTA DUPUIS   GA
of Saint Matthews Parish. She was born in 1755 in Purysburg,
South Carolina, and married John Adam Treutlen, who had migrated
from Austria with his parents to Saint Matthews Parish, now a
part of Effingham County. They had eight children. Mr. Treutlen
was a member of the First Provincial Congress of Georgia and was

II: SELECTED BIOGRAPHIES

a member of the Ebenezer Lutheran Church. In 1777 he was elected the first governor of Georgia. Governor Treutlen was aggressive in his campaign against the Tories and the British and became hated by them. In fact the British put a price on his head. Governor and Mrs. Treutlen mortgaged their property to raise money to support the Georgia troops in their fight for independence. Mrs. Treutlen died in 1777. Margueretta and her husband had made a great sacrifice for the cause of liberty. (Submitted by George M. Norton, Cocoa Beach, FL)

TRIST, ELIZABETH   PA
of Philadelphia. On December 19, 1782, Thomas Jefferson left Monticello for Philadelphia with his daughter, Patsy, aged ten. His wife, Martha, had died on September 6, 1782. Jefferson arrived in Philadelphia on December 27 and was scheduled to sail on the French frigate Romulus for France, having been appointed minister plenipotentiary. But the Romulus was locked in ice below Baltimore, and Jefferson had to spend almost a month in Philadelphia awaiting the arrival of the vessel.

Jefferson stayed at the home of Elizabeth Trist. Patsy and Mrs. Trist became great friends. Finally Jefferson left for Baltimore and arrived there on January 31, 1783, but British warships were off the Capes, awaiting to attack the Romulus once it left Baltimore. The Congress held up Jefferson's commission, and he returned to Philadelphia, then to Monticello, with his daughter.

Nicholas P. Trist was executor of Jefferson's will. (ST)

TRUMBULL, EUNICE BACKUS   CT
of Lebanon. She was the wife of Col. Jonathan Trumbull, Jr. On his trip from his headquarters in New Windsor, New York, to Providence, Rhode Island, Gen. Washington passed through Hartford on March 4, 1781, accompanied by Governor Jonathan Trumbull and his son, Col. Trumbull, according to Governor Trumbull's Diary. Washington and his party dined in Bolton (records show payment of $540) and apparently spent the night of March 4 in Lebanon at the home of Col. and Mrs. Jonathan Trumbull, although there is a tradition that Washington may have spent the night of March 4 in Hebron, but this has not been verified. Col. Trumbull was secretary to General Washington from 1781 to 1783.

The Duke de Lauzun was in winter quarters in Lebanon at the time, and Lebanon was the home of Governor Trumbull and his son Col. Trumbull, so it is more likely that he stayed in Lebanon. On March 5, Washington proceeded to Norwich. (Some information from Diane Norman, Otis Library, Norwich, CT) Governor Trumbull's wife had died in May 1780, so it is believed that Gen. Washington was entertained by Mrs. Jonathan Trumbull, Jr.

TRUMBULL, FAITH ROBINSON   CT
of Lebanon. The daughter of the Rev. John Robinson of Duxbury, Massachusetts, she was born in 1718. She married Jonathan Trumbull on December 9, 1735, who served as governor of Connecticut

from 1769 to 1784. He was the only colonial governor to side with the rebels at the outbreak of the American Revolution. They had four sons and two daughters.

In December 1777 the North Parish of New London took a collection for the benefit of the soldiers in the Continental Army. At this point there was great suffering among men encamped at Valley Forge. At this meeting Faith Trumbull arose and removed a beautiful cloak which had been given to her by the Comte de Rochambeau. This was her donation to the rebel cause. Later the cloak was cut into strips and used as trimming on the soldiers' uniforms. She died in May 1780.

The Trumbulls' son Joseph served as commissary general of the Continental Army from 1775 to 1777. Their son Jonathan served as governor of Connecticut from 1797 until his death in 1809, and their son John became a famous artist. The Norwich chapter of the Daughters of the American Revolution is named in her honor. (CG; DB)

George Washington spent the night of March 17, 1781, with Governor Trumbull. (BI)

TUCKER, ELIZABETH GOULD   NJ
of Trenton. She was the daughter of Ann and James Gould. Elizabeth married Samuel Tucker, sheriff of Hunterdon County, who was president of the Provincial Congress of New Jersey, 1775-1776. As the British forces were marching to Philadelphia, John Adams fled to Trenton and on September 19, 1777, lodged at the Tuckers'. Adams walked with Mr. Duane to Gen. Philemon Dickinson's home and saw the desolation there caused by Hessian soldiers. Elizabeth died in 1787, aged fifty-seven years. (BA)

TUCKER, MARY GATCHELL   MA
of Marblehead. She married Samuel Tucker who was born on November 1, 1747. He commanded the schooner Franklin of Washington's fleet in 1776 and then commanded the Hancock and took several prize vessels. Tucker was commissioned a captain in the Continental Navy on March 15, 1777. Later he commanded the Boston and sailed on February 15, 1778, for France with two illustrious passengers, John Adams and his eleven-year-old son, John Quincy Adams (later both men became presidents of the United States). Later Tucker commanded the Thorn and was captured on August 19, 1782, by HMS Arethusa and taken to Saint Johns, Prince Edward Island. He escaped, returned to Marblehead, and commanded the six-gun sloop Live Oak. (CN)

TUFTS, ANNE ADAMS   MA
of Boston. She was born in 1729, the daughter of Joseph Adams of Quincy, Massachusetts. On April 19, 1750, she married Peter Tufts II (1728-1791), and they lived in Charlestown, Massachusetts. Anne had eleven children. Her husband was a minuteman at the Battle of Lexington on their twenty-fifth wedding anniversary. Her husband and son Peter Jr. fought at the Battle of Bunker Hill.

II: SELECTED BIOGRAPHIES 193

After the battle, Anne Tufts nursed and cared for the wounded soldiers. The Somerville, Massachusetts, chapter of the Daughters of the American Revolution is named in her honor. (GP) Anne Tufts died on February 13, 1813.

TURNBULL, MRS. CHARLES   PA
of Philadelphia. Her husband was captain lieutenant of the 4th Continental Artillery and was taken prisoner by the British on April 13, 1777, at Bound Brook, New Jersey. While still a prisoner, he was promoted to captain on June 15, 1777. He was finally exchanged in April 1780 and served until September 1783.

Mrs. Turnbull was an active member of the ladies' relief association for the welfare of the American soldiers. (Pennsylvania Gazette, June 12, 1780; FW)

TURNER, KERENHAPPUCK NORMAN   VA
was born in 1692 and married James Turner. During the Revolutionary War she received word that her son was badly wounded on the Guilford Courthouse battleground in North Carolina on March 15, 1781. Mrs. Turner rode on horseback to Guilford, a distance of three hundred miles. There she bore holes in a tub which was filled with water and suspended from rafters. The cool water slowly dripping on her son's wounds and body lessened the fever (like the ice packs of today). Mrs. Turner also nursed the other soldiers.

Gen. Nathaniel Greene suffered a defeat by the British troops under Lord Cornwallis, but then Cornwallis withdrew to Wilmington, North Carolina. The Guilford Battleground Company erected a bronze statue to Mrs. Turner's memory, located near Greensboro, North Carolina. Mrs. Turner died in 1807, aged 115 years. (DAR) She supplied provisions for the army during the war. (Halifax County, VR, Ctf. 1)

V

VALENTINE, MRS.   NY
of Valentine's Hill (now in Yonkers). She was the wife of Thomas Valentine. In October 1776 Gen. Washington and his army were camped on Valentine's Hill. He left there on October 22 for White Plains, where he spent the night at the home of Ann Fisher Miller in North Castle.

On July 2, 1781, Gen. Washington left the home of Cornelia Beekman in Peekskill and returned to Valentine's Hill. Washington left there on July 4 and established his headquarters in the Appleby House near Dobbs Ferry (now Ardsley).

VAN ALLEN, MRS. HENRY   NJ
of Oakland. After he left the Schuyler House (home of Esther Schuyler Colfax) in Pompton, New Jersey, Gen. Washington rode to the Van Allen farmhouse in the Campgaw Mountains and was

there from July 14 to 15, 1777. As of 1957 this house was still
standing at Page's Corner in Oakland. (Ramsay Journal, chap.
2, July 1957)

VAN ALLEN, MRS. JOHN   NJ
of Ramapaugh (now Darlington). After he left the Henry Van Allen
farmhouse on July 16, 1777, Gen. Washington stopped briefly at
the home of Mr. and Mrs. John Van Allen. This house was about
two and a half miles north of the Hopper House, where Washington
had his headquarters from July 23 to 25, 1777. On July 16 Washington wrote to Sir Henry Howe, the British general, about an
exchange of prisoners. (FW; Ramsay Journal, July 1957)

VAN ALSTYNE, NANCY QUACKENBUSH   NY
of Canajoharie was born about 1733. She married Martin J. Van
Alstyne in 1751, and they settled in the Van Alstyne family mansion in the valley of the Mohawk. She had fifteen children. In
August 1780 she learned that a party of Tories and Indians were
encamped nearby, so she took her children and seven neighboring
families to an island owned by her husband across the river. Meanwhile the Indians burned the homes of the neighbors, but the home
of Mrs. Van Alstyne was spared. She died at Wampsville, Madison
County, in 1831 at the age of ninety-eight. (CD; FH)

VAN CORTLANDT, JOANNA LIVINGSTON   NY
from near Peekskill. She was the wife of Pierre Van Cortlandt,
who was lieutenant governor of New York from 1777 to 1795. Gen.
Washington made several visits to the Van Cortlandt Manor House,
but according to historians, the actual hostess was Mr. Van Cortlandt's daughter, Cornelia Van Cortlandt Beekman.

VANDENBERG, HELENA CLARK   NY
of Fishkill. She was the wife of Col. James Vandenberg. On his
trip from Fishkill, New York, to Newport, Rhode Island, Gen.
Washington was entertained for dinner at her home on March 2,
1781. On another trip to Wethersfield, Connecticut, on May 25,
1781, Gen. Washington dined with the Vandenbergs. (FW)

VAN DOREN, MARTHA LOTT   NJ
of Millstone (formerly Somerset Court House). She was born in
1728 and married John Van Doren. In 1776, when her husband
was away, a Hessian raiding party looking for provisions hanged
Mrs. Van Doren by her heels, and she still refused to talk. As
the Hessians were about to hang her by the neck, her husband
arrived in time to save her.
    On January 3, 1777, Gen. Washington spent the night with
the Van Dorens on his way to Princeton. She died in 1805. (BI;
BJ)

VAN HOOK, HANNAH WILSON   KY
of Ruddell's Station. Her first husband was named Williams. They

II: SELECTED BIOGRAPHIES

had children, but then her husband was killed by Indians. Later she married Samuel Van Hook (1733-1809). In the summer of 1780 a large force from Detroit, consisting of six hundred Indians and Canadians under the command of Col. Bird (or Byrd), invaded Kentucky. The army included six pieces of artillery, brought down the Big Miami River and up Licking as far as the town of Falmouth at the Forks of Licking, where it was unloaded. From this point Col. Bird and one hundred men, accompanied by the artillery, marched to Ruddell's Station. The enemy approach was not discovered until June 22, 1780, just before the fort was attacked. Unfortunately, the Americans had very little gunpowder, and Capt. Ruddell was forced to surrender, but made the proviso that the Americans would be prisoners of the British and not of the Indians.

When the gates were opened, the Indians rushed in and each grabbed someone, claiming him or her as his own prize. The women were separated from their husbands, and children were separated from their parents. The Indians then captured Martin's Station, about five miles away.

The Van Hooks and other Americans were taken to Detroit and held there as prisoners. The Van Hooks were released about 1783, and moved to Higgins's blockhouse on the Licking River in 1786. On June 12, 1786, the fort was attacked by Indians. Mrs. Van Hook's son, E. E. Williams, escaped secretly and summoned help. (CH; DAR)

VAN VEGHTEN, SARAH MIDDAH   NJ
lived between Bound Brook and Somerville, on the banks of the Raritan River. Sarah was the wife of Dirck Van Veghten. About March 15, 1779, while their home was the headquarters of Gen. and Mrs. Nathaniel Greene, the Greenes had a little party for Gen. Washington, who spent three hours dancing with Catherine Greene. (BI)

VARNUM, MOLLY BUTLER   MA
of Dracut. She was born on June 4, 1750, and married Joseph Bradley Varnum (1750-1821). Her husband was a captain of militia during the Revolutionary War. Molly weaved cloth for clothing for the soldiers and knitted socks for the troops. Her husband later became a major general, member of Congress, speaker of the House, and a United States senator. She died on April 17, 1833. The Lowell, Massachusetts, chapter of the Daughters of the American Revolution is named in her honor. (DAR; GP; suggested by Ruth Marshall, Boston Public Library)

VEACH, ELIZA   SC
is listed on the rolls of Capt. Philip Waters' Company, Col. Thomas's Regiment, Gen. Sumter's Brigade. (ESC)

VER PLANCK, EFFIE BEEKMAN   NY
of Van Courtland. She was the wife of Philip Ver Planck (1736-

1777), who was a patriot during the Revolutionary War. Their
manor house at Ver Planck's Point was destroyed by the British
sloop of war Vulture. He died at Fishkill on June 20, 1777.
(FP1)

VOORHIES, MINNIE   NJ
of New Brunswick. On July 2, 1778, Gen. Washington in his general orders stated: "The General Court Martial ordered to sit this
day for the trial of Major General Lee will sit tomorrow eight o'clock
at the house of Mrs. Voorkees [sic] in the Town of New Brunswick."
(FW)

W

WADE, MRS. FRANCIS   PA
of Philadelphia. Her husband, Capt. Francis Wade, was deputy
quartermaster general. On January 11, 1777, Wade was ordered
by Gen. Washington "to collect all the Beef, Pork, Flour, Spirituous
Liquors etc. not necessary for the Subsistence of the Inhabitants,
in all parts of East Jersey, lying below the Road leading from Brunswick to Trenton, and as fast as the Stores are collected, to be
removed to Newtown, Bucks County, Pennsylvania, and, there
stored, and formed into proper Magazines."
    Mrs. Wade was an active member of the ladies' association
for the benefit and welfare of the American soldiers. (Pennsylvania
Gazette, June 12, 1780; FW)

WAGLUN, JIMMIE   NJ
of Trenton. Late in 1776 Gen. Washington decided to attack the
British forces at Princeton, New Jersey, and needed some person
who knew the back roads in order to surprise the enemy. Mrs.
Waglun offered her services and led Washington's army to Princeton.
In a surprise attack on January 3, 1777, Washington succeeded in
forcing the enemy to retreat to New Brunswick, New Jersey. (CP)

WALKER, ESTHER GASTON   NC
of Rocky Mount. After hearing gunshot and cannon fire on July 13,
1780, at Rocky Mount, Esther and her sister-in-law decided to
ride to witness the conflict. On their way they met two fleeing
cowards and convinced the men to return to the battle. Esther
dressed the wounds of the injured soldiers and fetched water for
them. The following week she attended the wounded at the Waxhaw
church during the battle of Hanging Rock. Later she married
Alexander Walker. (CD) She was born in 1761 and died in 1809.
(DAR)

WALLACE, MARY MADDOX   NJ
of Somerville (previously Raritan), about four miles from Middlebrook,

II: SELECTED BIOGRAPHIES

now Bound Brook, New Jersey. Mary married John Wallace, and
they had two sons and one daughter. Gen. Washington established
his headquarters there on December 11, 1778, and remained here
until December 22, 1778. While here on December 14, Gen. Washington issued in his general orders:

"Much of the sickness among the Troops seems to have been
occasioned by the improper method adopted in forming many of the
Hutts last Winter; Some being sunk in the ground and others covered
with Earth ... That they be roofed with boards, slabs or large
shingles; That the men be not suffered to dig into the ground (except so far as to level the surface), or to cover their hutts with
earth or turf."

Gen. Washington returned to Middlebrook on February 5, 1779.
John Wallace gave a receipt to Maj. Gibbs on June 4, 1779, for
the use of their house, furniture, etc. (FW) When the New York
campaign against the Indians was planned, Lord Stirling came from
Bound Brook, Gen. Knox from Pluckemin and Gen. Greene from
Finderne to map out their strategy in the Wallace home. (BJ)

Mrs. Wallace died on January 9, 1794. The home is located
at 38 Washington Place, Somerville. (Information from Jim Sommerville, Somerville, NJ)

WALTON, DORTHEA CAMBER   GA
of Savannah. In 1775 she married George Walton, who later was
a signer of the Declaration of Independence. They had two sons.
Her father was a loyal British subject, but Dorothy was well known
for her patriotic views on independence for the colonies.

In December 1778 the British Lt. Col. Archibald Campbell
landed near Savannah with 3,500 soldiers and was attacked by
some 850 men under the American Gen. Robert Howe. In that disastrous battle, over half of Howe's troops were killed, wounded,
or taken prisoner. George Walton served under Howe, and Walton
was wounded and taken prisoner. Later Walton was imprisoned
at Sunbury, Georgia. He was exchanged in September 1779 for
a captain in the Royal Navy. (FG) Walton served as governor
of Georgia from November 1779 until January 1780. Meanwhile Dorothy was taken prisoner, sent to the West Indies, and later released.
(DAR Magazine, July 1921)

Her husband was chief justice of Georgia, 1783-1789, then
served a second term as governor. (DB)

WAMPOLE, CATHERINE MAGDELENA ROTH   PA
of Towamencin Township. Gen. Washington had his headquarters
in the Wampole's home on October 9, 1777. On this date Washington
wrote to Brig. Gen. James Potter in part: "A Person by the name
of Patterson, an Inhabitant of Wilmington, can give you a particular
Acct. of the Situation, strength & ca. of the Enemy at that place;
from whence you may judge the practicability of attempting something by way of Surprize, if your numbers are adequate, upon

the garrison. After having made every necessary enquiry proper for an enterprize of this kind let me know the result by an Officer and whether the undertaking is feasible with, or without, a little aid from hence." (FW)

Catherine was the wife of Frederick Wampole (1717-1800). Their home was in Kulpsville. Washington had his headquarters there until October 16, 1777. (BI)

WARD, NANCY   TN
of Chota. A Cherokee Indian, she was born about 1738, the daughter of Tame Doe, who was the daughter of the Raven of Chota. Her great-grandfather was the famous Cherokee chief Moytoy. Nancy was called "Nanye'hi," which later was anglicized to Nancy. She married Kingfisher, and they had a daughter, Catherine, and a son, Fivekiller.

Kingfisher was killed in 1755 while fighting the Creek Indians at the Battle of Taliwa, near the present city of Canton in northern Georgia. With the death of Kingfisher, it seemed the battle would be lost. But according to custom, Nanye'hi and the other Cherokee women followed the men into battle for the purpose of preparing lead bullets to make them more deadly. After Kingfisher was killed, Nancy noticed the lack of leadership, and holding her husband's rifle, she urged on the Cherokees, and they won the battle. The Creeks were defeated and never returned to northern Georgia. For her display of valor, the Indian chiefs elevated her to the position of Ghi-ga-u, or "Most Beloved Woman of the Cherokee Nation."

After her husband's death, Nancy operated an inn on Womankiller Ford, at a point where the old Unicoy Pike crossed the Ocoee River. In those days the pike formed a part of the main road from Knoxville into northern Georgia.

Bryan Ward of North Carolina, an Indian trader, about 1758 became the second husband of Nancy. He was born in Ireland and served in the British army during the Colonial Wars. After his service ended he remained in America and became a trader among the Cherokees. Bryan and Nancy had a daughter, Elizabeth. Some time before 1774 Bryan left Nancy and took a second wife, since the land deeds of Georgia from July 20, 1774, until June 4, 1776, show transfers of property between Bryan and Ann Ward and others. These land records also show transfers of property between 1785 and 1793 between Ward and others.

Nancy Ward sided with the Peace Party group of Cherokee chiefs against her cousin, Dragging Canoe, leader of the War Party. In July 1776 Nancy sent a message to Col. John Sevier of a planned pro-British Cherokee attack on the settlers in North Carolina. The attack took place at Eaton's Station on July 20/21, 1776. In retaliation, the North Carolina militia destroyed a neighboring Cherokee village.

Nancy's daughter Elizabeth married Brig. Gen. Joseph Martin II and left many descendants. Bryan Ward on September 21, 1785,

II: SELECTED BIOGRAPHIES

was granted land by the State of Georgia on the Tugaloo River, which forms the boundary between Georgia and South Carolina. William Martin, the son of Brig. Gen. Martin, stated in the Draper manuscripts that Nancy Ward visited Bryan and Ann on several occasions in 1790 and was received with great respect by Ward's white family. Gen. and Betty Ward Martin had a daughter, Nancy, and a son, James.

Nancy Ward died in 1822, and her grave is located on a knoll adjacent to U.S. Highway #411, just south of Benton, Tennessee. She is buried between her brother, Longfellow, and her son, Fivekiller, a veteran of the War of 1812. A plaque was erected on her burial place by the Tennessee and Polk County American Revolution Bicentennial Commission:

THE WILD ROSE OF THE CHEROKEE

Nancy Ward, Princess and prophetess of the Cherokee Nation. Pocahontas of Tennessee, constant friend of the American Pioneer, had as her major objective promoting peace between the Cherokees and Pioneers. In 1776 she warned the settlers on the Watauga and Holston rivers of the impending attack by the Cherokees. She also saved Mrs. William Beam from being burned at the stake. During the Indian outbreak of 1780, she helped many prisoners escape and often supplied starving pioneers with food. She was queenly and commanding in appearance and manner, tall, erect, and beautiful with the imperious yet kindly air. The Beloved Woman operated an inn near Womankiller Ford on the Ocoee river in Polk County. Here she is buried, beside her are her son Fivekiller and her brother, Longfellow.

There is also a highway sign on U.S. Highway #411 about one mile south of Benton, Tennessee:

NANCY WARD

High priestess of the Cherokees and a friend of the whites, is buried on the ridge to the west. She repeatedly prevented massacres of settlers and several times saved captives from death at her people's hands. She is credited with introducing milk cows and many other improvements in home-making into Cherokee economy.

The Chatanooga chapter of the Daughters of the American Revolution is named in her honor. (EW; HS; additional information supplied by James O. Sanders, Kailua, HI) In 1923 the Nancy Ward Chapter of the DAR erected a tablet on the monument of the grave of Nancy Ward.

WARD, PHEBE GREENE   RI
of Westerly. Phebe was born on March 20, 1760, the daughter of

Catherine Ray and Governor William Greene of Rhode Island. Catherine Greene was a friend of Benjamin Franklin. On March 8, 1778, Phebe Greene married Col. Samuel Ward II of Westerly, the son of Anna Ray and Governor Samuel Ward of Rhode Island. He was a delegate to the Continental Congress, but died of smallpox in March 1776 in Philadelphia and was replaced by William Ellery who signed the Declaration of Independence. Phebe and Samuel had ten children.

Col. Ward commanded a regiment in the defense of Rhode Island in 1778 and was with Washington's army in New Jersey. After the war they lived in East Greenwich, Rhode Island, and then in Jamaica, Long Island, New York. Phebe Ward died in New York City on October 11, 1828. She is listed as a patriot in the DAR Patriot Index. Her granddaughter was Julia Ward Howe who wrote the words of the "Battle Hymn of the Republic." The Phebe Greene Ward Chapter of the Daughters of the American Revolution is in Westerly, RI. (Submitted by Sally P. Small, Barrington, RI)

WARLICK, BARBARA SCHINDLER   NC
of Lincoln County. She was born in 1720 in Pace County, North Carolina, and married Daniel Warlick who was born in Poole, Pennsylvania. He was killed in an Indian raid in North Carolina in 1772. Barbara furnished supplies to the military of North and South Carolina during the Revolutionary War. She died in North Carolina in 1784. Both Barbara Warlick and her daughter, Barbara Reinhardt, are listed as patriots in the DAR Patriot Index. (Submitted by May Goodman, Memphis, TN)

WARNE, MARGARET VLIET   NJ
of Washington. The daughter of Geertruitje Springsteen and Capt. Daniel Vliet of Bethlehem Township, Hunterdon County, New Jersey, she was born in 1751. Peggy had five brothers who served in the Revolutionary War. One of the best known was Maj. Gen. Daniel Vliet. Peggy married Joseph Warne and they lived in Sussex County, now Warren County, New Jersey. They had nine children.

According to the "Medical History of the County of Warren," she was the most skillful, successful, and widely known midwife and nurse of Sussex and Hunterdon counties. She kept a horse ready at all times of the day and night to ride in drifting snow and rainstorms whenever she was summoned.

During the Revolutionary War, Peggy Warne cared for the wounded soldiers, and acted as a nurse in many outlying districts. Clement C. Moore, who wrote "A Visit from Saint Nicholas," immortalized Peggy Warne in a poem called the "Florence Nightingale of New Jersey."

Peggy Warne died at age eighty-nine. A small sandstone building on a country road past Pohatcong Creek bears a plaque to her memory. This is where she stored her herbs and prepared medicines. Peggy was buried in Old Mansfield Cemetery, Washington, New Jersey. Her grave is marked by a boulder and bronze

II: SELECTED BIOGRAPHIES

tablet erected by the Daughters of the American Revolution. The Phillipsburg, New Jersey, chapter of the Daughters of the American Revolution is named the Peggy Warne Chapter. (CP; DC)

WARREN, MERCY OTIS   MA
of Plymouth. The daughter of Mary Allyne and James Otis, she was born on September 14, 1728, in Barnstable, Massachusetts. On November 14, 1754, she married James Warren. During the Revolution she was a political activist and feminist, and corresponded with John and Samuel Adams, John Dickinson (president of the Supreme Executive Council of Delaware in 1781 and later president of the Supreme Executive Council of Pennsylvania), Elbridge Gerry (a signer of the Declaration of Independence), Thomas Jefferson, Gen. Henry Knox, and James Winthrop (Harvard librarian from 1772 to 1787).

As a result, Mercy Warren accumulated a great deal of information on the American Revolution between 1775 and 1783. She was a strong supporter of the Revolution and referred to the Tories as the "malignant party." In 1805 Mercy Warren published her three-volume History of the Rise, Progress and Termination of the American Revolution. In her history Mrs. Warren was critical of John Adams, and stated "his passions and prejudices were sometimes too strong for his sagacity and judgment." This caused a rift between Adams and Mrs. Warren, who felt that Adams favored a monarchy.

Elbridge Gerry interceded between Adams and Mrs. Warren and was able to reconcile the two antagonists, who then wrote loving letters to each other. They even exchanged locks of their hair as mementoes of peace. Mercy Warren died on October 19, 1814. (DB; DR) There is a Mercy Otis Chapter of the Daughters of the American Revolution in Des Moines, Iowa.

WASHINGTON, JANE RILEY ELLIOTT   VA
was the wife of Lt. Col. William Washington (1752-1810) of the 3rd Continental Dragoons. On May 21, 1779, Gen. Washington ordered Lt. Col. Washington to join the Southern Army. On June 28, Gen. Washington wrote a short note to Lt. Col. Washington to apply to Gen. Charles Scott for future directions.

Lt. Col. Washington was wounded at Cowpens, South Carolina, in January 1781 and was voted a silver medal by Congress. He was wounded and taken prisoner at Eutaw Springs, South Carolina, in September 1781. (DAR; FW)

WASHINGTON, MARTHA DANDRIDGE CUSTIS   VA
the daughter of Frances Jones and John Dandridge, she was born on June 2, 1731, in New Kent County. In 1749 she married Daniel Parke Custis and lived in the "White House" on a Pamunkey River plantation. Her husband died in 1758, and two children survived-- a son Jackie and a daughter Patsy.

On January 6, 1759, Martha married George Washington, and they resided at Mount Vernon, Virginia. Her daughter Patsy died in 1773 and Jackie in 1781, so they raised Jackie's two younger children: George Washington, and Martha Custis.

Martha Washington was a camp follower. She was with her husband in November 1777 at Whitemarsh when the British occupied Philadelphia, and was with him at Valley Forge during the winter of 1777/78. While there the women camp followers tanned goat skins for drumheads, and some risked their lives in espionage. Martha gave comfort to the commander-in-chief, and sustained him during his trials. She was also with him at Middlebrook, New York, during the winter of 1778/79 and later with him at Newburgh, New York.

Martha Washington died at Mount Vernon on May 22, 1802. (DB; BW)

WASHINGTON, MARY BALL   VA
of Fredericksburg. The daughter of the Widow Johnson and Joseph Ball, she was born in 1708 at Epping Forest, Lancaster, Virginia. Early in 1730 Mary Ball married Augustine Washington, a widower who had two sons--Lawrence and Augustine--by his first wife. Mary went to live on her husband's plantation "Wakefield." Mary and Augustine had four sons and two daughters, although one daughter died in infancy. Her first son was named George Washington in honor of Maj. George Eskridge, her guardian in her childhood. George later became commander-in-chief of the Continental Army and the first president of the United States. Her husband died on April 12, 1743, and Mary was left with seven children to raise.

After her children married and left her, Mary Washington lived alone at "Pine Grove." Mary believed in honesty and loyalty to God and country. She considered it a disaster that her four sons should resist the will of their king. Later Mary relented and knitted socks for the American soldiers, and so is included in this book as a patriot. Meanwhile she lived near Fredericksburg, close to "Kenmore," the mansion of her daughter, Betty Washington Lewis.

While at Mount Vernon, on April 14, 1789, Gen. Washington received official notice of his election as the first president of the United States. Accompanied by one servant, Washington set out on horseback for Fredericksburg to say farewell to his mother. This was the last time he saw her.

Mary Ball Washington died on August 25, 1789, attended by Betty Lewis and Dr. Charles Mortimer. Efforts to erect a monument over her grave failed several times, but through the efforts of the widow of Chief Justice Waite this was finally accomplished and dedicated by President Grover Cleveland on May 10, 1894. (GP, vol. 50)

WATTS, ANN WALKER   PA
of Turbut Township, Northumberland County. She married James Watts, Sr. (1733-1779), who was a sergeant in the Northumberland militia. They had four sons and two daughters. Her sons Frederick,

II: SELECTED BIOGRAPHIES

John, and Francis also served in the local militia and her son James Jr. was a soldier in the Pennsylvania Regiment of the Continental Line and served at the Battle of Long Island and at the Wyoming massacre.
In the summer of 1779 the Watts family took refuge in Fort Freeland on Farrior Run, several miles from the Susquehanna River, since British troops and Indians were raiding the local settlements. On the morning of July 28, 1779, Ann's husband, James, left the fort to look for his sheep which had strayed. About a hundred yards from the fort an Indian jumped from ambush and killed James with his tomahawk. About a hundred British rangers and some two hundred Indians descended upon the fort and demolished it. The women and children were released, but the men were taken prisoners, including her sons John and Francis. Later that same day Francis managed to escape, but John was held for several years. Ann Watts died about April 1794. (Submitted by Mrs. Paul H. Schalles, Jersey Shore, PA)

WATTS, JEAN MURRAY   PA
lived on a farm on the Juniata River. Jean Murray was born about 1725 in Ireland. In 1749 she married Frederick Watts, and the couple emigrated to Pennsylvania bout 1760. He was made a lieutenant colonel of the 1st Battalion which met in Lancaster, Pennsylvania, on July 4, 1776. Col. Watts was captured at the surrender of Fort Washington, New York, on November 16, 1776. After his release, he was justice of the peace in 1778, representative to the Pennsylvania assembly in 1779, and appointed a brigadier general of the Pennsylvania militia in 1782. They had several children.
During the Revolutionary War, Mrs. Watts and her neighbors made clothing for the American soldiers. She died about 1800.
(EP)

WEBB, ABIGAIL CHESTER   CT
of Wethersfield. She was born in 1749 and married Joseph Webb. Generals George Washington, Henry Knox, and Duportail stayed in her home from May 19 to 21, 1781. On May 21, the Comte de Rochambeau and the Marquis de Chastellux arrived in Wethersfield and stayed at Stillman's tavern. Generals Washington and Rochambeau held a strategy conference in the home of Mrs. Webb on May 22, 1781. Previously Washington stayed next door in the home of Mrs. Deane in 1775. The Webb house is now a museum and headquarters of the Colonial Dames of America in the State of Connecticut. Mrs. Webb died in 1815. The Wetherfield chapter of the Daughters of the American Revolution is named in her honor.
(CG)

WEBB, CATHERINE HOGEBOOM   CT
of Wethersfield. She was the wife of Lt. Col. Samuel Blatchley Webb (1753-1807) of an additional Continental Regiment, who was taken prisoner by the British on December 10, 1777, while on an

expedition with Col. John Ely to Long Island. He was the younger
brother of Joseph Webb. On January 27, 1779, Gen. Washington
wrote to Joseph Webb: "I have your favr. of the 18th instant
accompanied by one from Mr. Barrel [Joseph Barrell of Boston,
Mass, a brother-in-law of Lt. Col. Webb] owner of the Privateer
Vengeance. It gives me pleasure that the success of this Vessel
has put it in your power to make an agreement to procure the
Exchange of your Brother Colo. Saml. Webb. If you can effect
it for any of the Gentlemen captured in the Eagle packet, I shall
not have the least objection, as I apprehend the owners of the
privateer have a right, in disposing of their prisoners, to give
a preference for their friends."
Webb was exchanged in February 1779. (DAR; FW)

WEBB, MARY EDMONDSON   VA
of Essex County. She was born there about 1715 and married
James Webb in 1731. Mary supplied material aid to the army dur-
ing the Revolutionary War. Her son, Pvt. William Webb, married
Frances Young. Mary died on May 5, 1795, in Granville County,
North Carolina. (Submitted by Nelda Watson Willmig, Libertyville,
IL; VR, 2:158)

WEBSTER, ABIGAIL EASTMAN   NH
of Franklin. She was born in July 1737 in Salisbury, New Hampshire. Abigail became the second wife of Ebenezer Webster (1739-
1806), who had four children by his first wife, Mehitable Smith.
"Nabby" Eastman, as she was called, and Ebenezer had six children (one of whom was Daniel Webster, the famous orator), so
she had ten children to raise. While her husband was in the army,
Nabby was left in the wilderness to care for her family. Capt.
Ebenezer Webster guarded the tent of Gen. Washington on the very
night that the treason of Benedict Arnold was discovered. Capt.
Webster was personally commended by the "Father of His Country."
The Abigail Webster Chapter of the Daughters of the American
Revolution is named in her honor. (GP; submitted by Elizabeth
Knowles Folsom, New Hampshire DAR Historian, 1924-1931)

WENTZ, ROSANNA MARGARETTA   PA
of Worcester Township, twenty miles from Philadelphia. She was
the wife of Peter Wentz. Gen. Washington had his headquarters
there on October 3, 1777, and from October 16 to 20, 1777. On
October 3, 1777, Gen. Washington wrote, in part, in his general
orders: "At the northward every thing wears the most favourable
aspect, every enterprise has been successful, and in capital action,
the left wing only of General Gates's army maintained its ground,
against the main body of the enemy; commanded by General Burgoyne in person; our troops behaving with the highest spirit and
bravery, during the whole engagement; which lasted from one o'clock
'till dark. In short, every circumstance promises success in that
quarter, equal to our most sanguine wishes." (FW)
On October 17, 1777, from the Orderly Book: "The General

II: SELECTED BIOGRAPHIES 205

has his happiness completed relative to the success of the Northern
army. On the 14th instant General Burgoyne and his whole army
surrendered themselves prisoners of war. Let every face brighten,
and every heart expand with grateful joy and praise to the Supreme
Disposer of all events, who has granted us this signal success.
The chaplains of the army are to prepare short discourses, suited
to the occasion, to deliver to their several corps and brigades
at five o'clock this afternoon." (BI)

WESTMORELAND, ANN (NANCY) LENOIR   SC
of Spartanburg. She was born about 1735 in Brunswick County,
Virginia, and married Robert Westmoreland, who was born about
1735 in the same county. Later they lived in Spartanburg. Her
husband was beaten to death by Tories for refusing to give information on where supplies were hidden or where the American troops
were encamped. She is credited with rendering aid as a patriot.
Nancy Westmoreland died at Spartanburg sometime after 1823. (Submitted by Joyce Littlepage Keck, Laredo, TX)

WESTON, HANNAH WATTS   ME
of Jonesborough (formerly Chandler's River). The daughter of
Capt. Samuel Watts, who served in the French and Indian Wars,
she was born on November 22, 1758, in Haverhill, Massachusetts.
The family moved to Chandler's River in 1769. In October 1774
Hannah married Josiah Weston.

On June 11, 1775, Jeremiah O'Brien of Machias, Maine, with
forty men, seized the Tory sloop <u>Unity</u> in Machias Harbor and set
out to capture the British four-gun schooner <u>Margaretta</u>. Josiah
Weston was one of the men who responded to the call for help.
Hannah realized that the men would need ammunition, and so collected all the pewter spoons, lead, and powder she could obtain
from all her neighbors and for miles around Chandler's River. After
she had collected about thirty or forty pounds of metal and powder,
she set out on June 12, 1775, with her sister-in-law, Rebecca Weston
(later Mrs. Libby), to carry the supplies to the men in Machias
Harbor, a distance of sixteen miles. After they turned in their
bounty to the store of Smith and Stillman, the girls were given
as a reward twelve yards of camlet valued at Ł2.8.6 which the
storekeepers charged to the Committee of Safety at Machias. Hannah Weston died on December 12, 1855. (AM)

WETHERILL, RACHEL FITZ RANDOLPH   NJ
of Kingston. Rachel was born on January 31, 1742/43, in Princeton
and married Thomas Wetherill (or Wetheral) on March 18, 1764.
They had one son and six daughters.

Gen. Washington had his headquarters in the Wetherill home
on June 25, 1778. On this date Washington wrote to the Marquis
de Lafayette: "You are immediately to proceed with the detachment
commanded by General Poor and form a junction as expeditiously
as possible with that under the command of General Scott. You
are to use the most effectual means for gaining the enemy's left

flank and rear, and giving them every degree of annoyance." (FW; some information from Rebecca B. Colesar, New Jersey State Library, Trenton)

WHEATLEY, PHYLLIS   MA
of Boston. She was born in Africa about 1753 and brought to America in a slave ship. Phyllis was a servant in the home of John Wheatley. Phyllis wrote poetry which was published in 1773 in London. She was an American patriot and wrote a poem in tribute to Gen. Washington. Phyllis sent the poem to him, which Washington graciously acknowledged. A portion of her poem reads as follows:

> Fix'd are the eyes of nations on the scales,
> For in their hopes Columbia's arm prevails,
> Anon Britannia droops the pensive head,
> While round increase the rising hills of dead.
> Ah! cruel blindness to Columbia's state!
> Lament the thirst of boundless power too late,
> Proceed, great chief, with virtue on thy side,
> Thy ev'ry action let the goddess guide.
> A crown, a mansion, and a throne that shine,
> With gold unfading, WASHINGTON! be thine.

On February 28, 1776, Washington wrote to Phyllis from his camp at Cambridge, Massachusetts: "I thank you sincerely for your polite notice of me, in the elegant Lines you enclosed, and however undeserving I may be of such encomium and panegyrick, the style and manner exhibit a stricking proof of your great practical Talents. In honour of which, and as a tribute justly due to you, I would have published the Poem, had I not been apprehensive, that, while I only meant to give the World this new instance of your genius, I might have incurred the imputation of Vanity. This and nothing else, determined me not to give it place in the public Prints."

Phyllis married a black man named John Peters. She died on December 5, 1784. (FW)

WHEATLEY, SUBMITT PECK   NH
of Lebanon. The daughter of Mary and Benjamin Peck, she was born on August 1, 1722, at Franklin, Connecticut. About 1739 she married Lt. Aaron Cook and they had one son, Jesse Cook. Her husband was killed in the French and Indian War, but before he died he asked his friend John Wheatley to befriend his young wife. When John returned to Connecticut, he married the young widow in 1742/43, when he was twenty-three years of age and his bride was aged twenty. John and Submitt had seven children.

John and Submitt lived in Boston and Norwich, Connecticut, before they moved to Lebanon, New Hampshire, in 1764. John served on the Committee of Safety during the Revolutionary War and held other public offices in Lebanon. Four of their sons served during the war, and two of them died in service. The family

II: SELECTED BIOGRAPHIES   207

homestead is located on Campbell Street in Lebanon Center. Mrs.
Wheatley was buried in the Old Pine Cemetery in West Lebanon.
The local chapter of the Daughters of the American Revolution
is named in her honor. (Submitted by Ruby M. Towle, Farmington, and Anna R. Tenney, Newport, NH)

WHETTEN, MARGARET TODD   NY
of New York City. She was born in 1736 and married William Whetten. In 1776 they moved to New Rochelle, New York. One day
British troops broke into her home and ransacked her house, so
they moved back to New York City, whereupon her husband died.
Mrs. Whetten and her daughters visited the British prison ships
in New York Harbor and took food to the American prisoners. At
one point Mrs. Whetten concealed a spy in her home, which became
known as the "Rebel Headquarters." After the war Gen. Washington visited Mrs. Whetten to have breakfast and thank her for her
good deeds. Margaret died in March 1809 and was buried in the
churchyard of Saint George's Chapel in New York City. A chapter
of the Daughters of the American Revolution was named in her
honor. (DAR; GP)

WHITAKER, ELIZABETH OGDEN   NY
of Orange County. She was born in 1744 and married Squire Whitaker. They moved to Wyoming Valley, Pennsylvania. During the
great massacre there on July 3, 1778, Elizabeth nursed and cared
for the wounded soldiers. In the 1780s they moved to Deposit,
New York. (Information from Eleanor Josd, Matamoras, PA) Mrs.
Whitaker died in 1833. (DAR)

WHITALL, ANN COOPER   NJ
of Woodbury. She was the wife of James Whitall. They were Quakers and had nine children. In 1777 Fort Mercer was built in the
Whitall apple orchard just north of the Whitall's home on the Delaware River. During the Battle of Red Bank and the attack on
Fort Mercer on October 22, 1777, Ann Whitall refused to leave her
home. Other members of her family fled to Woodbury, but Mrs.
Whitall climbed the stairs to her attic to spin. Her only companion
was a loyal black servant. A cannonball hit the attic, so Mrs.
Whitall and her servant carried the spinning wheel to the basement.
A young man who was restoring the house in the twentieth century
discovered where the cannonball struck the attic, just below the
west window. He could see how repairs were made to the site.
    After the battle, Mrs. Whitall and her servant cared for and
nursed the wounded American and Hessian soldiers. Mrs. Whitall
was in her late sixties at the time and died on September 27, 1797,
at the age of eighty-one. Mrs. Whitall and her husband are interred
in the grounds of the Woodbury Friends Meeting House. Their
site is marked by a marble memorial inserted in the wall. The
Woodbury chapter of the Daughters of the American Revolution
is named in her honor. (Information from Jeanne G. Ruddick,
Woodbury, NJ)

WHITCHER, HANNAH MORRILL   NH
of Woodsville. The fourth of eleven children, she was born in
1753 in Amesbury, Massachusetts. In 1777 she married Chase Whitcher, who served in Capt. Henry Dearborn's Company, General
Stark's Regiment, in the Battle of Bunker Hill on June 17, 1775.
Mr. and Mrs. Whitcher built their cabin at the foot of Mount
Moosilauke at Warren. He served in the army until December 6,
1777. Mrs. Whitcher was the mother of eleven children. The local
chapter of the Daughters of the American Revolution is named in
her honor. (Submitted by Ruby M. Towle, Farmington, NH)

WHITE, MRS. EBENEZER   NJ
of Basking Ridge. Her first husband was Samuel Brown, and after
his death she married Ebenezer White. After his death she operated
a tavern in Basking Ridge known as the Widow White's Tavern. After
the disastrous defense of Fort Washington, the American Gen. Charles
Lee fled to New Jersey and spent the night of December 12/13,
1776, in Mrs. White's Tavern. That morning a cavalry attack on
the tavern was led by Sir Banastre Tarleton who learned that Gen.
Lee was there.

    Mrs. White took Lee upstairs and tried to hide him between
the chimney and the breastwork over the fireplace, but it was
too small for the general. So Lee went downstairs and surrendered
to the British, but credit must be given to Mrs. White who tried
to hide him. (DD; J. H. Van Horn, Historic Somerset, 1965; Susan
Tegge, Basking Ridge, NJ)

WHITE, MERCY HATHAWAY   NH
of Hopkinton. She was born in Taunton, Massachusetts, in 1746
and married John White, who was born in Rochester, Massachusetts,
on February 13, 1729. He was a fifth-generation descendant of
Susanna Fuller and William White of the Mayflower. They spent
their early years in Freetown, Massachusetts, then went to New
Boston, New Hampshire, and then settled in Hopkinton. John White
served as a sergeant in the Revolutionary War and then later as
town clerk in Hopkinton.

    Nancy White followed her husband to war, dodged bullets,
once killed a bear that came her way, and cared for the sick and
wounded.

    John White died on April 3, 1812, and Mary on August 1,
1816. Both are buried in the Stumpfield cemetery section of Contoocook, in the town of Hopkinton. They had one daughter, Hope
White Bartlett (1775-1859), who left many descendants now living
in the Bradford and Warner area of New Hampshire. (Submitted
by Mrs. Clarence Jeffrey, Contoocook, NH)

    The Warner, New Hampshire, chapter of the Daughters of
the American Revolution is named in her honor.

WILKINSON, ELIZA   SC
of Yonges Island. June 3, 1780, was a day of terror for Eliza,
a patriotic American. The British troops entered her house with

II: SELECTED BIOGRAPHIES

drawn swords and pistols in their hands crying, "Where're these women rebels?" They plundered her house, taking everything they thought was of value. The ladies' trunks were split open, and the soldiers even took their clothing. They took the earrings off her sister's ears, and a wedding ring from a friend. (Letters of Eliza Wilkinson, New York, 1839)

WILLIAMS, MARY TRUMBULL   CT
of Lebanon. She was born in 1746, the daughter of Jonathan Trumbull, who served as governor of Connecticut from 1769 to 1784. In 1771 Mary married William Williams. He was elected to the Continental Congress in 1775 and was a signer of the Declaration of Independence. During the war she fed and clothed soldiers, and her house was open to them. In 1781 they opened their house to the army and took quarters elsewhere. They had two sons and one daughter. Mary Williams died in 1831 in Lebanon. (GP)

WILSON, ELEANOR   NC
of Steel Creek, Mecklenburg County. She was born about 1724 and married Robert Wilson (ca. 1720-ca. 1810), who had left Pennsylvania about 1760 with his three brothers and settled in Mecklenburg County. Seven of her eleven sons served in the Revolutionary War. On August 16, 1780, at Camden, South Carolina, the American forces under Gen. Gates were defeated by Lord Cornwallis. But after the patriot victory at King's Mountain, North Carolina, on October 7, 1780, Gen. Cornwallis decided to abandon his invasion of North Carolina and marched northward from South Carolina. During his march, about October 14, the British army halted for the night at the Wilson's plantation near Steel Creek.
    The British general and Col. Banastre Tarleton requested dinner of Mrs. Wilson, which she was forced to serve to them. Mrs. Wilson asked Lord Cornwallis for the release of her husband and their son John who had been captured by the British. The British general informed Mrs. Wilson that if she could induce her husband and son to give up the rebel cause and fight for the king, he would have them released. She told him that the men had embarked in the holy cause of liberty, and had fought for it for five years. Then she told him, "I have seven sons who are now, or have been bearing arms ... Sooner than see one of my family turn back from the glorious enterprise, I would take these boys [pointing to her younger sons] and with them would myself enlist under Sumter's standard, and show my husband and sons how to fight, and if necessary, to die for my country!" Later Eleanor's husband escaped from the British, but her son John was imprisoned about two years.
    Both Eleanor and her husband died about 1810 at Steel Creek. (EW; submitted by Mary Holland Lancaster, Florence, AL, and Helen S. Henry, Pueblo, CO) There is a DAR chapter in Washington, D.C., named in her honor.

WILSON, RACHEL BIRD   PA
of Philadelphia. On November 5, 1771, she married James Wilson

of Reading, Pennsylvania, an attorney. They had six children.
In 1775 he was elected to the Second Continental Congress and
voted for independence on July 2, 1776. The Wilsons moved to
Philadelphia in 1778. Wilson was a delegate to the 1787 Constitutional Convention and was a signer of the United States Constitution.
   Mrs. Wilson was active in the ladies' relief association for
the welfare of the American soldiers. (<u>Pennsylvania Gazette</u>, June
12, 1780) Mrs. Wilson died in 1786.

WINTHROP, HANNAH FAYERWEATHER MA
of Cambridge. Her first husband was Farr Tolman, and in 1756
she became the second wife of John Winthrop, the astronomer,
who was also a professor at Harvard. On November 11, 1777,
Mrs. Winthrop wrote to Mercy Warren about captured Americans:

> I never had the least idea that the creation produced
> such a sordid set of creatures in human figure--poor,
> dirty, emaciated men, great numbers of women, who
> seemed to be the beasts of burden, having a bushel basket
> on their backs, by which they were bent double--the
> contents seemed to be pots and kettles, various sorts
> of furniture--children peeping thro' gridirons and other
> utensils, some very young infants who were born on the
> road, the women with bare feet, cloathed in dirty rags
> ... After a noble looking advanced guard Gen. J. Burgoyne headed this terrible group on horseback. The
> other general also, cloathed in blue cloaks. Hessians,
> Anspachers, Brunswickers, etc. followed on. The Hessian
> general gave us a polite bow as they passed. Not so
> the British. Their baggage waggons were drawn by poor
> half starved horses ...
> Surprising that our general or any of our colonels
> should insist on the first University in America being
> disbanded for their more genteel accommodations, and
> we poor oppressed people seek asylum in the woods against
> a piercing winter! ... It is said we shall have not less
> than seven thousand persons to feed in Cambridge and
> its environs, more than its inhabitants. Two hundred
> and fifty cord of wood will not serve them a week. Think
> then how we must be distressed. I never thought I could
> lie down to sleep surrounded by these enemies, but we
> strongly become enured to those high things which appear
> difficult when distant." (CS)

   There is a Hannah Winthrop Chapter of the Daughters of
the American Revolution in Cambridge, Massachusetts.

WITHERSPOON, ELIZABETH MONTGOMERY NJ
of Princeton. On September 2, 1748, she married the Rev. John
Witherspoon, a Presbyterian minister. They had ten children,

II: SELECTED BIOGRAPHIES

but five of them died in infancy. In 1768 he became president of the College of New Jersey (now Princeton University). In 1776 he signed the Declaration of Independence. On December 6, 1776, the Witherspoons were forced to leave Princeton when the British army approached the town. They had to abandon their home, most of their household goods, sheep, cows, and fowl, but they took with them four colts. The Witherspoons fled to Pequea, a village in Lancaster County, Pennsylvania.

Mrs. Witherspoon returned to her home in the summer of 1777 and found her house had been ransacked and plundered by the British and the Tories. Their eldest son, James, was killed in action in November 1777. This is another sample of the suffering endured by patriotic American women and their sons. (DD)

WOLCOTT, LAURA COLLINS   CT
of Litchfield. The daughter of Lois Cornwall and Capt. Daniel Collins of Guilford, Connecticut, she was married on January 21, 1755, to Oliver Wolcott of Litchfield. They had five children. He was made a colonel in the militia in 1774. Mr. Wolcott was a delegate to the Continental Congress in 1776 but was absent in July because of illness.

At Bowling Green in New York there stood a gilded lead statue of King George III, which was raised by the Sons of Liberty. Wolcott signed the Declaration of Independence and left Philadelphia on October 1, 1776. On his return home he visited New York City, where the Sons of Liberty gave him the statue, which he took to Litchfield, where Mrs. Wolcott and her children, assisted by neighbors, turned it into 42,088 bullets for the Continental Army. (See also Ruth Marvin, above) (CG)

On his way from Hartford to West Point on the evening of September 24, 1780, Gen. Washington was entertained in the home of Gen. and Mrs. Oliver Wolcott. (BI)

WOODHULL, RUTH FLOYD   NY
of Wantagh, Long Island. She was a sister of William Floyd, who signed the Declaration of Independence. In 1761 she married Nathaniel Woodhull of Suffolk County, New York, who was a colonel in the French and Indian Wars. After the counties of Queens and Suffolk raised an army for the Continental forces, he was made a general. While unarmed, Woodhull was captured by a detachment of seven hundred British soldiers. He was slashed repeatedly across his arm by a British officer with a broadsword, and his arm was nearly cut off.

Woodhull was sent to the old church in New Utrecht which was used as a prison. He was permitted to write to his wife and asked her to bring all the money she could procure. She did so, and he distributed the money to his fellow prisoners. A few hours after her arrival, on September 28, 1778, he died of gangrene. The death of Gen. Woodhull was considered wanton murder, not justified by the rules of warfare, and incensed the Americans.

The Woodhulls had one daughter, who married Henry Nicoll.

After his death she became the wife of Gen. John Smith. (GP, vol. 2)

WOODS, HANNAH WALLACE   KY
of Gilbert's Creek. She married Capt. Michael Woods (1740-1800) of Virginia, then they moved to Gilbert's Creek Station. In 1783, when the Indians attacked the stockade, one Indian forced his way into the house before the women and a slightly crippled Negro managed to bar the door against the other Indians. The Negro grappled with the intruder but was getting the worst of it when Hannah Woods, or her daughter Hannah, struck the Indian with an ax and killed him. Within an hour help arrived, but the Indians were gone. (Talbert, Benjamin Logan)

WOOSTER, MARY CLAP   CT
of New Haven. The daughter of the Rev. Thomas Clap, the fourth president of Yale University, she was born in 1729 in Windham, Connecticut. In 1745 in her father's house in New Haven, she married Capt. David Wooster, commander of the sloop Defense. During the Revolutionary War, she paid his officers and men from the family means of her husband, since money was not forthcoming from the Continental Congress. Capt. Wooster was mortally wounded on April 27, 1777.

On July 5, 1779, Mrs. Wooster's home was ransacked by British soldiers, and she lost all her possessions. Mrs. Wooster spent her last days in poverty and died in 1807. A New Haven chapter of the Daughters of the American Revolution is named in her honor. (CG)

WRIGHT, PHEBE QUINBY   NY
of North Castle. She was the wife of Reuben Wright of Wright's Mills, later known as Cox Mills, then Robbias Mills, and later as Old Kensico Village.

Gen. Washington in July 1778 crossed the Hudson River from Kings Ferry to Verplancks Point and established his headquarters in the Wright House from July 20 to 27. On July 22 Washington wrote to the Marquis de Lafayette to march with his troops to Rhode Island to subject himself to the orders of Maj. Gen. Sullivan to attack the British at Newport. (FW)

In 1784 Reuben Wright purchased some land in Cortlandt Manor and moved his family there.

Wright's Mills is now buried beneath the waters of the Kensico Reservoir. In 1932 the Daughters of the American Revolution placed a marker on the east side of the reservoir denoting the location of Wright's Mills as "beneath the water of this lake about 1,200 feet southwest of the long bridge which spans the connection between the waters of the old Rye Lake and the main reservoir property." (Some information from Susan Swanson, Westchester County Historian, White Plains, NY; Richard N. Lander, North Castle Historian, Armonk, NY)

II: SELECTED BIOGRAPHIES

WRIGHT, PRUDENCE CUMMINGS   MA
of Pepperell, Middlesex County. She was born on November 26, 1740, and married David Wright. After Col. William Prescott's minutemen sounded the alarm of 1775, Mrs. Wright together with Mrs. Job Shattuck of Groton, Massachusetts, and the neighboring women donned their husband's clothing and armed with muskets and pitchforks, defended Jewett's Bridge over the Nashua River. They were determined no Tory or British soldier would cross the bridge. When Capt. Leonard Whiting of Hollis, New Hampshire, a noted Tory, crossed the bridge, the women arrested him. In his boots they located dispatches from Canada to the British in Boston. The women sent Capt. Whiting to Oliver Prescott of Groton, and his dispatches were sent to the local Committee of Safety. Mrs. Wright died on December 2, 1823. (CD; DAR) There is a Prudence Wright Chapter of the Daughters of the American Revolution in Pepperell.

Near the bridge stands a granite tablet bearing the inscription: "Near this spot a party of patriotic women under the leadership of Mrs. David Wright of Pepperell, in April 1775, captured Leonard Whiting, a Tory who was carrying treasonable dispatches to the enemy in Boston. He was taken prisoner to Groton and the dispatches were sent to the Committee of Safety at Cambridge." (GP, vol. 2)

WYCKOFF, POLLY   NJ
of Allentown. She was the daughter of Gertrude Shipman and Samuel Wyckoff and was named Mary but had the nickname of Polly. She was born in February 1770 and apparently was visiting friends in Bogartsfield (now in Cresswell), New Jersey. According to tradition, she spotted Redcoats on the morning of November 20, 1776, after they had climbed the Palisades and were marching southward to Fort Lee. Polly told her mother, who then apparently told Peter Bogart, who rode to warn the American troops that the British were coming.

Some people believed that Polly issued the warning, but she was too young to have ridden horseback alone. Peter Bogart is immortalized in a poem, "The Lone Countryman from Closter," by Alma Jacobson Shadirons. Mary Wyckoff is buried in Allentown, New Jersey. (Information submitted by Mrs. Earl A. Mosley of Tenafly, NY, who regards issue as unsettled) The local chapter of the Daughters of the American Revolution is named the Polly Wyckoff Chapter.

WYCKOFF, SARAH HART   NJ
of Monmouth County. She was the wife of Jacob Wyckoff. Mrs. Wyckoff was an active member of the ladies' relief association for the welfare of the American soldiers. (<u>New Jersey Gazette</u>, July 4, 1780)

WYTHE, ELIZABETH TALIAFERRO   VA
of Williamsburg. The daughter of Elizabeth and Richard Taliaferro,

about 1755 she became the second wife of George Wythe. Elizabeth and George had one child who died in infancy. His first wife, Ann Lewis, died in 1748. George Wythe was a signer of the Declaration of Independence.

Lord Cornwallis and his army marched into Virginia in 1781. The manager of the Wythe plantation turned over all the slaves and the personal property of the Wythes to the British. Their home was plundered, and the Wythes lost most of their fortune. This is another example of the suffering of the patriotic men and women of the Revolutionary War.

Mrs. Wythe died in 1787. Mr. Wythe was a professor of law at the College of William and Mary, and a great legal mind. At age eighty-one he freed his slaves a few days before he was poisoned by a grandnephew who was eager to inherit. He died in 1806 in Richmond, Virginia. (FG)

General Washington had his headquarters in Williamsburg at the Wythe homestead from September 14 to November 5, 1781. During this time, on October 19, 1781, Lord Cornwallis surrendered at Yorktown, Virginia. (BI)

Y

YARD, SARAH   PA
of Philadelphia. On August 29, 1774, Robert Treat Paine, John Adams, and delegates to the First Continental Congress from Massachusetts lodged at the home of Mrs. Yard. From August 31 to September 3, Adams lodged at Jane Port's house on Arch Street, but then moved back to Mrs. Yard's home and stayed there until the spring of 1777. On this date, August 31, 1774, John Adams met Dr. Benjamin Rush, establishing a friendship which lasted for thirty-eight years until the death of Dr. Rush.

In 1774 John Adams met Caesar Rodney, the delegate from Delaware, and made the following comment in his diary: "Caesar Rodney is the oddest looking Man in the World. He is tall--thin and slender as a Reed--pale--his Face is not bigger than a large Apple. Yet there is a Sense and Fire, Spirit, Wit and Humor in his Countenance." (BA)

PART III: COMPLETE LISTING

The names in this section include patriotic services of women from the thirteen original colonies plus Maine (then a part of Massachusetts), Vermont (then a part of New Hampshire), and parts of Virginia and North Carolina (now the states of Kentucky, Tennessee, and West Virginia)--representing a total of eighteen states.

Over 90 percent of the entries are from official state records on nonmilitary patriotic services. Abbreviations are listed on pages xv-xviii, above.

New Hampshire has receipts for provisions supplied, but they are signed by the selectmen of each town and not by the individuals who supplied the provisions.

There are no official records for nonmilitary services available for New York State nor for Delaware (Revolutionary War material is not indexed or cataloged).

AARON, ELIZABETH   NC
   Wife of Isaac Aaron. She supplied provisions for the army (RA, K:123A).
ABBOTT, ALICE FULLER   PA
   Her house and barn were burned by the enemy. See Biographies.
ABERLAY, ANN   SC
   She supplied funds for the army (AA, 1:13), and also provisions (SI, Y-Z:161).
ABNEY, MARTHA   SC
   She supplied funds for the army (AA, 1:34).
ACREE, REBECCA   VA
   Hanover County. She performed a public service (VR, 111:162).
ADAIR, ELIZABETH   SC
   She supplied provisions for the army (SI, R-T:101).
ADAIR, MARY
   Born circa 1730. Married William Adair. She died in 1819 and is listed as a patriot in the DAR Patriot Index.
ADAIR, SARAH   SC
   She supplied provisions for the army (SI, R-T:162).

ADAMS, ABIGAIL SMITH   MA
    She was a strong patriot for American independence and an
    early advocate of women's rights. See Biographies.
ADAMS, CATHERINE   NC
    She supplied provisions for the army (RA, 8:87, fol. 3; 4:99-102).
ADAMS, ELIZABETH   VA
    Witham County. She performed a public service (VR, 3:238).
ADAMS, ELIZABETH WELLS   MA
    The wife of Samuel Adams, they were impoverished by the Revo-
    lutionary War. See Biographies.
ADAMS, KATHERINE   NC
    She supplied provisions for the army (RA, 5:1, fol. 2).
ADAMS, MARGARET   NC
    She supplied provisions for the army (RA, A:197).
ADAMS, MARTHA   VA
    Pittsylvania County. She performed a patriotic service (VR,
    5:1).
ADAMS, MARY   SC
    She provided funds for the army (AA, 1:66).
ADAMS, RHODA   MD
    Charles County. She supplied wheat for the army May 10, 1783
    (IM, 25453; submitted by Richard H. Richardson, Annapolis, MD).
ADAMS, SARAH   SC
    She supplied provisions for the army (SI, U-W:25).
ADAMS, SUSANNA BOYLSTON   MA
    Braintree. She was the wife of John Adams and the mother
    of John Adams who signed the Declaration of Independence,
    and of Elihu Adams who commanded a company of militia during
    the alarm of April 19, 1775. Elihu Adams died in camp at Cam-
    bridge in August 1775 during an epidemic of dysentery at the
    camp. Elihu Adams left a wife and three small children.
ADDISON, MARY   SC
    She provided funds for the army (AA, 1:103, 105).
ADKINS, LUCY   VA
    Sussex County. She performed a public service (VR, 5:197).
ADKINS, MARY   VA
    Goochland County. She performed a public service (Court Book-
    let, p. 4).
ADMEREST, JANE. See WESTERVELT
AIKEN, MOLLY   NH
    Antrim. Molly was the wife of Deacon James Aiken who served
    in the war. She was the first white woman to settle in Antrim.
    The local chapter of the Daughters of the American Revolution
    is named in her honor (submitted by Ruby M. Towle, Farming-
    ton, NH).
AIRY, MARY   NC
    She supplied provisions for the army (RA, A:105).
AKIN, ANN   SC
    She provided funds for the army (AA, 1:120).
ALCORN, CATHERINE   SC
    She provided funds for the army (AA, 1:128) and provisions
    (SI, Y-Z:161).

III: COMPLETE LISTING

ALDRICH, HANNAH TILSON   RI
    Cumberland. She was born in 1741 and married Abel Aldrich. Hannah provided food supplies for the army in December 1778. She died in 1819 (MR, p. 40:19; submitted by Phyllis Silva, Pawtucket, RI; DAR).

ALEXANDER, AGNES BREWSTER   VA
    She spun, knitted, wove, and cooked for the soldiers. See Biographies.

ALEXANDER, ELIZABETH   NC
    She supplied provisions for the army (RA, 11:82; A:197).

ALEXANDER, HANNAH   MD
    Talbot County. She supplied bacon for the army, June 12, 1778 (IM, 7243; submitted by Richard H. Richardson, Annapolis, MD).

ALEXANDER, MARGARET CLARKE   PA
    Born 1743. She married James Ross, then James Alexander. She died in 1809 and is listed as a patriot in the DAR Patriot Index.

ALEXANDER, SARAH LIVINGSTON. See LADY STIRLING

ALEXANDER, SUSANNA   VA
    King George County. She performed a patriot service (VR, 2:383).

ALLAN, MARY PATTON   ME
    She was taken prisoner by the British. See Biographies.

ALLEN, AGNES   SC
    She provided funds for the army (AA, 1:175).

ALLEN, ANN   VA
    King and Queen County. She performed a patriotic service (VR Lists, 4:3).

ALLEN, ELIZABETH PARSONS   MA
    Six of her sons fought in the Revolutionary War. See Biographies.

ALLEN, JANE   VA
    Elizabeth City County. She performed a patriotic service (VR Court Booklet, p. 14).

ALLEN, JEAN   VA
    Elizabeth City. She performed a public service (VR Court Booklet, p. 7).

ALLEN, KATHY   VA
    Frederick County. She performed a public service (VR, 2:168).

ALLEN, MARGARET   NC
    She supplied provisions for the army (RA, A:144).

ALLEN, MARTHA   VA
    Essex County. She performed a patriotic service (VR, 2:140).

ALLEN, MARY   CT
    Her property was destroyed in the Groton raid by the British (CAR, 1:79a).

ALLEN, MARY   VA
    Hanover County. She performed a patriotic service (VR, 2:140).

ALLEN, MARY ALDIS. See DRAPER

ALLEN, MARY BAKER   CT
    Her son, Ethan Allen, was captured by the British and imprisoned. See Biographies.

ALLEN, MARY BROWNSON   VT
  On June 23, 1762, Mary Brownson of Roxbury (Woodbury), CT, married Ethan Allen of Cornwall, VT. While residing in the New Hampshire Grants (now Vermont), Ethan Allen commanded the Green Mountain Boys. During the expedition to Canada in December 1775 he was captured by the British and imprisoned until 1778 (submitted by Dorothy Durham, Shoreham, VT).

ALLEN, RHODA   NC
  She supplied provisions for the army (RA, 6:42, fol. 3).

ALLEN, URSULA WITHERS   VA
  Fauquier County. She was born on September 19, 1709, and married John Allen. They had four sons and one daughter. Her husband died before the Revolution. Mrs. Allen gave supplies to the troops during the war, and died in September 1793 (submitted by Frances Vivian Moore, Monroe, LA).

ALLEN, WIDOW   NC
  She supplied provisions for the army (RA, 5:46, vol. 1).

ALLIN, RACHEL   NJ
  Hackensack. Her property was destroyed by the British (CDB, claim 105; submitted by Bette Marie Baker, Trenton, NJ).

ALLISON, DOROTHY   SC
  She provided funds for the army (AA, 2:4, 5).

ALLISON, ELIZABETH   MD
  She supplied wheat for the army, May 31, 1781 (IM, 17050).

ALLISON, MARY   MD
  She nursed the wounded soldiers in 1777 (IM, 3302).

ALLISON, RACHEL   SC
  She provided funds (AA, 2:7, 9) and also provisions for the army (SI, Y-Z:319).

ALLISON, RUTH   NJ
  Bordentown. Her property was damaged by the British (CDB, B:15).

ALLISON, SARAH   SC
  She provided funds for the army (AA, 2:10).

ALLSTON, ELIZABETH   SC
  She provided funds for the army (AA, 2:32).

ALLSTON, RACHEL   SC
  She provided funds for the army (AA, 2:34).

ALMY, ANN   RI
  She provided cordwood for the army in August 1777 (MR, 27:7; submitted by Phyllis Silva, Pawtucket, RI).

ALRICHS, ANN WEST. See LOWREY

ALSOP (ALSOF), SARAH   VA
  Spotsylvania County. She performed a public service (VR, 5:1).

ALSTON, HANNAH   NJ
  Woodbridge. Her property was damaged by the British (CDB, B:80; submitted by Bette Marie Baker, Trenton, NJ).

ALSTON, RACHEL   NJ
  Woodbridge. Her property was damaged by the British (CDB, B:54).

III: COMPLETE LISTING

ALSTON, THEODOSIA BURR. See BURR
ALTMAN, SARAH   SC
   She supplied funds (AA, 2:35, 37) also provisions for the army
   (SI, L-N:3).
ALVORD, MARY   CT
   Her property was destroyed in the Fairfield raid by the British
   (CAR, 153di, 63ps). She was a Western Land Grantee (submitted
   by Carolyn M. Picciano, Hartford, CT).
ALVORD, MARY HAMILTON   MA
   Northampton. She married Elisha Alvord (1731-1807), and they
   had five sons who served in the Revolutionary War. She died
   on January 2, 1791 (FP, 2).
AMBLER, MARY   VA
   James City. She performed a public service (VR Court Booklet,
   p. 1).
AMBLER, REBECCA BURWELL   VA
   She was active in the ladies' association for the welfare of the
   soldiers. See Biographies.
AMBROSE, CATHERINE   MD
   Frederick. She supplied beef for the army (IM, 18862).
AMIS, MARY   NC
   She supplied provisions for the army (RA, 5:59, fol. 4).
AMIS, MRS. WILLIAM   NC
   She supplied provisions for the army (RA, 1-6:331).
ANDERSON, ANN   SC
   She supplied provisions for the army (SI, B:68).
ANDERSON, ELIZABETH   VA
   Louisa County. She performed a public service (VR, 3:338).
ANDERSON, JANE   VA
   King and Queen County. She performed a public service (VR,
   3:214).
ANDERSON, JUDITH   VA
   Louisa County. She performed a public service (VR, 3:337).
ANDERSON, MARGARET   SC
   She was the wife of Capt. George Anderson. She supplied funds
   for the army (AA, 2: 64, 65).
ANDERSON, MARGARET   SC
   The widow of Thomas Anderson, she supplied funds for the
   army (AA, 2:112).
ANDERSON, MARGARET   VA
   Frederick County. She performed a public service (Court Booklet,
   p. 48).
ANDERSON, MARY   GA
   Liberty County. The wife of David Anderson, they had two
   daughters, Sarah and Mary. She supplied one barren cow for
   Gen. Wayne (WA, p. 170; submitted by Joanne Smalley, Atlanta,
   GA).
ANDERSON, MARY   VA
   Louisa County. She performed a public service (VR Lists, 1:6).
ANDERSON, NANCY STEPHENSON   SC
   Born circa 1750, she married William Anderson, then Daniel

Green. She died in 1820. She is listed as a patriot in the DAR Patriot Index

ANDERSON, PRISCILLA　　　　　MD
  She supplied wheat for the army in 1780 (IM, 13832).

ANDERSON, REBECCA　　　　　SC
  She refused to take the oath of loyalty to the Crown and was banished from Charleston. See Biographies.

ANDERSON, RUTH　　　　　SC
  She provided funds for the army (AA, 2:66, 67).

ANDERSON, SALLY　　　　　VA
  King and Queen County. She performed a public service (VR, 4:333).

ANDERSON, SARAH　　　　　NC
  She supplied provisions for the army (RA, 9:20, fol. 3).

ANDERSON, SARAH　　　　　VA
  Mecklenburg. She performed a public service (VR, 4:31).

ANDERSON, SARAH CARNEY　　　　　SC
  She supplied provisions for the army. See Biographies.

ANDERSON, MRS. T.　　　　　NJ
  Sussex County. She collected funds for the army (New Jersey Gazette, July 4, 1780).

ANDREWS, ABIGAIL　　　　　CT
  She suffered loss of property during the New Haven raid by the British (CAR, 1:63d, 91g). She was a Western Lands Grantee.

ANDREWS, ANN　　　　　VA
  Accomack County (VR, 1:21; Southampton County, 5:173). She performed a patriotic service.

ANDREWS, CHARITY　　　　　NC
  She supplied provisions for the army (RA, C:159).

ANDREWS, ELIZABETH　　　　　VA
  Prince George County. She performed a patriotic service (VR, 51:248).

ANDREWS, JANE　　　　　SC
  She supplied funds (AA, 2:127) and also provisions for the army (SI, L-N:57).

ANDREWS, JOICE　　　　　VA
  Essex County. She performed a public service (VR, 2:140).

ANDREWS, LYDIA　　　　　CT
  New Britain. The wife of Moses Andrews, six of her sons served during the Revolutionary War, and she made their clothing before they went off to battle (CG).

ANDREWS, MARGARET　　　　　VA
  Accomack County. She performed a public service (VR, Ctf 1).

ANDREWS, SARAH　　　　　CT
  She suffered loss of property in the Fairfield raid (CAR, 1:53a, 63c). She was a Western Lands Grantee.

ANDREWS, SUSANNA　　　　　NC
  She supplied provisions for the army (RA, B:273).

ANGELL, SUSANNAH　　　　　RI
  She supplied provisions for the army (MR, p. 15:19, 21; 21:18, 20).

III: COMPLETE LISTING

ANNAS, ELIZABETH   SC
She supplied provisions for the army (SI, 1:65).

APPLEBY, MRS. JOSEPH   NY
General Washington had his headquarters here. See Biographies.

APPLESMITH, ELIZABETH   VA
Isle of Wight. She performed a public service (VR, 2:312).

APTHROP, MRS. CHARLES WARD   NY
Gen. Washington stayed in her home. See Biographies.

ARCHER, MARY   VA
Hanover County. She performed a public service (VR Court Booklet 1, p. 9).

ARDEN, CATHERINE BEEKMAN   NY
Gen. Washington had breakfast at the home of Mrs. Arden. See Biographies.

ARMISTEAD, MRS.   VA
Elizabeth City. She performed a public service (VR, 2:160).

ARMISTEAD, MARY   VA
New Kent City. She performed a public service (VR, 55:130).

ARMOUR, ABIGAIL   CT
She suffered loss of property in the Greenwich raid by the British (CAR, 1:63c, 74a). She was a Western Lands Grantee.

ARMS, SUSANNAH WILLARD   VT
Born 1720, she married John Arms and died in 1793. She is listed as a patriot in the DAR Patriot Index.

ARMSTRONG, CATHERINE   NY
At age sixteen she was captured in May 1781 at Herkiman by Indians and released from Fort Ticonderoga on July 18, 1782 (MR).

ARMSTRONG, ELIZABETH   VA
Cumberland County. She performed a patriotic service (VR, 1:214).

ARMSTRONG, FRANCES   NC
She supplied provisions for the army (RA, B:182).

ARMSTRONG, MARY   PA
She was captured by Indians and taken to Montreal where she worked for Mr. Magins to support herself (MR).

ARMSTRONG, MARY   NC
She supplied provisions for the army (RA, 12:16, fol. 2, A 211).

ARMSTRONG, REBECCA LYON   PA
She organized a group of women making clothing for the soldiers. See Biographies.

ARNEST, EVE   PA
She was captured by the British and Indians in July 1781 along with her husband and taken to Montreal (MR).

ARNETT, HANNAH WHITE   NJ
She called on the men to fight the British. See Biographies.

ARNETT, JANE   SC
She supplied provisions for the army (SI, R-T:56).

ARNETT, SUSANNA   VA
Louisa County. She performed a public service (VR, 3:338).

ARNOLD, ANNE HENDRICKS			SC
 Born 1731, she married Benjamin Arnold, and died 1806. She is listed as a patriot in the DAR Patriot Index.
ARNOLD, ELIZABETH HITT			KY
 Frankfort. She was born on March 12, 1751 and married Capt. John Arnold of Virginia, who commanded a company of spies during the war. In 1783 he settled a station on the waters of Little Benson Creek, about seven miles above the present site of Frankfort. Mrs. Arnold is listed as a patriot in the DAR Patriot Index (CH).
ARNOLD, ELIZABETH TUTTLE			NJ
 Gen. Washington had his headquarters there. See Biographies.
ARNOLD, HANNAH			RI
 She supplied provisions for the army (MP, 23:47).
ARNOLD, HANNAH WATERMAN			CT
 She was a patriot, but her son was a traitor. See Biographies.
ARNOLD, PATIENCE BROWN			RI
 Born 1729, she was the first wife of Caleb Arnold, Sr. (1725-1784). She died on September 3, 1780. Mrs. Arnold is listed as a patriot in the DAR Patriot Index.
ARNOLD, PEGGY SHIPPEN. See SHIPPEN
ARNOLD, SARAH			RI
 East Greenwich, the wife of Capt. Thomas Arnold. She supplied corn, pork, veal, butter, sugar, cordwood, etc., for the army between December 10, 1776, and March 16, 1777 (MP, 30:1).
ARNOLD, ZIBA			NJ
 Morris County. She suffered damage by American troops (CDB, A, claims 41, 50, 59).
ARNST, MARIA			SC
 She supplied provisions for the army (SI, U-W:203).
ASDELL, MARY			VA
 Augusta County. She performed a patriotic service (VR, 2:359).
ASH, ELIZABETH			VA
 Fauquier County. She performed a patriotic service (VR, 2:233).
ASHBURN, BETSY GRISCOM. See ROSS
ATCHISON, ANN			PA
 At age thirty she was captured by the British and Indians on July 11, 1779, and taken to Quebec. Ann was sent home on August 22, 1782 (MR).
ATCHISON, ELIZABETH			MD
 Somerset County. She supplied bacon to the army in 1780 (IM, 13029).
ATCHISON, MARY			SC
 She supplied provisions for the army (SI, B:62).
ATCHISON (AITCHISON), REBECCA VA
 Princess Anne County. She performed a public service (VR, 4:209).
ATCHISON, WIDOW			PA
 At age twenty-eight she (with her daughter) was captured by Tories and Indians on March 1, 1779. They killed her husband (MR).

III: COMPLETE LISTING

ATKINS, MRS. ELISHA SC
  She supplied provisions for the army (SI, U-W:305).
ATKINS, LEA NC
  She supplied provisions for the army (RA, 8:68, fol. 2).
ATKINSON, ELIZABETH NJ
  Burlington County. She suffered loss of property in the British raid (CDB, B:51).
ATKINSON, JOYCE VA
  Henry County. She performed a public service (VR Court Booklet, 35).
ATKINSON, MARY VA
  Goochland County. She performed a public service (VR, 3:58).
ATLEE, SARAH RICHARDSON PA
  She provided meals for soldiers. See Biographies.
ATTOY, MARY SC
  She supplied provisions for the army (SI, Y-Z:111).
ATWATER, ELIZABETH BASSETT CT
  Born 1719, she married David Atwater and died in 1783. She is listed as a patriot in the DAR Patriot Index.
ATWATER, MARY SALTONSTALL CT
  She witnessed bonds for privateer captains. See Biographies.
ATWOOD, PHEBE NJ
  Newark. She suffered losses due to a British raid (CDB, claims 36, 38).
ATWOOD, SARAH LIGON VA
  The wife of Benjamin Atwood, Sarah died in 1785. She is listed as a patriot in the DAR Patriot Index.
AUSTIN, ELIZABETH RI
  She supplied beef, pork, corn, cheese, and sugar for the army in 1777 (MP, p. 36:8).
AUSTIN, ELIZABETH SC
  She was the wife of Bartholemew Austin, and died in 1803. Elizabeth supplied provisions for the army (SI, U-W:204).
AUSTIN, MARY CT
  She suffered damage in the British raid on Greenwich (CAR, 1:65c, 74a). She was a Western Lands Grantee.
AVERET, ANNA NC
  She supplied provisions for the army (RA, 4:54, fol. 2).
AVERETTS, MILDRED NC
  She supplied provisions for the army (RA, 7:24, fol. 1).
AVERIT, HANNAH CT
  She was a patriot who also signed the oath of fidelity under the Articles of Confederation. See Biographies.
AVERY, DEBORAH CT
  She suffered losses in the Groton raid by the British (CAR, 1:79a).
AVERY, DEBORAH LOTHROP. See PUTNAM
AVERY, ELIZABETH CT
  She suffered losses in the British raid on Groton (CAR, 1:63q, 79a). She was a Western Lands Grantee.

AVERY, GRACE DENISON   CT
    Groton. On December 10, 1748, she became the second wife
    of Parke Avery and bore him eleven children. Grace had five
    sons who served in the Revolutionary War. On September 6,
    1781, British forces under Benedict Arnold attacked Fort Gris-
    wold, and Mrs. Avery lost two sons and one grandson in the
    engagement. She died at Groton on August 13, 1800 (informa-
    tion from Elizabeth Anne Reiter, Groton, CT).
AVERY, LYDIA   CT
    She suffered losses in the British raid on Groton (CAR, 1:63q,
    79a). She was a Western Lands Grantee (submitted by Carolyn
    M. Picciano, Hartford, CT).
AVERY, MARY   CT
    Norwalk. She suffered losses during the British raid (CAR,
    1:63k, 98e). She was a Western Lands Grantee.
AVERY, PHEBE   CT
    Groton. She suffered losses during the British raid (CAR,
    1:63q, 79a). She was a Western Lands Grantee.
AVERY, PRUDENCE. See MORGAN
AXSON, ELIZABETH   SC
    She supplied provisions for the army (SI, B:3, 42).
AYER, FRANCES   SC
    She provided funds for the army (AA, 3:13).
AYERS, RACHEL   NJ
    Woodbridge. She suffered losses in a British raid (CDB, B:92).
AYLETT, MARY   VA
    King William County. She performed a public service (VR, 3:238).
AYRES, MARGARET   SC
    She provided funds for the army (AA, 3:15).

B

BABB, ANN   VA
    Isle of Wight. She performed a public service (VR, 4:331).
BABB, BLANCHE MERCER   VA
    Frederick County, born 1742. She married Thomas Babb. Mrs.
    Babb performed a public service (VR Court Booklet, p. 21).
    She died in 1821 (DAR).
BABB, MARY   SC
    Born about 1737, she married Joseph Babb. She provided funds
    (AA, 3:17) also provisions for the army (SI, R-T:164). Mrs.
    Babb died in December 1818 (DAR).
BABILITMAN, ZABA   SC
    She supplied provisions for the army (SI, R-T:9).
BACHE, SARAH FRANKLIN   PA
    The natural daughter of Benjamin Franklin, she was president
    of the ladies' association for the welfare of the soldiers, 1780-
    1783. See Biographies.
BACON, ABIGAIL SWAIN   MA
    Needham. She was born in 1724 and married John Bacon. He

III: COMPLETE LISTING 225

was killed at West Cambridge on April 19, 1775 during the Battle
of Lexington (FP2).
BACON, AGNES HOBSON   GA
   She carried a message to Gen. Greene in North Carolina. See
   Biographies.
BACON, MRS. JEREMIAH   VA
   She was captured by the British and Indians along with her
   six children in 1778 at Cherry Valley and later exchanged (MR).
BACON, MARY   VA
   Lunenburg County, born about 1723, she married Lydall Bacon,
   Sr. She performed a public service (VR, 4:4). Mary died
   in 1816 (DAR).
BACON, SARAH JOHNSON   CT
   She married Jacob Bacon (1754-1844), who served as surgeon
   on the privateer Jason. Dr. Bacon was captured by the British
   on October 22, 1781, but not imprisoned (CN).
BACOT, MARY   SC
   She provided funds (AA, 3:32) and also provisions for the army
   (SI, B:27).
BAGAS, SARAH   VA
   Rockingham County. She performed a public service (VR, 5:106,
   108, 109, 119).
BAGGS, SALLY   VA
   Hampshire County. She performed a public service (VR Lists,
   p. 6).
BAGLEY, DICEY   VA
   Amelia County. She performed a public service (VR, 1:39).
BAGNAL, MRS.   VA
   She was captured by the British and Indians at Cherry Valley
   in 1778 along with her four children and taken to Quebec. Later
   she was exchanged (MR).
BAGWELL, JANE   SC
   She supplied provisions for the army (SI, L-N:6).
BAILEY, ANN HENNIS   WV
   She was a scout for the Americans. See Biographies.
BAILEY, ANNA WARNER   CT
   She nursed wounded soldiers. See Biographies.
BAILEY, ELIZABETH   CT
   She suffered losses in the Groton raid by the British (CAR,
   1:79a).
BAILEY, JUDITH   VA
   New Kent County. She performed a public service (VR Court
   Booklet, p. 17).
BAILEY, MARY   NC
   She supplied provisions for the army (RA, 8:11, fol. 2).
BAILEY, MARY   VA
   Fauquier County. She performed a public service (VR, 2:235).
BAILLE, JOURDINA CUNNINGHAM   GA
   Savannah. The French troops under the Comte d'Estaing raided
   her farm at Bethesda and took thirteen steers, ten cows, five
   sheep, thirty-nine hogs, fifty fowl, and twenty gallons of Jamaica

rum. This is an example of the suffering of the women patriots. Her original bill is in the Archives Nationales in Paris.

BAILLIE, MRS.   GA
She supplied a hundred bushels of rough rice for the army (WA, p. 121; submitted by Joanne Smalley, Atlanta, GA).

BAILS, ELIZABETH   SC
She provided funds (AA, 3:50-52), also provisions for the army (SI, 1:66).

BAIRD, MRS. WINIFRED   SC
She provided funds for the army (AA, 3:55).

BAKER, CATHARINE   VA
King George County. She performed a public service (VR, 2:333).

BAKER, CHARLOTTE BOHUN   SC
She provided funds (AA, 3:71), also provisions for the army (SI, B:59).

BAKER, DESIRE HURLBURT   VT
Arlington. On April 3, 1760, she married Remember Baker, and they had one son, Ozi. In 1764 they settled in the New Hampshire Grants (now Vermont). Baker commanded a company of Green Mountain Bays. He was killed by Indians on August 21, 1775, near Saint Johns, New York. Later Mrs. Baker married Thomas Butterfield of Colchester, Vermont. She died on May 3, 1802 (FP4).

BAKER, ELIZABETH E.   SC
She supplied provisions for the army (SI, B:137).

BAKER, ELIZABETH NICKELSON   VA
York County. The wife of George Baker, she performed a public service (VR, 4:272).

BAKER, MRS. GEORGE   PA
She was captured by the British at Fort Pitt along with her husband and five sons on July 27, 1777, and later taken to Fort Chambly, Quebec (MR).

BAKER, JANE
Mecklenburg County. She performed a public service (VR, 4:36).

BAKER, LUCY   VA
Surry County. She performed a public service (VR, 5:165).

BAKER, MARGARET   NC
She supplied provisions for the army (RA, A:174).

BAKER, MARY   CT
She suffered losses in the British raid on Groton (CAR, 1:63q, 79a). She was a Western Lands Grantee.

BAKER, MARY   SC
When Charleston fell, Mrs. Baker refused to sign the oath of fidelity to the Crown and so was banished from the city (SC).

BAKER, MARY HILLSMAN   NC
She married Samuel Ely, then William Baker. Mary supplied provisions for the army (RA, 8:18, vol. 1).

BALDRIDGE, ISABELLA LUCKEY   NC
Born in 1761, she married John Baldridge. She is listed as a patriot in the DAR Patriot Index 2.

III: COMPLETE LISTING

BALDWIN, ELIZABETH PITNEY   NJ
Gen. Washington spent a night in her home. See Biographies.

BALDWIN, EUNICE JENNISON   NH
Hillsboro. On December 31, 1761, she married Isaac Baldwin of East Sudbury, Massachusetts. They had six children. In 1776 they moved to Hillsboro. As soon as he heard about the Alarm at Lexington, Capt. Baldwin fought at Bunker Hill, where he was killed. The local chapter of the Daughters of the American Revolution is named in her honor (submitted by Thaida J. Gruenler, Hillsboro, NH).

BALDWIN, MARGARET   NC
She supplied provisions for the army (RA, 5:54, fol. 3), also Margrit (RA, 11:93, fol. 2).

BALDWIN, MARY FITZ RANDOLPH. See DISSOWAY

BALDWIN, PHEBE   NJ
Wardsession, Essex County. Widow of Jabez Baldwin, she suffered losses in a British raid (CDB, B, claim 21).

BALDWIN, PRUDENCE   NJ
Orange Township, Orange County. She suffered losses in a British raid (CDB, B, claim 48).

BALFOUR, ELIZABETH TODD DAYTON   NC
She supplied provisions for the army. See Biographies.

BALFOUR, MARGARET   NC
She supplied provisions for the army (RA, 4:61, fol. 3).

BALL, AGATHA   VA
Lancaster County. She performed a public service (VR, 3:206).

BALL, ANN   VA
Northumberland County. She performed a public service (VR Court Booklet, p. 5).

BALL, EASTER   NJ
Connecticut Farms, Essex County. She suffered losses in a British raid (CDB, B, claim 62).

BALL, ELIZABETH   SC
She provided funds (AA, 3:96) and also provisions for the army (SI, B:p. 44).

BALL, ELIZABETH   VA
Chesterfield County. She performed a public service (VR, 2:19).

BALL, HANNAH   VA
Norfolk. She performed a public service (VR Court Booklet, p. 18).

BALL, MARGARET   VA
Westmoreland County. She performed a public service (VR, 5:217).

BALL, MARY   VA
Lancaster County. She performed a public service (VR, 3:267).

BALL, MARY REED   KY
Born 1762, she married Thomas Ball and died in 1822. She is listed as a patriot in the DAR Patriot Index.

BALL, PATIENCE   VA
Essex County. She performed a public service (VR, 2:140).

BALL, PRUDENCE and MARY NJ
  Morristown. They knitted socks for Lt. Bethuel Farrand's company (DW).
BALL, REBECCA VA
  Campbell County. She performed a public service (VR, 4:301).
BALLARD, ANN VA
  Hansford County. She performed a public service (VR, 4:148, 150).
BALLARD, ELIZABETH VA
  Hansemond County. She performed a public service (VR, 4:149).
BAMPFIELD, REBECCA SC
  She provided funds (AA, 3:127-130) and also provisions for the army (SI, B:162, 208).
BANCART, MARY SC
  She supplied provisions for the army (SI, B:137).
BANKS, CHARITY CT
  She suffered losses in the British raid on Greenwich (CAR, 1:63c, 74a). She was a Western Lands Grantee.
BANKS, ELIZABETH VA
  Warwick County. She performed a public service (VR, 5:211).
BANTA, ANNE (ANTIE) NJ
  Hackensack. Widow of David Banta, she suffered losses in a British raid (CDB, B, claim 80).
BANTA, ELIZABETH NJ
  Hackensack. Widow of Hendrick Banta. She suffered losses in a British raid (CDB, B, claim 62).
BARBER, MARY SC
  She provided funds (AA, 3:142) and also provisions for the army (SI, 1:66).
BARBEY, MARY NC
  She supplied provisions for the army (RA, C:54).
BARCLAY, MARY HOOPS PA
  Gen. Washington had his headquarters there. See Biographies.
BARE, MRS. JOHN CHRISTOPHER SC
  She provided funds for the army (AA, 3:143).
BARECROFT, SUSANNAH VA
  Northumberland County. She performed a public service (VR, 4:113).
BAREFIELD, CATHARINE VA
  Botetourt County. She performed a public service (VR Court Booklet, p. 26).
BARHAM, MARY VA
  Southampton County. She performed a public service (VR, 5:173).
BARKER, LUCY CT
  She suffered losses in a British raid on New Haven (CAR, 1:63e, 91h). She was a Western Lands Grantee.
BARKER, LUCY VA
  Surry County. She performed a public service (VR Court Booklet, pp. 1, 15).

III: COMPLETE LISTING 229

BARKER, PENELOPE PAGETT   NC
When the British attempted to steal her horses, she cut the reins with her husband's sword. See Biographies.

BARNARD, TABITHA   MA
Amesbury. She was a widow. In 1780 Tabitha provided Ł280 to support the militia (Joseph Merrill, History of Amesbury and Merrimac).

BARNES, CATHARINE   MD
She supplied wheat for the army (IM, 20098).

BARNES, SARAH   VA
Princess Anne County. She performed a public service (VR, 4:209).

BARNET, SARAH   NC
She supplied provisions for the army (RA, D:52).

BARNETT, ANN SPRATT   NC
She nursed wounded soldiers and cared for Gen. Sumter and his invalid wife. See Biographies.

BARNEY, ANNE BEDFORD   MD
Baltimore. The daughter of Gunning Bedford of Philadelphia, in 1780 she married Lt. Joshua Barney of the Continental Navy, who was the seventh of fourteen children of Frances Holland and William Barney of Baltimore. After their marriage, Barney was captured by the British for a third time and confined in the Mill Prison in Plymouth, England for a year, then escaped, but was recaptured. Later he escaped again, using various disguises, arriving in Boston in December 1781 and in Baltimore in March 1782. Meanwhile Mrs. Barney was living in Philadelphia with her infant son, born during his imprisonment (CN; DB).

BARNS, MARY   NJ
Hunterdon County. The daughter of Thomas Barns, she suffered losses in an American battle (CDB, A, claim 44).

BARNUM, MARY   CT
She suffered losses in a British raid on Danbury (CAR, 1:51a, 63a). She was a Western Lands Grantee.

BARR, CATHERINE   PA
She gave a gun to the Committee of Safety on November 3, 1776. The receipt was signed by John M. Nesbitt (RP, roll 11, frame 106).

BARRETT, MARY   VA
Louisa County. She performed a public service (VR Lists, 1:6, 29, 34).

BARRETT, MRS. SMITH   VA
Norfolk County. She performed a public service (VR, Ctf 1).

BARRON, REBECCA   SC
She supplied provisions for the army (SI, 1:66).

BARRON, SARAH   SC
She supplied provisions for the army (SI, B:127).

BARROTT, SARAH   VA
Northumberland County. She performed a public service (VR, 4:112).

BARRS, MARY   VA
    Northumberland County. She performed a public service (VR, 4:112).
BARRY, ABIA M.   GA
    She gave seven horses to the legion (WA, p. 115).
BARRY, MARGARET CATHERINE MOORE   SC
    She was a scout and guide for the army. See Biographies.
BARTLETT, HANNAH BARKER   MA
    Marblehead. She married Nicholas Bartlett, Jr., who was commissioned in 1776 to command the brigantine America. While in command of the General Glover in October 1779, Bartlett was captured by the British. After a long period of confinement, he was finally exchanged (CN).
BARTLETT, HOPE. See MERCY WHITE
BARTLETT, MARY   WV
    Berkeley County. She performed a patriotic service (VR, Ctf 1).
BARTLETT, MARY BARTLETT   NH
    The Tories burned her home to the ground. See Biographies.
BARTLETT, SUSANNAH   VA
    Spotsylvania County. She performed a public service (VR, 4:258).
BARTON, MARGARET GALBRAITH   WV
    She warned the Americans of an impending enemy attack. See Biographies.
BARTON, PHOEBE CARLTON   MA
    Sutton. She was born on January 7, 1725, and married Bezaleel Barton who was killed at the Battle of Bunker Hill on June 17, 1775 (FP2).
BASEY, ANN   VA
    Culpeper County. Wife of Edward Basey. She performed a public service (VR Court Booklet, 1:51).
BASS, ELIZABETH   VA
    Amelia County. She performed a public service (VR, 1:40).
BASS, FRANCES   VA
    Chesterfield County. She performed a public service (VR, 2:13, 20).
BASSETT, ANN   NJ
    Acquacanunk, Essex County. Her property was destroyed by the British (CDB, B, claim 15).
BASSETT, ANNE MARIE DANDRIDGE   VA
    Gen. Washington was at her home. See Biographies.
BASSETT, SARAH   CT
    She suffered a loss of property in the Danbury raid by the British (CAR, 1:51c, 63x). She was a Western Lands Grantee.
BATCHELOR, MARY   SC
    She supplied provisions for the army (SI, B:22).
BATTAIL (BATTAILE), HANNAH   VA
    Culpeper County. She performed a public service (VR, Ctf 1), also Caroline County (Court Booklet, 2:2, 9), and Spotsylvania County (Court Booklet, p. 30).

III: COMPLETE LISTING

BATTLE, ANN   NC
    She supplied provisions for the army (RA, A:183).
BATTLE, MARY   NC
    She supplied provisions for the army (RA, 5:44, fol. 1).
BAUGH, ELIZABETH   VA
    Chesterfield County. She performed a public service (VR, 2:18).
BAUGH, RACHEL   VA
    Powhatan County. She performed a public service (VA Lists, p. 17).
BAXTER, GRACE   VA
    Botetourt County. She performed a public service (VR, 1:157).
BAXTER, MARY   SC
    She supplied provisions for the army (SI, Y-Z:313).
BAYLET, LUCY   SC
    She supplied provisions for the army (SI, X, pt. 1:145).
BAYLEY, HANNAH   VA
    Elizabeth City. She performed a public service (VR Court Booklet, p. 5).
BAYLISS, ELIZABETH LINCOLN   MA
    She was the wife of Maj. Hodijah Bayliss who was an aide to Gen. Benjamin Lincoln. Bayliss was taken prisoner in May 1780 when Charleston, South Carolina, surrendered to the British. After his exchange he was a lieutenant colonel and an aide to Gen. Washington from May 1782 to December 1783 (FW).
BAYNARD, ELIZA   SC
    She supplied provisions for the army (SI, Y-Z:210).
BAYNE (BAINE), ELIZABETH   VA
    Westmoreland County. She performed a public service (VR Lists, pp. 1, 3).
BEACH, DEBORAH COONE   CT
    Her husband, James Coone, was killed by Indians in September 1780, Salisbury. She went to New York and married Zerah Beach (CAR, 37:105).
BEACH, MARTHA   NJ
    Newark. Her property was damaged by the British (CDB, B, claim 6).
BEAL, ANN   VA
    Isle of Wight. She performed a public service (VR, 2:313), also listed in Albemarle County (VR, 2:345).
BEALE, ANN   VA
    Orange County. She performed a public service (VR, 4:173).
BEALE, ELEANOR   MD
    Charles County. She supplied wheat for the army in 1781 (IM, 19817).
BEALE, EUNICE   SC
    After Charleston fell to the British on May 12, 1780, she refused to sign an oath of fidelity to the Crown and was banished from the city (SC).
BEAM, MRS. WILLIAM   TN
    She was captured by the Cherokee Indians and was saved from being burned at the stake by Nancy Ward. See Biographies.
BEAN, ANN   NC
    She supplied provisions for the army (RA, J:179).

BEARD, ELIZABETH   PA
   At age twenty-three she was captured by Indians in July 1778
   and taken to Canada. She was sent home on August 22, 1782
   (MR).
BEARD, ELIZABETH   VA
   Bedford County, wife of John Beard. She supplied provisions
   for the army (VR, Ctf 1) and also listed as Campbell County
   (VR, Ctf 1, pp. 277, 278).
BEARD, MAGDALENE   VA
   At age forty-three she was captured by Indians along with her
   daughter, Barbara, aged eleven, and sent to the Saint Lawrence
   suburbs (MR).
BEARD, MARY   SC
   She supplied provisions for the army (SI, 1:104).
BEARFIELD, SARAH   NC
   She supplied provisions for the army ((RA, 5:49, fol. 3).
BEARS, MRS. ISAAC
   New Haven. On their way to Philadelphia, John Adams and
   members of the First Continental Congress from Massachusetts
   spent the night of August 18, 1774, at the Bears' Tavern. The
   next day they had breakfast with the Bryants in Milford, Con-
   necticut (BA).
BEASLEY, ANN   VA
   Caroline County, the wife of William Beasley. She performed
   a public service (VR Court Booklet, 2:3).
BEASLEY, ELIZABETH   NC
   She signed the agreement against drinking British tea. See
   Background.
BEASLEY, SARAH   NC
   She signed the agreement against drinking British tea. See
   Background.
BEASON, LYDIA   NC
   She supplied provisions for the army (RA, A:180).
BEAVER, MARGARETTA BARBARA STEINBRENNER   PA
   Born in 1725, she married John Beaver, and died in 1816. She
   is listed as a patriot in the DAR Patriot Index.
BECK, JUDITH   VA
   Powhatan County. She performed a public service (VR Lists,
   p. 10).
BECK, SARAH   NJ
   Burlington. She suffered a loss in a British raid (CDB, B:70).
BECKEL, LIESEL   PA
   She nursed the Marquis de Lafayette back to health. See
   Biographies.
BECKHAM, MRS.   SC
   She lived near the Pacolet River. In 1781 Col. Tarleton and
   his officers stayed in her home, then let his men pillage every
   room. When Col. Tarleton ordered his men to set fire to her
   home, she convinced the colonel to let it stand (CD).
BEDFORD, MERCY RAYMOND   NC
   She was a patriot, but her husband was a Tory. See Biographies.

III: COMPLETE LISTING 233

BEDINGER, MAGDALENE   WV
   Berkeley County. She supplied provisions for the army (VR, 1:187).
BEEBE, ELIZABETH   CT
   She suffered property damage in the British raid on New London (CAR, 1:63k, 95e). She was a Western Lands Grantee.
BEEBE, HANNAH   CT
   She suffered property damage in the British raid on New London (CAR, 1:63g, 95d). She was a Western Lands Grantee.
BEEBE, JOANNA   CT
   New London. She suffered property damage in the British raid (CAR, 1:63g, 95a). She was a Western Lands Grantee.
BEEBE, LYDIA   CT
   She suffered damage in the British raid on New London (CAR, 1:63g, 95a). She was a Western Lands Grantee.
BEEKMAN, CORNELIA VAN COURTLANDT   NY
   She refused to give a secret valise to a Tory. See Biographies.
BEEKMAN, MARTHA   NJ
   Somerset County. She suffered damage in the British raid (CDB British, p. 177).
BEERS, LUCY   CT
   She suffered damage in the British raid on Fairfield (CAR, 1:53d, 63p). She was a Western Lands Grantee.
BEETS, ELIZABETH   VA
   Southampton County. She performed a public service (VR, 5:173).
BEGGS, SARAH BARNES. See RUDDELL
BELCH, MARY   NC
   She provided provisions for the army (RA, C:35).
BELL, ABIGAIL   CT
   She suffered damage in the British raid on New London (CAR, 1:63g, 95a). She was a Western Lands Grantee.
BELL, ANN   VA
   Frederick County. She performed a public service (VR, 2:173).
BELL, DOROTHY CRIM   NY
   She married Frederick Bell, Jr., and died about 1778. She is listed as a patriot in the DAR Patriot Index.
BELL, FLORENCE   VA
   Augusta County. She performed a public service (VR Court Booklet, p. 17).
BELL, HEPSIBATH TYLER. See JOHNSTON
BELL, JUDITH   VA
   Buckingham County. She performed a public service (VR Court Booklet, pp. 5, 42).
BELL, MARTHA McFARLAND   NC
   She served as a nurse and as a spy. See Biographies.
BELL, MARY   NC
   She supplied provisions for the army (RA, 5:26, fol. 1; 5:40-42, etc.).
BELL, MARY   VA
   Orange County. She performed a public service (VR, 4:180, 181).

BELL, MATCHIA   NC
   She supplied provisions for the army (RA, D:112).
BELL, MILDRED   VA
   Sussex County. She performed a public service (VR, Ctf 1).
BELL, SYLVIA   VA
   The wife of Michael Bell, she died in 1789. She is listed as a
   patriot in the DAR Patriot Index.
BELLAMY, MARY   NC
   She supplied provisions for the army (VR, 7:63, fol. 2).
BELLERIGEAN, CHARITY TUCKER. See BRITTAIN
BELLOWS, ABIGAIL STEARNS   NH
   Walpole. She was the first wife of Benjamin Bellows, the founder
   of Walpole. Four of her sons were officers or soldiers in the
   war. The Abigail Stearns Chapter of the Daughters of the
   American Revolution is named in her honor (submitted by Ruby
   M. Towle, Farmingham, NH).
BELVER, CATHERINE   NC
   She supplied provisions for the army (RA, 12:103, fol. 4).
BENBOW, MARTHA   SC
   She supplied provisions for the army (SI, O-Q:114).
BENBURY, RUTH   NC
   She signed the agreement against drinking British tea. See
   Background.
BEND, ELIZABETH   NY
   In 1776 she made flags for the regiments of the New York Line.
   See Biographies.
BENEDICT, JERUSHA STARR   CT
   Danbury. She was born on April 26, 1726, and married Elisha
   Benedict, who was a captain of the New York militia in 1775.
   He was taken prisoner in 1780 and held for two and a half years.
   Mrs. Benedict died on July 22, 1799 (FP4).
BENEDICT, MARY   CT
   She suffered in the British raid on Norwalk (CAR, 1:63j, 98c,
   100b). She was a Western Lands Grantee.
BENEDICT, SARAH   CT
   She suffered a loss in the British raid on Danbury (CAR, 1:
   51a, 63a). She was a Western Lands Grantee.
BENEZET, JOYCE MARRIOTT   PA
   She was a member of the ladies' association for the welfare of
   the soldiers. See Biographies.
BENJAMIN, SARAH MATTHEWS   NY
   She baked bread for the soldiers. See Biographies.
BENJAMIN, WIDOW   PA
   At age thirty-six on May 24, 1778, she and her children were
   captured by Tories and Indians and taken to Quebec. They
   killed her husband (HP).
BENNET, ELIZABETH KROESEN   PA
   Northampton Township, Bucks County. She was born in 1704
   and married Isaac Bennet, Jr., and they had nine children.
   Her husband died in 1747. Her four sons and a son-in-law

III: COMPLETE LISTING 235

served during the war. Her son, Lt. Matthew Bennet, was taken prisoner when Fort Washington fell to the British on November 16, 1776 (submitted by Edward L. Woodyard, Armonk, NY).

BENNETT, CATHARINE   VA
King George County. She performed a public service (VR, 2:333).

BENNETT, FRANCES   VA
Bedford County. She performed a public service (VR Court Booklet, p. 7).

BENNETT, LYDIA   NC
She supplied provisions for the army (RA, 10:80, fol. 4).

BENNETT, MARTHA JACKSON   PA
Born in 1731, she married Thomas Bennett. She died in 1810. Martha is listed as a patriot in the DAR Patriot Index.

BENSON, MARGARET   NC
She supplied provisions for the army (RA, 1:96, fol. 2).

BENSON, MARY LYDECKER   NJ
Hackensack. Formerly the widow of Cornelius Lydecker, she suffered property damage (CDB British claim, p. 32).

BERELEY, JANE WILEY   VA
Caroline County. She performed public services (VR Lists, 2:20, 28; Ctf. 1, 1:241, 255).

BERESFORD, DOROTHY   SC
She supplied provisions for the army (SI, B:34).

BERESFORD, SARAH   SC
She supplied provisions for the army (SI, B:18, 105, 110).

BERGEN, MARGARET   NJ
Rocky Hill, Somerset County. The widow of Jacob Bergen, she suffered property damage (CDB British claim, p. 136).

BERRIEN, MARGARET EATON   NJ
Gen. Washington had his headquarters there. See Biographies.

BERRY, ELIZABETH   NC
She supplied provisions for the army (RA, A:186).

BERRY, ELIZABETH GILMORE   PA
Born in 1757, she married John Berry, a private. Elizabeth died in 1824. She is listed as a patriot in the DAR Patriot Index.

BERRY, SARAH SHARP   KY
Born in 1754, Sarah, her husband Francis, son, and daughter were captured by Tories and Indians on June 22, 1780, and taken to Canada. She died in 1834 (HP; DAR).

BERRY, MRS. SIDNEY   NJ
Hunterdon County. Her husband was the assistant deputy quartermaster general. Mrs. Berry was active in the ladies' association for the welfare of the soldiers (New Jersey Gazette, July 4, 1780).

BERRYMAN, SARAH DISHMAN   VA
King George County. The wife of James Berryman, she performed a public service (VR Court Booklet, p. 3).

BERWICK, ANN   SC
    She supplied provisions for the army (SI, Y-Z:217).
BESSONETT, PARTHENA BRELSFORD   PA
    Born in 1755, she married Charles Bessonett, and died in 1839.
    Mrs. Bessonett is listed as a patriot in the DAR Patriot Index.
BIBB, ANN   VA
    The wife of Benjamin Bibb, she died in 1789. She is listed
    as a patriot in the DAR Patriot Index.
BIBB, SARAH MARTIN   VA
    Amherst County, the wife of Thomas Bibb. She performed a
    public service (VR Court Booklet, p. 4).
BIBB, SUSANNAH BIGGER   VA
    Goochland County. The wife of John Bibb, she performed a
    public service (VR, 3:60).
BICKERSTAFF, MARY   NC
    The wife of Capt. John Bickerstaff, she supplied provisions
    for the army (RA, A:215).
BIDDLE, MARY RICHARDSON   PA
    She cooked meals for the soldiers. See Biographies.
BIDDLE, MARY SCULL   PA
    Her son, Nicholas Biddle, commander of the Randolph, was killed
    in a naval battle. See Biographies.
BIGELOW, ANNA FISKE   MA
    Born in 1731, she married Abraham Bigelow and died in 1810.
    She is listed as a patriot in the DAR Patriot Index.
BIGELOW, ELIONER   NJ
    Burlington. The wife of Samuel Bigelow, she suffered losses
    in a British raid (CDB British, p. 106).
BILL, ELIZABETH   VA
    Augusta. She performed a public service (VR Lists, 3:1).
BILLUPS, SARAH   VA
    Gloucester County. She performed a public service (Court Book-
    let, pp. 11, 26).
BILYOU, LEDEA   NJ
    Somerset County. She suffered losses in a British raid (CDB
    British, p. 12).
BINGLEY, ANN   VA
    James City. She performed a public service (VR Court Booklet,
    p. 2).
BINGLEY, HANNAH   CT
    She suffered losses in the British raid on New London (CAR,
    1:63a, 91d). She was a Western Lands Grantee.
BINGLEY, JUDITH   VA
    Powhatan County. She performed a public service (VR, 4:231).
BINNS, ELIZABETH   VA
    Surry County. She performed a public service (VR, 5:165).
BIRD, BARBARA   VA
    King and Queen County. She performed a public service (VR,
    3:214).
BIRD, MARY LEE   VA
    Middlesex County. The wife of Philemon Bird, she performed

III: COMPLETE LISTING   237

a public service (VR, Ctf. 1). Also shown as King and Queen
County (VR, 3:214) and Hansemond County (VR, 4:351). She
died in 1809 (DAR).
BIRDSALL, HANNAH MANDEVILLE   NY
Gen. Washington had his headquarters there. See Biographies.
BISCOE, ELIZABETH   VA
Lancaster County. She performed a public service (VR Court
Booklet, p. 17).
BISHOP, ESTHER   NJ
Middlesex County. She suffered damage in the British raid
(CDB British, p. 102).
BISHOP, RACHEL RUGGLES   VT
She repelled attacking Indians by burning hay and wheat stocks.
See Biographies.
BISSELL, ESTHER HAYDEN   CT
Windsor. She was the wife of Ebenezer Fitch Bissell who was
taken prisoner at the Battle of Long Island (FP1).
BISSITT, MARGARET   VA
Dinwiddie County. She performed a public service (VR, 1:319).
BLACK, SARAH   VA
Augusta County. She performed a public service (VR Lists,
2:21).
BLACKBURN, ELIZA   NC
She supplied provisions for the army (RA, 4:16-2).
BLACKBURN, ELIZABETH   VA
Powhatan County. She performed a public service (VR, 4:231).
BLACKBURN, MARY   VA
Middlesex County. She performed a public service (VR, 4:88,
89).
BLACKLEY, FRANCES   VA
Middlesex County. She performed a public service (VR Court
Booklet, p. 1; Lists, pp. 1, 4).
BLACKMORE, JEMIMA   VA
Lancaster County. She performed a public service (VR, 3:266).
BLACKMORE, SUSANNA   NC
She supplied provisions for the army (RA, 7:93, fol. 1).
BLACKNALL, MARY   VA
Gloucester County. She performed a public service (VR, 4:286).
BLACKWELDER, BETSEY PHIFER   NC
Born in 1724, she married Caleb Blackwelder. She is listed
as a patriot in the DAR Patriot Index 2.
BLACKWELDER, MARY DECKER   NC
The wife of Caleb Blackwelder, she is listed in the DAR Patriot
Index.
BLACKWELL, ELIZABETH   VA
Fauquier County. She performed a public service (VR Court
Booklet, p. 7).
BLAIR, BARBARA   SC
She provided funds (AA, 3:52), also provisions for the army
(SI, 1:660).
BLAIR, JANE   NJ
Somerset County. She owned half of a forty-ton sloop with

Jeremiah Van Deventer. She suffered losses in the British raid (CDB British, p. 26).

BLAIR, JANE (JEAN)　　　　　　　NJ
Raritan Landing, Middlesex County. She suffered losses in the British raid (CDB British, p. 133).

BLAIR, JEAN GAMBLE　　　　　　NC
She opposed the drinking of British tea. See Background.

BLAIR, SIBBIAH EARL　　　　　　GA
Born in 1754, she married William Blair and died in 1815. She is listed as a patriot in the DAR Patriot Index.

BLAIR, SUSAN SHIPPEN　　　　　PA
She was a member of the ladies' association for the welfare of the soldiers. See Biographies.

BLAISDELL, ANNA SANBORN　　　ME
Pictou, Nova Scotia. She was the wife of Moses Blaisdell. In 1776 they moved from New England to Nova Scotia. Anna had twelve children. Moses was an American rebel, and in 1783 he was outlawed for "over acts." Their property at Gagetown was seized and his family forced to flee. They finally reached Verona Island on the Penobscot River where they settled (DAR Magazine, , February 1983).

BLAKESLEE, MARY ANDREWS　　　CT
Born in 1766, she married Joseph Blakeslee, Jr. Mary died in 1853. She is listed as a patriot in the DAR Patriot Index.

BLANCHARD, JUDITH　　　　　　GA
She supplied seven head of cattle for the troops (WA, p. 114).

BLANCHFIELD, ALICE　　　　　　NC
She supplied provisions for the army (RA, 5:54, fol. 1; II:12, fol. 1).

BLAND, JUDITH　　　　　　　　　VA
Amelia County. She performed a public service (VR Court Booklet, 1:53).

BLAND, MARY　　　　　　　　　　VA
Fauquier County. She performed a public service (VR Lists, pp. 3, 7).

BLAND, RACHEL　　　　　　　　　VA
Botetourt County. She performed a public service (VR, 1:157).

BLANSETT (BLANCIT), RHODA　　VA
Prince William County. She performed a public service (VR, 4:193).

BLAUVELT, ANNA MARIA DE WINT　NY
General Washington had his headquarters in her household. See Biographies.

BLAUVELT, MARY　　　　　　　　NJ
Harrington Township, Bergen County. She suffered losses in a British raid (CDB, British claim, p. 22).

BLEDSOE, ANN　　　　　　　　　VA
Orange County. She performed a public service (Lists, p. 16).

BLEDSOE, KATHERINE MONTGOMERY　NC
She carried a message to Gen. Washington. See Biographies.

III: COMPLETE LISTING

BLEDSOE, MARY RAMSAY   TN
   Born in 1734, she married Col. Anthony Bledsoe of Virginia
   and died in 1808. She is listed as a patriot in the DAR Patriot
   Index.
BLEWER, MRS. JOSEPH   PA
   She was a member of the ladies' association for the welfare of
   the soldiers. See Biographies.
BLEWS, MARY   NC
   She supplied provisions for the army (RA, 1-6:197).
BLINOOR, ANN   VA
   Northumberland County. She performed a public service (VR,
   4:113).
BLISS, ANN   CT
   East Windsor. The Widow Bliss supplied a blanket for the army
   (CAR, 11:17a).
BLISS, ANN   NJ
   Bordentown. The widow of Thomas Bliss, she suffered losses
   in a British raid (CDB British, p. 3).
BLISS, ELIZABETH BARRETT BARTLETT   MA
   She was the wife of Capt. Thomas Theodore Bliss of the 15th
   Continental Artillery. He was taken prisoner at the Cedars in
   May 1776 and exchanged later. In January 1777 Bliss was made
   captain of the 2nd Continental Artillery, but then was taken
   prisoner a second time in June 1778 in Monmouth, New Jersey,
   and not released until January 1781 (FW).
BLISS, RUTH LOWELL   VT
   Newbury. She was the wife of Pelatiah Bliss, Jr., of Lebanon,
   Connecticut. When a detachment of British troops set out to
   capture Gen. Jacob Bailey of Johnson Village, they captured
   Minuteman Bliss (FP1).
BLODGET, HEPIABAH BROWN   MA
   Brimfield. She was born on Mary 16, 1759, and became the
   second wife of Pvt. Solomon Blodget, who was captured by the
   Hessians. He managed to escape on May 17, 1779 and served
   in the army again. She died on February 17, 1793 (FP4).
BLOODGOOD, ISABEL. See MUNDY
BLOOMFIELD, ABIGAIL   NJ
   Woodbridge. She suffered losses in a British raid (CDB British,
   pp. 102, 113).
BLOOMFIELD, MARY McILVAINE   NJ
   Burlington. She was active in the ladies' association for the
   welfare of the soldiers. See Biographies.
BLOOMFIELD, PHEBE   NJ
   Middlesex County. She suffered losses in a British raid (CDB
   British, p. 98).
BLOOMFIELD, SARAH   NJ
   Woodbridge, widow of Thomas Bloomfield. She suffered losses
   in a British raid (CDB British, p. 108).
BLOUNT, ANNE HALL   NC
   She refused to drink British tea. See Background.

BLOUNT, LYDIA BONNER   NC
    She refused to drink British tea. See Background.
BLOUNT, MARY   NC
    She refused to drink British tea. See Background.
BLOUNT, PATIENCE   NC
    She supplied provisions for the army (RA, 5:58, fol. 3).
BLOW, MARTHA   VA
    Southampton County. She performed a public service (VR, 5:174).
BLUNT, ANN   VA
    Southampton County. She performed a public service (VR Court Booklet, p. 12).
BLUNT, PRISCILLA   VA
    Southampton County. She performed a public service (VR, 5:173).
BOARDMAN, MARY WARD   CT
    Middletown. Born on October 21, 1753, she married Timothy Boardman who was a carpenter on the privateer Oliver Cromwell. He was captured by the British on June 5, 1779, and imprisoned. She died in December 1836 (FP2).
BOATRIGHT, MARY   VA
    Cumberland County. She performed a public service (VR Lists, p. 7).
BOGART (BOGERT), ANNATJE   NJ
    Franklin Township, Bergen County. The Widow Bogart suffered losses in a British raid (CDB, British claim 28).
BOGART, CATERINE   NJ
    Franklin Township, Bergen County. She suffered losses in a British raid (CDB, British claim 6).
BOGART, MARY   NJ
    Hackensack, the widow of Gillam Bogart, she suffered losses in a British raid (CDB, British claim 68).
BOHANNAN, ANN   VA
    King and Queen County. She performed a public service (VR, Ctf 1).
BOICE, JANE   NJ
    Middlesex County. She suffered losses in a British raid (CDB British, p. 318).
BOLLES, MARGARET   RI
    Wife of John Bolles. She supplied corn, beef, pork, and sugar for the army in 1777 and 1778 (MP, 36:5).
BOLLING (BOWLING), ANN   VA
    Fairfax County. She performed a public service (VR, 2:221).
BOLLING, MARY MARSHALL   VA
    The British occupied her home and placed her under arrest. See Biographies.
BOLLING, SUSANNA   VA
    She warned Lafayette of an impending enemy attack. See Biographies.
BOLTON, AGNES   SC
    She supplied provisions for the army (SI, Y-Z:12).

III: COMPLETE LISTING   241

BOLTON, HANNAH   CT
   She suffered losses in the British raid on New London (CAR,
   1:63g, 95a). She was a Western Lands Grantee.
BOND, SARAH   NC
   She supplied provisions for the army (RA, A:63).
BOND, SARAH   VA
   Lancaster County. She performed a public service (VR, 3:266).
BOND, SARAH CARRUTHERS   NC
   Wife of Vineyard Bond, she supplied provisions for the army
   (RA, 11:15, fol. 4).
BOND, SUSANNA   NJ
   Bound Brook. Wife of Jacob Bond, she suffered losses in a
   British raid (CDB British, p. 11).
BONDFIELD, REBECCA   NC
   She refused to drink British tea. See Background.
BONDS, SARAH   NC
   She supplied provisions for the army (RA, 5:2, fol. 3).
BONNEAU, ANN   SC
   She supplied provisions for the army (SI, R-T:106).
BONNEL, EUNICE   NJ
   Connecticut Farms, Essex County. She suffered losses in a
   British raid (CDB, British claim 49).
BONNEL, REBECCA   NJ
   Connecticut Farms, Essex County. She suffered losses in a
   British raid (CDB, British claim 33). Her second husband was
   Jonathan Ogden.
BONNER, RUTH   GA
   She placed a claim for a mare taken by order of Col. Clarke
   (WA, p. 156).
BONNEY, JANE   VA
   Princess Anne County. She performed a public service (VR,
   4:210).
BONOS, SARAH   NC
   She supplied provisions for the army (RA, 5:85, fol. 1).
BONTICOU, ELEANOR   CT
   New Haven. She suffered losses in a British raid, in 1779 (CAR,
   15:234e, 269c). She was a Western Lands Grantee.
BONTICOU, SUSANNAH   CT
   New Haven. She suffered losses in a British raid (CAR, 15:234e).
BOOBE, SARAH   SC
   She supplied provisions for the army (SI, B:56).
BOONE, MARTHA BRYAN   KY
   Boonesborough. The daughter of Martha Strode and Morgan
   Bryan, she was the sister of Rebecca Bryan, who married Daniel
   Boone. Martha married Edward Boone, a Baptist preacher,
   who was a brother of Daniel Boone. Martha had two sons and
   two daughters. In 1775 they joined the expedition to Kentucky.
   On October 6, 1780, Preacher Boone was killed by Indians at
   Blue Licks. Martha died in 1783 in Fayette County, Kentucky
   (submitted by Katherine Blaylock, Winston-Salem, NC).

BOONE, REBECCA BRYAN   KY
   Her husband, Daniel Boone, was captured by Indians. See
   Biographies.
BOONE, SARAH DAY   KY
   Her son was killed at the Battle of Blue Licks. See Biographies.
BOONE, SARAH MORGAN   KY
   The mother of Daniel Boone, one son and three sons-in-law
   were killed by Indians. See Biographies.
BOOTH, EUNICE   CT
   Newtown. The Widow Booth supplied a blanket for the army
   in 1777 (CAR, 11:466b).
BOOTH, LUCY   VA
   Essex County. She performed a public service (VR Lists, pp.
   8, 12. Also King William County 3:240).
BOOTH, MAY   SC
   She supplied provisions for the army (SI, O-Q:179).
BOOTH, REBECCA   VA
   Brunswick County. She performed a public service (VR, 1:106).
BORDEN, ELIZABETH ROGERS   NJ
   Her home was burned by the British. See Biographies.
BORDEN, MARY HATHAWAY   MA, RI
   Freetown. She was born on May 26, 1757, and married Thomas
   Borden. He was captured in the British invasion of 1778, and
   their home and mills were destroyed at the time of the British
   invasion of Rhode Island. She died on February 18, 1824 (FP4).
BORDEN, SARAH   RI
   She supplied provisions for the army (MP, 23:36).
BOSWELL, MARGARET   VA
   Accomack County. She performed a public service (VR, 1:21).
BOUDE, ALICE AMELIA. See ATLEE
BOUDENOT, RACHEL   NJ
   Somerset County. She suffered losses in a British raid (CDB
   British, p. 67).
BOUDINOT, CATHERINE SMITH   NJ
   She was a member of the ladies' association for the welfare of
   the soldiers. See Biographies.
BOUGHTON, CATHARINE   CT
   Norwalk. She suffered losses in a British raid (CAR, 1:63i,
   98b, 100b). She was a Western Lands Grantee.
BROUGHTON, SARAH   CT
   Norwalk. Her house was destroyed in a British raid in October
   1780 (CAR, 19:190, 191).
BOUNETHEAU, MARY   SC
   She supplied provisions for the army (SI, B:220).
BOURNE, MARY   VA
   Caroline County. She performed a public service (VR Lists,
   2:16, 24).
BOURQUIN, JANE   GA
   She supplied forage for public use (WA, p. 126).
BOUTWELL, ANN   VA
   Elizabeth City. She performed a public service (VR Court Booklet, p. 7).

III: COMPLETE LISTING 243

BOUTWELL, MARY VA
Caroline County. She performed a public service (VR, pp. 240, 264, 272).

BOW, CATHARINE VA
Hanover County. She performed a public service ((VR, 3:167).

BOWDEN, SARAH VA
King and Queen County. She performed a public service (VR, 3:215; Lists 4:2).

BOWDOIN, GRACE VA
Northampton County. She performed a public service (VR Lists, p. 1).

BOWEN, ELIZABETH RI
Providence. On June 2, 1781, Joseph Cooke obtained a letter of marque to command the sloop Hope with ten guns and a crew of forty men. Elizabeth witnessed the Continental bond (CN).

BOWEN, LILY McILHANEY VA
She performed a public service during the war. See Biographies.

BOWEN, MARGARET LOUISA SMITH VA
She shouldered a rifle to deter Indians from attacking the fort. See Biographies.

BOWEN, RACHEL PENNINGTON NJ
Bridgeton. She was the wife of Jonathan Bowen, an assemblyman. Mrs. Bowen was active in the ladies' assocation for the welfare of the soldiers (New Jersey Gazette, July 4, 1780; information on Bridgeton women received from Patricia W. McCulley, Bridgeton).

BOWEN, SARAH BROWN RI
Gen. Washington had his headquarters here. See Biographies.

BOWER, KATHERINE SC
She supplied provisions for the army (SI, B:139).

BOWERS, MRS. DANIEL MD
She sent Gen. Washington a cloth made of buffalo hair. See Biographies.

BOWERS, HANNAH BOWERS MA
She married her cousin David Bowers, Jr. In 1778 Bowers was prize master on the Angelica and was captured by the British. On July 7, 1778, he was confined in the Fortun Prison at Gosport, England (CN).

BOWERS, MARY VA
Hanover County. She performed a public service (VR, 3:168).

BOWERS, SYLVANA SC
She supplied provisions for the army (SI, O-Q:273).

BOWIE, MARY VA
Caroline County. She performed a public service (VR Court Booklet, 2:4).

BOWIE, SARAH VA
Caroline County. She performed a public service (VR Court Booklet, 2:2).

BOWLES, MARY VA
Hanover County. She performed a public service (VR, 3:168).

BOWMAN, GRACE GREENLEE NC
Born in 1750, she married Capt. Charles Bowman, then Charles

McDowell. She died in 1823. She supplied provisions for the army (RA, A:189; DAR).

BOWMAN, MARY HITE   VA
Gen. Washington stayed here. See Biographies.

BOWMAN, SARAH   SC
She supplied provisions for the army (SI, R-T:165).

BOWYE (BOWIE), ISABEL   MD
Charles County. She supplied wheat for the army (IM, 25452).

BOX, MARGARET   SC
She supplied provisions for the army (SI, U-W:248).

BOX, MARY   SC
She supplied provisions for the army (SI, R-T:163).

BOYD, ELIZABETH   SC
She supplied provisions for the army (SI, B:153).

BOYD, LUCY   VA
King and Queen County. She performed a public service (VR Lists, 4:2).

BOYD, MARGARET   VA
Northumberland County. She performed a public service (VR, 4:113).

BOYD, MARTHA   SC
She supplied provisions for the army (SI, R-T:9).

BOYES, ISABELLA STUART   ME
Robbinston. She was born at Georgetown on December 7, 1754, the daughter of Mary Stinson and Charles Stuart. On April 19, 1775, she married Samuel Boyes (Boice) who was wounded at Cambridge, Massachusetts, and died in February 1776. Isabella had one daughter. On July 3, 1795, she married Abel Brooks. She is buried in the Brewer Cemetery in Robbinston, Maine (submitted by Dee C. Brown, Readfield, ME).

BOYLES, MARTHA   SC
She supplied provisions for the army (SI, U-W:152).

BOYS, ELIZABETH   GA
She supplied cattle for the army (WA, p. 163).

BOYS, ISABELLA STUART   ME
A patriot.

BRACKFIELD, CATHARINE   VA
Botetourt County. She performed a public service (VR, 1:156).

BRADFORD, EDITH HOWE   NH
She was born on November 11, 1744, and married Ens. Timothy Bradford. She is credited with patriotic service in the DAR Patriot Index. She died in 1822 (DAR).

BRADFORD, MARY   MD
Worcester County. She supplied corn for the army (IM, 12421).

BRADFORD, MARY   NC
She supplied provisions for the army (RA, C:44).

BRADINGFIELD, SARAH   NC
She supplied provisions for the army (RA, 7:79, fol. 2).

BRADLEE, ANN DUNLAP   MA
She painted her husband's face to look like an Indian for the Boston Tea Party. See Biographies.

III: COMPLETE LISTING

BRADLEY, ELIZABETH   VA
   Charles City. She performed a public service (VR Court Booklet, p. 23).
BRADLEY, ELIZABETH PELHAM   NC
   Born in 1724, she married James Bradley, and died in 1788. She is listed as a patriot in the DAR Patriot Index.
BRADLEY, ELIZABETH QUIGLEY   PA
   Born in 1735, she married John Bradley and died in 1783. She is listed as a patriot in the DAR Patriot Index.
BRADLEY, MARGARET   SC
   She supplied provisions for the army (SI, O-Q:46).
BRADLEY, MARY   VA
   Hansemond County. She performed a public service (VR, 4:148, 149). Also Mary Bradley in Norfolk County (VR, 4:146).
BRADLEY, MARY BOONE   KY
   Boone's Station. The daughter of Sarah Day and Samuel Boone, a brother of Daniel Boone, she married Leonard K. Bradley who was captured on May 12, 1780, when the British took Charleston, South Carolina.
BRADLEY, SARAH   VA
   Charles City. She performed a public service (VR Court Booklet, p. 21).
BRADLEY, WIDOW   NC
   She supplied provisions for the army (RA, C:137).
BRAME, MELICHIA   VA
   Caroline County. She performed a public service (VR, 1:242).
BRAMLETT, ANNE   VA
   Bedford County. She performed a public service (VR Lists, 2:7).
BRAMLETT, MARGARET   VA
   Fauquier County. She performed a public service (VR, 2:235).
BRANCH, OLIVE   VA
   Bedford County. She performed a public service (Lists 2:14).
BRANDON, MRS. AGNEW   SC
   She supplied provisions for the army (SI, X, pt. 1:142, 196).
BRANDON, REBECCA   VA
   Halifax County. She performed a public service (VR, 2:253).
BRASSFIELD, ELIZABETH   NC
   She supplied provisions for the army (RA, D:44).
BRASWELL, ELIZABETH   NC
   She supplied provisions for the army (RA, A:80).
BRASWELL, SARAH   NC
   She supplied provisions for the army (RA, 12:59, fol. 4).
BRATTON, MARTHA ROBINSON   SC
   She exploded ammunition her husband had stored to prevent its being taken by the enemy. See Biographies.
BRAXTON, ELIZABETH CORBIN   VA
   Her home was burned by the British. See Biographies.
BRAY, ELIZABETH   NC
   She supplied provisions for the army (RA, 10:26, fol. 2, A 55).

BRAZELL, HANNAH   SC
  She supplied provisions for the army (SI, L-N:6; SI, R-T:8).
BREARLY, ELIZABETH MULLEN   NJ
  Trenton. She was the wife of David Brearly, an attorney. In
  1775 he was arrested for his rebel speeches, but a mob of
  patriotic citizens stormed the jail and released Brearly. Later
  he served as chief justice of New Jersey and was a signer of
  the Constitution of the United States (DB).
BRECKENRIDGE, LETTICE   VA
  Botetourt County. She performed a public service (VR, 1:155,
  156).
BREDDMAN, SARAH   VA
  Amelia County. She performed a public service (VR, 1:40).
BREED, PRISCILLA AVERY   SC
  Born April 29, 1715, she married Joseph Breed. She supplied
  provisions to the army (SI, X, pt. 1:142).
BREEDEN, ELIZABETH   VA
  Greenbrier County. She performed a public service (VR Court
  Booklet, p. 5).
BREEDEN, MARGARET.   See STUCKER
BREESTEAD, SABINA   NJ
  Saddle River. She suffered loss of property by the British
  (CDB, British claim 33).
BREMMIL (BROMMIL), ELIZABETH   VA
  Gloucester County. She performed a public service (VR Court
  Booklet, pp. 11, 17).
BRENDT, ANN   VA
  Prince William County. She performed a public service (VR,
  4:193), and also listed in Stafford County (VR, 5:187).
BRENDT, BETSY AMBLER   VA
  She was the daughter of Rebecca Burwell and Jacquelin Ambler.
  In a letter of March 1809 to Nancy Fisher, Betsy wrote that
  their education in 1776 was interrupted by the war, and instead
  of their morning lessons, they had to knit stockings for the
  soldiers (NL).
BRENT, JUDITH   VA
  Lancaster County. She performed a patriotic service (VR, 3:266,
  267; 4:347).
BRENT, MARGARET   VA
  Charlotte County. She performed a public service (VR, 1:296).
BREVARD, JEAN McWHORTER   NC
  The wife of John Brevard, Sr. She is listed as a patriot in
  the DAR Patriot Index.
BREWER, BRIGET   NJ
  New Barbadoes, Bergen County. She suffered damage by the
  British (CDB, p. 50).
BREWER, CATHERINE   NJ
  Saddle River. She suffered damage caused by the Americans
  during the war (CDB, sec. 2, claim 43).
BREWER, ELIZABETH   NJ
  New Barbadoes, Bergen County. She suffered damage caused
  by the British (CDB, p. 50).

III: COMPLETE LISTING 247

BREWER, ELIZABETH NJ
  Saddle River. She suffered damage caused by the Americans (CDB, sec. 2, claim 30).
BREWER, MARY
  She supplied provisions for the army (RA, C:56).
BREWSTER, LOIS BREWSTER CT
  Norwich. She married Zadock Brewster. In July 1776 he served as first lieutenant on the galley Shark. They were captured by the British in February 1777 and imprisoned (CN; information on Norwich women received from Diane Norman of Norwich).
BREWSTER, MARY VA
  Loudon County. She performed a public service (VR Court Booklet, p. 26).
BREWTON, JEMIMA JOHNSON. See FONTAINE
BREWTON, MARY SC
  When Charleston fell, she refused to sign the oath of fidelity to the Crown and so was banished from the city (SC).
BRIANT, HANNAH NJ
  Springfield, Essex County. She suffered damage caused by the British (CDB, claim 14).
BRIANT, MARY NJ
  Connecticut Farms, Essex County. She suffered damage caused by the British (CDB, claim 63).
BRICE, MARGARET LOCKHARDT SC
  She supplied provisions for the army (SI, Y-Z:206).
BRICKNEL, RACHEL NC
  She supplied provisions for the army (RA, 9:73, fol. 3).
BRIDGER, MARTHA VA
  Isle of Wight. She performed a public service (VR, 2:312).
BRIDGES, MARY SC
  She supplied provisions for the army (SI, L-N:265).
BRIEZENDINE, ELIZABETH VA
  Essex County. She performed a public service (VR Lists, pp. 2, 4).
BRIGHT, MARY NC
  She supplied provisions for the army (RA, D:136).
BRINCKERHOFF, GEERTIE WYCOFF NY
  Gen. Washington stayed there. See Biographies.
BRINCKERHOFF, JANNETJIE VAN VOORHIES NY
  Gen. Washington stayed there. See Biographies.
BRINK, HUSELTY (URSULA) WV
  She supplied provisions for the army. See Biographies.
BRINKERHOFF, MARY NJ
  New Barbadoes, Bergen County. The widow of Henry Brinkerhoff, she suffered damage caused by the British (CDB, claim 25). Her second husband was named Duryea (Deryea).
BRINKERHOFF, MECASEY NJ
  Hackensack. The wife of Derrick Brinkerhoff (?), she suffered damage caused by the British (CDB, claim 26).
BRINKLEY, MRS. WILLIAM NC
  She supplied provisions for the army (RA, 1-6:331).

BRINSFIELD, ELIZABETH   MD
    Dorchester County. She supplied wheat for the army (IM, 22027).
BRISCOE, MARY   NC
    She supplied provisions for the army (RA, 10:21, fol. 1).
BRITTAIN, CHARITY TUCKER   NC
    She married a Mr. Bellerigean, then Joseph Brittain, and died
    in 1790. She is listed as a patriot in the DAR Patriot Index.
BROADBERRY, AGNES   NJ
    Woodbridge. She suffered damage caused by the British (CDB,
    p. 36).
BROADHEAD, ELIZABETH DEPUI   PA
    She made clothing for the soldiers. See Biographies.
BROADNAX, SARAH   VA
    Amelia County. She performed a public service (VR, 1:90).
BROCKET, FRANCES   NC
    She supplied provisions for the army (RA, 4:24, fol. 2).
BROCKETT, MARY   CT
    Wallingford. The Widow Brockett supplied a blanket for the
    army in 1777 (CAR, 11:208a).
BROOKE, LYDIA   VA
    Essex County. She performed a public service (VR 2:141).
BROOKE, MARGARET   MD
    She supplied wheat for the army (IM, 25269).
BROOKING, FRANCES UPSHAW   VA
    The wife of Charles Brooking, she died in 1804. She is listed
    as a patriot in the DAR Patriot Index 2.
BROOKS, ANITA   VA
    Halifax County. She performed a public service (VR, 2:258).
BROOKS, MARY. See ISABELLA STUART BOYES
BROOKS, SARAH BOONE   KY
    When the Indians attacked, she was one of the women who went
    for water. See Biographies.
BROUGHTON, ANN   SC
    She supplied provisions for the army (SI, B:20).
BROW, ELIZABETH   NC
    She supplied provisions for the army (RA, C:29).
BROWN, MRS. See MRS. EBENEZER WHITE
BROWN, ALICE   VA
    Stafford County. She performed a public service (VR Ctf 1).
BROWN, AMELIA   VA
    Norfolk County. She performed a public service (VR, 4:126).
BROWN, ANN   NC
    She supplied provisions for the army (RA, A:62).
BROWN, ANNA   NC
    She supplied provisions for the army (RA, 5:65, fol. 1).
BROWN, ANNE   NC
    She supplied provisions for the army (RA, 10:5, fol. 4).
BROWN, DINAH   NY
    In 1776 she was listed as a matron in the General Hospital. In
    1785 she petitioned the United States for land in return for
    her military service as a nurse (FH).

III: COMPLETE LISTING 249

BROWN, ELEANOR   VA
  Richmond County. She performed a public service (VR, 5:94).
BROWN, ESTHER   VA
  Rockbridge County. She performed a public service (VR, 5:70).
BROWN, FRANCES   CT
  New Haven. She suffered damage in a British raid (CAR, 1:63y, 91a). She was a Western Lands Grantee.
BROWN, MRS. GRIZELL   SC
  She supplied provisions for the army (SI, X, pt. 1:143).
BROWN, HANNAH   CT
  Norwalk. She suffered damage in a British raid (CAR, 1:63k, 98e). She was a Western Lands Grantee.
BROWN, HANNAH   NJ
  Somerset County. She suffered damage in a British raid (CDB, p. 149).
BROWN, IVEY   VA
  Norfolk. She performed a public service (VR, 4:126).
BROWN, JANE   NJ
  Bordentown. She suffered damage in a British raid (CDB, p. 31).
BROWN, MARGARET   NC
  She supplied provisions for the army (RA, 1:35, fol. 4, A 97).
BROWN, MARY   CT
  Norwalk. She suffered damage in a British raid (CAR, 1:63k, 98f, 100a). She was a Western Lands Grantee.
BROWN, MARY   RI
  Wife of Kingsley Brown. She supplied one fifty-eighth of cheese for the army in 1777 (MP, 36:6).
BROWN, MARY   VA
  Prince Edward County (VR, 5:38), she performed a public service.
BROWN, MILLEY   VA
  Norfolk. She performed a public service (VR Court Booklet, p. 15).
BROWN, PHEBE   CT
  New Haven. She suffered damage in a British raid in July 1779 (CAR, 234bi). She was a Western Lands Grantee.
BROWN, REBECCA   CT
  Stamford. The Widow Brown sent money in 1779 to the Continental Loan Office. She suffered losses in the British raid in 1781 (CAR, 22:296a, 297).
BROWN, REBEKAH   NC
  She supplied provisions for the army (RA, A:202).
BROWN, RHODA   NJ
  Connecticut Farms, Essex County. She suffered losses in a British raid (CDB, British claim 42).
BROWN, SARAH   CT
  New Haven. She suffered losses in the 1779 British raid (CAR, 15:269e).
BROWN, SARAH   NJ
  Burlington County. She suffered losses in a British raid (CDB, p. 82).

BROWN, SARAH SC
She supplied provisions for the army (SI, L-N:262).
BROWN, SARAH VA
Hanover County. She performed a public service (VR Lists, 1:15, 22). Also Sarah Brown in Prince George County (VR, 4:249).
BROWN, SIBYLE OLNEY RI
Smithfield. She was born on August 17, 1759, and married Othniel Brown, a private and then a marine on the Providence. Brown was captured by the British on May 12, 1780, when they took Charleston, South Carolina. Mrs. Brown died on June 8, 1825 (FP2).
BROWN, SUSANNAH VA
Hanover County. She performed a public service (VR, 3:169).
BROWNE, MARY VA
James City. She performed a public service (VR Ctf 1).
BROWNE, OLIVE VA
Southampton County. She performed a public service (VR, 5:174).
BROWNLEA, ELIZABETH PA
Elizabeth and her daughter were captured by Indians. See Biographies.
BROWNLEY, SARAH VA
Gloucester County. She performed a public service (VR, 4:286).
BRUMFIELD, ELIZABETH SC
She supplied provisions for the army (SI, O-Q:48).
BRUMFIELD, SUSANNA VA
King William County. She performed a public service (Lists, 1:18).
BRUSH, DEBORAH CT
Greenwich. The Widow Brush suffered losses in British raids in March 1779 and December 1783 (CAR 36:19b I 63c). She was a Western Lands Grantee.
BRUSH, DORTHEA PLATT NY
She was born in 1751 and married Jesse Brush, and died in 1835. She is listed as a patriot in the DAR Patriot Index.
BRYAN, ANN VA
Northampton County. She performed a public service (VR Court Booklet, p. 6).
BRYAN, ELIZABETH NC
She supplied provisions for the army (RA, 5:25, fol. 3, A 83).
BRYAN, LYDIA BALL. See SIMMONS
BRYAN, MARY BOONE KY
When the Indians attacked, she was one of the women who left the fort to obtain water. See Biographies.
BRYAN, MARY HUNTER NC
She opposed drinking British tea. See Background.
BRYANT, HANNAH SEARING NJ
She was born in 1718 and married Simeon Bryant, and died in 1785. She is listed as a patriot in the DAR Patriot Index.

III: COMPLETE LISTING 251

BRYANT, SARAH   CT
Fairfield. She suffered losses in a British raid (CAR, 1:53h, 63r). She was a Western Lands Grantee.

BRYANT, SARAH   SC
She supplied provisions for the army (SI, L-N:264).

BUCK, MRS.   NJ
Cumberland County. The wife of Attorney Buck, she collected funds for the army (New Jersey Gazette, July 4, 1780).

BUCK, ELIZABETH   VA
Charles City. She performed a public service (VR Court Booklet, p. 24).

BUCKINGHAM, ANN   CT
Milford. The wife of Josiah Buckingham, her house was plundered in November 1782 by Tories from Long Island (CAR, 29:290a).

BUCKNER, ELIZABETH   VA
Caroline County. She performed a public service (VR, 1:241, 254, 264). Also Elizabeth Buckner in Spotsylvania County (Court Booklet, pp. 3, 10).

BUCKNER, JUDITH   VA
Gloucester County. She performed a public service (VR, 4:286).

BUDD, ANN HAWKHURST   NY
Westchester County. She married Dr. Thomas Budd who served as surgeon on the Randolph commanded by Nicholas Biddle. On March 7, 1778, Dr. Budd was killed when a shot from HMS Yarmouth struck the powder magazine of the Randolph, which then exploded (CN; FP1).

BUDD, PHEBE   NJ
Morris County. She suffered damage by the Americans (CDB, claim 4).

BUDD, SUSANNAH   SC
She supplied provisions for the army (SI, Y-Z:62).

BUFORD, MARGARET   VA
Amherst County. She performed a public service (VR Court Booklet, p. 13).

BUGG, ELIZABETH HOBSON   GA
Wife of Capt. Sherwood Bugg, she provided forage, etc., for the army (WA, p. 171). She died in 1799 (DAR). Also shown in South Carolina (SI, Y-Z:126).

BULKELEY, ABIGAIL   CT
Fairfield. The Widow Bulkeley suffered damage in the British raid of July 1779 (CAR, 15:267). She was a Western Lands Grantee.

BULKELEY, ANN   CT
New London. The Widow Bulkeley suffered losses in the British raid (CAR, 27:331b). She was a Western Lands Grantee.

BULKELEY, JANE   CT
Fairfield. Her house was burned in the British raid (CAR, 15:259).

BULKELEY, OLIVE   CT
Fairfield. She suffered losses in the British raid of July 1779 (CAR, 15:251a; 19:73a).

BULKELEY, SARAH   CT
Wethersfield. She housed army officers in 1781 (CAR, 33:402, 403, 416).

BULL, MARY PHILLIPS   PA
She defied Lord Howe. See Biographies.

BULLOCK, MARY   GA
She supplied provisions for the army (WA, p. 137) and also funds (p. 180).

BUNBURY, ELIZABETH   VA
King George County. She performed a public service (VR, 2:333).

BUNCH, MARY   VA
Louisa County. She performed a public service (VR, 3:340).

BUNTZ, MARGARET   GA
Wife of Urban Buntz. She supplied a horse for the troops under orders of Gen. Wayne (WA, p. 111).

BURCH, ELIZABETH   VA
Caroline County. She performed a public service (VR, 1:242).

BURCH, REBECCA   MD
Charles County. She supplied wheat for the troops in 1782 (IM, 23663).

BURCHFIELD, BELIAH   NC
She supplied provisions for the army (RA, A:189).

BURCHFIELD, BERELLA   NC
She supplied provisions for the army (RA, A:220).

BURD, SARAH SHIPPEN   PA
She made clothes for the soldiers and cared for the wounded. See Biographies.

BURGES, MARY   CT
Windsor. She supplied a blanket for the army in 1777 (CAR, 11:59a).

BURGIN, ELIZABETH   NY
She operated an escape line for American prisoners of war from 1776 to 1779 (FH).

BURKE, ELIZABETH   SC
She supplied provisions for the army (SI, Y-Z:217).

BURKE, MARY FREEMAN   NC
Her husband, the governor, was captured by Tories. See Biographies.

BURKHAM, REBECCA   MD
She supplied wheat for the army in 1781 (IM, 18989).

BURLEY, SARAH   CT
Greenwich. The Widow Burley suffered losses in the British raid in 1779 (CAR, 36:19c, I 74a, 95a).

BURLINGAME, SUSAN   RI
East Greenwich. The wife of William Burlingame, she supplied corn, rye, cheese, and shoes for the army in 1777 and 1778 (MP, 30:15).

BURNET, MARY CAMP   NJ
She was a member of the ladies' association for the welfare of the soldiers. See Biographies.

III: COMPLETE LISTING 253

BURNETT, AMY VA
Essex County. She performed a public service (VR, 4:304).
BURNETT, MARGARET VA
Amherst County. She performed a public service (VR Ctf 1).
BURNEY, MRS. NJ
Essex County. The wife of Dr. Burney, she collected funds for the army (New Jersey Gazette, July 4, 1780).
BURNS, MARY SC
The wife of John Burns, she supplied provisions for the army (SI, R-T:166).
BURR, ABIGAIL CT
Fairfield. She suffered losses in the British raid in July 1779 (CAR, 15:250h, 261a). She was a Western Lands Grantee.
BURR, ABIGAIL, JR. CT
Fairfield. In the British raid of July 1779 she suffered losses (CAR, 15:250i, 261a). She was a Western Lands Grantee.
BURR, AMELIA CT
Fairfield. She suffered losses in the July 1779 raid by the British (CAR, 15:250g, 251a). She was a Western Lands Grantee.
BURR, EUNICE DENNIE CT
Her home was burned by the British. See Biographies.
BURR, HEPHA CT
Stratford. The Widow Burr gave a gun to the army (CAR, 3:267a).
BURR, PRISCILLA CT
Fairfield. She suffered losses in the July 1779 raid by the British (CAR, 15:251a; 19:73a). She was a Western Lands Grantee.
BURR, RUTH CT
Fairfield. She suffered losses in the British raid of July 1779 (CAR, 15:250h, 251a). She was a Western Lands Grantee.
BURR, THEODOSIA BARTOW NJ
She supplied information for the American army. See Biographies.
BURRAS, ELIZABETH VA
King William County. She performed a public service (VR, 3:239).
BURRELL, SARAH CT
New Haven. She suffered losses in the July 1779 raid by the British (CAR, 15:234a).
BURRINGTON, ELIZABETH SC
She supplied provisions for the army (SI, B:127).
BURROWS, DIANA VA
Caroline County. She performed a public service (VR Lists, 1:34).
BURROWS, SARAH CT
Groton. Her husband was killed at Fort Griswold in September 1781. His company's arms were taken by the British (CAR, 24:202, 204).
BURRUS, MARY VA
Orange County. She performed a public service (VR List, 1:16).

BURTON, ISABELLE   NC
   She supplied provisions for the army (RA, 11:84, fol. 1).
BURWELL, CHRISTINA BLAIR   VA
   She opposed the British tax on imported tea. See Background.
BURWELL, JOANNA   PA
   At age twenty-two in March 1782 she was captured by Indians
   at Big Island and released from Fort Ticonderoga on July 18,
   1783 (MR).
BURWELL, MARY   VA
   Mecklenburg. She performed a public service (VR, 4:40). Also
   Mary Burwell, Prince William County (VR, 4:193).
BUSH, MARTHA   VA
   James City. She performed a public service (VR Court Booklet,
   p. 2).
BUSH, MARY   NJ
   New Barbadoes, Bergen County. The wife of Casparis Bush,
   she suffered damage caused by the British (CDB, claim 48).
BUSH, RUTH LYON   NY
   Gen. Israel Putnam had his headquarters there. See Biographies.
BUTEAU, MARY   VA
   Orange and Hampshire Counties. She performed a public service
   (List, p. 9).
BUTLER, ABIGAIL. See PRATT
BUTLER, JANE   SC
   She supplied provisions for the army (SI, B:87).
BUTLER, MARY SIMPSON   SC
   96th District. She married James Butler of Prince William County,
   Virginia, and they had eight children. About 1772 they moved
   to South Carolina. In 1781 her husband and second son, James,
   were killed at Cloud's Creek by the notorious Tory leader, "Bloody
   Bill" Cunningham (DB).
BUTLER, MRS. SAMUEL   NC
   The wife of Capt. Butler, she supplied provisions for the army
   (RA, 11:9, fol. 3).
BUTLER, SARAH   SC
   She supplied provisions for the army (SI, B:36).
BUTT, ANNE   VA
   Norfolk. She performed a public service (VR, 4:125, 141).
BUTT, HANNAH   VA
   Norfolk. She performed a public service (VR, 4:125).
BUTTERFIELD, DESIRE HURLBURT. See BAKER
BUTTERS, ELIZABETH   PA
   At age sixteen on July 17, 1781, she was captured by Indians
   and taken to the Saint Lawrence suburbs (MR).
BUTTERS, JEAN   PA
   At age fifty-six she was captured by Indians on July 17, 1781,
   and taken to the Saint Lawrence suburbs (MR).
BUTTS, ELENOR   VA
   Culpeper County. She performed a public service (VR, 2:97).
BUTTS, ELIZABETH   VA
   Southampton County. She performed a public service (VR Court
   Booklet, p. 3).

III: COMPLETE LISTING 255

BUTTS, MARY VA
  Dinwiddie County. She performed a public service (VR, 1:321).
BUXSLEY, JANE VA
  Caroline County. She performed a public service (VR Court Booklet, p. 18).
BUXTON (BUCKSTON), JOICE VA
  Buckingham County. She performed a public service (VR, 1:191).
BUZZARD, ELIZABETH SC
  She supplied provisions for the army (SI, X, pt. 2:27).
BYERLY, BEATRICE GULDEN PA
  She nursed wounded American soldiers. See Biographies.
BYRD, MARY VA
  Charles City. She performed a public service (VR, 1:308-309). Also Middlesex County (VR, 4:88, 90).
BYRNE, ELIZABETH NC
  She supplied provisions for the army (RA, 5:48, fol. 3).

C

CADWALADER, ELIZABETH NJ
  She was a member of the ladies' association. See Biographies.
CADWALADER, HANNAH LAMBERT NJ, PA
  Trenton. The daughter of Thomas Lambert, Jr., she married Dr. Thomas Cadwalader of Philadelphia in 1738. Their son, Lambert Cadwalader, was appointed colonel of the 4th Pennsylvania Battalion and was taken prisoner on November 16, 1776, at the Battle of Fort Washington in New York City (DB).
CAESAR, HANNAH SC
  She supplied provisions for the army (SI, B:116).
CAHOON, MRS. SAMUEL VA
  Hansemond County. She performed a public service (VR, 4:353).
CAIN, REBECCA. See McDONALD
CAIRY, ELIZABETH VA
  Prince George County. She performed a public service (VR, 4:361-362).
CALDWELL, MRS. A. PA
  Philadelphia. She was an active member of the ladies' association for the welfare of the soldiers (Pennsylvania Gazette, June 12, 1780).
CALDWELL, ANN CT
  Fairfield. She suffered losses in the July 1779 raid by the British (CAR, 15:251a; 19:73a). She was a Western Lands Grantee.
CALDWELL, HANNAH OGDEN NJ
  She cared for the sick and wounded soldiers, but was killed by a stray bullet. See Biographies.
CALDWELL, MARTHA ROUNDS PA
  Philadelphia. She was the wife of Samuel Caldwell, paymaster for troops. Mrs. Caldwell was an active member of the ladies' association for the welfare of the troops (Pennsylvania Gazette, June 12, 1780).

CALDWELL, MARY   CT
    Hartford. On February 7, 1781 Nathan Sage of Middletown obtained a letter of marque to command the ship Hunter with eighteen guns and a hundred men. Bonders included Charles Caldwell, and Mary Caldwell witnessed the bond (CN).
CALDWELL, MARY   SC
    She supplied provisions for the army (SI, U-W:65).
CALDWELL, MARY   VA
    Charlotte. She performed a public service (VR Court Booklet, pp. 19, 45).
CALDWELL, RACHEL CRAIGHEAD   NC
    She helped an American courier escape. See Biographies.
CALDWELL, REBECCA PARKS   SC
    The wife of William Caldwell, she died in 1806. She is listed as a patriot in the DAR Patriot Index.
CALDWELL, MRS. S.   PA
    Philadelphia. She was a member of the ladies' association for the welfare of the soldiers (Pennsylvania Gazette, June 12, 1780).
CALLIS, SUSANNAH   VA
    Gloucester County. She performed a public service (VR Court Booklet, pp. 11, 27).
CALLOWAY, ELIZABETH HOY   KY
    Her two daughters were captured by Indians. See Biographies.
CALLOWAY, JEMIMA BOONE   KY
    of Boonesborough. The daughter of Rebecca Bryan and Daniel Boone, she was born in 1762. For the life of this little girl at Boonesborough, see Biographies: Boone, Rebecca. Later Jemima married Flanders Calloway. She died in 1834.
CALMES, LUCY NEVILLE   VA
    She furnished beef for the army. See Biographies.
CALVERT, SARAH   VA
    Prince William County. She performed a public service (VR, 4:195).
CAMBLE (CAMPLE), CATHERINE   NJ
    Hackensack. The wife of John, she suffered losses in a British raid (CDB, claim 51).
CAMFIELD, MARY   NJ
    Newark. She suffered losses in a British raid (CDB, claim 58).
CAMFIELD, PHEBE   NJ
    Orange. She suffered losses in a British raid (CDB, claim 33).
CAMFIELD, SARAH   NJ
    Orange. She suffered losses in a British raid (CDB, claim 40).
CAMP, HANNAH   NC
    She supplied provisions for the army (RA, 7:54, fol. 3).
CAMP, LYDIA   NJ
    The wife of Caleb Camp, she was a member of the ladies' association. See Biographies.
CAMP, MARY   CT
    Salisbury. She furnished pork for the Salisbury furnace (CAR, 17:256).

III: COMPLETE LISTING 257

CAMP, MARY   NJ
   Newark. She suffered losses in a British raid (CDB, claim 54).

CAMP, MARY BAKER   VA
   Halifax County. The wife of Samuel Camp, she performed a public service (VR, 2:264). Also James City (Court Booklet, p. 4).

CAMP, MELICENT BALDWIN. See PORTER

CAMP, PHEBE   NJ
   Newark. She suffered losses in a British raid (CDB, claim 54).

CAMP, SARAH   CT
   Salisbury. She furnished pork for the Salisbury furnace (CAR, 17:285, 287).

CAMP, WIDOW   CT
   Norwalk. She suffered losses in a British raid in July 1779 (CAR, 15:379a, 380).

CAMPBELL, MRS.   MA
   She was a member of the Daughters of Liberty. See Background.

CAMPBELL, ANNA   VA
   Princess Anne County. She performed a public service (VR, 4:212).

CAMPBELL, CATHERINE   NC
   She supplied provisions for the army (RA, 5:60, fol. 2).

CAMPBELL, ELIZABETH   SC
   She refused to sign an oath of fidelity to the Crown and so was banished from Charleston. See Biographies.

CAMPBELL, ELIZABETH   VA
   Hansemond County. She performed a public service (VR, 4:152).

CAMPBELL, ISBELL   VA
   Rockingham County. She performed a public service (VR, 5:133).

CAMPBELL, JANE   NC
   She supplied provisions for the army (RA, 5:63, fol. 4).

CAMPBELL, JANE CANNON   NY
   She was captured by Seneca Indians. See Biographies.

CAMPBELL, MRS. JOHN   VA
   She was captured by the British and Indians at Cherry Valley in 1778 along with her husband, Col. John Campbell, children, and grandchild and taken to Quebec. Later Mrs. Campbell and her children were exchanged, but Col. Campbell was held prisoner at Quebec (MR).

CAMPBELL, MARGARET   NC
   She supplied provisions for the army (RA, C:67).

CAMPBELL, MARIA HULL HALE   CT
   Coventry. She was the daughter of Nathan Hale, who was hanged as a spy on September 22, 1776, in New York City near the present site of Grand Central Terminal. Mrs. Campbell suffered with the loss of her father.

CAMPBELL, MARTHA   VA
   Loudoun County. She performed a public service (VR, 3:288).

CAMPBELL, RACHEL   NJ
    Woodbridge. She suffered losses in a British raid (CDB, claim 67).
CAMPBELL, REBECCA   CT
    She supplied funds for the ship Defence account (CAR, 9:246f).
CAMPBELL, REBECCA   VA
    Bedford County. She performed a public service (VR Court Booklet, p. 8). Also shown in Shenandoah County (VR, 5:354).
CAMPBELL, MRS. ROBERT   SC
    She is listed on the rolls of Capt. Francis Moore's Company, Col. Middleton's Regiment, during the Revolutionary War (ESC).
CAMPBELL, ROSANNAH   VA
    Orange County. She performed a public service (VR, 5:181).
CAMPBELL, SARAH   NJ
    Woodbridge. She suffered losses in a British raid (CDB, claim 299).
CAMPBELL, SARAH   VA
    Essex County. She performed a public service (VR, 4:304). Also shown in King and Queen County (VR, 3:217).
CAMPBELL, LADY SARAH IZARD   SC
    She supplied provisions for the army. See Biographies.
CAMPBELL, TABITHA   VA
    Amherst County. She performed a public service (VR Court Booklet, p. 14).
CAMRON, FRANCES   NC
    She supplied provisions for the army (RA, 6:14, fol. 1).
CANFIELD, WIDOW   CT
    Derby. She furnished a blanket in 1777 for the army (CAR, 9:105a).
CANNON, ELEANOR McKINNEY   NY
    Born in 1717, she married Matthew Cannon and died in 1778. She is listed as a patriot in the DAR Patriot Index.
CANNON, MARGARET   VA
    Caroline County. She performed a public service (VR Court Booklet, 2:6).
CANNON, MARY   NC
    She supplied provisions for the army (RA, 5:43, fol. 3).
CANNON, MRS. MARY   SC
    Also spelled Camon. She supplied provisions for the army (SI, B:102).
CANNON, MARY   VA
    Caroline County. She performed a public service (VR, 1:245).
CANTRELL, SARAH   VA
    Bedford County. She performed a public service (VR Court Booklet, p. 20).
CAPRON, MARGARET   RI
    East Greenwich. The wife of Jonathan Capron, she furnished mutton, corn, butter, and cordwood for the army in 1778 (MP, 30:25).
CARDIN, JUDITH   SC
    She supplied provisions for the army (SI, B:161).

III: COMPLETE LISTING

CARDWELL, OBEDIENCE　　　　　　VA
　Dinwiddie County. She performed a public service (VR, 1:324).
CARDY, MRS. ANN　　　　　　SC
　She supplied provisions for the army (SI, B:40).
CAREY, MARY　　　　　　MD
　Frederick. In 1781 she provided wheat for the army (IM, 24879).
CARMEL, ISABEL　　　　　　PA
　Donegal. In June 1777 at age fourteen she was captured by Indians at Fort Ligonier and released from Fort Ticonderoga on July 18, 1783 (MR).
CARMER, ISABEL. See MUNDY
CARMICHAEL, MRS.　　　　　　NJ
　Morris County. She collected funds for the army (New Jersey Gazette, July 4, 1780).
CARMICHAEL, RUTH　　　　　　MD
　Queen Anne County. In March 1778 she provided a bull for the army (IM, 6154).
CARNEY, SARAH　　　　　　VA
　Norfolk. She performed a public service (VR, 4:128).
CARNEY, SUSANNA　　　　　　VA
　Norfolk. She performed a public service (VR, 4:127).
CARPENTER, ANN　　　　　　VA
　Rockingham County. She performed a public service (VR, 5:111).
CARPENTER, HOPE　　　　　　NJ
　Connecticut Farms. Essex County. The wife of James Carpenter, she suffered losses in a British raid (CDB, claim 13).
CARR, BARBARA　　　　　　MD
　She supplied paper in 1779 for the army (IM, 8318).
CARR, BARBARA　　　　　　VA
　Louisa County. She performed a public service (VR, 3:343).
CARR, ELIZABETH　　　　　　VA
　Albermarle County. She performed a public service (VR Court Booklet, pp. 10, 18, 39).
CARR, GRACE HASTINGS　　　　　　GA
　Sunbury. She provided provisions and forage for public use (WA, p. 118).
CARR, JANE　　　　　　SC
　She supplied provisions for the army (SI, Y-Z:172).
CARR, LENAH　　　　　　GA
　She supplied provisions for public service (WA, p. 168), also beef and flour (p. 175).
CARR, MARTHA　　　　　　VA
　Goochland County. She performed a public service (Lists, 3:2, 3, 15).
CARR, MARY　　　　　　VA
　Hansemond County. She performed a public service (VR, 4:151-152).
CARR, SUSANNA　　　　　　VA
　Albemarle County. She performed a public service (Court Booklet, p. 24).

CARRAN, SUSANNA   VA
  Loudoun County. She performed a public service (VR, 3:288).
CARRELL, JUDITH   VA
  Henry County. She performed a public service (VR, 3:132, 134).
CARRIGAN, ELIZABETH   NC
  She supplied provisions for the army (RA, 11:30, fol. 4).
CARRIGAN, WIDOW   NC
  She supplied provisions for the army (RA, C:141).
CARRINGTON, ANNE ADAMS   VA
  She married Mayo Carrington who served in Virginia Regiments, 1777-1779, then was made a captain and deputy quartermaster of the Southern Army in December 1779. He was captured and imprisoned when the British took Charleston in 1780 (FW).
CARROLL, ELINOR   MD
  She supplied wheat for the army in 1780 (IM, 13835).
CARROLL, MARY   SC
  She supplied provisions for the army (SI, Y-Z:173).
CARRUTHERS, MARTHA   NC
  She supplied provisions for the army (RA, 5:32, fol. 4).
CARSWELL, MARTHA SIMPSON   NY
  Salem. She was the wife of David Carswell who was captured by the British and Indians on October 10, 1780, at Fort Ann, New York. He was taken to Montreal with about 150 other prisoners. He managed to escape, but six days later was recaptured and placed in irons for six months. He was then taken to an island prison in the Saint Lawrence River where he was finally released on June 10, 1782. After the war Martha and David moved to Sandusky, Ohio, where she died in 1853 (submitted by Col. Jeffry L. Cooke, Oakland Park, FL).
CARTER, MRS. EDWARD   VA
  Thomas Jefferson stayed at her home. See Biographies.
CARTER, ELIZABETH   VA
  Charles City. She performed a public service (VR Court Booklet, p. 4).
CARTER, HANNAH BENEDICT   CT
  She opened her home to military officers to plan strategy. See Biographies.
CARTER, MARY   VA
  Bedford County. She performed a public service (VR, 4:292).
CARTER, REBECCA CUTTER   CT
  She was born in 1712 and married Zachariah Hill, then Capt. Samuel Carter, and died in 1797. She is listed as a patriot in the DAR Patriot Index.
CARTER, SARAH RAND   MA
  She was born in 1777 and married Samuel Carter, a private in the war, and died in 1842. She is listed as a patriot in the DAR Patriot Index.
CARTLIDGE (CARTLEDGE), MRS. EDMUND GA
  She supplied one horse for the legion (WA, p. 115).

III: COMPLETE LISTING 261

CARY, ANN VA
　　Gloucester County. She performed a public service (VR Court Booklet, pp. 11, 24).
CARY, ANNE VA
　　Hansemond County. She performed a public service (VR, 4:151).
CASEY, JANE MONTGOMERY KY
　　Her cabin was attacked by Indians. See Biographies.
CASH, MARY VA
　　King George County. She performed a public service (VR, 2:334).
CASON, ROSEY SC
　　She supplied provisions for the army (SI, R-T:12).
CASON, SUSANNA VA
　　Spotsylvania County. She performed a public service (VR, 4:259).
CASTELAW, ANN SC
　　She supplied provisions for the army (SI, R-T:70).
CATHCART, MARGARET NC
　　She opposed drinking British tea. See Background.
CATHEY, ESTHER NC
　　She supplied provisions for the army (RA, A:135).
CATLETT, POLLY VA
　　Frederick County. Recognized for public service (VR, 2:175).
CATTELL, SABINA SC
　　She supplied provisions for the army (SI, B:159).
CAVE, ELIZABETH CRAIG KY
　　She went for water when the Indians attacked. See Biographies.
CAVEN, SARAH NC
　　She supplied provisions for the army (RA, A:12).
CAVENAUGH, JOICE NC
　　Wife of Covenant Cavenaugh. She supplied provisions for the army (RA, B:266).
CAVENAUGH, SARAH VA
　　Norfolk. She performed a public service (Court Booklet, p. 1).
CAVILIER, MRS. JOHN NJ
　　Somerset. She suffered damage in a British raid (CDB, claim 52).
CAW, RACHEL SC
　　She supplied provisions for the army (SI, O-Q:178).
CAWLEY, ELKANA VA
　　Prince Edward County. Recognized for public service (VR, 5:47).
CHADWICK, ABIGAIL CT
　　Hartford. She made shirts for Capt. Mattock's company in 1778 (CAR, 11:565).
CHALMERS, ANN SC
　　She supplied provisions for the army (SI, B:130).
CHALMERS, ELIZABETH SC
　　She supplied provisions for the army (SI, B:80).
CHALMERS, MARTHA SC
　　She supplied provisions for the army (SI, B:130).

CHAMBERLAIN, JANE   MD
    She boarded Capt. James Nicholson in 1776 (IM, 1298).
CHAMBERLAYNE, AGNES DANDRIDGE   VA
    She was the wife of Edward Pye Chamberlayne, who served
    as midshipman of the brig Musqueto, 1776-1777. His brothers
    1st. Lt. Byrd and 2nd Lt. George also served on this brig.
    The vessel was captured by the British on August 8, 1777,
    and all three brothers were confined in the Fortun Prison in
    Gosport, England. The brothers escaped, but were recaptured
    on October 12, 1777. Later they escaped again and returned
    to Virginia (CN).
CHAMBERLAYNE, MARY   VA
    Buckingham County. Public service recognized (VR, 1:195;
    2:365). Also in New Kent County (Court Booklet, p. 17).
CHAMBERS, ANN   MD
    She supplied wheat on 1781 for the army (IM, 16482).
CHAMBERS, ELINOR   NC
    She supplied provisions for the army (RA, 11:75, fol. 2).
CHAMBERS, RUTH   NJ
    Brunswick. The wife of Capt. David Chambers, she suffered
    damages caused by the British (CDB, p. 245).
CHAMIER, MRS. ACHSAH   NY
    She was an American patriot. See Biographies.
CHAMPION, DEBORAH. See GILBERT
CHAMPION, ESTHER   CT
    She supplied provisions for the army in 1780 (CAR, 35:177a).
CHAMPION, LYDIA DUNK   MA
    West Springfield. She was the wife of Dr. Reuben Champion,
    who joined the Continental Army in 1775 as a surgeon. Dr.
    Champion cared for the sick and wounded at Fort Ticonderoga,
    where he contracted a fever and died there on March 29, 1777
    (FP1).
CHAMPLIN, MARY RICHARD ELY   CT
    New London. She married Lodowick Champlin, who commanded
    the sloop Richard in 1780 and was captured and imprisoned by
    the British (CN).
CHANDLER, JOYCE   VA
    Henry County. She performed a public service (VR Court Book-
    let, p. 36).
CHANDLER, POLLY   CT
    Newton. She lodged American officers in 1776 (CAR, 5:472c).
CHAPIN, MARGARET PYNCHON COLTON   VA
    Alexandria. She was born on October 24, 1738, and married
    Dr. Benjamin Chapin of Springfield, Massachusetts. He served
    as surgeon on the privateer Tartar and on March 9, 1780, was
    captured by the British and imprisoned on a prison ship, where
    Chapin died in 1785 (CN; FP2).
CHAPMAN, ABIGAIL   CT
    She suffered losses in a British raid in July 1779 (CAR, 15:250g,
    251e, I 53a, 63g). She was a Western Lands Grantee.

III: COMPLETE LISTING 263

CHAPMAN, DEBORAH   NC
   She supplied provisions for the army (RA, 4:91; fol. 2, etc.).
CHAPMAN, ELIZABETH   VA
   King and Queen County. Recognized for public service (VR, 3:217, 223).
CHAPMAN, ESTHER   CT
   Her husband was killed at Fort Griswold, Groton, in September 1781 (CAR, 26:295a).
CHAPMAN, MARY   CT
   Tolland. She supplied a blanket for the army (CAR, 11:18).
CHAPMAN, MERCY BEAUMONT   PA
   Col. Alexander Hamilton had his headquarters in her home. See Biographies.
CHAPMAN, SARAH   CT
   Hebron. She supplied a rifle for the army (CAR, p. 320b) and also boarded Roger Sherman and servant, 1779-1780 (CAR, 33:103).
CHAPMAN, SARAH   VA
   Montgomery County. She performed a public service (VR, 4:98).
CHAPMAN, SARAH KETCHUM   CT
   Her husband and son were captured by the British. See Biographies.
CHAPMAN, SARAH LEWIS. See MOREHOUSE
CHAPMAN, TABITHA   NC
   She supplied provisions for the army (RA, 12:84, fol. 2, A 97).
CHAPPEL, MARY   VA
   Sussex County. She performed a public service (VR, 5:199).
CHAPPEL, PHOEBE   VA
   Amelia County. Recognized for public service (VR, 1:46).
CHAPPELL, ELIZABETH   VA
   Amelia County. Recognized for public service (VR Court Booklet, 2:61).
CHARLTON, ABIGAIL   NC
   She opposed drinking British imported tea. See Background.
CHASE, JUDITH   MD
   Charles County. She supplied wheat for the army in 1781 and 1782 (IM, 14471, 19417, 19523, 19742).
CHASTAIN, CHARLOTTE   VA
   Powhatan County. She performed a public service (VR, 4:242).
CHAVERS, WINIFRED   NC
   She supplied provisions for the army (RA, K:123a).
CHEADLE, JUDITH   VA
   Caroline County. Recognized for public service (VR, 1:244).
CHEATHAM, ELIZABETH   VA
   Mecklenburg. She performed a public service (VR, 4:43).
CHENEY, FAITH   NC
   She supplied provisions for the army (RA, 11:99, fol. 4).
CHESSHIRE, ANNE   WV
   Hampshire County. She supplied provisions for the army (VR, 3:116).

CHESSMAN, MRS.   PA
  Philadelphia. She boarded Oliver Ellsworth of Connecticut while
  he was a delegate to the Continental Congress in 1779 (CAR,
  33:161, 163).
CHESTER, EUNICE   CT
  Groton. She suffered losses in a British raid (CAR, 1:79a).
  She was a Western Lands Grantee.
CHESTER, HANNAH   CT
  Danbury. She suffered losses in a British raid (CAR, 28:296).
CHEW, ELIZABETH OSWALD   PA
  Gen. and Mrs. Washington stayed in her house. See Biographies.
CHEW, LUCY MILLER   CT
  New London. She married Samuel Chew, who commanded the
  ship Alfred and was killed in battle on March 4, 1778 (CN).
CHILDRESS, ANN   VA
  Amherst County. She performed a public service (Court Booklet,
  p. 19).
CHILDRESS, LUCY   VA
  Amherst County. Recognized for public service (Ctf 1).
CHILES, ELIZABETH FAULKNER   VA
  She was killed by the enemy. See Biographies.
CHILES, FANNY   VA
  Orange County. She performed a public service (VR, 4:181).
CHILES, JEMIMA   VA
  Caroline County. She performed a public service (VR Lists,
  1:34; II:21, 30).
CHILTON, SABELLAH   VA
  Westmoreland County. Recognized for public service (VR Ctf 1).
CHINN, SARAH BRYAN   KY
  She left the fort to get water when the Indians attacked. See
  Biographies.
CHISHOLM, RACHEL   VA
  Hanover County. She performed a public service (VR, 3:172).
CHISMAN, DIANA   VA
  York County. Recognized for public service (VR, 4:273).
CHOATE, MARY GIDDINGER   MA
  She was born in 1732 and married William Choate, and died in
  1810. She is listed as a patriot in the DAR Patriot Index 2.
CHRISTIAN, POLLY   VA
  Gloucester County. She performed a public service (VR, 4:286).
CHRISTOPHERS, ELIZABETH   CT
  New London. She suffered damage in a British raid (CAR,
  1:63g, 95b) and was a Western Lands Grantee.
CHURCH, HANNAH   CT
  Danbury. In 1777 her husband went over to the British and
  died, but she was loyal, and her son served in the Continental
  Army, 1779-1782 (CAR, 23:364, 365).
CHURCH, PRISCILLA   NC
  She supplied provisions for the army (RA, 5:61, fol. 4).
CHURCHILL, THANKFUL HEWITT   VT
  Hubbardton. She was the wife of Samuel Churchill, who was

III: COMPLETE LISTING

taken prisoner at the Battle of Hubbardton and sent to Fort Ticonderoga. Later he escaped (FP1).

CILLEY, ELSE NH
Two of her sons and two grandsons served in the war. See Biographies.

CLAGHORN, THANKFUL DEXTER MA
Her home was burned by the British. See Biographies.

CLAIBORNE, ELIZABETH VA
King William County. She performed a public service (VR, 3:241-242).

CLAN, NANCY RI
Providence. Wife of Robert Clan. She supplied beef, pork, corn, rye, sugar, butter, cordwood, etc., for the troops (MP, 48:25).

CLAPP, PHEBE
Greenwich widow. She suffered losses in a British raid (CAR, 24:276).

CLARK, MRS. NJ
Gloucester County. She was the wife of Col. Clark. She collected funds for the army (New Jersey Gazette, July 4, 1780).

CLARK, ANNA CT
Fairfield. Her husband, Capt. Daniel Clark, was killed in battle in 1778 at Saratoga and his money for payment of the soldiers was stripped from his body by the enemy (CAR, 14:206, 210).

CLARK, BETTY NJ
Westfield, Essex County. The wife of Azariah Clark, she suffered losses in a British raid (CDB, claim 27).

CLARK, MRS. BOLLING VA
Dinwiddie County. She performed a public service (VR Ctf 1).

CLARK, COMFORT CT
Stamford widow. She suffered losses in the British raid of 1781 (CAR, 22:214).

CLARK, ELIZABETH NJ
Westfield, Essex County. She suffered damage in a British raid (CDB, claim 6).

CLARK, ELIZABETH ZANE WV
She left the fort to get ammunition when the Indians attacked. See Biographies.

CLARK, HANNA CT
She supplied forage for an express rider in 1779 (CAR, 16:432).

CLARK, HANNAH ARRINGTON GA
She accompanied her husband on a campaign. See Biographies.

CLARK, JANE LARDNER NJ
The wife of Lt. Col. Elijah Clark, she was active in the ladies' association for the welfare of the soldiers (New Jersey Gazette, July 4, 1780).

CLARK, JOHANNA NC
She supplied provisions for the army (RA, 1:96, fol. 4, A 218).

CLARK, PHEBE CT
Middletown. She was the widow of Lt. Othneil Clark, who was killed July 1782 in service (CAR, 36:69, 70).

CLARK, PHEBE NJ
Connecticut Farms, Essex County. She suffered damage by the British (CDB, claim 60).

CLARK, PRUDENCE VA
Brunswick County. She performed a public service (VR, 1:109).

CLARK, RACHEL NJ
Westfield. She suffered losses in a British raid (CDB, claim 75).

CLARK, SARAH NJ
Westfield. She suffered losses in a British raid (CDB, claim 44).

CLARK, SARAH. See MARY HITE BOWMAN

CLARK, SARAH BARNARD MA
Harwich. She was the Widow Morrill when she married Seth Clark, who commanded the Continental vessel Unity. Clark was captured on September 17, 1776, by the British schooner Porcupine (CN; FP2).

CLARK, SARAH HATFIELD NJ
Her two sons were captured and imprisoned on the ship Jersey in New York Harbor. See Biographies.

CLARK, SUSANNA NC
She was the wife of Col. Thomas Clark of the 1st North Carolina Regiment, who was wounded at Stone Ferry on June 20, 1779. He was taken prisoner on May 12, 1780, when Charleston fell to the British (FW).

CLARK, SUSANNA VA
Essex County. She performed a public service (VR, 2:144).

CLARK, TEMPERANCE VA
Dinwiddie County. Recognized for public service (VR Ctf 1).

CLARKE, CHARITY NY
A friend supplied Charity with homespun yarn, and she knitted stockings for the soldiers and felt "Nationaly" (NL).

CLARKE, LUCY VA
Surry County. She performed a public service (VR, 5:166).

CLARKE, MARTHA VA
Surry County. Recognized for public service (VR, 5:166).

CLARKE, MARY GA
She supplied two cattle for the army (WA, 170).

CLARKE, MARY REYNOLDS MD
She was born in 1768 and married Joseph Clarke. Mary is listed as a patriot in the DAR Patriot Index.

CLARKSON, MRS. PA
Philadelphia. She was an active member of the ladies' association for the welfare of the soldiers (Pennsylvania Gazette, June 12, 1780).

CLARKSON, MARY BONDE PA
She was a member of the ladies' association. See Biographies.

CLAUSON, RUTH CT
Stamford widow. She suffered damage in the British raid of 1781 (CAR, 22:295, 300).

III: COMPLETE LISTING

CLAY, ALICE   VA
Lunenburg County. She performed a public service (Court Booklet, 1:16).
CLAY, ANN LEGARDIRE   GA
She nursed wounded American soldiers. See Biographies.
CLAY, ELEANOR   VA
Chesterfield County. She performed a public service (VR, 2:22).
CLAY, ELIZABETH   VA
Hanover County. Recognized for public service (VR Lists, 2:6).
CLAY, PATIENCE   CT
New London. Her son was in the army and died at sea (37:57, 58).
CLAYPOOLE, BETSY GRISCOM. See ROSS
CLAYTON, ELIZABETH   NJ
Burlington. She suffered losses in a British raid (CDB, claim 29).
CLAYTON, GRACE   NC
She refused to drink British tea. See Background.
CLELAND, MARY   GA
She supplied two steers for the army (WA, p. 168).
CLEMENT, SUSANNAH HILL   VA
She helped manufacture gunpowder for the army. See Biographies.
CLEMENTS, ELIZABETH   VA
Southampton County. She performed a public service (VR Ctf 1).
CLEMENTS, MARTHA   VA
Pittsylvania County. Filed claim for services with certificate of John Buckley.
CLEMENTS, SARAH   VA
Goochland County. Recognized for public service (VR, 3:61).
CLEMENTS, SUSANNAH   VA
Pittsylvania County. Recognized for public service (VR, 5:6).
CLEMONS (CLEMONDS), CATHARINE   VA
Augusta County. She performed a public service (VR Lists, 1:2, 5).
CLERK, JANET   NC
She supplied provisions for the army (WA, C:9).
CLIFFORD, PHEBE   RI
She supplied provisions for the army (MP, 53:6).
CLIFTON, MARY   NC
She supplied food for the army (RA, 6:20, fol. 1).
CLIFTON, MILDRED   VA
King George County. She performed a public service (VR, 2:334).
CLINGAN, JANE ROAN   PA
She would marry only a patriot. See Biographies.
CLINTON, ANNA   CT
West Haven. She suffered damage by the British in 1781 (CAR, 24:16a; I:63c, 91h). She was a Western Lands Grantee.

CLOKE, ELIZABETH COOK   DE
    She molded bullets for the soldiers. See Biographies.
CLOSE, DEBORAH   CT
    Greenwich. She suffered losses in a British raid (CAR, 1:63c, 74b). She was a Western Lands Grantee.
CLOSE, HANNAH   CT
    Greenwich. She suffered damage in a British raid (CAR, 15:271a; I:63c, 74b). She was a Western Lands Grantee.
CLOUGH, ELIZABETH   VA
    Amelia County. She performed a public service (VR, 1:45).
CLUVERUS, MARTHA   VA
    Gloucester County. Recognized for public service (VR, 4:286).
CLYATT, HANNAH   SC
    She supplied provisions for the army (SI, Y-Z:173).
CLYMER, ELIZABETH MEREDITH   PA
    The British ransacked her home. See Biographies.
COALE, ANN   MD
    She supplied cattle for the army in 1783 (IM, 26278).
COAS, SUSANNA PARSONS   MA
    Gloucester. She was the wife of William Coas, Jr., commander of the ship General Stark. On October 8, 1781, Coas was captured by HMS Chatham and imprisoned (CN).
COATES, ELIZABETH AVERY   PA
    She was born in 1724 and married a Mr. Evans, then Moses Coates. Elizabeth died in 1790. She is listed as a patriot in the DAR Patriot Index.
COATES, LYDIA SAUNDERS   PA
    She was active in the ladies' association. See Biographies.
COBB, AMY   RI
    Wife of Thomas Cobb, she supplied corn and wool for the army in 1779 (MP, 41:11).
COBB, AVERILLA   VA
    King and Queen County. She performed a public service (VR, 3:217).
COBB, JUDITH   SC
    She supplied food for the army (SI, R-T:106).
COBBS, JUDITH   VA
    Hanover County. Recognized for public service (VR, 3:171, 174).
COBBS, SUSANNA   VA
    Hanover County. She performed a public service (VR, 3:167, 171).
COCHRAN, GERTRUDE SCHUYLER   NY
    She entertained Col. Alexander Hamilton. See Biographies.
COCHRAN, PHOEBE GRAY   SC
    She married Daniel Cochran, then Maj. John Hearst, and died in 1807. She is listed as a patriot in the DAR Patriot Index.
COCK, AGNES   VA
    The wife of George Cock, she is listed as a patriot in the DAR Patriot Index.

III: COMPLETE LISTING 269

COCKBURN, MARY NC
She supplied provisions for the army (RA, D:53).

COCKE, ANN VA
Goochland County. She performed a public service (VR, 3:61, 69; IV:313). Also Ann Cocke listed in Southampton County (5:181) and Surry County (Court Booklet, p. 5).

COCKE, ELIZABETH VA
Prince George County. Recognized for public service (VR Court Booklet, p. 11).

COCKE, JANE VA
Charles City. She performed a public service (VR, 1:310).

COCKE, REBECCA HUBBARD VA
Charles City. Recognized for public service (VR, 1:309; 4:302).

COCKER, JOANNA VA
Gloucester County. She performed a public service (VR, 4:286).

COCKFIELD, MARY SC
She supplied food for the soldiers (SI, B:140).

COCKRILL, ANN ROBERTSON TN
She defended Fort Watagua while the Indians attacked. See Biographies.

CODDINGTON, MARY RI
She provided provisions for the troops (MP, 23:38).

COFFIELD, ELIZABETH VA
Hansemond County. She performed a public service (VR, 4:153).

COFFIN, RUTH MA
The wife of Richard Coffin, she died in 1779. She is listed as a patriot in the DAR Patriot Index.

COGSWELL, MARY BACKUS CT
Gen. Washington had breakfast with the Cogswells. See Biographies.

COLE, MRS. NC
She supplied provisions for the army (RA, 4:72, fol. 3).

COLE, EFFIE NJ
Harrington Township, Bergen County. She suffered damage due to a British raid (CDB, claim 46).

COLE, ELIZABETH MD
She supplied flour for the army (IM, 10699).

COLE, MRS. JAMES NC
She supplied provisions for the army (RA, E-G:2).

COLE, SARAH MD
Charles County. In 1782 she supplied wheat for the army (IM, 23953).

COLE, SARAH PA
At age thirteen she was captured in July 1778 by the Indians and taken to Canada. She was sent home on August 22, 1782 (MR).

COLE, WIDOW VA
Hansemond County. Recognized for public service (VR, 4:352-353).

COLEMAN, ANN VA
Caroline County. She performed a public service (VR Court Booklet, 2:2).

COLEMAN, ELIZABETH   VA
   Amherst County. Recognized for public service (VR, 4:282).
COLEMAN, HANNAH   VA
   Caroline County. She performed a public service (VR, 1:246).
COLEMAN, MARTHA   NJ
   Orange. She suffered losses in a British raid (CDB, claim 2).
COLEMAN, MILDRED   VA
   King and Queen County. She performed a public service (VR, 4:333).
COLEMAN, NICEY   VA
   Spotsylvania County. Recognized for public service (VR, 4:259).
COLEMAN, PATIENCE   VA
   Cumberland County. She performed a public service (VR, 4:293).
COLEMAN, REBECCA   VA
   Buckingham County. She performed a public service (VR, 1:295).
COLEMAN, UNITY   NC
   She supplied provisions for the army (RA, A:2).
COLES, LUCY   VA
   Hanover County. Recognized for public service (VR, 3:170).
COLES, MILDRED   VA
   Halifax County. She performed a public service (VR Court Booklet, p. 58).
COLFAX, ESTHER SCHUYLER   NJ
   She entertained Gen. Washington. See Biographies.
COLLETON, MARGARET SWAINTON   SC
   She provided funds for the army (AA, 3:162).
COLLIER, JENNET   CT
   Hartford. She provided for prisoners from Fort Ticonderoga (CAR, 3:633ab) and entertained the governor and his council (CAR, 3:612a).
COLLIER, SARAH   MD
   Worcester County. She supplied corn in 1780 for the army and then beef (IM, 13423, 13466).
COLLINGS, HANNAH TURNER   MA
   Cape Ann. She married Charles Collings who served as 1st Lt. on the <u>Black Princess</u> with his brother, Isaac, as 2nd Lt. They were captured by the British on October 20, 1781, and committed to the Mill Prison at Plymouth, England. Also spelled Collins. (CN).
COLLINS, ELIZABETH   VA
   Pittsylvania County. She performed a public service (VR, 5:7).
COLLINS, FRANCES   VA
   Princess Anne County. Recognized for public service (VR, 4:212).
COLLINS, MARGARET   VA
   Caroline County. She performed a public service (VR, 1:244).
COLLINS, MARY   SC
   She supplied provisions for the troops (SI, R-T:106).
COLLINS, MARY   VA
   Orange County. She performed a public service (VR, 4:174). Also listed in Pittsylvania County (VR, 5:6).

III: COMPLETE LISTING 271

COLLINS, MARY PARRISH   PA
    Philadelphia. On September 1, 1774, John Adams and other members of the First Continental Congress dined with the Collinses (BA).

COLLINS, PEGGY   VA
    Caroline County. She performed a public service (VR Lists, 1:34).

COLLINS, RUTH   CT
    Guilford. She supplied a blanket in 1777 for the army (CAR, 11:283).

COLLINS, SARAH   MD
    Montgomery County. The Widow Collins supplied wheat in 1781 for the army (IM, 17141).

COLLINS, SARAH WHITMAN. See HOOKER

COLOMBE, MARGARET MOORE DE LA
    Her husband was taken prisoner in 1778. After the war he was imprisoned with Lafayette in Austria. See Biographies.

COMPTON, MARY   NJ
    Woodbridge. She suffered damage by the British (CDB, p. 63).

COMPTON, SARAH   NJ
    Middlesex County. She suffered losses in a British raid (CDB, p. 52).

CONCIL, ELIZABETH   SC
    She supplied provisions for the army (SI, L-N:271).

CONDICT, HULDA   NJ
    Morris County. She suffered damage by the Americans (CDB, claim 162).

CONDICT, RHODA   NJ
    Orange. She suffered losses in a British raid (CDB, claims 21, 43).

CONDIT, JEMIMA CONDICT   NJ
    Morris County. She married her cousin, Capt. Jonathan Condit (different spellings). She was a member of the ladies' association for the welfare of the soldiers (New Jersey Gazette, Jly 4, 1780).

CONE, KEZIAH BARBER   GA
    Her husband was captured by the British and imprisoned. See Biographies.

CONGER, MARY   NJ
    Middlesex County. She suffered losses in a British raid (CDB, p. 55).

CONKEY, DINAH DICK   NY
    She was born in 1738 and became the first wife of Capt. Joshua Conkey, Sr., and died in 1792. She is listed as a patriot in the DAR Patriot Index.

CONKLIN, ESTHER   CT
    Groton. She suffered damage in a British raid (CAR, 1:63q, 70a). She was a Western Lands Grantee.

CONKLING, ELIZABETH   CT
    New London. She married Edward Conkling commander of the sloop Eagle, who was captured on May 8, 1779, off Stonington, Connecticut, by the British and murdered (CN).

CONN, JANE　　　　　　　　　　MD
　　Montgomery County. She supplied wheat in 1780 for the army (IM, 13636).

CONNELL, MARY　　　　　　　　SC
　　She supplied provisions for the army (SI, L-N:268).

CONTURIER, MARTHA　　　　　　SC
　　She supplied provisions for the army (SI, L-N:9).

CONWAY, ELIZABETH RICHARDSON　KY
　　Elizabeth and her children were captured by the British and Indians. See Biographies.

CONWAY, JANE　　　　　　　　NJ
　　Woodbridge. The wife of Col. John Conway, she suffered losses in a British raid (CDB, p. 111).

CONYERS, MARY WITHERSPOON　　SC
　　She was born in 1764 and married Capt. Daniel Conyers, and died in 1831. She is listed as a patriot in the DAR Patriot Index.

CONYNGHAM, ANN HOCKLEY　　　　PA
　　Her husband was twice captured by the British and imprisoned. See Biographies.

COOK, MRS.　　　　　　　　　NJ
　　Morris County. The wife of Col. Cook, she collected funds for the army (New Jersey Gazette, July 4, 1780).

COOK, AMY　　　　　　　　　NC
　　She supplied provisions for the army (RA, 10:37; fol. 3).

COOK, ANNE　　　　　　　　　VA
　　York County. She performed a public service (VR Court Booklet, 2:10).

COOK, CHARLOTTE　　　　　　　VA
　　Pittsylvania County. Recognized for public service (Court Booklet, p. 53).

COOK, ELIZABETH　　　　　　　VA
　　Gloucester County. She performed a public service (VR, 3:39).

COOK, LUCY ELY　　　　　　　NJ
　　Morristown. The wife of Col. Ellis Cook, she was a member of the ladies' association for the welfare of the soldiers (New Jersey Gazette, July 4, 1780).

COOK, MARGARET　　　　　　　SC
　　She supplied provisions for the army (SI, B:67).

COOK, MARY　　　　　　　　　VA
　　Hanover County. Recognized for public service (VR, 3:170, 173) and in King and Queen County (VR Ctf 1).

COOK, REBECCA　　　　　　　　SC
　　She supplied provisions for the army (SI, B:67).

COOK, SUBMITT PECK. See WHEATLEY

COOKE, MRS. SAMUEL　　　　　CT
　　John and Abigail Adams stayed in her home. See Biographies.

COOKE, SARAH SIMPSON　　　　PA
　　She turned her home into a hospital for wounded soldiers. See Biographies.

III: COMPLETE LISTING 273

COOKUS, CATHARINE WV
   Berkeley County. She performed a public service (VR Ctf 1).
COOLIDGE, DOROTHY MA
   She took down the portrait of King George III from her tavern walls and put up a portrait of General Washington. See Biographies.
COOLIDGE, EUNICE STRATTON MA
   Watertown. She was born on December 27, 1727, and married Joseph Coolidge who was killed during the Battle of Lexington on April 19, 1775. She died in 1801 (FP4).
COOPER, ELIZABETH NJ
   Harrington, Bergen County. The wife of Richard Cooper, she suffered loss of property caused by Americans (CDB, claim 44).
COOPER, ELIZABETH SC
   She supplied provisions for the army (SI, L-N:269).
COOPER, ELIZABETH WV
   Berkeley County. She performed a public service (VR Ctf 1).
COOPER, JANE VA
   Norfolk. Recognized for public service (VR, 4:144).
COOPER, MARY SC
   She supplied provisions for the army (SI, B:95).
COOPER, MARY VA
   Hansemond County. She performed a public service (VR, 4:15).
COOPER, PATIENCE NC
   She supplied provisions for the army (RA, 4:68, fol. 2).
COOPER, POLLY NY
   She served Gen. Washington for seven years and refused pay for her services. See Biographies.
COOPER, SARAH GA
   She supplied six head of beef cattle (WA, p. 160).
COPELAND, JANE VA
   Surry County. She performed a public service (VR Court Booklet, p. 11).
COPELAND, JEAN VA
   Surry County. Recognized for public service (VR Ctf 1).
CORBEN, ELIZABETH SC
   She supplied provisions for the army (SI, Y-Z:212).
CORBIN, HANNAH LEE VA
   She supplied provisions for the army and tried to get the right of widows to vote. See Biographies.
CORBIN, MARGARET COCHRAN PA
   "Captain" Molly was injured in battle. See Biographies.
CORDES, ANN SC
   She supplied provisions for the army (SI, B:80).
CORNELISEN, CATHERINE COOPER NY
   Nyack. After her husband was imprisoned in 1777, she took food to him (FH).
CORNELL, ANNIE NJ
   Somerset County. The wife of Albert Cornell, she suffered losses in a British raid (CDB, p. 169).

CORNELL, HANNAH FINCH   NY
   Her husband was captured by Indians. See Biographies.
CORTLEYOU, MARY   NJ
   Somerset County. Wife of Hendrick Cortleyou, she suffered
   damages caused by a British raid (CDB, p. 148).
COTTHEEN, CHARITY   SC
   She supplied provisions for the army (SI, U-W:226).
COTTON, MARY   WV
   Greenbrier County. She performed a public service (VR, 4:313).
COUCH, JANE   VA
   Buckingham County. Recognized for public service (VR, 1:196).
COUENHOVEN, ANNATIE KOEME   NY
   She entertained Gen. Washington. See Biographies.
COUNOVER, EVA   NJ
   Hackensack. Widow of Samuel Counover, she suffered damage
   by the Americans (VDB, p. 5).
COVENER, JOICE   NC
   She supplied provisions for the army (RA, A:81).
COVENHOVEN, DEBORAH   NJ
   Middlesex County. Widow of William Covenhoven of Penns Neck,
   she suffered losses in a British raid (CDB, p. 284).
COVENHOVEN, ELIZABETH   NJ
   Somerset County. Widow of Stoffel Probasco, she suffered losses
   in a British raid (CDB, p. 4).
COVENHOVEN, MRS. PETER   NJ
   Monmouth County. She was a member of the ladies' association
   for the welfare of the soldiers (New Jersey Gazette, July 4,
   1780).
COVENHOVER, LIDYA   WV
   Berkeley County. Recognized for public service (VR Ctf 2).
COVERT, LEHA   NJ
   Somerset County. Wife of Tunis Covert. The British stole
   a stored chest of Peter Staats (CDB, p. 42).
COWEN, JANE   SC
   She supplied provisions for the army (SI, B:190).
COWLES, SARAH   VA
   James City. She performed a public service (VR Court Booklet,
   pp. 4, 25).
COWLEY, MARY   VA
   York County. Recognized for public service (VR Court Booklet,
   1:3).
COWNE (COWN), ELIZABETH   VA
   Hanover County. She performed a public service. Also in
   King William County (VR Court Booklet, p. 16).
COWPER, MARY   VA
   Hansemond County. Recognized for public service (VR Court
   Booklet, 1:3).
COWPER, PATIENCE   NC
   She supplied provisions for the army (RA, 8:88, fol. 3).
COX, ANNA   VA
   Northumberland County. Recognized for public service (VR,
   4:113) and Chesterfield County (Ctf 2).

III: COMPLETE LISTING 275

COX, CATHERINE NC
She supplied provisions for the army (RA, 5:58, fol. 1).

COX, ESTHER BOWES NJ
She entertained Gen. Washington and Lafayette in her home. See Biographies.

COX, HETTY NJ
She was a member of the ladies' association for the welfare of the soldiers. See Biographies.

COX, JUDITH VA
Chesterfield County. She performed a public service (VR, 2:21, 25).

COXE, MRS. CHARLES NJ
Hunterdon County. She was an active member of the ladies' association for the welfare of the soldiers (New Jersey Gazette, July 4, 1780).

CRAFFORD, ELIZABETH VA
Surry County. Recognized for public service (VR Court Booklet, p. 8).

CRAFT, SARAH NJ
Burlington County. She suffered losses caused by the British (CDB, p. 20).

CRAFTS, ELIZABETH ALLEN MD
Born in 1734, she married Samuel Samples, then Lt. Col. Eleazer Crafts. She died in 1824 and is listed as a patriot in the DAR Patriot Index.

CRAFTS, NABBY MA
While the British occupied Boston, she rode there to obtain needles to make blankets and stockings for the soldiers. See Biographies.

CRAIG, ELEANOR SC
She supplied provisions for the army (SI, R-T:170).

CRAIG, ELIZABETH JOHNSON KY
She went for water when the Indians were attacking. See Biographies.

CRAIG, LUCY HAWKINS KY
Bryan's Station. When the Tories and Indians attacked on August 15, 1782, she was one of the women who went for water. Her name is inscribed on the monument erected in 1896 by the Lexington Chapter, Daughters of the American Revolution.

CRAIG, MARY HAWKINS KY
She went for water when the Indians attacked the fort. See Biographies.

CRAIG, SALLY PAGE KY
She went for water when the Indians attacked. See Biographies.

CRANE, ANN VA
King and Queen County. She performed a public service (VR Ctf 1).

CRANE, ESTHER NJ
Westfield. Widow of Benjamin Crane, she suffered losses in a British raid (CDB, claim 45).

CRANE, HANNAH NJ
Orange. She suffered damage by the British (CDB, claim 45).

CRANE, HANNAH CLARK   NJ
    Westfield. She suffered damage by the British (CDB, claim 44).
CRANE, PATIENCE   NJ
    Westfield. She suffered damage caused by the British (CDB, claim 37).
CRANE, SARAH   NJ
    Orange. She suffered losses in a British raid (CDB, claim 8).
CRANSTON, RACHEL   RI
    She nursed the wounded prisoners (MP, 57:4).
CRAVEN, PENELOPE PAGETT. See BARKER
CRAVENS, MARGARET HIATT   VA
    She was born in 1727 and married William Dyer, then John Cravens, then Dennis Lanahan, and died in 1826. She performed a public service (VR, 5:112; DAR).
CRAVENS, MARY HARRISON   VA
    Rockingham County. Born in 1696, she married Robert Cravens, Sr., and died in 1781. She performed a public service (VR, 5:112-113; DAR).
CRAWFORD, ANN   VA
    Amherst County. She was born in 1708, married David Crawford and died in 1802. She is recognized for public service (VR Court Booklet, p. 11; DAR).
CRAYCRAFT, CHARITY   MD
    Charles County. In 1783 she supplied wheat for the army (IM, 25400).
CREACY, ELIZABETH   NC
    She opposed drinking British tea. See Background.
CREACY, MARY   NC
    She opposed drinking British tea. See Background.
CREECH, ANN   SC
    She supplied provisions for the army (SI, Y-Z:12).
CREECY, MARY   NC
    She supplied provisions for the army (RA, K:132c).
CREIGHTON, ELIZABETH   SC
    She supplied provisions for the army (SI, Y-Z:253).
CRENSHAW, MARY   VA
    Amelia County. She performed a public service (VR, 1:41).
CRESSMUR, HARRIOTT   VA
    Norfolk. Recognized for public service (VR, 4:145).
CRICKET, ELIZABETH   NC
    She opposed drinking British tea. See Background.
CRILLY, RHODA   NJ
    Connecticut Farms, Essex County. Wife of John Crilly, she suffered damage caused by the British (CDB, claim 16).
CRIM, LENA STEELE   NY
    Born in 1733, she married Paul Crim and died in 1802. She is listed as a patriot in the DAR Patriot Index.
CHRISTMAN, SUSANNA KEELY   PA
    Born in 1750, she married Henry Cristman and died in 1823. She is listed as a patriot in the DAR Patriot Index.

III: COMPLETE LISTING

CROFOOT, REBECCA CT
  Danbury. The wife of Seth Crofoot, she suffered damage in a British raid (CAR, 1:51b).
CROGHAN, LUCY CLARK VA
  She was the wife of Maj. William Croghan, who was taken prisoner on May 12, 1780, when Charleston fell to the British (FW).
CROKER, ANN PA
  Philadelphia. On January 3, 1782, Walter Conner obtained a letter of marque to command the brigantine Saint John Nepomuceno with eight guns and twenty-five men. Ann Croker witnessed the bond (CN).
CRONBERGER, ELIZABETH GA
  Wife of Jacob Cronberger, she supplied forage and provisions for public use (WA, p. 128).
CROSBY, HANNAH SC
  The wife of Dennis Crosby, she provided provisions for the army (SI, O-Q:278). She died in 1785.
CROSS, ELIZABETH VA
  Loudoun County. She performed a public service (VR Lists, p. 1).
CROUCH, MARY SC
  She supplied provisions for the army (SI, Y-Z:126).
CROUCH, SUSANNA VA
  Goochland County. Recognized for public service (VR, 3:88).
CROUCHER, ELIZABETH VA
  Caroline County. She performed a public service (VR, 1:244).
CROW, MARTHA NJ
  Amboy, Middlesex County. She suffered losses in a British raid (CDB, p. 56).
CRUMBELL, CATHERINE VA
  Frederick County. Recognized for public service (VR, 2:178).
CRUMP, SARAH VA
  New Kent County. She performed a public service (Court Booklet, p. 11).
CRUTCH, JUDITH VA
  Norfolk. Recognized for public service (VR, 4:127-128).
CRUTE, HANNAH VA
  Amelia County. She performed a public service (VR, 1:46).
CULBERTSON, MARTHA THOMAS SC
  She loaded muskets for the men while under attack. See Biographies.
CULLOM, MARGARET FOSS. See GERRISH
CULVER, JOANNA CT
  New London. She suffered losses in a British raid (CAR, 1:63g, 95a). She was a Western Lands Grantee.
CUMMINGS, JANE NJ
  Hunterdon County. She suffered damage caused by Americans (CDB, claim 38).
CUNNINGHAM, ANN WV
  Berkeley County. She performed a public service (VR Ctf 1).

CUNNINGHAM, SARAH PRICE   VA
   The wife of Edward Cunningham, she is listed as a patriot in
   the DAR Patriot Index.
CUNNINGHAM, TERESA   NC
   She opposed drinking British tea. See Background.
CURD, SARAH   VA
   Goochland County. Recognized for public service (VR, 3:60-
   61).
CURRIE, CATHERINE   NC
   She supplied provisions for the army (RA, 6:4, fol. 2).
CURRY, MARY   NC
   She supplied provisions for the army (RA, A:166).
CURTIS, JEANNE   VA
   Middlesex County. Recognized for public service (VR Court
   Booklet, p. 2).
CURTIS, MARTHA COWLES   CT
   Norfolk. She was born in 1741 and married Thomas Curtis who
   died in 1776 of smallpox in the army camp at Stillwater, New
   York. Mrs. Curtis died on December 5, 1829 (FP4).
CURTIS, RUTH PEABODY   MA
   She was born in 1744 and married John Curtis, then Bartholomew
   Trask. She died in 1829 and is listed as a patriot in the DAR
   Patriot Index.
CUSHING, ABIGAIL. See SHEFFIELD
CUSHING, ANN WAINWRIGHT   MA
   The wife of James Cushing, she died in 1810. She is listed
   as a patriot in the DAR Patriot Index.
CUSHING, HANNAH PHILLIPS   MA
   She opposed buying British goods. See Background.
CUSHMAN, DESIAH BRANCH   VT
   Born in 1752, she married Charles Cushman and died in 1849.
   She is listed as a patriot in the DAR Patriot Index.
CUSTIS, ELEANOR CALVERT   VA
   She was the daughter-in-law of Martha Washington. See Biogra-
   phies.
CUTCHIN, PRISCILLA   VA
   Isle of Wight. She performed a public service (VR, 2:315-316).
CUTLER, DINAH LEE   NJ
   Morristown. The wife of private Abijah Cutler, she suffered
   his loss when he died of exposure at Valley Forge (FP1).
CUTLER, ELIZABETH ROCKWOOD   MA
   She kept open the Cutler Inn so the officers' horses could be
   stabled. See Biographies.
CUTLER, ESTHER   CT
   New London. She suffered losses in a British raid (CAR, 1:63q,
   95b). She was a Western Lands Grantee.
CUTLER, MARY   CT
   Fairfield. She suffered damage in the British raid (CAR, 1:53e,
   63p). She was a Western Lands Grantee.
CUTTER, MARY   NJ
   Woodbridge. She suffered losses in a British raid (CDB, p. 217).

III: COMPLETE LISTING

CUTTER, TABITHA NJ
  Woodbridge. She suffered losses in a British raid (CDB, p. 219).
CUYLER, JEANNE GA
  She was born in 1738 and married Telemon Cuyler and died
  in 1779. She is listed as a patriot in the DAR Patriot Index.

D

DAGGETT, POLLY MA
  She destroyed a flagpole so it would not fall into the hands
  of the British. See Biographies.
DAGWORTHY, MARY. See HUNT
DAILEY, MARCY RI
  Wife of Field Dailey. She supplied corn, rye, beef, sugar,
  butter, and cordwood for the troops in 1778 (MP, 48:26).
DAILEY, MARY VA
  Hanover County. She performed a public service (VR, 3:175-176).
DAINGERFIELD, MRS. VA
  Spotsylvania County. Recognized for public service (VR Court
  Booklet, p. 35).
DAINGERFIELD, HANNAH VA
  New Kent County. She performed a public service (VR, Court
  Booklet, p. 9).
DALBY (DOLBY), MARY VA
  Hanover County. Recognized for public service (VR Court Booklet, 1:20).
DALE, ROSE VA
  King George County. She performed a public service (VR Lists,
  pp. 3, 4, 11).
DALTON, MRS. VA
  At age thirty she was captured with her husband, Capt. Dalton,
  and three children at Fort Vincent by the British and Indians
  and taken to Niagara, then arrived at Montreal on October 4,
  1782, then ordered to Three Rivers (MR).
DALTON, NANCY VA
  She was captured by Indians at Fort Vincent in September 1782
  by Indians along with Hannah Dalton, aged five, and released
  from Fort Ticonderoga on July 18, 1783 (MR).
DALY, ELIZABETH GREEN NC
  Edentown. She signed the resolution banning British tea. Later
  she married Capt. John Daly (DAR).
DAMAREST, ELIZABETH NJ
  Hackensack. She suffered losses in a British raid (CDB, claim 45).
DAMAREST, MARY NJ
  Hackensack. She suffered damages in a British raid (CDB,
  claim 46).
DANA, SUSANNAH HUNTINGTON PA
  Wyoming Valley. She was born on June 23, 1730, and married

Andrew Dana of Pomfret, Connecticut. The family moved to the Wyoming Valley in 1772. During the massacre by Tories and Indians in 1778, Susannah, her husband, and children were killed, although a son, Anderson Dana, survived and left descendants (FP1).

DANIEL, ANN   VA
New Kent County. She performed a public service (VR Court Booklet, p. 9).

DANIEL, CELIA   NC
She provided provisions for the troops (RA, C:78).

DANIEL, ELIZABETH   VA
Caroline County. She performed a public service (VR Court Booklet, 2:9). Also in Orange County (Court Booklet, p. 8).

DANIEL, SARAH   VA
Stafford County. Recognized for public service (VR, 5:188).

DANIELSON, SARAH WILLIAMS   CT
She was a camp follower. See Biographies.

DANNELL, RACHEL   NC
She supplied two cows for the army. See Biographies.

DARBY, ELIZABETH   SC
She provided funds for the army (AA, 3:28).

DARBY, MARY   NJ
Woodbridge. She suffered damage in a British raid (CDB, p. 301).

DARDEN, ANNE   VA
Hansemond County. She performed a public service (VR, 4:154).

DARDEN, ELIZABETH   VA
Hansemond County. Recognized for public service (VR, 4:353).

DARDON, ELIZABETH   VA
Isle of Wight. She performed a public service (VR, 2:317).

DARKE, SARAH DELAYEA   WV
Charles Town. She was a widow when she married William Darke, a captain in the militia. Darke was captured at the Battle of Germantown in October 1777 and was confined in a prison ship in New York Harbor until November 1780 (DB).

DARLEY, MARTHA   VA
Dinwiddie County. She performed a public service (VR Ctf 1).

DARLING, MARY   SC
She supplied provisions for the army (SI, 10, pt. 2:56).

DARNEL, RACHEL   NC
She provided provisions for the army (RA, A:195).

DARRAGH, LYDIA BARRINGTON   PA
She carried a message of an impending British attack. See Biographies.

DARRELL, FRANCES   SC
She supplied provisions for the army (SI, 1:17).

DARRELL, SARAH   VA
Fairfax County. Recognized for public service (VR, 2:224).

DART, AMELIA   SC
She supplied provisions for the army (SI, 1:117).

III: COMPLETE LISTING

DARVILLE, ANN CATHERINE　　　VA
  Dinwiddie County. She performed a public service (VR, 1:326).
DASHER, ANN CHRISTINA MEYER　　GA
  She provided supplies for Gen. Wayne (WA, p. 113).
DATON (DAYTON), SARAH　　　NC
  She provided supplies for the army (RA, C:111).
DAUGHERTY, MARY　　　SC
  She supplied provisions for the army (SI, L-N:275).
DAVENPORT, ANN　　　NC
  She supplied food for the army (RA, A:247).
DAVENPORT, CATHERINE　　　VA
  Halifax County. Recognized for public service (VR, 2:267, 320).
DAVENPORT, DEBORAH　　　CT
  Stamford. The daughter of Hannah and Joseph Davenport, she was born on January 30, 1757. On December 17, 1781, Ebenezer Jones obtained a letter of marque to command three Connecticut boats, and Deborah Davenport witnessed the bond (CN).
DAVENPORT, MEHITABLE COGGESHALL　　CT
  She witnessed a letter of marque. See Biographies.
DAVENPORT, SARAH　　　CT
  New Haven. She suffered damage in a British raid in July 1779 (CAR, 15:234f).
DAVIDSON, CATHARINE MARTIN　　PA
  She nursed wounded soldiers. See Biographies.
DAVIDSON, ELIZABETH　　　VA
  Rockbridge County. She performed a public service (VR, p. 72).
DAVIDSON, MARGARET　　　NC
  She supplied provisions for the troops (RA, A:238).
DAVIDSON, MARY　　　NC
  She provided food for the army (RA, 4:54, fol. 2).
DAVIDSON, MARY BREVARD　　　NC
  She was the wife of Lt. Col. William Lee Davidson of the 5th North Carolina Regiment, and later promoted to brigadier general. He was killed at Cowna's Ford, North Carolina on February 1, 1781 (FW; DAR). She supplied provisions for the army (RA, 5:30-3).
DAVIDSON, SARAH　　　SC
  She supplied provisions for the army (SI, 10, pt. 1:65, 152).
DAVIDSON, VIOLET WINSLOW WILSON　　NC
  She was born in 1741 and married Maj. John Davidson. She died in 1818, and is listed as a patriot in the DAR Patriot Index.
DAVIS, AGNES　　　SC
  She provided provisions for the troops (SI, 1:38).
DAVIS, ANN　　　VA
  Essex County. She performed a public service (VR Court Booklet, p. 4). Also an Ann Davis in Amelia County (Court Booklet, 2:26).

DAVIS, ANN SIMPSON   PA
 She carried messages for Gen. Washington. See Biographies.
DAVIS, DEVOTION   NC
 She supplied provisions for the army (RA, 4:87, fol. 3).
DAVIS, ELIZABETH   MD
 Charles County. She provided wheat in 1782 for the army (IM, 24367).
DAVIS, ELIZABETH   PA
 At age seven she was captured by Indians in September 1780 and taken to Montreal (MR).
DAVIS, ELIZABETH   VA
 Chesterfield County. She performed a public service (VR, 2:25). Also an Elizabeth Davis in Prince Edward County (VR, 5:40), and one in Richmond County (Court Booklet, p. 1).
DAVIS, EUNICE   CT
 Litchfield. Her husband joined the British army but she remained loyal to the U.S. and signed a petition of loyalty (CAR, 13:307-311).
DAVIS, HANNAH   VA
 Shenandoah County. She performed a public service (VR, 5:155, 363).
DAVIS, JANE   NC
 She provided provisions for the troops (RA, C:43).
DAVIS, JANE   SC
 She supplied provisions for the army (SI, O-Q:106).
DAVIS, MARGARET   NC
 She supplied provisions for the troops (RA, 5:61, fol. 3).
DAVIS, MARGARET DOZIER   KY
 She suffered an attack by Indians. See Biographies.
DAVIS, MARY   NC
 She supplied food for the troops (RA, D:179).
DAVIS, MARY   SC
 She supplied provisions for the troops (SI, R-T:70; also Y-Z: 15, 215).
DAVIS, MARY   VA
 Gloucester County. She performed a public service (VR, 4:286). Also a Mary Davis on the Hanover County Lists (1:15, 22).
DAVIS, ROSE   NC
 She provided provisions for the troops (RA, A:245).
DAVIS, SARAH   CT
 New London. She suffered damage in a British raid (CAR, 1:63h, 95b). She was a Western Lands Grantee.
DAVIS, SARAH   NJ
 Newark. Widow of Thomas Davis, she suffered losses in a British raid (CDB, claim 36).
DAVIS, SARAH   NJ
 Orange. She suffered losses in a British raid (CDB, claim 7).
DAVIS, SARAH   NJ
 Wardsession, Essex County. She suffered damage in a British raid (CDB, claim 18).
DAVIS, VARINA HOWELL. See KEZIAH HOWELL

III: COMPLETE LISTING

DAVISON, MARY — NC
She supplied provisions for the troops (RA, 7:44, fol. 3).

DAWKINS, CHLOE — SC
She supplied provisions for the army (SI, 10, pt. 1:151).

DAWKINS, ELIZABETH — SC
She was a widow when she provided funds for the army (AA, 3:57), and also provisions (SI, 10, pt. 2:127).

DAWLEY, ELIZABETH — VA
Princess Anne County. She performed a public service (VR, 4:213).

DAWLEY, RHODA — VA
Princess Anne County. Recognized for public service (VR, 4:213).

DAWNEY, SARAH — SC
She provided provisions for the troops (SI, 1:81).

DAWS, MARGARET — SC
She supplied provisions for the army (SI, 1:239).

DAWSON, ANN — VA
Gloucester County. She performed a public service (VR, 3:41).

DAWSON, LYDIA DEXTER — RI
Providence. On December 12, 1780, Oliver Bowen obtained a letter of marque to command the sloop *Argo* with six guns and fourteen men. Lydia Dexter witnessed the bond. Later she married James Dawson (CN; DAR).

DAWSON, MARGARET — VA
Surry County. She performed a public service (VR Court Booklet, p. 10).

DAWSON, PENELOPE — NC
She opposed drinking British tea. See Background.

DAY, HANNAH — NJ
Westfield, Essex County. She suffered damage caused by a British raid (CDB, claim 35).

DAY, MARY — NJ
Hackensack. She suffered losses in a British raid (CDB, claim 81).

DAY, MARY — NJ
Hackensack. A widow, she suffered damage in a British raid (CDB, claim 113).

DEAN, ELIZABETH — NJ
Orange. She suffered damages in a British raid (CDB, claim 45).

DEANE, ELIZABETH SALTONSTALL — CT
Gen. Washington spent the night in her home. See Biographies.

DEARBORN, MARY BARTLETT — NH
Nottingham Square. In 1771 she married Dr. Henry Dearborn. He led a company of musketmen but was captured during the assault on Quebec on December 31, 1775. He was exchanged in March 1777. Dearborn spent the winter of 1777/78 at Valley Forge and served at Yorktown. Mary died in 1779. In 1780 Dearborn married the widow Dorcas Osgood Marble, and on her death he married the widow Sarah Bowdin in 1813 (DB).

DEARE, FRANCES   NJ
New Brunswick. She was the wife of Jonathan Deare, an attorney, who served as sheriff of Middlesex County, 1778-1794. Mrs. Deare was a member of the ladies' association for the welfare of the soldiers (New Jersey Gazette, July 4, 1780).

DEBREW, HANNAH   NC
She supplied provisions for the troops (RA, C:69).

DeCAMP, DEBORAH   NJ
Westfield. The wife of John DeCamp, she suffered damage caused by the British (CDB, claim 88).

DECATUR, ANN OINE   RI
She was the wife of Stephen Decatur, who commanded the galley Retaliation in 1779, the brig Fair American in 1780, and the Rising Sun in 1781. Then Decatur was captured by the British and imprisoned. They were the parents of Stephen Decatur, hero of the War of 1812 (CN).

DEDERICK, FIETJE   NJ
Saddle River. The wife of Christian Dederick, later she was Mrs. Credare Hoagland. She suffered damage caused by American troops (CDB, sec. 2, claim 46).

DEDMAN, SARAH   NC
She provided provisions for the troops (RA, 4:97, fol. 2).

DEFOREST, REBECCA   CT
Norwalk. She suffered damage in the British raid (CAR, 1:63m, 98h, 99b). She was a Western Lands Grantee.

DEFORREST, SARAH   VA
York County. She performed a public service (VR, Ctf 2:29).

DEGGE (DEGGES), MARY   VA
Gloucester County, the wife of Augustine Degge. Recognized for public service (VR, 3:39; 4:287).

DEGROAT (DEGRATE), SARAH   NJ
Hackensack. She suffered losses in a British raid (CDB, claim 92).

DE HART, HANNAH   VA
Botetourt County. She performed a public service (VR, 1:162).

DEHART, MARY   NJ
Somerset County. The wife of Hendrick Dehart, she suffered damage caused by the British (CDB, claim 138).

DEITZ (DIETZ), DORTHEA WERNER (WEINER)   NY
She was born in 1723 and married Capt. William Dietz, and died in 1781. She is listed as a patriot in the DAR Patriot Index.

DEITZ, ENGELTIE WEINER   NY
The wife of Johannes Peter Deitz, she died in 1782. She is listed as a patriot in the DAR Patriot Index.

De KALB, ANNA ELIZABETH EMILIE VAN ROBAIS   PA
Her husband, Baron Johann de Kalb, was killed in 1780 during the Battle of Camden, South Carolina (DB).

DELANEY, ELIZABETH   SC
She supplied provisions for the troops (SI, 1:18).

DELAVAN, AGNES TYLER   NY
Gen. Washington had breakfast in her home. See Biographies.

III: COMPLETE LISTING

DELAVON, MARY W.   NJ
Burlington. She suffered losses in a British raid (CDB, p. 150).

DELLINGER, MAGDALENE   VA
Shenandoah County. The wife of Christian Dellinger, she performed a public service (VR Court Booklet, p. 3).

DEMAREST, ANATJE   NJ
Harrington Township, Bergen County. The wife of Peter D. Demarest, she suffered losses caused by the Americans (CDB, claim 40).

DEMELT, ELIZABETH   NJ
Millstone, Somerset County. Her chest, hidden in John Staat's barn, was stolen by the British (CDB, p. 35).

DENISON, RHODA   CT
New Haven. She suffered losses in a British raid (CAR, 1:63b, 91d). She was a Western Lands Grantee.

DENMAN, ELIZABETH   NC
She supplied provisions for the troops (RA, 11:56, fol. 1).

DENNIS, JANE   VA
Amelia County. Recognized for public service (VR Lists, 1:12).

DENNIS, MARY   NJ
New Brunswick. The wife of John Dennis, she suffered damage in a British raid (CDB, p. 336).

DENNIS, RACHEL   NC
She provided food for the troops (RA, 9:85, fol. 1).

DENNIS, SUSANNAH   MD
Worcester County. She supplied wheat and beef in 1780 for the army (IM, 13668).

DENT, SARAH   MD
Charles County. She supplied wheat in 1782 for the troops (IM, 23942).

DENTON, ELIZABETH   KY, VA
At age thirty she was captured in June 1780 by Indians at Licking Creek along with her husband, John Denton, and three sons and a daughter, Jane, aged eight. They were released from Fort Ticonderoga on July 18, 1783 (MR).

DE PRE, MARY ELIZABETH   SC
She supplied provisions for the troops (SI, 10, pt. 2:128).

DE SAUSSURE, JANE   SC
She provided food for the soldiers (SI, Y-Z:130).

DESHON, MARY ANN PACKWOOD   CT
New London. She married Daniel Deshon, Jr. While in command of a vessel in 1776, he was captured by the British and sent to Newport, but was recaptured by the Continental brig <u>Andrea Doria</u>. Deshon then commanded the brig <u>Old Defense</u>, but was captured a second time and taken to Jamaica (CN).

DE VANE, ANN ROBINSON   NC
Her husband was captured and imprisoned. See Biographies.

DEVIER (DIVER), MARGARET   VA
Rockingham County. She performed a public service (VR, 5:116).

DE VOE, ELIZABETH PARCELLS   NJ
   Her home was plundered by the British. See Biographies.
DE VOE, POLLY   NJ
   Hackensack. The wife of Abraham DeVoe, she suffered damages by the British (CDB, claim 23).
DE WAR, ELIZABETH   SC
   She supplied provisions for the troops (SI, 1:11).
DEWBRY (DUBERRY), REBECCA   VA
   Elizabeth City. She performed a public service (VR, 4:307).
DEWEES, SARAH   SC
   After Charleston fell on May 12, 1780, she refused to sign an oath of fidelity to the Crown and was banished from the city (SC).
DE WINT, MRS. JOHANNES   NY
   Gen. Washington had his headquarters here. See Biographies.
DEY, HANNAH PIERSON   NJ
   Bergen County. The wife of Maj. Richard Dey of the New Jersey Militia, she was an active member of the ladies' association for the welfare of the soldiers (New Jersey Gazette, July 4, 1780).
DEY, HESTER SCHUYLER   NJ
   Gen. Washington had his headquarters here. See Biographies.
DICK, MARY   SC
   She provided food for the soldiers (SI, Y-Z:76).
DICK, MARY ROY   VA
   She made cartridges for the army. See Biographies.
DICK, SARAH SINNICKSON   NJ
   She was a member of the ladies' association. See Biographies.
DICKEN, FANNY   VA
   Mecklenburg. She performed a public service (VR, 4:47).
DICKERSON, MARY   VA
   Isle of Wight. Recognized for public service (VR, 2:317).
DICKERSON, SARAH   NJ
   Morris County. The widow of Peter Dickerson, she suffered damage caused by the Americans (CDB, claim 154).
DICKERSON, SARAH   SC
   When Charleston fell to the British on May 12, 1780, Sarah was asked to sign an oath of fidelity to the Crown. She refused to do so and was banished from the city (SC).
DICKINSON, DEBORAH   CT
   Norwalk. She suffered losses in a British raid (CAR, 1:63j, 98d, 100c). She was a Western Lands Grantee.
DICKINSON, HANNAH   CT
   Norwalk. She suffered damage in a British raid (CAR, 1:63m, 98j, 100g). She was a Western Lands Grantee.
DICKINSON, MARY   VA
   Isle of Wight. She performed a public service (VR Court Booklet, p. 6).
DICKINSON, MARY MORRIS   PA
   She entertained Gen. Washington and the Comte de Rochambeau. See Biographies.

III: COMPLETE LISTING 287

DICKINSON, POLLY VA
   Isle of Wight. Recognized for public service (VR, 4:331).
DICKINSON, REBECCA CADWALADER NJ
   John Adams visited her property to see the damage done by
   the British. See Biographies.
DICKSON, AGNES CARSON SC
   She was born in 1747, married Matthew Dickson, and died in
   1826. She is listed as a patriot in the DAR Patriot Index.
DICKSON, ELIZABETH NJ
   Bound Brook. She suffered damage in a British raid (CDB,
   p. 20).
DICKSON (DIXON), ELIZABETH VA
   Hansemond County. She performed a public service (VR Court
   Booklet, 1:6).
DICKSON, SARAH NC
   She supplied provisions for the army (RA, A:240).
DIGGINOS (DIGGINS), ANN VA
   Powhatan County. Recognized for public service (VR, 4:233).
DIKEMAN, ESTHER SCRIBNER CT
   She was born in 1763, married Hezekiah Dikeman, and died in
   1840. She is recognized as a patriot in the DAR Patriot Index.
DILLARD, MARY RAMAGE SC
   She warned the Americans of an impending British attack. See
   Biographies.
DILWORTH, JANE NC
   She provided food for the army (RA, A:260).
DIMON, ANN CT
   Fairfield. She suffered losses in a British raid (CAR, 1:53a,
   63c). She was a Western Lands Grantee.
DISBROW, ABIGAIL CT
   Fairfield. She suffered damage in a British raid (CAR, 1:53h,
   63r). She was a Western Lands Grantee.
DISHMAN, SARAH VA
   Essex County. She was born about 1730, married Peter Dishman,
   and died in 1808. She performed a public service (VR, 2:144;
   DAR).
DISSOWAY, MARY FITZ RANDOLPH NY
   She was born in 1748 and married Jones Baldwin. She then
   became the second wife of Cornelius Dissoway, and died in 1808.
   She is listed as a patriot in the DAR Patriot Index.
DITMARS, CATRINE NJ
   Somerset Courthouse. The wife of Abraham Ditmars, she suf-
   fered damage in a British raid (CBA, p. 120).
DITMARS, LENA VAN LIEW NJ
   Hillsborough, Somerset County. Born in 1724, she married
   Rem Ditmars and died in 1778. She is listed as a patriot in
   the DAR Patriot Index (CDB, claim p. 40).
DIUGUID, ANN VA
   Powhatan County. Recognized for public service (VR Ctf 2).
DIXON, MARTHA RI
   She supplied a peck of Indian meal for the troops in 1777 (MP,
   36:3).

DIXON, MARTHA WYNN NC
She was the wife of Lt. Col. Henry Dixon, who died in 1782.
She supplied provisions for the army (RA, 4:48, fol. 2).

DOBBIN, RACHEL NC
The wife of Thomas Dobbin, she died in 1797. She supplied provisions for the army (RA, A:66).

DOBBINS, MARGARET NC
She provided provisions for the troops (RA, A:148).

DOBIN, ELIZABETH SC
She supplied provisions for the troops (SI, O-Q:173).

DOBSON, GRACE VA
Gloucester County. Recognized for public service (VR Court Booklet, p. 26).

DODD (DOD), SARAH NJ
Orange. She suffered losses in a British raid (CDB, claim 54).

DODGE, MARY CT
Groton. She suffered damage in a British raid (CAR, 1:63q, 79a). She was a Western Lands Grantee.

DODGE, MARY HUNTER PA
After an Indian attack, she rode to obtain ammunition. See Biographies.

DOLES, MRS. VA
King William County. She performed a public service (VR Court Booklet, p. 11).

DOLLARSON, HANNAH NC
She supplied provisions for the troops (RA, D:52).

DONAHUE, MARGARET VA
Loudoun County. The widow Donahue is recognized for public service (VR, 3:292; Court Booklet, p. 46).

DONALDSON, MARY PA
Born about 1745, she married Moses Donaldson, and died on June 12, 1778. She is listed as a patriot in the DAR Patriot Index.

DONATHAN (DONIPHAN), MARY VA
King George County. She performed a public service (VR, 4:339).

DONE, SARAH MD
Somerset County. She supplied rations for the troops in 1777 (IM, 4572).

DONELLY, FRANCES NC
She provided provisions for the army (RA, W, no. 1:38).

DONNALLY, JANE McCREARY VA
Born about 1750, she married Col. Andrew Donnally and died about 1784. She is listed as a patriot in the DAR Patriot Index.

DONNOM (DUNHAM), SUSAN SC
She supplied provisions for the soldiers (SI, 1:183).

DOOLEY, DINAH GA
She supplied provisions for the troops (WA, p. 166) and forage (p. 171).

DOOLEY, REBECCA VA
Bedford County. She was born about 1740, married Capt.

Thomas Dooley, and died in 1783. She performed a public service (VR Court Booklet, p. 7; DAR).

DOOLITTLE, ABIGAIL CT
Wallingford. She supplied a blanket for the troops (CAR, 11: 204b).

DOOLITTLE, DEBORAH CT
Ridgebury. She lodged the commissioners in 1781 (CAR, 34:430).

DOOLITTLE, MARGARET CT
Chatham. After her son contracted smallpox in the army, he returned home and died. Her husband and four other children then died in May 1779 (CAR, 4:244-245).

DOREMUS, ANN NJ
Acquacanunk, Essex County. She suffered losses in a British raid (CDB, claim 13).

DOREMUS, ANNE NJ
New Barbadoes, Bergen County. She suffered damage in a British raid (CDB, claim 12).

DOREMUS, CAROLINE NJ
Morris County. She suffered damages caused by Americans (CDB claim, 101).

DOREMUS, MRS. PETER NJ
Gen. Washington spent the night in her home. See Biographies.

DORRANCE, MRS. CT
She entertained Gen. Washington. See Biographies.

DORSETT, WIDOW CT
New London. She suffered losses in a British raid (CAR, 1:63j, 95h). She was a Western Lands Grantee.

DORSEY, RUTH DORSEY MD
Howard County. She was born in 1743 and married Ely Dorsey, who was a member of the Committee of Observation in 1775, which had full power to rule the county. He served as captain of the 2nd Maryland Company and was taken prisoner at Staten Island on August 22, 1777 (FP2).

DORTON, ANNE VA
Mecklenburg. She performed a public service (VR, 4:49).

DOWELL, REBEKAH VA
Hanover County. Recognized for public service (VR Lists, 1:9).

DOUGHERTY, ELIZABETH KY
She was captured by Indians. See Biographies.

DOUGHTY, ELIZABETH SC
She supplied provisions for the troops (SI, 1:78).

DOUGHTY, MARY SC
She supplied provisions for the army (SI, 1:78).

DOUGLAS, HANNAH CT
Branford. The widow of Col. Douglas, she supplied clothing for the troops in 1780 (CAR, 35:249c).

DOUGLAS, SUSANNA VA
Northumberland County. She performed a public service (VR, 4:115).

DOWDY, BETSY   NC
 She warned the Americans of an impending attack. See Biographies.

DOWNEMAN, ANN   VA
 Prince William County. Recognized for public service (VR, 4:196).

DOWNER, JOHANNA   CT
 Preston. She supplied pork in 1781 for the army (CAR, 35:6).

DOWNER, MARGARET CARRUTHERS   CT
 She was born in 1742 and married Richard Downer, and died in 1829. She is listed as a patriot in the DAR Patriot Index.

DOWNS, JANE DOUGLAS   SC
 She donated $60,000 for the American cause. See Biographies.

DRAFFIN, MARGARET   NC
 She supplied provisions for the troops (RA, 12:25, fol. 4; A:134).

DRAKE, CHARITY   NJ
 Middlesex. The widow of Daniel Drake, she suffered losses in a British raid (CDB, p. 319).

DRAKE, ESTHER (EASTER)   NJ
 Woodbridge. She suffered damage caused by the British (CDB, p. 63). Also Easter Drake of Woodbridge, daughter of Easter Drake (British claim CDB, p. 63).

DRAKE, MARGARET   NJ
 Middlesex County. Widow of Henry Drake, she suffered losses caused by the British (CDB, p. 44).

DRAKE, MARTHA   CT
 Hartford. In 1778 she cared for wounded soldiers (CAR, 11:591).

DRAKE, PHOEBE REYNOLDS   NY
 She warned the Americans of an impending attack. See Biographies.

DRAKE, SARAH. See MERRILL

DRAPER, MARY ALDIS   MA
 She donated pewter to make bullets. See Biographies.

DRIEKEL, SARAH   NC
 Wife of David Driekel, she supplied provisions for the army (RA, 1:87, fol. 4).

DRINKER, ANN SWENT   PA
 She refused to care for a wounded British captain. See Biographies.

DRISKETT, MARY   VA
 Spotsylvania County. She performed a public service (Court Booklet, p. 40).

DROZE, MARY   SC
 She supplied provisions for the troops (SI, Y-Z:114).

DRY, MARY JANE   NC
 She provided provisions for the troops (RA, 5:51, fol. 2).

DRYDEN, AGNES   VA
 Rockbridge County. Recognized for public service (VR, 5:72).

DRYER, ELIZABETH   NC
 She supplied provisions for the army (RA, 11:82, fol. 1 and A:194).

III: COMPLETE LISTING

DRYSDALE, MARGARET MD
    She boarded Capt. George Cook of the ship Defence in 1776 (IM, 287).

DUBERIAS, WIDOW SC
    After Charleston fell to the British, she refused to sign the oath of fidelity to King George III and so was banished from the city (SC).

DU BOIS, AMEY GREENMAN NJ
    She performed a public service. See Biographies.

DUDGEON, MARY VA
    Charlotte County. Recognized for public service (VR, 1:298).

DUDLEY, MARY VA
    Middlesex County. She performed a public service (VR, 4:92).

DUDLEY, REBECCA VA
    Warwick County. Recognized for public service (VR, 5:212, 215).

DUETT, MARY KY
    She was captured by Indians. See Biographies.

DUGGAN, ELIZABETH KY, VA
    At age sixty in June 1780 she was captured by Indians at Licking Creek and released from Fort Ticonderoga on July 18, 1783 (MR).

DUKE, BETTY VA
    Louisa County. She performed a public service (VR, 3:347).

DUKE, ELIZABETH VA
    Hanover County. Recognized for public service (VR, 3:176). Also Elizabeth Duke in Louisa County (VR, 4:344).

DUKE, MARY NC
    She provided provisions for the troops (RA, 28:32).

DUNBAR, MARY REED NJ
    Hunterdon County. The daughter of Clolworty Reed, she suffered damage caused by the Americans (CDB, claim 48).

DUNCAN, AGNES NC
    She supplied provisions for the army (RA, A:66).

DUNCAN, ELINOR SHARP KY
    She was born in 1742 and married Capt. John Duncan. On June 26, 1780, Elinor, her husband, two sons, and six daughters were captured by the Tories and Indians and taken to Quebec (HP).

DUNCAN, MARGARET NY
    She spun clothing for the American troops (FH).

DUNCAN, MARGARET PA
    Philadelphia. She was a widow with three sons in the service. Two sons were captured by the enemy--one taken to Quebec and the other taken to New York. The enemy broke into her house on 2nd Street and did considerable damage. She appealed for help to the Council of Safety on January 22, 1777 (RP roll 11, frame 1072-74).

DUNDING, ELIZABETH VA
    Hansemond County. She performed a public service (VR, 4:154).

DUNHAM, JANE NJ
    Burlington. She suffered damage in a British raid (CDB, p. 90).

DUNHAM, MRS. JOHN NJ
Gen. Washington had breakfast here. See Biographies.
DUNLAP, JOHANNA VA
Gloucester County. Recognized for public service (VR, 3:39-40). Also shown in Greensville (Ctf 1).
DUNLAP, MARGARET SC
She supplied provisions for the troops (SI, 1:17).
DUNLAP, MARY VA
Rockbridge County. She performed a public service (VR, 5:73).
DUNLAP, NANCY CRAIGHEAD SC
Born in 1740, she married the Rev. William Richardson, then Capt. George Dunlap, and died in 1790. She is recognized as a patriot in the DAR Patriot Index.
DUNLEVY, MARY CRAIG KY
Bryan's Station. She was born in 1765 and married Francis Dunlevy, a sergeant in the war. On August 15, 1782, the Indians attacked Bryan's Station (for details, see Biographies: Craig, Polly). Mary died in 1828 and is listed in the DAR Patriot Index.
DUNN, ELINOR BREWSTER VA
She spun, wove and knitted clothing for the soldiers. See Biographies.
DUNN, ELIZABETH VA
Essex County. She performed a public service (VR Court Booklet, p. 8).
DUNN, JANE NJ
Piscataway. She suffered losses caused by the British (CDB, p. 208).
DUNN, MARY SHEFFIELD NC
The wife of Isaac Dunn, she died in 1862. She is listed as a patriot in the DAR Patriot Index.
DUNN, SARAH VA
Norfolk. Recognized for public service (VR, 4:128).
DUNNING, ELIZABETH CT
Norwalk. She suffered damage in a British raid (CAR, 1:63m, 98h, 99b). She was a Western Lands Grantee.
DUNSTON, MARY VA
Gloucester County. She performed a public service (VR, 3:41).
DUPUY, JUDITH VA
Amelia County. Recognized for public service (VR Court Booklet, 1:31).
DURN, ELIZABETH SC
She supplied provisions for the army (SI, U-W:261).
DURYEA, MARY. See BRINKERHOFF
DURYEA (DURIE), SARAH NJ
Harrington Township, Bergen County. The wife of John Duryea, she suffered losses by the British (CDB, claim 11).
DUSTIN, RACHEL WV
Berkeley County. She performed a public service (VR Ctf 1).
DWIGHT, SIBBIL
Gen. Washington spent the night in her household. See Biographies.

III: COMPLETE LISTING

DYER, ANNE   RI
    She stored cartridges and sacks of powder for the troops in 1778 (MP, 21:11; 43:3).
DYER, MARGARET HIATT.   See   CRAVENS
DYER, MARY   RI
    She nursed sick and wounded soldiers in 1776 (MP, 57:8).
DYKE, MARY   VA
    Essex County. Credited with public service (VR Court Booklet, p. 7).
DYSON, MARY   MD
    Montgomery County. She supplied wheat in 1781 for the army (IM, 16871).

E

EAGLES, MARY   NJ
    Newark. The wife of Thomas Eagles, she suffered losses in the British raid (CDB, claim 29).
EAPS, FRANCES   NC
    She supplied provisions for the troops (RA, 10:16, fol. 3).
EARL (EARLE), ELIZABETH   NC
    She provided provisions for the army (RA, 5:49, fol. 3; 11:88, fol. 4).
EARLE, MARY   NJ
    New Barbadoes, Bergen County. The wife of Morris Earle, she suffered damage caused by the British (CDB, claim 29).
EARLY, MARY   VA
    Bedford County. She performed a public service (VR Ctf 2). Aso Mary Early in Campbell County (VR Court Booklet, pp. 2, 3).
EASLEY, MRS. HANNAH   VA
    Chesterfield County. Credited with public service (VR Ctf 2).
EASTIN (EASTEN), ELIZABETH   VA
    Orange County. Recognized for public service (VR, 4:175, 182).
EASTLAND, SARAH   VA
    Mecklenburg. Credited with public service (VR, 4:50, 51).
EASTMAN, MARY BUTLER   NH
    She was known for "Mary Butler's Ride." See Biographies.
EASTON, SARAH   NJ
    Woodbridge. Widow of John Easton, she suffered damage caused by the British (CDB, p. 87).
EATON, ELIZABETH THORNE   ME
    Pemaquid, now Bristol. She was born on December 29, 1740, and married Jacob Eaton, who was captured by the British and taken to England on the man-of-war Boyne. Later Eaton escaped and returned home destitute. She died on March 15, 1804 (FP2).
EATON, REBEKAH   NC
    She supplied provisions for the army (RA, B:145).

EDDINGS, ANNE   VA
    Lunenburg County. She performed a public service (VR, 4:9).
EDDY, OLIVE MORSE   ME
    She was taken prisoner by the British. See Biographies.
EDELIN, SUSANNAH   MD
    Charles County. In 1783 she supplied wheat for the army (IM,
    25457).
EDGAR, MARY   NJ
    Middlesex County. The widow of Samuel Parker, she suffered
    damage caused by the British (CDB, p. 84).
EDGAR, RACHEL   IL
    She convinced her husband to desert the British navy. See
    Biographies.
EDGAR, RACHEL   NY
    At age forty she was captured by Indians along with her daughter,
    Rachel, aged nine, at Fort Ann and taken to the Saint Lawrence
    suburbs (MR).
EDLOE, ANNE   VA
    Charles City. She performed a public service (VR, 1:311).
EDMONDS, SARAH   CT
    New London. She suffered damage in a British raid (CAR,
    1:63h, 95c). She was a Western Lands Grantee.
EDMONDSON, LEAH   VA
    Essex County. Recognized for public service (VR Ctf 1).
EDMONDSON, SARAH   VA
    Essex County. Credited with public service (VR, 2:146).
EDSALL, CATHRINE   NJ
    Hackensack. The wife of Jacob Edsall, she suffered damage
    caused by the Americans (CDB, claim 34).
EDWARDS, ANN   VA
    Northumberland County. The wife of Richard Edwards, she
    is recognized for her public service (VR Ctf 1).
EDWARDS, ANN   VA
    Northumberland County. The wife of Robert Edwards, she per-
    formed a public service (VR Ctf 1).
EDWARDS, ANNE   VA
    Northumberland County. Credited for public service (VR, 4:115-
    116).
EDWARDS, ELIZABETH   SC
    She supplied provisions for the army (SI, R-T:189).
EDWARDS, ELIZABETH   VA
    Northumberland County. She performed a public service (VR,
    4:116).
EDWARDS, ELIZABETH   VA
    Southampton County. Credited with public service (VR, 5:175-
    176; Court Booklet, p. 4).
EDWARDS, MARGARET   SC
    She provided provisions for the troops (SI, B:185).
EDWARDS, MARY (ESTATE)   NC
    She supplied provisions for the army (RA, A:96).

III: COMPLETE LISTING 295

EDWARDS, MARY   SC
  She provided provisions for the troops (SI, B:185).
EDWARDS, MARY   VA
  York County. She performed a public service (VR, 4:274).
EDWARDS, MARY   VA
  York County. Recognized for public service (VR Ctf 1).
EDWARDS, RACHEL PARSONS   MA
  Northampton. She was the wife of Oliver Edwards, who was
  captured on December 31, 1775, by the British on the attack
  on Quebec. Years later he was exchanged and joined the Mas-
  sachusetts militia (FP1).
EDWARDS, REBECCA   SC
  She supplied provisions for the army (SI, B:100).
EDWARDS, SARAH   SC
  She provided provisions for the troops (SI, B:52).
EELLS, LOIS BENEDICT   CT
  Norwalk. She was the wife of Ens. Jeremiah Beard Eells of
  the 9th Company of the 9th Regiment of the Connecticut militia.
  He was captured by a Tory raiding party on March 15, 1777
  (FP1).
EFFORD, CATHERINE   VA
  Northumberland County. Credited with public service (VR,
  4:116).
EGEE, DOROTHY   VA
  Henrico County. Recognized for public service (VR, 3:98).
EGGLESTON, ELIZABETH   VA
  Hanover County. She performed a public service (VR, 3:177).
  Also shown in James City (VR Court Booklet, p. 4).
EGGLESTON, FRANCES   VA
  James City. Recognized for public service (VR Court Booklet,
  pp. 4, 19).
EGGLESTON, JUDITH   VA
  Amelia County. She performed a public service (VR 1:51, 91).
EIKESTER, MARY   SC
  She supplied provisions for the troops (SI, B:71).
ELBERT, ELIZABETH RAE   GA
  Savannah. She married Samuel Elbert, and they had six children.
  In the spring of 1777 Col. Elbert led an expedition to Florida
  and landed on Amelia Island, but his supplies were low so he
  returned to Georgia. Elbert was captured at the Battle of Briar
  Creek in Georgia on March 3, 1779, and imprisoned. He was
  exchanged in 1781 (DB).
ELDER, MARY   VA
  Dinwiddie County. Credited with public service (VR, 1:328).
ELDER, SARAH   PA (?)
  She was captured by Indians in 1780 and taken to Montreal (MR).
ELDRIDGE, ABIGAIL   NJ
  Burlington. She suffered damages caused by the British (CDB,
  p. 147).
ELIOT, ABIGAIL   CT
  New London. She suffered losses in a British raid (CAR, 1:63h,
  95c). She was a Western Lands Grantee.

ELISS (ELLIS), DORTHEA   NC
    She supplied provisions for the army (RA, 7:63, fol. 4).

ELKINS, ANN   SC
    She provided provisions for the troops (SI, O-Q:280).

ELKINS, MARY HAILES   MA
    Marblehead. She married Thomas Elkins, who was commissioned in 1778 to command the schooner Spring Bird, but he was captured and confined in the Fortun Prison at Gosport, England. After his exchange in 1781, he commanded the privateer Hercules but was captured for a second time in January 1782 (CN).

ELLEGOOD, MARY   VA
    Princess Anne County. The wife of Jacob Ellegood, she performed a public service (VR, 4:214).

ELLERY, ABIGAIL CAREY   RI
    Her home was burned by Tories. See Biographies.

ELLETT, MARTHA   VA
    King William County. Recognized for public service (Lists, 1:13, 15).

ELLETT, MARY   NJ
    Hunterdon County. She suffered losses caused by the Americans (CDB, claim 7).

ELLETT, MARY   VA
    King William County. Recognized for public service (VR Court Booklet, p. 27).

ELLINGTON, AMARINTHIA   SC
    She supplied provisions for the troops (SI, B:85).

ELLIOTT, CATHERINE   VA
    Washington County. Credited with public service (VR, 4:269).

ELLIOTT, RUTH   NC
    She supplied provisions for the troops (RA, A:200).

ELLIOTT, MARTHA   VA
    Dinwiddie County. Recognized for public service (VR, 1:328).

ELLIOTT, MARY   SC
    She supplied provisions for the army (SI, B:35).

ELLIOTT, RUTH   NC
    She provided provisions for the troops (RA, A:221).

ELLIOTT, SABINA   SC
    She supplied provisions for the army (SI, L-N:288).

ELLIOTT, SARAH   SC
    She provided provisions for the troops (SI, B:117).

ELLIOTT, SUSANNAH SMITH   SC
    She embroidered two standards for the South Carolina army. See Biographies.

ELLIOTT, WIDOW   VA
    York County. She performed a public service (VR Court Booklet, 2:2, 5).

ELLIS, MRS.   NJ
    Gloucester County. The wife of Col. Ellis, she collected funds for the soldiers (New Jersey Gazette, July 4, 1780).

ELLIS, ELIZABETH   SC
    She supplied provisions for the army (SI, O-Q:310).

III: COMPLETE LISTING

ELLIS, ELIZABETH   VA
 Hanover County. She performed a public service (VR, 3:177).
ELLIS, LOVIE   NC
 She supplied food for the troops (RA, 8:84, fol. 4).
ELLIS, MARY   SC
 She provided provisions for the troops (SI, B:30, 45).
ELLIS, MARY   VA
 Amelia County. Credited with public service (VR, 1:50).
ELLISON, ELIZABETH POTTS   SC
 She was molested by Tories. See Biographies.
ELLISON (ELLYSON), MARY   VA
 New Kent County. Recognized for public service (VR, 4:108).
ELLISON, MRS. THOMAS   NY
 Gen. Washington had his headquarters there. See Biographies.
ELLSWORTH, MARTHA   CT
 She supplied clothing for the army in 1780 (CAR, 35:249d).
ELLSWORTH, SUSANNAH   SC
 When Charleston fell on May 12, 1780, to the British she refused
 to sign an oath of fidelity to the Crown and so was banished
 from the city (SC).
ELMER, MARY SEELY   NJ
 Bridgeton. The wife of Dr. Jonathan Elmer of Cedarville, New
 Jersey, he was a delegate to the Continental Congress, 1776-
 1778. Mrs. Elmer was a member of the ladies' association for
 the welfare of the soldiers (New Jersey Gazette, July 4, 1780).
ELMORE, JANE   VA
 Henrico County. She performed a public service (VR, 3:97,
 98).
ELSTONE, SUSANNAH   NJ
 Westfield. She suffered damage caused by the British (CDB,
 claim 59).
ELY, EVE   GA
 She provided forage for Gen. Wayne's troops (WA, p. 127).
ELY, MARY HILLSMAN. See BAKER
ELY (ELEY), SARAH   VA
 Isle of Wight. Recognized for public service (VR, 2:318).
ELY, SARAH WORTHINGTON   CT
 She was the wife of Col. John Ely. While on an expedition to
 Long Island with Col. Samuel Blatchey Webb, the men were taken
 prisoners by the British on December 10, 1777 (FW; DAR).
ELZEY, MARGARET   MD
 Calvert County. On February 28, 1778, she made a loan to
 the Continental Congress (IM, 6142).
EMERSON, NAOMI BLAISDELL   ME
 She was forced to flee from Nova Scotia to Maine for her patriotic
 beliefs. See Biographies.
EMERY, MARY   VA
 Charles City. She performed a public service (VR Court Book-
 let, p. 24).
EMLEN, MRS. GEORGE   PA
 Gen. Washington had his headquarters there. See Biographies.

EMLEY, ANN ATKINSON. See HOLCOMBE
EMMONS, LUCRETIA   NJ
   She was a black woman who loaded muskets for her employer.
   See Biographies.
ENTELWEIN, MARTHA   SC
   She provided provisions for the troops (SI, B:23).
EPPES (EPPS), AMEY   VA
   Prince George County. Recognized for public service (VR,
   4:250).
EPPES (EPPS), ELIZABETH   VA
   Prince George County. She performed a public service (VR,
   4:250). Also shown in Dinwiddie County (VR Ctf 1).
EPPES, MARY   VA
   Charles City. Credited for public service (VR, 1:311).
EPPS (EPPES), PHOEBE   VA
   Greensville. Born about 1739, she married Francis Epps, and
   died in 1782. She performed a public service (VR Court Booklet,
   p. 9).
ERSKINE, ELIZABETH   NJ
   She was a member of the ladies' association. See Biographies.
ERVIN, ELIZABETH ELLISON   SC
   The wife of John Ervin, she died in 1795. She is listed as
   a patriot in the DAR Patriot Index 3.
ERVIN, ELIZABETH JAMES   SC
   The wife of James Ervin, she died in 1782 and is listed as a
   patriot in the DAR Patriot Index 3.
ERVIN, JANE WITHERSPOON   SC
   Born in 1753, she married John Ervin and died in 1790. She
   is listed as a patriot in the DAR Patriot Index 3.
ERWIN, HANNAH   NC
   She supplied provisions for the army (RA, A:246).
ERWIN, SARAH ANNE ROBINSON   NC
   Born in 1750, she was the first wife of Alexander Erwin. She
   died in 1785 and is listed as a patriot in the DAR Patriot Index.
ESPY, JEAN   PA
   She molded bullets for soldiers. See Biographies.
ESTES, ANN   VA
   Spotsylvania County. Recognized for public service (VR, 4:260).
ESTES, MARY   VA
   Halifax County. She performed a public service (VR, 2:268).
ESTES, URSULA   VA
   Louisa County. The wife of John Estes, she is credited with
   public service (VR, 4:245).
ESTILL, RACHEL WRIGHT   KY
   Estill's Station, Madison County. She married James Estill of
   Augusta County, Virginia. About 1776 he founded Estill's Sta-
   tion. On March 18, 1782, Estill and a few men pursued some
   Wyandot Indians across the Kentucky River into Montgomery
   County, where a bloody battle took place on Little Mountain.
   Estill was killed. Estill County, Kentucky, was named in his
   honor (CH).

III: COMPLETE LISTING

ESTILL, REBECCA   VA
   Augusta County. Recognized for public service (VR Ctf 1).
ESTOR, MARGARET   VA
   Norfolk. She performed a public service (VR, 4:329).
ETHERIDGE, ANNE   VA
   Norfolk. Credited with public service (VR, 4:145).
ETHERIDGE, SARAH   VA
   Norfolk. Recognized for public service (VR, 4:129).
ETHERINGTON, MRS. CHRISTOPHER   VA
   Westmoreland County. Credited with public service (VR Lists, p. 3).
EUBANK, SUSANNA   VA
   King and Queen County. She performed a public service (VR Court Booklet, p. 17).
EVANS, ANN   VA
   Halifax County. Recognized for public service (VR, 2:267).
EVANS, ANN MESHOW   SC
   She married Thomas Rigdon, then George Evans, and died in 1799. She is listed as a patriot in the DAR Patriot Index.
EVANS, ELEANOR   PA
   Philadelphia. The wife of Daniel Evans, she supplied hardware for wheels for Mr. Saller's schooner docked at Arch Street Wharf in 1777 (RP roll 13, frames 61, 62).
EVANS, ELIZABETH   MD
   Worcester County. In 1780 she supplied beef for the army (IM, 13765).
EVANS, ELIZABETH   NJ
   Middlesex County. She suffered losses in a British raid (CDB, p. 76).
EVANS, MRS. ELIZABETH   SC
   She supplied provisions for the troops (SI, L-N:12).
EVANS, ELIZABETH   VA
   Essex County. She performed a public service (VR Lists, p. 8).
EVANS, ELIZABETH AVERY. See COATES
EVANS, MARY   VA
   Loudoun County. Recognized for public service (VR, 3:293).
EVANS, SARAH   NC
   She supplied provisions for the troops (RA, 10:36, fol. 3).
EVENS, CATHERINE   NJ
   Woodbridge. She suffered damage in a British raid (CDB, p. 56).
EVENS, ELIZABETH   NJ
   Woodbridge. Wife of David Evens, she suffered losses in a British raid (CDB, p. 35).
EVERIT, ANN   NC
   She supplied provisions for the troops (RA, K:198).
EVERITT, MARY   VA
   Hansemond County. Recognized for public service (VR, 4:155).
EVERSLY, SARAH   CT
   Norwalk. She suffered damage in a British raid (CAR, 1:63k, 98f, 100d).

EWING, ELIZABETH VA
  Frederick County. Credited with public service (VR, 2:183).
EYRE, MRS. G. R. PA
  Philadelphia. She was a member of the ladies' association for the welfare of the soldiers (Pennsylvania Gazette, June 12, 1780).
EYRE, MARGARET VA
  Northampton County. Recognized for public service (VR Lists, 1).

F

FAESCH, MRS. NJ
  Morris County. She collected funds for the army (New Jersey Gazette, July 4, 1780).
FAIRCHILD, ABIGAIL NJ
  Morris County. She suffered damage caused by the Americans (CDB, claim 29).
FAIRCHILD, ALICE NJ
  Morris County. The wife of Phineas Fairchild, she suffered losses caused by the Americans (CDB, claim 24).
FAIRCHILD, MARTHA CT
  Fairfield. She suffered damage in a British raid in July 1779 (CAR, 19:73).
FAIRCHILD, THEODOSIA NJ
  Morris County. She suffered damage caused by the Americans (CDB, claim 157).
FAIRLEY, SARAH NC
  She supplied provisions for the troops (RA, A:67).
FALCONBURY, MARY NC
  She supplied provisions for the army (RA, 12:106, fol. 2).
FALCONER, JOICE CRAIG KY
  The family had to flee from an Indian attack. See Biographies.
FALLS, ISABELLA NC
  She supplied provisions for the army (RA, 12:17, fol. 4).
FANNING, ANNE BREWSTER CT
  A chapter of the Daughters of the American Revolution was named in her honor. See Biographies.
FANNING, ELIZABETH SMITH CT
  She was the wife of Nathaniel Fanning, a midshipman, who was captured by the British and confined in the Mill Prison in Plymouth, England. After his exchange in 1779, Fanning served on the Bon Homme Richard commanded by John Paul Jones. In 1782 Fanning commanded the privateer Ranger, but was captured by the British for a second time. Sometime later he escaped and returned to America (CN).
FANNING, PRUDENCE STANTON CT
  She married Roger Fanning, who served as sailing master on the galley Shark and was captured by the British in 1777 and imprisoned. His brother, John Fanning, Jr., served in the Continental Navy and was captured by the British in 1781. His

III: COMPLETE LISTING 301

brothers Joshua and Simeon were killed in the explosion of the frigate Randolph in 1782. His brothers Nathaniel and Gilbert were also captured by the British and imprisoned (CN).

FARGUSON (FERGUSON), ELIZABETH   VA
Culpeper County. She performed a public service (VR, 2:74, 85).

FARLEY, ELIZABETH   NC
She supplied provisions for the troops (RA, A:127).

FARLEY (FARLER), HANNAH   VA
Dinwiddie County. She performed a public service (VR, 1:328).

FARLEY, HANNAH   VA
Amelia County. Recognized for public service (VR Lists, 1, 6). Also in Charles City (VR Ctf, p. 9), and Halifax County (VR, 2:269-270).

FARLEY, MARY   VA
Charlotte County. Credited with public service (VR Court Booklet, p. 16).

FARLING, ELIZABETH M.   VA
Westmoreland County. She performed a public service (VR, 5:219).

FARLOW, SARAH   NC
She supplied provisions for the troops (RA, D:49).

FARMER, MRS.   NJ
John Adams and other Massachusetts members of the First Continental Congress on their way to Philadelphia spent the night of August 21, 1774, at her home. Adams remarked in his diary that the road from Elizabethtown, now Elizabeth, was as fine a road as he had ever traveled on (BA).

FARMER, ELIZABETH   VA
Halifax County. Recognized for public service (VR Court Booklet, p. 73).

FARMER, SARAH   VA
Lunenburg County. She performed a public service (VR, 4:12).

FARNEL (FERNEL), ELIZABETH   NC
She supplied provisions for the troops (RA, 10:36, fol. 3).

FARRAND, RHODA SMITH   NJ, VT
After Gen. Washington told her that cabbage would prevent scurvy, she collected cabbage for the army. See Biographies.

FARRIS, MARY   VA
New Kent County. She performed a public service (VR Court Booklet, p. 14).

FARROW, ROSANNA WATERS   SC
She rode miles to save her sons from execution. See Biographies.

FAULKNER, MARY   VA
King and Queen County. Credited with public service (VR, 3:220).

FAULTERNOY, CATHARINE   VA
Caroline County. Recognized for public service (VR, 1:249).

FAUST, MRS.   SC
She supplied provisions for the troops (SI, O-Q:311).

FEBIGER, ELIZABETH CARSON   PA
Philadelphia. The daughter of William Carson, Elizabeth and

her sister Mary (later Mrs. O'Hara) made clothing for the soldiers.
She married Col. Christian Febiger (EP).
FELDER, SARAH SC
She provided provisions for the troops (SI, O-Q:228).
FELL, MRS. JONATHAN PA
Gen. Washington pitched his tent on her property. See
Biographies.
FELL, SUSANNA MARSCHALK NJ
Gen. Washington had his headquarters there. See Biographies.
FELLON, ANN NC
She provided provisions for the troops (RA, K:132c).
FELTON, ANNA MARIA NC
She supplied provisions for the troops (RA, 9:110, fol. 3).
FENIMORE, SARAH NJ
Burlington. She suffered damage caused by the British (CDB, claim 315).
FENNER, MARTHA RI
Wife of Daniel Fenner. She provided corn, pork, beef, sugar, tallow, etc., for the troops (MP, 53:3).
FERGUSON, ELIZABETH SC
She supplied provisions for the army (SI, 1:45).
FERGUSON, ELIZABETH GREENE PA
She cared for American prisoners. See Biographies.
FERGUSON, MARY SC
She provided supplies for the troops (SI, 1:45).
FERNS, SARAH NC
She supplied provisions for the army (RA, K:35).
FERRALL, JANE NC
She provided supplies for the troops (RA, 7:51, fol. 3).
FERRIS, ANN TRIP NY
Gen. Washington had his headquarters there. See Biographies.
FERRIS, CHARITY THOMAS NY
Born in 1734, she married James Ferris. She died in 1809.
Mrs. Ferris is listed as a patriot in the DAR Patriot Index.
FERRIS, KEZIAH CT
Greenwich widow. She suffered damage in the British raid of July 1779 (CAR, 24:274, 275).
FERRIS, MARY CT
Greenwich widow. She suffered losses in the July 1779 raid of the British (CAR, 24:274c).
FERYAR, MRS. WINNY NC
She supplied provisions for the army (RA, 11:8, fol. 3).
FEW, MARY WHEELER NC
The British seized her cattle and horses. See Biographies.
FFORD, HANNAH BALDWIN NJ
She was born in 1701 and married Jacob Fford, Sr., and died on July 30, 1777. She is recognized as a patriot in the DAR Patriot Index.
FICKLIN, MARY HERNDON KY
Bryan's Station. She was born in 1745 and married Thomas Ficklin. When the Tories and Indians attacked on August 15,

III: COMPLETE LISTING 303

1782, Mary and her daughter Philadelphia Ficklin were among the women who went for water. Their names are inscribed on the monument erected by the Lexington DAR. She died in 1816. Mrs. Ficklin is listed as a patriot in the DAR Patriot Index.

FIELD, ANN   VA
Culpeper County. She performed a public service (VR, 2:84). Also an Ann Ferris shown in Rockingham County (VR Court Booklet, 2:12).

FIELD, JEMIMA   VA
Loudoun. The wife of Thomas Field, she is recognized for public service (VR, 3:295).

FIELD, MARY PEELE. See READ

FIELD, PHEBE   NJ
Piscataway. She suffered damage in a British raid (CDB, claim 17).

FIELDS, MARY   NC
She supplied provisions for the troops (RA, B:186).

FIELDS, SARAH   VA
Fauquier County. Recognized for public service (VR Ctf 1).

FINCH, REBECCA   VA
New Kent County. Credited with public service (VR Court Booklet, p. 11).

FINK, ANN MARGARET   GA
She supplied forage for the army (WA, p. 136).

FINNEY, MARY   VA
Amelia County. She performed a public service (VR, 1:53).

FISHBURN, HENRIETTA MARIA HACK   PA
Born in 1763, she married a Mr. Hadin, then Pvt. Philip Fishburn, and died in 1854. She is listed as a patriot in the DAR Patriot Index.

FISHER, MRS.   VA
At age thirty-five she was captured on June 24, 1780, by Indians and taken to Canada. She was sent home on August 22, 1782 (MR).

FISHER, MARY CROSURE   PA
She was the first wife of Capt. Samuel Fisher. Mrs. Fisher is listed as a patriot in the DAR Patriot Index.

FISHER, MRS. MEIRS   PA
Philadelphia. On September 7, 1774, John Adams dined at the Fishers' home. Among the guests were two former governors of Rhode Island--Hopkins and Ward--and Caesar Rodney of Delaware (BA).

FISHER, SARAH   SC
She supplied provisions for the army (SI, R-T:22).

FITCH, ANNA   CT
Guilford. In 1777 she supplied a blanket for the army (CAR, 11:283).

FITCH, ELIZABETH MARY MIX   CT
She witnessed a privateer Continental bond. See Biographies.

FITCH, HANNAH   CT
Norwalk. She suffered damage in a British raid (CAR, 20:379b, 380b).

FITCH, MRS. JABEZ   CT
   Stamford. On August 19, 1774, John Adams and other delegates
   from Massachusetts to the First Continental Congress on their
   way to Philadelphia breakfasted with the Fitches. Adams reported
   that the Congregational Church there had no minister (BA).
FITCH, LYDIA   CT
   Norwalk. She suffered damage in a British raid (CAR, 1:63i,
   98g, 99a). She was a Western Lands Grantee.
FITCH, REBEKAH   CT
   Norwalk. She suffered losses in a British raid (CAR, 20:379be,
   380be). She was a Western Lands Grantee.
FITCH, SUSANNA   CT
   Norwalk. She suffered damage in a British raid (CAR, 20:379bg,
   380bh). She was a Western Lands Grantee.
FITHIAN, ELIZABETH BEATTY   NJ
   She spun wool and linen for clothing for the soldiers. See
   Biographies.
FITZHUGH, ANNE FRISBY   MD
   She fired on the Tories. See Biographies.
FITZHUGH, ELIZABETH   VA
   Prince George County. She performed a public service (VR
   Ctf 3). Also shown in Dinwiddie County (VR, 1:329).
FITZHUGH, ELIZABETH CROWLEY CHEW   MD
   Patuxent. She married Peregrine Fitzhugh, cornet of the 3rd
   Continental Dragoons who was taken prisoner in September 1778
   at Tappan, New York, and not exchanged until October 1780.
   In 1781 he was made a lieutenant colonel and an aide to Gen.
   Washington (FW).
FITZ RANDOLPH, RUTH   NJ
   Piscataway. She suffered damage in a British raid (CDB, claim
   121).
FITZ RANDOLPH, STELLA   NJ
   Piscataway. Wife of Ephriam Fitz Randolph. She suffered losses
   in a British raid (CDB, p. 288).
FLACK, JANE McCUISTON   NC
   Wife of Thomas Flack, she supplied provisions for the army
   (RA, A:277).
FLAGLER, MARGARET GREGG   SC
   She married Samuel Scott, then William Gordon, then William
   Flagler, and died about 1790. She is listed as a patriot in the
   DAR Patriot Index.
FLANAGAN, MRS.   SC
   She supplied provisions for the army (SI, L-N:279).
FLEARABOOM, JEAN   NJ
   Harrington County. Wife of Jacobus Flearaboom. She suffered
   damage in a British raid (CDB, claim 49).
FLEET, MARY   CT
   Norwalk. She suffered losses in a British raid (CAR, 1:63m,
   98h, 99a). She was a Western Lands Grantee.
FLEMING, MARY   VA
   Goochland County. She performed a public service (VR, 4:314).

III: COMPLETE LISTING

FLETCHER, REBECCA   VA
     Prince George County. Recognized for public service (VR, 4:251).

FLING, ELIZABETH   VA
     Loudoun County. Credited with public service (VR, 3:245).

FLIPPER, MARY   VA
     Cumberland County. The wife of Robert Flipper, she performed a public service (VR Lists, p. 7).

FLIPPO, SARAH   VA
     Caroline County. Recognized for public service (VR, 1:249).

FLOOD, ANN   NJ
     Woodbridge. Wife of Stephen Flood, she suffered damage caused by the British (CDB, p. 71).

FLOURNOY, ELIZABETH   VA
     Powhatan County. She performed a public service (VR, 4:234).

FLOURY, NELLY   NC
     She supplied provisions for the troops (RA, 6:61, fol. 1).

FLOYD, HANNAH JONES   NY
     Her home was looted by the British. See Biographies.

FLOYD, JANE BUCHANAN   KY
     Her husband was killed by Indians. See Biographies.

FLOYD, MARY   CT
     On March 28, 1782, Ebenezer Dayton obtained a letter of marque to command the New York Boat <u>Suffolk</u> with one gun and nine men. Witnesses to the bond were Nicoll Floyd and Mary Floyd (CN).

FLOYD, SARAH   VA
     Charles City. Recognized for public service (VR Court Booklet, p. 20; I:312).

FOGLE, BARBARA   SC
     She provided provisions for the troops (SI, 1:72).

FOLK, RACHEL   NJ
     Harrington. Her husband, Henry Folk, was a prisoner in New York for seven months (CDB, claim 57).

FONCHES, CATHERINE   SC
     She supplied provisions for the army (SI, O-Q:281).

FONTAINE, ELIZABETH   VA
     Hanover County. She performed a public service (VR, 3:178).

FONTAINE, JEMIMA JOHNSON   SC
     She married Francis Fontaine, then Benjamin Brewton. She is listed as a patriot in the <u>DAR Patriot Index</u>.

FOOT, MARY DEDMAN   MA
     She married Caleb Foot who was prize master on the <u>Black Prince</u> and was captured by the British. On February 18, 1779, Foot was committed to the Fortun Prison at Gosport, England (CN).

FOOTE, BETSEY   CT
     In October 1775 she recorded in her diary that she spun ten knots of wool and "felt Nationaly in the bargain." She felt proud that her homespun wool would help the nation in the war effort (NL).

FORBES, MARTHA HALL   MA
Upton. The daughter of Martha Gibbs and the Honorable Willis Hall, she was born in Sutton, Massachusetts. On July 25, 1771, Martha married Absolom Forbes and they had four sons. Absolom was killed in the Battle of White Plains in 1778. On November 21, 1782, Martha married Joel White at Northbridge, Massachusetts, and they had several children. She died on March 26, 1828 (submitted by Verna Forbes Willson, Farmington, NM).

FORD, ANNE   RI
She provided corn, rye, beef, pork, sugar, coffee, butter, etc., for the troops (MP, 48:18).

FORD, ELIZABETH   KY, VA
In June 1780 at age twenty-nine she and her husband and six children were captured by Indians at Licking Creek and released from Fort Ticonderoga on July 18, 1783 (MR).

FORD, ELIZABETH   VA
Goochland County. She performed a public service (VR, 3:63).

FORD, GRACE   NJ
Morris County. She suffered damage caused by the Americans (CDB, claim 135).

FORD, MARY   NJ
Piscataway. She suffered losses in a British raid (CDB, pp. 282, 297).

FORD, MARY   VA
Amelia County. Credited with public service (VR, 1:52).

FORD, SARAH   NJ
Middlesex County. The widow of Lewis Evans, she suffered damage caused by the British (CDB, p. 76).

FORD, THEODOSIA JOHNES   NJ
Gen. Washington had his headquarters here. See Biographies.

FORDHAM, ALICE   NC
She supplied provisions for the troops (RA, 11:25, fol. 3).

FOREMAN, IVY   VA
Norfolk. She performed a public service (VR, 4:130, 143).

FORKER, SARAH   NJ
Burlington. She suffered damage caused by the British (CDB, p. 77).

FORKS, FRANCES   NC
She supplied provisions for the army (RA, 11:86, fol. 4).

FORMAN, ANN MARSH   NJ
She was a member of the ladies' association for the welfare of the soldiers. See Biographies.

FORMAN, CATHERINE PARKER   WV
Hampshire County. She was the wife of Capt. William Forman of Virginia (his second wife). She supplied provisions for the troops (VR, 3:117).

FORMAN, MARY LEDYARD   NJ
Born in 1758, she became the second wife of Lt. Col. Jonathan Forman. She is listed as a patriot in the DAR Patriot Index.

FORNEY, MARIA BERGNER   NC
All her provisions were taken by the British. See Biographies.

III: COMPLETE LISTING 307

FORRESTER, RACHEL HAWTHORNE MA
   Salem. She married Simon Forrester, who was commissioned in 1776 to command the eighteen-gun sloop Rover, and later other ships. In 1782 he commanded the twenty-gun ship Exchange but was captured by the British and confined on a prison ship in New York Harbor (CN).

FORT, SUSANNAH TOMLINSON GA
   She was born in 1755 and married William Whitehead, then Capt. Arthur Fort, Jr. She died in 1820. Mrs. Fort is listed as a patriot in the DAR Patriot Index.

FOSDICK, ANN CT
   New London. She suffered losses in a British raid (CAR, 1:63h, 95ci). She was a Western Lands Grantee.

FOSTER, AMEY VA
   Albemarle County. Credited with public service (VR, 2:346).

FOSTER, ELIZABETH VA
   Gloucester County. She performed a public service (VR Court Booklet, 2:30).

FOSTER, LEAH RI
   She provided corn, rye, beef, salt, etc., for the troops (MP, 40:15).

FOSTER, LYDIA NJ
   Burlington. She suffered losses in a British raid (CDB, p. 154).

FOSTER, MARGARET NC
   She supplied provisions for the army (RA, 7:60, fol. 1).

FOSTER, MARY CT
   The army used her lead mine (CAR, 12:38).

FOSTER, MARY VA
   Amelia County. Credited with public service (VR, 1:54).

FOSTER, MARY RUSSELL. See HURD

FOSTER, PHEBE CT
   She supplied forage for state teams in 1779 (CAR, 35:236).

FOSTER, PRISCILLA RI
   Wife of William Foster. She supplied beef, mutton, salt, coffee, sugar, etc., for the troops (MP, 48:22).

FOWLER, ELIZABETH VA
   Isle of Wight. She performed a public service (VR, 2:319).

FOWLER, MARY CT
   She received money from public funds which she sent to prisoners in New York City in 1777 (CAR, 12:289a).

FOWLER, MARY BRUNDAGE NY
   She married Moses Fowler, and died in 1815. She is listed as a patriot in the DAR Patriot Index.

FOX, ANN VA
   Caroline County. Credited with public service (VR, 1:254).

FOX, MARY SC
   She supplied provisions for the troops (SI, O-Q:71).

FRANCIS, ANNE WILLING PA
   She was a member of the ladies' association. See Biographies.

FRANK, LEA NC
  The widow of Edward Frank, she supplied provisions for the army (RA, B:65).
FRANK, MARY NC
  She provided provisions for the troops (RA, D:144).
FRANKLIN, DEBORAH MORRIS PA
  She was born in 1736 and married John Franklin of New York. She died in 1787. Deborah is listed as a patriot in the DAR Patriot Index.
FRANKLIN, JERUSHA HICOCK PA
  She was born in 1740 and became the first wife of Lt. Col. Roswell Franklin, and died in 1781. Credited as a patriot in the DAR Patriot Index.
FRANKLIN, MARY RI
  She supplied provisions for the troops (MP, 23:5).
FRANKLIN, MARY CLEVELAND NC
  Surry County. She married Bernard Franklin. Their third son, Jesse Franklin, served as a captain of a rebel company in 1776, commanded by his uncle, Col. Benjamin Cleveland. Later Jesse was captured by Tories and hanged by his own bridle to a tree, where they left him. But the bridle broke and Jesse escaped. He served as a United States senator from 1799 to 1805 (DB).
FRANKLIN, PRISCILLA MD
  Charles County. In 1781 and 1783 she supplied wheat for the army (IM, 19226; 25426).
FRANKLING, FRANCES B. MD
  Charles County. In 1782 she supplied wheat for the troops (IM, 21377; 21670).
FRASHERS, ANN SC
  She supplied provisions for the troops (SI, Y-Z:52).
FRAZEE, CATHARINE. See FREEMAN
FRAZEE, ELIZABETH NJ
  Westfield. She suffered losses by the British (CDB, claim 31).
FRAZEE, PHEBE NJ
  Westfield. She was the widow of John Little and the wife of Benjamin Frazee. She suffered damage caused by a British raid (CDB, claims 12, 30, 53).
FRAZEE, SUSANNAH NJ
  Westfield. She suffered losses by the British (CDB, claim 6).
FRAZER, ELIZABETH SC
  She provided provisions for the troops (SI, B:92).
FRAZER, MARY WORALL TAYLOR PA
  She collected food and clothing for the soldiers at Valley Forge. See Biographies.
FREEAR, WINIFRED NC
  She supplied provisions for the army (RA, 4:75, fol. 4).
FREEMAN, CATHARINE NJ
  Middlesex County. The widow of Samuel Frazee, she suffered damage caused by the British (CDB, p. 95).

III: COMPLETE LISTING 309

FREEMAN, MARY NJ
   Burlington. She suffered losses in a British raid (CDB, claim 280).
FREEMAN, MARY. See ROSS
FREEMAN, PHEBE NJ
   Morris County. She suffered losses caused by the Americans (CDB, claim 150).
FREEMAN, SARAH NJ
   Woodbridge. She suffered damage by the British (CDB, p. 108).
FREER, ANN SC
   She supplied provisions for the army (SI, B:224).
FRENCH, MARY VA
   Henry County. The wife of John French, Sr., she performed a public service (VR, 3:137). She died in 1815 (DAR).
FRENCH, RACHEL DREW NY
   She locked British soldiers in her cellar. See Biographies.
FREYER, ELIZABETH GA
   She supplied ten head of cattle for public use (WA, p. 158).
FRIEND, SARAH VA
   Chesterfield County. Credited with public service (VR, 2:28).
FRIERSON, MARY SC
   She provided provisions for the troops (SI, B:156).
FRINK, RUTH PINCKNEY SC
   She was born in 1737 and married Jabeah Frink, and is listed as a patriot in the DAR Patriot Index 2.
FRIPP, ELIZABETH SC
   She supplied provisions for the army (SI, B:30).
FRISBIE, PHOEBE GAYLORD PA
   She was born in 1767, married Levi Frisbie, and died in 1852. She is recognized as a patriot in the DAR Patriot Index.
FRITCH, ELIZABETH MD
   Frederick County. In 1778 she supplied bacon for the troops (IM, 6835).
FRIZZEL, LYDIA NC
   She supplied provisions for the army (RA, A:98).
FROST, ANNA FUNCH MA
   Her son was captured and imprisoned by the British. See Biographies.
FRY, ELIZABETH NC
   She supplied provisions for the army (RA, A:240).
FULFORD, LOVY VA
   Norfolk. She performed a public service (VR, 4:136, 141, 142).
FULLER, MRS. JOHN NY
   She was captured along with her husband and two children and taken to Niagara, then to Montreal on December 24, 1782 (MR).
FULLER, JUDITH SC
   She provided provisions for the troops (SI, B:127).
FULTON, JANE PA
   In May 1781, at age forty-five, she was captured at Waldair with her husband, John, and daughter, Jane aged fourteen,

by Indians and taken northward. They were released on July
18, 1783, from Fort Ticonderoga (MR).

FULTON, SARAH BRADLEE   MA
She applied an Indian disguise on her husband for the Boston
Tea Party. See Biographies.

FURMAN, SARAH WHITE   NJ
Trenton. She was a Philadelphia belle when she married Moore
Furman, who served as deputy quartermaster general. He was
the first mayor of Trenton under the charter of 1782. Mrs.
Furman was treasurer of the ladies' association for the welfare
of the soldiers (New Jersey Gazette, July 4, 1780).

G

GACH, JEANET   NJ
Middlesex County. She suffered damage in a British raid (CDB,
p. 12).

GADDIS, CHRISTINA   SC
She supplied provisions for the army (SI, Y-Z:175).

GAGE, JENNET PIKE   NJ
Her husband was a Tory, but she was a patriot. See Biographies.

GAINES, BETTY   VA
King and Queen County. She performed a public service (VR
Lists, 4:2k).

GAINS, MARY   NH
Portsmouth. On July 10, 1782, William Parker obtained a letter
of marque to command the brigantine Hermoine with six guns
and sixteen men. Witnesses to the bond were Mary Gains and
George Gains, who was selectman in Portsmouth in 1776. His
first wife, Mary Dame Gains, died in 1780 (CN).

GALBREATH, ELIZABETH   VA
Berkeley County. Credited with public service (VR Court Booklet, 1:7).

GAMBELL, MARY   NC
She supplied provisions for the troops (RA, A:195).

GAMBLE, AGNES   VA
Augusta County. Credited with public service (VR Lists, 1:11).

GAMBLE, CATHERINE GRATTON   VA
She was the wife of Robert Gamble. In August 1780 Capt. Gamble
was taken prisoner in Camden (FW; DAR).

GANNETT, DEBORAH SAMPSON   NY
She served in the army. See Biographies.

GARDINER, ALICE FULLER. See ABBOTT

GARDINER, ELIZABETH MUMFORD   PA
She was born in 1743 and married John Gardiner, and died in
1834. She is listed as a patriot in the DAR Patriot Index.

GARDINER, MARY   CT
New London. She suffered damage in a British raid (CAR,
1:63h, 95c). She was a Western Lands Grantee.

III: COMPLETE LISTING

GARDNER, MRS.   NC
She provided provisions for the troops (RA, A:27).
GARDNER, ANNE   VA
Hansemond County. She performed a public service (VR, 4:156).
GARDNER, JEMIMA   NC
She supplied provisions for the army (RA, A:266).
GARDNER, LUCY   SC
She supplied provisions for the troops (SI, B:243; U-W:268).
GARDNER, MARTHA   NC
She provided provisions for the troops (RA, B:47).
GARDNER, SALLY   CT
New London. On October 16, 1781, James Young obtained a letter of marque to command the schooner Black Slover with one gun and twenty-five men. Witnesses to the bond were Gurdon Saltonstall and Sally Gardner. She also witnessed bonds for Asa Palmer of Stonington and for Ludowick Champlin of New London (CN).
GARLAND, ELIZABETH   VA
Gloucester County. Recognized for public service (VR, 3:44).
GARLICK, MARY   VA
King William County. She performed a public service (VR, 3:246).
GARNET, ANN   VA
Essex County. Credited with public service (VR, 2:148).
GARNETT, CATHERINE   VA
Culpeper County. Recognized for public service (VR Court Booklet, 1:40).
GARNETT, JUDITH   VA
Essex County. She performed a public service (VR, 2:149).
GARNETT, MARGARET   VA
Essex County. Recognized for public service (VR, 2:149, 150).
GARRETT, ELIZABETH   VA
Louisa County. Credited with public service (VR, 3:349).
GARRISON, ELIZABETH   VA
Stafford County. She performed a public service (VR, 5:189).
GARRITSE, EVA   NJ
Franklin Township, Bergen County. The former widow of Peter Van Derlinden, she suffered damage by the British (CDB, claim 24).
GARY, ELIZABETH   VA
Prince George County. Recognized for public service (VR Court Booklet, p. 2).
GASKILL, RHODA   NJ
Burlington. She suffered damage in a British raid (claim 222).
GASKINS, MOLLY   VA
Northumberland County. Credited with public service (VR, 4:116).
GASTON, ESTHER WAUGH   SC
The wife of John Gaston, she died in 1789. Mrs. Gaston is recognized as a patriot in the DAR Patriot Index.
GASTON, MARTHA   SC
She was born in 1741 and married Joseph Gaston, and died

in 1826. She is listed as a patriot in the DAR Patriot Index.

GATES, MARY VALENCE   NY, WV
She opened her home as a hospital for wounded soldiers. See Biographies.

GATEWOOD, MARY   VA
Essex County. She performed a public service (VR, 4:305).

GATEWOOD, RACHEL   VA
Essex County. Recognized for public service (VR Court Booklet, 2:12).

GATLIFF, CHRISTINA McGUIRE   KY
Mrs. Gatliff and her five children were held as prisoners by the Canadians and Indians. See Biographies.

GATLIFF, MARTHA   WV
Greenbrier County. She was the wife or widow of Lt. James Gatliff when she provided provisions for the militia in October 1781 (VR, 3:7).

GATTS, CATHARINE   NY
At age forty-six she was captured along with her husband, Michael, one son, and three daughters (Margaret, aged twelve; Polly, aged eight; and Charity, aged six) by Indians at Schoharie and released from Fort Ticonderoga on July 18, 1783 (MR).

GAUSE, MARGARET   NC
She supplied provisions for the army (RA, A:118).

GAY, PATIENCE. See DEBORAH GANNETT

GAYLORD, KATHERINE COLE   CT, PA
After the Battle of Wyoming, she fled with her three children. See Biographies.

GEIGER, EMILY   SC
She carried a message from Gen. Greene to Gen. Sumter. See Biographies.

GELBRAITH, ELIZABETH   WV
Berkeley County. She supplied provisions for the army (RW).

GEORGE, BETHIAH   NC
She provided provisions for the troops (RA, A:22).

GEORGE, MARGARET WHITSON   VA
Fauquier County. The wife of Nicholas George, she performed a public service (VR, 2:239).

GERE, REBEKAH   MD
She supplied wheat in 1781 for the army (IM, 16849).

GERRISH, MARGARET FOSS   ME
Kittery. Her first husband was named Gullom, then she married Samuel Gerrish, who commanded the brigantine Aurora. But on June 14, 1780, he was captured by the British vessel Cerebus and confined in the Mill Prison, near Plymouth, England. On December 28, 1780, he escaped and returned to America (CN; FP4).

GERRITSE, LANA   NJ
Somerville. She suffered losses in a British raid (CDB, pp. 100, 107).

III: COMPLETE LISTING 313

GERRITSE, PHEBE NJ
    Somerville. She suffered damage by the British (CDB, pp. 87, 107).

GEST, SARAH SC
    She supplied provisions for the army (SI, Y-Z:52).

GETTINGS, MARY MD
    Kent County. In August 1779 her property was stolen by the British (IM, 8326, 10411).

GEYER, MARY PA
    She was born in 1735 and married Peter Geyer. She is listed as a patriot in the DAR Patriot Index.

GHOLSTON, MARY VA
    Halifax County. She performed a public service (VR, 2:271).

GIBBONS, HANNAH MARTIN GA
    Near Sunbury. The wife of Joseph Gibbons, she supplied rice for the Continental troops (WA, pp. 111, 144), and also forage (p. 119).

GIBBONS, MARGERY HANNUM PA
    She took food to imprisoned American soldiers. See Biographies.

GIBBONS, REBECCA VA
    The wife of John B. Gibbons, she is credited as a patriot in the DAR Patriot Index.

GIBBONS, SARAH GA
    Gen. Pulaski spent the night at her home. See Biographies.

GIBBS, ANN VA
    Frederick County. She performed a public service (VR, 2:184).

GIBBS, ELIZABETH NJ
    Burlington. The wife of Mablon Gibbs, she suffered damage in a British raid (CDB, p. 60).

GIBBS, FRANCES NJ
    Burlington. She suffered losses in a British raid (CDB, p. 59).

GIBSON, ANNE WEST PA
    She supplied flour for the army. See Biographies.

GIBSON, MARGARET NC
    She supplied provisions for the troops (RA, A:141).

GIBSON, MARGARET WEIR. See HOUSTON

GIBSON, MARY NC
    She supplied provisions for the army (RA, 1:49, fol. 4).

GIGNILLIAT, MARY MAGDALEN SC
    She provided provisions for the troops (SI, B:11).

GIGNILLIAT, SUSAN SC
    She supplied provisions for the troops (SI, B:12).

GILBERD, ELIZABETH PA
    While a widow aged fifty-five she was captured by the British at Fort Allen along with her daughters on April 22, 1780, and taken to Montreal. They were sent home on August 22, 1782 (MR).

GILBERD, JOYCE PA
    At age twenty-one she was captured on April 22, 1780 at Fort Allen and sent home on August 22, 1782 (MR).

GILBERD, REBECCA   PA
At age seventeen she was captured on April 22, 1780, at Fort Allen and taken to Montreal. She was sent home on August 22, 1782 (MR).

GILBERD, SARAH   PA
At age nineteen she was captured on April 22, 1780, at Fort Allen and taken to Montreal and sent home on August 22, 1782 (MR).

GILBERT, DEBORAH CHAMPION   CT
She carried messages to Gen. Washington. See Biographies.

GILBERT, LYDIA   CT
Ridgefield. She suffered losses in the British raid of April 1777 (CAR, 8:391a, 63m). She was a Western Lands Grantee.

GILBERT, POLLY. See DEBORAH GANNETT

GILES, SARAH ELLENWOOD   MA
Beverly. She married Eleazer Giles, commander of the Saratoga, in 1780, but he was captured by the British and imprisoned (CN).

GILL, ELIZABETH   VA
Charles City. Recognized for public service (VR, 1:310).

GILL, SALLY   VA
Northumberland County. Recognized for public service (VR Court Booklet, p. 6).

GILL, SARAH   VA
Northumberland County. Credited with public service (VR, 4:116).

GILLAM, ELIZABETH CALDWELL   SC
She married Capt. Robert Gillam, Jr., and died in 1851. She is recognized as a patriot in the DAR Patriot Index.

GILLESPIE, ELIZABETH MAXWELL. See STEELE

GILLESPIE (GALISPIE), FRANCES   VA
Prince Edward County. Recognized for public service (VR, 5:44).

GILLETT, ELIZA   CT
Her husband was captured and imprisoned. See Biographies.

GILLISON, JANE   NC
She supplied provisions for the army (RA, A:241).

GILLON, MARY CRIPPS   SC
She refused to sign an oath of fidelity to the Crown. See Biographies.

GILMAN, REBECCA IVES   NH
Samuel Adams spent the night in her home. See Biographies.

GILMORE, SALLY   WV
Hampshire County. She performed a public service (VR Ctf 1).

GILMORE, SARAH   WV
Hampshire County. Credited with public service (VR, 4:325).

GINGLES, MARGARET   NC
She supplied provisions for the army (RA, A:151).

GIRMAN, ELIZABETH   NC
She provided provisions for the troops (RA, A:191).

III: COMPLETE LISTING

GLAZE, ANN　　　　　　　　　SC
　After Charleston fell to the British on May 12, 1780, she refused to sign an oath of fidelity to King George III and so was banished from the city (SC).

GLEADOW, MARY　　　　　　　SC
　When Charleston was captured by the British on May 12, 1780, she refused to sign an oath of fidelity to the Crown and so was banished from the city (SC).

GLIDDEN, ALICE MILLS　　　　NH
　She hunted game with her flintlock. See Biographies.

GLINES, ELIZABETH WILLIAMS　NH
　She was born in 1763 and married William Glines who was a private during the war. She died on May 20, 1822. Mrs. Glines is credited with patriotic service during the war (DAR Patriot Index).

GLOSTER, MARGARET　　　　　SC
　She supplied funds for the army (AA, 1:141).

GODDARD, ELIZABETH BRITTON.　See JENKINS

GODDARD, MARY KATHERINE　　CT, MD
　She printed the official broadside of the Declaration of Independence. See Biographies.

GODDING, ELIZABETH　　　　　VA
　New Kent County. She performed a public service (VR Court Booklet, p. 8).

GODFREY, ANN　　　　　　　　CT
　Fairfield. She suffered losses in the British raid of April 1777 (CAR, 15:261c). She was a Western Lands Grantee.

GODLY, MARY　　　　　　　　NC
　She provided provisions for the troops (RA, 5:44, fol. 2).

GODWIN, ANNE　　　　　　　　VA
　Hansemond County. She performed a public service (VR, 4:354).

GODWIN, CHARLOTTE　　　　　VA
　Hansemond County. Recognized for public service (VR, 4:150).

GODWIN, ELIZABETH　　　　　VA
　Hansemond County. Credited with public service (VR, 4:156).

GODWIN, LEAH　　　　　　　　VA
　Hansemond County. She performed a public service (VR, 4:354).

GODWIN, PHEBE COLE　　　　　NJ
　Gen. Washington held a court-martial here. See Biographies.

GODWIN, SUSANNAH　　　　　　VA
　Warwick County. Credited with public service (VR, 5:312; Court Booklet, p. 13).

GOE, REBECCA BOONE　　　　　KY
　Boonesborough. The daughter of Rebecca Bryan and Daniel Boone, she was born in 1768. In September 1775 Daniel Boone and his family moved to Kentucky. For details on the experience of this seven-year-old girl in Kentucky, see Biographies: Boone, Rebecca Bryan. Rebecca Boone Goe died in 1805.

GOETCHIUS, MAGDALENE　　　　NJ
　Hackensack. She suffered damage in a British raid (CDB, p. 89).

GOLDSMITH, SARAH   CT
New Haven. In a British raid of July 1779 she suffered damages (CAR, 15:234, 269). She was a Western Lands Grantee.

GOODE, MARTHA JEFFERSON   VA
Powhatan County. She was born in 1719 and married Bennett Goode, and died in 1797. Mrs. Goode is recognized as a patriot in the DAR Patriot Index (also in VR, 4:234).

GOODELL, RHODA GRANT   NH
Lyme. She was the wife of Titus Goodell, a corporal in the militia. While substituting for a man absent on leave, he was killed in October 1777 during a night skirmish shortly before the surrender of Gen. Burgoyne at Saratoga (FP1).

GOODFAITH, MARY   CT
New London. She suffered damage in a British raid (CAR, 1:63h, 95c). She was a Western Lands Grantee.

GOODGAME, ELIZABETH   GA
She supplied nine head of steers for the army (WA, p. 152).

GOODRICH, ANN. See STORY

GOODRICH, MARY ANN WOLCOTT   CT
Litchfield. In 1776 Mary Ann Wolcott assisted her mother, Laura Collins Wolcott, in molding 42,088 bullets from the lead statue of King George III. Later she married Chauncey Goodrich of Hartford (BD).

GOODWIN, ANNA   CT
She furnished supplies for the army (CAR, 35:153k).

GOODWIN, ELIZABETH   VA
Dinwiddie County. She performed a public service (VR, 1:329).

GOODWIN, MARGARET   VA
Isle of Wight. Recognized for public service (VR, 2:319).

GOODWIN, REBECCA   VA
York County. Credited with public service (VR Lists, p. 5). Also King William County (VR, 3:246; 4:336).

GORDON, ELIZABETH   VA
King George County. She performed a public service (VR, 2:335).

GORDON, MARGARET   SC
She supplied provisions for the army (SI, Y-Z:150).

GORDON, MARGARET GREGG. See FLAGLER

GORDON, MARY   VA
Prince George County. Credited with public service (VR, 4:251).

GORDON, RACHEL ST. JOHN   VA
Essex County. Wife of John Gordon, she performed a public service (VR, 4:304-305).

GORDON, RUTH   CT
New Haven. She suffered damages in a British raid (CAR, 15:269b). She was a Western Lands Grantee.

GORDON, SUSANNAH   NC
She provided provisions for the troops (RA, 6:22, fol. 1).

GORE, MARGARET   SC
She supplied provisions for the troops (SI, Y-Z:41).

III: COMPLETE LISTING

GORE, RACHEL NEIGHBORS   SC
   The wife of Thomas Gore, Sr., she supplied provisions for the
   army (SI, L-N:14).
GORHAM, REBECCA CALL   MA
   The British burned her home. See Biographies.
GOSS, ELIZABETH   NJ
   Piscataway. The sister of Benjamin and Joseph Goss, she suf-
   fered losses in a British raid (CDB, p. 307).
GOSS, ELIZABETH   PA
   The wife of George Goss, she died in 1810. She is listed as
   a patriot in the DAR Patriot Index.
GOUGE, ELIZABETH   VA
   Caroline County. Credited with public service (VR Lists, 1:14,
   29).
GOULD, ELIZABETH   CT
   Fairfield. She suffered damage in British raids, 1779-1780
   (CAR, 15:251). She was a Western Lands Grantee.
GOULD, PHEBE   NJ
   Morris County. She suffered damages caused by the Americans
   (CDB, claim 109).
GOULD, SARAH ANTHONY   RI
   Portsmouth. The daughter of Susanna Albro and John Anthony,
   she was born there on August 1, 1697. On October 17, 1723,
   she married Anthony Gould. They had one son and two daugh-
   ters. The Goulds had sheep taken during the war. Sarah
   died on January 10, 1797, and is listed as a patriot in the
   DAR Patriot Index (submitted by Sally P. Small, Barrington,
   RI).
GOWEN (GOING), MARY   VA
   Gloucester County. She performed a public service (VR, 3:43).
GRAAF, MRS. JACOB   PA
   In her home Thomas Jefferson wrote the Declaration of Independ-
   ence. See Biographies.
GRACE, MARIA SARGENT   MA
   She was born in 1762 and married Joseph Grace, and died in
   1844. She is listed as a patriot in the DAR Patriot Index.
GRAHAM, ELIZABETH   NJ
   Bound Brook. The wife of Ennis Graham, she suffered damages
   caused by the British (CDB, p. 1).
GRAHAM, ELIZABETH   VA
   Augusta County. Recognized for public service (VR Court Book-
   let, p. 10).
GRAHAM, ELIZABETH NORTON. See JOYNER
GRAHAM, SARAH   SC
   She provided provisions for the troops (SI, Y-Z).
GRAHAM, SARAH   VA
   Caroline County. She performed a public service (VR, 1:249,
   250).
GRAHAM, SARAH MERWIN   NY
   She was the wife of Dr. Chauncey Graham who served as surgeon

on the ship Recovery. On March 23, 1780, they were captured by HMS Galatea and delivered to a prison ship in New York Harbor (CN).

GRAINGER, MARY   NC
She supplied provisions for the troops (RA, 5:6, fol. 1).

GRANDER, MARY   NC
She supplied provisions for the troops (RA, 4:78, fol. 1).

GRANT, ELIZABETH BOONE   KY
She helped defend the fort. See Biographies.

GRAVES, ANN DAVENPORT   VA
At age eighty-five she supplied provisions for the army. See Biographies.

GRAVES, SARAH   VA
Chesterfield County. Recognized for public service (VR, 2:32, 33).

GRAY, ABIGAIL WALES   CT
She was the wife of Dr. Thomas Gray, who served as surgeon's mate on the Oliver Cromwell, 1776-1777. But in May 1777 they were captured by the British and imprisoned (CN).

GRAY, ELEANOR   VA
Botetourt. She performed a public service (VR, 1:163).

GRAY, ELIZABETH   NC
She provided provisions for the troops (RA, 5:49, fol. 3).

GRAY, ELIZABETH   VA
Southampton County. Recognized for public service (VR Court Booklet, p. 25).

GRAY, ELIZABETH CHIPMAN   MA
Salem. She was born in 1756 in Marblehead, Massachusetts, and in 1782 she married William Gray, a millionaire. They had six children. Mrs. Gray was charitable and donated funds for the American soldiers. She died in Boston on September 24, 1823 (CD).

GRAY, GRACE   VA
King William County. Recognized for public service (VR, 3:p. 246).

GRAY, MARTHA IBBETSON   PA
She was born in 1734 and married George Gray. She was a nurse during the war, and died on June 27, 1781. She is listed as a patriot in the DAR Patriot Index.

GRAY, MARY   CT
Ridgefield. In the raid of April 1777 by the British she suffered damages (CAR, 7:391b). She was a Western Lands Grantee.

GRAY, MARY   SC
She supplied provisions for the troops (SI, L-N:253).

GRAY, SARAH   NJ
Westfield. She suffered losses in a British raid (CDB, claim 59).

GRAYDON, RACHEL MARKS   PA
She was born in 1723 and married Alexander Graydon. Her son, Alexander Graydon, Jr., was a captain of the 3rd Pennsylvania Regiment and was taken prisoner by the British. In May 1777 Mrs. Graydon obtained a pass from Gen. Philip Schuyler to visit her son in prison. She died in 1807 (FW).

III: COMPLETE LISTING

GREEN, ALICE KOLLACK — PA
She sold her jewelry for gold for her imprisoned husband and other seamen. See Biographies.

GREEN, AMY — CT
New London. In the British raid of September 1782 she suffered damages (CAR, 23:164).

GREEN, ANN — NC
She supplied provisions for the troops (RA, 11:99, fol. 2).

GREEN, ANN — VA
Culpeper County. She performed a public service (VR, 2:87). Also shown in Fauquier County (Ctf 1).

GREEN, ELEANOR — VA
Culpeper County. Recognized for public service (VR, 5:231).

GREEN, ELIZABETH — NC
She refused to drink British tea. See Background.

GREEN, ELIZABETH — NJ
Hunterdon County. The wife of Joseph Green, she suffered damages caused by the Americans (CDB, claim 38).

GREEN, ELIZABETH ROADS — MA
Marblehead. She married Samuel Green, who commanded the ship *Pilarne* in 1777. Green was captured by the British on September 17, 1777, and imprisoned in Rhode Island. Several months later Capt. Mark Workman volunteered to be exchanged for Capt. Green (CN).

GREEN, LUCY — VA
Amelia County. She performed a public service (VR, 1:56).

GREEN, LYDIA — CT
New London. She suffered damages in a British raid (CAR, 1:63i, 95e). She was a Western Lands Grantee.

GREEN, MARGARET — CT
New London. She suffered losses in the British raid of September 1781 (CAR, 23:164).

GREEN, MARY — VA
Princess Anne County. Recognized for public service (VR, 4:215).

GREEN, MARY ANN — VA
Caroline County. Credited with public service (VR Court Booklet, 1:8, 12).

GREEN, NANCY STEPHENSON. See ANDERSON

GREEN, REBECCA SPOONER — CT
Middletown. On April 7, 1780, Sanford Thompson obtained a letter of marque to command the schooner *Bunker Hill* with ten guns and forty-five men. Timothy Green and Rebecca Green witnessed the bond (CN).

GREEN, WIDOW — CT
Middletown. She supplied a blanket for the army (CAR, 6:179).

GREENE, CATHERINE RAY — RI
She opened her home to refugees, and Benjamin Franklin's sister stayed at her place. See Biographies.

GREENE, CATHERINE LITTLEFIELD — RI
She turned her home into a hospital. See Biographies.

GREENE, CELIA RI
   East Greenwich. On February 7, 1781, Isaac Freeborn of Newport obtained a letter of marque to command the brig Minerva with fourteen guns and forty-five men. Witnesses to the bond were William Greene and Celia Greene (CN).
GREENSTATE, MARY CT
   Danbury. In the British raid of April 1777 she suffered damages (CAR, 8:382).
GREENWELL, MARY SC
   She supplied provisions for the troops (SI, O-Q:233).
GREER, ANN NC
   She supplied provisions for the army (RA, 1:80, fol. 4).
GREER, ANN PORTER VA
   Bedford County. The wife of William Greer, she supplied provisions for the army (VR Court Booklet, p. 8), and died in 1810 (DAR).
GREGORY, HANNAH CT
   Norwalk. She suffered damages in a British raid (CAR, 1:63e, 98g, 99a).
GREGORY, JAMIMA VA
   Charles City. Recognized for public service (VR Ctf 1).
GREGORY, LYDIA CT
   Norwalk. She suffered losses in a British raid (CAR, 1:98a).
GREGORY, MARY VA
   Gloucester County. Recognized for public service (VR, 3:44).
GREGORY, NINA ANN VA
   Charles City. Credited with public service (VR Court Booklet, p. 22).
GREGORY, RACHEL CT
   Danbury. She suffered losses in a British raid in April 1777 (CAR, 8:382b). She was a Western Lands Grantee.
GREGORY, RUTH NC
   She supplied provisions for the army (RA, C:15).
GRESHAM, ANN MD
   Kent County. In 1780 she supplied wheat for the army (IM, 10833, 11074).
GRIEFT, MARY MD
   She supplied mlik for the ship Defence (IM, 3512).
GRIFFEY, PRUDENCE NJ
   Burlington. She suffered damage in a British raid (CDB, claim 300).
GRIFFIN, ELIZABETH CT
   New London. She suffered losses in a British raid (CAR, 1:63h). She was a Western Lands Grantee.
GRIFFIN, JUDITH VA
   Richmond County. Credited with public service (VR Ctf 1).
GRIFFIN, MARY SC
   She supplied provisions for the army (SI, O-Q:150).
GRIFFIN, SARAH MD
   Charles County. In 1781 she supplied wheat for the army (IM, 19305).

III: COMPLETE LISTING

GRIFFING, SARAH STILWELL   NJ
She appealed to Gen. Washington for a pass, and she rode to New York and contacted Gen. Clinton, who released her imprisoned husband. See Biographies.

GRIFFIS, BARBARA   SC
She provided provisions for the troops (SI, B:6).

GRIFFITH (GRIFFY), MARGARET   VA
Bedford County. She performed a public service (Court Booklet, p. 10).

GRIGG (GREGG), ANNE   CT
Greenwich widow. She suffered losses in the British raid of April 1777 (CAR, 24:276b).

GRIGGING, SARAH. See STILWELL

GRIGGS, ANNE   CT
Greenwich. She suffered damage in a British raid (CAR, 50: 63d, 74b). She was a Western Lands Grantee.

GRIGGS, MARY   VA
Westmoreland County. Recognized for public service (VR, 5:219).

GRIGGS, MERCY   CT
Tolland. She supplied a blanket for the army (CAR, 11:18).

GRIMBALL, SARAH   SC
She supplied provisions for the army (SI, O-Q:284).

GRIMES, AGNES   NC
She provided provisions for the troops (RA, 9:27, fol. 3).

GRIMES, ELIZABETH   NC
She supplied provisions for the army (RA, 5:62, fol. 3).

GRIMES, SARAH   VA
Norfolk. She performed a public service (VR, 4:130).

GRIMES, SUSANNAH   NC
She provided provisions for the troops (RA, 5:47, fol. 1).

GRISWOLD, ELIZABETH CHENEY   CT
Bolton. She was the wife of White Griswold, a private, who was taken prisoner on October 4, 1777, at the Battle of Germantown, and died a prisoner in Philadelphia on December 2, 1777 (FP1).

GRISWOLD, WIDOW   CT
New Haven. In 1777 she supplied a blanket for the army (CAR, 11:143).

GRIZZARD, LUCY   VA
Sussex County. Credited with public service (VR, 5:200).

GROOM, MARY   VA
King and William County. Recognized for public service (VR 3:221).

GROSS, MARY   CT
She received money from a fund to send to prisoners in New York in 1777 (CAR, 12:284a).

GROUP, ELIZABETH   NC
She supplied provisions for the troops (RA, 9:28, fol. 1).

GRUBB, ELIZABETH   NC
She supplied provisions for the army (RA, 9:107, fol. 4). Also shown as Elizabeth Grupp (RA, A:111).

GUENIN, JAMIMA　　　　　　　　　NJ
　　Morris County. The wife of Vincent Guenin, she suffered damage
　　caused by the Americans (CDB, claim 67).
GUERRAUD, ELIZABETH　　　　　　SC
　　After Charleston fell to the British on May 12, 1780, she refused
　　to sign an oath of fidelity to King George III and so was banished
　　from the city (SC).
GUESS, MRS.　　　　　　　　　　VA
　　Loudoun County. Recognized for public service (VR, 3:298).
GUPBELL, ELIZABETH　　　　　　　SC
　　She provided provisions for the troops (SI, O-Q:283).
GUTHRIE, MARY　　　　　　　　　VA
　　She performed a public service (VR, 3:222).
GUTHRIE, PATIENCE　　　　　　　CT
　　Danbury. In the British raid of April 1777 she suffered damages
　　(CAR, 8:382b).
GUTRA, ANN　　　　　　　　　　　MD
　　Baltimore. She lodged Capt. George Cook of the ship Defence
　　in 1777 (IM 4077).
GUTRIDGE, MOLLY　　　　　　　　MA
　　She was a member of the Daughters of Liberty. See Biographies.
GUY, ELIZABETH　　　　　　　　　VA
　　Accomack County. Recognized for public service (VR, 1:24).
GUYTON, MARGARET McCURDY　　　SC
　　She was born in 1773, married Aaron Guyton, and died in 1860.
　　Margaret McCurdy is listed as a patriot in the DAR Patriot
　　Index.
GWATHNEY, HANNAH　　　　　　　VA
　　King William County. She performed a public service (VR, 4:336).
GWIN, ISABELLA　　　　　　　　　NC
　　She provided provisions for the troops (RA, 1:89, fol. 4).
GWINNETT, ANN BOURNE　　　　　GA
　　Her home was seized by the British, and she disappeared. See
　　Biographies.
GWYNN, MARY　　　　　　　　　　RI
　　She nursed wounded prisoners in 1776 (MP, 57:15, 11:42).

H

HACKET, MARY ANN　　　　　　　VA
　　Princess Anne County. She performed a public service (VR
　　Court Booklet, p. 5).
HACKNEY, ELIZABETH　　　　　　　VA
　　Middlesex County. Recognized for public service (VR, 4:93).
HACKNEY, RACHEL　　　　　　　　NC
　　She provided provisions for the troops (RA, 11:94, fol. 4).
HADDEN, JENNETT　　　　　　　　SC
　　She supplied provisions for the army (SI, O-Q:78).
HADDEN, MARY　　　　　　　　　SC
　　She provided provisions for the troops (SI, Y-Z:128).

III: COMPLETE LISTING

HADDEN, MARY VA
  Middlesex County. She performed a public service (VR, 4:93).
HADDOCK, HANNAH MA
  Boston. On May 4, 1782, Nathan Plimpton obtained a letter of marque to command the sloop Count de Grasse with eight guns and thirty-five men. Hannah Haddock witnessed the bond (CN).
HADDOCK, SARAH SC
  She provided funds for the army (AA, 2:92), and also provisions (SI, R-T:108).
HADIN, HENRIETTA MARIA HACK. See FISHBURN
HADLEY, JANE FISKE MA
  She was born in 1733, married Josiah Hadley, and died in 1819. She is recognized as a patriot in the DAR Patriot Index.
HAGAR, ELIZABETH NC
  She supplied provisions for the troops (RA, 6:38, fol. 4).
HAGGIDORN, MARY NY
  Schoharie. When men under Sir John Johnston attacked the upper fort of Schoharie in 1780, Mary refused to go to the cellar with the other women. She took a spear to help Capt. Hager defend the fort successfully (CD).
HAILEY (HALEY), MARY VA
  Caroline County. She performed a public service (VR, 1:251).
HAINS, ANN NJ
  Burlington. The wife of Jonathan Hains, she suffered damage by the British (CDB, p. 46).
HAINS, CATHERINE WV
  Berkeley County. With Catherine Cookus she supplied provisions for the army (VR Ctf 1).
HAKES, HANNAH CT
  Stonington. She supplied provisions for the army in 1777 (CAR, 30:125b).
HALBERT, ELIZABETH HILL VA
  She was born in 1747, married Lt. William Halbert, and died in 1836. She is recognized as a patriot in the DAR Patriot Index.
HALE, ABIGAIL GROUT NH
  She was an original advocate of women's suffrage. See Biographies.
HALE, ELIZABETH STRONG
  The mother of Nathan Hale. See Background.
HALEY, MARY SC
  She supplied provisions for the army (SI, B:18).
HALL, ANN VA
  Gloucester County. Recognized for public service (VR, 3:46).
HALL, BETSY CT
  Norwalk. She suffered losses in a British raid (CAR, 1:63k, 98f, 100d). She was a Western Lands Grantee.
HALL, ELIZABETH NC
  She provided provisions for the troops (RA, 1:65, fol. 4).

HALL, FRANCES HICKS   NC
She refused to drink British tea. See Background.
HALL, HANNAH   VA
Stafford County. Credited with public service (VR, 5:190).
HALL, JOYCE   VA
Northumberland County. She performed a public service (VR, 4:118).
HALL, LYDIA   CT
She supplied cattle and other provisions for the troops in 1780 (CAR, 35:106b, 108ab).
HALL, MARY   NC
She supplied provisions for the army (RA, 1:82, fol. 4).
HALL, MARY   SC
She provided provisions for the troops (SI, B:217).
HALL, MARY ANN   SC
She supplied provisions for the army (SI, Y-Z:42).
HALL, MARY OSBORNE   GA
Her home was confiscated by the British. See Biographies.
HALL, PERSIS TOWER LINCOLN   MA
When the British occupied Boston, she crossed the bay to Gloucester to obtain provisions. See Biographies.
HALL, SUSAN T.   SC
She supplied provisions for the army (SI, B:43, 84).
HALL, SUSANNA   VA
Gloucester County. Recognized for public service (VR Court Booklet, 2:9).
HALSEY, ABIGAIL HOWELL   NJ
She was the third wife of Dr. Silas Halsey and died on March 26, 1777. She is recognized as a patriot in the DAR Patriot Index.
HAMBLIN, ELIZABETH   VA
Prince Edward County. She performed a public service (VR, 5:50).
HAMILTON, ANNE KENNEDY   SC
She warned the Americans of an impending attack. See Biographies.
HAMILTON, ELIZABETH SCHUYLER. See GERTRUDE SCHUYLER COCHRAN
HAMILTON, JANE   VA
Loudoun County. Recognized for public service (VR, 3:302).
HAMILTON, MARY   NJ
Burlington. She suffered damage in a British raid (CDB, p. 144).
HAMILTON, NANCY   VA
Rockbridge County. Recognized for public service (VR, 5:76).
HAMILTON, RACHEL   SC
She supplied provisions for the troops (SI, Y-Z:122).
HAMILTON, TEMPERANCE ARNOLD   SC
She was born in 1762, married Thomas Hamilton, and died in 1849. She is listed as a patriot in the DAR Patriot Index.
HAMLIN, SARAH   VA
Sussex County. Recognized for public service (VR, 5:201).

III: COMPLETE LISTING

HAMMETT, CHARLOTTE BENNETT   SC
    Charleston. She was born there in 1752. On November 3, 1776, Charlotte married Thomas Hammett, Sr., and they had two sons and two daughters. Thomas was a defender of Charleston and was taken prisoner when that city fell to the British on May 12, 1780 (submitted by Edith H. Benter, Macon, GA).

HAMMOND, ANN "NANCY" WILEY   NY
    Gen. Washington had his headquarters there. See Biographies.

HAMMOND, MARY SCOTT   RI
    Newport. She was a niece of Benjamin Franklin, and in 1754 she married John Arnold Hammond, captain of a privateer during the war. He was captured by the British and died in June 1781 in a prison ship in New York Harbor (CN).

HAMMOND, REBECCA   GA
    She supplied cattle for public use (WA, p. 162).

HAMMOND, SARA CLEMENT   KY
    Bryan's Station. She was the wife of John Hammond. When the Tories and Indians attacked on August 15, 1782, she was one of the women who went for water. Her name is inscribed on the monument erected in 1896 by the Lexington Chapter of the Daughters of the American Revolution.

HAMPTON, ELIZABETH PRESTON   SC
    She was born in 1710 and married Anthony Hampton. Elizabeth and her husband were killed in July 1776. She is recognized as a patriot in the DAR Patriot Index.

HAMPTON, MARY   VA
    Frederick County. She performed a public service (VR Ctf 1).

HAMPTON, MARY COLSTON   VA
    She was born in 1731 and married private George Hampton. Mary and her husband were killed in 1778. She is listed as a patriot in the DAR Patriot Index.

HAMPTON, MARY FALCONER   KY
    The Indians burned their fort to the ground. See Biographies.

HANBY, MRS. JEREMIAH   SC
    She provided provisions for the troops (SI, R-T:220).

HANBY, SUSANNAH   SC
    She supplied provisions for the army (SI, R-T:220).

HANCKLE, BARBARA   WV
    Hampshire County. Recognized as a patriot (RW).

HANCOCK, ANN   CT
    New London. She suffered losses in a British raid (CAR, 1:63i, 95d). She was a Western Lands Grantee.

HANCOCK, DOROTHY QUINCY   MA
    Her home was seized and occupied by British Gen. Gage. See Biographies.

HANCOCK, RACHEL   NC
    She supplied provisions for the troops (RA, 9:23, fol. 4).

HANCOCK, SUSANNAH   NC
    She provided provisions for the troops (RA, C:47).

HAND, MRS.   NJ
    Cape May. She was the wife of Attorney Hand. Mrs. Hand collected funds for the army (New Jersey Gazette, July 4, 1780).

HAND, CATHERINE EWING   PA
    She nursed wounded soldiers. See Biographies.
HAND, ELIZABETH   VA
    Shenandoah County. Recognized for public service (VR Court Booklet, p. 20).
HANDY, HANNAH HUNTER   VT
    The wife of Robert Handy, she is listed as a patriot in the DAR Patriot Index.
HANFORD, HANNAH   CT
    Norwalk. She suffered damage in a British raid (CAR, 1:63j, 98d, 100c). She was a Western Lands Grantee.
HANNA, MRS.   NJ
    Hunterdon County. She collected funds for the army (New Jersey Gazette, July 4, 1780).
HANNA, ELIZABETH   PA
    She was captured by the British and Indians at Fort Pitt in 1777 and taken to Montreal (MR).
HANNA, JANE   PA
    Captured in 1777 by the British and Indians at Fort Pitt, she was taken to Montreal (MR).
HANSFORD, ELIZABETH   VA
    York County. Recognized for public service (VR Court Booklet, 2:1, 2a, 5).
HANSON, ELIZABETH   VA
    York County. She performed a public service (VR, 4:276).
HAPPER (HOPPER), MARY   VA
    Norfolk. The wife of William Happer, she performed a public service (VR, 4:138, 140).
HARDEN, ELIZABETH   SC
    She supplied provisions for the army (SI, Y-Z:177).
HARDEN, ELIZABETH SEALY. See WALKER
HARDIMAN, DOROTHY   NC
    She provided provisions for the troops (RA, 1:52, fol. 2).
HARDIMAN, DOROTHY   VA
    Pittsylvania County. Recognized for public service (VR, 5:15).
HARDING, AMY GARDNER   PA
    She survived the Wyoming Massacre. See Biographies.
HARDING, JANE   NJ
    Mount Holly. She suffered damage by the British (CDB, p. 149).
HARDWICK, MARY   VA
    Richmond. She performed a public service (VR, 5:97).
HARDY, DEBORAH   NC
    She supplied provisions for the army (RA, D:276).
HARE, ELIZABETH   VA
    Hansemond County. Recognized for public service (VR, 4:158).
HARGINS, MRS.   VA
    At age twenty she was captured by Indians on March 3, 1782, and taken to Canada. She was sent home on August 22, 1782 (MR).
HARGROVE, ELIZABETH   VA
    Hansemond County. Credited with public service (VR, 4:354, 355).

III: COMPLETE LISTING

HARGROVE, MARY   VA
　Surry County. She performed a public service (VR Court Booklet, p. 7).
HARING, CORNELIA   NJ
　Harrington Township, Bergen County. The wife of Abraham Haring, she suffered damage by the British (CDB, claim 19).
HARING, ELIZABETH   NJ
　Harrington Township, Bergen County (British CDB, claim 16).
HARLAND, ELONER   WV
　Berkeley County. Recognized for public service (VR Ctf 1).
HARLESTON, ANN ASHBY   SC
　She provided provisions for the troops (SI, Y-Z:121).
HARMON, BARBARA TETER.   See   HINKLE
HARPER, HANNAH   VA
　Amelia County. Credited with public service (VR, 1:63).
HARPER, MARY   VA
　Prince Edward County. She performed a public service (VR, 5:50).
HARPER, PHOEBE VERNON   PA
　She was the wife of John Harper, who was appointed brigade major of Washington's Guard on June 2, 1777. Harper was taken prisoner at the Battle of Brandywine on September 11, 1777, and was not exchanged until November 1780 (FW, DAR).
HARRINGTON, MARY   RI
　She provided supplies for the troops in 1778 (MP, 35:6), and corn and wool in 1779 (MP, 24:6).
HARRIS, ALTJE SCHENCK   NJ
　She carried a message to Washington's staff. See Biographies.
HARRIS, ANN EPPS   VA
　Powhatan County. The wife of Benjamin Harris, she died in 1787. She performed a public service (VR, 4:235; DAR).
HARRIS, BRIDGET   CT
　New London. She suffered damage in a British raid (CAR, 1:63h, 95d). She was a Western Lands Grantee.
HARRIS, FRANCES   VA
　Buckingham County. Recognized for public service (VR, 1:202; 2:166).
HARRIS, GRACE   CT
　New London. She suffered losses in a British raid (CAR, 1:63h, 95d). She was a Western Lands Grantee.
HARRIS, HANNAH STEWART   PA
　Gen. Washington stayed in her home. See Biographies.
HARRIS, JUDITH   VA
　Mecklenburg County. Credited with public service (VR, 4:57).
HARRIS, LAMETJE   NJ
　Saddle River. She suffered damage caused by the Americans (CDB, claims 15, 41).
HARRIS, LYDIA   CT
　New London. The widow of Ebenezer Harris, she suffered damage in the British raid of September 1781 (CAR, 23:182; 28:182-185, 163h, 95d). She was a Western Lands Grantee.

HARRIS, MARY   NC
   She provided provisions for the troops (RA, A:147).
HARRIS, MEHITABLE   MA
   Salem. On June 29, 1782, David Smith obtained a letter of marque
   to command the ship Patty with eight guns and twenty men.
   Mehitable Harris witnessed the bond. She also witnessed a bond
   for John Brewer (CN).
HARRIS, RUTH   CT
   New London. She suffered damage in a British raid (CAR,
   1:63h, 95c). She was a Western Lands Grantee.
HARRIS, RUTH OGDEN   NJ
   Bridgeton. The wife of Dr. Isaac Harris, a surgeon in the
   war, she was active in the ladies' association for the welfare
   of the soldiers (New Jersey Gazette, July 4, 1780).
HARRIS, SARAH   CT
   New London. She suffered damage in a British raid (CAR,
   1:63h, 95d). She was a Western Lands Grantee.
HARRIS, SARAH   NC
   She supplied provisions for the troops (RA, 9:107, fol. 1).
HARRIS, SARAH   VA
   Hanover County. She performed a public service (VR, 3:183).
HARRIS, TYRA   NC
   She supplied provisions for the troops (RA, C:67).
HARRISON, AGNES   VA
   Halifax County. Recognized for public service (VR, 2:277).
HARRISON, ANN   VA
   Prince George County. Credited with public service (VR, 4:252).
HARRISON, ANNA. See SYMMES
HARRISON, ELEANOR   VA
   Westmoreland County. Credited with public service (VR, 5:220).
HARRISON, ELIZABETH BASSETT   VA
   Their shipyard was burned by the British. See Biographies.
HARRISON, JANE   VA
   Dinwiddie County. She performed a public service (VR, 1:332).
HARRISON, JANE   VA
   Fauquier County. Credited with public service (VR, 2:240).
HARRISON, JOANNA   NJ
   Orange. The wife of Daniel Harrison, she suffered damage by
   the British (CDB, claim 38).
HARRISON, LYDIA   NJ
   Orange. The wife of Jonathan Harrison, she suffered losses
   caused by the British (CDB, claim 29).
HARRISON, LYDIA   NJ
   Wardsession, Essex County. She suffered damages by the
   British (CDB, claim 18).
HARRISON, MARGARET   VA
   Isle of Wight. She performed a public service (VR, 2:321, 322).
   Also Peggy Harrison (VR Court Booklet, p. 10).
HARRISON, MARY GRAY   VA
   She provided provisions during the war. See Biographies.

III: COMPLETE LISTING

HARRISON, REBECCA   VA
   Prince George County. Recognized for public service (VR Court
   Booklet, p. 11).
HARRISON, SARAH   VA
   Culpeper County. Credited with public service (VR Court Booklet,
   1:2).
HART, ANN   SC
   She supplied provisions for the army (SI, B:112).
HART, DEBORAH SCUDDER   NJ
   She died during a Hessian attack. See Biographies.
HART, LYDIA REDMOND   NJ
   The wife of Nathaniel Hart, she died in 1816 and is listed as
   a patriot in the DAR Patriot Index.
HART, NANCY MORGAN   GA
   She held British soldiers at bay with a rifle. See Biographies.
HART, PENELOPE ANDERSON   NJ
   She carried provisions to her husband hiding from the British.
   See Biographies.
HART, RUTH COLE   CT
   Her husband was captured and confined. See Biographies.
HART, SARAH SIMPSON   KY
   Transylvania. In 1760 she married Capt. Nathaniel Hart of
   North Carolina, and they had several children. On March 17,
   1775, as an agent for Col. Richard Henderson, Hart purchased
   Transylvania from the Indians. In 1779 he brought his family
   there, but on August 11, 1782, Capt. Hart was killed and scalped
   by Indians. Sarah Hart died in 1784 (CH).
HARTZOG, CATHERINE SNELL   SC
   She provided beef and sheep for the soldiers. See Biographies.
HARVERY, ELIZABETH   VA
   Culpeper County. She performed a public service (VR Court
   Booklet, 1:2).
HARVEY, MARY BONNER   NC
   Mary Bonner agreed not to drink British tea. Later she mar-
   ried John Harvey. See Background.
HARVIE, MARTHA GAINES   VA
   Amherst County. She was born in 1719 and married John Harvie.
   She performed a public service (VR Court Booklet, p. 13) and
   died in 1802 (DAR).
HARWOOD, AGNES   VA
   King and Queen County. Recognized for public service (VR,
   3:224).
HARWOOD, ELIZABETH   VA
   Charles City. Credited with public service (VR Court Booklet,
   p. 11).
HARWOOD, MARGARET   VA
   Charles City. She performed a public service (VR Ctf 1).
HARWOOD, MARTHA   VA
   Warwick County. Recognized for public service (VR, 5:213).
HARWOOD, MARY   VA
   Warwick County. She performed a public service (VR Court
   Booklet, p. 5).

HASALGROVE, MRS.   VA
    Spotsylvania County. Recognized for public service (VR Court Booklet, p. 19).

HASBROUCK, TRYNTJE DEBOIS   NJ
    Gen. Washington had his headquarters there. See Biographies.

HASKELL, DOROTHY ROBINSON   MA
    Rochester. Her first husband's name was Peckham, and after his death she married Elnathan Haskell. They had five sons and one daughter. Her son Elnathan Haskell was a colonel at the Battle of Saratoga and witnessed the surrender of Gen. Burgoyne. Her son Nathan was a lieutenant in the Continental Marines and was killed in action on the ship Mars off the coast of France in 1780 when he was only twenty years old (CN).

HASKELL, ELIZABETH   MA
    Gloucester. On November 14, 1776, Philemon Haskell obtained a letter of marque to command the schooner Speedwell with three guns and twelve men. Elizabeth Haskell witnessed the bond (CN).

HASKINS, SARAH   NC
    She refused to drink British tea. See Background.

HASKITT, MARY   NC
    She provided provisions for the troops (RA, C:9).

HASSENCLEVER, MARY   PA
    Philadelphia. She collected money for the ladies' association for the welfare of the soldiers (Pennsylvania Gazette, June 12, 1780).

HATFIELD, HANNAH DE MONEY   NJ
    Gen. Washington issued her a pass to secure her husband's release. See Biographies.

HATH, ELIZABETH   NC
    She provided provisions for the troops (RA, K:221).

HAVERIN, EVE   GA
    She supplied sundry articles for the army (WA, p. 117).

HAWKINS, CATHARINE   MD
    Charles County. She supplied wheat for the army in 1781 (IM, 18706, 19401).

HAWKINS, DOROTHY   MD
    Montgomery County. She supplied wheat in 1781 for the troops (IM, 16913).

HAWKINS, MARGARET   VA
    Essex County. She performed a public service (VR, 2:151; 4:305).

HAWKINS, MARTHA   VA
    Frederick County. Recognized for public service (VR Court Booklet, p. 32).

HAWKINS, SARAH   VA
    Orange County. Credited with a public service (VR Court Booklet, p. 30).

HAY, ELIZABETH   CT
    New Haven. In the British raid of July 1779 she suffered damage (CAR, 15:234i).

III: COMPLETE LISTING

HAY, MARTHA SMITH
Gen. Washington was here. See Biographies.

HAYBEY, MARY   VA
Caroline County. She performed a public service (VR Lists, 2:13).

HAYDON, MARY   VA
Lancaster County. Credited with public service (VR, 3:274).

HAYES, ELINORAH   CT
New Haven. She suffered losses in a British raid (CAR, 1:63b, 91e). She was a Western Lands Grantee.

HAYES, HANNAH   CT
Greenwich. She suffered losses in the July 1779 raid by the British (CAR, 15:271b). She was a Western Lands Grantee.

HAYES, MARY   CT
Ridgefield. She suffered in the 1777 British raid (CAR, 8:391b). She was a Western Lands Grantee.

HAYES, SARAH   CT
She supplied provisions for the army (CAR, 35:44b).

HAYMAN, RACHEL   MD
Worcester County. In 1780 she supplied pork for the troops (IM, 13821).

HAYNE (HAINES), SUSAN   SC
She supplied provisions for the army (SI, L-N:255).

HAYNES, LUCY BASSETT   VA
Warwick County. Recognized for public service (VR, 5:212).

HAYS, MARY. See McCAULEY

HAYS, SUSANNA BOONE   KY
Boonesborough. The daughter of Rebecca Bryan and Daniel Boone, she was born in 1760. Early in 1775 Boone built a fort at Boonesborough. For the life of this fifteen-year-old girl in Kentucky, see Biographies: Boone, Rebecca Bryan. Later Susanna married William Hays. Susanna died in 1800.

HAYWARD, HANNAH FARRAND   NJ
Morristown. She was the daughter of Rhoda Smith and Bethul Farrand. In 1778 Hannah and her sister, Bet, together with their mother, knitted socks for the soldiers. Later she married Capt. Newton Hayward (DW).

HAYWARD, SARAH   MD
Worcester County. In 1781 she supplied beef for the army (IM, 19286).

HAYWOOD, ROSANNA   RI
In 1778 she supplied beef and mutton for the troops (MP, 40:24).

HAZELTINE, RUTH LADD   MA
She was born in 1712, married James Hazeltine, and died in 1796. She is recognized as a patriot in the DAR Patriot Index.

HAZELWOOD, MARY   VA
James City. Credited for public service (VR Court Booklet, p. 6).

HEADIN (HADING), SARAH   NC
She supplied provisions for the army (RA, C:54).

HEAPS, SARAH   SC
   The wife of Benjamin Heaps, she supplied provisions for the
   troops (SI, R-T;203; DAR).
HEARD, JOYCE   VA
   Henry County. She performed a public service (VR Court Booklet, p. 43).
HEARN (HYRNE), MARY   SC
   She supplied provisions for the army (SI, B:37).
HEARST, PHOEBE GRAY. See COCHRAN
HEATH, MRS.   NC
   She supplied provisions for the army (RA, D:199).
HEATH, ETHEL   SC
   She provided provisions for the troops (SI, U-W:168, 174).
HEDDEN, HANNAH   NJ
   Orange. She suffered damages by the British (CDB, claim 8).
HEDDEN, SARAH CANFIELD   NJ
   Newark. She was the wife of Joseph Hedden, Jr., commissioner
   for the seizure and sale of forfeited estates for Royalists. He
   died on September 27, 1780, a victim of British cruelty (FP1).
HEDGEMAN, ELEANOR   NJ
   Somerville. Michael Hedgeman was executor of her estate and
   put in for damages caused by a British raid (CDB, p. 139).
HEDLEY, CATHARINE   NJ
   Morris County. She suffered damages caused by Americans
   (CDB, claim 57).
HEGERMAN, SARAH   PA
   At age fifty-four in October 1778 she was captured by Tories
   and Indians and taken to Quebec (HP).
HELM, LUCY NEVILLE. See CALMES
HEMPHILL, MARY ANN MACKEY   NC
   The British tried to take her sheep. See Biographies.
HENCH, CHRISTINA SCHNEIDER   PA
   The wife of John Hench, she is recognized as a patriot in the
   DAR Patriot Index.
HENDEE, HANNAH HUNTER   VT
   She rescued her son and other boys from the Indians. See
   Biographies.
HENDEN, LYDIA   NC
   She provided provisions for the troops (RA, 5:45, fol. 4).
HENDERSON, ELIZABETH CALLAWAY   NC
   She was born in 1760 and married Maj. Samuel Henderson. She
   is listed as a patriot in the DAR Patriot Index.
HENKLE, BARBARA   VA
   Hampshire County. She performed a public service (VR, 3:119).
HENLEY, NOWDINIA   VA
   Princess Anne County. Recognized for public service (VR,
   4:216).
HENLY, ELIZABETH   VA
   James City. Credited with public service (VR Court Booklet,
   p. 21).

III: COMPLETE LISTING

HENNING, ELEANOR   VA
   Culpeper. The wife of Samuel Henning, she died in 1782. She
   supplied provisions for the army (VR, 2:90; DAR).
HENRY, ELEANOR   NJ
   Middlebush, Somerville. She suffered damage caused by the
   British (CDB, p. 139).
HENRY, ELIZABETH   CT
   Danbury. She suffered losses in a British raid (CAR, 1:51b,
   63u). She was a Western Lands Grantee.
HENRY, JANE   VA
   Charlotte. She performed a public service (VR Court Booklet,
   p. 38).
HENRY, JOICE   VA
   Charlotte. She performed a public service (VR, 1:299).
HENRY, MARGARET   NC
   She provided provisions for the troops (RA, A:183).
HENRY, MARTHA   NC
   She supplied provisions for the army (RA, 9:98, fol. 2).
HENRYS, ELIZABETH   CT
   Danbury. In the British raid of April 1777 she suffered damage
   (CAR, 8:382a).
HEPBORN, ANN (NANCY) ROGERS   NJ
   Burlington. Daughter of Samuel Rogers of Bordentown, later of
   Morris County. She suffered damage in a British raid (CDB,
   p. 47).
HEPBURN, CRECY COVENHOVEN   PA
   She cared for the sick and wounded soldiers. See Biographies.
HERBERT, ELIZABETH   NJ
   Middlesex County. She suffered damage in a British raid (CDB,
   p. 175).
HERNDON, ROSANNAH   VA
   Goochland County. Recognized for public service (VR Lists,
   2:2).
HERRIMAN, SUSANNA   NJ
   Elizabeth. She suffered damage in a British raid (CDB, claim 1).
HERRING, MARY   NC
   She provided provisions for the troops (RA, A:143).
HERRIOT, RACHEL   NJ
   Amboy. She suffered losses in a British raid (Claim, p. 275).
HESTER, ANNE RAGLAND   VA
   Mecklenburg. The wife of Abraham Hester, she performed a
   public service (VR, 4:57).
HESTER, BARBARA   VA
   Mecklenburg. Credited with public service (VR, 4:58).
HEWES, DEBORAH   PA
   Gen. Washington had his headquarters there. See Biographies.
HEWITT, SUSANNA   VA
   Stafford County. Recognized for public service (VR, 5:190).
HEWLETT, MARY   VA
   Hanover County. She performed a public service (VR, 3:184).

HEWS, SARAH   CT
   Fairfield. She suffered damage in the British raids of 1779-
   1780 (CAR, 15:251d).
HEYWARD, ELIZABETH MATHEWES   SC
   She refused to light up her house when the British took Charles-
   ton in 1780. See Biographies.
HIATT, SARAH   VA
   Orange County. Recognized for public service (VR, 4:184).
HICKEY, MARY   VA
   Henry County. Credited with public service (VR, 3:140).
HICKMAN, ANN   VA
   King William County. She performed a public service (VR, 3:247).
HICKMAN, ELIZABETH   VA
   Frederick County. Recognized for public service (VR Ctf 1).
HICKOK, BETSY HURLBURT   CT
   She was born in 1769, married Noah Hickok, and died in 1850.
   She is recognized as a patriot in the DAR Patriot Index.
HICKS, ELIZABETH   NC
   She supplied provisions for the army (RA, C:133).
HICKS, JANE   SC
   She provided provisions for the troops (SI, L-N:325).
HICKS, MARY   VA
   Goochland County. She performed a public service (VR, 3:65).
HICKS, THANKFUL   NC
   She provided supplies for the troops (RA, 11:86, fol. 2).
HIERS, BARBARA MAGDALENE   SC
   She was born in 1711 and married Jacob Hiers, Sr. She is
   recognized as a patriot in the DAR Patriot Index 2.
HIGGINS, JUDITH   VA
   Berkeley County. Credited with public service (VR, 1:240).
HIGGINS, MRS. ROBERT H.   VA
   She was Mrs. Wright before she married Mr. Higgins, who was
   a lieutenant in the 8th Virginia Regiment. He was taken prisoner
   at the Battle of Germantown in October 1777. After his release
   in February 1782, he became a captain and later a major (FW;
   DAR).
HIGH, ABEY (ABBY)   NC
   The wife of Capt. Robert High, she provided provisions for
   the troops (RA, C:160).
HIGHTOWER, SUSANNA   VA
   Amelia County. Recognized for public service (VR, 1:88).
HILDRETH, DORCAS   NJ
   She was the wife of Jonathan Hildreth. Mrs. Hildreth was an
   active member of the ladies' association for the welfare of the
   soldiers (New Jersey Gazette, July 4, 1780; some information
   supplied by Hannah R. Swain, Cape May Court House, NJ).
HILDRETH, MARTHA   RI
   The wife of Samuel Hildreth, she supplied corn and cheese for
   the army (MP, 35:7).
HILL, MRS.   PA
   Philadelphia. She provided funds for the army (Pennsylvania
   Gazette, June 12, 1780).

III: COMPLETE LISTING 335

HILL, ANN NC
 She supplied provisions for the troops (RA, C:99).
HILL, BARBARA NC
 She supplied provisions for the army (RA, E-G:29).
HILL, BETTY VA
 Lancaster County. She performed a public service (VR, 2:90, 119).
HILL, ELIZABETH NC
 She provided provisions for the troops (RA, C:40).
HILL, ELIZABETH VA
 Lancaster County. Recognized for public service (VR, 3:273).
HILL, HANNAH SC
 She supplied provisions for the army (SI, B:221).
HILL, HANNAH GORTON RI
 At age eight she cared for wounded soldiers. See Biographies.
HILL, MRS. HENRY PA
 Gen. Washington had his headquarters there. See Biographies.
HILL, MARGARET NC
 She provided provisions for the troops (RA, 10:1, fol. 1).
HILL, MARGARET VA
 Greensville. She performed a public service (VR, 3:24). Also a Margaret Hill in Sussex County (VR, 5:207).
HILL, MARY NH
 Portsmouth. She was the wife of Capt. Elisha Hill. On August 4, 1778, Kinsman Peverly obtained a letter of marque to command the five-gun schooner Hero. Mary died on August 6, 1785, in Berwick, Maine, in her sixty-eighth year and was survived by twelve children and sixty-three grandchildren. She witnessed the Continental bond for Peverly. (Information from Richard E. Winslow III, Portsmouth, NH).
HILL, MARY SC
 She supplied provisions for the army (SI, U-W:153).
HILL, MILLY SC
 She provided supplies for the troops (SI, R-T:202).
HILL, REBECCA CUTTER. See CARTER
HILL, SUSANNA VA
 Prince Edward County, credited with public service (VR, 5:51).
HILL, VIOLET VA
 Henry County. She performed a public service (VR, 3:139, 141).
HILLEGAS, HENRIETTA BOUDE PA
 She was a member of the ladies' association for the welfare of the soldiers. See Biographies.
HILLHOUSE, WIDOW CT
 New Haven. She supplied a blanket for the army (CAR, 11:129).
HILLIARD, MARGARET NC
 She supplied provisions for the troops (RA, 1:12, fol. 2).
HILTON, AMY SC
 She provided supplies for the troops (SI, Y-Z:164).
HINCKLEY, SUSANNAH HEWES MA
 Boston. She married Thomas Hinckley, a private in the army,

who was captured by the British when Fort Washington fell to
the enemy on November 16, 1776 (FP1).
HINDS, HANNAH　　　　　　　　　NJ
Westfield. The wife of John Hinds, she suffered losses in a
British raid (CDB, claim 77).
HINKLE, BARBARA TETER　　　　VA
The daughter of Margaret Ludman and George Teter, she was
born in 1734 and married Jacob Hinkle (Henckle). After his
death she married David Harmon. Barbara is listed as a patriot
in the DAR Magazine, January 1988 (submitted by C. Pauline
Walters, Crawfordsville, IN).
HINMAN, ABIGAIL DOLBEAR　　　CT
New London. The daughter of George Dolbear, she was married
on March 1, 1777, to Capt. Elisha Hinman of the Continental
Navy. He commanded the ship *Alfred*; in March 1778 he was
captured by two British men-of-war and was confined in the
Fortun Prison at Gosport, England. On July 25, 1778, Hinman
escaped to France and then managed to return to America (CN).
HINMAN, JOANNA HURD　　　　　PA
Her husband was killed by Indians. See Biographies.
HINMAN, MABEL　　　　　　　　　CT
Woodbury. In 1780 she supplied cattle for the army (CAR,
35:96).
HITCH, SALLY　　　　　　　　　MD
In 1781 she supplied beef for the troops (IM, 18483).
HITCHCOCK, JANE　　　　　　　　CT
Norwalk. She suffered damage in a British raid (CAR, 1:63j,
98d). She was a Western Lands Grantee.
HITE, ELIZABETH ERICKSON　　　VA
She was the wife of Abraham Hite, Jr., captain of the 8th Virginia Regiment. On May 12, 1780, Capt. Hite was captured
by the British when Charleston, South Carolina, surrendered
to the enemy (FW).
HIZER, MARGARET　　　　　　　　PA
At age thirteen in April 1781 she was captured, along with her
brother, on the Monongahela River by Indians and finally released
from Fort Ticonderoga on July 18, 1783 (MR).
HOAGHLAND, FRANSEINTIE　　　NJ
Hackensack. The wife of Cornenius Hoaghland, she suffered
damages caused by the British (CDB, claim 3).
HOAGLAND, FIETJE. See DEDERICK
HOBBS, AMEY　　　　　　　　　VA
Prince George County. She performed a public service (VR,
4:252, 253).
HOBBS, LAMMA　　　　　　　　VA
Amelia County. Recognized for public service (VR Lists, 1:18).
HOBBY, LOIS　　　　　　　　　CT
Greenwich. In the British raid of 1780 she suffered losses (CAR,
19:80b).
HOBSON, JOANNA　　　　　　　VA
Cumberland County. Credited with public service (VR, 1:224).

III: COMPLETE LISTING 337

HOBSON, SARAH VA
  Cumberland County. The wife of John Hobson, she performed a public service (VR Ctf 1).
HOCKADAY, REBECCA VA
  New Kent County. Recognized for public service (VR Court Booklet, p. 9).
HODGE, ELEANOR VA
  Rockbridge County. Credited with public service (VR, 5:76).
HODGE, SARAH MA
  She witnessed twenty-three privateer bonds. See Biographies.
HODGES, LUCY VA
  Goochland County. Performed a public service (VR, 3:66).
HODGES, MARY VA
  Norfolk. Recognized for public service (VR, 4:143).
HODGES, REBECCA SC
  She provided provisions for the troops (SI, L-N:324).
HODGSON, PENELOPE PAGETT. See BARKER
HODGSON, SARAH NJ
  Middlesex County. The widow of Daniel Noe, she suffered losses in a British raid (CDB, p. 78).
HODNETT, MARY McGHEE VA
  Pittsylvania County. The wife of Ayres Hodnett, she performed a public service (VR, 5:113).
HODSDEN, MARY SC
  She supplied provisions for the army (SI, B:97).
HOFF (HUFF), ELIZABETH VA
  Brunswick County. Recognized for public service (VR, 1:114).
HOFF, SARAH WV
  Hampshire County. Credited with public service (VR Court Booklet, p. 22).
HOFFMAN, CATHERINE SC
  She supplied provisions for the army (SI, 1:76).
HOGAN, HANNAH NC
  She provided provisions for the troops (RA, 12:8, fol. 2).
HOGG, MILDRED VA
  Gloucester County. She performed a public service (VR Court Booklet, 2:26).
HOGSHEAD, ANN VA
  Augusta County. Recognized for public service (VR Ctf 1).
HOLBROOK, EDITH VA
  Goochland County. Credited with public service (VR, 3:65).
HOLBROOK, RUTH CT
  Pomfret. She supplied a blanket for the army (CAR, 3:448a).
HOLCOMB, LUCY LITTLEBURY SC
  She furnished a horse for the soldiers. See Biographies.
HOLCOMBE, MARY HARVEY NJ
  Gen. Washington had his headquarters there. See Biographies.
HOLDEN, ANN VA
  Accomack County. Recognized for public service (VR, 1:25).
HOLDEN, ROSE RI
  She supplied provisions for the army (MP, 57:3).

HOLDSWORTH, REBECCA VA
  Surry County. She performed a public service (VR, 5:167).
HOLIDAY, RUTH CT
  Groton. She suffered damages in a British raid (CAR, 1:63q, 79b). She was a Western Lands Grantee.
HOLLADAY, MRS. VA
  Spotsylvania County. Credited with public service (VR Court Booklet, p. 20).
HOLLADAY, ANNE VA
  Hansemond County. Performed a public service (VR, 4"158, 159).
HOLLADAY, MILDRED VA
  Spotsylvania County. Recognized for public service (VR, 4:261).
HOLLAND, ESTHER VA
  Hansemond County. Performed a public service (VR, 4:159).
HOLLEY, LOIS CT
  Greenwich widow. In the British raid of March 1779 she suffered damage (CAR, 36:19c).
HOLLIMAN, ANN VA
  Southampton County. Recognized for public service (VR, 5:181).
HOLLIS, ELIZABETH VA
  New Kent County. Credited with public service (VR Court Booklet, p. 7).
HOLLOWAY, BETTY VA
  Caroline County. She performed a public service (VR Ctf 1).
HOLLOWAY, ELIZABETH CAMMACK VA
  Caroline County. The wife of George Holloway, she died in 1783. She performed a public service (VR Court Booklet, 2:14; DAR).
HOLLOWAY, MARTHA NC
  She supplied provisions for the troops (RA, 12:74, fol. 4).
HOLLOWAY, MARY NC
  She supplied provisions for the army (RA, A:184).
HOLMAN, JANE VA
  Powhatan County. Recognized for public service (VR Lists, p. 11).
HOLMAN, LUCY VA
  Mecklenburg. She performed a public service (VR, 4:59).
HOLMAN (HALLMAN), MARY ANN SC
  Lexington County. In 1752 she married Conrad Holman of Orangeburg County. They moved to Lexington County where he operated a tavern and a grain mill. During the war she supplied corn and other grain for the troops. They had one daughter and two sons, and changed the name to Hallman. She died in 1784 (submitted by Mary Frances Hallman Hilton, Alamo, TX).
HOLMEN, ELIZABETH VA
  Prince William County. Recognized for public service (VR, 4:199).
HOLMES, FRANCES NC
  She supplied provisions for the troops (RA, 19:154).
HOLT, ABIGAIL (NABBY) CT
  New London. She suffered damage in a British raid (CAR, 1:63h, 95a). She was a Western Lands Grantee.

III: COMPLETE LISTING

HOLT, CATHERINE   NC
 She provided provisions for the army (RA, 4:86, fol. 5).

HOLT, KATHERINE   NC
 She supplied provisions for the troops (RA, B:135).

HOLT, MARTHA   CT
 In the British raid of September 1781, the enemy killed her husband, John Holt (CAR, 23:180cd, 181).

HOLTZCLAW, CATHERINE JAMES   VA
 Fauquier County. The wife of Joseph Holtzclaw, she performed a public service (VR Lists, p. 1).

HONEYMAN, MARY HENRY   NJ
 Her husband was a spy for Gen. Washington but was considered a traitor by the neighbors. See Biographies.

HOOD, ELIZABETH   VA
 Sussex County. Recognized for public service (VR Ctf 1).

HOOD, MARY KIMBALL   MA
 Topsfield. She was the wife of John Hood, who was a mariner on a privateer and captured. He was taken to Halifax, Nova Scotia, and from there to the Mill Prison, Plymouth, England. On November 21, 1781, he attempted to escape but was recaptured (FP1).

HOOKER, HANNAH   CT
 Norwalk. In a British raid she suffered damages (CAR, 1:63i, 98b, 100b). She was a Western Lands Grantee.

HOOKER, MARTHA   GA
 She supplied cattle for public use (WA, p. 136).

HOOKER, SARAH WHITMAN   CT
 She supplied a blanket for the army. See Biographies.

HOOP, MARY   VA
 Shenandoah County. She performed a public service (VR Court Booklet, p. 11).

HOOP, WIDOW   VA
 Shenandoah. Recognized for public service (VR, 5:157).

HOOPER, ANNE CLARK   NC
 Her home was destroyed by the British. See Biographies.

HOOPER, ELIZABETH   VA
 Hanover County. Recognized for public service (VR, 3:181, 183).

HOOPER, HANNAH   CT
 New Haven. In the British raid of 1779 she suffered losses (CAR, 15:269e).

HOOPS, MRS. ROBERT   NJ
 She was a member of the ladies' association for the welfare of the soldiers. See Biographies.

HOPE, ANN   VA
 Accomack County. She performed a public service (VR, 1:25).

HOPE, SARAH DURHAM   NJ
 She was born in 1741, married Adam Hope, and died in 1826. Recognized as a patriot in the DAR Patriot Index.

HOPKINS, ELIZABETH   VA
 Louisa County. Credited with public service (VR, 3:353).

HOPKINS, JAMIMA VT
  Bennington. She advanced funds to Connecticut during the Revolutionary War (CAR, 36:279).
HOPKINS, MARY CT
  Windsor. In 1777 she supplied a blanket for the army (CAR, 11:59a).
HOPKINS, SARAH SC
  She provided provisions for the troops (SI, O-Q:285).
HOPKINS, SARAH VA
  Princess Anne County. She performed a public service (VR, 4:215).
HOPKINSON, ANN BORDEN NJ
  Her home was plundered by the enemy. See Biographies.
HOPPER, MRS. ANDREW NJ
  Gen. Washington had his headquarters there. See Biographies.
HOPPER, ELIZABETH NC
  She supplied provisions for the troops (RA, C:114).
HOPSON, MONACA NC
  She provided provisions for the army (RA, B:295).
HORD, MRS. VA
  Caroline County. Recognized for public service (Lists, 2:28, 31).
HORD, LUCY VA
  Caroline County. Credited with public service (VR, 1:252).
HORN, ELIZABETH NC
  She provided provisions for the troops (RA, C:139).
HORN, LEAH NJ
  Hillsborough, Somerville. She suffered losses by the British (CDB, p. 77).
HORNBACK, MARY WV
  Hampshire County. She performed a public service (VR Court Booklet, p. 16).
HORNBLOWER, ELIZABETH KINGSLAND NJ
  She was a member of the ladies' association for the welfare of the soldiers. See Biographies.
HORNIBLOW, ANNE NC
  She refused to drink British tea. See Background.
HOROUGH, MARGARET NC
  She supplied provisions for the troops (RA, B:191).
HORTON, MRS. VA
  Stafford County. Recognized for public service (VR Court Booklet, 2:3).
HORTON, MARY CT
  New Haven. In the British raid of July 1779 she suffered damage (CAR, 15:234a, 269d). She was a Western Lands Grantee.
HORTON, SARAH NC
  She supplied provisions for the troops (RA, C:116).
HOSKINS, DOLLY VA
  Halifax County. She performed a public service (VR, 2:276).
HOSKINS, DOROTHY VA
  Halifax County. She is credited for public service (VR Court Booklet, p. 49).

III: COMPLETE LISTING

HOSKINS, WINIFRED WIGGINS   NC
   The wife of Richard Hoskins, she died in 1807. She is listed
   as a patriot in the DAR Patriot Index.
HOTCHKISS, ABIGAIL   CT
   She made bags for the army in 1780 (CAR, 35:112a).
HOTCHKISS, HANNAH   CT
   New Haven. In the British raid of 1777 she suffered damage
   (CAR, 15:269b). She was a Western Lands Grantee.
HOTCHKISS, SUSANNAH JONES   CT
   New Haven. She was the wife of John Hotchkiss, who was killed
   on July 5, 1779, during the New Haven alarm (FP1; CAR, 15:269e).
   She was a Western Lands Grantee.
HOTCHKISS, TAMAR RICHARDSON   CT
   She prepared meals for the soldiers. See Biographies.
HOUGH (HUFF), MARY   VA
   Henry County. She performed a public service (VR, 3:141).
HOUGHTON, ANNE   NC
   She refused to drink British tea. See Background.
HOUSE, ELIZABETH   NY
   At age twenty-four she was captured by Indians, along with
   her infant son, and sent to the Saint Lawrence suburbs. She
   was still there in July 1782 (MR).
HOUSE, MARY   CT
   She boarded Jesse Root, a member of the Continental Congress
   in 1779 (CAR, 33:276, 279).
HOUSE, MARY   VA
   Brunswick County. Recognized for public service (VR, 1:214).
HOUSTON, MARGARET WEIR   VA
   She married George Houston, then George Gibson, and died
   in 1800. She is listed as a patriot in the DAR Patriot Index.
HOVEY, LYDIA   CT
   Windham. She took care of a soldier (CAR, 10:381-382).
HOWARD, ANNE MYERS   PA
   She warned of an impending Tory attack. See Biographies.
HOWARD, ELIZABETH   NJ
   Morris County. She suffered damage caused by the Americans
   (CDB, claim 150).
HOWARD, JANE   VA
   Buckingham County. Recognized for public service (VR, 1:202;
   2:166).
HOWARD, JANE   VA
   Powhatan County. Credited with public service (VR Lists, pp.
   11, 16).
HOWARD, MARTHA   VA
   York County. The wife of Henry Howard, she performed a
   public service (VR Ctf 1).
HOWCUTT, SARAH   NC
   She refused to drink British tea. See Background.
HOWE, HANNAH   CT
   New Haven. In the British raid of 1779 she suffered damages
   (CAR, 15:269a). She was a Western Lands Grantee.

HOWE, JANE DUNLAP — SC
   She was born in 1743, married John Howe, and died in 1804. She supplied provisions for the army (SI, U-W:153).

HOWE, SARAH — CT
   New Haven. In the British raid of 1779 she suffered losses (CAR, 15:269c). She was a Western Lands Grantee.

HOWE, SARAH — NC
   She refused to drink British tea. See Background.

HOWELL, ELIZABETH — VA
   Southampton County. She performed a public service (VR, 5:176).

HOWELL, KEZIAH BURR — NJ
   Her husband was a spy for Gen. Washington and was accused of being a Tory. See Biographies.

HOWELL, MARGARET — VA
   Loudoun County. The wife of Hugh Howell, she was recognized for public service (VR, 3:300).

HOWELL, MARTHA EPPES — SC
   She provided provisions for the troops (SI, Y-Z:177; O-Q:228; U-W:69).

HOWELL, MARY — MA
   Marblehead. On March 29, 1782, Benjamin Ashton obtained a letter of marque to command the schooner *Montgomery* with four guns and fifteen men. Witnesses to the bond included John Howell and Mary Howell (CN).

HOWELL, MARY — MD
   Charles County. In 1782 she provided wheat for the army (IM, 20366).

HOWELL, MARY — NJ
   Hunterdon County. Mother of Arthur Howell, she suffered damages caused by the Americans (CDB, claim 43).

HOWELL, REBECCA — VA
   Hansemond County. She performed a public service (VR, 4:157, 159).

HOWELL, WIDOW — VA
   Hansemond County. Recognized for public service (VR Court Booklet, 1:18).

HOWLAND, LYDIA — CT
   Norwich. On May 27, 1772, she married Joseph Howland. On July 3, 1782, William Waters obtained a letter of marque to command the brigantine *Thetis* with six guns and twenty men. Lydia Howland witnessed the bond (CN).

HOWLET, HANNA — VA
   Gloucester County. Credited with public service (VR, 3:45).

HOWLETT, JOHANNA — VA
   Gloucester County. She performed a public service (VR Court Booklet, 2:25).

HOWSON, ANN — NC
   She supplied provisions for the army (RA, B:198).

HOYLAND, ANNA M. — SC
   She provided provisions for the troops (SI, B:102).

III: COMPLETE LISTING 343

HOYLES, ELIZABETH   VA
   King George County. Recognized for public service (VR Lists, pp. 6, 14).
HOYT, MARY   CT
   Danbury. Her husband joined the British army but she remained loyal to the American cause (CAR, 8:148, 156).
HOYT, RUTH   NC
   She supplied provisions for the army (RA, A:215).
HOYT, SARAH   CT
   Greenwich. In the British raids of March 1779 and December 1783 she suffered damage (CAR, 36:19a, I-63d, 74c). She was a Western Lands Grantee.
HUBBARD, ABIGAIL   SC
   She supplied provisions for the army (SI, R-T:200).
HUBBARD, EUNICE   CT
   Windham. She supplied a blanket for the army (CAR, 3:451b).
HUBBARD, LUCY STEARNS   MA
   She was born in 1727 and married Elisha Hubbard. She is listed as a patriot in the DAR Patriot Index.
HUBBARD, MRS. MANOAH   SC
   She supplied provisions for the troops (SI, L-N:322).
HUBBARD, MARY   CT
   New Haven. She suffered damage in the British raid of July 1779 (CAR, 15:234d, 269a). She was a Western Lands Grantee.
HUBBARD, SARAH   VA
   Halifax County. She performed a public service (VR, 308).
HUBBELL, ABIGAIL   CT
   Fairfield. In the British raids of 1779-1780 she suffered losses (CAR, 15:250e, 251a). She was a Western Lands Grantee.
HUDDY, MARY   NJ
   Her husband was hanged by the British. See Biographies.
HUDSON, JANE   VA
   Amelia County. Recognized for public service (VR, 1:61, 63).
HUDSON, MARY   NC
   She supplied provisions for the troops (RA, 4:56, fol. 1).
HUDSON, NANCY   NC
   She supplied provisions for the army (RA, 12:18, fol. 4).
HUDSON, SUSANNAH   VA
   Prince Edward County. Credited with public service (VR, 5:50).
HUFF, MARY   VA
   Brunswick County. Recognized for public service (VR, 1:114).
HUGDEN, ELIZABETH   VA
   Gloucester County. She performed a public service (VR Ctf 1).
HUGER, MARTHA   SC
   She provided provisions for the army (SI, B:193).
HUGER, MARY ESTHER KINLOCH   SC
   Lafayette and the Baron de Kalb spent the night at her home. See Biographies.
HUGG, MRS.   NJ
   Gloucester County. The wife of Col. Hugg, she was a member

of the ladies' association for the welfare of the soldiers (New Jersey Gazette, July 4, 1780).

HUGGINS, ANN   VA
Gloucester County. Recognized for public service (VR Court Booklet, 2:10).

HUGGINS, MARY   SC
She provided provisions for the troops (SI, O-Q:106).

HUGGINS, SARAH   VA
Princess Ann County. Credited with public service (VR, 4:216).

HUGHES, ABIGAIL   CT
New Haven. In the British raid of July 1779 she suffered losses (CAR, 15:234g, 269d).

HUGHES, ANN   VA
Powhatan County. Recognized for public service (VR, 4:235).

HUGHES, ELIZABETH   VA
Mecklenburg. Credited with public service (VR, 4:57).

HUGHES, HANNAH HOLSTEIN   PA
Gen. Washington had his headquarters here. See Biographies.

HUGHES, MAGDALANE   NJ
Burlington. The widow of Capt. Charles P. Hughes, she suffered damage caused by the British (CDB, p. 155).

HUGHES, MARTHA   VA
Goochland County. Recognized for public service (VR, 3:65).

HUGHES, MARTHA   VA
Powhatan County. She performed a public service (VR, 4:235).

HUGHES, PATTY   NJ
Burlington. She suffered damages by the British (CDB, p. 155).

HUGHES, SARAH   CT
Fairfield. She suffered damages in a British raid (CAR, 1:53e, 63g). She was a Western Lands Grantee.

HULIN, SARAH   NC
She supplied provisions for the troops (RA, A:196).

HULL, ANN   CT
Fairfield. In the British raid of 1780 she suffered losses (CAR, 19:73a).

HULL, ANNA   CT
Fairfield. In the British raid of July 1779 she suffered damage (CAR, 15:251a). She was a Western Lands Grantee.

HULL, SARAH   NC
She supplied provisions for the troops (RA, 5:48, fol. 4).

HULSE, ELIZABETH   WV
Berkeley County. With Samuel John Hulse, she performed a public service (VR Ctf 1).

HUMASTON, ABI BLACKESLEE   CT
She chopped up some flannel and turnips and made fake sausages, which she fed to the Tories. See Biographies.

HUMASTON, HANNA   CT
New Haven. In 1777 she supplied a blanket for the army (CAR, 110:142).

HUME, FRANCES SUSANNA QUASH. See PINCKNEY

III: COMPLETE LISTING

HUMPHREY, PHOEBE CT
  She put a Hessian soldier to flight with her bread shovel. See Biographies.
HUMPHREYS, SARAH RIGGS CT
  Four of her sons served in the Revolutionary War. See Biographies.
HUMPHRIES, REBECCAH NC
  She supplied provisions for the troops (RA, 6:20, fol. 5).
HUNDLEY, ANN VA
  Essex County. Credited with public service (VR Court Booklet, p. 1).
HUNDLEY, JANE VA
  Hanover County. She performed a public service (VR, 3:181).
HUNGERFORD, ANN VA
  Westmoreland County. Recognized for public service (VR, 5:220).
HUNT, ANNE VA
  Bedford County. She performed a public service (VR Court Booklet, p. 10).
HUNT, ELEANOR NC
  She provided provisions for the troops (RA, 11:61, fol. 2).
HUNT, MRS. JOHN NJ
  Gen. Washington had his headquarters there. See Biographies.
HUNT, MARY DAGWORTHY NJ
  She was secretary of the ladies' association for the welfare of the soldiers. See Biographies.
HUNT, SARAH CT
  New Haven. In the British raid of July 1779 she suffered damage (CAR, 15:234q, 269b). She was a Western Lands Grantee.
HUNTER, AGNES NC
  She provided provisions for the army (RA, A:170).
HUNTER, ANN LEVIS PA
  She was the wife of Capt. John Hunter, who was captured by the enemy at Fort Montgomery, New Jersey, in October 1777 (FW; DAR).
HUNTER, ELIZA NC
  She supplied provisions for the army (RA, C:129).
HUNTER, ELIZABETH VA
  Fairfax County. Recognized for public service (VR Court Booklet, p. 2).
HUNTER, ELIZABETH VA
  Princess Anne County. She performed a public service (VR, 4:216-217).
HUNTER, EUNICE MD
  She supplied wheat, 1782-1783, for the army (IM, 24628).
HUNTER, MARGARET NC
  She provided provisions for the army (RA, C:57).
HUNTER, MARGARET VA
  James City. Recognized for public service (VR Court Booklet, p. 6).
HUNTER, MARY VA
  Gloucester County. Credited with public service (VR, 3:44).

HUNTINGDON, SELINA SHIRLEY, COUNTESS OF   SC
   She supplied provisions for the American troops. See Biographies.
HUNTINGTON, EUNICE   CT
   Norwich. In 1746 she married Jonathan Huntington. On November 27, 1779, Nicoll Fosdick obtained a letter of marque to command the brigantine Defiance with ten guns and sixty men. Eunice witnessed the bond. She also witnessed a bond on October 10, 1780, for Samuel Smedley (CN).
HUNTINGTON, FAITH TRUMBULL   CT
   She nursed wounded American soldiers. See Biographies.
HUNTINGTON, SUSAN KENT   CT
   She was the wife of Hezekiah Huntington who was captured by the enemy and confined on the prison ship Jersey in New York Harbor. This vessel was loaded with prisoners stricken with smallpox (FP2).
HUNTINGTON, WIDOW   CT
   Windham. She supplied a blanket for the army in 1777 (CAR, 11:102a).
HUPP, ANN HOWE   PA
   She was born in 1757, married John Hupp, Sr., and died in 1823. She is listed as a patriot in the DAR Patriot Index.
HURD, MARY RUSSELL   MA
   She married first Isaac Foster, then Col. John Hurd. She is listed as a patriot in the DAR Patriot Index.
HURLBURT, HANNAH   CT
   Groton. She suffered losses in a British raid (CAR, 27:333a). She was a Western Lands Grantee.
HURLBURT, MARY   CT
   New London. She suffered damage in a British raid (CAR, 1:63h, 95c). She was a Western Lands Grantee.
HURT, ANNE   VA
   Caroline County. She performed a public service (VR, 1:252).
HUSSEY, MARY JESSUP   NC
   She was born in 1740 and married John Hussey. Credited with public service (RA, 12:19, fol. 2; DAR).
HUTCHINGS, ANNEY   VA
   Pittsylvania County. Recognized for public service (VR, 5:113).
HUTCHINGS, ELIZABETH   VA
   Southampton County. Credited with public service (VR, 5:177).
HUTCHINSON, LETITA WRIGHT   NC
   The wife of John Hutchinson, she is listed as a patriot in the DAR Patriot Index.
HUTCHINSON, LYDIA BIDDLE   PA
   She was a member of the ladies' association for the welfare of the soldiers. See Biographies.
HUTTO, ANN   SC
   The wife of Charles Hutto, she performed a public service (SI, I:76; DAR).
HUYLER, EVA   NJ
   Hackensack. She suffered damages in a British raid (CDB, claim 70).

III: COMPLETE LISTING 347

HUYLER, MARY NJ
  Hackensack. She suffered losses in a British raid (CDB, claim 70).

HYDE, ABIGAIL CT
  Hartford. On April 17, 1782, Gideon Olmstead obtained a letter of marque to command the General Greene with sixteen guns and a hundred men. Witnesses to the bond were John Trumbull and Abigail Hyde (CN).

HYDE, MARTHA NJ
  Kingston, Somerville. She suffered damages in a British raid (CDB, p. 189).

HYDE, MARTHA NJ
  Middlesex County. She suffered losses in a British raid (CDB, p. 230).

HYERS, SARAH MA
  Newburyport. On August 1, 1780, George Thompson obtained a letter of marque to command the schooner Iris Gimblet with four guns and twenty-five men. Sarah Hodge and Sarah Hyers witnessed the bond (CN).

HYLER, CATHY NJ
  Morris County. The wife of Nicholas Hyler, she suffered damages caused by the Americans (CDB, claim 77).

HYLTON, MRS. DANIEL VA
  Thomas Jefferson spent the night with the Hyltons. See Biographies.

HYRNE (HEARN), SARAH ANN SC
  She supplied provisions for the army (SI, Y-Z:53, 168).

HYSLOP, ANNE VA
  Northampton County. She performed a public service (VR Court Booklet, p. 13).

I

IGLE, HANNAH GA
  She supplied leather and corn for the troops (WA, p. 110).

INABNET, MARGARET NEGLY SC
  The wife of John Inabnet, she provided provisions for the troops (SI, R-T:211). She is listed in the DAR Patriot Index 3.

INGERSOL, ELIZABETH CT
  Greenwich. In the British raids of March 1779 and December 1783, she suffered damages (CAR, 15:271b). She was a Western Lands Grantee.

INGERSOL, MERCY CT
  She advanced funds for the army in 1779 (CAR, 16:376b).

INGERSOLL, ANNE CT
  Greenwich. In a British raid she suffered damage (CAR, 1:63a, 74c). She was a Western Lands Grantee.

INGLE, RACHEL VA
  Buckingham County. She performed a public service (VR, 1:202).

INGRAHAM, MARY   CT
  Stonington. She provided supplies for the army, 1777-1781 (CAR, 30:1b, 5b).
INGRAM, FRANCES   VA
  Shenandoah County. Recognized for public service (VR Court Booklet, p. 1).
INMAN, SARAH   RI
  The wife of Elisha Inman, she supplied a cow and pork for the army (MP, 35:2).
INNES, CATHERINE   NY
  At age eighteen, she was captured by Indians on July 11, 1780, and taken to Quebec (MR).
INSLEE, GRACE MOORE   NJ
  Woodbridge. The wife of Jonathan Inslee, she suffered damages caused by the British (CDB, p. 93).
IRBY, ANN   VA
  Amelia County. Recognized for public service (VR, 1:66).
IREDELL, HANNAH JOHNSTON   NC
  She cared for William Hopper, a signer of the Declaration of Independence, when he fled from the British army. See Biographies.
IRVIN, JENNET BREWSTER   VA
  She sewed, spun, knitted, wove, cooked meals, and made bullets for the soldiers. See Biographies.
IRVINE, ANNE CALLENDER   PA
  During her husband's army duty she ran the flour mill to supply the army. See Biographies.
IRVINE, SARAH HAINES   PA
  She spun and made clothing for the soldiers. See Biographies.
ISRAEL, HANNAH ERWIN   DE
  Despite musket shots by the British, she drove her cattle home. See Biographies.
IVERSON, LUCY   VA
  King and Queen County. Recognized for public service (VR, 3:225).
IVES, MABEL   CT
  New Haven. She supplied a blanket for the army (CAR, 11:131).
IZARD, MRS. CHARLOTTE   SC
  She supplied provisions for the troops (SI, B:108).

J

JACK, ISABEL   NJ
  Burlington. She suffered damage by the British (CDB, claim 251).
JACK, MARY. See ANN SPRATT BARNETT
JACKSON, AMEY   VA
  Amelia County. She performed a public service (VR, 1:66).
JACKSON, AMY   SC
  She supplied provisions for the army (SI, X, pt. 2:134).

III: COMPLETE LISTING

JACKSON, ANN   VA
Culpeper County. Recognized for public service (VR, 2:94).
JACKSON, ANNE   VA
York County. Credited with public service (VR Lists, p. 3).
JACKSON, ELIZABETH CUMMINS   VA
She was born in 1724, married John Jackson, and died in 1825. She is listed as a patriot in the DAR Patriot Index.
JACKSON, ELIZABETH HUTCHINSON   SC
She brought food and clothing to the soldiers on board a prison ship. See Biographies.
JACKSON, FRANCES   VA
Sussex County. She performed a public service (VR Ctf 1).
JACKSON, MARY   NJ
Middlesex. The wife of Charles Jackson, she suffered damages by the British (CDB, pp. 45, 210).
JACKSON, MARY   VA
Dinwiddie County. Recognized for public service (VR, 1:333).
JACKSON, RACHEL DONELSON   TN
At age fourteen, she assisted in defending Fort Nashborough. See Biographies.
JACKSON, SARAH   MD
Talbot County. In 1781 she supplied wheat for the army (IM, 18896).
JACOBS, ELIZABETH   MD
Frederick County. In 1781 she supplied wheat for the army (IM, 18960).
JACOBS, MARY ANN   NC
She provided provisions for the troops (RA, 1:76, fol. 4).
JACQUELIN, MARTHA   VA
Listed as a patriot (VR).
JACQUES, MARY   CT
Stonington. In 1777 she provided supplies for the army (CAR, 30:125b).
JAMES, MRS. AMERICA   SC
She supplied provisions for the army (SI, L-N).
JAMES, ANN   VA
King and Queen County. Recognized for public service (VR, 3:225).
JAMES, CATHERINE "CATY"   VA
Fauquier County. In 1780 she supplied brandy for the militia (County Ctf; submitted by H. Lee Capps, Jefferson City, MO).
JAMES, DINAH   VA
Fauquier County. Credited with public service (VR, 2:241).
JAMES, ELIZABETH   VA
Princess Anne County. She performed a public service (VR, 4:218). Also Lancaster County (VR Court Booklet, p. 15).
JAMES, ELIZABETH, JR.   VA
Lancaster County. Recognized for public service (VR Court Booklet, p. 16).
JAMES, ELIZABETH ANN   SC
She supplied provisions for the army (SI, B:103).

JAMES, NANCY   VA
    King and Queen County. Recognized for public service (VR
    Court Booklet, p. 13).
JAMES, SARAH   NJ
    Burlington. She suffered damage in a British raid (CDB, p.
    166).
JAMES, SARAH   VA
    Lancaster County. Recognized for public service (VR Court
    Booklet, p. 16).
JAMES, SARAH MOORE   SC
    She was born in 1747 and married John James. She supplied
    provisions for the army (SI, L-N:328). After her husband
    died, she married Reuben Long (DAR).
JAMESON, MARY CANTY. See SUMTER
JARRELL, ELIZABETH   NC
    She supplied provisions for the troops (RA, D:51).
JARRELL, MARY   VA
    Southampton County. Recognized for public service (VR, 5:178).
JARRETT, MARY   VA
    Sussex County. She performed a public service (VR, 5:202).
JARVIS, BETTY   CT
    Norwalk. She suffered damage in a British raid (CAR, 1:63m,
    98j, 100d). She was a Western Lands Grantee.
JARVIS, MARY   CT
    Norwalk. She suffered losses in the 1780 British raid (CAR,
    19:76b, 78b).
JAY, SARAH. See LIVINGSTON
JEFFERSON, MARTHA WAYLES   VA
    The British plundered the Jefferson's plantation. See Biographies.
JEFFERSON, PATSY. See ELIZABETH TRIST
JEFFORDS, ANN TOWNSEND   SC
    She married private John Jeffords, Jr., then Dr. Thomas Ken-
    nedy, then Duncan Littlefield, and died in 1796. She is listed
    as a patriot in the DAR Patriot Index.
JEFFREYS, JEMIMA   NJ
    Springfield. She suffered damage in a British raid (CDB, claim
    27).
JENCKES, HANNAH   RI
    In 1778 she provided food supplies for the army (MP, 40:23).
JENKINS, MISS   PA
    Philadelphia. She was a member of the ladies' association for
    the welfare of the soldiers (Pennsylvania Gazette, June 12, 1780).
JENKINS, BETHIA HARRIS   PA
    She took money and food to the American prisoners. See
    Biographies.
JENKINS, ELIZABETH BRITTON   SC
    She was born in 1741 and married William Goddard, then Samuel
    Jenkins, Sr. She is listed as a patriot in the DAR Patriot
    Index.3.
JENKINS, MARTHA   VA
    Monongalia County. Recognized for public service (VR Court
    Booklet, p. 24).

III: COMPLETE LISTING 351

JENKINS, PHOEBE SC
   She supplied provisions for the troops (SI, O-Q:3).
JENNINGS, ABIGAIL CT
   Fairfield. In the British raids of 1779-1780 she suffered losses
   (CAR, 15:250g, 251c). She was a Western Lands Grantee.
JENNINGS, HANNAH WILLIAMS VA
   Fauquier County. The wife of Augustine Jennings, she is listed
   for public service (VR, 2:241).
JENNINGS, MARTHA CT
   Fairfield. In the British raids of 1779-1780 she suffered damage
   (CAR, 15:250i, 251d). She was a Western Lands Grantee.
JENNINGS, REBECCA CT
   Fairfield. In the 1779-1780 British raids she suffered losses
   (CAR, 15:250f, 251b). She was a Western Lands Grantee.
JENNINGS, WIDOW CT
   She spun clothes for the soldiers in 1777 (CAR, 35:234cd).
JESPER, CATHARINE VA
   Richmond County. She performed a public service (VR, 5:98).
JETER, WINIFRED VA
   Amelia County. Recognized for public service (VR, 1:67, 93;
   2:354).
JEWEL, RACHEL NJ
   Connecticut Farms, Essex County. She suffered damages in
   a British raid (CDB, claim 56).
JEWETT, LUCRETIA ROGERS CT
   Lyme. She was the wife of Capt. Joseph Jewett of Col. Hunt-
   ington's regiment. After his troops surrendered at the Battle
   of Long Island, Capt. Jewett gave up his sword, but then was
   cut down by several bayonet thrusts into his body. He lingered
   on for a few days and died on August 29, 1776 (FP1).
JILES, VIRGINIA NC
   She supplied provisions for the army (RA, A:173).
JOB, SARAH NJ
   Middlesex County. The wife of Joel Job, she suffered losses
   in a British raid (CDB, p. 240).
JOHNS, LUCY VA
   Charlotte. She performed a public service (VR Court Booklet,
   p. 30). She was the wife of John Johns.
JOHNS, MARY VA
   Amherst County. Credited with public service (VR, 1:5). Also
   Caroline County (VR, 1:252).
JOHNSON, ANN ROBERTSON TN
   She poured hot water on the Indians climbing the stockade.
   See Biographies.
JOHNSON, CHARITY VA
   Southampton County. Recognized for public service (VR, 5:178).
JOHNSON, DORTHEA VA
   Louisa County. Credited with public service (VR Lists, 1:13).
JOHNSON, ELIZABETH VA
   Culpeper County. She performed a public service (VR Ctf 2).
   Also Louisa County (VR Lists, 1:6).

JOHNSON, ELIZABETH CRAIG   KY
    She went for water when the Indians attacked Bryan's Station.
    See Biographies.
JOHNSON, ELSA AUTEN   NJ
    Somerville. The sister of Aaron Auten, she suffered damages
    when the British attacked (CDB, p. 123).
JOHNSON, EVE   WV
    Botetourt County. Recognized for public service (VR Court
    Booklet, p. 27).
JOHNSON, MRS. GRISSETT   SC
    She supplied provisions for the troops (SI, L-N:330).
JOHNSON, JANE FALCONER   KY
    She was one of the women who went for water when the Indians
    attacked. See Biographies.
JOHNSON, JEMIMA SUGGETT   KY
    She led the women to obtain water when the Indians attacked
    Bryan's Station. See Biographies.
JOHNSON, LUCY   VA
    Louisa County. She performed a public service (VR Court Book-
    let, p. 40).
JOHNSON, LYDIA   CT
    New Haven. In the British raid of July 1779 she suffered damage
    (CAR, 15:269q). She was a Western Lands Grantee.
JOHNSON, MABEL   CT
    New Haven. She suffered losses in the British raid of July
    1779 (CAR, 15:234f, 269a). She was a Western Lands Grantee.
JOHNSON, MARY   VA
    Mecklenburg. She performed a public service (VR, 4:63).
JOHNSON, MARY CHARLTON. See SULLIVAN
JOHNSON, MARY WHITMORE   CT
    Middletown. The wife of Col. Jonathan Johnson, in 1777 she
    made clothing for the soldiers (CG).
JOHNSON, PRISCILLA   CT
    Woodstock. She supplied a blanket for the army (CAR, 3:453b).
JOHNSON, SARAH   CT
    Norwalk. She suffered damages in a British raid (CAR, 1:63j,
    98d, 100c). She was a Western Lands Grantee.
JOHNSON, SARAH NIGHTINGALE   SC
    She was born in 1751, married William Johnson, and died in 1825.
    She is listed as a patriot in the DAR Patriot Index.
JOHNSTON, ABIGAIL   NJ
    Newark. The wife of John Johnston, she suffered damages
    in a British raid (CDB, claim 8).
JOHNSTON, ALICE ERWIN   PA
    She gathered supplies for the troops at Valley Forge. See
    Biographies.
JOHNSTON, ANN ROBERTSON. See COCKRILL
JOHNSTON, EASTHER   NC
    She supplied provisions for the troops (RA, 10:4, fol. 4).
JOHNSTON, HEPSIBATH TYLER   VT
    She is credited with patriotic service. See Biographies.

III: COMPLETE LISTING

JOHNSTON, LYDIA CT
  New London. She suffered damage in a British raid (CAR, 1:95d).
JOHNSTON, MARTHA SC
  She provided provisions for the troops (SI, Y-Z:122).
JOHNSTON, MOLLY VA
  Frederick County. She performed a public service (VR Ctf 1).
JOHNSTON, SARAH SC
  She provided provisions for the troops (SI, X, Pt. 1:162).
JOHNSTON, SARAH KNOX PA
  She was born in 1751, married John Johnston, and died in 1835. She is listed as a patriot in the DAR Patriot Index.
JONES, MRS. NJ
  Morris County. The wife of Parson Jones, she collected funds for the army (New Jersey Gazette, July 4, 1780).
JONES, AGNES VA
  Amelia County. She performed a public service (VR, 1:66). Also Campbell County (VR, 1:287).
JONES, ANN NC
  She supplied provisions for the troops (RA, 11:89, fol. 5).
JONES, ANN VA
  Bedford County. She performed a public service (VR Lists, 1:11). Also Campbell County (VR, 1:287) and Caroline County (VR, 1:252).
JONES, CATHERINE VA
  Culpeper County. Recognized for public service (VR Ctf 1).
JONES, DOROTHY CHAMBERLAYNE VA
  Amelia County. The wife of Peter Jones, she is credited with public service (VR Ctf 1; 1:67).
JONES, ELIZABETH SC
  She provided provisions for the army (SI, X, pt. 1:73).
JONES, ESTHER CT
  Groton. She suffered damage in a British raid (CAR, 1:79b).
JONES, HENRIETTA GA
  She supplied boat hire and forage for the army (WA, p. 119).
JONES, JANE VA
  Hanover County. She performed a public service (VR, 3:184).
JONES, JOANNA NJ
  Orange. The wife of Cornelius Jones, she suffered damage caused by the British (CDB, claim 50).
JONES, JUDITH VA
  Northumberland County. Credited with public service (VR, 4:118).
JONES, LETTICE VA
  Amelia County. Recognized for public service (VR, 1:66, 93).
JONES, LUCRETIA VA
  Lunenburg County. Recognized for public service (VR Court Booklet, p. 26).
JONES, LUCY VA
  Lunenburg County. Credited with public service (VR, 4:17).

JONES, MARGARET　　　　　　　NC
　　She supplied provisions for the army (RA, B:218).
JONES, MARTHA　　　　　　　　NC
　　She provided provisions for the troops (RA, A:38; VR, B:202).
JONES, MARY　　　　　　　　　NC
　　She provided supplies for the army (RA, 5:27, fol. 5).
JONES, MARY　　　　　　　　　NJ
　　Somerville. She suffered damages by the British (CDB, p. 146).
JONES, MARY　　　　　　　　　VA
　　Amherst County. She performed a public service (VR Court Booklet, p. 3). Also Gloucester County (VR, 3:46); Hanover County (VR Lists, 2:5, 6); Hansemond County (VR, 4:160); and Warwick County (VR, 5:213).
JONES, NANCY　　　　　　　　NJ
　　Connecticut Farms, Bergen County. She suffered damage caused by the British (CDB, claim 36).
JONES, PHEBE　　　　　　　　NJ
　　Orange. She suffered losses in a British raid (CDB, claim 58).
JONES, PRUDENCE　　　　　　　VA
　　Southampton County. Recognized for public service (VR, 5:178).
JONES, RACHEL　　　　　　　　NC
　　She supplied provisions for the troops (RA, D:144).
JONES, MRS. ROSS　　　　　　VA
　　Middlesex County. Credited with public service (VR, 4:94).
JONES, SARAH　　　　　　　　VA
　　Amelia County. She performed a public service (VR, 93). Also Princess Anne County (VR, 4:218).
JONES, SARAH DAVIS　　　　　GA
　　Her husband was imprisoned in Saint Augustine. See Biographies.
JONES, SUSANNA　　　　　　　NC
　　She provided provisions for the army (RA, 5:8, fol. 1).
JONES, SUSANNA　　　　　　　NJ
　　Westfield. She suffered damages by the British (CDB, claim 108).
JONES, TABITHA　　　　　　　VA
　　Mecklenburg. Recognized for public service (VR, 4:63).
JORDAN, ANN　　　　　　　　　NC
　　She supplied provisions for the troops (RA, C:81).
JORDAN, ELIZABETH　　　　　　VA
　　Hansemond County. She performed a public service (VR, 4:160, 161).
JORDAN, MARY　　　　　　　　VA
　　Amelia County. Recognized for public service (VR, 1:67).
JORDAN, SARAH　　　　　　　　VA
　　Louisa County. Credited with public service (VR, 3:354, 355, 357).
JORDAN, SARAH O'NEAL　　　　GA
　　She married Dempsey Jordan and is listed as a patriot in the DAR Patriot Index 2.

III: COMPLETE LISTING 355

JOYNER, ELIZABETH NORTON   GA
    She rode to the enemy camp to obtain the release of her son.
    See Biographies.
JUDD, BETHIA   CT
    Danbury. In the British raid of April 1777 she suffered losses
    (CAR, 8:382b).
JULIAN, MRS.   VA
    Spotsylvania County. She performed a public service (VR,
    4:261).
JUSTICE, MARY   NJ
    Burlington. She suffered damage caused by the British (CDB,
    claim 145).
JUSTIN, MARY   RI
    The wife of Philip Justin, she supplied eight yards of tow cloth,
    coffee, and butter for the troops (MP, 48:10).

K

KABLER, IONA   VA
    Culpeper County. She performed a public service (VR, 2:100).
KARR, MARGARET   VA
    She was the wife of Richard Karr, a soldier who was killed at
    the Battle of Guilford Court House on March 15, 1781. They
    had several children (submitted by Mary Ann Barnes, Rockville,
    MD).
KATE, BONNY. See CATHERINE SHERRILL SEVIER
KEARNEY, ELIZABETH ELLIOTT. See TABB
KEEBLER, ELIZABETH   GA
    She provided provisions for Gen. Wayne's troops (WA, p. 128).
KEELER, JAMIMA   CT
    Ridgefield. In the British raid of April 1777 she suffered damages
    (CAR, 8:391b). She was a Western Lands Grantee.
KEELER, MARGARET   CT
    Fairfield. In the British raids of 1779-1780 she suffered losses
    (CAR, 15:251d). She was a Western Lands Grantee.
KEELER, MARTHA   CT
    Ridgefield. In the British raid of April 1777 she suffered damage
    (CAR, 8:391b). She was a Western Lands Grantee.
KEELING, ELIZABETH (BETTY)   VA
    Princess Anne County. Recognized for public service (VR,
    4:218).
KEENE, SARAH   VA
    Mecklenburg. She performed a public service (VR Court Book-
    let, p. 8).
KEEVE, MRS. THOMAS   VA
    Northumberland County. Credited with public service (VR,
    4:119).
KEITH, ELIZABETH WILSON   PA
    Gen. Washington had his headquarters there. See Biographies.

KEITH, MARGARET   SC
   She provided provisions for the troops (SI, L-N:331).
KEITH, MARY LAFOONE   SC
   She rode miles to warn the Americans that the British were coming. See Biographies.
KELLEBREW, MRS.   NC
   She supplied provisions for the army (RA, D:331).
KELLEY, HANNAH BARTLETT   MA
   She provided funds for the army. See Biographies.
KELLEY, MARGARET   SC
   She supplied provisions for the troops (SI, R-T:224).
KELLOGG, RHODA CALLENDER   MA
   Sheffield. She was the wife of Daniel Kellogg, who was a private on the expedition to Quebec. He was killed in action in December 1775 (FP1).
KELLOGG, WIDOW   CT
   Hartford. She supplied a blanket in 1777 for the army (CAR, 11:291).
KELLY, ANN   MD
   She boarded Capt. James Nicholson from May to September 1776 (IM, 1445, 2367).
KELLY, MRS. JAMES   SC
   She is listed on the rolls of Capt. Ross's Company, Col. Middleton's Regiment, during the Revolutionary War (ESC).
KELSAL, MARY ELIZABETH   SC
   She provided provisions for the troops (SI, B:137).
KELSICK, MARY   VA
   Richmond County. She performed a public service (VR, 5:98).
KEMBRO, TABITHA   NC
   She supplied provisions for the army (RA, 9:91, fol. 4).
KEMP, ELIZABETH   VA
   Gloucester County. Credited with public service (VR, 3:46, 47).
KEMP, HANNAH   NC
   She provided provisions for the troops (RA, 6:29, fol. 4).
KEMP, MARY   VA
   Middlesex County. Recognized for public service (VR, 4:94, 348).
KENAN, ELEANOR   NC
   She supplied provisions for the army (RA, 5:49, fol. 1).
KENAN, ELIZABETH   NC
   She provided provisions for the troops (RA, 5:43, fol. 3).
KENAN (KEENAN), ELIZABETH JOHNSTON   VA
   Northumberland County. Wife of Thomas Kenan. She performed a public service (VR, 4:119).
KENDALL, WIDOW   CT
   Suffield. In 1777 she supplied a blanket for the army (CAR, 11:411a).
KENDRICK, ELIZABETH   NY
   Albany. At age forty-three in 1783 she was captured by Indians on the Mohawk River and released from Fort Ticonderoga on July 18, 1783 (MR).

III: COMPLETE LISTING 357

KENDRICK, HULDA PEASE MA
  Wareham. She was the wife of John Kendrick, who commanded the brigantine Count d'Estaing. About November 1779 Kendrick was captured by the British and imprisoned (CN).
KENNADAY, ELIZABETH NJ
  Somerville. She suffered damage by the British (CDB, p. 27).
KENNADAY, ESTHER VA
  Bedford County. The wife of John Kennaday, she performed a public service (VR Court Booklet, pp. 8, 22).
KENNAN, MARY ANN SC
  She supplied provisions for the army (SI, B:101).
KENNEDY, ANN TOWNSEND. See JEFFORDS
KENNEDY, ESTHER NC
  She supplied provisions for the troops (RA, 7:94, fol. 1).
KENNEDY, MARGARET WHITE SC
  She was born in 1756, married Lt. James Kennedy, and died in 1820. She is listed as a patriot in the DAR Patriot Index.
KENNELLEY, ELIZABETH SC
  She supplied provisions for the troops (SI, I:78).
KENNER, MARGARET ESKRIDGE VA
  Fauquier County. The wife of Howson Kenner, she provided provisions for the army (VR, 2:242).
KENT, CHARITY NJ
  Piscataway. The widow of John Kent, she suffered damage by the British (CDB, p. 193).
KENT, SIBBIL DWIGHT MA
  She entertained Gen. Washington. See Biographies.
KENTON, MARTHA DOWDEN KY
  Her husband was tortured by Indians. See Biographies.
KERFOOT, MARGARET VA
  Frederick County. The wife of George Kerfoot, she performed a public service (VR, 2:193).
KERR, ANNE NC
  She supplied provisions for the troops (RA, 9:6, fol. 2).
KERR, ELIZABETH NC
  She supplied provisions for the army (RA, A:160).
KERR, ELIZABETH VA
  Sussex County. Recognized for public service (VR, 5:203).
KERR, MARGARET NC
  She supplied provisions for the army (RA, A:160).
KERR, ROSANNAH VA
  Goochland County. She performed a public service (VR Lists, 1:4).
KESSEL, MRS. SC
  She provided provisions for the army (SI, R-T:212).
KESTER, THEODOSIA NJ
  Burlington. The wife of Peter Kester, she suffered damage by the British (CDB, claim 128).
KETTLE, ELIZABETH SC
  She supplied provisions for the troops (SI, O-Q:290).

KEY, TANDY   VA
   Fluvanna County. She performed a public service (VR, 1:359, 366).
KIBLER, LUCRETIA   SC
   She provided provisions for the army (SI, 1:79).
KILBY, MARY   CT
   New Haven. In the July 1779 raid by the British she suffered losses (CAR, 15:234d, 269c).
KIMBALL, WIDOW   CT
   Windham. In 1777 she supplied a blanket for the army (CAR, 11:102a).
KIMBERLY, LYDIA   CT
   New Haven. In the British raid of July 1779 she suffered damage (CAR, 15:234g). She was a Western Lands Grantee.
KIMBERLY, MARY   CT
   New Haven. In the July 1779 raid by the British she suffered losses (CAR, 15:234i).
KIMBERLY, MARY   CT
   West Haven. In the 1781 British raid she suffered losses (CAR, 24:18ab).
KIMBERLY, SARAH   CT
   New Haven. In the July 1779 British raid she suffered damage (CAR, 15:234e, 269b). She was a Western Lands Grantee.
KIMBOROUGH (KIMBRO), ELEANOR NC
   The wife of Robert Kimborough, she supplied provisions for the army (RA, B:286).
KIMBRO, LEANAH   NC
   She provided provisions for the troops (RA, C:62).
KING, AVERILLA   VA
   Princess Anne County. She performed a public service (VR Court Booklet, p. 10).
KING, ELIZABETH   CT
   New Haven. In the July 1779 British raid she suffered losses (CAR, 15:234f).
KING, ELIZABETH   NC
   She provided provisions for the army. See Biographies.
KING, HANNAH. See ARNOLD
KING, MARGARET. See ANN ROBINSON DE VANE
KING, MARY   VA
   Hansemond County. Recognized for public service (VR, 4:16).
KING, MRS. MARY   VA
   Surry County. Credited with public service (VR Ctf 1).
KING, RACHEL See PENNINGTON
KING, SUSANNAH BLAKE   MD
   She was the wife of Benjamin King, who commanded the armed boat Plater and then the brig Maryland. In September 1780 this brig was captured by the British, and King was imprisoned (CN).
KINGFISHER, NANCY. See WARD
KINLOCH, ANN   SC
   She supplied provisions for the army (SI, B:11).

III: COMPLETE LISTING 359

KINSLER, ELIZABETH NC
   The wife of Herman Kinsler, Sr., she is listed as a patriot in
   the DAR Patriot Index 2.
KIPP, LEA NJ
   Hackensack. The wife of Isaac N. Kipp, she suffered damage
   by the British (CDB, claim 36).
KIRBY, RUTH MARVIN CT
   She molded bullets for the army. See Biographies.
KIRK, ELIZABETH VA
   Fauquier County. Recognized for public service (VR, 2:242).
KIRK, MARY STORY PA
   She was born in 1720 and married Moses Kirk, and died in 1804.
   She is listed as a patriot in the DAR Patriot Index.
KIRKLAND, SUSANNAH SC
   She supplied provisions for the troops (SI, 1:79).
KIRKPATRICK, LYDIA LEWIS NJ
   She supplied food for the soldiers. See Biographies.
KIRTLAND, CONSTANT CT
   Wallingford. She supplied a blanket for the army in 1777 (CAR,
   11:208a).
KITCH, SUSANNA NC
   She supplied provisions for the troops (RA, 1:109, fol. 4).
KNAPP, EUNICE CT
   Greenwich. In the British raids of March 1779 and December
   1783, she suffered damage (CAR, 15:271b; 36:19a). She was
   a Western Lands Grantee.
KNAPP, MARY SC
   She supplied provisions for the army (SI, B:35).
KNIGHT, CATHERINE SC
   She provided provisions for the troops (SI, U-W:71).
KNIGHT, ELIZABETH NJ
   Burlington. The wife of Henry Knight, she suffered damage
   by the British (CDB, claim 94).
KNIGHT, MARY WORRELL PA
   She brought food to the soldiers at Valley Forge. See Biographies.
KNOWLES, PRUDENCE BENTON CT
   Wethersfield. On April 3, 1768, she married James Knowles
   who was an ensign in Capt. Hanchette's Company on the expedi-
   tion to Quebec. Later Knowles went to sea and was captured
   in battle early in 1777. Knowles was taken to Halifax, Nova
   Scotia, where he died on June 1, 1777. Mrs. Knowles died
   on August 17, 1839, in Pittsfield, Massachusetts (FP4; submitted
   by E. Jeannette Ryan, Norwich, CT).
KNOX, MRS. PA
   Philadelphia. She provided funds for the army (Pennsylvania
   Gazette, June 12, 1780).
KNOX, ANN NC
   She provided provisions for the army (RA, A:134).
KNOX, ELIZABETH SC
   She supplied provisions for the troops (SI, B:4).

KNOX, LUCY FLUCKER　　　　　MA
　　She was a camp follower and danced with Gen. Washington.
　　See Biographies.
KNOX, MARY　　　　　　　　　NC
　　She provided provisions for the troops (RA, 9:18, fol. 5).
KNOX, ROSE T.　　　　　　　　MD
　　Charles County. She supplied wheat for the army in 1783 (IM, 25424).
KNOX, SARAH　　　　　　　　　SC
　　She supplied provisions for the troops (SI, U-W:70).
KOONCE, ELIZABETH　　　　　　NC
　　She supplied provisions for the troops (RA, D:197a).
KROSEN, CATHERINE　　　　　　NJ
　　Somerville. She suffered damage in a British raid (CDB, p. 99).
KUNTZ, MARY　　　　　　　　　NC
　　She provided provisions for the troops (RA, A:175).
KUYENDAEL, FERMMETJE DECKER　NY
　　Port Jervis. She was the wife of Peter Kuyendael. They donated their home as a frontier fort during the Revolutionary War (FP1).
KUYENDALL, CATHARINE　　　　VA
　　Hampshire. Recognized for public service (VR, 4:326).
KUYENDALL, KATHERINE　　　　WV
　　Berkeley County. She supplied provisions for the army (RW).
KUYPER, MRS.　　　　　　　　NJ
　　Bergen County. She collected funds for the army (New Jersey Gazette, July 4, 1780).

L

LA BOUCH, SARAH　　　　　　　VA
　　Chesterfield County. She performed a public service (VR, 2:38; 4:302).
LACEY, ELIZABETH LEE　　　　　MD
　　She was born in 1764, married George Lacey, and died in 1864. She is listed as a patriot in the DAR Patriot Index.
LACKMAN, MRS. JOHN　　　　　　VA
　　She was captured by the British and Indians along with her three children in 1778 at Cherry Valley and later exchanged (MR).
LACY, MARTHA COCKER　　　　　VA
　　Pittsylvania County. The wife of Theophilus Lacy, she performed a public service (VR, 5:17).
LADD, JUDITH　　　　　　　　　VA
　　Charles City. Recognized for public service (VR, 1:313).
LADD, SARAH　　　　　　　　　VA
　　Charles City. She performed a public service (VR Court Booklet, pp. 18, 23).

III: COMPLETE LISTING

LADD, URSULA ELLYSON   VA
   Mecklenburg. The wife of William Ladd, Jr., she is recognized for public service (VR, 4:65).
LADNER, RACHEL   NJ
   Somerville. She suffered damages by the British (CDB, p. 30).
LADSON, ELIZABETH   SC
   She supplied provisions for the army (SI, B:217).
LAFAYETTE, ADRIENNE   PA
   She was a member of the ladies' association and contributed funds for the soldiers. See Biographies.
LA FORCE, WIDOW   KY
   At age fifty-two in June 1780 she and her children were captured by Tories and Indians and taken to Quebec (HP).
LAKE, MARY BIRD   NY
   She married Archibald Lake and died in 1796. She is listed as a patriot in the DAR Patriot Index.
LA LUZERNE, COUNTESS DE   PA
   She was a member of the ladies' association and contributed funds for the soldiers. See Biographies.
LAMB, MARY   NJ
   Westfield. The widow of John David Lamb, she suffered damages caused by the British (CDB, claim 10).
LAMMOND (HAMMOND), REBECCA GRANT   KY
   Bryan's Station. She was the daughter of William Grant, one of the founders of Bryan's Station. When the Tories and Indians attacked on August 15, 1782, she was one of the women who went for water. Her name is inscribed on the monument erected in 1896 by the Lexington Chapter of the Daughters of the American Revolution.
LAMPKIN (LAMPSON), MARY   VA
   Culpeper. Recognized for public service (VR, 2:82).
LANAHAN, MARGARET HIATT. See CRAVENS
LANCE, ANN M.   SC
   She supplied provisions for the troops (SI, B:116).
LANDRUM, NELLY   VA
   Caroline County. Credited with public service (VR, 1:256).
LANE, ANNA MARIA   VA
   She worked as a nurse in the soldiers' barracks in Richmond. See Biographies.
LANE, CATHERINE   SC
   She provided provisions for the troops (SI, B:139).
LANE, MARGARET   NJ
   Piscataway. She suffered losses in a British raid (CDB, claim 124).
LANE, SARAH RICHARDSON   PA
   She was born in 1732, married Edward Lane, and died in 1818. Mrs. Lane is recognized as a patriot in the DAR Patriot Index.
LANE, TIDENCE   NC
   She supplied provisions for the army (RA, B:283).
LANGLEY, BRIDGET   VA
   Princess Anne County. She performed a public service (VR, 4:220).

LANGLEY, ELIZABETH　　　　　　VA
　　Warwick County. Recognized for public service (VR, 5:215).
LANGSTON, ANN　　　　　　　　SC
　　She provided provisions for the troops (RA, K:96).
LANIER, ELIZABETH CHAMBERLAIN. See SMITH
LANKFORD, ELIZABETH　　　　　VA
　　Southampton County. Credited with public service (VR, 5:179).
LARKEN, MAY　　　　　　　　　MD
　　She boarded Capt. George Cook of the Defence in 1777 (IM, 3439).
LA ROCHE, ELIZABETH　　　　　SC
　　She supplied provisions for the army (SI, B:71).
LA TEMREUF, EVE　　　　　　　RI
　　She supplied provisions for the troops in 1780 (MP, 11:17).
LATHAM, ELIZABETH　　　　　　CT
　　Groton. She suffered damage in a British raid (CAR, 1:63r, 79b). She was a Western Lands Grantee.
LATHAM, ELIZABETH　　　　　　MD
　　She married John Manley, then John Latham, and died in 1782. She is recognized as a patriot in the DAR Patriot Index.
LATHAM, EUNICE FORSYTHE　　 CT
　　She despised Benedict Arnold. See Biographies.
LATHAM, LYDIA　　　　　　　　CT
　　Groton. She suffered losses in a British raid (CAR, 1:63r, 79b). She was a Western Lands Grantee.
LATHAM, MARY　　　　　　　　 CT
　　Groton. She suffered damage in a British raid (CAR, 1:63r, 79b). She was a Western Lands Grantee.
LATHAM, MARY　　　　　　　　 NC
　　She supplied provisions for the troops (RA, C:157).
LATIMER, LYDIA　　　　　　　　CT
　　New London. She suffered losses in a British raid (CAR, 1:63i, 95a). She was a Western Lands Grantee.
LA TOUR, SUSAN　　　　　　　 SC
　　She supplied provisions for the army (SI, B:126).
LAWRENCE, AMY　　　　　　　　VA
　　Hansemond County. She performed a public service (VR, 4:162).
LAWRENCE, ANN　　　　　　　　NC
　　She provided provisions for the troops (RA, 1:96, fol. 2).
LAWRENCE, MARY　　　　　　　 VA
　　Hansemond County. Recognized for public service (VR, 4:161, 162).
LAWRENCE, SARAH　　　　　　　NY
　　Long Island. She furnished supplies for the army in Connecticut (CAR, 28:133-135).
LAWSON, MARY　　　　　　　　 VA
　　Lancaster County. She performed a public service (VR, 3:274).
LAWSON, SARAH　　　　　　　　VA
　　Richmond County. Recognized for public service (VR, 5:98).
LAYBOYTEUX, ELIZABETH　　　　NJ
　　New Brunswick. She suffered damage in a British raid (CDB, pp. 78, 96).

III: COMPLETE LISTING 363

LEA, FANNY SANDERS　　　　　　KY
　　Bryan's Station. She was born in 1748 and married Francis
　　Wainwright Lea. When the Tories and Indians attacked on August 15, 1782, she was one of the women who went for water.
　　Her name is inscribed on the monument erected in 1896 by the
　　Lexington Chapter of the Daughters of the American Revolution.

LEACH, CATHARINE　　　　　　NJ
　　Burlington. She suffered losses in a British raid (CDB, p.
　　140).

LEACH, MARY　　　　　　MD
　　Montgomery County. In 1781 and 1782 she supplied wheat for
　　the army (IM, 17781, 20721).

LEACH, REBECCA BUGBEE　　　　　　MA
　　Wenham. She was the wife of Pvt. Richard Leach, who was
　　captured by the enemy on November 16, 1776, when the British
　　took Fort Lee, New Jersey (FP2).

LEAR, EVE. See PIPER

LEDYARD, ABIGAIL HEMPSTEAD. See MOORE

LEDYARD, ANNE WILLIAMS　　　　　　CT
　　She suffered property damage in a British raid, and also the
　　loss of her husband. See Biographies.

LEDYARD, BRIDGET　　　　　　CT
　　Her husband was killed at Fort Griswold, Groton, during the
　　British attack led by Benedict Arnold in September 1781 (CAR,
　　26:295b). She was a Western Lands Grantee.

LEDYARD, FANNY. See PETERS

LEE, AGNES DICKINSON　　　　　　CT
　　She fired a cannon to warn the British were coming. See
　　Biographies.

LEE, ALICE　　　　　　NJ
　　Burlington. She suffered damage caused by the British (CDB,
　　claim 236).

LEE, ANN　　　　　　SC
　　She was born in 1750, married William Lee, and died in 1797.
　　She is listed as a patriot in the DAR Patriot Index.

LEE, ANNE　　　　　　MD
　　Baltimore. She boarded sick seamen of the Defence in December
　　1776 and nursed the sailors in February 1777 (IM, 3053, 3660).

LEE, ANNE GASKINS　　　　　　VA
　　She went through many trying times. See Biographies.

LEE, BETHIAH　　　　　　NJ
　　Morris County. She suffered damages caused by American troops
　　(CDB, claim 30).

LEE, BETTY　　　　　　VA
　　Northumberland County. Credited with public service (VR,
　　4:319).

LEE, BETTY PAGE　　　　　　VA
　　Goochland County. The wife of John Lee, she performed a
　　public service (VR Court Booklet, p. 34).

LEE, HANNAH　　　　　　VA
　　Fauquier County. Recognized for public service (VR Lists,
　　p. 7).

LEE, MARTHA   NC
    She supplied provisions for the troops (RA, A:45).
LEE, MARY   MD
    Dorchester County. In 1782 she supplied wheat for the army
    (IM, 22930).
LEE, MARY ANN CUSTIS. See ELEANOR CUSTIS
LEE, MARY DIGGS   MD
    She mobilized women to support the ladies' association for the
    welfare of the soldiers. See Biographies.
LEE, NANCY ANN WILSON   SC
    She was born in 1759 and married Andrew Lee, then Nicholas
    Vaughan. She is listed as a patriot in the DAR Patriot Index.
LEE, RACHEL HOOPER   MA
    Cape Ann. She was the wife of Isaac Lee, who commanded the
    sixteen-gun ship Polly. On July 4, 1782, Lee was captured
    by the British frigate Ceres near the Georges Bank and imprisoned
    (CN).
LEE, SARAH   SC
    She provided funds for the army (AA, 1:60).
LEE, SUSANNA   VA
    Essex County. She performed a public service (VR, 2:152).
LEECH, ANNA HERRICK   MA
    Beverly. She was the wife of Nathan Leech. On September 1,
    1780, Israel Ober obtained a letter of marque to command the
    sloop Fish Hawk with eight guns and sixteen men. Anna Leech
    witnessed the bond (CN).
LEECH, MARY   NC
    She provided provisions for the troops (RA, 5:53, fol. 4).
LEEDS, ANNA   CT
    Groton. She suffered damage in a British raid (CAR, 1:63r,
    79b). She was a Western Lands Grantee.
LEEK, ELIZABETH   MD
    She supplied wheat in 1781 for the army (IM, 16155).
LEETE, MEHITABLE   CT
    New London. She suffered damage in a British raid (CAR,
    1:63k, 95i). She was a Western Lands Grantee.
LEETE, MERCY   CT
    Guilford. In 1777 she supplied a blanket for the army (CAR,
    11:283).
LEFORGE, RACHEL   NJ
    Piscataway. The wife of John Leforge, she suffered damage
    in a British raid (CDB, p. 308).
LEGARE, ELIZA BASNETT   NC
    She was born in 1734, married Thomas Legare, and died in 1798.
    She is listed as a patriot in the DAR Patriot Index.
LEMANT, MARTHA SMYTHE   SC
    She married James Lemant, then John Walker, Sr. She is listed
    as a patriot in the DAR Patriot Index.
LEMAY, SUSANNA   VA
    Hanover County. She performed a public service (VR, 3:187).
    Also listed in New Kent County (Ctf 1).

III: COMPLETE LISTING

LENUD, ELIZABETH   SC
She supplied provisions for the army (SI, Y-Z:5).

LEONARD, MARY   VA
Henrico County. Recognized for public service (VR Court Booklet, p. 10).

LESESNE, MARY   SC
She provided provisions for the troops (SI, B:54; R-T:148; X, pt. 1:225).

LESTER, DOROTHY   CT
Groton. She was widowed by a British attack and suffered loss of property (CAR, 27:333a).

LETTS, CATHARINE   NJ
Amboy. She suffered losses in a British raid (CDB, p. 153).

LETTS, HANNAH   NJ
South Amboy. The mother of Elisha Letts, she suffered damage in a British attack (CDB, p. 28).

LEVE, JANE   NC
She provided provisions for the troops (RA, B:262).

LEWELLEN (LEWELLYN), ELIZABETH   VA
Norfolk. She performed a public service (VR, 4:132).

LEWIS, ANNE MONTGOMERY   VA
She was born in 1736, married Col. William Lewis, and died in 1808. She is listed as a patriot in the <u>DAR Patriot Index</u>.

LEWIS, BETTY WASHINGTON   VA
She knitted socks for the soldiers. See Biographies.

LEWIS, DEBORAH   CT
Groton. She was widowed by the British attack on Fort Griswold in September 1781 and suffered loss of property (CAR, 27:333a).

LEWIS, ELEANOR   SC
She supplied provisions for the army (SI, R-T:225).

LEWIS, ELIZABETH ANNESLEY   NY
She was captured and imprisoned by the British. See Biographies.

LEWIS, LUCY TALIFERRO   VA
Caroline County. The wife of Charles Lewis, she performed a public service (VR, 1:256).

LEWIS, MARY   CT
New London. She suffered damage in a British raid (CAR, 1:63i, 95a). She was a Western Lands Grantee.

LEWIS, MARY   MD
In 1781 she supplied wheat for the army (IM, 16529).

LEWIS, MARY   VA
Albemarle County. Recognized for public service (VR Court Booklet, p. 28).

LEWIS, MARY   VA
Goochland County. Recognized for public service (VR, 3:69). Also shown in Mecklenburg (VR, 4:65).

LEWIS, MARY JOHN   VA
She was the wife of Capt. William Lewis, major of the 10th Virginia Regiment, who was taken prisoner on May 12, 1780, when Charleston fell to the British. He remained a prisoner to the close of the war (FW).

LEWIS, MELICENT BALDWIN.   See PORTER
LIBBEY, MEHITABLE SEAVY   NH
  Rye. She was the wife of Samuel Libbey, a soldier and mariner.
  He went on four privateering cruises and twice was captured
  and imprisoned (FP1).
LIBBY, REBECCA WESTON   ME
  Jonesborough. With her sister-in-law, Hannah Watts Weston,
  Rebecca rode sixteen miles to Machias to take some thirty pounds
  of metal and gunpowder to aid the men in an attempt to capture
  the British schooner Margaretta, which the men did. Later
  she married Reuben Libby. Rebecca died in 1819 (AM; DAR).
LIGAN, ANN   VA
  Charlotte. She performed a public service (VR Ctf 1).
LIGHTFOOT, MARY   VA
  James City. Recognized for public service (VR Court Booklet,
  p. 7).
LIGON, ANN   VA
  Powhatan. Credited with public service (VR, 4:237).
LIGON, JUDITH STEWART   VA
  Chesterfield County. The wife of Capt. Joseph Ligon, Sr.,
  she died in 1784. Mrs. Ligon is credited with public service
  (VR, 2:38; DAR).
LIGON, SARAH   VA
  Prince Edward County. Recognized for public service (VR,
  5:52).
LILBORN, MARY   WV
  Berkeley County. With Colbert Anderson she supplied provisions for the army (VR Ctf 1).
LINCEY, MARGARET   NY
  At age twenty-three on July 15, 1780, she was captured with
  her son by Indians and sent to the Saint Lawrence suburbs
  (MR).
LINCH, MARY   NC
  She supplied provisions for the troops (RA, 1:15, fol 1).
LINCOLN, MARY CUSHING   MA, NJ
  Gen. and Mrs. Lincoln entertained Gen. Washington and the
  Comte de Rochambeau for dinner. See Biographies.
LINCOLN, PERSIS TOWER. See HALL
LIND, AGNES   SC
  She provided provisions for the army (SI, B:138).
LINDSAY, ANNE KENNEDY   KY
  Her husband was killed by Indians. See Biographies.
LINDSAY, DINAH   NC
  She provided provisions for the troops (RA, 10:20, fol. 4).
LINDSEY, JOANNA   NJ
  Orange. The wife of Jedidiah Lindsey, she suffered damage
  in a British attack (CDB, claim 4).
LINING, SARAH   SC
  She supplied provisions for the army (SI, B:15).
LINK, MARGARET   KY, VA
  She was the wife of John Link. At age thirty-six she was

III: COMPLETE LISTING 367

    captured, along with her daughters Cathy aged ten, Molly aged eight, Sarah aged six, and one son, by Indians in June 1780 at Licking Creek and released from Fort Ticonderoga on July 18, 1783 (MR).
LINN, MARY   SC
    She provided provisions for the troops (SI, O-Q:5).
LINSEY, ELIZABETH   VA
    James City. She performed a public service (VR Court Booklet, p. 7).
LIPPINCOTT, ANNE   NJ
    Burlington. She suffered damage caused by American troops (CDB, p. 3).
LIPSCOMB, ANN   VA
    King William County. Credited with public service (VR, 3:249).
LIPSCOMB, ELIZABETH   VA
    King William County. She performed a public service (VR, 3:250-251).
LIPTON, MARY   SC
    She provided provisions for the troops (SI, Y-Z:264).
LISTON, MARTHA   SC
    She provided provisions for the army (SI, B:44).
LITTLE, MRS.   NC
    She provided provisions for the army (RA, D:71).
LITTLE, ELIZABETH   NJ
    Springfield. She suffered damage by the British (CDB, claim 27-2).
LITTLE, HANNAH LOVELL   MA
    She was the wife of Luther Little, who was a midshipman on the Protector. This vessel was taken by the British in May 1781, and Little was imprisoned (CN).
LITTLE, MARY   SC
    She supplied provisions for the troops (SI, Y-Z:264).
LITTLE, PHEBE. See FRAZEE
LITTLE, SUSANNAH   NJ
    Westfield. The widow of John Little, she suffered losses caused by the British (CDB, claim 53).
LITTLEDIE, MARY   NC
    She refused to drink British tea. See Background.
LITTLEJOHN, ANN TOWNSEND. See JEFFORDS
LITTLEJOHN, SARAH BLOUNT   NC
    The wife of William Littlejohn, she was born in 1747 and died in 1807. She is listed as a patriot in the DAR Patriot Index.
LITTON, MARTHA   KY, VA
    At age twenty-seven she was captured with her husband, Solomon, by Indians in June 1780 on Licking Creek and released from Fort Ticonderoga on July 18, 1783 (MR).
LIVINGSTON, CHRISTINA TEN BROEK   NY
    Her home was plundered by the British. See Biographies.
LIVINGSTON, ISABEL   NC
    She provided provisions for the troops (RA, A:192).

LIVINGSTON, SUSANNA FRENCH   NJ
She refused a guard to protect her home. See Biographies.

LIZENBY, ELLEN   VA
Lancaster County. Recognized for public service (VR, 3:274).

LLOYD, ANNA MARIE   MD
Talbot County. In 1780 she supplied wheat for the army (IM, 10884).

LLOYD, MRS. RICHARD B.   NY
She carried messages to and from Gen. Washington. See Biographies.

LLOYD, SARAH   CT
Stonington. On March 6, 1778, Joseph Dodge obtained a letter of marque to command the ship Beaver with twelve guns and forty-five men. Sarah Lloyd witnessed the bond (CN).

LLOYD, SARAH   NC
She provided provisions for the troops (RA, K:94).

LOBB, ELIZABETH   VA
Spotsylvania County. She performed a public service (VR Court Booklet, p. 8).

LOCKE, POLLY   NH
She was the New Hampshire champion weaver. See Biographies.

LOCKHART, ELIZABETH   VA
Norfolk. She performed a public service (VR Court Booklet, p. 28).

LOCKHART, ISABELLA   VA
Augusta County. She performed a public service (VR Court Booklet, p. 2).

LOCKHART, SARAH BARRETT   NC
Her husband, Samuel Lockhart, was a major in the 3rd North Carolina Regiment and was promoted to lieutenant colonel on October 12, 1777, by George Washington and assigned to the 8th North Carolina Regiment. Lt. Col. Lockhart was taken prisoner on May 12, 1780, when the British captured Charleston, South Carolina (DAR; FW).

LOCKWOOD, MRS.   CT
Danbury. She supplied lead for the army in 1777 (CAR, 11:518).

LOCKWOOD, HANNAH   CT
Danbury. She suffered damage in the British raid of April 1777 (CAR, 8:382b). She was a Western Lands Grantee.

LOCKWOOD, HANNAH   CT
Greenwich. The widow Lockwood suffered damage in the British raids of March 1779 and December 1783 (CAR, 36:19c). She was a Western Lands Grantee.

LOCKWOOD, MARY   CT
Greenwich. The Widow Lockwood suffered damage in the March 1779 and December 1783 raids by the British (CAR, 36:19e).

LOCKWOOD, MARY   CT
Norwalk. She suffered damage in a British raid (CAR, 1:63k, 98e, 100a). She was a Western Lands Grantee.

LOCKWOOD, RUTH   CT
Greenwich. She suffered damage in the British raid of December 1783 (CAR, 24:274f).

III: COMPLETE LISTING

LOCKWOOD, SARAH   CT
   Stanford. She suffered damage in 1781 by a British raid (CAR, 22:296b).
LODGE, SARAH   NC
   Wife of Levi Lodge. She supplied provisions for the army (RA, K:93).
LOGAN, ANN MONTGOMERY   KY
   She molded bullets. See Biographies.
LOGAN, ELIZABETH   SC
   She supplied provisions for the army (SI, B:147).
LOGAN, MRS. JAMES   PA
   Gen. Washington had his headquarters in her home. See Biographies.
LOGAN, MARTHA   SC
   She provided supplies for the army (SI, B:4).
LOMAX, JUDITH   VA
   Essex County. Credited with public service (VR Lists, p. 5).
LONG, CHARITY   NJ
   Middlesex County. She suffered damage caused by the British (CDB, p. 99).
LONG, ROSY   VA
   Hampshire County. She performed a public service (VR Lists, p. 17).
LONG, SARAH   NC
   She supplied provisions for the troops (RA, 9:97, fol. 2).
LONG, SARAH BROWN   VA
   Culpeper County. The wife of Brumfill Long, she is credited with public service (VR, 2:101).
LONG, SARAH MOORE. See JAMES
LONGEST, MARTHA   VA
   Essex County. She performed a public service (VR, 2:152).
LONGSTAFF, MARY   NJ
   Piscataway. The wife of John Longstaff, she suffered damage in a British raid (CDB, p. 296).
LONNON, SARAH   NC
   She supplied provisions for the army (RA, A:224).
LOOTHOLTS, SARAH   SC
   She supplied provisions for the troops (SI, O-Q:176).
LORD, BEATRICE GULDEN. See BYERLY
LORD, ESTHER   CT
   Fairfield. She suffered damage in a British raid (CAR, 1:53e, 63q). She was a Western Lands Grantee.
LORING, KEZIAH GOVE   MA
   Her husband was captured and imprisoned by the British. See Biographies.
LOTHROP, ABIGAIL HUNTINGTON   CT
   Norwich. On his trip from Cambridge to New York, on April 8, 1776 Gen. Washington had dinner with Gov. Jonathan Trumbull and Col. Jedediah Huntington in the tavern of Mr. & Mrs. Azariah Lothrop. Washington was here again in March 1781.
LOVE, ELIZABETH HAWLING   VA
   Brunswick. Credited with public service (VR, 1:121).

LOVETT, REBECCA   MA
    She was born in 1707 and married Josiah Lovett. Rebecca died
    in 1787. She is credited as a patriot in the DAR Patriot Index.
LOW, ELIZABETH   VA
    Augusta County. Credited with public service (VR Court Booklet,
    p. 8).
LOW, MARY   NC
    She supplied provisions for the troops (RA, A:195).
LOWDON, MARY   VA
    Frederick County. Credited with public service (Ctf 1).
LOWE, FRANCES SIMPSON   GA
    She supplied funds for the army (WA, p. 164).
LOWENS, ANN   VA
    Culpeper County. She performed a public service (VR, 2:102).
LOWENS, MARGARET   VA
    Culpeper County. Credited with public service (VR, 2:102).
LOWRANCE, ANN   NC
    She supplied provisions for the troops (RA, A:113).
LOWREY, ANN WEST   PA
    She spun material and collected clothing for the soldiers. See
    Biographies.
LOWREY, ESTHER FLEMING   NJ
    She was active in the ladies' association for the welfare of the
    soldiers. See Biographies.
LOWRY, ELIZABETH   NC
    Credited with supply provisions for the troops (RA, 7:24, fol.
    4).
LOWRY, ISABELLA   NC
    She supplied provisions for the army (RA, A:89).
LOWRY, JANE   SC
    She supplied provisions for the troops (SI, U-W:155).
LOWRY, MARTHA   VA
    Caroline County. Credited with public service (VR, 1:273).
LOWRY, MARY   VA
    Gloucester County. She performed a public service (VR Court
    Booklet, 3:24).
LOWRY, SARAH SPENCER   NJ
    She was the wife of Stephen Lowry (1747-1821), who was assistant
    deputy commissary of purchases in 1776. He was captured by
    the British, and on April 19, 1778, Gen. Washington arranged
    for an exchange between a Mr. Higgins and Stephen Lowry (DAR;
    FW).
LOYALL, BETHSHEBA   VA
    Cumberland County. She performed a public service (VR Court
    Booklet, pp. 26, 29).
LUCAS, MARGARET   MD
    She made clothing for the seamen on the ship Defence, April 12,
    1777 (IM, 4075).
LUCAS, REBECCA   VA
    Greensville. Credited with public service (VR, 3:26).

III: COMPLETE LISTING

LUCE, LYDIA CLEVELAND   MA
Boston. She was the wife of Elijah Luce who commanded the brigantine Eagle. Luce was captured by the British, and on October 20, 1778, he was confined in the Fortun Prison at Gosport, England (CN).

LUCK, MARY   MD
She supplied wheat for the army in 1780 (IM, 12787).

LUCK, SARAH   VA
She supplied provisions for the army. See Biographies.

LUCKIE, MARY   NC
She provided supplies for the troops (RA, A:204).

LUCKLAND, MRS. BARNABAS   VA
She was captured by the British and Indians at Cherry Valley in 1778, along with her husband and child, and later exchanged (MR).

LUDINGTON, SYBIL   NY
She spread the alarm that the British were coming. See Biographies.

LUKE, BETTY (ESTATE)   VA
Princess Anne County. She is credited with public service (VR, 4:219a).

LUMPKIN, SARAH   VA
King and Queen County. She performed a public service (Lists, 4:2).

LUNDY, ELIZABETH   VA
Southampton County. Credited with public service (VR, 5:179).

LUNN, ABIGAIL   NJ
Connecticut Farms, Essex County. The wife of Stephen Lunn, she suffered damage caused by the British (CDB, claim 59).

LUSK, SARAH   NC
She supplied provisions for the troops (RA, A:246).

LUX, MRS. WILLIAM   MD
John Adams and other signers of the Declaration of Independence dined at her home. See Biographies.

LYDECKER, MARY. See BENSON

LYLE, FANNY   VA
Rockbridge County. She performed a public service (VR, 5:80).

LYMAN, MARY   CT
New Haven. She supplied 141 horses for the militia (CAR, 18:8-11) and provided blankets for the troops, 1775-1778 (CAR, 11:620-623).

LYMAN, MEHITABLE   CT
Hartford. In 1778 she supplied a blanket for the militia (CAR, 12:213).

LYNCH, HANNAH MOTTE. See MOULTRIE

LYNCH, MRS. JOHN   PA
Philadelphia. On August 31, 1774, John Adams dined with the Lynches. Adams reported that Mr. Lynch was a solid, firm, judicious man, and that Mrs. Lynch inquired about the health of Mrs. Adams (BA).

LYNCH, MARY   NC
    She supplied provisions for the troops (RA, 2:15, fol. 1).
LYNE, MARY   VA
    Richmond County. Credited with public service (VR, 5:98).
LYON, JOANNA   NJ
    Connecticut Farms, Essex County. She suffered damage caused
    by the British (CDB, claim 60).
LYON, RUTH. See BUSH
LYTLE, SUSANNAH PERKINS   NC
    She sassed a British colonel. See Biographies.

M

MABIE, ELIZABETH BLAUVELT
    Gen. Washington was here. See Biographies.
MABSON, MARY   NC
    She provided supplies for the army (RA, 5:63, fol. 2).
MacATEE, ELIZABETH   MD
    Charles County. In 1783 she supplied wheat for the army (IM,
    25212).
MacDONALD, SUSANNA OGLE   WV
    Botetourt County. The wife of Bryan MacDonald (or McDonald),
    she died in 1801. Susanna supplied provisions for the army
    (RW).
MACHAN, MRS.   VA
    At age fifty she was captured by the British and Indians on
    June 26, 1780, and taken to the Saint Lawrence suburbs (MR).
MACHAN, ELIZABETH   VA
    At age twenty-five she was captured by the British and Indians
    on June 26, 1780, and taken to the Saint Lawrence suburbs
    (MR).
MACHAN, ISABEL   VA
    At age nineteen she was captured by the British and Indians
    on June 26, 1780, and taken to the Saint Lawrence suburbs
    (MR).
MACHEN, MARGARET   VA
    Gloucester County. Recognized for public service (VR Court
    Booklet, 3:9, 42).
MACKARY, JENNETT   GA
    She provided six head of cattle for Mr. Gwinnett's expedition
    (WA, p. 129).
MACKAY, MARY   GA
    Midway. The wife of Capt. James Mackay. She supplied tobacco
    and deer skins for the Continental Army (WA, p. 120), also
    beef (p. 132), and a thousand bushels of corn (p. 152).
MACKEY (MACKNEY), MRS.   VA
    Rockbridge County. She performed a public service (VR, 5:85).
MACKS, MARY   VA
    Hanover County. She performed a public service (Court Booklet,
    pp. 31, 32, 37).

III: COMPLETE LISTING

MADDEN (MADDIN), MALBRA   VA
Frederick County. She performed a public service (VR, 2:200, 201).

MADDOX, SARAH   MD
Charles County. On April 15, 1783, she supplied wheat for the troops (IM, 25222).

MADISON, NELLY. See MARY HITE BOWMAN

MADRIS, HANNAH   NC
She supplied provisions for the troops (RA, 10:16, fol. 5).

MAGDALEN, MARY   SC
She provided supplies for the army (SI, U-W:210).

MAGEE, ANNE   NC
She provided provisions for the troops (RA, 9:90, fol. 2).

MAGEE, ELIZABETH   NC
She supplied provisions for the troops (RA, 9:25, fol. 3).

MAGGOT, MARGARET   VA
Shenandoah. She performed a public service (VR Court Booklet, p. 4).

MAHON, AGNES LA FORCE   KY
At age nineteen Agnes, her husband, and children were captured by Tories and Indians in June 1780 (HP).

MAHON, SUSANNA   CT
New Haven. She suffered property damage in a British raid (CAR, 1:63c, 91e). She was a Western Lands Grantee.

MAID, ANN   SC
She supplied provisions for the troops (SI, 1:65).

MAIN, RACHEL   SC
After Charleston fell, she refused to sign an oath of fidelity to the Crown and so was banished from the city (SC).

MAJOR, CHRISTIANA   VA
Dinwiddie County. Recognized for public service (VR, 1:336).

MAJOR, MARY   VA
King and Queen County. She performed a public service (Lists, 4:3).

MALCHER (MALCHET), MARY   NJ
Middlesex County. She suffered damage in a British raid (CDB, p. 21).

MALIN, MRS. JOSEPH   PA
Gen. Washington spent the night with the Malins. See Biographies.

MALLARD, SUSAN   SC
She supplied provisions for the troops (SI, R-T:45).

MALLIN, MARY   NJ
Harrington County. She suffered damage in a British raid (CDB, claim 13).

MALLONEE, REBECCA   MD
She was the second wife of John Mallonee (Malone), who was born in France. John was a soldier and was captured by the British. He was imprisoned on the ship Jersey in New York Harbor and died on August 2, 1783, as a result of the abuses on that old prison ship (submitted by Ruth Smith Stell, Gunnison, CO).

MALLORY, LYDIA   VA
    Hanover County. She performed a public service (VR, 3:191).

MALONE, ANN   VA
    Dinwiddie County. Recognized for public service (VR, 1:337).

MALONE, MARY   VA
    Dinwiddie County. She performed a public service (VR, 1:347; 5:238).

MALTBY, ELIZABETH   SC
    When Charleston fell to the British on May 12, 1780, she refused to sign an oath of fidelity to the Crown and so was banished from the city (SC).

MANA, MAREITT   NJ
    Hackensack. The wife of Philip Mana, she suffered damage in a British raid (CDB, claim 2).

MANLEY, ELIZABETH. See LATHAM

MANLEY, MARTHA HICKMAN   MA
    Boston. She was the wife of John Manley, who was commissioned as a captain in the Continental Navy in 1776. In December 1778 Manley commanded the Cumberland, but was captured by the British and taken to Barbados. Later Manley escaped, and in June 1779 he commanded the ship Jason, but was captured for a second time and sent to prison in England (CN).

MANN, PHOEBE   VA
    Halifax County. Recognized for public service (VR Court Booklet, pp. 6, 7, 29, 49).

MANN, SUSANNA   SC
    She provided provisions for the troops (SI, O-Q:183).

MANNING, EFFIE   NJ
    Middlesex County. She suffered damage in a British raid. Her second husband was Nicholas Munday (CDB, p. 295).

MANNING, MARY   NJ
    Middlesex County. The widow of Samuel Stone, she suffered damage in a British raid (CDB, p. 91).

MANNING, MARY   RI
    The wife of Joseph Manning, she supplied beef, pork, mutton, cordwood, corn, rye, salt, cheese, butter, etc., for the troops (MP, 48:17).

MANSFIELD, ESTHER   CT
    New Haven. In the July 1779 British raid, she suffered damage (CAR, 15:234b, 269c). She was a Western Lands Grantee.

MANSFIELD, HANNAH   CT
    New Haven. In the July 1779 British raid she suffered damages (CAR, 15:234c, 269c). She was a Western Lands Grantee.

MANSFIELD, SARAH   MD
    In 1782 she supplied wheat for the troops (IM, 20386).

MAPLES, SARAH   NC
    The wife of Thomas Maples, she died in 1831. During the war Sarah provided provisions for the army (RA, 5:56, fol. 1).

MARBERSON, EVE   NJ
    Somerville. She suffered damages in a British raid (CDB, p. 196).

III: COMPLETE LISTING 375

MARCHENT (MARCHANT), CATHERINE   NC
    She supplied provisions for the troops (RA, C:4).
MARION, CATHERINE   SC
    She supplied provisions for the army (SI, B:69).
MARIOTT, MARY   NJ
    Burlington. She suffered damage caused by the Americans (CDB, p. 11).
MARKHAM, KATY   VA
    Fauquier County. Recognized for public service (VR, 2:244).
MARR, ELIZABETH   SC
    She supplied provisions for the troops (SI, Y-Z:169).
MARRIOTT, ELIZABETH   VA
    Surry County. Recognized for public service (VR Court Booklet, pp. 7, 8, 14).
MARSDEN, MARY   VA
    Hanover County. Recognized for public service (VR, 3:190).
MARSDON, LUCY   VA
    Culpeper County. She performed a public service (VR Court Booklet, 1:50, 51).
MARSE (MIRAS), MARTHA   NJ
    Woodbridge. She suffered damage in a British raid (CDB, p. 304).
MARSH, MRS.   PA
    Philadelphia. She collected money for the welfare of the soldiers (Pennsylvania Gazette, June 12, 1780).
MARSH, ANNE   NJ
    Westfield. She suffered damages in a British raid (CDB, claim 107).
MARSH, MRS. E.   VA
    She was captured by the British and Indians along with her husband and four children at Cherry Valley in 1778 and later exchanged (MR).
MARSH, ESTHER SKINNER   NJ
    New Brunswick. Her husband, Daniel Marsh, was quartermaster general of New Jersey. She was a member of the ladies' association for the welfare of the soldiers (New Jersey Gazette, July 4, 1780).
MARSH, MINNEY   VA
    Northumberland County. She performed a public service (VR, 4:120).
MARSHALL, ELIZABETH   VA
    Rockingham County. She performed a public service (VR, 5:128).
MARSHALL, ELIZABETH   VA
    Caroline County. Recognized for public service (VR, 1:274).
MARSHALL, JUDITH   VA
    Amelia County. Credited with public service (VR, 1:74).
MARSHALL, MARGARET   PA
    Philadelphia. She boarded Richard Law of Milford, Connecticut, Revolutionary War patriot, 1781-1782 (CAR, 33:184, 186, 193).
MARSHALL, MARY   SC
    She provided provisions for the troops (SI, O-Q:3; Y-Z:134).

MARSHALL, MARY   VA
   King George County. She performed a public service (VR,
   4:339).
MARSHALL, MARY RANDOLPH KEITH   VA
   Washington Parish, Westmoreland County. She was the wife
   of Thomas Marshall, who was colonel of the 3rd Virginia Regiment, 1777-1779. Later he succeeded as commander of troops
   on the death of Gen. Mercer, but Marshall was captured by
   the British when Charleston, South Carolina, fell to the enemy
   on May 12, 1780 (FP1).
MARSHALL, NAOMI   CT
   Windsor. She supplied a blanket for the army in 1777 (CAR,
   p. 159a).
MARSHALL, POLLY AMBLER   VA
   Henrico County. She was the daughter of Rebecca Burwell
   and Jacquelin Ambler. With her sister, Betsy Ambler, the two
   girls in 1776 had to knit stockings for the American soldiers,
   and so the two girls missed their morning lessons (NL). Later
   the girls married men named Marshall and Brent.
MARSHALL, RACHEL   CT
   Greenwich. In the 1779 British raid, she suffered damage (CAR,
   1:63e, 74d; 15:271b). She was a Western Lands Grantee.
MARSHALL, SARAH   SC
   She supplied provisions for the troops (SI, U-W:72).
MARSHALL, SUSANNAH   MD
   Baltimore. She boarded Capt. James Nicholson of the Continental
   Navy in 1776 (IM, 1360).
MARSHE, SUSANNAH   NJ
   Morris County. She suffered damage caused by the Americans
   (CDB, claim 161).
MARTIN, MRS.   NJ
   Somerset County. The wife of Col. Martin, she collected funds
   for the army (New Jersey Gazette, July 4, 1780).
MARTIN, AGNES   WV
   Botetourt County. Performed a public service (VR, 1:171).
MARTIN, ELEANOR   VA
   Pittsylvania County. Credited with public service (VR Court
   Booklet, p. 54).
MARTIN, ELIZABETH   GA
   She supplied beef for the troops (WA, p. 168).
MARTIN, ELIZABETH   VA
   Fluvanna County. Credited with public service (VR Court Book-
   let, pp. 17, 31).
MARTIN, ELIZABETH. See NANCY WARD
MARTIN, ELIZABETH MARSHALL   SC
   She was born in 1726 and married John Smith, Jr., then Abraham
   Martin. Elizabeth died in 1797 and is recognized as a patriot
   in the DAR Patriot Index.
MARTIN, GRACE WARING   SC
   She captured a British courier. See Biographies.

III: COMPLETE LISTING 377

MARTIN, JANE VA
   Rockbridge County. She performed a public service (VR, 5:85).
MARTIN, KATHERINE NJ
   She was a member of the ladies' association for the welfare of the soldiers. See Biographies.
MARTIN, LUCY VA
   King George County. Recognized for public service (VR, 2:337).
MARTIN, MARGARET WV
   Berkeley County. She supplied provisions for the troops (see VR Ctf 1, with Thomas Vilet).
MARTIN, MARIA STAATS NY
   She was born in 1744 and married Peter Martin. Maria is listed as a patriot in the DAR Patriot Index.
MARTIN, MARY GA
   She supplied provisions for the troops (WA, p. 152).
MARTIN, MARY NC
   She supplied provisions for the troops (RA, A:224).
MARTIN, MARY NJ
   Bonhamtown, Middlesex County. She suffered damage caused by the British (CDB, p. 38).
MARTIN, MARY SC
   She provided supplies for the army (SI, R-T:213).
MARTIN, RACHEL CLAY SC
   She captured a British courier. See Biographies.
MARTIN, SALLIE CLAY GA
   She was born in 1764 and married Matthew Martin. Sallie is listed as a patriot in the DAR Patriot Index.
MARTIN, SARAH NC
   She supplied provisions for the troops (RA, A:195).
MARTIN, SUSANNAH PA
   Northumberland. She was captured by the British and Indians in July 1782 and taken to Montreal (MR).
MARTIN, SUSANNAH SC
   She supplied provisions for the army (SI, O-Q:261).
MARVIN, RUTH WELCH CT
   She molded bullets for the army. See Biographies.
MASCOLL, HANNAH DEAN MA
   Salem. She was the wife of Stephen Mascoll who was commissioned on December 7, 1775, to command the schooner Boston Revenge. This was the second privateer bond issued by Massachusetts. In August 1776 he commanded the eight-gun General Putnam, but in an engagement with the British ship Nancy and Betsey on January 1, 1777, Mascoll was killed (CN).
MASON, ELEANOR SC
   She supplied provisions for the troops (SI, U-W:286).
MASON, ELIZABETH VA
   Bedford County. She performed a public service (VR Court Booklet, pp. 8, 10). Also listed in Caroline County (VR, 4:299).
MASON, MARGARET NC
   The wife of John Mason, she supplied provisions for the army (RA, 30:47).

MASON, MARGARET CHAMPLIN. See VERNON
MASON, MARTHA SC
She supplied provisions for the troops (SI, L-N:341).
MASON, MARY VA
Gloucester County. Credited with public service (VR, 4:288).
MASTEN, SARAH MD
Charles County. In 1782 she provided wheat for the troops (IM, 22637).
MASTERS, CATHERINE NJ
Morris County. The wife of Edward Masters, she suffered damages caused by the Americans (CDB, claim 40).
MATHEWS, MARY MD
Charles County. In April and December 1782 she supplied wheat for the army (IM, 21466, 24501).
MATHIAS, MRS. JOHN NC
She supplied provisions for the troops (RA, D:294).
MATTHEWS, ANN CALHOUN SC
She was born in 1755 and married Isaac Matthews. Ann died in 1830 and is recognized as a patriot in the DAR Patriot Index.
MATTHEWS, ANNA NJ
Orange. She suffered damage in a British raid (CDB, claim 23).
MATTHEWS, ANNE VA
Henrico County. Credited with public service (VR Court Booklet, p. 16).
MATTHEWS, DEBORAH NJ
Orange. The wife of William Matthews, she suffered damages caused by the British (CDB, claim 16).
MATTHEWS, DOROTHY VA
Gloucester County. Recognized for public service (VR Court Booklet, 3:24).
MATTHEWS, ELIZABETH NC
She supplied provisions for the troops (RA, K:2).
MATTHEWS, SARAH NY
She donned her husband's coat and acted as a sentinel. See Biographies.
MATTOOKS, RACHEL NC
She supplied provisions for the army (RA, 9:72, fol. 1).
MAUREY, MARY VA
Albemarle County. She performed a public service (VR Court Booklet, pp. 18, 40).
MAURICE, MAUDIE NC
She supplied provisions for the troops (RA, 7:25, fol. 4).
MAXWELL, ELIZABETH
She was captured by the British and Indians and taken to Montreal where she worked as a servant for Mr. Franks to support herself (MR).
MAXWELL, ELIZABETH MD
She supplied wheat in 1780 for the army (IM, 13718).
MAXWELL, NANCY ROBBINS WV
She made bullets for the soldiers. See Biographies.

III: COMPLETE LISTING

MAXWELL, SARAH SC
   She supplied provisions for the troops (SI, U-W:284).
MAY, AGNES SMITH WV
   Botetourt County. She was born in 1722 and married John May. Agnes died in 1805 (DAR). She supplied provisions for the army (VR Court Booklet, pp. 3, 41).
MAY, PRISCILLA VA
   Charlotte. She performed a public service (VR Court Booklet, p. 30).
MAYES (MAYLS), LYDIA VA
   Norfolk. Credited with public service (VR, 4:134).
MAYHEW, SARAH VAN METER NJ
   She was a member of the ladies' association for the welfare of the soldiers. See Biographies.
MAZYCK, MARY SC
   She supplied provisions for the troops (SI, B:155).
McADOO (McADOE), MARGARET NC
   She supplied provisions for the army (RA, A:25). Also spelled McAdow (RA, B:184).
McALLISTER, WIDOW NC
   She provided provisions for the troops (RA, 7:83, fol. 4).
McALLISTER, ELIZABETH (ESTATE) VA
   Louisa County. Credited with public service (VR Court Booklet, p. 32).
McBRIDE, JANE NC
   She supplied provisions for the army (RA, C:131).
McCABB, CATHERINE NC
   She provided supplies for the troops (RA, 9:11, fol. 1).
McCAKEY, MARGARET NC
   Provided provisions for the troops (RA, 5:56, fol. 3).
McCALEB, CATHERINE NC
   Supplied provisions for the army (RA, A:259).
McCALL, MARGARET HEXT SC
   The wife of John McCall, she died in 1784 and is listed as a patriot in the DAR Patriot Index.
McCALLA, MARY ADAIR SC
   She was born in 1755 and married John Nixon, then David McCalla. She died in 1807 and is listed as a patriot in the DAR Patriot Index.
McCALLS, SARAH WAYNE GARDINER SC
   She gave information about Lord Cornwallis's army to Gen. Morgan. See Biographies.
McCAMBY, MRS. DAVID NJ
   New Brunswick. On his trip north from Philadelphia to Braintree, Massachusetts, John Adams spent the night of November 16, 1777, at the McCambys' home (BA).
McCARROLL, ELIZABETH NC
   Provided provisions for the troops (RA, 11:74, fol. 1).
McCARTY, FLORENCE NC
   The wife of Capt. Florence McCarty, she supplied provisions for the army (RA, D:122).

McCARTY, MARTHA   SC
  She provided supplies for the troops (SI, 10, pt. 2:158).
McCARTY, MARY   PA
  At age twenty she was captured by Indians in 1779 and sent
  to the Saint Lawrence suburbs (MR, p. 29). George McCarty
  was taken on September 2, 1779, at Fort George.
McCAULEY, MARY HAYS   NJ
  She was a soldier called "Molly Pitcher." See Biographies.
McCAW, MARY   VA
  Powhatan County. Recognized for public service (VR, 4:240).
McCAY, SUSANNA   NC
  The wife of Spruce McCay, she provided supplies for the troops
  (RA, J:175).
McCHESNEY, MARY   NJ
  South Amboy. She suffered damage in a British raid (CDB,
  p. 244).
McCLELLAN, SARAH LOWRY   KY
  Her husband was killed by Indians. See Biographies.
McCLENACHAN, MRS. BLAIR   PA
  She was an active member of the ladies' association for the
  welfare of the soldiers. See Biographies.
McCLEUR, MARY   SC
  She supplied provisions for the troops (SI, L-N:40).
McCLURE, ISABELLA   VA
  Rockbridge County. She performed a public service (VR, 5:82,
  83).
McCLURE, MARY GASTON   SC
  She was born in 1712 and married James McClure. Mary died
  in 1802 and is listed as a patriot in the DAR Patriot Index.
McCOLLUM, MARY   NC
  The wife of Daniel McCollum, she died in 1783. Mary supplied
  provisions for the troops (RA, 11:73, fol. 1).
McCONCHY, MARGARET   GA
  She gave four head of cattle for the army (WA, p. 151).
McCONNELL, SUSANNA SNAVELY   VA
  She was the wife of George McConnell. Susanna wove blankets
  for the soldiers of the Revolutionary War (submitted by Clara
  Hayes, Coeburn, VA).
McCORD, MRS. SOPHIANISBA   SC
  She provided supplies for the army (SI, U-W:283).
McCORMACK, CATHERINE   PA
  At age fifteen in October 1782 she was captured by Indians
  at Bedford and released on July 18, 1783, from Fort Ticonderoga
  (MR).
McCORMICK, MARTHA SANDERSON   VA
  She supplied produce for the army. See Biographies.
McCOUN, MARY
  Somerville. The wife of Alexander McCoun, she suffered damage
  in a British raid (CDB, p. 24).
McCOY, ANN   NC
  She provided supplies for the troops (RA, 5:55, fol. 4).
  Also Mrs. Ann McCoy (RA, 8:50, fol. 3).

III: COMPLETE LISTING 381

McCOY, ELIZABETH NJ
  Somerville. She suffered damage caused by the British (CDB, p. 24).
McCOY, MARGARET NC
  She supplied provisions for the troops (RA, 5:55, fol. 3).
McCRAW, MRS. VA
  Mecklenburg. She performed a public service (VR Ctf 1).
McCUISTON, JANE. See FLACK
McCULLOCH, MARY NJ
  Middlesex County. The wife of Robert McCulloch, she suffered damage in a British raid (CDB, p. 263).
McCULLOCH, MARY MITCHELL WV
  Her husband's heart was cut out and eaten by Indians. See Biographies.
McCULLOCH, SARAH INSKEEP VA
  Her son was killed by Indians. See Biographies.
McCULLOGH, PHOEBE BOYD GA
  She was the wife of Daniel McCullough, who commanded the privateer Rattlesnake and was captured by the British. On April 15, 1778, he was confined in the Fortun Prison at Gosport, England. After a long imprisonment, he escaped and returned to America (CN).
McCURDY, ANNE LORD CT
  Gen. Washington stayed here. See Biographies.
McCURDY, MARY WATSON SC
  The wife of Robert McCurdy, she died in 1803. Mary is listed as a patriot in the DAR Patriot Index.
McDANIEL, ANNA VA
  Halifax County. Credited with public service (VR, 2:282).
McDANIEL, LUANN McDONNELL PA
  She was born in 1759 and married Robert McDaniel. Luann died in 1850 and is listed as a patriot in the DAR Patriot Index.
McDANIEL, TEMPERANCE NC
  She supplied provisions for the army (RA, A:267).
McDONALD, ANN VA
  Frederick County. She performed a public service (VR, 2:199, 201). Also Anne McDonald (VR, 2:282).
McDONALD, ELIZABETH GA
  She supplied thirty-seven head of cattle for Gen. Wayne's troops (WA, p. 165). Her first husband was named McDonald, then on December 9, 1786, she was married for a second time, to William McDonald (DAR).
McDONALD, ELIZABETH NC
  She supplied provisions for the troops (RA, A:67).
McDONALD, ELIZABETH OGLE VA
  She was born in 1726 and married Joseph McDonald. Elizabeth died in 1795. She is recognized as a patriot in the DAR Patriot Index.
McDONALD, MARGARET FORSYTH GA
  Frederica, Saint Andrews Parish. The wife of Charles McDonald, she provided cattle for the army (WA, p. 178).

McDONALD, MARY WV
 Botetourt County. Recognized for public service (Lists, pp. 2, 6, 10).

McDONALD, RACHEL SC
 She supplied provisions for the troops (SI, O-Q:11).

McDONALD, REBECCA SC
 She nursed American soldiers on a prison ship. See Biographies.

McDONALD, SUSANNA OGLE. See MacDONALD

McDOUGAL (McDOUGLE), ANN VA
 Hanover County. Credited with public service (VR, 3:188, 190).

McDOWELL, ELIZABETH VA
 Rockbridge County. Credited with public service (VR, 5:82).

McDOWELL, ELLEN NC
 Ellen assisted her husband in making gunpowder. See Biographies.

McDOWELL, GRACE GREENLEE. See BOWMAN

McDOWELL, MARGARET O'NEAL NC
 She furnished food and supplies for the soldiers. See Biographies.

McDOWELL, MARY McCLUNG KY
 She was born in 1734 and married Col. Samuel McDowell of Virginia. She died in 1826 and is recognized as a patriot in the DAR Patriot Index.

McDUGALL, MOLLY NC
 She supplied provisions for the troops (RA, 5:60, fol. 3).

McELVEEN, MARY SC
 Provided supplies for the army (SI, R-T:151).

McEVESS, CATHERINE NJ
 Bound Brook. She suffered damage in a British raid (CDB, p. 29).

McEWEN, MARGARET HOUSTON NC
 She was born in 1758 and married Alexander McEwen. Margaret died in 1831 and is listed as a patriot in the DAR Patriot Index.

McFALL, BARBARA KY
 She was held captive by Indians for fourteen years. See Biographies.

McFALL, MARY NC
 Furnished provisions for the troops (RA, 5:59, fol. 2).

McFARLAND (McFARLANE), JANE VA
 Fairfax County. Recognized for public service (VR, 2:226).

McFARLAND, MARGARET NC
 The wife of Robert McFarland, she supplied provisions for the troops (RA, C:65).

McFARLANE, ELIZABETH VA
 Westmoreland County. She performed a public service (VR Court Booklet, p. 2).

McFEA, ELLONER NY
 At age thirty-one she was captured along with her husband, Alexander, and her three children by Indians at Bowman Creek in 1783 and released from Fort Ticonderoga on July 18, 1783 (MR).

McGEE, MARTHA McFARLAND. See BELL

III: COMPLETE LISTING

McGILL, HANNAH   SC
　She supplied provisions for the troops (SI, O-Q:184).
McGINTY, ANN KENNEDY. See POGUE
McGOUCH, SARAH   NC
　She furnished provisions for the army (RA, A:137).
McGREGOR, MRS. WILLIAM
　She was captured with her husband and two children in 1782 and taken to the Saint Lawrence suburbs (MR).
McGUIRE, MARY SHIRLEY   KY
　At age eighteen in June 1780 Mary, her husband, William, and son were captured by Tories and Indians (HP). She died in 1845 (DAR).
McGUIRE, NELLY   NC
　Furnished supplies for the troops (RA, 1:15, fol. 4).
McHARD, ELIZABETH   VA
　Mecklenburg. She performed a public service (VR, 4:69).
McILVAIN, MRS. JOHN   PA
　Gen. Washington had his headquarters in her home. See Biographies.
McILVEEN, MARY   SC
　She provided supplies for the troops (SI, O-Q:183).
McINSMITH, CATHERINE   SC
　Furnished provisions for the troops (SI, 10, pt. 1:173).
McINTOSH, ANNE   CT
　New London. She performed a service for the state (CAR, 28:114-116).
McINTOSH, GEORGIANA   GA
　She supplied six head of cattle for public use (WA, p. 143).
McINTOSH, SARAH THREADCRAFT   GA
　The British refused to let Mrs. McIntosh and her five children leave Savannah during the bombing of that city. See Biographies.
McINTOSH, SUSANNA MARSCHALK. See FELL
McJUNKIN, ANN JANE THOMAS   SC
　She was born in 1757 and married Maj. Joseph McJunkin. Ann died in 1826 and is listed as a patriot in the DAR Patriot Index.
McKAY, ANN   NC
　Furnished provisions for the troops (RA, 9:8, fol. 3).
McKAY, MRS. CABTON   SC
　Supplied provisions for the army (SI, Y-Z:135).
McKAY, MARGARET   NC
　Provided supplies for the troops (RA, 9:116, fol. 4).
McKAY, SUSANNAH   NC
　Furnished provisions for the troops (RA, 6:4, fol. 4).
McKEAN, SARAH ARMITAGE   PA
　She was an active member of the ladies' association for the welfare of the soldiers. See Biographies.
McKEE, MARTHA   NC
　She supplied provisions for the army (RA, A:90).
McKEE, MARTHA HODGE   PA
　She spun flax to make clothes for the soldiers. See Biographies.

McKEE, MARY   NC
　　She provided supplies for the troops (RA, A:229).
McKELVEN, MARY   SC
　　She provided provisions for the troops (SI, U-W:146).
McKENDRICK, CATHERINE   SC
　　She provided provisions for the army (SI, 10, pt. 1:173).
McKILLIP, MRS. ARCHIBALD   VA
　　She was captured by the British and Indians along with her husband at Cherry Valley in 1778 and later exchanged (MR).
McKINLY, JANE RICHARDSON   DE
　　Her husband was the president of Delaware and was taken prisoner by the British. See Biographies.
McKINSEY, HANNAH   CT
　　Fairfield. She suffered damage in a British raid (CAR, 1:53e, 63q). She was a Western Lands Grantee.
McKISICK, JANE WILSON   NC
　　She was born in 1749 and married Capt. Daniel McKisick. Jane died in 1818 and is recognized as a patriot in the DAR Patriot Index.
McKNEEL, MARY   NJ
　　Middlebush, Somerset County. She suffered damage in a British raid (CDB, p. 185).
McLAUGHLIN, ELIZABETH DUNCAN VA
　　She was born in 1762 and married Thomas McLaughlin. Elizabeth died in 1850 and is listed as a patriot in the DAR Patriot Index.
McLAUGHLIN, ELIZABETH ZANE. See CLARK
McLAURINE, ELIZABETH   VA
　　Powhatan County. She performed a public service (VR, 4:239).
McLEAN, JANE   SC
　　When Charleston fell to the British on May 12, 1780, she refused to sign an oath of fidelity to the Crown and so was banished from the city (SC).
McLEOD, ELIZABETH   GA
　　She supplied cattle for the army (WA, p. 178).
McLEOD, ELIZABETH   GA
　　She supplied provisions for the troops (RA, 7:24, fol. 3).
McMACKEN, JANE   NJ
　　Somerville. The wife of Andrew McMacken, she suffered damage in a British raid (CDB, p. 192).
McMANAS, SARAH   NJ
　　Westfield. The wife of James McManas, she suffered damage in a British raid (CDB, claim 100).
McMILLAN, MRS. SETH   VA
　　Prince William County. Credited with public service (VR Court Booklet, p. 11).
McMILLIN, JANE McDOWELL   SC
　　She was born in 1769 and married Hugh McMillin. Jane is listed as a patriot in the DAR Patriot Index.
McMYER, MARY   NJ
　　New Brunswick. The widow of Capt. Andrew McMyer, she suffered damage in a British raid (CDB, p. 78).

III: COMPLETE LISTING

McNAIR, MARGARET   NC
The wife of Daniel McNair, she supplied provisions for the troops (RA, J:175).

McNEALE, FANNY   NC
The wife of James McNeale, she provided supplies for the troops (RA, K:197).

McNEELY, MARGARET   NC
She supplied provisions for the army (RA, 12:73, fol. 4).

McNEIL, ABIGAIL HARVEY   MA
Charlestown (Boston). In 1772 she became the second wife of Daniel McNeil who commanded the privateer vessel Hancock in 1776, the America in 1777, the General Mifflin in 1778, and others. While in command of the Wasp, about November 1782, he was captured by the Stag and imprisoned until the end of the war (CN).

McNEIL, MARY   NC
She provided provisions for the troops (RA, 5:54, fol. 1). Also a Mary McNell (RA, 11:92, fol. 3).

McOWEN, FRANCES   NC
She provided supplies for the army (RA, C:4).

McPHERSON, ABIGAIL   NC
She supplied provisions for the troops (RA, 6:1, fol. 1).

McPHERSON, CHLOE   MD
Charles County. She provided wheat in 1782 for the troops (IM, 23658).

McPHERSON, SARAH   SC
She supplied provisions for the army (SI, Y-Z:192).

McREE, MARTHA   NC
She provided provisions for the troops (RA, 1:76, fol. 4).

McTYRE, ELIZABETH FIZZEL   VA
Lancaster County. The wife of Robert McTyre, she is recognized for public service (VR, 3:275).

McWARE, MARY   VA
At age twenty she was captured by the British and Indians on June 26, 1780, and taken to the Saint Lawrence suburbs (MR).

McWHARTER, ELIZABETH   SC
She supplied provisions for the troops (SI, B:221).

MEACHAM, MARGARET   VA
Gloucester County. Recognized for public service (VR, 3:49).

MEAD, ABIGAIL   CT
Greenwich. In the British raids of March 1779 and December 1783 she suffered damage (CAR, 36:19d). She was a Western Lands Grantee.

MEAD, ANN   CT
Greenwich. She suffered damage in a British raid (CAR, 21:55ab).

MEAD, ANN   VA
York County. She performed a public service (VR Court Booklet, 2:2, 5).

MEAD, DELIVERANCE   CT
Greenwich. In the British raids of March 1779 and December

1783 she suffered damage (CAR, 15:271b). She also loaned money to Oliver Wolcott for his militia (CAR, 17:376, 380).

MEAD, ELIZABETH   CT
Greenwich. In the British raid of 1779 she suffered damage (CAR, 15:271b). She was a Western Lands Grantee.

MEAD, HANNAH   CT
Greenwich. In a British raid she suffered damage (CAR, 1:63e, 74d). She was a Western Lands Grantee.

MEAD, JAMIMA   CT
Greenwich. In the British raid of 1779 she suffered damage (CAR, 15:271b). She was a Western Lands Grantee.

MEAD, JERUSHA   CT
Greenwich. In the British raids of March 1779 and December 1783 she suffered damage (CAR, 36:19a). She was a Western Lands Grantee.

MEAD, MARY   CT
Greenwich. The wife of John Mead, she suffered damage in a British raid (CAR, 21:55ab).

MEAD, RUTH   CT
Greenwich widow. She suffered damage in a British raid (CAR, 24:274f, 276c).

MEAD, SARAH   CT
Greenwich widow. In the British raids of March 1779 and December 1783 she suffered damage (CAR, 15:271b). She was a Western Lands Grantee.

MEAD, SYBIL   CT
She suffered losses in Tory raids. See Biographies.

MEADOWS, HANNAH   NC
The wife of William Meadows, she provided supplies for the army (RA, D:223).

MEAG, MRS.   CT
Woodbury. She provided lodging for the troops (CAR, 3:138a).

MEANLY, ELIZABETH   VA
Goochland County. She performed a public service (VR, 3:72).

MEASE, MRS. JOHN   PA
She contributed funds for the army. See Biographies.

MEATON, SARAH   MD
Baltimore County. She provided lodging in 1777 for Capt. George Cook, commander of the twenty-two-gun ship <u>Defence</u> (IM, 4078; CN).

MECOM, JANE FRANKLIN   MA
Her son was killed at the Battle of Bunker Hill. See Biographies.

MEEKER, ELIZABETH   NJ
Connecticut Farms, Essex County. The wife of Michael Meeker, she suffered damage in a British raid (CDB, claims 38, 43).

MEHELM, JOANNA BEEKMAN   NJ
Gen. Washington stayed in her home. See Biographies.

MEIGS, GRACE STARR   CT
She made clothing for the soldiers. See Biographies.

MELTON, LETTICE   VA
Albemarle County. The wife of William Melton, she is recognized for public service (VR Court Booklet, p. 16).

III: COMPLETE LISTING

MELVILE, JANE SC
She supplied provisions for the troops (SI, B:91; Y-Z:82).

MELVIN, MARTHA SC
After Charleston fell to the British on May 12, 1780, Martha refused to sign an oath of fidelity to the Crown and so was banished from the city (SC).

MERCER, GRACE SC
She provided supplies for the army (SI, B:133).

MERCER, ISABELLA GORDON VA
Fredericksburg. She married Dr. Hugh Mercer, who practiced medicine in what is now Mercersburg, then moved to Fredericksburg. Gen. Mercer was in charge of the Flying Camp, which was composed of the militia from Delaware, Maryland, New Jersey, and Pennsylvania. On January 3, 1777, during the Battle of Princeton, Gen. Mercer's horse was shot from under him. Then he was clubbed on the head by a British soldier with the breech of a musket, knocked down, and bayoneted in seven places. General Mercer died on January 12, 1777 (DB).

MERCHANT, KATHERINE NC
She provided supplies for the army (RA, 10:21, fol. 1).

MEREWETHER, MARGARET VA
Albemarle County. She performed a public service (VR Court Booklet, pp. 25, 26).

MERITHEW, PATIENCE BURGESS MA
She refused to take an oath of allegiance to the Crown. See Biographies.

MERMINGHAM, SARAH MD
In April and November 1776 she boarded Capt. James Nicholson of the Continental Navy. He was a resident of Chestertown, Maryland (IM, 1359, 2759).

MERRIAM, WIDOW CT
Litchfield. She supplied a gun for the militia (CAR, 6:182a).

MERRICK, ANN VA
Southampton County. Credited with public service (VR, 5:179).

MERRICK, HANNAH VA
Loudoun County. Recognized for public service (VR, 3:31).

MERRILL, ANNA BELDING CT
West Hartford. She was the wife of Titus Merrill (1756-1785), a private in the 8th Regiment, Connecticut Militia. He was taken prisoner by the British at the Cedars, Canada, on May 19, 1776 (FP4).

MERRILL, SARAH NJ
Middlesex. The widow of John Drake, she suffered damage in a British raid (CDB, p. 120).

MERRIT, MARTHA MD
In 1780 she supplied wheat for the army (IM, 11588).

MERRITT, REBEKAH CT
Greenwich widow. She suffered damage in the 1783 raid by the British (CAR, 24:276c).

MERRY, CATHARINE. See SUGGETT

MESSICK (MEYSICK), MARY NC
She supplied provisions for the troops (RA, 3:106, fol. 2).

MESSROLL, ANNE   NJ
    Somerville. She suffered damage caused by the British (CDB, p. 91).
MESSROLL (MESSROOL), MAGDELAIN   NJ
    Somerville. She suffered property loss caused by the British (CDB, pp. 92, 160).
MIADS, SARAH   SC
    She supplied provisions for the troops (SI, U-W:224).
MICKIE, ELIZABETH   VA
    Louisa County. She performed a public service (VR, 3:360).
MIDDLETON, ELIZABETH   NC
    She supplied provisions for the army (RA, 5:50, fol. 1).
MIDDLETON, ELIZABETH   NJ
    Burlington. She suffered damage in a British raid (CDB, p. 131).
MIDDLETON, MARY   NC
    She provided provisions for the army (RA, D:49).
MIDDLETON, MARY IZARD   SC
    Mrs. Middleton, her husband, and children were captured by the British. See Biographies.
MIERS, MARY   VA
    Berkeley County. The Widow Miers is recognized for public service (VR, 1:143).
MIFFLIN, SARAH MORRIS   PA
    She nursed sick and wounded soldiers. See Biographies.
MILAN, ANNE   VA
    Bedford County. Recognized for public service (VR Court Booklet, p. 8).
MILES, ALICE   CT
    New Haven. She suffered damage in a British raid (CAR, 1:63z, 91c). She was a Western Lands Grantee.
MILES, MARGARET. See STUCKER
MILES, MARY   CT
    New Haven. In the July 1779 British raid she suffered losses (CAR, 15:234c, 269b). She was a Western Lands Grantee.
MILLER, ANN FISHER   NY
    Gen. Washington had his headquarters here. See Biographies.
MILLER, CATHERINE   NY
    She was captured by Indians in July 1780 on the Mohawk River and taken to Montreal (MR).
MILLER, CHARLOTTE. See ALLAN
MILLER, EVE   NY
    She was captured by Indians in July 1780 on the Mohawk River and taken to Montreal (MR).
MILLER, HANNAH   CT, MA
    Boston. She fled to Pomfret, Connecticut, and supplied rum and coffee in 1779 for the army (CAR, 13:402-404).
MILLER, JANE   SC
    She provided provisions for the troops (SI, R-T:90).
MILLER, MARY   SC
    She provided supplies for the army (SI, R-T:158).

III: COMPLETE LISTING

MILLER, MARY   VA
   Goochland County. She is recognized for public service (VR, 3:72).
MILLER, MARY HEATH   VA
   She married Capt. William Miller. Mary is listed as a patriot in the DAR Patriot Index.
MILLER, PHOEBE   CT
   New Haven. In the 1779 British raid she suffered losses (CAR, 15:269e). She was a Western Lands Grantee.
MILLER, SARAH   VA
   Southampton County. She performed a public service (VR, 5:179).
MILLER, SUSAN TWITTY   NC
   She was born in 1763 and married Ens. John Miller. Susan died in 1825 and is recognized as a patriot in the DAR Patriot Index
MILLS, MRS.   VA
   Hanover County. Credited with public service (VR, 1:17).
MILLS (MILLES), ANN   NC
   She supplied provisions for the troops (RA, 1:94, fol. 4).
MILLS, ELIZABETH   GA
   She provided a mare for the army (WA, p. 175).
MILLS, ELIZABETH   VA
   Middlesex County. She performed a public service (VR, 4:95).
MILLS, ELIZABETH COLLIER MD
   She was born in 1751 and married Benjamin Mills. Elizabeth died in 1822 and is recognized as a patriot in the DAR Patriot Index.
MILLS, HANNAH   CT
   Groton. She suffered damage in a British raid (CAR, 1:79b).
MILLS, LUCY   VA
   Albemarle County. Recognized for public service (VR Court Booklet, p. 36).
MILLS, MARY   VA
   Albemarle County. Credited with public service (VR, 2:349). Also Hanover County (VR, 3:188-190).
MILLS, MARY   WV
   Botetourt County. She supplied provisions for the troops (VR, 1:171-172).
MILLS, MARY GILL   SC
   She was born in 1758 and married Capt. John Mills (1757-1795). Mary led a band of eleven women who set out to gather crops for the militia and traveled from farm to farm to collect the provisions. She died in 1841 (GP).
MILLS, PATIENCE   NJ
   Westfield. The wife of Elias Mills, she suffered damage in a British raid (CDB, claim 60).
MINER, PRUDENCE   CT
   Groton. She suffered losses in a British raid (CAR, 1:63q, 79b). She was a Western Lands Grantee.

MINER, REBECCA CT
   Groton. She was widowed by action at Fort Griswold and suffered losses in the British raid (CAR, 26:295e). She was a Western Lands Grantee.
MINGE, CHRISTIANA VA
   Charles City County. Recognized for public service (VR, 1:314-315).
MINGHAM, ELIZABETH VA
   Elizabeth City County. She performed a public service (VR Ctf 1).
MINIS, ABIGAIL GA
   She provided provisions and forage for the army for the siege of Savannah (WA, p. 117).
MINIS, SARAH GA
   She lent out "Negro Smith" for hire by the quartermaster's department (WA, p. 117).
MINNICH, REBECCA SC
   She supplied provisions for the army (SI, R-T:213).
MINOR, JEMIMA VA
   Fairfax. She performed a public service (VR, 2:227).
MINOR, MARY VA
   Gloucester County. Credited with public service (VR, 3:48).
MINSKY, MARY ANNE MD
   In 1777 she supplied blankets for the army (IM, 4236).
MINTER, MRS. SC
   She supplied provisions for the troops (SI, R-T:282).
MITCH (MITCHELL), SUSANNAH NC
   She provided supplies for the troops (RA, 1:114, fol. 2).
MITCHELL, AGNES VA
   Rockbridge County. Credited with public service (VR, 5:83).
MITCHELL, JANE VA
   Culpeper County. Recognized for public service (VR, 2:122).
MITCHELL, MRS. JOHN PA
   She was an active member of the ladies' association for the welfare of the soldiers. See Biographies.
MITCHELL, RACHEL NC
   She supplied provisions for the troops (RA, 12:19, fol. 4).
MITCHELL, SUSANNA VA
   King and Queen County. Credited with public service (VR, 3:228).
MITCHUM, SUSAN ALLEN VA
   She was born in 1759 and married Dudley Mitchum. Susan died in 1833 and is recognized as a patriot in the DAR Patriot Index.
MIX, HANNAH CT
   New Haven. In the 1779 British raid she suffered losses (CAR, 15:269f). She was a Western Lands Grantee.
MIX, PATIENCE CT
   New Haven. Suffered losses in a British raid (CAR, 1:63c, 91f). She was a Western Lands Grantee.
MIXON, FRANCES SC
   She supplied provisions for the troops (SI, 10, pt. 1:14).

III: COMPLETE LISTING 391

MOBLEY, MARY NC
She provided supplies for the army (RA, 11:32, fol. 4).
MOFFETT, SARAH MARTHA McDOWELL VA
The wife of Col. George Moffett, she is listed as a patriot in the DAR Patriot Index.
MOGER, ABIGAIL CT
Stratford. In 1778 she supplied a blanket for the army (CAR, 12:93a).
MONFORE, CORNELIA NJ
Somerville. Her goods stored in the home of Cornelius Lott were taken by the British (CDB, p. 121).
MONROE, JEMIMA SMITH VA
Westmoreland County. The wife of William Monroe, she supplied provisions for the troops (VR, 5:221).
MONROE, MARGARET VA
Westmoreland County. She performed a public service (VR Lists, p. 3).
MONTAYNE, SARAH NJ
Hackensack. The wife of John Montayne, she suffered losses in a British raid (CDB, claim 47).
MONTGOMERY, JANE PATTERSON KY
She had a rifle ready when the Indians attacked. See Biographies.
MONTGOMERY, JANET LIVINGSTON NY
Her husband was killed in the attack on Quebec. See Biographies.
MONTGOMERY, KATHERINE. See BLEDSOE
MONTGOMERY (MUMGUMMRY), MARY MD
Charles County. In 1782 she supplied wheat for the army (IM, 24041).
MONTGOMERY, RACHEL RUSH PA
She supplied food and clothing for the soldiers. See Biographies.
MONTGOMERY, SARAH BOONE. See BROOKS
MOODY, MARY NC
She supplied provisions for the troops (RA, 5:29, fol. 1).
MOONE, ELSA NJ
South Brunswick. The wife of Martin Moone, a wine merchant, she suffered losses in a British raid (CDB, p. 260).
MOOR, MARTHA NC
She provided provisions for the army (RA, 12:106, fol. 2).
MOORE, ABIGAIL HEMPSTEAD NY
She was born in 1728 and married John Ledyard, then Micah Moore. Abigail died in 1805 and is recognized as a patriot in the DAR Patriot Index.
MOORE, ANN CT
East Windsor. In 1778 she supplied a blanket for the army (CAR, 12:222a).
MOORE, ANN NC
She supplied provisions for the troops (RA, 8:23, fol. 4).
MOORE, ANN NJ
Burlington. She suffered damage in a British raid (CDB, p. 159).

MOORE, BEHETHLAND FOOTE   SC
   She warned the Americans of an impending British attack. See Biographies.
MOORE, CATHARINE   NC
   She supplied provisions for the troops (RA, 5:53, fol. 2).
MOORE, CATHARINE   VA
   King William County. She performed a public service (VR, 3:253).
MOORE, DOLLEY   SC
   The wife of James Moore, she provided supplies for the troops (SI, O-Q:41).
MOORE, ELIZABETH   CT
   Groton. She suffered losses in a British raid (CAR, 1:63q, 79b). She was a Western Lands Grantee.
MOORE, ELIZABETH   CT
   Greenwich. In the 1779 British raid she suffered property damage (CAR, 15:271b). She was a Western Lands Grantee.
MOORE, ELIZABETH   NJ
   Hackensack. The wife of Samuel S. Moore, she suffered damage in a British raid (CDB, claim 31).
MOORE, ELIZABETH CRESWELL WHITEHALL   PA
   She was born in 1733 and married James Moore. Elizabeth died in 1815. She is listed as a patriot in the DAR Patriot Index.
MOORE, JANE   VA
   Princess Anne County. Credited with public service (VR, 4:220).
MOORE, JOANNA   VA
   King William County. She performed a public service (VR Lists, 2:1).
MOORE, MARGARET   VA
   Hansemond County. Credited with public service (VR, 4:357).
MOORE, MARTHA   NC
   She supplied provisions for the troops (RA, A:109).
MOORE, MARY   CT
   Groton. She suffered losses in a British raid (CAR, 1:63r, 79b). She was a Western Lands Grantee.
MOORE, MARY   NC
   She supplied provisions for the army (RA, 5:44, fol. 3).
MOORE, MARY   NJ
   Hackensack. The wife of Samuel Moore, she suffered losses in a British raid (CDB, claim 83).
MOORE, MARY   VA
   Brunswick. She performed a public service (VR, 1:222).
MOORE, MARY   VA
   York County. Credited with public service (VR Court Booklet, 2:1, 7).
MOORE, MARY HARPER   NY
   She was born in 1733 and married James Moore. Mary died in 1798 and is recognized as a patriot in the DAR Patriot Index.

III: COMPLETE LISTING

MOORE, NANCY CT
Groton. She suffered damage in a British raid (CAR, 1:63q, 79b). She was a Western Lands Grantee.

MOORE, RACHEL NC
She supplied provisions for the troops (RA, 11:81, fol. 1).

MOORE, SARAH NC
She provided supplies for the army (RA, 5:64, fol. 3).

MOORE, SARAH SC
She supplied provisions for the troops (SI, U-W:73).

MOORE, TEMPERANCE CT
New London. She suffered damage in a British raid (CAR, 1:63k, 95i). She was a Western Lands Grantee.

MOORE, THANKFUL SC
When Charleston fell on May 12, 1780, to the British, she refused to sign an oath of fidelity to the Crown and so was banished from the city (SC).

MOORES, GRACE NJ
Woodbridge. She suffered losses in a British raid (CDB, p. 90).

MOORES, JEAN ROSS SC
She married Henry Moores, and they had twelve children. He served as a lieutenant of the 4th South Carolina Regiment, 1777-1780, and was captured by the British when Charleston fell on May 12, 1780 (submitted by Charles W. True, Jr., El Paso, TX).

MORECOCK, MILDRED VA
Charles City County. Credited with public service (VR, 1:316).

MOREHOUSE, ELIZABETH CT
Fairfield. In 1777 she supplied a blanket for the army (CAR, 11:188a).

MOREHOUSE, EUNICE CT
Fairfield widow. She suffered losses in the 1779-1780 British raids (CAR, 15:250a). She was a Western Lands Grantee.

MOREHOUSE, HANNAH CT
Fairfield. She suffered damages in the 1779-1780 British raids (CAR, 15:250g). She was a Western Lands Grantee.

MOREHOUSE, LUCRETIA CT
New Fairfield. In 1781 she supplied provisions for the army (CAR, 35:185a).

MOREHOUSE, SARAH CT
Norwalk. She suffered losses in a British raid (CAR, 1:63i, 98h). She was a Western Lands Grantee.

MOREHOUSE, SARAH CT
Ridgefield. She suffered damage in the April 1777 British raid (CAR, 8:391a). She was a Western Lands Grantee.

MOREHOUSE, SARAH LEWIS CT
She was born in 1748 and married Josiah Morehouse, then Benjamin Chapman. Recognized as a patriot in the DAR Patriot Index.

MOREL, MRS. JOHN   GA
   French troops ransacked her plantation. See Biographies.
MORELAND, ELIZABETH   VA
   Surry County. She performed a public service (VR Court Booklet, p. 13).
MORFORD, ELIZABETH   NJ
   Middlesex County. The widow of Joseph Morford, she suffered damage in a British raid (CDB, p. 279).
MORGAN, MRS.   CT
   Gen. Washington stayed here. See Biographies.
MORGAN, MRS.   NC
   She supplied provisions for the troops (RA, 4:73, fol. 1).
MORGAN, ABIGAIL BAILEY   VA
   Her husband was taken prisoner at Quebec. See Biographies.
MORGAN, ANN   VA
   New Kent County. Recognized for public service (VR Court Booklet, pp. 10, 19).
MORGAN, ELIZABETH   SC
   She supplied provisions for the army (SI, L-N:337).
MORGAN, ESTHER   VA
   Bedford County. The wife of Thomas Morgan, she performed a public service (VR Lists, 1:21).
MORGAN, JANE   WV
   Berkeley County. She supplied provisions for the troops (VR Ctf 1).
MORGAN, MARY BAYNTON   NJ
   She was active in the ladies' association for the welfare of the soldiers. See Biographies.
MORGAN, MARY HOPKINSON   PA
   Philadelphia. She was the wife of Dr. John Morgan. On October 14, 1774, John Adams dined with the Morgans. Adams mentioned that Messrs. Middleton, Mifflin, William Russell, and the two Rutledges dined with them, and that Mrs. Morgan was a sprightly pretty lady (BA).
MORGAN, PRUDENCE   CT
   Groton. She was born in 1732 and married Joseph Morgan, then Elijah Avery. Prudence died in 1809 (DAR). She suffered losses in a British raid (CAR, 1:63q, 79a). She was a Western Lands Grantee.
MORGAN, SARAH   NC
   She supplied provisions for the troops (RA, 2:58, fol. 2).
MORGAN, SARAH   VA
   Pittsylvania County. Recognized for public service (VR, 5:19).
MORGAN, TEMPERANCE AVERY   CT
   She was born in 1725 and married William Morgan. Temperance died in 1801 and is listed as a patriot in the DAR Patriot Index.
MORISON, MRS. THOMAS   NH
   She supplied breakfast for her husband and son as they left for the war. See Biographies.
MORREAU (MORRER), MARY   SC
   She supplied provisions for the troops (SI, I:83).

III: COMPLETE LISTING

MORRILL, SARAH BARNARD. See CLARK
MORRIN, MARY   VA
   Loudoun. Credited with public service (VR, 3:311).
MORRIS, MRS.   NJ
   Somerset County. She was the wife of Gen. Morris. She collected funds for the army (New Jersey Gazette, July 4, 1780).
MORRIS, ANN   MD
   Charles County. She supplied wheat for the army, May 8, 1783 (IM, 25395).
MORRIS, ELIZABETH   VA
   New Kent County. She performed a public service (VR Court Booklet, p. 14).
MORRIS, EUNICE   NJ
   Wardsession, Essex County. The widow of John Morris, she suffered damage in a British raid (CDB, claim 20).
MORRIS, MRS. JAMES   PA
   Gen. Washington had his headquarters there. See Biographies.
MORRIS, LUCRETIA RUSSELL   CT
   She was the wife of Andrew Morris, who served as midshipman on the armed ship Oliver Cromwell, and later as third lieutenant. On June 5, 1779, he was captured by the British and imprisoned (CN).
MORRIS, MARGARET   NJ
   She cared for sick and wounded soldiers. See Biographies.
MORRIS, MARY   NC
   She supplied provisions for the troops (RA, 11:99, fol. 2).
MORRIS, MARY   VA
   James City County. She performed a public service (VR Ctf 1).
MORRIS, MARY PHILIPSE   NY
   Gen. Washington had his headquarters there. See Biographies.
MORRIS, MARY WALTON   PA
   Her home was vandalized by the enemy. See Biographies.
MORRIS, MARY WHITE   PA
   She collected funds for the soldiers. See Biographies.
MORRIS, PENELOPE   NC
   She supplied provisions for the troops (RA, 7:49, fol. 1).
MORRIS, SARAH CHAFFEE   CT
   She was the wife of Isaac Morris, who was a private in the 8th Continental Line. During the winter of 1777/78 at Valley Forge, he suffered from exposure and died on January 10, 1778 (FP1).
MORRISON, ANN   VA
   Brunswick. She performed a public service (VR Lists, p. 6).
MORRISON, ANNA   VA
   Prince George County. Credited with public service (VR, 4:254).
MORRISON, MARY   NY
   In 1780 she went to New York City to arrange a parole for her son (FH).
MORRISON, PENELOPE. See MORRIS
MORRISON, PHEBE   NJ
   Orange. She suffered damages in a British raid (CDB, claims 45, 51, 53).

MORROW, MRS. JAMES   VA
   She was captured with her husband and one child by the British
   and Indians on June 20, 1780, and taken to the Saint Lawrence
   suburbs, Canada (MR).
MORROW, JANE PEDEN   SC
   She married a Mr. Morton, then Samuel Morrow. Jane is listed
   as a patriot in the DAR Patriot Index.
MORROW, MARGARET   KY
   At age twenty-one Margaret and her husband were captured
   by Tories and Indians in June 1780 (MR).
MORROW, RACHEL REED   NC
   The wife of William Morrow, she supplied provisions for the
   army (RA, 6:2, fol. 5).
MORROW, SARAH   NC
   She provided provisions for the troops (RA, 11:30, fol. 4).
MORTON, AGNES WOODSON   VA
   Charlotte. The wife of Joseph Morton, she supplied provisions
   for the army (VR Court Booklet, p. 44).
MORTON, ANN JUSTIS   PA
   Mrs. Morton, her five daughters, and three sons had to flee
   from an invading army. See Biographies.
MORTON, JANE   VA
   Fairfax. She performed a public service (VR, 2:228).
MORTON, JANE PEDEN. See MORROW
MORTON, MRS. JOHN   NJ
   She nursed wounded soldiers. See Biographies.
MOSEBY, ELIZABETH. See ELIZABETH BOONE GRANT
MOSELEY, PATIENCE   CT
   Southbury. She provided lodging for the soldiers in 1776 (CAR,
   5:274e).
MOSS, JANE   VA
   Goochland County. Credited with public service (VR Ctf 1).
MOSS, MARGARET   NC
   She supplied provisions for the troops (RA, 6:23, fol. 3).
MOSSE, DOROTHY PHOEBE NORTON   SC
   Her husband was captured by the enemy. See Biographies.
MOTLEY, MARTHA ELLINGTON   VA
   She was the first wife of Joseph Motley, Jr., and died about
   1780. Martha is recognized as a patriot in the DAR Patriot
   Index.
MOTT, NANCY   VA
   Northumberland County. Credited with public service (VR,
   4:120).
MOTTE, REBECCA BREWTON   SC
   She nursed wounded soldiers. See Biographies.
MOULSON, MARY   VA
   Amelia County. She performed a public service (VR, 1:75).
MOULTRIE, HANNAH MOTTE   SC
   Her husband was imprisoned by the British. See Biographies.
MOUNT, ANNE ANDERSON   NC
   She opposed drinking British tea. See Background.

III: COMPLETE LISTING

MOUNTCASTLE, ANNE VA
  Charles City County. The wife of Joab Mountcastle, she is credited with public service (VR Court Booklet, p. 23).

MOURSE, ELEANOR VA
  She was captured by the British and Indians along with her child in 1778 at Cherry Valley and later exchanged (MR).

MUCKLEWAIN, MARY SC
  She supplied provisions for the troops (SI, Y-Z:132).

MUDGE, MARY CT
  Windham. In 1777 she supplied a blanket for the army (CAR, 11:120a).

MUHLENBERG, ANNE VA
  Shenandoah County. Recognized for public service (VR Court Booklet, p. 14).

MUIR, PHOEBE VA
  Loudoun County. The wife of Robert Muir, she performed a public service (VR, 3:314).

MULFORD, HANNAH NJ
  Connecticut Farms, Essex County. The widow of Thomas Mulford, she suffered damage in a British raid (CDB, claim 34).

MULLEN, ELIZABETH NJ
  Burlington. The wife of Joseph Mullen, she suffered property loss in a British raid (CDB, claim 248).

MULLINS, DOROTHY VA
  Gloucester County. She performed a public service (VR Court Booklet, 3:24).

MUMFORD, FRANCES RI
  The wife of Nathaniel Mumford, in January 1782 she supplied rations for the troops (MP, 23:36).

MUMFORD, JANE VA
  Amelia County. Recognized for public service (VR, 1:74).

MUN, JANE NJ
  Orange. She suffered damage in a British raid (CDB, claim 3).

MUNDAY, ANN NJ
  Piscataway. The wife of Isaac Munday, she suffered losses in a British raid (CDB, p. 247).

MUNDAY, EFFIE. See MANNING

MUNDROE, FLORA NC
  She supplied provisions for the troops (RA, 5:53, fol. 1).

MUNDY, ISABEL NJ
  Middlesex County. She was born in 1730 and married Stephen Cramer, then Moses Bloodgood, then Edward Mundy. Isabel died in 1809 (DAR). She suffered losses in a British raid (CDB, p. 60).

MUNROE, MRS. VT
  Bennington. After the Battle of Bennington, she carried buckets of milk and water to the wounded American and Hessian soldiers lying on the field of battle (submitted by Dorothy Wilcox, Durham, NH).

MUNROE, ANN NC
  She supplied provisions for the troops (RA, 5:62, fol. 4).

MUNROW (MUNROE), ABIGAIL   CT
  The Widow Abigail supplied the clothing which was lost when
  her husband was killed in the New Jersey campaign in 1777 (CAR,
  11:574d, 576).

MUNSON, DESIRE   CT
  Wallingford. In 1777 she supplied a blanket for the army (CAR,
  11:208a).

MURDEN, ELIZABETH   VA
  Norfolk. She performed a public service (VR, 4:133).

MURDEN, SARAH   VA
  In April 1779 she was captured by Tories and Indians (MR).

MURDOCK, MARY   VA
  Fauquier County. She was credited for public service (VR,
  2:244). Also King George County (VR Court Booklet, pp. 2,
  10).

MURPHY, SARAH DUKE   SC
  She was born in 1733 and married Simon Murphy. Sarah died
  in 1818 (DAR). She provided supplies for the army (SI, 10,
  pt. 2:136).

MURRAY, ANN   VA
  Prince George County. Credited with public service (VR, 4:254).

MURRAY, ANNE BOLLING   VA
  She was born in 1710 and married James Murray. Anne died
  in 1800 and is listed as a patriot in the DAR Patriot Index.

MURRAY, MARY LINDLEY   NY
  She delayed the British army for two hours, giving Gen. Putnam
  and his men a chance to escape. See Biographies.

MURRAY, RACHEL   VA
  Middlesex County. Recognized for public service (VR, 4:348).

MUSE, CHARITY   NC
  She supplied provisions for the troops (RA, 5:55, fol. 4).

MUSE, JANE   VA
  Westmoreland County. Credited for public service (VR, 5:221).

MUSICK, MARY   NC
  She supplied provisions for the troops (RA, A:223).

MUSSIN, JEAN   WV
  Botetourt County. Recognized for public service (VR Court
  Booklet, p. 30).

MUSSLEWHITE, MILLY   NC
  She provided supplies for the army (RA, 5:60, fol. 4).

MYER, CATRINA   NJ
  Harrington Township, Bergen County. She suffered damage in
  a British raid (CDB, claim 22).

MYERS, HANNAH   NY
  At age five she was captured by Indians in June 1780 and taken
  to Montreal (MR).

MYERS, MARY   NC
  Her second husband was Michael Myers, and she died in 1784.
  Mary is listed as a patriot in the DAR Patriot Index 2.

MYERS, MARY   SC
  She supplied provisions for the troops (SI, 1:82).

III: COMPLETE LISTING 399

MYERS, MARY WV
   Berkeley County. She performed a public service (VR Court Booklet, 1:35).

N

NAGLE, MARY FISH. See SILLIMAN
NAIL, SARAH VA
   Hansemond County. Recognized for public service (VR, 4:164).
NAILOR, ELIZABETH VA
   At age twenty-three she was captured in October 1779 by Indians at Holston with Jane Nailor (aged six) and released from Fort Ticonderoga on July 18, 1782 (MR).
NANCE, ELIZABETH SC
   She supplied provisions for the troops (SI, O-Q:294).
NARON, SARAH NC
   She provided supplies for the army (RA, 12:72, fol. 2).
NASH, REBECCA CT
   Fairfield. In the British raid of April 1777 she suffered damage (CAR, 15:261c). She was a Western Lands Grantee.
NASH, SARAH NC
   She supplied provisions for the troops (RA, 8:35, fol. 3).
NASH, SARAH MOORE NC
   She was the wife of Brig. Gen. Francis Nash who was wounded at the Battle of Germantown, Pennsylvania, on October 4, 1777, and died of his wounds on October 7, 1777 (DAR; FW).
NAYLOR, JANE VA
   Elizabeth City County. She performed a public service (VR, 2:163).
NEALE, JANE VA
   King William County. Credited with public service (VR, 3:254).
NEALS, MARY VA
   In August 1780 she was captured by Tories and Indians (MR).
NEELY, SARAH MORGAN SC
   She was born in 1730 and married William Neely (or Niely). Sarah died in 1796 (DAR). She provided supplies for the army (SI, U-W:187).
NEIL, ELIZA NJ
   Acquacanunk, Essex County. She suffered damage in a British raid (CDB, claim 58).
NEIL, ELIZABETH MALLAM NJ
   She sent a piece of buffalo cloth to Gen. Washington. See Biographies.
NEILSON, CATHERINE VOORHEES NJ
   She was a member of the ladies' association for the welfare of the soldiers. See Biographies.
NEILSON, CHARLOTTE VA
   Middlesex County. She performed a public service (VR, 4:96, 349).

NEILSON, GANNITTE HARRISON   NJ
She was a member of the ladies' association for the welfare of the soldiers. See Biographies.
NEILSON, GRACE CARWILL   NJ
She was a member of the ladies' association. See Biographies.
NELMS, SARAH   NC
She supplied provisions for the troops (RA, 8:70, fol. 1).
NELSON, AGNES   NC
She provided provisions for the army (RA, A:266).
NELSON, ANN   NC
She supplied provisions for the army (RA, A:281).
NELSON, ELIZABETH   VA
Hanover County. She performed a public service (VR, 3:191).
NELSON, ELIZABETH   VA
Warwick County. Credited with public service (VR, 5:214). Also York County (VR Lists, p. 5).
NELSON, HARRIET MORGAN   KY
Bryan's Station. She married Edward Nelson. When the Tories and Indians attacked on August 15, 1782, she was one of the women who went for water. Her name is inscribed on the monument erected in 1896 by the Lexington DAR. She is listed as a patriot in the DAR Patriot Index.
NELSON, LUCY GRIMES   VA
The Nelsons spent their own money for the Revolutionary cause. See Biographies.
NELSON, MARY   VA
Cumberland County. The wife of Matthew Nelson, she died in 1789 (DAR). She is recognized for public service (VR, 1:230).
NELSON, SARAH   NC
She supplied provisions for the troops (RA, A:214).
NETHEROUT, SARAH   NC
She provided supplies for the army (RA, 5:22, fol. 2).
NEWBERRY, MARY   CT
New London. She suffered losses in a British raid (CAR, 1:63i, 95f). She was a Western Lands Grantee.
NEWCOMB, ELIZABETH   CT
New London. She suffered damage in a British raid (CAR, 1:63i, 95e). She was a Western Lands Grantee.
NEWELL, MRS. JONATHAN   NJ
Monmouth County. The wife of Capt. Jonathan Newell, she was a member of the ladies' association for the welfare of the soldiers (New Jersey Gazette, July 4, 1780).
NEWGENT, ANN   VA
Fauquier County. Recognized for public service (VR, 2:244).
NEWLEY (NEWLY), ELIZABETH   NC
She provided provisions for the army (RA, 11:6, fol. 4; RA, 4:73, fol. 1).
NEWPORT, JANE   VA
Mecklenburg. She performed a public service (VR, 4:70). Also Jean Newport of Mecklenburg (VR Ctf 1).

III: COMPLETE LISTING

NEWSON, BERTHA NC
She supplied provisions for the troops (RA, 3:62, fol. 2).

NEWSUM, LUCY VA
Brunswick. Recognized for public service (VR Lists, p. 6).

NEWSUM, LUCY VA
Dinwiddie County. Credited with public service (VR, 1:338).

NEWSUM, PATIENCE VA
Southampton County. Credited with public service (VR, 5:180).

NEWSUM, TABITHA VA
Southampton County. Recognized for public service (VR, 5:179-180).

NEWTON, ANN NC
She supplied provisions for the troops (RA, 5:48, fol. 4).

NEWTON, ANNA VA
Princess Anne County. She performed a public service (VR, 4:222).

NEWTON, ELIZABETH NC
She supplied provisions for the army (RA, 5:44, fol. 1).

NEWTON, JANE SC
She provided supplies for the army (SI, R-T:46).

NEWTON, MARY VA
Caroline County. Credited with public service (VR Lists, 2:18, 26).

NEWTON, SARAH VA
Norfolk. She performed a public service (VR, 4:134).

NICHOLAS, MARGARET NJ
Newark. The wife of Moses Nicholas, she suffered losses in a British raid (CDB, claim 45).

NICHOLS, MARY VA
Halifax County. Credited with public service (VR, 2:283a).

NICHOLS, SARAH CT
East Windsor. She supplied a blanket for the army (CAR, 11:12a).

NICHOLSON, ELIZABETH MD, VA
Chestertown, Maryland. The wife of John Nicholson, some time before 1776 they moved to Virginia. In 1779 he was captain of the Continental frigate Deane and later the Hornet, then he was captured by the British and imprisoned. Some time later he escaped and returned to America. His brothers James, Samuel, and William were also naval officers from Maryland. James and William were also captured by the British. Samuel was the most successful; in 1777, with Capt. Lambert Wickes, he captured eighteen enemy vessels (CN).

NICHOLSON, FRANCES WITTER MD
Chestertown. She married James Nicholson, who on June 6, 1776, was commissioned a captain in the Continental Navy. In January 1778 he commanded the frigate Virginia out of Baltimore, but was captured by the British and imprisoned on the ship Jersey in New York Harbor. This ship was ridden with smallpox and other diseases (CN).

NICHOLSON, LUCY NC
She supplied provisions for the troops (RA, A:60).

NICHOLSON, SARAH   VA
    Southampton County. Credited with public service (VR, 5:179).
    Also Sussex County (VR, 5:198, 205).
NICKSON (NIXON), BATHANA   NC
    She provided supplies for the army (RA, C:127).
NIXON, MARY ADAIR. See McCALLA
NOBLIN, MARTHA   VA
    Warwick County. She performed a public service (VR, 5:214).
NOE, SARAH. See HODGSON
NOELL, OLIVE   VA
    Caroline County. Recognized for public service (VR Court Booklet, 2:20-21). Also Essex County (VR, 4:305).
NOELL, SARAH   VA
    Essex County. Credited with public service (VR, 4:154).
NOLES, MARY   SC
    After the fall of Charleston on May 12, 1780, all women who were heads of households were required to take an oath of fidelity to the Crown. Mrs. Noles refused to do so, and was banished from the city along with 120 other women and 264 children (SC).
NORMENT, ELIZABETH   VA
    Caroline County. She performed a public service (VR, 1:275; Court Booklet, 2:35).
NORTH, NAOMI DAVIS   PA
    She was born in 1762 and married Thomas North. Naomi died in 1844 and is listed as a patriot in the DAR Patriot Index.
NORTHRUP, ANNE   CT
    Danbury. In the British raid of April 1777 she suffered damage (CAR, 8:382b). She was a Western Lands Grantee.
NORTON, MARY GODFREY   GA
    Savannah. She was the wife of William Norton, who was captured by the British when they took the city on December 29, 1778. His sister, Elizabeth Norton Joyner, rode on horseback to the enemy camp to secure his release. Since the soldier was ill, she was successful in bringing him home to Mrs. Norton (submitted by George Norton, Cocoa Beach, FL).
NORVEL, MARY   VA
    Hanover County. She performed a public service (VR Court Booklet, 1:11).
NOTT, MARY   CT
    The Widow Nott in 1779 spun yarn for the army (CAR, 35:228ij, 234c).
NOVELTON, MRS.   SC
    She supplied provisions for the troops (SI, Y-Z:207).
NOX (KNOX), MARY   NC
    She provided supplies for the army (RA, A:112).
NUNNERY, LUCY   VA
    Halifax County. Recognized for public service (VR, 2:282).

III: COMPLETE LISTING

O

O'BANNON, ABIGAIL   SC
  She supplied provisions for the troops (SI, Y-Z:176).
O'BANNON, MATILDA. See MORGAN, ABIGAIL
OBENDORF, MARGARET   PA, NY
  She was captured by Indians in 1780 along with her son and taken to Montreal (MR).
OBERKERSH, FRANCES   NC
  She supplied provisions for the troops (RA, B:190).
O'BRIEN, ELIZABETH FITZPATRICK   ME
  Kittery. She married Jeremiah O'Brien who commanded the sloop Unity in 1775 and captured the British schooner Margaretta. O'Brien sailed on April 8, 1780, on the Hannibal, but was captured by the British and imprisoned in New York. He was then taken to the Mill Prison, Plymouth, England. O'Brien escaped and returned to America (CN).
ODELL, MARTHA BOWDOIN   NC
  She was born in 1768 and married Isaac Odell. Martha died in 1800 and is listed as a patriot in the DAR Patriot Index.
ODOM (ODUM), ELIZABETH   GA
  She provided ferriage and provisions to detachments of Gen. Wayne's army (WA, 114), and ferriages in 1777-1778 (p. 156).
ODUM, MARGARET   SC
  She supplied provisions for the troops (SI, R-T:289).
OGDEN, ANNE   NJ
  Morris County. The wife of Stephen Ogden, she suffered damages caused by the Americans (CDB, claim 26).
OGDEN, JANE STURGES   CT
  Fairfield. The daughter of Abigail Bradley and Solomon Sturges, she was born there on April 6, 1729. On April 5, 1750, she married David Ogden III. Two of her sons served in the war. Her father was killed in the Battle of Fairfield in 1779. The family moved to Greenfield, Connecticut, in 1776 when her husband died. Jane died on October 26, 1807 (submitted by Edward L. Woodyard, Armonk, NY).
OGDEN, MARY   CT
  Fairfield. The widow of Samuel Ogden, she suffered losses in the April 1777 raid by the British (CAR, 15:261a).
OGDEN, MARY GOUVERNEUR   NJ
  She was active in the ladies' association for the welfare of the soldiers. See Biographies.
OGDEN, REBECCA. See BONNEL
OGDEN, SARAH   CT
  Fairfield. She suffered damage in a British raid (CAR, 1:53h, 63r). She was a Western Lands Grantee.
OGDEN, TABITHA   NC
  She supplied provisions for the troops (RA, 11:89, fol. 3).
OGLE, AGNES   MD
  Frederick County. In 1781 she supplied wheat for the army (IM, 18850).

O'HARA, MARY CARSON   PA
  She made clothing and knitted socks for the soldiers. See Biographies.
OKIE, MARY   NJ
  New Brunswick. The widow of Abraham Okie, she suffered damage in a British raid (CDB, p. 96).
OLIPHANT, CATHERINE   SC
  She supplied provisions for the troops (SI, Y-Z:315).
OLNEY, ANN PAGET   RI
  Providence. She married Joseph Olney who commanded the Continental brig Cabot in 1776. But then on March 25, 1777, Olney was captured by HMS Milford and taken to Halifax, Nova Scotia, where he was imprisoned (CN).
ORD, MRS.   PA
  Philadelphia. She collected money for the soldiers (Pennsylvania Gazette, June 12, 1780).
ORMOND, ELIZABETH P.   NC
  She opposed drinking British tea. See Background.
ORMOND, MARY   NC
  She supplied provisions for the troops (RA, A:162).
ORNE, LUCY   MD
  In 1781 she supplied bacon for the army (IM, 17336).
ORR, ELIZABETH   NC
  She provided supplies for the army (RA, 6:37, fol. 1).
ORR, MILDRED (MILDRIDGE)   NC
  She supplied provisions for the troops (RA, A:139).
ORRELL, ALICE   MD
  Charles County. In 1782 she supplied wheat for the army (IM, 22984).
ORTH, ROSINA KUCHER   PA
  She made clothing for the soldiers. See Biographies.
OSBORN, ABIGAIL   CT
  Fairfield widow. She suffered damage in a British raid (CAR, 15:250i, 251b). She was a Western Lands Grantee.
OSBORN, MABEL   CT
  Fairfield. She suffered losses in a British raid (CAR, 1:53b, 63o). She was a Western Lands Grantee.
OSBORN, MARY   MD
  Montgomery County. In 1781 she provided wheat for the army (IM, 16037).
OSBORN, MEHITABLE   CT
  New Haven. She suffered damage in a British raid (CAR, 1:63z, 91c). She was a Western Lands Grantee.
OSBORN, SARAH MATTHEWS. See BENJAMIN
OSGOOD, HANNAH   NH
  She was the only woman in American history to sign the "Association Test." See Biographies.
OSWALD, MARGARET   SC
  She supplied provisions for the troops (SI, L-N:26).
OTIS, ELIZA L.   MA
  Barnstable. On December 26, 1782, Ebenezer Crocker obtained

III: COMPLETE LISTING 405

a letter of marque to command the sloop Sally with two guns
and ten men. Samuel A. Otis, Jr., and Eliza L. Otis witnessed
the bond (CN).
OTIS, MERCY. See WARREN
OUTWATERS, JOANNA   NJ
Orange. She suffered damage in a British raid (CDB, claim
47).
OVERSTREET, SARAH BOOTH   SC
She was commended by the president of the United States for
her war effort. See Biographies.
OWEN, ELIZABETH   SC
After the fall of Charleston on May 12, 1780, all women who
were heads of households were required to take an oath of fidelity
to the Crown. Mrs. Owen refused to do so, and was banished
from the city along with 120 other women and 264 children (SC).
OWENS, MARGARET   VA
Spotsylvania County. She performed a public service (VR,
5:243).

P

PACA, ANNE HARRISON   MD
Mr. and Mrs. Paca spent a fortune of their own money supplying
troops. See Biographies.
PACK, MARY   MD
She supplies wheat in 1781 for the army (IM, 17569).
PADRICK, SUSANNAH   NC
She supplied provisions for the troops (RA, C:21).
PAGAN, JENNETT   SC
She provided supplies for the army (SI, L-N:53).
PAGE, MARY MASON   VA
Gloucester County. She performed a public service (VR, 2:51).
PAGETT, SARAH MATTHEWS   NC
Sarah Matthews opposed drinking British tea. Later she married
Thomas Pagett. See Background.
PAGGETT (PAGETT), SARAH   SC
She provided funds for the army (AA, p. 35).
PAINE (PANE), MARY   NJ
Woodbridge. The wife of Capt. John Paine, she suffered damage
in a British raid (CDB, p. 110).
PAINTER, ELIZABETH   CT
New Haven. In the British raid of July 1779 she suffered losses
(CAR, 15:234ai).
PALMER, ABIGAIL   CT
Groton. In the July 1779 British raid she suffered damage (CAR,
29:107ad). She was a Western Lands Grantee.
PALMER, ANN   VA
King William County. Recognized for public service (VR, 3:255).
PALMER, DESIRE PALMER   CT
Stonington. She was the wife of Roswell Saltonstall Palmer, who

was commissary of Connecticut troops during the war. Later he was a marine on the privateer Pilgrim and was captured by the British in 1781. Palmer was confined on the prison ship Jersey in New York Harbor for eighteen months (FP1).

PALMER, E. AMY SMITH   CT
Stonington. She married Joshua Palmer, who servied as a midshipman in the Continental Navy on the ship Oliver Cromwell, until he was captured by the British on June 5, 1779, and imprisoned (CN).

PALMER, ELIZABETH   VA
King William County. Credited with public service (CR, 3:255).

PALMER, HANNAH   VA
Greensville. She performed a public service (VR, 3:29).

PALMER, HANNAH PALMER   CT
Stonington. She married Andrew Palmer as his second wife. Andrew commanded the schooner Fortune in 1776; on February 3, 1777, he was captured by the British frigate Amazon and imprisoned in New York City, where he died in 1780 (CN).

PALMER, LOIS STANTON   CT
Stonington. She married Asa Palmer, who commanded the sloop America in 1777. On July 18, 1777, Palmer and his crew were captured by the British and taken to Newport, Rhode Island, as prisoners (CN).

PALMER, LOVE ADAMS   NH
Portsmouth. She married Thomas Palmer, who commanded the privateer Enterprize in 1776 and the ship Portsmouth in 1780. In June 1780 the ship was captured by the British, and Palmer was imprisoned (CN).

PALMER, MILDRED   VA
Caroline County. Recognized for public service (VR, 1:275-276).

PALMERLY, MARGARET   NJ
Westfield. She suffered damage in a British raid (CDB, claim 78).

PALMORE, ELINOR   MD
In 1781 she supplied wheat for the army (IM, 17780).

PARDEE, LYDIA   CT
New Haven. In the British raid of July 1779 she suffered damage (CAR, 15:234g, 269f). She was a Western Lands Grantee.

PARDEE, MARY   CT
New Haven. She suffered losses in the British raid of July 1779 (CAR, 15:234g, 269f). She was a Western Lands Grantee.

PARDEE, MERCY   CT
New Haven. She suffered damage in the July 1779 British raid (CAR, 15:234g, 269f).

PARHAM, ELIZABETH   VA
Sussex County. She performed a public service (VR, 5:206).

PARK, PRESSEY   NC
The Widow Park supplied provisions for the troops (RA, B:266).

PARKER, MRS.   NC
She provided supplies for the army (RA, 9:26, fol. 1).

PARKER, ABIGAIL GROUT. See HALE

III: COMPLETE LISTING 407

PARKER, ANN　　　　　　　　GA
　She supplied provisions and forage for the troops (WA, p. 136).
PARKER, MARY　　　　　　　VA
　Frederick County. Credited with public service (VR, 2:205).
PARKER, MARY. See EDGAR
PARKER, SARAH　　　　　　VA
　Charles City County. Recognized for public service (VR Court Booklet, p. 23).
PARKER, THANKFUL　　　　　CT
　She supplied provisions for the army in 1780 (CAR, 35:108a).
PARKINSON, REBECCA　　　　NC
　She provided supplies for the troops (RA, 7:46, fol. 2).
PARMELE, SARAH　　　　　　CT
　New Haven. The widow of Jeremiah Parmele, she suffered damage in the July 1779 British raid (CAR, 15:234j, 269d).
PARSONS, PHEBE　　　　　　MA
　She opposed the tax on British imported goods. See Background.
PARSONS, SARAH　　　　　　CT
　Greenwich. In the 1779 British raid she suffered damage (CAR, 15:271b). She was a Western Lands Grantee.
PARSONS, SARAH　　　　　　VA
　Chesterfield County. Credited with public service (VR, 2:44).
PARSONS, SUSAN　　　　　　SC
　She supplied provisions for the troops (SI, L-N:26).
PARSONS, SUSANNA　　　　　VA
　Henrico County. Recognized for public service (VR, 3:105).
PARTRIDGE, JEMIMA　　　　　VA
　Westmoreland County. She performed a public service (VR, 5:223).
PATE, MARY　　　　　　　　NC
　She supplied provisions for the troops (RA, A:232).
PATERSON, CORNELIA BELL　　NJ
　She was active in the ladies' association for the welfare of the soldiers. See Biographies.
PATTEN, SUSANNAH McCLINTOCK　NC
　She was the wife of Col. John Patten of the 2nd North Carolina Regiment. He was taken prisoner at Charleston on May 12, 1780, when the city fell to the British (DAR; FW).
PATTERSON, ANN　　　　　　NC
　The wife of Gilbert Patterson, she supplied provisions for the troops (RA, J:144).
PATTERSON, ELIZABETH　　　NC
　She opposed drinking British tea. See Background.
PATTERSON, ISABELLA　　　　VA
　Augusta County. She performed a public service (VR, 2:359).
PATTERSON, JANE　　　　　　NC
　She supplied provisions for the troops (RA, C:133).
PATTERSON, JANE SHANK　　　NJ
　North Brunswick. The daughter of John Shank, she suffered damage in a British raid (CDB, pp. 124-125).

PATTERSON, JANET   VA
    Henry County. Recognized for public service (VR, 3:150).
PATTERSON, MARY   NJ
    North Brunswick. The daughter of Jane Patterson, she suffered losses in a British raid (CDB, p. 125).
PATTERSON, MARY   VA
    Buckingham County. Credited with public service (VR Ctf 1). Also Chesterfield County (VR, 2:44).
PATTERSON, MARY ANN   CT
    Woodbury. She lodged a prisoner of war (CAR, 5:438b).
PATTERSON, SARAH   NC
    She supplied provisions for the troops (RA, 1:66, fol. 2).
PATTISON, SARAH   NC
    She provided supplies for the army (RA, 6:49, fol. 2).
PATTON, JANE   GA
    She provided corn for the troops (WA, p. 174).
PATTON, JANE   SC
    She supplied provisions for the troops (SI, L-N:304).
PATTON, MARY   NJ
    Burlington. She suffered losses in a British raid (CDB, pp. 3, 24).
PATTON, MARY   TN
    She made gunpowder for the men. See Biographies.
PATTON, MARY McNABB   DE
    She was the wife of Capt. John Patton of a Delaware regiment. He was promoted to major in December 1779, and was taken prisoner at the Battle of Camden, South Carolina, in August 1780 (DAR; FW).
PATTON, SARAH   SC
    She supplied provisions for the army (SI, Y-Z:158).
PAUL, ELIZABETH   NC
    She provided supplies for the army (RA, 9:33, fol. 4).
PAUL, MARY   NJ
    Connecticut Farms, Essex County. She suffered damage in a British raid (CDB, claim 69-2).
PAYNE, ANN   VA
    Fauquier County. She performed a public service (VR Lists, p. 13).
PAYNE, ELIZABETH   VA
    Fairfax. Recognized for public service (VR Ctf 1).
PAYNE, ELIZABETH JOHNSON   KY
    She saved the life of her baby brother, who later became vice president of the United States. See Biographies.
PAYNE, M.   NC
    She opposed drinking British tea. See Background.
PEACE, MARY   NC
    She supplied provisions for the troops (RA, 5:27, fol. 3).
PEACOCK, LYDIA BENNETT   NC
    Lydia Bennett opposed drinking British tea. Later she became the second wife of Isham Peacock, a soldier in the Revolutionary War (DAR). See Background.

III: COMPLETE LISTING 409

PEAKE, MARY VA
Fauquier County. She performed a public service (VR, 2:245).

PEARSON, ELIZABETH NJ
Burlington. She suffered damage in a British raid (CDB, pp. 29, 152).

PEARSON, MARGARET NC
She supplied provisions for the troops (RA, 9:108, fol. 2).

PEARSON, MARY RAIFORD SC
The wife of John Pearson, she is listed as a patriot in the <u>DAR Patriot Index</u>.

PEARSON, TABITHA JEACOCKS SC
She was born in 1749 and married Enoch Pearson. During the war she supplied provisions for the army (SI, Y-Z:200). Her second husband was John Townsend (DAR).

PEASE, MARY CT
New Haven. In the July 1779 British raid she suffered damage (CAR, 15:234g, 269c). She was a Western Lands Grantee.

PEATROSS, AMEY VA
Caroline County. She performed a public service (VR, 1:275-276). Also Hanover County (VR, 3:186).

PEBBLES, AMELIA NC
She supplied provisions for the troops (RA, 7:62, fol. 3).

PECHIN, CHRISTIANA BRIGHT PA
She was born in 1747 and married Christopher Pechin. She died in 1835 and is listed as a patriot in the <u>DAR Patriot Index</u>.

PECK, ABIGAIL CORBIN CT
She was born in 1747 and married Phineas Peck. Abigail died in 1848 and is listed as a patriot in the <u>DAR Patriot Index</u>.

PECK, CATHERINE CT
Greenwich. In the March 1779 and December 1783 British raids, she suffered damage (CAR, 36:19b). She was a Western Lands Grantee.

PECK, MARGARET PA
She was born in 1737 and married John Peck. Margaret died in 1814 and is listed as a patriot in the <u>DAR Patriot Index</u>.

PECK, MARY CT
Greenwich. In the British raids of March 1779 and December 1783 she suffered damage (CAR, 36:19b). She was a Western Lands Grantee.

PECK, SARAH CT
Danbury. In the April 1777 British raid she suffered losses (CAR, 8:382b). She was a Western Lands Grantee.

PECK, SARAH MD
Charles County. In 1781 she provided wheat for the army (IM, 18465).

PECKHAM, RUTH RI
On October 6, 1776, she nursed wounded prisoners (MR, 57:5).

PEDDRICK, LURANNAH NC
She supplied provisions for the troops (RA, 6:26, fol. 3).

PEED (PUD), SARAH VA
King George County. The wife of John, she performed a public service (VR, 5:227).

PIERSON, MARY   NJ
   Connecticut Farms, Essex County. The wife of Samuel Pierson, she suffered damage in a British raid (CDB, claim 32).

PELOT, CATHERINE STOLL SCREVEN   SC
   She provided provisions for the army. See Biographies.

PELOT, FRANCES   SC
   She supplied provisions for the troops (SI, U-W:150).

PELOT, MARY   SC
   She provided supplies for the army (SI, U-W:150).

PEMBERTON, MARGARET   NC
   The wife of Edward Pemberton, she supplied provisions for the troops (RA, 5:46).

PENDARVIS, SARAH   SC
   She supplied provisions for the troops (SI, Y-Z:44).

PENDER, MARTHA   VA
   Hansemond County. Recognized for public service (VR, 4:164).

PENDER, PATTY   VA
   Hansemond County. Credited with public service (VR, 4:358).

PENDLETON, ALICE ANN WINSTON   VA
   She was born in 1769 and married Henry Pendleton, a soldier. Alice died in 1813 and is listed as a patriot in the <u>DAR Patriot Index</u>.

PENFIELD, MARY   CT
   Fairfield. In the British raids of 1779-1780 she suffered damage (CAR, 15:250f, 251d). She was a Western Lands Grantee.

PENFIELD, SARAH   CT
   Fairfield. In the British raids she suffered damage (CAR, 1:53f, 63g). She was a Western Lands Grantee.

PENN, POLLY MASTERS   PA
   Her home was the headquarters of Benedict Arnold when he was still a loyal American general. See Biographies.

PENNEY, ANN   SC
   She supplied provisions for the troops (SI, U-W:77).

PENNINGTON, HANNAH BOONE STEWART   KY
   Her husband was killed by Indians. See Biographies.

PENNYPACKER, HANNAH GERBERT   PA
   Gen. Washington had his headquarters there. See Biographies.

PENROSE, SARAH BIDDLE   PA
   Philadelphia. She was the wife of James Penrose. Their son, Clement Biddle Penrose, as a boy was a standard-bearer of a Philadelphia company and he suffered through the hardships at Valley Forge. Mrs. Penrose was an active member of the ladies' association for the welfare of the soldiers (<u>Pennsylvania Gazette</u>, June 12, 1780).

PERCIVAL, MARY FULLER   CT
   She turned her home into a hospital for sick and wounded soldiers See Biographies.

PERKINS, ABIGAIL   CT
   Groton. She suffered damage in a British raid (CAR, 1:79b).

PERKINS, ANN   VA
   New Kent County. She performed a public service (VR Court Booklet, p. 7).

III: COMPLETE LISTING

PERKINS, ANNA LATHROP   CT
She married Jabez Perkins. On March 8, 1776, Capt. Jabez Perkins, Jr., was captured and taken to Antigua. Jabez Perkins III served as captain of marines on the ship Oliver Cromwell; on June 5, 1779, the Oliver Cromwell was captured by the British (CN).

PERKINS, ELIZABETH   CT
Groton. Her husband was killed by the British at Fort Griswold in September 1781 (CAR, 27:333a; 26:295e).

PERKINS, FREELOVE   CT
Groton. In the September 1781 British raid she suffered damage (CAR, 38).

PERKINS, GRACE   VA
Frederick County. She performed a public service (VR, 2:204).

PERKINS, JUDITH   VA
Goochland County. Credited with public service (VR, 3:76, 79, 89).

PERKINS (PURKINS), MARY   VA
Essex County. Recognized for public service (VR Court Booklet, p. 7).

PERKINS, MARY   VA
Goochland County. The widow of Stephen Perkins, she performed a public service (VR Ctf 2; VR, 3:75, 78).

PERKINS, SARAH   CT
Groton. In the September 1781 British raid she suffered damage (CAR, 27:333a).

PERKINS, SEBRA   GA
She supplied three horses for public use (WA, p. 169), cattle (p. 174), provisions and forage (p. 127).

PERKINS, SUSANNAH   VA
Gloucester County. Credited with public service (VR, 3:51).

PERKINS, SUSANNA   VA
King William County. She performed a public service (VR Lists, 1:11, 14).

PERRIN, JANE   VA
Halifax County. She performed a public service (VR Court Booklet, p. 73).

PERRY, AGNES   VA
Dinwiddie County. Credited with public service (VR Court Booklet, p. 34).

PERRY, ANNE PRESTON   CT
Woodbury. She was the wife of Nathaniel Perry, who served in the Connecticut Militia. He was captured when the British took Fort Washington on November 16, 1776. Perry died at New Milford (FP1).

PESOUD, ELIZABETH   VA
York County. Recognized for public service (VR, 4:278).

PESTINPOST, BARBARA   NC
She supplied provisions for the troops (RA, A:105).

PETERS, FANNY LEDYARD   NY
She nursed wounded soldiers at Groton, Connecticut. See Biographies.

PETERS, PHYLLIS. See WHEATLEY

PETERS, SARAH ROBINSON   PA
Philadelphia. In August 1776 she married Richard Peters, an attorney. The Peterses resided at "Belmont," his estate on the Schuykill River. Sarah was an active member of the ladies' association for the welfare of the soldiers (Pennsylvania Gazette, June 12, 1780).

PETERSON, KATHERINE   CT
New London. On February 1, 1781, William Havens obtained a letter of marque to command the brigantine Jay with twelve guns and seventy men. Katherine Peterson witnessed the bond (CN).

PETERSON, LUCY   VA
Dinwiddie County. She performed a public service (VR, 1:339).

PETTUS, ANN   VA
Hanover County. Recognized for public service (VR, 3:183, 193).

PETTWAY, HINCHIA   VA
Greensville. Credited for public service (VR Court Booklet, p. 25).

PETTY, ELIZABETH   SC
She supplied provisions for the troops (SI, U-W:189).

PEYTON, MARGARET   VA
Prince William County. She performed a public service (VR, 4:204).

PEYTON, MRS. SETH   VA
Prince William County. Credited with public service (VR Court Booklet, p. 12).

PHELPS, LORENA. See KATHERINE GAYLORD

PHILIPS, ELIZABETH   SC
She provided supplies for the army (SI, O-Q:16).

PHILIPS, MARGARET   CT
She supplied baize material for the army (CAR, 31:265).

PHILIPS, MARY   VA
Bedford County. Recognized for public service (VR Court Booklet, p. 8).

PHILIPS, MARY   VA
At age sixteen she was captured by Indians in March 1779 at Washington and released from Fort Ticonderoga on July 18, 1783 (MR).

PHILLIPS, HANNAH   NJ
Hunterdon County. She suffered damage caused by the Americans (CDB, claim 25).

PHILLIPS, PHOEBE FOXCRAFT   MA
Andover. She was the wife of Samuel Phillips, co-founder of Andover Academy with his uncle. During the Revolutionary War, Mrs. Phillips made bandages and clothing for the soldiers (CD).

PHILLIPS, RACHEL FRIZZELL   MD
She married James Phillips, who served as a lieutenant on the Angelica and was captured by the British. On July 7, 1778,

III: COMPLETE LISTING

he was confined in the Fortun Prison at Gosport, England. Later Phillips escaped and returned to America (CN).

PHIPP, HANNAH   VA
Norfolk. She performed a public service (VR Court Booklet, p. 1).

PHIPPS, MARY ENGLISH   CT
New Haven. She married David Phipps, who was commissioned a lieutenant in the Continental Navy in 1776. He was captured three times, imprisoned, and later exchanged (CN).

PIATT (PYATT), MARY   SC
She supplied provisions for the troops (SI, 10, pt. 1:186).

PICKENS, REBECCA CALHOUN   SC
She was born in 1745 and married Andrew Pickens. Rebecca died in 1814. She is listed as a patriot in the DAR Patriot Index 2.

PICKETT, DEBORAH   CT
Norwalk. She suffered damage in a British raid (CAR, 1:63j, 98a).

PICKETT, ELIZABETH COOKE   VA
Fauquier. She was born in 1712 and married William Pickett. Elizabeth died in 1808 (DAR). She performed a public service (VR, 2:245).

PICKETT, MARTHA   VA
Fauquier County. Recognized for public service (VR, 4:311).

PIERSON, EXPERIENCE   NJ
Morris County. The wife of Samuel Pierson, she suffered damage caused by the Americans (CDB, claim 12).

PIERSON, MARY   NJ
Woodbridge. She suffered losses in a British raid (CDB, p. 201).

PIERSON, MARY   VA
Chesterfield County. Credited with public service (VR Court Booklet, p. 62).

PIERSON, PHEBE   NJ
Orange. The wife of Dr. Matthias Pierson, she suffered damage caused by the British (CDB, claim 52).

PIKE, ELIZABETH   NJ
Woodbridge. She suffered damage in a British raid (CDB, p. 87).

PIKE, HANNAH   NJ
Woodbridge. She suffered losses caused by the British (CDB, p. 87).

PIKE, ISABELLA BROWN   NJ
Trenton. She married Zebulon Pike and was the mother of Zebulon Montgomery Pike, the explorer. Pike's Peak is named after him. She was an active member of the ladies' association for the welfare of the soldiers (New Jersey Gazette, July 4, 1780).

PILAND, MARY   VA
Surry County. She performed a public service (VR, 5:168).

PILES, ANN   VA
Augusta County. Credited with public service (VR Court Booklet, p. 8).

PINCHAM, MRS.　　　　　　　　　VA
　　Amelia County. Recognized for public service (VR, 1:80).
PINCKARD, ANNE GASKINS. See LEE
PINCKNEY, ELEANOR LAURENS　　SC
　　Her father was captured and imprisoned in the Tower of London.
　　See Biographies.
PINCKNEY, ELIZABETH MOTTE　　SC
　　Her home was burned by the British. See Biographies.
PINCKNEY, FRANCES SUSANNA QUASH　　SC
　　She was born in 1743 and married Robert Hume, then Roger
　　Pinckney. Frances died in 1822. She is listed as a patriot
　　in the DAR Patriot Index 2.
PINER, SARAH　　　　　　　　　MD
　　Kent County. In 1780 she supplied wheat for the army (IM,
　　10827).
PINNEY, SUSANNA LATHROP　　　CT
　　Ellington. She was the wife of Capt. Benjamin Pinney. Mr.
　　and Mrs. Pinney gave their own money to supply his troops
　　during the Revolutionary War. He was captured by the British
　　and died on a prison ship in 1777 (FP1).
PIPER, EVE LEAR　　　　　　　　CT
　　She gave gold to buy clothing and shoes for the soldiers.
　　See Biographies.
PITCHER, MOLLY. See McCAULEY, MARY HAYS; CORBIN, MAR-
　　GARET
PITKIN, ANNE　　　　　　　　　CT
　　Hartford. In 1777 she supplied a blanket for the army (CAR,
　　11:420).
PITMAN, AMEY　　　　　　　　　VA
　　Stafford County. Recognized for public service (VR, 5:192).
PITMAN, PRISCILLA　　　　　　　SC
　　She supplied provisions for the troops (SI, L-N:27).
PITT, PATIENCE　　　　　　　　　VA
　　Hansemond County. She performed a public service (VR, 4:165).
PLATT, ANNE　　　　　　　　　CT
　　New Haven. In the 1779 British raid she suffered damage (CAR,
　　15:269g). She was a Western Lands Grantee.
PLUMMER, MARY　　　　　　　　NC
　　She supplied provisions for the troops (RA, 1:12, fol. 2).
POAGUE, ANN KENNEDY. See LINDSAY
POE, ELIZABETH CAIRNES　　　MD
　　She was born in 1756 and married David Poe. Elizabeth died
　　in 1838. She is listed as a patriot in the DAR Patriot Index.
POE, HANNAH　　　　　　　　　NC
　　She supplied provisions for the troops (RA, B:277).
POINDEXTER, ELIZABETH PLEDGE　NC
　　She sewed warning letters in the petticoats of her daughter,
　　who delivered them to the Americans. See Biographies.
POLK, DELIAH TYLER　　　　　KY
　　Mrs. Polk and her four children were captured by Indians.
　　See Biographies.

III: COMPLETE LISTING

POLLARD, FRANCES VA
   Gloucester County. She performed a public service (VR, 3:51).
POLLOCK, ABIGAIL RI
   She supplied provisions for the troops (MP, 21:12).
POMEROY, SARAH CT
   New Haven. She suffered damage in the British raid of 1779
   (CAR, 269e). She was a Western Lands Grantee.
PON, ELIZABETH SC
   She provided supplies for the army (SI, R-T:51, 214).
POOL, SARAH CT
   New London. She suffered losses in a British raid (CAR, 1:63i,
   95f). She was a Western Lands Grantee.
POPE, ANN VA
   Southampton County. Recognized for public service (VR, 5:184).
POPE, MARY NC
   The wife of West Pope, she provided provisions for the troops
   (RA, K:97).
PORT, JANE PA
   Philadelphia. She lived on Arch Street between Front Street
   and 2nd Street. On August 31, 1774, as a delegate to the First
   Continental Congress, John Adams took up residence in her
   home until September 3, then moved back to the home of Mrs.
   Yard (CS).
PORTER, ELIZABETH KY
   She was captured by the British and Indians. See Biographies.
PORTER, MAGDALEN VA
   Powhatan County. Credited with public service (VR, 4:241).
PORTER, MARY CT
   Wethersfield. She cared for prisoners of war for Connecticut
   in 1776 (CAR, 28:1-3).
PORTER, MEHITABLE HINE CT
   She cooked meals for the soldiers. See Biographies.
PORTER, MELICENT BALDWIN NJ
   She cooked meals for the soldiers. See Biographies.
PORTER, REBECCA HENRY MA
   Boston. She married David Porter, who commanded the privateer
   sloop Delight in 1778 and the ship Tartar in 1779. In 1781 Porter
   was captured by the British and taken to New York City. She
   was the mother of David Porter, commander of the Essex during
   the War of 1812, and grandmother of Adm. David D. Porter,
   naval hero of the Civil War.
PORTLOCK, ANNE VA
   Norfolk. She performed a public service (VR, 4:138).
POSEY, RACHEL PECK PA
   She was born in 1766 and married Maj. Micajah Posey. Rachel
   died in 1868 and is listed as a patriot in the DAR Patriot Index
   2.
POST, MARCELA NJ
   Acquacanunk, Essex County. She suffered damage in a British
   raid (CDB, claim 36).

POSTON, PRISCILLA   MD
Charles County. She supplied wheat for the army, 1781-1783 (IM, 17418, 22719, 24392, 25213).

POTTER, ABIGAIL   CT
New Haven. In the July 1779 British raid she suffered damage (CAR, 15:234b, 269d). She was a Western Lands Grantee.

POTTER, AMIE   NC
She supplied provisions for the army (RA, 5:60, fol. 1).

POTTER, DEBORAH REYNOLDS   RI
Gen. Washington was entertained by the Potters. See Biographies.

POTTER, ELIZABETH WILLIAMS   NY
She was born in 1728 and married Dr. Gilbert Potter. Elizabeth died in 1811 and is listed as a patriot in the DAR Patriot Index.

POTTER, HANNAH   NJ
Westfield. She suffered damage in a British raid (CDB, claim 31).

POTTER, LYDIA BARNES   PA
She spun, wove, cut, and made clothing for the soldiers. See Biographies.

POTTER, MARGARET   NJ
Westfield. She suffered losses caused by the British (CDB, claim 31).

POTTHRESS, MARY   VA
Dinwiddie County. She performed a public service (VR, 5:239). Also shown for Prince George County (VR Court Booklet, p. 12).

POTTHRESS, PATSY   VA
Dinwiddie County. Credited with public service (VR, 1:340).

POTTS, ELEANOR   SC
She supplied provisions for the troops (SI, U-W:132).

POTTS, FRANCES ANN   VA
Northumberland County. The wife of Robert Potts, she performed a public service (VR, 4:121).

POTTS, MRS. ISAAC   PA
Gen. Washington had his headquarters there. See Biographies.

POTTS, MARY   NC
She supplied provisions for the troops (RA, 12:19, fol. 2).

POULISEN, LEA   NJ
Harrington, Bergen County. The wife of Poulis Poulisen, she suffered damages caused by the British (CDB, claim 68).

POWELL, ELIZABETH   SC
She provided supplies for the army (SI, L-N:304).

POWELL, ELIZABETH   VA
King William County. Credited with public service (VR Lists, 2:2).

POWELL, ELIZABETH WILLING   PA
She entertained Gen. and Mrs. Washington. See Biographies.

POWELL, MARY   VA
Gloucester County. Recognized for public service (VR Court Booklet, p. 50).

III: COMPLETE LISTING 417

POWELL, SARAH   SC
    She supplied provisions for the troops (SI, Y-Z:192).
POWELL, SARAH   VA
    Accomack County. Credited with public service (VR, 1:29).
POWERS, ANNA KEYES   NH
    She had four sons who served in the Revolutionary War. See Biographies.
PRATT, ABIGAIL BUTLER   NH
    She opposed the drinking of British tea. See Biographies.
PRATT, ELIZABETH HAGAR   MA
    She repaired abandoned British cannons for the American army. See Biographies.
PRATT, MARGARET   VA
    King George County. Credited with public service (VR, 2:337).
PRATT, MARY   CT
    In 1779 she supplied clothing for the army (CAR, 35:227b).
PRATT, MARY   SC
    She supplied provisions for the troops (SI, U-W:79).
PRATT, SARAH   MD
    In 1777 she supplied stockings and blankets and did laundering for the army and in 1781 provided wheat for the militia (IM, 3298, 4794, 19378).
PRENTICE, ABIGAIL   CT
    Stonington. In 1777 she supplied a blanket for the army (CAR, 12:117).
PRENTICE, SARAH SARTEL   MA
    Boston. She was a protagonist of religious freedom and a member of the Daughters of Liberty, who sewed and knitted clothing for the American soldiers. She had ten children (HC).
PRESCOTT, ESTHER   SC
    She supplied provisions for the troops (SI, U-W:131, 149).
PRESLEY, MARY   MD
    Baltimore. She nursed sick soldiers on the ship Defence in November 1777 (IM, 5252).
PREVOST, THEODOSIA. See BURR
PRICE, ELIZABETH   NJ
    Springfield. She suffered damage caused by the British (CDB, claim 1).
PRICE, JERUSHA PENICK   VA
    Prince Edward County. The wife of Pugh Price, she performed a public service (VR, 5:58).
PRICE, MARY   VA
    Cumberland County. Credited with public service (VR, 4:294).
PRICE, MARY   VA
    King George County. Recognized for public service (VR, 2:337).
PRIDE, MRS. FRANCIS   VA
    Amelia County. She performed a public service (VR, 1:79).
PRIGGS, ELIZA   SC
    She supplied provisions for the troops (SI, U-W:155).
PRINTER, MARGARET   SC
    She supplied provisions for the army (SI, R-T:294).

PRIOR, MILDRED VA
Charlotte. She performed a public service (VR Court Booklet, p. 8).
PROBASCO, ELIZABETH. See COVENHOVEN
PROSSER, ANN VA
King William County. She performed a public service (VR Court Booklet, p. 11).
PROVANCE, SARAH YARDS PA
She was born in 1748 and became the second wife of John William Provance. Sarah died in 1796 and is listed as a patriot in the DAR Patriot Index 2.
PROVINCE, SARAH WV
Monongalia County. Credited with public service (VR Court Booklet, p. 8).
PROVOST, MRS. (BURR, THEODOSIA BARTOW) NY
Gen. Washington had his headquarters there. See Biographies.
PRYOR, ANN HARDEN NC
The wife of Phillip Pryor, she is recognized for public service (RA, C:47).
PRYOR, MARGARET GAINES NC
She was born in 1706 and married John Pryor. Margaret supplied provisions for the troops (RA, 11:44, fol. 3). She died in 1790 (DAR).
PUGH, HANNAH NC
She provided supplies for the army (RA, J:223).
PUGH, MARY VA
Hansemond County. She performed a public service (Court Booklet, 1:6).
PUGH, SARAH VA
Westmoreland County. Credited with public service (VR, 5:223).
PUNCH, MARY SC
She supplied provisions for the troops (SI, Y-Z:192).
PURNELL, MARY MD
In 1781 she supplied beef for the army (IM, 18790).
PURNELL, SARAH MD
In 1780 she supplied corn for the army and in 1781 beef (IM, 11265, 19079).
PURVIANCE, MRS. SAMUEL MD
She entertained John Adams and other signers of the Declaration of Independence. See Biographies.
PURYSAR, SARAH VA
Mecklenburg. She performed a public service (VR, 4:73).
PURYSAR, SUSANNA VA
Henrico County. Recognized for public service (VR Court Booklet, p. 15).
PUTNAM, DEBORAH LATHROP CT
She spun flax for shirts for the soldiers and entertained Gen. and Mrs. Washington. See Biographies.
PUTNEY, SUSANNAH FRENCH MA
She inoculated smallpox patients. See Biographies.

III: COMPLETE LISTING

Q

QUARLES, DOROTHY   VA
   King William County. She performed a public service (VR Lists, 1:7).

QUATTLEBAUM, RACHEL DERRIN   SC
   She was born in 1748 and married Matthias Quattlebaum. Rachel is listed as a patriot in the DAR Patriot Index.

QUINCE, ANN   NC
   She supplied provisions for the troops (RA, 5:64, fol. 3).

QUINCY, ELIZA SUSAN. See MORTON

R

RADFORD, ANN   NJ
   Burlington. The wife of Samuel Radford, she suffered damage in a British raid (CDB, claim 9).

RAINS, MARY   NC
   She supplied provisions for the army (RA, C:158).

RAMSAY, ANN McCARTY   VA
   She was born in 1731 and married William Ramsay. Ann died in 1785 and is listed as a patriot in the DAR Patriot Index.

RAMSAY, MARGARET JANE PEALE   MD
   She nursed wounded soldiers. See Biographies.

RAMSAY, MARTHA LAURENS   SC
   Her father was imprisoned by the British. See Biographies.

RAMSEY, MARY   NC
   She supplied provisions for the troops (RA, A:208).

RAMSEY (RAMSAY), MARY   VA
   Princess Anne County. Credited with public service (VR, 4:223).

RAND, MARY SMITH   NY
   Rye. She married Ephraim Rand, who served as a private in the war. He died of smallpox in December 1777 while camped at Chatangay, New York (FP2).

RANDALL, WIDOW   RI
   She went reconnoitering with Maj. Cortland on the Western Shore (MP, 39:21).

RANDOLPH, ANNA HARRISON   VA
   She was active in the ladies' association. See Background.

RANDOLPH, MRS. BENJAMIN   PA
   She entertained Thomas Jefferson. See Biographies.

RANDOLPH, BETTY   VA
   Charlotte. She performed a public service (VR Court Booklet, p. 20). Also shown in James City (VR Ctf 1).

RANDOLPH, CATHARINE   NJ
   Middlesex County. She suffered damage in a British raid (CDB, p. 213).

RANDOLPH, ELIZABETH HARRISON   VA
   While president of the Continental Congress, her husband

dropped dead at the dinner table in the presence of Thomas
Jefferson. See Biographies.
RANDOLPH, ELIZABETH NICHOLAS VA
    She supplied horses, cattle, and crops for the Americans before
    the Battle of Yorktown. See Biographies.
RANDOLPH, LUCY BOLLING   VA
    She supplied provisions for the army. See Biographies.
RANSOM, ESTHER LAWRENCE   PA
    Her husband was killed by Indians. See Biographies.
RANSOME, LETTIA   VA
    Gloucester County. Credited with public service (VR, 3:52).
RANSON, AMEY   NC
    She supplied provisions for the troops (RA, 7:71, fol. 2).
RAPPLEYEA, STYNTJE   NJ
    Somerville. The wife of Derick Rappleyea, she suffered damage
    caused by the British (CDB, p. 16).
RATCLIFF, ANN   VA
    New Kent County. She performed a public service (VR Court
    Booklet, p. 12).
RATCLIFF, ZAPHANIA   VA
    Prince William County. Credited with public service (VR, 4:204).
RATHBURN, WIDOW   CT
    Greenwich. In the 1783 British raid she suffered losses (CAR,
    24:274j).
RATLIFF (RATCLIFF), ANN   VA
    Bedford County. She performed a public service (VR Lists,
    1:18).
RAVENAL, DEMARIS ELIZABETH   SC
    She supplied provisions for the army (SI, L-N:29; Y-Z:275;
    10, pt. 1:23, 24).
RAWLEY, HANNAH   CT
    She purchased state notes to help the war effort (CAR, 32:84,
    193).
RAWLINGS, MARGARET   VA
    Prince William County. Credited with public service (VR, 4:207).
RAY, LYDIA   NC
    She supplied provisions for the troops (RA, C:73).
RAY (ROY), MARTHA   CT
    New Haven. In the 1779 British raid she suffered losses (CAR,
    p. 269b).
RAYMOND, ABIGAIL   CT
    Norwalk. She suffered damage in a British raid (CAR, 1:63i,
    98a). She was a Western Lands Grantee.
READ, ELIZABETH   NJ
    Burlington. She suffered damage in a British attack (CDB,
    p. 146).
READ (REED), ELIZABETH   VA
    Bedford County. She performed a public service (VR Lists,
    1:4).
READ, GERTRUDE ROSS   DE
    She escaped from the British. See Biographies.

III: COMPLETE LISTING   421

READ, MARY, JR.   VA
   Charlotte. She performed a public service (VR Court Booklet,
   p. 21).
READ, MARY PEELE   NJ
   She was active in the ladies' association for the welfare of the
   soldiers. See Biographies.
READ, SARAH MATTHEWS. See BENJAMIN
READING, HANNAH   SC
   She supplied provisions for the troops (SI, U-W:149).
READS, ELIZABETH   VA
   Middlesex County. Recognized for public service (VR, 4:96).
REDD, MRS.   GA
   She supplied one horse for the legion (WA, p. 115).
REDFIELD, LUCRETIA   CT
   Fairfield. She suffered damage caused by the British (CAR,
   1:53f, 63q). She was a Western Lands Grantee.
REDFIELD, SARAH   CT
   Fairfield. In the British raid she suffered losses (CAR, 1:53f,
   63q). She was a Western Lands Grantee.
REDMAN, ALICE   MD
   She nursed Governor Thomas Sim Lee during his 1779 illness
   (IM, 8328).
REED, MRS.   NJ
   Burlington. The wife of Capt. Reed, she was secretary of the
   ladies' assocation, which collected money for the army (New
   Jersey Gazette, July 4, 1780).
REED, ELIZABETH   CT
   Salisbury. In 1778 she supplied a blanket for the army (CAR,
   11:631a).
REED, ELIZABETH   VA
   Hampshire County. She performed a public service (VR Lists,
   p. 17).
REED, ESTHER DE BERDT   PA
   She founded the ladies' association for the welfare of the soldiers.
   See Biographies.
REED, MARY   CT
   Norwalk. In the British raid she suffered losses (CAR, 1:631,
   98g). She was a Western Lands Grantee.
REED, MARY   NC
   She supplied provisions for the troops (RA, 7:73, fol. 4).
REED, RACHEL   MD
   Queen Anne County. In 1778 she supplied bacon for the army
   (IM, 6434).
REEKLESS, ANN   NJ
   Burlington. The wife of Isaac Reekless, she suffered losses
   caused by the British (CDB, p. 39).
REESE, AMY   VA
   Dinwiddie County. Recognized for public service (VR, 1:341).
REESE, MARY   VA
   Southampton County. She performed a public service (VR Court
   Booklet, p. 11).

REEVES, ANN					SC
   She supplied provisions for the troops (SI, 1:86).
REGGS, ELIZABETH				SC
   She supplied provisions for the army (SI, 10:pt. 1:104).
REID, ISABEL					NC
   She supplied provisions for the troops (RA, 5:55, fol. 1).
REID (REED), MARTHA				VA
   Amherst County. She performed a public service (VR Court
   Booklet, p. 17).
REID, MARY WOODBURN				NH
   She took charge of her farm while her husband, a general,
   spent eight years in the army. See Biographies.
REILY, BRIDGET					MD
   In 1777 she boarded the guests of Capt. Jonathan Morris (IM,
   4026).
REILY, ELIZABETH				MD
   In 1781 she supplied wheat for the army (IM, 16653).
REILY, ELIZABETH MYER				PA
   She made clothing and sent food to the soldiers at Valley Forge.
   See Biographies.
REINHARDT, BARBARA WARLICK			NC
   She secreted Adam Reep in her home. See Biographies.
REMSEN, MRS. WILLIAM				NJ
   Morristown. Her husband was captain of the Monmouth Light
   Horse in 1777. Later Col. and Mrs. Remsen moved to Morris
   County, where she was an active member of the ladies' association
   for the welfare of the soldiers (New Jersey Gazette, July 4,
   1780).
RENTZ, CATHERINE				SC
   She married George Rentz. Catherine is listed as a patriot
   in the DAR Patriot Index 2.
REYNOLDS, MRS.					VA
   Also spelled Raynald, Renalds, and Ranalds. At age thirty-
   two she was captured by Indians along with her daughters Mary,
   Elizabeth, Sarah, and four sons on March 22, 1780, and taken
   to the Saint Lawrence suburbs (MR).
REYNOLDS, AMY					CT
   Greenwich. In the British raids of March 1779 and December
   1783 she suffered damage (CAR, 36:19b). She was a Western
   Lands Grantee.
REYNOLDS, ANN					CT
   Greenwich. She suffered losses in the British raids of March
   1779 and December 1783 (CAR, 36:19b). She was a Western
   Lands Grantee.
REYNOLDS, ANNE					CT
   Greenwich. In the British raids she suffered damage (CAR,
   1:63f, 74f). She was a Western Lands Grantee.
REYNOLDS, ELIZABETH				VA
   Caroline County. She performed a public service (VR, 1:262).
REYNOLDS (RENOLDS), FRANCES			NC
   She supplied provisions for the troops (RA, 11:82, fol. 2).

III: COMPLETE LISTING

REYNOLDS (RAYNOLDS), MRS. FRANCIS   VA
   Richmond County. Credited with public service (VR Court Booklet, p. 3).
REYNOLDS, JOANNA   CT
   Greenwich. In the British raids of March 1779 and December 1783, she suffered damage (CAR, 36:19b). She was a Western Lands Grantee.
REYNOLDS, MARGARET SMITH   MD
   She was born in 1748 and married Capt. John Reynolds, Jr. Margaret died in 1783 and is listed as a patriot in the DAR Patriot Index.
REYNOLDS, SUSANNA   CT
   Greenwich. In the March 1779 British attack she suffered damage (CAR, 105:271c). She was a Western Lands Grantee.
REYNOLDS, SUSANNAH LANGFORD   VA
   Henry County. The wife of George Reynolds, she performed a public service (VR, 3:152).
RHODES, ELIZA   NC
   She supplied provisiosn for the troops (RA, 5:65, fol. 4).
RHODES, ELIZABETH   NC
   She provided supplies for the troops (RA, 5:47, fol. 2).
RHODES, ELIZABETH   SC
   She provided provisions for the troops (SI, Y-Z:96).
RHODES, HOPE   CT
   Ridgefield. In the April 1777 British raid she suffered losses (CAR, 8:391b). She was a Western Lands Grantee.
RICE, ABIGAIL HARTMAN   PA
   She cared for the sick and wounded soldiers at the Yellow Springs Hospital. See Biographies.
RICE, ANN   VA
   Rockingham County. She performed a public service (VR, 5:130).
RICE, SARAH NELMS   VA
   Culpeper County. The wife of William Rice, whe is recognized for public service (VR, 2:110).
RICH, HANNAH   CT
   Greenwich. In the British raids of March 1779 and December 1783 she suffered damage (CAR, 36:19b). She was a Western Lands Grantee.
RICH, MARY   CT
   Greenwich. In the March 1779 and December 1783 British raids she suffered losses (CAR, 36:19c). She was a Western Lands Grantee.
RICHARDS, MRS.   PA
   Philadelphia. She collected money for the soldiers (Pennsylvania Gazette, June 12, 1780).
RICHARDS, ABIGAIL   CT
   Washington. Her property was destroyed by Indians (CAR, 6:84).
RICHARDS, ANN   CT
   New London. In a British attack she suffered losses (CAR, 1:63j, 95f). She was a Western Lands Grantee.

RICHARDS, CECILLA   VA
   King William County. Credited with public service (VR, 3:257).
RICHARDS, ELIZABETH BAIRD   PA
   Philadelphia. The wife of William Richards, she was an active member of the ladies' association for the welfare of the soldiers (Pennsylvania Gazette, June 12, 1780).
RICHARDS, HULDA HOPKINS   CT
   She furnished clothing for the soldiers. See Biographies.
RICHARDS, MARY   CT
   New London. She suffered losses in a British raid (CAR, 1:63j, 95f). She was a Western Lands Grantee.
RICHARDS, MARY   VA
   King and Queen County. She performed a public service (VR, 3:230).
RICHARDS, MILLICENT   VA
   Essex County. Recognized for public service (VR, 4:306).
RICHARDSON, CATHARINE   VA
   Albemarle County. Credited with public service (VR, 2:349).
RICHARDSON, DORCAS NELSON   SC
   She defied British officers. See Biographies.
RICHARDSON, LUCY   VA
   Bedford County. She performed a public service (VR Court Booklet, p. 25).
RICHARDSON, LYDIA   VA
   Norfolk. Recognized for public service (VR, 4:144).
RICHARDSON, MARY PRENTICE   MA
   Woburn. She was the wife of Moses Richardson, who was killed at the Battle of Lexington on April 19, 1775 (FP1).
RICHARDSON, NANCY CRAIGHEAD. See DUNLAP
RICHMAN, REBECCA KEEN   NJ
   She nursed wounded soldiers. See Biographies.
RICKENBACKER (RICONBAKER), ANN   SC
   She supplied provisions for the troops (SI, 1:86).
RICKETTS, SARAH   MD
   In 1781 she supplied wheat for the army (IM, 17300, 19060).
RICKS, ANN   VA
   Southampton County. She performed a public service (VR, 5:180).
RICKS, MARY   VA
   Southampton County. Recognized for public service (VR, 5:180).
RIDDICK, MARY   NC
   She supplied provisions for the troops (RA, K:52).
RIDDLE, REBECCA   VA
   Caroline County. Credited with public service (VR, 1:262-263).
RIDGE, WINNIFRED   NC
   She provided provisions for the army (RA, 1:14, fol. 4).
RIDINGS, MARY POINDEXTER   NC
   She was born in 1775 and married Jesse Ridings. Mary died in 1863. She is listed as a patriot in the DAR Patriot Index.

III: COMPLETE LISTING 425

RIDLEY, SARAH   VA
  Southampton County. She performed a public service (VR, 5:180).
RIFE, ANN   VA
  Rockingham County. She performed a public service (VR Court Booklet, 1:2).
RIFFLE, ELEANOR   WV
  Monongalia County. Credited with public service (VR, 2:342).
RIGDON, ANN MESHOW. See EVANS
RIGGS, ARANNAH   NJ
  Orange. She suffered damage in a British raid (CDB, claim 5).
RIGGS (RIGS), MARY   NC
  She supplied provisions for the troops (RA, 11:72, fol. 4).
RILEY, ANN   SC
  She was born in 1750 and married Patrick Riley (or Reiley) (DAR). She supplied provisions for the army (SI, L-N:30).
RING, MRS. BENJAMIN   PA
  Gen. Washington had his headquarters there. See Biographies.
RINGGOLD, ANN   MD
  Kent County. In 1780 she supplied wheat for the army (IM, 11283).
RINGGOLD, MARY   MD
  Kent County. She supplied wheat in 1781 for the army (IM, 11290).
RINKER, MOM   PA
  She was an American spy. See Biographies.
RITCHIE, MARY   SC
  She is listed as a soldier. See Biographies.
RITTENHOUSE, ELIZABETH BULL   MD
  She was born in 1753 and was the first wife of Capt. Benjamin Rittenhouse. She is listed as a patriot in the DAR Patriot Index.
RIVES, ELIZABETH BRIGGS MASON VA
  Sussex County. The wife of Christopher Rives, she is recognized as a patriot (VR, 5:206).
RIVES, HANNAH WILLIAMSON   VA
  Greensville. The wife of Simon Rives, she performed a public service (VR, 3:29).
ROACH, PHEBE   NY
  She was captured with her husband, Michael, and taken to Montreal. On November 3, 1782, they recovered a child and their niece from Indians on Carleton's Island (MR).
ROACH, SUSANNA   NC
  The wife of Joseph Roach, she provided provisions for the army (RA, D:141).
ROASBOROUGH, MARY   NC
  She supplied provisions for the troops (RA, 11:59, fol. 3).
ROBARDS, RACHEL DONELSON. See JACKSON
ROBB, MRS. FRANCIS   VA
  Lancaster County. She performed a public service (VR, 4:347).

ROBB, LOUISA ST. CLAIR   PA, OH
   She was the daughter of Gen. Arthur St. Clair. At age eighteen
   Louisa was a crack shot and a splendid horsewoman, and over
   the years braved many dangers with the Indians. She married
   Mr. Robb, a violinist. After the defeat of her father in 1791,
   they returned to Pennsylvania (DAR Magazine, July 1921).
ROBBINS (ROBINS), SARAH   NC
   She supplied provisions for the troops (RA, 11:99, fol. 1).
ROBERDEAU, MARY BOSTWICK   PA
   She entertained John Adams. See Biographies.
ROBERTS, ANNA   VA
   Northampton County. Recognized for public service (VR Lists,
   p. 1).
ROBERTS, ELIZABETH   NC
   She opposed drinking British tea. See Background.
ROBERTS, ELIZABETH   VA
   Chesterfield County. Credited with public service (VR Ctf
   1). Also Frederick County (VR, 4:309).
ROBERTS, ESTHER   CT
   She supplied clothing for the army (CAR, 23:230).
ROBERTS, HANNAH   VA
   York County. She performed a public service (VR, 4:279).
ROBERTS, JANE   VA
   Halifax County. Recognized for public service (VR, 2:286,
   288).
ROBERTS, MARY   SC
   She supplied provisions for the troops (SI, R-T:208).
ROBERTS, SARAH   VA
   Culpeper County. Credited with public service (VR, 2:111).
ROBERTSON, ANNE   VA
   Halifax County. She performed a public service (VR, 2:289).
ROBERTSON, CHARLOTTE REEVES   TN
   She warned the Americans of an impending attack on Fort Nash-
   borough. See Biographies.
ROBERTSON, MARY   VA
   Amelia County. Credited with public service (VR Lists, 1:5,8).
ROBERTSON, NANCY   VA
   Halifax County. Recognized for public service (VR, 4:321).
ROBESON, ELIZABETH   NC
   She supplied provisions for the troops (RA, 6:53, fol. 2).
ROBESON (ROBERTSON), SUSANNA NC
   She supplied provisions for the army (RA, 11:14, fol. 3; RA,
   5:12, fol. 2).
ROBINS, ELIZABETH   VA
   Northampton County. Credited with public service (VR Court
   Booklet, p. 9).
ROBINSON, ANN   SC
   She provided supplies for the army (SI, I:83).
ROBINSON, ELEANOR   VA
   Lancaster County. She performed a public service (VR Court
   Booklet, p. 16).

III: COMPLETE LISTING 427

ROBINSON, ELIZABETH (ESTATE)   VA
   Middlesex County. Credited with public service (VR Court Booklet, p. 5; Lists, pp. 1, 4, 5).
ROBINSON, HANNAH   CT
   Danbury. In the British raid of April 1777 she suffered damage (CAR, 8:382c).
ROBINSON, JANE   GA
   She supplied cattle for public use (WA, p. 157).
ROBINSON, MARTHA   CT
   New Haven. In the July 1779 British raid she suffered losses (CAR, 15:234k).
ROBINSON, NANCY   SC
   She supplied provisions for the troops (SI, B:102).
ROBINSON, SARAH   NC
   She provided supplies for the army (RA, A:175).
ROBINSON (ROBERTSON), SARAH   VA
   Hansemond County. She performed a public service (VR, 4:166).
ROCHE, ANN   NJ
   Acquacanunk. The widow of Dr. Nicholas Roche, she suffered damage in a British raid (CDB, claim 29).
ROCHESTER, FRANCES   MD
   Queen Anne County. In 1778 she supplied bacon for the army (IM, 6805).
ROCK, MARY   NJ
   Windsor, Middlesex County. The widow of James Rock, she suffered damage in a British attack (CDB, p. 246).
ROCKHILL, REBECKAH   NJ
   Burlington. The wife of Solomon Rockhill, she suffered losses in a British raid (CDB, claim 131).
ROCKWELL, ABIGAIL   CT
   In 1780 she supplied cattle for the army (CAR, 35:142ab).
RODDIN, PHOEBE   VA
   Greensville. She performed a public service (VR, 4:318).
RODES (RHODES), MARY   VA
   Albemarle County. Recognized for public service (VR Lists, p. 5).
RODGERS, ELIZABETH   NC
   She supplied provisions for the troops (RA, 9:30, fol. 1).
RODGERS, HANNAH   NJ
   Morris County. She suffered damages caused by the Americans (CDB, claims 1, 9).
ROE, ELIZABETH ELTUNGE   NY
   She was born in 1749 and married James Roe. Elizabeth died in 1793 and is listed as a patriot in the DAR Patriot Index.
ROE, JAMIMA   VA
   Westmoreland County. Credited with public service (VR, 5:223).
ROGERS, AGNES   VA
   Amelia County. She performed a public service (VR, 1:83).
ROGERS, ELIZABETH   CT
   Norwalk widow. She suffered damage in a British raid (CAR, 18:269a). She was a Western Lands Grantee.

ROGERS, ELIZABETH, II   CT
   Norwalk. She suffered losses in a British raid (CAR, 1:63i, 98d). She was a Western Lands Grantee.
ROGERS, ELIZABETH   NC
   She supplied provisions for the troops (RA, 5:48, fol. 4).
ROGERS, HANNAH   VA
   James City County. She performed a public service (VR Court Booklet, p. 8).
ROGERS, MRS. JOHN   NC
   She provided supplies for the army (RA, 5:63, fol. 4).
ROGERS, LUCY   VA
   Spotsylvania County. Credited with public service (VR, 4:264).
ROGERS, MARY LARABEE   CT
   Her property was burned by the British. See Biographies.
ROGERS, RUTH   MD
   Baltimore. Her husband was taken by the British, and she wrote to the governor on December 26, 1777 (IM, 5536).
ROGERS, SARAH   NC
   She supplied provisions for the troops (RA, 6:53, fol. 1).
ROICE, ANN   NC
   She provided provisions for the army (RA, 11:98, fol. 3).
ROLING, SUSANNAH   NJ
   Middlesex County. She suffered damage caused by the British (CDB, p. 179).
ROLINSON (ROWLISON), HANNAH   NJ
   Hackensack. The wife of Benjamin, she suffered damage in a British raid (CDB, claims 39, 44).
ROLINSON (ROWLISON), SARAH   NJ
   Saddle River. The wife of Jacob, she suffered damage caused by the Americans (CDB, claims 15, 41).
ROOK, ELIZABETH   PA
   She was captured by Indians and taken to Montreal on December 24, 1782. She decided to remain there until she could locate her children (MR).
ROOTES, FANNY   VA
   King and Queen County. She performed a public service (VR, 3:229).
ROPER, ELEANOR   VA
   Charles City County. Credited with public service (VR Court Booklet, p. 23).
ROSCOE, MARY   CT
   Norwalk. She suffered damage in a British raid (CAR, 1:63j, 98a). She was a Western Lands Grantee.
ROSE, CHRISTIANA   CT
   Danbury. She suffered losses in a British raid (CAR, 1:51b, 63u). She was a Western Lands Grantee.
ROSEBOROUGH, MARY   NC
   The wife of William Roseborough, she supplied provisions for the troops (RA, A:122).
ROSS, BETSY   NJ
   Westfield. She suffered damage in a British raid (CDB, claim 10).

III: COMPLETE LISTING

ROSS, BETSY GRISCOM   PA
     She made flags for the Pennsylvania navy. See Biographies.

ROSS, ELIZABETH   MD
     Baltimore. While the British occupied Philadelphia, the Continental Congress moved to Baltimore. John Adams stayed at her home on Market Street from February 5 to February 27, 1777 (BA).

ROSS, ELIZABETH   SC
     She married Hugh Ross and died in 1805 (DAR). Elizabeth supplied provisions for the troops (SI, L-N:58).

ROSS, ELIZABETH GOODWIN   MA
     Salem. She married William Ross who commanded the privateer Wasp. On December 22, 1776, Ross was captured by the British man-of-war Hind and imprisoned (CN).

ROSS, ISABEL   NC
     She supplied provisions for the troops (RA, 11:60, fol. 1, A:68).

ROSS, MARY   NJ
     Middlesex County. The widow of Jonathan Freeman, she suffered damage in a British raid (CDB, p. 44).

ROSS, MARY   VA
     Caroline County. She performed a public service (VR Court Booklet, 2:24).

ROSS, SARAH   VA
     York County. Recognized for public service (VR, 4:279).

ROSS, SARAH GIRDLER   MA
     Newburyport. She married Alexander Ross, who served as mate on the Dalton, which was captured in December 1776 by the Reasonable. In June 1777 Ross was confined in the Mill Prison at Plymouth, England. On December 19, 1778, he escaped and returned to America. In 1780 he commanded the privateer Fox, and in January 1781 Ross was captured for a second time and imprisoned again (CN).

ROSS, TALMAGE   NJ
     Westfield. The wife of Ichabod Ross, she suffered damage in a British raid (CDB, claim 1).

ROSSITER, MARY ELIZABETH STEPHENS   PA
     She was born in 1761 and married Samuel Rossiter. Mary died in 1839 and is listed as a patriot in the DAR Patriot Index.

ROULAIN, SUSAN   SC
     She supplied provisions for the troops (SI, B:163).

ROUNDSEVAL (ROUNSEVAL), SARAH   NC
     She provided supplies for the army (RA, 7:41, fol. 3; 6:3, fol. 4).

ROUNTREE, ELIZABETH   NC
     She supplied provisions for the troops (RA, C:12).

ROUSBY, ANNE FRISBY. See FITZHUGH

ROUSE, DEBORAH   SC
     She provided provisions for the army (SI, Y-Z:95).

ROUSE, ELIZABETH   NC
     She supplied provisions for the troops (RA, 5:19, fol. 4).

ROUSE, MARY VA
Dinwiddie County. She performed a public service (VR, 1:341).

ROUTE, MRS. ALEXANDER VA
Northumberland County. Credited with public service (VR Ctf 1).

ROWDUS, ELIZABETH SC
She supplied provisions for the troops (SI, U-W:79).

ROWE, MRS. (ESTATE) VA
Caroline County. Credited with public service (VR Lists, 2:19, 27).

ROWE, MARGARET MD
Baltimore. She boarded Capt. James Nicholson in May 1776 (IM, 1513).

ROWE, REBECCAH VA
Gloucester County. She performed a public service (VR, 3:52, 53; 4:288).

ROWE, SUSANNA VA
Caroline County. Recognized for public service (VR, 1:263).

ROWLAND, LETTY NJ
New Brunswick. The wife of James Rowland, she suffered damage in a British attack (CDB, p. 164).

ROWLEY, RACHEL VA
Accomack County. She performed a public service (VR, 1:30).

ROWS, DEBORAH SC
She provided supplies for the army (SI, 1:25).

ROY, ANN VA
Caroline County. She performed a public service (VR Court Booklet, 2:16, 23).

RUBLE (RUBEL), JANE VA
Frederick County. Credited with public service (VR, 2:206).

RUCKER, BETTY VA
Amherst County. She performed a public service (VR Ctf 1).

RUCKER, ELIZABETH VA
Culpeper County. Recognized for public service (VR, 2:112).

RUDDELL, ELIZABETH BOWMAN KY
She was captured by the British and later taken to Quebec. See Biographies.

RUDDELL, SARAH BARNES VA
She was the wife of Thomas Beggs, then became the second wife of Stephen Ruddell. Sarah is listed in the DAR Patriot Index.

RUDSPATH, ELIZABETH NC
She supplied provisions for the troops (RA, 2:14, fol. 4).

RUFFIN, MRS. VA
King William County. She performed a public service (VR Court Booklet, p. 7).

RUFFIN, MARY VA
King William County. Credited with public service (VR, 4:337, 338).

RUFFIN, MARY VA
New Kent County. Credited with public service (VR Lists, 1:3, 5).

III: COMPLETE LISTING

RUNDALL, AMY   CT
  Greenwich. She suffered damage in a British raid (CAR, 1:63f, 74f). She was a Western Lands Grantee.

RUNDEL, ABIGAIL   CT
  Greenwich. In the March 1779 and December 1783 British raids she suffered damage (CAR, 36:19a). She was a Western Lands Grantee.

RUNDEL, HANNAH   CT
  Greenwich. In the March 1779 and December 1783 British raids she suffered damage (CAR, 36:19b). She was a Western Lands Grantee.

RUSH, JULIA STOCKTON   PA
  She was active in the ladies' association for the welfare of the soldiers. See Biographies.

RUSHING, SABRINA   SC
  She supplied provisions for the troops (SI, U-W:294).

RUSK, MARGARET   VA
  Augusta. The wife of John Rusk, she performed a public service (VR Court Booklet, pp. 4, 14).

RUSSELL, ANN   VA
  Princess Anne County. Credited with public service (VR, 4:223).

RUSSELL, ELIZABETH HENRY CAMPBELL   VA
  She was the wife of Col. William Russell, Sr., of the 5th Virginia Regiment. On May 12, 1780, Col. Russell was captured by the British when Charleston, South Carolina, fell to the enemy (FW).

RUSSELL, HANNAH   CT
  New Haven. In the British raid of July 1779 she suffered damage (CAR, 15:269b). She was a Western Lands Grantee.

RUSSELL, JUNE   NC
  She supplied provisions for the troops (RA, C:93).

RUSSELL, MARY   NC
  She provided supplies for the army (RA, 1:94, fol. 4; RA, 1:65, fol. 4).

RUSSELL, RACHEL   CT
  New Haven. She suffered damage in a British raid (CAR, 1:63d, 91f). She was a Western Lands Grantee.

RUSSELL, RACHEL   VA
  At age seventeen she was captured in October 1779 at Holston by Indians and released from Fort Ticonderoga on July 18, 1738 (MR).

RUST, ANN   VA
  Campbell County. She performed a public service (VR, 1:291).

RUST, ELIZABETH   VA
  Westmoreland County. Credited with public service (VR, 5:223).

RUTGERS, ELIZABETH   NY
  The British seized her brewery. See Biographies.

RUTHERFORD, MRS.   NC
  She supplied provisions for the army (RA, 5:53, fol. 3).

RUTLEDGE (ROUTLEDGE), CATHERINE   NC
  She supplies provisions for the troops (RA, 5:50, fol. 3).

RUTLEDGE, HENRIETTA MIDDLETON   SC
   Her husband was imprisoned by the British. See Biographies.
RUTLEDGE, SARAH HEXT   SC
   Her home was plundered by the British. See Biographies.
RYALS, SARAH   NC
   She supplied provisions for the army (RA, 9:95, fol. 4).
RYERSON, ELENA   NJ
   Saddle River. The wife of John Ryerson, she suffered damage caused by the American troops (CDB, claim 37).

S

SACKETT, HANNAH   CT
   New Haven. In the July 1779 British raid she suffered damage (CAR, 15:234i, 269c). She was a Western Lands Grantee.
SAGE, ESTHER HALL   CT
   Middletown. She married Giles Sage, who commanded the privateer sloop Lucy. On February 6, 1779, he was captured by HMS Mars and taken to New York as a prisoner. But on February 21, 1779, the American prisoners overpowered the British and took the vessel. They beached the vessel at Guilford, Connecticut. The Mars was renamed the Guilford and commanded by William Nott of Milford, Connecticut (CN).
SAGE, FRANCES   CT
   New Haven. She suffered damage in a British raid (CAR, 1:63a, 91c). She was a Western Lands Grantee.
ST. CLAIR, PHOEBE BAYARD   PA
   Gen. and Mrs. St. Clair advanced their own funds to support the army. See Biographies.
ST. JOHN, ESTHER   CT
   Norwalk. In a British raid she suffered damage (CAR, 1:63k, 98e). She was a Western Lands Grantee.
ST. JULIAN, SUSAN   SC
   She supplied provisions for the troops (SI, B:181).
SALE, HANNAH   VA
   Caroline County. She performed a public service (VR, 4:300).
SALE, MARY   VA
   Essex County. She performed a public service (VR Court Booklet, p. 8).
SALISBURY, ABIGAIL   RI
   She knitted socks for the soldiers. See Biographies.
SALISBURY, MARTHA SAUNDERS   MA
   She was born in 1704 and married Nicholas Salisbury. Martha died in 1792. She is listed as a patriot in the DAR Patriot Index.
SALLEE, ELIZABETH   NJ
   Connecticut Farms, Essex County. The wife of Puch Sallee, she suffered damage in a British attack (CDB, claim 36).
SALLER, ELIZABETH   SC
   She supplied provisions for the troops (SI, 10, pt. 1:31).

III: COMPLETE LISTING 433

SALTER, CLARISSA NC
  She provided supplies for the army (RA, A:55).
SALTONSTALL, ANN CT
  New London. The daughter of Rebeckah and Gurdon Saltonstall, she was born on February 29, 1739/40. On November 20, 1778, Edward Conckling obtained a letter of marque to command the six-gun sloop Eagle. Ann witnessed the bond. In 1781 she also witnessed a bond for Jeremiah Simmons of Philadelphia to command the six-gun Connecticut schooner Mayflower (CN).
SALTONSTALL, MARY. See ATWATER
SALTUS, MARY SC
  She supplied provisions for the troops (SI, R-T:154).
SAMPLES, ELIZABETH ALLEN. See CRAFTS
SAMPSON, DEBORAH. See GANNETT
SAMPSON, MARY VA
  Culpeper County. She performed a public service (VR Court Booklet, 50:2, 41).
SAMUEL, ANN NC
  She supplied provisions for the troops (RA, 9:26, fol. 2). Also Anne Samuel (RA, 5:13, fol. 3).
SAMUEL, ELIZABETH VA
  Caroline County. Recognized for public service (VR, 1:259).
SANDELL, MAGDALENE SC
  The wife of Peter Sandell, she died in 1782. She is listed as a patriot in the DAR Patriot Index 2.
SANDERLIN (SANDERLING), DEVOTION NC
  She supplied provisions for the troops (RA, C:20, 25).
SANDERS, ANN MD
  In 1778 she provided sheep and vegetables for Capt. Berrill Matthews of the Independence (IM, 7553).
SANDERS, ANN NC
  She supplied provisions for the army (RA, A:235).
SANDERS, CATHERINE VA
  Spotsylvania County. She performed a public service (VR Court Booklet, p. 3).
SANDERS, MARGARET SC
  She supplied provisions for the troops (SI, 10, pt. 1:51).
SANDERS, MARY NC
  She provided provisions for the army (RA, 10:24, fol. 1).
SANDERSON, ANN VA
  Cumberland County. Credited with public service (VR, 1:233, 234).
SANDRIDGE, ELIZABETH GRAVES VA
  She supplied provisions for the army. See Biographies.
SANDS, ANN MD
  In 1776 and 1777 she made clothing for the army (IM, 285, 5377).
SANFORD, MARGARET VA
  Westmoreland County. Recognized for public service (VR, 5:224).
SANGER, BRIDGET NJ
  Middlesex County. She suffered damage in a British attack (CDB, p. 33).

SATCHELL, SARAH   VA
    Northampton County. Recognized for public service (VR Lists, p. 2).
SATTERWHITE, ANN   VA
    Essex County. She performed a public service (VR, 2:157). She was the wife of John Satterwhite.
SAUNDERS, ANN   SC
    She provided provisions for the army (SI, B:20).
SAUNDERS, BETTY   VA
    Lancaster County. Recognized for public service (VR Court Booklet, p. 15).
SAUNDERS, ELEANOR   GA
    She supplied cattle for public use (WA, p. 157).
SAUNDERS, ELIZABETH   VA
    Lancaster County. Credited with public service (VR, 3:278).
SAUNDERS, JANE CRAIG   KY
    Bryan's Station. She was the wife of John Saunders. When the Tories and Indians attacked on August 15, 1782, Jane and her daughters Polly, Betsy, and Lydia were among the women who went for water. Their names are inscribed on the monument erected in 1896 by the Lexington Daughters of the American Revolution.
SAUNDERS, MARY   NC
    She supplied provisions for the troops (RA, C:7).
SAUNDERS, NANCY   NC
    She provided provisions for the army (RA, A:203).
SAUNDERS, SARAH   VA
    Loudoun County. Credited with public service (VR, 3:323).
SAVAGE, MARTHA   SC
    She supplied provisions for the troops (SI, B:85).
SAVAGE, RUTH   SC
    She supplied provisions for the army (SI, B:100).
SAVAGE, SARAH   CT
    Middletown. She supplied blankets for the army (CAR, 5:53-58).
SAWYER, MARGARET   NC
    She supplied provisions for the troops (RA, 6:61, fol. 3).
SAYLOR, ELIZABETH   SC
    She provided supplies for the army (SI, R-T:217).
SAYRES, SARAH   NJ
    Connecticut Farms, Essex County. She suffered damage in a British attack (CDB, claim 40).
SCALES, MARY   NC
    She supplied provisions for the troops (RA, A:88).
SCANDRET, SARAH   VA
    Essex County. She performed a public service (VR Court Booklet, pp. 2, 5).
SCANLAN, DEBORAH   SC
    She provided supplies for the army (SI, B:129).
SCHELL, MARIA SCHELL   NY
    She was born in 1735 and married Christian Schell. Maria died

III: COMPLETE LISTING

in 1790 and is listed as a patriot in the DAR Patriot Index.

SCHMILIE, ELIONAR NJ
Burlington. She suffered damage caused by the Americans (CDB, claim 158).

SCHOLL, LIVINIA BOONE KY
Boonesborough. The daughter of Rebecca Bryan and Daniel Boone, she was born in 1766. Daniel Boone moved his wife and daughters to Boonesborough in 1775. Livinia Boone Scholl died in 1802. For the story of this nine-year-old girl in the wilds of Kentucky, see Biographies: Boone, Rebecca.

SCHREIBER, REBECCA RACHEL NY
Mrs. Schreiber and her three children were captured by Indians. See Biographies.

SCHUYLER, CATHERINE VAN RENSSELAER NY
She set fire to her grain fields to stop Gen. Burgoyne. See Biographies.

SCHUYLER, MARGARET NY
Tories plundered her home. See Biographies.

SCOGGIN, FRANCES NC
She provided provisions for the army (RA, 11:47, fol. 1).

SCOTHORN, ELIZABETH BROWN VA
The wife of Joseph Scothorn, she died in 1789. Elizabeth is listed as a patriot in the DAR Patriot Index 2.

SCOTT, ANNE VA
Princess Anne County. She performed a public service (VR Court Booklet, p. 11).

SCOTT, ELIZABETH HARRISON VA
Fauquier County. The wife of Capt. James Scott, she performed a public service (VR, 2:246).

SCOTT, FRANCES SC
She supplied provisions for the troops (SI, B:118).

SCOTT, JOYCE JANE CALLIHAM SC
The wife of Samuel Scott, she is listed as a patriot in the DAR Patriot Index.

SCOTT, MARGARET GREGG. See FLAGLER

SCOTT, MARY VA
Gloucester County. Credited with public service (VR, 3:53).

SCOTT, SARAH CT
She supplied provisions for the militia (CAR, 35:44b).

SCOTT, SARAH VA
Amelia County. She performed a public service (VR, 1:94). Also Cumberland County (VR, 1:234).

SCREVEN, REBECCA SC
She provided supplies for the army (SI, B:162).

SCRUGGS, TABITHA VA
Cumberland County. Credited with public service (VR, 1:234).

SCUDDER, ISABELLA ANDERSON NJ
She was active in the ladies' association for the welfare of the soldiers. See Biographies.

SCUDDER, PRISCILLA   CT
    Greenwich. In the 1779 and 1783 British raids she suffered
    damage (CAR, 1:63d, 91f). She was a Western Lands Grantee
    (CAR, 36:19e).
SEABURN, MARTHA   VA
    Sussex County. Recognized for public service (VR, 5:207)'.
SEABURY, ELIZABETH   CT
    Groton. In the British attack she suffered losses (CAR, 1:63s,
    79c). She was a Western Lands Grantee.
SEADAM, HANNAH   PA
    At age twenty-one she was captured in February 1782 by Indians
    at Fiskany and released from Fort Ticonderoga on July 18, 1783
    (MR).
SEARING, ANN   NJ
    Connecticut Farms, Essex County. The wife of John Searing,
    she suffered damage in a British attack (CDB, claim 48).
SEARLE, ANN SMITH   PA
    She was active in the ladies' association for the welfare of the
    soldiers. See Biographies.
SEARS, REBECCA KELLEY   MA
    Amesbury. While single she provided L75 for the militia. Later
    she married Enos Sears (Joseph Merrill, History of Amesbury
    and Merrimac).
SEAVY (SEAY), AMY   VA
    Fluvanna County. Recognized for public service (VR, 1:364).
SEBRE, MARY   VA
    Spotsylvania County. Credited with public service (VR, 5:244).
SEGLER, ESTHER   NJ
    Somerville. She suffered damage in a British attack (CDB,
    p. 2).
SEIGLER, MARY   SC
    She supplied provisions for the troops (SI, 1:88).
SELDEN, ELIZABETH ELY   CT
    She was the wife of Samuel Selden, who was a major in the 3rd
    Regiment of Connecticut militia in 1775. Later he was a colonel.
    When the British attacked New York City on September 15, 1776,
    Selden was captured and taken prisoner. He died in prison
    on October 11, 1776 (FP1).
SELDEN, MARY   VA
    Lancaster County. She performed a public service (VR Court
    Booklet, p. 17).
SEMPLE, ELIZABETH   VA
    King and Queen County. Recognized for public service (VR,
    3:232).
SERGEANT, MARGARET SPENCER   NJ
    With her infant child she fled from the British army. See
    Biographies.
SESCAT, DESIRE   CT
    Norwalk. In a British raid she suffered losses (CAR, 1:63k,
    98e). She was a Western Lands Grantee.

III: COMPLETE LISTING 437

SETCHELL, SARAH   CT
   New London. She suffered damage in a British raid (CAR, 1:63j, 95h). She was a Western Lands Grantee.
SETTLES, MARY   VA
   Westmoreland County. She performed a public service (VR Court Booklet, p. 2).
SEVIER, CATHERINE SHERRILL   TN
   "Bonny Kate" made clothes for her husband and five sons to serve in the army. See Biographies.
SEWELL, ANNE   MA
   Exeter. On September 29, 1779, William Friend of Newburyport, Massachusetts, obtained a letter of marque to command the ship Postillion with eight guns and twenty men. Rebecca Gilman and Anne Sewell witnessed the bond. She also witnessed a bond for William Preston (CN).
SEXTON, MRS.   NJ
   Hunterdon County. She collected funds for the army (New Jersey Gazette, July 4, 1780).
SEXTON, ANNA LARSON   NJ
   The wife of Jared Sexton, she was an active member of the ladies' association for the benefit of the soldiers (New Jersey Gazette, July 4, 1780).
SEYMOUR, ABIGAIL   CT
   Hartford. In 1781 she lodged guards for prisoners (CAR, 31:156, 161).
SEYMOUR, ANNA   CT
   Norwalk. In the 1779 British raid she suffered losses (CAR, 20:379). Also Anne Seymour listed (CAR, 1:63jk, 98de). She was a Western Lands Grantee.
SEYMOUR, HANNAH   CT
   Ridgefield. In the April 1777 raid by the British she suffered losses (CAR, 8:391a). She was a Western Lands Grantee.
SEYMOUR, LYDIA ST. JOHN   CT
   The wife of Lt. William Seymour, she died in 1829 and is listed as a patriot in the DAR Patriot Index.
SHACKELFORD, FRANCES   VA
   King and Queen County. She performed a public service (VR Court Booklet, p. 3).
SHACKELFORD, JUDITH   VA
   Hanover County. Credited with public service (VR, 3:166, 199, 201).
SHAFFER, ELIZABETH WARNER   NY
   She was born in 1760 and married Henry Shaffer. Elizabeth is listed as a patriot in the DAR Patriot Index.
SHANKLAND, MRS. WILLIAM   VA
   In 1778 she was captured by the British and Indians along with her husband and four children and later exchanged (MR).
SHANKLIN, MARY   NC
   She supplied provisions for the troops (RA, C:70).
SHAPLEY, ELIZABETH   CT
   New London. She suffered damage in a British raid (CAR, 1:63j, 95g). She was a Western Lands Grantee.

SHARP, ANN   NJ
   Burlington. The wife of John Sharp, she suffered damage in
   a British attack (CDB, p. 98).
SHARPE, JEMIMA ALEXANDER   NC
   She carried food, clothing, and medicine to prison ships in Charleston Harbor, South Carolina. See Biographies.
SHATTUCK, SARAH HARTWELL   MA
   She captured a British courier. See Biographies.
SHAW, LUCRETIA HARRIS   CT
   She entertained Gen. Washington and turned her home into a hospital for sick and wounded soldiers. See Biographies.
SHAW (SCHAW), MARY   NC
   She supplied provisions for the troops (RA, 5:53, fol. 3).
SHEAD, ELEANOR   SC
   After the fall of Charleston on May 12, 1780, she refused to sign an oath of fidelity to the Crown and so was banished from the city (SC).
SHEAFFE, MARIA   MA
   Boston. On January 11, 1781, James Brown obtained a letter of marque to command the ten-gun brigantine Success with thirty men. The bond was witnessed by Maria and Sarah Sheaffe (CN).
SHEAFFE, SARAH   MA
   Boston. On January 11, 1781, James Brown obtained a letter of marque to command the brigantine Success. The bond was witnessed by Sarah and Maria Sheaffe (CN).
SHED, HANNAH   MA
   Salem. On May 15, 1782, Samuel Croel obtained a letter of marque to command the sixteen-gun ship General Greene with eighty men. Witnesses to the bond were James Shed and Hannah Shed (CN).
SHEFFIELD, ABIGAIL   RI
   The widow of Samuel Cushing, she supplied provisions for the army (MP, 23:45; 19:11).
SHELBY, ISABEL   NC
   She provided supplies for the army (RA, A:99).
SHELBY, SUSANNA HART   KY
   Her husband was killed by Indians. See Biographies.
SHELDON, MRS. SAMUEL   CT
   She entertained Gen. Washington. See Biographies.
SHELL, ELIZABETH   NC
   She supplied provisions for the troops (RA, 6:41, fol. 1).
SHELL, ELIZABETH PETRIE   NY
   She loaded flintlocks for her husband and sons. See Biographies.
SHELLY (SHILLEY), DREWSELLA   SC
   She provided provisions for the army (SI, U-W:157).
SHEPARD, ANNE   CT
   Danbury. She suffered losses in a British raid (CAR, 1:63u).
SHEPHERD, CATHERINE VAN WINKLE   NJ
   After her father was hanged by the British, she cut him down. She also carried warning messages. See Biographies.

III: COMPLETE LISTING 439

SHEPHERD, LYDIA   VA
  Hansemond County. She performed a public service (VR Court Booklet, 1:22).
SHEPHERD, MARTHA   NC
  She supplied provisions for the troops (RA, 7:78, fol. 4).
SHERMAN, ANN   VA
  Lancaster County. Credited with public service (VR, 3:278).
SHERMAN, REBECCA PRESCOTT   CT
  Assisted by Mrs. Wolcott, she made the first flag in Connecticut. See Biographies.
SHERROD (SHEROD), SUSANNAH   NC
  She supplied provisions for the troops (RA, 11:94, fol. 1).
SHERWOOD, ANN   CT
  Danbury. She suffered damage in a British raid (CAR, 1:51b).
SHIELDS, MARY   NC
  She provided supplies for the army (RA, A:100; RA, 12:72, fol. 4).
SHILOUT, MARGERY   VA
  King George County. She performed a public service (VR, 5:227).
SHINHOLSTER, MRS.   SC
  She supplied provisions for the troops (SI, R-T:296).
SHIP, ELIZABETH   NC
  She provided provisions for the army (RA, A:80).
SHIPMAN, ELIZABETH   VA
  Rockingham County. Credited with public service (VR, 5:116).
SHIPPEN, ALICE LEE   PA
  She was active in the ladies' association for the welfare of the soldiers. See Biographies.
SHIPPEN, MARGARET FRANCES   PA
  She entertained Gen. Washington. See Biographies.
SHIRLEY, MARY   VA
  King William County. Credited with public service (VR, 3:258).
SHIVERS, CATHERINE   WV
  Hampshire County. She performed a public service (VR Court Booklet, p. 6).
SHOEMAKER, BLANDINA VAN CAMPEN   PA
  Philadelphia. She was born in 1750 and married Henry Shoemaker, a lieutenant of riflemen. He was captured in the Battle of Long Island on August 27, 1776, and was confined on a prison ship in New York Harbor. Later Shoemaker managed to escape (FP1).
SHOEMAKER, ELIZABETH   SC
  She supplied provisions for the troops (SI, O-Q:92, 248).
SHOLES, LUCRETIA   CT
  Groton. She suffered damage in the British attack (CAR, 1:63r, 79c). She was a Western Lands Grantee.
SHORT, JOANNA   CT
  New London. In the British attack, she suffered losses (CAR, 1:63k, 95i).
SHORT, MARY   NC
  She supplied provisions for the troops (RA, A:21).

SHORT (SHORTE), PATTY   NC
    She supplied provisions for the army (RA, 7:62, fol. 1).
SHOTWELL, NANCY   NJ
    Middlesex County. In the British attack she suffered damage (CDB, p. 90).
SHREVE, SARAH   NJ
    Burlington. In the British raid she suffered losses (CDB, pp. 76, 78).
SHRIVER, SARAH   PA
    She was captured by British and Indians on April 16, 1778, and taken to Montreal (MR).
SIBERY, MARY   VA
    Spotsylvania County. She performed a public service (VR Court Booklet, p. 17).
SIBLEY, ANNA   NH
    While pregnant with her third child, she hoed three acres of corn. See Biographies.
SIBLEY, HANNAH MARSH   MA
    Sutton. She was the wife of Capt. John Sibley, who served as surgeon's mate. While taking care of the sick and wounded he died of typhus on November 27, 1778 (FP1).
SICKLES, ELIZABETH   NY
    New York City. In 1776 she was listed as a matron in the General Hospital. She cared for the wounded soldiers (RW).
SIDMAN, WIDOW   NY
    Gen. Washington stopped several times at her tavern. See Biographies.
SIKES, SUSANNA   VA
    Gloucester County. She performed a public service (VR, 3:53).
SILLIMAN, MARY FISH   CT
    She hid the church communion silver in her home. See Biographies.
SILSBE, SARAH   CT
    Ridgefield. She suffered losses in a British raid (CAR, 1:63n). She was a Western Lands Grantee.
SILVESTER, ANNE   VA
    Norfolk. Recognized for public service (VR, 4:142).
SIMMONS, ABIGAIL   NC
    She supplied provisions for the troops (RA, A:46).
SIMMONS, ANN   CT
    New London. She suffered damage in a British raid (CAR, 1:63j, 95h). She was a Western Lands Grantee.
SIMMONS, ELIZABETH   NC
    She provided supplies for the army (RA, 9:5, fol. 1).
SIMMONS, ELIZABETH   VA
    Norfolk. She performed a public service (VR Ctf 1).
SIMMONS, LYDIA BALL   SC
    She was born in 1757 and married Edward Simmons. Later she became the second wife of John Bryan. Lydia died in 1842 and is listed as a patriot in the DAR Patriot Index.

III: COMPLETE LISTING

SIMMONS, MARTHA VA
  Brunswick County. Recognized for public service (VR, 1:129).
SIMMONS, MARY NJ
  Burlington. She suffered damage in a British attack (CDB, p. 115).
SIMMONS, MARY SC
  She supplied provisions for the troops (SI, B:45, 46).
SIMMONS, REBECCA VA
  Surry County. Credited with public service (VR Court Booklet, p. 4).
SIMMONS, SARAH (ESTATE) VA
  Southampton County. She performed a public service (VR Court Booklet, p. 11).
SIMMONS, SUSANNA VA
  Brunswick County. The wife of Henry Simmons, she is recognized for public service (VR Lists, p. 6).
SIMMS, SARAH DICKINSON NC
  Her home was burned by Tories. See Biographies.
SIMONJON, PHEBE NJ
  Griggs Township, Somerset County. She suffered damages in a British attack (CDB, pp. 165, 181).
SIMPSON, ANN MD
  Baltimore. In April 1777 she lodged Lt. Ritter of the ship Defence and provided nursing in March 1777 for the seamen (IM, 3089, 3907).
SIMPSON, ISABEL SC
  She supplied provisions for the troops (SI, 10, pt. 1:178).
SIMPSON, MARGARET MURRAY PA
  She supplied food and clothing for the soldiers at Valley Forge. See Biographies.
SIMPSON, MARY REMER SC
  She was born in 1743 and married Chaplain John Simpson. Mary died in 1812. She supplied provisions for the army (SI, 10, pt. 1:52).
SIMPSON, SOPHIA SC
  She supplied provisions for the troops (SI, R-T:216; Y-Z:182).
SIMS, ELIZABETH VA
  Greensville. She performed a public service (VR, 3:31).
SIMS, ISABELLA SC
  She nursed wounded soldiers. See Biographies.
SIMS, MARY VA
  Cumberland County. Credited with public service (VR, 1:233).
SIMSON, MARGARET NJ
  Middlesex County. The mother of Abraham Simson, she suffered damage in a British attack (CDB, p. 243).
SINCLAIRE, ELIZABETH WILSON VA
  She was the first wife of John Sinclaire, who was mate on the privateer Disdain and was captured by the British. On January 3, 1782, Sinclaire was committed to the Mill Prison at Plymouth, England (CN).

SINGLETON, ANN SC
   She provided supplies for the army (SI, O-Q:131; U-W:107).
SINGLETON, SARAH CRAIG KY
   She went for water when the Indians attacked. See Biographies.
SINGLEY, RACHEL SC
   She supplied provisions for the troops (SI, 10, pt. 1:83).
SKARRAT, MARGARET VA
   Amelia County. She performed a public service (VR Court Booklet, 1:25).
SKEATHS, MARY VA
   Spotsylvania County. Recognized for public service (VR Court Booklet, p. 10).
SKILLMAN, ANN NJ
   South Brunswick. The wife of Jacob Skillman, wine merchant, she suffered damage in a British raid (CDB, p. 249).
SKINNER, ELEANOR GLOVER MA
   She married Richard Skinner, who was mate on the privateer Phoenix and was captured by the British. On May 10, 1779, Skinner was committed to the Mill Prison near Plymouth, England. He escaped and served as mate on the Jason, but he was captured for a second time and imprisoned again (CN).
SKINNER, PRUDENCE CT
   She supplied a blanket for the army (CAR, 11:12a).
SKINNER, SARAH NJ
   Woodbridge. The widow of Capt. Richard Skinner, she suffered damage caused by American troops (CDB, claim 14).
SKIRVING, ELIZABETH SC
   She supplied provisions for the troops (SI, B:233).
SKIRVING, SARAH SC
   She provided supplies for the army (SI, B:87).
SLAPPY, ISABELLE SC
   She supplied provisions for the troops (SI, R-T:216).
SLAUGHTER, ANN VA
   Fairfax. She performed a public service (VR, 2:230).
SLAUGHTER, ANN VA
   King William County. Credited with public service (VR, 3:259).
SLAUSON, ELIZABETH CT
   Stamford. In the 1781 British attack she suffered losses (CAR, 22:296b).
SLINGSBY, MRS. NC
   She supplied provisions for the troops (RA, 6:100, fol. 2).
SLOAN, ANN VA
   Culpeper County. Credited with public service (VR, 2:116).
SLOCUM, MARY RI
   The wife of Ebenezer Slocum, she supplied goods in December 1776 for the militia (MP, 36:6).
SLOCUMB (SLCCOMB), MARY HOOKS NC
   She nursed wounded soldiers. See Biographies.
SLOPER, HANNAH NEWELL CT
   Her property was destroyed in a British attack. See Biographies.

III: COMPLETE LISTING 443

SLOT, MARRETJE VAN DUESEN   NY
   Gen. Washington had his headquarters here. See Biographies.
SMALLEY, ANN. See STORY
SMALLWOOD, MARY   MD
   On May 8, 1783, she supplied wheat for the army, Charles County, (IM, 25410).
SMALLWOOD, PRISCILLA   MD
   Charles County. In 1782 she supplied wheat for the army (IM, 21999).
SMALLWOOD, PRISCILLA   VA
   Culpeper County. Recognized for public service (VR, 2:116).
SMALLY (SMELLY), MARY   VA
   Isle of Wight. Credited with public service (VR, 2:326).
SMART, SUSANNAH BARNETT   NC
   She fed and cared for the soldiers. See Biographies.
SMITH, MRS.   NJ
   Hunterdon County. The wife of Judge Smith, she collected funds for the army (New Jersey Gazette, July 4, 1780).
SMITH, ALICE   VA
   Lancaster County. She performed a public service (VR, 3:277).
SMITH, ANN   VA
   Louisa County. Recognized for public service (VR Lists, 1:6).
SMITH, ANNA M.   SC
   She supplied provisions for the troops (SI, B:237).
SMITH, AVARILLA   VA
   Surry County. She performed a public service (CR Ctf 1).
SMITH, BETHIAH DOOLITTLE   CT
   She was born in 1746 and married Jonathan Smith. Bethiah died in 1842 and is listed as a patriot in the DAR Patriot Index.
SMITH, BETTY   VA
   Dinwiddie County. Recognized for public service (VR Court Booklet, pp. 24, 31).
SMITH, BRIDGET   VA
   Dinwiddie County. Credited with public service (VR, 1:344).
SMITH, CATHERINE   NC
   She supplied provisions for the troops (RA, 5:53, fol. 1).
SMITH, CATHERINE   PA
   Philadelphia. She was a gun borer and was buried in an unmarked grave.
SMITH, CATHERINE   SC
   She supplied provisions for the troops (SI, 1:70; Y-Z:103).
SMITH, CATHY   VA
   Prince George County. Credited with public service (VR, 4:256).
SMITH, CHARITY   NJ
   Morris County. She suffered damage caused by American troops (CDB, claim 156).
SMITH, MRS. CHRISTOPHER   SC
   She provided supplies for the army (SI, 10, pt. 1:181).
SMITH, CLARA   NC
   The wife of Benjamin Smith, she supplied provisions for the troops (RA, A:113).

SMITH, DEBORAH   NC
    She supplied provisions for the troops (RA, 4:74, fol. 4).
SMITH, DEBORAH KNAPP   CT
    She guarded British prisoners. See Biographies.
SMITH, DORCAS BARRETT   MA
    Boston. She married Isaac Smith, who commanded the six-gun ship Friendship in 1779 and the twelve-gun brigantine Thomas in 1780. In October 1781 Smith was captured by the Enterprise and imprisoned (CN).
SMITH, DOROTHY   VA
    Louisa County. Recognized for public service (VR, 3:366).
SMITH, MRS. E.   NC
    She provided supplies for the army (RA, 5:51, fol. 4).
SMITH, ELIZABETH   NC
    She supplied provisions for the troops (RA, 9:9, fol. 3).
SMITH, ELIZABETH   NJ
    The wife of William P. Smith, she suffered damage in a British attack (CDB, claim 6).
SMITH, ELIZABETH   PA
    At age forty-four she was captured in May 1779 by Indians near Fort Pitt and taken to Montreal (MR).
SMITH, ELIZABETH   VA
    Several women named Elizabeth Smith performed a public service in Virginia:
    Brunswick County (VR, 1:130)
    Hanover County (VR, 3:166, 199, 201)
    Henrico County (VR, 3:107)
    Isle of Wight (VR, 2:327)
    King George County (VR, 2:337)
    Louisa County (VR, 3:365, 367)
    Lunenburg County (VR, 4:24)
    Warwick County (VR, 5:214)
    Westmoreland County (VR, 5:225)
SMITH, ELIZABETH CARRAWAY   SC
    of Old 96 District. Elizabeth, her husband Captain Aaron Smith and five of their children were killed in the Cherokee Indian attack and massacred at Fort 96 on July 1, 1776. (Howe: History of the Presbyterian Church in South Carolina, 1870; submitted by Winifred G. Williams, Ellaville, GA).
SMITH, ELIZABETH CHAMBERLAIN   VA
    She married Sampson Lanier, then Cuthbert Smith. Elizabeth is listed as a patriot in the DAR Patriot Index.
SMITH, ELIZABETH MARSHALL. See MARTIN
SMITH, ESTHER   NC
    She supplied provisions for the army (RA, B:276).
SMITH, FRANCES   NC
    She provided supplies for the troops (RA, A:54).
SMITH, FRANCES   VA
    She married John Smith and died in 1783/84. Frances is listed as a patriot in the DAR Patriot Index.

III: COMPLETE LISTING 445

SMITH, GRACE   NC
   She supplied provisions for the troops (RA, 5:62, fol. 2).

SMITH, HANNAH   NJ
   Burlington. She suffered damage in a British raid (CDB, claim 187). Also Hannah Smith in Saddle River (British claim CDB, claim 28).

SMITH, ISABELLA   VA
   Henrico County. She performed a public service (VR, 3:106).

SMITH, IVEY   NC
   She provided supplies for the army (RA, 5:47, fol. 1).

SMITH (SMYTH), JAIMAMA   NC
   She supplied provisions for the troops (RA, C:55).

SMITH, JANE   NJ
   Saddle River. She suffered losses in a British raid (CDB, claim 28).

SMITH, JANET   SC
   She supplied provisions for the troops (SI, Y-Z:184).

SMITH, LUCY LANE   VA
   Surry County. The wife of William Smith, she performed a public service (VR, 5:169).

SMITH, MAGALENA   KY
   At age eleven she was captured in June 1780 by Indians at Licking Creek together with Elizabeth (Lissy) Smith, age eight (MR).

SMITH, MARGARET (ESTATE)   VA
   Middlesex County, credited with public service (VR, 4:96).

SMITH, MARTHA   CT
   Stamford. In the 1781 British raid she suffered damage (CAR, 22:300).

SMITH, MARTHA   VA
   Dinwiddie County. She performed a public service (VR, 1:345). Also Rockingham County (VR Court Booklet, 2:2).

SMITH, MARTHA I.   VA
   Hanover County. Credited with public service (VR, 3:199, 201).

SMITH, MARY   CT
   Fairfield. In the 1779-1780 British raids she suffered losses (CAR, p. 251a). She was a Western Lands Grantee.

SMITH, MARY   CT
   Norwalk. She suffered damage in a British raid (CAR, 1:63k, 98f). She was a Western Lands Grantee.

SMITH, MARY   NC
   She supplied provisions for the troops (RA, 1:80, fol. 2).

SMITH, MARY   NJ
   Middlesex County. The wife of John Smith, she suffered damage in a British raid (CDB, p. 168).

SMITH, MARY   PA
   At age thirty-five in April 1781 she was captured by Indians on the Monongahela River and released from Fort Ticonderoga on July 18, 1783 (MR).

SMITH, MARY   RI
  The widow of Arthur Smith, who was killed in action by the
  British (MP, 23:45).
SMITH, MARY   SC
  She was born in 1737 and married W. Robert Smith. Mary died
  in 1829 and is listed as a patriot in the DAR Patriot Index.
SMITH, MARY   SC
  She was born in 1729 and married Stephen Smith. Mary died
  in 1844 and is listed as a patriot in the DAR Patriot Index.
SMITH, MARY   VA
  Several women named Mary Smith performed a public service
  in Virginia:
  Botetourt County (VR Lists, pp. 2, 6, 10)
  Culpeper County (VR, 2:116)
  Loudoun County (VR, 3:324)
  Surry County (VR, 5:169)
  Westmoreland County (VR, pp. 224, 245)
SMITH, RACHEL   VA
  York County. Credited with public service (VR Court Booklet,
  2:1, 7).
SMITH, RACHEL STRONG   MA
  Amherst. The daughter of Miriam Shelton and Nathaniel Strong,
  Jr., she was born on February 5, 1732, in Northampton. In
  1763 she married Simeon Smith, who served as a second lieutenant
  in the 4th Hampshire County Regiment. Simeon was wounded
  during a skirmish in the Northern Department and died of his
  injuries on March 23, 1777. Mrs. Smith was left with five small
  children to raise (submitted by Edward L. Woodyard, Armonk,
  NY).
SMITH, REBECCA   CT
  Norwalk. She suffered damage in a British raid (CAR, 1:63j,
  98d). She was a Western Lands Grantee.
SMITH, REBECCA   MD
  Montgomery County. In 1781 she supplied wheat for the army
  (IM, 17166).
SMITH, SARAH   NY
  She took food to American prisoners. See Biographies.
SMITH, SARAH REYNOLDS   CT
  She was born in 1762 and married Lt. Josiah Smith. Sarah
  died in 1849. She is listed as a patriot in the DAR Patriot
  Index.
SMITH, SUSAN   SC
  She supplied provisions for the troops (SI, 10, pt. 1:29).
SMITH, SUSANNA   VA
  Henrico County. Recognized for public service (VR, 3:108).
SMITH, SUSANNAH BAYARD   PA
  She was active in the ladies' association for the welfare of the
  soldiers. See Biographies.
SMITH, TABITHA   VA
  Greensville. She performed a public service (VR Court Booklet,
  p. 8).

III: COMPLETE LISTING 447

SMITH, MRS. THOMAS PA
Philadelphia. On October 7, 1774, John Adams together with the Virginia delegates to the First Continental Congress dined with the Smiths. Mrs. Smith was an active member of the ladies' association for the welfare of the soldiers (Pennsylvania Gazette, June 12, 1780).

SMITH, MRS. WILLIAM MD
She entertained John Adams and Elbridge Gerry. See Biographies.

SMOCK, NELLY NJ
Somerville. She suffered damage in a British raid (CDB, p. 32).

SMOOT, ELIZABETH MD
Charles County. In 1781 she supplied wheat for the army (IM, 18656, 18751).

SNAVELEY, SABINA PA
The wife of Caspar Snaveley, she is listed as a patriot in the DAR Patriot Index.

SNEAD, TEMPERANCE NC
She supplied provisions for the troops (RA, 9:3, fol. 1).

SNEAK, ELIZABETH NY
She was captured by Indians in July 1780 on the Mohawk River and taken to Montreal (MR).

SNEDIKER, ALFEY MARTYNE NY
Orange County. "Affie" was the daughter of Affie Mabie and John Martyne. On June 7, 1747, she married Johannes Snediker, who was commissioned a captain of militia on June 29, 1776. He was captured by the British and confined in the Sugar House on Liberty Street in New York City, where he died of smallpox as a prisoner on September 28, 1779. Her son Garrett was also taken prisoner, but survived (submitted by Loyola T. Vuolo, Verona, NJ).

SNEED, MARY VA
Caroline County. She performed a public service (VR Court Booklet, 2:26, 27).

SNELGROVE, SARAH DUKE SC
She was born in 1753 and married Henry Snelgrove (or Swillgrove) (DAR). She supplied provisions for the troops (SI, 10, pt. 1).

SNELLING, ANN NC
The wife of Hugh Snelling, she provided supplies for the army (RA, D:45).

SNOW, APPHIA ATWOOD ME
Harpswell. She was the wife of Isaac Snow, who commanded the schooner America in 1776. He served on other privateer vessels and was captured by the British. On January 22, 1782, he was confined in the Mill Prison in Plymouth, England (CN).

SNOW, HANNAH SC
She supplied provisions for the troops (SI, U-W:139).

SNOWDEN, ANN MAUGRIDGE PA
She was the wife of William Snowden, a sea captain. She died about 1776 and is listed as a patriot in the DAR Patriot Index.

SNYDER, ELIZABETH CATHERINE MANN   NY
   She passed to the soldiers biscuits and rum laced with gunpowder
   "to divert them from fear." See Biographies.
SNYDER, MARY   SC
   She supplied provisions for the troops (SI, 1:89).
SOLLEDY (HOLLIDAY), HANNAH
   She was captured by Indians, taken to Montreal, and sent home
   on August 22, 1782 (MR).
SON, ELIZABETH   VA
   Augusta County. She performed a public service (VR Ctf 1).
SONES, MOLLY   VA
   King and Queen County. She performed a public service (VR
   Court Booklet, p. 17).
SOURLOCK, MIAH   NC
   She supplied provisions for the army (RA, 8:61, fol. 4).
SOURLOCK, SARAH   NC
   She provided supplies for the army (RA, 12:7, fol. 4).
SOUTHER, MARY   NC
   She supplied provisions for the troops (RA, A:199).
SOUTHMAYD, ANNA   CT
   On July 5, 1782, John Wilkinson obtained a letter of marque
   to command the one-gun galley Recompense with twelve men.
   Witnesses to the bond were Hannah Spencer and Anna South-
   mayd (CN).
SOUTHWELL, SARAH   SC
   Her husband was named Edward. Sarah died in 1783 and is
   listed as a patriot in the DAR Patriot Index 2.
SOUTHWICK, BETHIA   MA
   The wife of Joseph Southwick, she died in 1803. She is listed
   as a patriot in the DAR Patriot Index.
SPADER (SPEEDER), JANE   NJ
   Middlebush, Somerville. The wife of John, she suffered damage
   in a British raid (CDB, p. 87).
SPARROW, MARY   VA
   Norfolk. She performed a public service (VR, 4:139).
SPAULDING, GRACE   CT
   Fairfield. In the 1779-1780 British raids she suffered losses
   (CAR, 15:250ge). She was a Western Lands Grantee.
SPAULDING, MRS. LEVI   NH
   The wife of Capt. Spaulding, she helped make paper cartridges
   for sixty men in her husband's company (submitted by Dorothy
   Wilcox, Durham, NH).
SPEAK, HENRIETTA   MD
   Charles County. In December 1782 and April 1783 she supplied
   wheat for the army (IM, 24221, 24572).
SPEARS, MARY NEELY   NC
   She was born in 1761 and married George Spears. Mary died
   in 1852 and is listed as a patriot in the DAR Patriot Index.
SPEED, SARAH   VA
   Mecklenburg. Recognized for public service (VR, 4:59).

III: COMPLETE LISTING

SPEIGHT, ABIGAIL   NC
   The wife of William Speight, she died in 1781. Abigail furnished
   supplies for the army (RA, 6:37, fol. 2; DAR).
SPEIR, REBECCA   NJ
   Wardsession, Essex County. She suffered damage in a British
   raid (CDB, claim 34).
SPENCER, HANNAH   CT
   On July 5, 1782, John Wilkinson obtained a letter of marque
   to command the galley Recompense with one gun and twelve men.
   Witnesses to the bond were Anna Southmayd and Hannah Spencer
   (CN).
SPENCER, MARY   VA
   Buckingham County. Credited with public service (VR, 1:210).
SPINCKS, AMEY   NC
   She supplied provisions for the troops (RA, C:111).
SPINK, LYDIA   CT
   New London. In a British attack she suffered damage (CAR,
   1:63j, 95g). She was a Western Lands Grantee.
SPOTSWOOD, ELIZABETH   VA
   Middlesex County. Credited with public service (VR, 4:349).
SPRIGHTLY, ELIZABETH   MD
   On March 4, 1782, she signed a deposition against Tories James
   Vickers and James Stewart for their plundering activities (IM,
   20741).
SPRING, DOROTHY   SC
   She supplied provisions for the troops (SI, L-N:315).
SPRINGER, MARGARET   SC
   After the fall of Charleston on May 12, 1780, she refused to
   sign an oath of fidelity to the Crown and so was banished from
   the city (SC).
SPRINGFIELD, LAODICES LANGSTON   SC
   "Dicey" warned the Americans of an impending attack. See
   Biographies.
SPRINGSTONE, ELIZABETH   WV
   Monongalia County. Credited with public service (VR, 4:351).
SPROUL, KATHERINE   NC
   She supplied provisions for the troops (RA, 5:25, fol. 1).
SPROUT, SARAH SMITH   PA
   Philadelphia. Her husband, James Sprout, was a preacher and
   they lived on 3rd Street, a few doors from his meetinghouse.
   John Adams came to lodge here on September 15, 1777, but as
   the British forces approached Philadelphia, Adams fled on September 19, 1777 to Trenton, New Jersey (BA).
SPURLOCK, AGNES   VA
   Mecklenburg. She performed a public service (VR, 4:78).
SPURLOCK, ELIZABETH   SC
   She provided supplies for the troops (SI, 1:89).
SQUIRE, ANN   CT
   New London. In a British attack she suffered losses (CAR,
   1:63j, 95g). She was a Western Lands Grantee.

STAATS, SUSANNAH   NJ
    Millstone, Somerville. The wife of Peter Staats, she suffered
    damage in a British raid (CDB, p. 42).
STALLINGS, MARGARET   VA
    Hansemond County. Recognized for public service (VR, 4:168).
STANLEY, MARGARET   NC
    She supplied provisions for the troops (RA, 5:27, fol. 1).
STANTON, PRUDENCE   CT
    Groton. In the British attack, she suffered damage (CAR,
    28:296).
STANTON, THANKFUL   CT
    Her husband was killed during the British attack on Fort Griswold in September 1781, and she suffered property damage (CAR,
    27:198-200).
STANYARNE, ANN   SC
    She supplied provisions for the army (SI, B:83).
STANYARNE, ELIZABETH   SC
    She provided provisions for the troops (SI, B:203).
STARK, ELIZABETH PAGE   NH
    "Molly" spread the alarm through the countryside. See
    Biographies.
STARKE, MARY BOLLING   VA
    Richmond. The daughter of Robert Bolling of "Bollingbrook,"
    she was the sister of Lucy Bolling Randolph. Mary married
    William Starke. After his death she was active in the ladies'
    association, which opposed the importation of British tea (Virginia Gazette, July 27, 1769).
STARR, ABIGAIL   CT
    New Haven. In the British attack of July 1779 she suffered
    damage (CAR, 15:234g, 269f). She was a Western Lands
    Grantee.
STARR, CHRISTINA   CT
    Danbury. In the April 1777 raid she suffered losses (CAR,
    8:382b). She was a Western Lands Grantee.
STARR, HANNAH   CT
    Groton. In the British attack she suffered damage (CAR, 1:79c).
STARR, LUCY   CT
    New London. In the British raid she suffered damage (CAR, 1:
    63j, 95h). She was a Western Lands Grantee.
STATHAN, LOVE   VA
    Louisa County. Credited with public service (VR Lists, 1:17,
    27).
STEARNS, ABIGAIL. See BELLOWS
STEEL, AGNES   NC
    She supplied provisions for the troops (RA, A:150).
STEEL, ELIZABETH   NC
    She provided supplies for the army (RA, 5:17, fol. 3).
STEEL, JANE   VA
    Northumberland County. She performed a public service (VR,
    4:122).

III: COMPLETE LISTING 451

STEEL, KATHERINE FISHER SC
"Witty Kate" defended the fort when the men were away. See Biographies.

STEELE, BETHIA CT
In 1779 she supplied clothing for the army (CAR, 35:249q).

STEELE, ELIZABETH NC
She supplied provisions for the troops (RA, A:131).

STEELE, ELIZABETH MAXWELL NC
She gave two bags of money to Gen. Greene, who was desperate for funds. See Biographies.

STEELE, MRS. SALISBURY NC
She supplied provisions for the troops (RA, K:155).

STEEN, MRS. SC
She provided supplies for the army (SI, 10, pt. 1:180).

STEPHENS, MARY BOWMAN VA
She supplied provisions for the army. See Biographies.

STEPHENS, PRISCILLA THOMAS PA
The wife of Dr. Abijah Stephens, she is listed as a patriot in the DAR Patriot Index.

STEPHENSON, ANN WV
Berkeley County. Recognized for public service (VR, 1:149).

STEPHENSON, ESTHER SARAH WAITS VA
Rockingham County. She married John Taylor, then Capt. John Stephenson. Esther died in 1783 and is listed as a patriot in the DAR Patriot Index. She is credited with public service (VR, 5:130).

STERLING, JANE VA
King and Queen County. She performed a public service (VR Court Booklet, p. 11).

STEVENS, MRS. NJ
Hunterdon County. She was the vice president of the ladies' association, which collected funds for the soldiers (New Jersey Gazette, July 4, 1780).

STEVENS (STEPHENS), ANN VA
Lancaster County. She performed a public service (VR, 3:278).

STEVENS, CHARITY NC
She supplied provisions for the troops (RA, 5:25, fol. 3).

STEVENS, SARAH CT
New Haven. In the 1779 British raid she suffered damage (CAR, 15:269d). She was a Western Lands Grantee.

STEVENSON, MRS. VA
York County. Recognized for public service (VR Lists, p. 3).

STEWARD, ABIGAIL NJ
Westfield. In a British raid she suffered losses (CDB, claims 23, 25).

STEWARD, SARAH NJ
Westfield. She suffered damage in a British raid (CDB, claim 35).

STEWART, ELIZABETH GA
She supplied cattle for the army (WA, p. 178).

STEWART, ELIZABETH NC
    She supplied provisions for the troops (RA, 5:25, fol. 4).
STEWART, HANNAH BOONE. See PENNINGTON
STEWART, JANE ARMSTRONG PA
    She was born in 1760 and married William Stewart. Jane died in 1817 and is listed as a patriot in the DAR Patriot Index.
STEWART, MARGARET McBRIDE NC
    "Maggie" was born in 1769 and married Robert Stewart (DAR). She supplied provisions for the army (RA, 5:47, fol. 4).
STEWART, MARTHA VA
    Pittsylvania County. The wife of James Stewart, she performed a public service (VR Court Booklet, p. 56).
STEWART, SARAH. See PENNINGTON
STIGLER, MARY VA
    King George County. Credited with public service (VR, 2:337).
STILES, SARAH NJ
    Morris County. She suffered damage caused by American troops (CDB, claim 160).
STILES, SARAH CUTLER DENNIS NJ
    Elizabethtown (now Elizabeth). The wife of Richard Stiles, an attorney. On February 6, 1776, he was appointed captain of the Somerset County Militia. Stiles served in the Battle of Long Island and was wounded there on August 27, 1776. He died of his wounds in Elizabethtown on September 16, 1776 (FP1).
STILLMAN, ELIZABETH CT
    New Haven. In the 1779 British attack she suffered damage (CAR, 15:269b).
STILLMAN, PRUDENCE KINGSBURY CT
    Wethersfield. She married Allyn Stillman, who commanded the sloop Prudence, which sailed to the West Indies to obtain salt, essential for the preservation of meat since there was no refrigeration. Stillman returned to port on July 31, 1777, but on a later cruise he was captured by the British and imprisoned (CN).
STILLMAN, SUSANNAH CT
    In 1776 she provided a bed for a sick soldier with smallpox (CAR, 11:488, 490).
STILLWELL, MARY CT
    New Haven. In the July 1779 British attack she suffered losses (CAR, 15:234c, 269e).
STILLWELL, REBECCA NJ
    She fired a cannon to warn the Americans of an impending attack. See Biographies.
STILLWELL, WIDOW CT
    New Haven. In 1777 she provided barracks for the soldiers (CAR, 11:552). She was a Western Lands Grantee.
STILWELL, SARAH. See GRIFFING
STIRLING, ELIZABETH VA
    Princess Anne County. She performed a public service (VR Court Booklet, p. 10).

STIRLING, LADY
: The wife of Gen. Stirling, she was a major contributor to the ladies' association for the welfare of the soldiers. See Biographies.

STITES, MARY PREDMORE   NJ
: Lt. Col. Alexander Hamilton had his headquarters there. See Biographies.

STITH, ANN   VA
: King George County. Recognized for public service (VR, 2:338).

STITH, IVEY   NC
: She supplied provisions for the troops (RA, 11:86, fol. 4).

STITH, JOANNA   VA
: Hanover County. She performed a public service (VR Court Booklet, 1:19).

STITH, LUCY   VA
: Brunswick County. Credited with public service (VR Court Booklet, p. 60).

STOCKBRIDGE, PHEBE   NJ
: Morris County. She suffered damage caused by American troops (CDB, claim 128).

STOCKER, EUNICE   CT
: New Haven. In the July 1779 British raid she suffered losses (CAR, 15:234f).

STOCKER, MARY   CT
: Middletown. The Widow Stocker supplied military articles for the army (CAR, 32:250b).

STOCKLY, ANN   VA
: Accomack County. Recognized for public service (VR Ctf 1).

STOCKTON, ANNIS BOUDINOT   NJ
: She was imprisoned by the British. See Biographies.

STODDARD, EUNICE SANFORD   CT
: Her husband was killed in action. See Biographies.

STODDERT, ELIZABETH   MD
: Charles County. In 1782 she supplied wheat for the army (IM, 21272).

STODDERT, LETTY   MD
: Charles County. In 1782 she provided wheat for the army (IM, 21268).

STODDERT, SALLY   MD
: Charles County. She supplied wheat in 1782 for the army (IM, 23934).

STOKE, BRIDGET   RI
: From August 1, 1780, to December 31, 1781, she supplied provisions for the militia (MP 11:49; 13:40).

STOKES, ELIZABETH   VA
: She supplied beef and bacon for the troops. See Biographies.

STOLL, PHOEBE   SC
: She supplied provisions for the troops (SI, B:219).

STOLL, REBECCA   SC
: She provided supplies for the army (SI, Y-Z:32, 103).

STONE, LUCY   VA
: Henrico County. Credited with public service (VR, 3:106, 107).

STONE, MARY   MD
    Charles County. In 1781 and 1782 she supplied wheat for the
    army (IM, 19506, 23400).
STONE, MARY. See MANNING
STONE, PRUDENCE   VA
    Henrico County. Recognized for public service (VR, 3:107).
STONE, RUTH   SC
    She supplied provisions for the troops (SI, B:63).
STONE, SARAH   VA
    Chesterfield County. Credited with public service (VR, 2:48-
    50). Also in King and Queen County (VR Lists, 4:3).
STOOTHOFF, SARAH   NJ
    Somerville. She suffered damage in a British raid (CDB, p.
    149).
STORES, SUSANNA   VA
    Henrico County. She performed a public service (VR, 3:107).
STORY, ANN   VT
    Her home was a refuge for the Green Mountain Boys. See
    Biographies.
STORY, MEHETABLE WEBB   CT
    Norwich. She was the wife of Ebenezer Story, who served on
    the Continental frigate Confederacy, captured by the British on
    June 22, 1781. Story died on a prison ship some time between
    September 1781 and November 1782 (FP1).
STOUTENBERG, CATHERINE VAN VELECH   NY
    John Adams stayed in her home. See Background.
STOW, FREELOVE BALDWIN   CT
    She cared for soldiers suffering from smallpox. See Biographies.
STOWE, NAOMI OLDSTEAD   CT
    She married Samuel Stowe who served as third mate on the Oliver
    Cromwell, then as a lieutenant on the schooner Bunker Hill.
    On April 14, 1780, Lt. Stowe was killed in an engagement with
    the British privateer Dolphin (CN).
STOWERS, MRS.   VA
    Louisa County. She performed a public service (VR, 3:357).
STRAFF (STROFF), MARGARET   PA
    At age forty she was captured by Indians, along with her daugh-
    ter Mary, aged ten, on May 20, 1778, and taken to the Saint
    Lawrence suburbs (MR).
STRATTON, MARTHA   VA
    Powhatan County. Recognized for public service (VR, 4:244).
STRAWBRIDGE, ISABEL   NY
    At age twenty she was captured by Indians on July 11, 1780,
    along with Archibald and Stephen Strawbridge, and taken to
    Quebec (MR).
STREET, HANNAH   CT
    Norwalk. In the May 1780 British raid she suffered damage
    (CAR, 20:379g, 380g).
STRONG, MRS.   CT
    Gen. Washington spent the night at the home of the Widow Strong.
    See Biographies.

III: COMPLETE LISTING

STROP, MRS. JOHN   PA
She was captured with her husband and two children by Indians at Susquehanna in May 1780 and taken to the Saint Lawrence suburbs (MR).

STROTHER, ANN   VA
Culpeper County. Credited with public service (VR, 2:119, 121).

STROTHER, MARGARET   VA
King George County. Recognized for public service (VR, 2:357).

STROTHER, TABITHA   VA
King George County. She performed a public service (VR, 2:338).

STROZIER, MARGARET DOZIER   GA
She was born in 1740 and married Peter Strozier. Margaret died in 1842 at age 102. She is listed as a patriot in the DAR Patriot Index.

STRYKER, CORNELIA   NJ
Somerville. She suffered damage in a British raid (CDB, p. 144).

STUART, ISABEL   SC
She supplied provisions for the troops (SI, 10, pt. 1:53).

STUART, MARY   NJ
Woodbridge. She suffered losses in a British raid (CDB, p. 302).

STUART, MARY   SC
She furnished provisions for the army (SI, 10, pt. 1:48).

STUART, SARAH   NJ
Woodbridge. She suffered damage in a British raid (CDB, p. 302).

STUCKER, ANNA EVA MARIA   VA
The wife of Jacob Stucker, Sr., she died in 1795. She is listed as a patriot in the DAR Patriot Index.

STUCKER, MARGARET   VA
She married George Stucker, then John Miles, then Nathan Breeden. Margaret is listed as a patriot in the DAR Patriot Index.

STURDIVANT, ANN   VA
Prince George County. Credited with public service (VR, 4:256).

STURGES, ELIZABETH   CT
Fairfield widow. In the 1779-1780 British raids she suffered damage (CAR, 15:250c, 251a). She was a Western Lands Grantee.

STURGES, SARAH   CT
Fairfield. In the British raid on Danbury in April 1777 she suffered damage (CAR, 15:261c).

STURMAN, HANNAH CHILTON   VA
Westmoreland County. The wife of Foxhill Sturman, she performed a public service (VR, 5:225).

STURNSON, ESTHER   VA
Rockingham County. The wife of William Sturnson, she is credited with public service (VR, 5:131).

SUCUCK, URSULA SC
   She furnished provisions for the troops (SI, 1:91).
SUDDOTH, ELIZABETH VA
   Fauquier County. Recognized for public service (VR Lists, p. 15).
SUFFERN, MARY MEYERS NY
   Gen. Washington had his headquarters there. See Biographies.
SUFFRETT (SYFRETT), REBECCA SC
   She provided supplies for the troops (SI, 1:88).
SUGGETT (SUGGITT), ELIZABETH VA
   Richmond. She performed a public service (VR, p. 102).
SUGGETT, JEMIMA SPENCE KY
   She went for water when the Indians attacked. See Biographies.
SUGGETT, MILDRED DAVIS KY
   Bryan's Station. She was born in 1756 and married John Suggett. When the Tories and Indians attacked on August 15, 1782, she was one of the women who went for water. Mildred is listed as a patriot in the DAR Patriot Index. Her name is inscribed on the monument erected by the Lexington Daughters of the American Revolution.
SUGGS, MARY NC
   She supplied provisions for the troops (RA, 10:4, fol. 3).
SULLENS, ANN VA
   King William County. Credited with public service (VR, 3:260).
SULLIVAN, ABIGAIL COTTON NH
   The wife of Capt. Ebenezer Sullivan of the 15th Continental Infantry, a brother of Gen. Sullivan. Capt. Sullivan was taken prisoner at the Cedars on May 20, 1776, and not exchanged until 1778 (DAR; FW).
SULLIVAN, LYDIA WOOSTER NH
   Gen. and Mrs. Sullivan supplied their own funds for the army. See Biographies.
SULLIVAN, MARGERY BROWN NH
   Her three sons were officers in the army. See Biographies.
SULLIVAN, MARY VA
   Henrico County. Recognized for public service (VR, 3:105).
SULLIVAN, MARY VA
   Spotsylvania County. Credited with public service (VR Lists, p. 2).
SULLIVAN, MARY CHARLTON SC
   She was born on June 1, 1722, and married a Mr. Johnson, then Charles Sullivan. Mary died on December 20, 1837. She is listed as a patriot in the DAR Patriot Index.
SULLIVAN, MARY DUNKLIN SC
   She was born in 1770 and is listed as a patriot in the DAR Patriot Index. Mary married Hewlett Sullivan.
SULLIVANT, HANNAH VA
   Charlotte. She performed a public service (VR Court Booklet, p. 10).
SUMMERFORD, SARAH SC
   She supplied provisions for the troops (SI, O-Q:95).

III: COMPLETE LISTING

SUMMERS, RUTH   CT
Stratford. In 1778 she furnished a blanket for the army (CAR, 12:93a).

SUMMERS, SARAH   MD
On March 7, 1781, she lodged the Dorchester militia in her home (IM, 15652).

SUMNER, MRS. JOHN   CT
Middletown. The wife of Col. John Sumner, in 1777 she made clothing for the soldiers (CG).

SUMTER, MARY CANTY   SC
She was the wife of Gen. Sumter. See Biographies.

SUSS (SURS), SUSAN   SC
She provided supplies for the army (SI, Y-Z:97).

SUTHARD, MARGARET   NC
The wife of William Suthard, she provided provisions for the troops (RA, A:246).

SUTTLES (SETTLES), AMY   VA
King George County. The wife of William Suttles, she performed a public service (VR, 2:338).

SUTTON, MARY   VA
Campbell County. Recognized for public service (VR Court Booklet, p. 13).

SUTTON, SARAH   CT
Greenwich. In the 1783 British raid she suffered damage (CAR, 24:274j, 276d).

SWAIN, MELISCENT BARRETT   MA
She made bullet cartridges for the soldiers. See Biographies.

SWAN, JANE   NC
She furnished supplies for the army (RA, 5:62, fol. 3).

SWAN, JANET   VA
Powhatan County. Credited with public service (VR, 4:243).

SWAN, MARY   SC
She supplied provisions for the troops (R-T:155; Y-Z:33).

SWAN, RACHEL   NJ
Franklin Township, Bergen County. She suffered damage in a British raid (CDM, claim 21).

SWEARINGEN, HANNAH   VA
Hanover County. Recognized for public service (VR, 3:199).

SWEARINGEN, HANNAH   WV
Berkeley County. She provided provisions for the army (RW).

SWEARINGEN, MARGARET   MD
She supplied provisions for the army in 1781 (IM, 14646).

SWEET, KEZIAH   SC
She provided provisions for the troops (SI, U-W:140).

SWEET, LIDIA   RI
East Greenwich. The wife of Samuel Sweet, she furnished mutton, corn, rye, cordwood, etc., for the militia (MP, 30:19).

SWETLAND, HANNAH TIFFANY   PA
She made gunpowder for the men. See Biographies.

SWETLAND, LYDIA. See ABBOTT

SWIFT, FLOWER NC
　She furnished provisions for the troops (RA, 9:20, fol. 1).
SYDNOR, ANN VA
　Hanover County. Recognized for public service (VR, 3:199).
SYDNOR, ELIZABETH TAYLOR VA
　Northumberland. The wife of Anthony Sydnor, she supplied provisions for the army (VR, 4:122).
SYKES, MARY VA
　Isle of Wight. Credited with public service (VR, 4:333).
SYMMES, SUSAN LIVINGSTON NJ
　She saved important documents which the British failed to take. See Biographies.

T

TABB, ELIZABETH ELLIOT WV
　Berkeley County. She was married to Robert Tabb, then to James Kearney. Elizabeth died in 1799 (DAR). She provided provisions for the army (VR, 1:150).
TABB, HANNAH PHRIPP VA
　Princess Anne County. She performed a public service (VR Court Booklet, p. 5).
TABER, SUSANNA NJ
　Burlington. She suffered losses in a British raid (CDB, claim 146).
TAGART, MRS. NJ
　Salem County. She collected funds for the army (New Jersey Gazette, July 4, 1780).
TALBOT, ANNA RICHMOND RI
　Providence. She was the first wife of Silas Talbot, who served in the Continental Navy. Talbot commanded the ship General Washington, and was captured by the British. On March 31, 1781, Talbot was committed to the Mill Prison, Plymouth, England. He escaped twice, but was recaptured both times. Finally on October 16, 1781, he was exchanged for eight British prisoners held by the Americans (CN).
TALBOT, DRUCILLA VA
　Bedford County. Recognized for public service (VR Lists, 1:10).
TALIAFERRO, MARY VA
　Caroline County. Credited with public service (VR, 1:258, 260).
TALIAFERRO, MARY VA
　Spotsylvania County. She performed a public service (VR Court Booklet, p. 18).
TALLMAN, HANNAH NJ
　Burlington. She was the wife of Thomas Tallman, an attorney. Hannah collected funds for the army (New Jersey Gazette, July 4, 1780).
TANNER, ANN VA
　Amelia County. Recognized for public service (VR, 2:355).

III: COMPLETE LISTING

TANSELLER, MARY   SC
She supplied provisions for the troops (SI, 1:91).
TAPSCOTT, MARY   VA
Lancaster County. Credited with public service (VR, 3:279).
TARRANT, SARAH   MA
She sassed British soldiers. See Biographies.
TARRENT, MARY   VA
Henry County. The wife of Leonard Tarrent, she performed a public service (VR, 3:158).
TATE, AGNES   VA
Louisa County. Recognized for public service (VR, 3:372).
TATE, MRS. WILLIAM   VA
Louisa County. Credited with public service (VR Ctf 1).
TAYLOR, ANN   NJ
Burlington. The wife of Aaron Taylor, she suffered losses in a British raid (CDB, claim 6).
TAYLOR, ANN   SC
She supplied provisions for the troops (SI, O-Q:194).
TAYLOR, ELIZABETH   NC
She provided supplies for the army (RA, A:83).
TAYLOR, HANNAH   CT
Fairfield widow. In the British raids of 1779-1780 she suffered damage (CAR, 29:72b, 74b).
TAYLOR, HANNAH   VA
Hansemond County. She performed a public service (VR, 4:168).
TAYLOR, JANE   SC
She supplied provisions for the troops (SI, 10, pt. 1:35).
TAYLOR, JUDITH   VA
Fauquier County. Credited with public service (VR, 2:249).
TAYLOR, MARY   CT
New London. In a British attack she suffered damage (CAR, 1:63k, 95h). She was a Western Lands Grantee.
TAYLOR, MARY   NC
She furnished supplies for the army (RA, 5:13, fol. 4).
TAYLOR, SARAH   NC
She supplied provisions for the troops (RA, A:222).
TAYLOR, SARAH   SC
She furnished supplies for the army (SI, Y-Z:9).
TAYLOR, TEMPERANCE   VA
Southampton County. She performed a public service (VR, 5:182).
TEAGUE, ALICE (ALEE)   SC
The wife of Elijah Teague, she supplied provisions for the troops (SI, R-T:157; DAR).
TEAS, MARY HENDERSON   VA
The wife of William Teas, she died in 1790. Mary is listed as a patriot in the DAR Patriot Index 3.
TEMPLE, ANN   VA
King William County. She performed a public service (VR Lists, 1:3, 13, 18).

TENANT, ELIZABETH   VA
   Princess Anne County. Recognized for public service (VR Court
   Booklet, p. 5).
TENHAM, ELIZABETH   VA
   Louisa County. Credited with public service (VR Lists, 1:15).
TENHAM, MARY   VA
   York County. She performed a public service (VR Court Booklet,
   2:1a, 4a).
TENNANT, SUSAN   SC
   She supplied provisions for the troops (SI, L-N:313).
TENNENT, CATHERINE   SC
   She furnished supplies for the army (SI, B:91).
TERRANCE (TARRANCE), ANN   NC
   She supplied provisions for the troops (RA, A:127).
TERRANT, ELIZABETH   VA
   Princess Anne County. She performed a public service (VR,
   4:225).
TERRELL, ELIZABETH   SC
   She supplied provisions for the troops (SI, O-Q:96).
TERRELL, ELIZABETH   VA
   Louisa County. She is credited with public service (VR, 3:370).
TERRELL, PLEASANT   VA
   Caroline County. Recognized for public service (VR, 1:269).
TERRELL, SARAH   SC
   She furnished provisions for the troops (SI, L-N:34).
TERRY, GRACE   NJ
   Burlington. She suffered damage in a British raid (CDB, claim
   91).
TERRY, OLIVE   NC
   She provided supplies for the army (RA, 3:61, fol. 1).
THEBOUT (TEBOUT), SARAH   SC
   She supplied provisions for the troops (SI, 10, pt. 2:58, 82).
THIMS, MARTHA   NC
   She furnished supplies for the army (RA, 5:48, fol. 1).
THOMAS, ANN   SC
   She supplied provisions for the troops (SI, B:53).
THOMAS, ELIZABETH   NC
   She furnished supplies for the army (RA, A:213).
THOMAS, JANE BLACK   SC
   She loaded muskets for the men and carried a warning. See
   Biographies.
THOMAS, MARTHA   VA
   Southampton County. She performed a public service (VR Court
   Booklet, p. 12).
THOMAS, MARY   CT
   Newtown. In 1777 the Widow Thomas supplied a blanket for
   the army (CAR, 12:81b, 86).
THOMAS, MARY   NC
   She supplied provisions for the troops (RA, 8:2, fol. 1).
THOMAS, MARY   SC
   She furnished provisions for the army (SI, B:22).

III: COMPLETE LISTING 461

THOMAS, MARY   VA
  King William County. She performed a public service (VR, 4:338).
THOMAS, MARY LAMBEL   SC
  She supplied provisions for the troops (SI, U-W:162; O-Q:250).
THOMAS, ROSE   NC
  She furnished provisions for the army (RA, A:63).
THOMAS, SARAH   NC
  She provided supplies for the army (RA, 1:63, fol. 2).
THOMAS, SARAH   VA
  Orange County. She performed a public service (VR, 4:188).
THOMPSON, ABIGAIL   CT
  Fairfield. She suffered damage in a British raid (CAR, 1:53e, 63q). She was a Western Lands Grantee.
THOMPSON, AMEY   VA
  Mecklenburg. She performed a public service (VR, 4:82).
THOMPSON, ANN   VA
  Louisa County. Credited with public service (VR, 3:371).
THOMPSON, BYARA   VA
  Louisa County. Credited with public service (VR, 3:370).
THOMPSON, CATHERINE ROSS   PA
  She sent her crops to Washington's army. See Biographies.
THOMPSON, MRS. CHARLES   PA
  Philadelphia. On September 24, 1774, John Adams dined with the Thompsons, John Dickinson, his lady, and niece. Later Mrs. Thompson was an active member of the ladies' association for the welfare of the soldiers (Pennsylvania Gazette, June 12, 1780).
THOMPSON, ELIZABETH   SC
  She supplied provisions for the troops (SI, 10, pt. 1:185).
THOMPSON, HANNAH   NC
  She furnished supplies for the army (RA, 12:10, fol. 4).
THOMPSON, LYDIA   CT
  The wife of Gideon Thompson, she died in 1802. She is listed as a patriot in the DAR Patriot Index.
THOMPSON, MARGARET   VA
  Sussex County. Recognized for public service (VR, 5:208).
THOMPSON, MARY   CT
  Stratford. Widow of Joseph Thompson. In 1777 she supplied a blanket for the army (CAR, 11:422a).
THOMPSON, MARY   MD
  She cared for sick soldiers in 1776 (IM, 2850).
THOMPSON, MARY   NC
  She supplied provisions for the troops (RA, C:120).
THOMPSON, MARY   VA
  Amelia County. She performed a public service (VR Court Booklet, 1:47). Also Charles City (VR Court Booklet, p. 18).
THOMPSON, MARY TORR   NH
  She spun and wove clothing for the soldiers. See Biographies.
THOMPSON, PHOEBE SNOW   MA
  Lexington. She was the wife of Daniel Thompson, who was killed at the Battle of Lexington on April 19, 1775 (FP1).

THOMPSON, RACHEL VA
   Halifax County. Recognized for public service (VR, 2:294).
THOMPSON, RHODA VA
   Louisa County. Credited with public service (VR, 3:369).
THOMPSON, SARAH SC
   She supplied provisions for the troops (SI, U-W:161).
THOMPSON, THANKFUL BEARDSLEY CT
   New Haven. Her husband, Jeduthan Thompson, was killed during the defense of New Haven when attacked by troops of Governor Tryon of New York on July 5, 1779 (FP1). She also suffered property damage in the raid (CAR, 1:63d, 91g). She was a Western Lands Grantee.
THOMSON, MRS. NJ
   Sussex County. The wife of Col. Thomson, she collected money for the soldiers (New Jersey Gazette, July 4, 1780).
THOMSON, ELIZABETH VA
   Hanover County. She performed a public service (VR, 3:203).
THOMSON, MARY VA
   Hanover County. Recognized for public service (VR, 3:203, 206).
THORN, ELIZABETH SC
   She supplied provisions for the troops (SI, 10, pt. 1:185).
THORNE, ELIZABETH PITNEY. See BALDWIN
THORNHILL, ELIZABETH VA
   Culpeper County. Credited with public service (VR, 3:125).
THORNLEY, ANN VA
   King George County. Recognized for public service (VR, 5:227).
THORNTON, ELIZABETH VA
   Albemarle County. She performed a public service (VR, 2:350).
THORNTON, ELIZABETH VA
   Caroline County. Credited with public service (VR, 1:300; 4:300).
THORNTON, ELIZABETH VA
   Fauquier County. She performed a public service (VR, 2:249). Also King George County (VR, 2:338), and Richmond County (VR, 5:103).
THORNTON, ELIZABETH, SR. VA
   Caroline County. Credited with public service (VR Lists, 2:19, 27).
THORNTON, ELIZABETH, JR. VA
   Caroline County. Recognized for public service (VR Lists, 2:19, 22, 27).
THORNTON, ELIZABETH DAVIS VA
   The wife of Thomas Thornton, she died in 1794 and is listed as a patriot in the DAR Patriot Index.
THORNTON, ESTHER VA
   Gloucester County. She performed a public service (VR Court Booklet, 3:12).
THORNTON, MARY VA
   Spotsylvania County. Credited with public service (VR, 4:265). Also Stafford County (VR, 5:194).

III: COMPLETE LISTING

THORNTON, SARAH   GA
  She supplied provisions to a party of men on their march to join Gen. Wayne (WA, p. 123).

THORP, SARAH   CT
  Fairfield. In the British raids of 1779-1780 she suffered losses (CAR, 15:251d; 19:73d).

THORPE, MARTHA   VA
  Southampton County. She performed a public service (VR, 5:181, 182).

THORPE, PHOEBE   VA
  Southampton County. Credited with public service (VR, 5:182).

THRASHER, ELIZABETH   NC
  She supplied provisions for the troops (RA, 9:73, fol. 2).

THURSTON, ELIZABETH   RI
  In January 1778 she supplied a wheelbarrow for the army (MP, 27:12).

THURSTON, SARAH   VA
  Gloucester County. Credited with public service (VR, 4:259).

THURSTON, SARAH, JR.   VA
  Gloucester County. She performed a public service (Court Booklet, 3:4).

THWEAT, MARY   VA
  Brunswick County. Recognized for public service (VR Court Booklet, pp. 1, 21).

THWEATT, REBECCAH   VA
  Greensville. Credited with public service (VR, 3:32).

TICHENOR, ANNA   NJ
  Newark. The wife of Jedediah Tichenor, she suffered damage in a British raid (CDB, claim 47).

TICHENOR, JANE   NJ
  Connecticut Farms, Essex County. First the wife of Elias Whitehead, then the wife of Josiah Tichenor, she suffered losses in the British attack (CDB, claim 29).

TIDMORE, DOROTHY   SC
  She is listed as a patriot in the DAR Patriot Index.

TIDWELL, MRS.   NC
  She supplied provisions for the troops (RA, 5:53, fol. 3).

TIDWELL, ANN BARBARA   VA
  Westmoreland County. She performed a public service (VR, 5:225).

TILGHMAN, BELITHA   NC
  She furnished supplies for the army (RA, 2:41, fol. 1).

TILL, GERTRUDE ROSS. See READ

TILLERY, NANCY   NC
  She supplied provisions for the troops (RA, 8:70, fol. 1).

TIMPSON, SARAH   VA
  York County. The wife of Samuel Timpson, she performed a public service (VR, 4:279).

TINKER, TEMPERANCE   CT
  East Haddam. She was the wife of Jehiel Tinker, who commanded the state galley Crane. Tinker was captured in March 1777 by HMS Unicorn and imprisoned. He died in September 1780 (CN).

TINSLEY, MARTHA   VA
  Hanover County. Credited with public service (VR, 3:206).
TOBIAS, ELIZABETH   SC
  After the fall of Charleston on May 12, 1780, she refused to sign an oath of fidelity to the Crown and so was banished from the city (SC).
TODD, CATHERINE   VA
  King and Queen County. She performed a public service (VR, 3:233, 234).
TODD, MARY   VA
  Isle of Wight. Recognized for public service (VR Lists, p. 12).
TOLLER, MARY   SC
  She supplied provisions for the troops (SI, R-T:218).
TOLMAN, HANNAH. See WINTHROP
TOMKIES, MARY   VA
  Gloucester County. Credited with public service (VR, 3:54).
TOMLINSON, MRS. JOHN E.   NC
  She furnished supplies for the army (RA, D:98).
TOMLINSON, MARTHA CRAIG   KY
  Bryan's Station. The wife of William T. Tomlinson, they settled in Bryan's Station, which was attacked by Indians on August 15, 1782. Martha helped the ladies obtain water from the spring. See Biographies: Craig, Polly; Johnson, Jemima.
TOMPKINS, ANN   VA
  Caroline County. Credited with public service (VR, 1:269).
TOMPKINS, ANN   VA
  Northampton County. Public service (VR Lists, pp. 1, 2).
TOMPKINS, ANNE   VA
  Henrico County. Public service (VR Court Booklet, p. 22).
TOMPKINS, MRS. THOMAS   NY
  Gen. Washington had his headquarters here. See Biographies.
TOOKER, SARAH   NJ
  Burlington. She suffered damage in a British attack (CDB, claim 319).
TOOLEY, BETTY   VA
  Princess Anne County. She performed a public service (VR, 4:225).
TOOLEY, SARAH   VA
  Princess Anne County. Credited with public service (VR, 4:225).
TORR, MARY. See THOMPSON
TOSH, MARY   VA
  Botetourt County. Recognized for public service (VR, 1:183, 184).
TOUNLEY, PHEBE   NJ
  Connecticut Farms, Essex County. The wife of John Tounley, she suffered damage in a British raid (CDB, claims 24, 33).
TOURS, CATHSLYNA   NJ
  Saddle River. She suffered losses in a British raid (CDB, claim 42).

III: COMPLETE LISTING

TOWER, BETHIAH NICHOLS   MA
"Resolution Tower" cared for soldiers and civilians stricken with smallpox. See Biographies.
TOWLER, MARY   VA
Goochland County. Credited with public service (VR, 4:316).
TOWLER, WIDOW   VA
Goochland County. Credited with public service (VR Lists, 1:1).
TOWLES, ELIZABETH   VA
Spotsylvania County. Performed a public service (VR, 4:265).
TOWN, MARY   CT
Greenwich. In the British raids of March 1779 and December 1783 she suffered losses (CAR, 36:19).
TOWNSEND, MRS.   NJ
Cape May County. She collected funds for the army (New Jersey Gazette, July 4, 1780).
TOWNSEND, JEMIMA   MD
In 1776 her plantation was destroyed by Tories (IM, 306).
TOWNSEND, REBECCA. See HANNAH CORNELL
TOWNSEND, ROSE   MD
Charles County. In 1782 she supplied wheat for the army (IM, 22852).
TOWNSEND, SARAH   CT
New Haven. The wife of Jeremiah Townsend, Jr., she was abused in July 1779 by the British (CAR, 15:243).
TOWNSEND, SARAH   NY
She sent a message to her brother, a spy, that Benedict Arnold planned an attack on West Point. See Biographies.
TOWNSEND, TABITHA JEACOCKS. See PEARSON
TRACY, MRS.   CT
Gen. Washington was entertained at her home. See Biographies.
TRACY, LUCY SPRAGUE   MA
She was born on July 28, 1725, and married Thomas Tracy. Lucy died on March 6, 1826. She is listed as a patriot in the DAR Patriot Index.
TRAPLER, ELIZABETH   SC
She supplied provisions for the troops (SI, Y-Z:145).
TRASK, RUTH PEABODY. See CURTIS
TRAVIS, ANN   VA
Isle of Wight. Recognized for public service (VR, 2:329).
TRAVIS, MARGARET   VA
Stafford County. She performed a public service (VR, 5:195).
TREFETHEN, MADAM   NH
She attacked the British man-of-war Scarborough. See Biographies.
TREIT, PEGGE   NJ
Hackensack. She suffered losses in a British raid (CDB, claim 19).
TREUTLEN, ANNE UNSETT   GA
The Tories burned her home. See Biographies.

TREUTLEN, MARGUERETTA DUPUIS   GA
   Governor and Mrs. Treutlen spent their money to support the
   Georgia troops. See Biographies.
TREZEVANT, CHARLOTTE   SC
   She supplied provisions for the troops (SI, B:78).
TRICE, JANE   VA
   King and Queen County. Performed a public service (VR, 4:4).
TRICE, MARY   VA
   Louisa County. She performed a public service (VR, 3:370).
TRIGG, MARY   VA
   Southampton County. Credited with public service (VR Court
   booklet, p. 19). Also Spotsylvania County (VR, 4:265).
TRIGG, MARY CHRISTIAN   KY
   The wife of Stephen Trigg of Virginia, in 1780 they settled
   at a station at the mouth of Dick's River. Col. Trigg was killed
   on October 19, 1782, by Indians at the Battle of the Blue Licks.
   Trigg County, Kentucky, was named in his honor (CH).
TRIMBLE, SARAH   VA
   Rockbridge County. Recognized for public service (VR, 5:89).
TRIMMER, LUCY   VA
   Louisa County. Credited with public service (VR Lists, 1:14).
TRIPLETT, ELIZABETH   VA
   Loudoun County. Performed a public service (VR, 3:328).
TRIPLETT, SARAH   VA
   Fairfax. Recognized for public service (VR Court Booklet,
   p. 11).
TRIPP, MARY   NC
   She supplied provisions for the troops (RA, C:57).
TRIPPE, ELIZABETH   MD
   Talbot County. In 1778 she furnished bacon for the army (IM,
   6942).
TRIPPE, MARGARET   MD
   Dorchester County. In 1782 she supplied wheat for the army
   (IM, 23965).
TRIPPLET, ELEANOR   NC
   The wife of William Tripplet, she furnished provisions for the
   troops (RA, A:204). She died in 1782 (DAR).
TRIST, ELIZABETH   PA
   Thomas Jefferson stayed in her home. See Biographies.
TROTTER, ANN HENNIS. See BAILEY
TROTTER, ELIZABETH   VA
   Hansemond County. Performed a public service (VR, 4:169,
   359).
TROWBRIDGE, BETHIA RUSSICA   CT
   New Fairfield. The wife of Caleb Trowbridge, he was a captain
   in Colonel Huntington's regiment when taken prisoner at the
   Battle of Long Island on August 27, 1776 (FP2).
TROWBRIDGE, MRS. STEPHEN   VA
   She was captured along with her husband and one child on October
   11, 1780, by the British at Fort George and taken to the Saint
   Lawrence suburbs (MR).

III: COMPLETE LISTING

TRUE, ANN STEVENS BRADBURY   MA
She married Jonathan True, Sr., who was a soldier during the war. Her fifth son, Jacob True, was a captain in Arnold's expedition to Quebec in 1775. He was captured by the British during the assault on the fort on December 31, 1775, and was imprisoned (submitted by Charles W. True, Jr., El Paso, TX).

TRUMAN, SUSANNA   VA
Henrico County. Credited with public service (VR, 3:107, 108).

TRUMBULL, EUNICE   CT
Hartford. On July 12, 1781, George Church obtained a letter of marque to command the sloop John Michael with eight guns and twenty men. Eunice Trumbull witnessed the bond (CN).

TRUMBULL, FAITH ROBINSON   CT
She donated to the cause a cloak given to her by the Comte de Rochambeau. See Biographies.

TRUSS, MARY   VA
Norfolk. She performed a public service (VR, 4:136, 139).

TUBMAN, ELINOR   MD
Charles County. In 1782 she supplied wheat for the army (IM, 24482).

TUCKER, ELIZABETH GOULD   NJ
John Adams stayed in her home. See Biographies.

TUCKER, MARTHA   MD
Montgomery County. In 1781 she supplied wheat for the army (IM, 19493).

TUCKER, MARTHA   VA
Lunenburg County. Credited with public service (VR, 4:26).

TUCKER, MARY   VA
Halifax County. Performed a public service (VR, 2:295).

TUCKER, MARY GATCHELL   MA
Her husband was captured by the British. See Biographies.

TUCKER, RUTH   NJ
Little Egg Harbor. The wife of Ebenezer Tucker, she suffered damage in a British raid (CDB, claim 265).

TUFTS, ANNE ADAMS   MA
She nursed wounded soldiers. See Biographies.

TUGGLE, CATHARINE (ESTATE)   VA
Middlesex County. Credited with public service (VR, 4:97; VR Court Booklet, p. 6).

TULLINGTON, ANNE   VA
Hansemond County. Recognized for public service (VR, 4:168, 169).

TUNSTALL, MOLLY   VA
King and Queen County. Performed a public service (VR, 3:233).

TUNSTALL, SALLY   VA
King and Queen County. Credited with public service (VR Ctf 1).

TUNSTALL, SARAH   VA
King and Queen County. Recognized for public service (VR Lists, 1:3; 2:1; 3:1).

TURNBULL, MRS. CHARLES PA
She was a member of the ladies' association for the welfare of the soldiers. See Biographies.

TURNER, ANNE VA
Halifax County. Credited with public service (VR, 2:296).

TURNER, ELIZABETH NJ
Perth Amboy. She suffered damage in a British raid (CDB, p. 203).

TURNER, KERENHAPPUCK NORMAN MD
She devised a system to care for patients with fever. See Biographies.

TURNER, MARGARET NC
She supplied provisions for the troops (RA, 5:61, fol. 1).

TURNER, MARTHA NC
She furnished provisions for the army (RA, 5:60, fol. 4).

TURNER, NANCY NC
She provided supplies for the army (RA, 9:10, fol. 2).

TURNER, PLEASANT VA
Goochland County. Performed a public service (VR, 3:83).

TURNER, RACHEL VA
King William County. Credited with public service (VR, 3:260, 261).

TURNER, TERESHA VA
Amherst County. Recognized for public service (VR, 1:7).

TURNER, TERESHA, JR. VA
Amherst. Credited with public service (VR Court Booklet, p. 24).

TURNIDGE, SELAH SC
Chesterfield County. She married William Turnidge, who was born in Fredericksburg, Virginia. While a soldier in the war, he was captured at Charleston, South Carolina, when that city fell to the British on May 12, 1780. Their son left many descendants named Turnage (submitted by George M. Norton, Cocoa Beach, FL).

TUTTLE, ANNA CT
New Haven. In the July 1779 British attack she suffered losses (CAR, 15:234f).

TUTTLE, MEHITABLE NY
Southhold, Long Island, New York. The enemy landed in October 1777 and damaged her house (CAR, 8:81). She left Guilford, Connecticut for Long Island in January 1783.

TYLER, ALICE VA
Stafford County. Recognized for public service (VR, 2:9).

TYLER, HANNAH PEABODY MA
North Boxford. She was born on April 22, 1714, and became the wife of Asa Tyler, a minuteman who was killed at the Battle of Lexington on April 19, 1775 (FP2).

TYSON, SARAH SC
She supplied provisions for the troops (SI, L-N:35).

III: COMPLETE LISTING 469

U

UNDEAN, MARY E.   SC
  She furnished provisions for the troops (SI, U-W:196).
UNDERHILL, ANN ELIZABETH BOWNE   NY
  She was born in 1722 and married John Underhill. Ann died in 1786. She is listed as a patriot in the DAR Patriot Index.
UNDERWOOD, ANOMI   SC
  She provided supplies for the army (SI, Y-Z:60).
UTLEY, AMASA   NC
  She supplied provisions for the troops (RA, 4:74, fol. 3).
UTLEY, MARY   CT
  Windham. In 1777 she supplied a blanket for the army (CAR, 11:103).

V

VAIDEN, MARTHA   VA
  New Kent County. The wife of Joseph Vaiden, she performed a public service (VR Court Booklet, p. 13).
VAIL, ELIZABETH   NC
  She opposed drinking British tea. See Background.
VAIL, SUSANNA   NC
  She opposed drinking British tea. See Background.
VALENTINE, MAGDELANE   NJ
  Harrington Township. She suffered damage in a British raid (CDB, claim 38).
VALENTINE, PEGGY   NJ
  Harrington. She suffered losses in a British raid (CDB, claim 55).
VALENTINE, SARAH   NC
  She opposed drinking British tea. See Background.
VAN ALSTYNE, NANCY QUACKENBUSH   NY
  When she learned that Tories and Indians were camped nearby, she aroused her neighbors. See Biographies.
VAN ANTWERP, MARGARET COLLIER   NY
  Schenectady. She was born in 1733 and married Abraham Van Antwerp. Margaret had 800-weight of British musket balls stored in her home that she sold to the Committee of Safety in 1775 for Ŀ4. She died in 1811 (DAR; FH).
VAN BIBBER, MARGARET   SC
  She supplied provisions for the troops (SI, O-Q:134).
VANCE, MARY   NC
  She provided supplies for the army (RA, 4:56, fol. 2).
VAN CLEVE, MARY   NJ
  Hunterdon County. Her husband, Benjamin Van Cleve, was a captain in the militia. Mrs. Van Cleve was a member of the ladies' association for the welfare of the soldiers (New Jersey Gazette, July 4, 1780).

VAN CLIEF, JANE NJ
Somerset Courthouse. The widow of Lawrence Van Clief, she suffered damage in a British raid (CDB, p. 118).
VAN CLIEF, MARY NJ
Somerset. The sister of Dorcas Van Clief, she suffered losses in a British raid (CDB, pp. 41, 44, 65).
VAN COURTLANDT, JOANNA LIVINGSTON NY
Gen. Washington had his headquarters there. See Biographies.
VANDENBERG, HELENA CLARK NY
She entertained Gen. Washington. See Biographies.
VAN DERLINDEN, EVA. See GARRITSE
VANDERLINDER, MARSETIE NJ
New Barbadoes, Bergen County. The widow of Roeloff Vanderlinder, she suffered damage in a British raid (CDB, claims 35, 59).
VANDERSPIEGEL, MARGARET V. CT
Hartford. On April 6, 1778, Joseph Jauncey obtained a letter of marque to command the ship General McDougall with ten guns and thirty men. Margaret Vanderspiegel witnessed the bond (CN).
VANDERWALL, ANNE VA
Henrico County. She performed a public service (VR, 3:108).
VAN DEVENTER, ELIZABETH NJ
Somerville. She suffered damage in a British raid (CDB, p. 5).
VAN DOREN, ALTJE SCHENCK NJ
Somerville. In 1723 she married Christian Van Doren, and they lived in Middlebush. She was the mother of Benjamin Van Doren (BJ). Altje suffered damage by the British (CDB, p. 82).
VAN DOREN, ANNE VAN DYKE NJ
Griggstown. When a British officer invaded her home, Anne pounded the drunken officer on his head with a candlestick. Later she married Abraham Van Doren. Anne died in 1820 (DAR; BJ).
VAN DOREN, CATREGNTJE VOORHEES NJ
Somerset County. She was born on December 27, 1754, and married John Van Doren who was a private in the militia. John was captured at the Battle of Monmouth and held prisoner in New York City (FP2).
VAN DOREN, MARTHA LOTT NJ
The Hessians hanged her by her heels. See Biographies.
VAN DOREN, MARY NJ
Somerset Courthouse. The wife of John Van Doren, she suffered damage in a British raid (CDB, p. 176).
VAN DUERSEN, ANN NJ
She was born in 1745 and married William Van Duersen. Ann died in 1834 and is listed as a patriot in the DAR Patriot Index.
VAN DYKE, MARY NJ
Hackensack. She suffered losses in a British raid (CDB, claim 20).

III: COMPLETE LISTING 471

VAN DYKE, MARY   VA
   Mecklenburg. The wife of John Van Dyke, she is credited with public service (VR, 4:83).
VANEMBURGH, CATHARINE   NJ
   Saddle River. The wife of Gilbert Vanemburgh, she suffered damages caused by American troops (CDB, sec. 2, claim 27).
VAN HARLINGEN, EVA   NJ
   Brunswick. She suffered damage in a British attack (CDB, pp. 14, 34).
VAN HOOK, HANNAH WILSON   KY
   She was captured by Indians. See Biographies.
VAN HOUTEN, CATRYNA   NJ
   Saddle River. She suffered damage caused by American soldiers (CDB, claim 24).
VAN HOUTEN, HELMEGH   NJ
   Saddle River. The wife of Adrian Van Houten, she suffered damage caused by American soldiers (CDB, claims 13, 46).
VAN LIEW, ANNE   NJ
   Somerville. She suffered damages in a British raid (CDB, p. 97).
VAN NORDSTRAND, MAGDELAIN   NJ
   Somerville. The wife of Adrian Van Nordstrand, she suffered damage in a British raid (CDB, p. 92).
VAN NORSTRAND, ALTYE   NJ
   Saddle River. She suffered losses caused by the Americans (CDB, sec. 2, claim 8).
VAN NORTWICK, ELIZABETH   NJ
   Millstone, Somerville. The wife of Philip Van Nortwick, she suffered damage in a British raid (CDB, p. 84).
VAN NUYS, CATHERINE   NJ
   Hillsborough, Somerville. She suffered losses in a British raid (CDB, p. 41).
VAN ORDEN, MARY KONING   NJ
   Hackensack. The wife of Stephen Van Orden, she died in 1783. She suffered damage in a British raid (CDB, claims 4, 79).
VAN ORDEN, NELLY   NJ
   Franklin Township, Bergen County. The wife of Lawrence Van Orden, she suffered damage caused by the Americans (CDB, claims 14, 25).
VAN ORDER, SARAH   CT
   She received money from a fund to be sent to American prisoners in New York City (CAR, 12:289a).
VAN RIPER, ANNA   NJ
   Acquacanunk. She suffered damage by the British (CDB, claim 15).
VAN RIPER, JANE   NJ
   Acquacanunk. She suffered losses by the British (CDB, claim 49).
VAN RIPER, SOPHIAH   NJ
   Acquacanunk. She suffered damage by the British (CDB, claim 52-2).

VAN SAEN, RACHEL   NJ
  New Barbadoes, Bergen County. The wife of Jacob Van Saen,
  she suffered damage in a British attack (CDB, claim 30).
VAN SAEN (VAN ZEAN), RACHEL   NJ
  Saddle River. The wife of Cornelius, she suffered damage caused
  by American troops (CDB, sec. 2, claim 37). Also Rachel for
  Hackensack, British damage (CDB, claim 24).
VANSANT, MRS.   NJ
  Morris County. She collected funds for the soldiers (New Jersey
  Gazette, July 4, 1780).
VAN SWAN, MARRETYE   NJ
  Saddle River. She suffered damage caused by American troops
  (CDB, sec. 2, claim 14).
VAN TINE, MARY   NJ
  Middlesex County. The wife of John Van Tine, she suffered
  damage in a British raid (CDB, p. 168).
VAN TINE, SOPHIE   NJ
  Middlesex County. Property damaged by the British (CDB,
  p. 32).
VAN VARICK, EFFIE TEN EYCK   NY
  She was born in 1718 and married Andrew Van Varick. Effie
  died in 1782. She is listed as a patriot in the DAR Patriot
  Index.
VAN VEGHTEN, MARGARET   NJ
  Somerville. She suffered damage in a British raid (CDB, p.
  31).
VAN VEGHTEN, SARAH MIDDAH   NJ
  Gen. Washington had his headquarters there. See Biographies.
VAN VOORHES, MARY   NJ
  New Barbadoes, Bergen County. The wife of Daniel Van Voorhes,
  she suffered damage in a British raid (CDB, claim 21).
VAN VOORHIS, CRISYE   NJ
  Saddle River. The wife of Albert Van Voorhis (or Voorhes),
  she suffered damage caused by American soldiers (CDB, sec.
  2, claim 16).
VAN VOORHIS, CRISYE   NJ
  New Barbadoes, Bergen County. The wife of Peter Van Voorhis
  (or Van Vorhis), she suffered damage by the British (CDB,
  claim 5).
VAN WART, RACHEL STRONG   NY
  She was born in 1760 and married Isaac Van Wart. Rachel died
  in 1834 and is listed as a patriot in the DAR Patriot Index.
VAN WINKLE, ELLENOR   NJ
  Acquacanunk. She suffered damage by the British (CDB, clain 3).
VAN WINKLE, POLLY   NJ
  New Barbadoes, Bergen County. The wife of Henry Van Winkle,
  he was taken prisoner and held by the British for five months
  and five days (CDB, claim 1).
VAN WINKLE, THEODOSIA   NJ
  New Barbadoes, Bergen County. The wife of Theodore Van
  Winkle, she suffered damage in a British raid (CDB, claim 57).

III: COMPLETE LISTING

VAN ZANDT (VAN SANN), MANETYE   NJ
   New Barbadoes, Bergen County. The wife of Isaac, she suffered
   damage in a British raid (CDB, claim 56).

VAN ZANDT, SUSANNAH   NJ
   Middlesex County. She suffered damage in a British raid (CDB,
   p. 167).

VARNUM, MOLLY BUTLER   MA
   She wove cloth for clothing and knitted socks for the soldiers.
   See Biographies.

VAUGHN, JANE   NC
   She supplied provisions for the troops (RA, 7:80, fol. 1).

VAUGHAN, NANCY ANN WILSON.   See LEE

VAUX, ANN   SC
   She furnished supplies for the army (SI, Y-Z:201).

VEACH, ELIZA   SC
   She is listed on army rolls. See Biographies.

VEASEY (VEZE), ELIZA   NC
   She supplied provisions for the troops (RA, C:99).

VEEDER, ELIZABETH MARGRETTA SHANNON   NY
   She was born in 1755 and married Simon B. Veeder. Elizabeth
   served in the navy and is listed as a patriot in the DAR Patriot
   Index. She died in 1808.

VELT, DEBORAH   VA
   In 1781 she was captured by Tories and Indians (HP).

VENABLE, ELIZABETH   VA
   Campbell County. The wife of John Venable, she performed
   a public service (VR, 1:294).

VENABLE, ELIZABETH MICHAUS WOODSON   VA
   She was born in 1740 and married Nathaniel Venable. Elizabeth
   died in 1791 and is listed as a patriot in the DAR Patriot Index.

VENABLE, ELIZABETH SMITH   VA
   Prince Edward County. The wife of Charles Venable, she is
   recognized for public service (VR, 5:65).

VERBON, ELIZABETH   NJ
   Bound Brook. The wife of Nehemia Verbon, she suffered damage
   in a British raid (CDB, p. 193).

VER PLANCK, EFFIE BEEKMAN   NY
   Her home was destroyed by the British. See Biographies.

VERRE, MARY   SC
   She supplied provisions for the troops (SI, Y-Z:208).

VERVAL, DOROTHY   NC
   She provided supplied for the army (RA, 12:54, fol. 2).

VER VALIN, ALEDA   NJ
   Harrington. The wife of Abraham Ver Valin, she suffered losses
   in a British attack (CDB, claim 65).

VER VALIN, CATHRINA   NJ
   Harrington. She suffered damage in a British raid (CDB, claim
   18).

VER VALIN, ELIZABETH   NJ
   Harrington. She suffered damage in a British raid (CDB, claim
   10).

VICKERS, SARAH   MD
   In 1781 she provided wheat for the army (IM, 18988).
VILLEPONTOUX, JANE   SC
   She furnished provisions for the army (SI, B:5).
VINCENT, PHOEBE WARD   PA
   She was born in 1740 and married Cornelius Vincent. Phoebe
   died in 1800 and is listed as a patriot in the DAR Patriot Index.
VOBE, JANE   VA
   York County. Recognized for public service (VR Court Booklet,
   p. 4a).
VOLK, ADRANTYE   NJ
   Franklin Township, Bergen County. She suffered damage in a
   British raid (CDB, claim 2).
VOORHEIS (VOORHEESE), HELENA   NJ
   Somerville. The widow of Isaac Voorheese, she suffered damage
   in a British raid (CDB, p. 154).
VOORHEIS, HILEY   NJ
   Windsor, Middlesex County. The widow of Cornelius Voorheis,
   she suffered losses in a British raid (CDB, p. 198).
VOORHEIS (VOORHEESE), JANE   NJ
   Somerville. She suffered damage in a British raid (CDB, p.
   154).
VOORHEIS (VOORHEESE), JOHANNA   NJ
   New Brunswick. The wife of John Voorheese, she suffered
   losses in a British raid (CDB, p. 8).
VOORHIES, MINNIE   NJ
   The court-martial of Gen. Charles Lee was held in her home.
   See Biographies.
VREELANDT, CATHERINE   NJ
   Westfield. She suffered damage in a British raid (CDB, claim
   66).
VREELANDT, CHARITY   NJ
   Acquacanunk. She suffered damage in a British raid (CDB,
   claim 33).
VREELANDT, LEAH   NJ
   Acquacanunk. The wife of Peter H. Vreelandt, she suffered
   losses in a British raid (CDB, claim 8).
VREELANDT, MARY   NJ
   Acquacanunk. She suffered damage in a British raid (CDB,
   claim 6).
VROOM, ELIZABETH DE MOTT   NJ
   She was born in 1758 and married Hendrik D. Vroom. Elizabeth
   died in 1835 and is listed as a patriot in the DAR Patriot Index.
VROOMAN, ANGELICA   NY
   Schoharie. She was the wife of Peter Vrooman. When Sir John
   Johnson and his men in 1780 attacked Middle Fort, the Americans
   were badly in need of bullets. Mrs. Vrooman took the bullet
   mold of a ranger and an iron spoon and molded bullets for the
   soldiers, and the British were repulsed (CD).

VROOMAN, MARYTJE ACKERSON   NY
    The wife of Capt. Tunis Vrooman, she died in 1780. She is
    listed as a patriot in the DAR Patriot Index.

W

WADDY, MARGARET   VA
    Northumberland. The wife of Thomas Waddy, she performed
    a public service (VR, 4:123).
WADDY, REBECCA   VA
    Hanover. The wife of John Waddy, she is recognized for public
    service (VR, 3:211).
WADE, ELIZABETH   NJ
    Connecticut Farms, Essex County. She suffered damage in
    a British raid (CDB, claim 10).
WADE, ELIZABETH   VA
    Mecklenburg. The wife of George Wade, she performed a public
    service (VR, 4:85).
WADE, MRS. FRANCIS   PA
    She was an active member of the ladies' association for the
    welfare of the soldiers. See Biographies.
WADE, MARTHA   VA
    Mecklenburg. Credited with public service (VR, 4:86).
WADE, MARY   NJ
    Connecticut Farms, Essex County. She suffered damage in
    a British raid (CDB, p. 54).
WADE, PATTY   VA
    Mecklenburg. Recognized for public service (VR Court Booklet,
    p. 15).
WADE, RHODA   NJ
    Connecticut Farms, Essex County. The widow of David Wade,
    she suffered losses in a British raid (CDB, claims 1, 21).
WADSWORTH, ABIGAIL FLAGG   CT
    Farmington. She was the wife of Jonathan Wadsworth, who
    served as a captain in the militia. He was mortally wounded
    at Stillwater on September 19, 1777. Abigail advanced $2,200
    to the army (CAR, 36:298-300).
WADSWORTH, LOIS JUDD   CT
    Farmington. She was born in 1724 and married Hezekiah Wads-
    worth, who was taken prisoner at the surrender of Fort Wash-
    ington on November 16, 1776 (FP4).
WAGGONER, ELIZABETH   VA
    Gloucester County. She performed a public service (VR, 3:57).
WAGGONER, MARY   NC
    She supplied provisions for the troops (RA, A:224).
WAGLUN, JIMMIE   NJ
    She led Washington's army to Princeton. See Biographies.
WAGNER, MARY   NC
    She provided supplies for the army (RA, 1:67, fol. 4).

WAID (WADE), MARTHA   VA
Prince Edward County. The wife of Joseph Waid, she performed a public service (VR Court Booklet, p. 12).

WAKE, JOHANNA   VA
Middlesex County. Credited with public service (VR, 4:97).

WAKEMAN, RUTH   CT
Fairfield widow. In the 1779-1780 British raids she suffered damage (CAR, 15:250h; 19:73c).

WALDEN, ABBY LOWD   NH
She married Jacob Walden, who served as steward on the frigate Ranger. On May 12, 1780, this vessel was taken by the British, and Walden and the crew were imprisoned (CN).

WALDEN, SARAH   VA
Halifax County. Credited with public service (VR, 2:299).

WALDRON, UDA   NJ
North Brunswick. The wife of Leffert Waldron, she suffered losses in a British attack (CDB, p. 160).

WALES, MARY   CT
After her husband, Nathaniel Wales, died she took care of the state supply of saltpeter (CAR, 28:228a).

WALING, MARY   NJ
Harrington. She suffered losses in a British raid (CDB, claim 76).

WALKER, BERSHEBA   SC
She supplied provisions for the troops (SI, 1:14).

WALKER, CATHARINE   CT
She received money from the fund for the care of prisoners in New York City in 1777 (CAR, 12:289q).

WALKER, CATHERINE   VA
She married James Walker and died in 1786. She is listed as a patriot in the DAR Patriot Index.

WALKER, CATHERINE   VA
Pittsylvania County. The wife of Joseph Walker, she performed a public service (VR, 5:33).

WALKER, ELEANOR WHITE   SC
She was born in 1759 and married Lt. Alexander Walker. Eleanor died in 1839 (DAR). She provided provisions for the army (SI, Y-Z:222).

WALKER, ELIZABETH   SC
She supplied provisions for the troops (SI, Y-Z:177).

WALKER, ELIZABETH   VA
King and Queen County. The probable widow of Baylor Walker, she is recognized for public service (VR Lists, 4:1).

WALKER, ELIZABETH SEALY   SC
She married Henry Harden, then Robert Walker. Elizabeth died in 1794 (DAR). She supplied provisions for the troops (SI, B:245).

WALKER, ESTHER GASTON   NC
She nursed wounded soldiers. See Biographies.

WALKER, JANE LEMON LEMANT   SC
She was born in 1768 and married William Walker, a soldier. She is listed as a patriot in the DAR Patriot Index.

III: COMPLETE LISTING

WALKER, MARTHA　　　　　　　PA
  At age sixteen she was captured by Indians in August 1781
  and taken to Canada. She was sent home on August 22, 1782
  (MR).
WALKER, MARTHA　　　　　　　VA
  Prince Edward County. The wife of David Walker, she performed a public service (VR, 5:63, 66, 68).
WALKER, MARTHA SMYTHE. See LEMANT
WALKER, MARY　　　　　　　　NC
  She supplied provisions for the troops (RA, 5:14, fol. 4).
WALKER, MARY　　　　　　　　PA
  At age eighteen she was captured by Indians in August 1781
  and taken to Canada. She was sent home on August 22, 1782
  (MR).
WALKER, MARY　　　　　　　　VA
  Hanover County. She performed a public service (VR, 3:208,
  210, 211).
WALKER, SARAH　　　　　　　　VA
  Accomack County. The wife of John Walker, she is recognized
  for public service (VR Ctf 1).
WALKER, SARAH　　　　　　　　VA
  Charles City. The widow of Freeman Walker, she performed
  a public service (VR Court Booklet, pp. 4, 5).
WALKER, SARAH THOMAS　　　PA
  She was born in 1734 and became the first wife of Joseph Walker.
  Sarah died in 1792 and is listed as a patriot in the DAR Patriot
  Index.
WALKER, SUSAN　　　　　　　　SC
  She supplied provisions for the troops (SI, B:31).
WALKER, SUSANNA　　　　　　　VA
  Charles City. The wife of Capt. Robert Walker, she is recognized for public service (VR Court Booklet, p. 15).
WALL, MARY　　　　　　　　　　VA
  Greensville. The wife of James Wall, she is credited with
  public service (VR Court Booklet, pp. 8, 11).
WALL, ANN PARHAM　　　　　　SC
  She married Richard Wall, who was mate on the Richard and
  was captured by the British. On October 14, 1779, Wall was
  confined in the Fortun Prison at Gosport, England (CN).
WALLACE, FRANCES　　　　　　NC
  She furnished provisions for the troops (RA, 6:23, fol. 1).
WALLACE, JANE　　　　　　　　VA
  Augusta County. The wife of Samuel Wallace, she is recognized
  for public service (VR Lists, 1:12).
WALLACE, MRS. JOHN　　　　　NJ
  Gen. Washington had his headquarters there. See Biographies.
WALLACE, MARTHA　　　　　　　VA
  Norfolk. The wife of Thomas Wallace, she performed a public
  service (VR, 4:137).
WALLAN, JANE　　　　　　　　　VA
  Halifax County. Credited with public service (VR Court Booklet, p. 4).

WALLER, ANN   VA
    Caroline County. The wife of John Waller, she is recognized
    for public service (VR Court Booklet, 2:16, 33).
WALLING, MRS. JAMES   VA
    Montgomery County. She was Miss White when she married
    James Walling. In 1778 he was captain of the 13th Virginia Regi-
    ment and was captured by the British (FP4).
WALLIS, JANE   VA
    Halifax County. She performed a public service (VR, 2:298).
WALRATH, ELIZABETH BAUDER   NJ
    She was born in 1769 and married Peter J. Walrath. Elizabeth
    died in 1848 and is listed as a patriot in the DAR Patriot Index.
WALSWORTH, SARAH   CT
    Groton. She was widowed by action at Fort Griswold in 1781
    and suffered damage in the British attack (CAR, 27:333b).
WALTER, MRS.   SC
    She provided supplies for the troops (SI, B:88).
WALTERS, MARY   SC
    She supplied provisions for the army (SI, L-N:35).
WALTERS, SARAH   MD
    In 1781 she supplied wheat for the army (IM, 17051).
WALTON, DORTHEA CAMBER   GA
    She was captured by the British and taken to the West Indies.
    See Biographies.
WALTON, MARTHA   VA
    Cumberland County. The wife of George Walton, she performed
    a public service (VR, 1:238).
WALTON, MARTHA COX   VA
    She wife of Thomas Walton, she is listed as a patriot in the
    DAR Patriot Index.
WALTON, MARY   NC
    She supplied provisions for the troops (RA, 9:5, fol. 2).
WALTON, MARY   VA
    Hanover County. The wife of Edward Walton, she is credited
    with public service (VR, 3:213).
WALTON, MARY SIMS   VA
    The wife of John Walton, Sr., she died in 1781. She is listed
    as a patriot in the DAR Patriot Index 2.
WAMPOLE, CATHERINE ROTH   PA
    Gen. Washington had his headquarters here. See Biographies.
WANZER, ELIZABETH   CT
    New Fairfield. In 1777 she supplied a blanket for the army
    (CAR, 11:366).
WARD, ABIGAIL   CT
    She furnished milk for the militia (CAR, 4:155a).
WARD, ANN   VA
    Isle of Wight. Credited with public service (VR, 2:331).
WARD, CATHARINE   NC
    She furnished provisions for the troops (RA, A:228).
WARD, ELIZABETH   VA
    Norfolk. She performed a public service (VR, 4:137).

III: COMPLETE LISTING 479

WARD, EUNICE NJ
Orange. The widow of Nathaniel Ward, she suffered damage in a British attack (CDB, claims 51, 53).

WARD, EXPERIENCE CT
Groton. In the British attack, she suffered damage (CAR, 27:333b).

WARD, HANNAH NJ
Orange. The wife of Bethuel Ward, she suffered damage in a British attack (CDB, claim 49).

WARD, HANNAH NJ
Wardsession, Essex County. The wife of Abel Ward, she suffered losses in a British attack (CDB, claim 15).

WARD, MARTHA VA
Prince Edward County. The widow of Joseph Ward, she performed a public service (VR, 5:49).

WARD, MARY CT
In 1779 she supplied clothing for the army (CAR, 35:249b). She was a Western Lands Grantee.

WARD, MARY NJ
Newark. The wife of Ebenezer Ward, she suffered damage in a British attack (CDB, claim 43).

WARD, NANCY TN
Princess Nanye'hi warned the Americans of an impending Indian attack. See Biographies.

WARD, PHEBE BREENE RI
She is listed as a patriot in the DAR Patriot Index. See Biographies.

WARD, SARA McCALL SC
She was born in 1740 and married Joseph Ward. Sara died in 1810. She is listed as a patriot in the DAR Patriot Index.

WARD, SARAH CT
Middletown. She furnished a blanket for the army (CAR, 6:179).

WARD, SUSAN SC
She supplied provisions for the troops (SI, O-Q:252).

WARDINBROUGH, MARY RI
Newport. The widow of Christopher Wardinbrough, she gave a hundred pistols to Robert Riles, captain of the schooner Spy (CAR, 27:377-380).

WARE, ELIZABETH NC
The wife of George Ware, she supplied provisions for the army (RA, 30:81).

WARE, JANE VA
King and Queen County. The widow of John Ware, she performed a public service (VR Lists, 4:2).

WARE, SUSANNA VA
King William County. The wife of Thomas Ware, she is credited with public service (VR Lists, 1:9).

WARHAM, MARY SC
She supplied provisions for the troops (SI, B:187).

WARING, DOROTHY SC
She provided supplies for the army (SI, B:14).

WARING, JULIET SC
  She furnished provisions for the army (SI, B:14).
WARING, MARY SC
  She supplied provisions for the troops (SI, B:61).
WARLICK, BARBARA SCHINDLER NC
  She furnished provisions for the army. See Biographies.
WARNE, MARGARET VLIET NJ
  She cared for wounded soldiers. See Biographies.
WARNER, ANN CT
  She supplied funds for the militia (CAR, 32:190a).
WARREN, CATHARINE VA
  King and Queen County. Credited with public service (VR, 3:235).
WARREN, ELIZABETH VA
  Prince George County. Recognized for public service (VR, 4:257).
WARREN, ELIZABETH HOOTEN MA
  Boston. At age fourteen in 1764 she married Dr. Joseph Warren. On April 18, 1775, Dr. Warren sent Paul Revere, Prescott, and Dawes on their ride to warn Adams and Hancock of their danger of capture. Later Warren was made a general. On August 23, 1775, he was killed at the Battle of Bunker Hill (Breed's Hill). Elizabeth had four children, but only one son, Joseph Warren, left descendants (GP).
WARREN, MARGARET NC
  She supplied provisions for the troops (RA, 9:33, fol. 1).
WARREN, MERCY OTIS MA
  She kept a record of the Revolutionary War from 1775 to 1783 and then published her history. See Biographies.
WARSHAN, MRS. VA
  Pittsylvania County. She performed a public service (VR, 5:32).
WARTHEN, ELIZABETH VA
  Prince George County. She is recognized for public service (VR Court Booklet, p. 6).
WARTHEN, MARY VA
  Prince George County. The wife of James Warthen, she performed a public service (VR, 4:257).
WASH, MARY VA
  Louisa County. The wife of William Wash, she is recognized for public service (VR, 3:373, 375).
WASHBURN, ELIZABETH VA
  Culpeper County. The widow of Thomas Washburn, she is credited with public service (VR, 2:129).
WASHINGTON, JANE RILEY VA
  Her husband was wounded in battle. See Biographies.
WASHINGTON, MARTHA DANDRIDGE CUSTIS VA
  She was a camp follower and was with Gen. Washington as much as possible. See Biographies.
WASHINGTON, MARY VA
  Spotsylvania County. The wife of Charles Washington, she performed a public service (VR Lists, p. 2).

III: COMPLETE LISTING   481

WASHINGTON, MARY BALL   VA
  She was loyal to the Crown, but finally knitted socks for the
  soldiers. See Biographies.
WASHINGTON, SUSANNAH   VA
  Westmoreland County. The wife of John Washington, she per-
  formed a public service (VR, 5:226).
WASSON, ESTHER   CT
  Norwalk. She suffered damage in a British attack (CAR, 1:63i,
  98h). She was a Western Lands Grantee.
WASSON, REBECCA   CT
  Norwalk. She suffered losses in a British raid (CAR, 1:63k,
  98e). She was a Western Lands Grantee.
WATERBURY, MARY WATERBURY   CT
  She married David Waterbury who was a captain of Marines in
  the Continental Navy. David was captured by the British in
  October 1776 during the Battle of Lake Champlain, New York.
  After his release in October 1778 he served as a brigadier gen-
  eral in the Connecticut Militia (CN).
WATERBURY, SARAH   CT
  Stamford widow. In the 1781 British raid she suffered damage
  (CAR, 22:296a).
WATERMAN, JEMIMA   VA
  Princess Anne County. Recognized for public service (VR Court
  Booklet, p. 11).
WATERMAN, MARTHA   RI
  The wife of S. N. Waterman, she furnished supplies for the
  army (MP 23:45).
WATERS, ROSANNA. See FARROW
WATJUBS, MARY HUDSON   VA
  The wife of John Watjubs, she is listed as a patriot in the DAR
  Patriot Index.
WATKINS, ELIZABETH   VA
  King William County. Credited with public service (VR, 3:262).
WATKINS, MARY   VA
  Henrico County. Recognized for public service (VR, 3:108).
WATKINS, PRISCILLA   VA
  Isle of Wight. She performed a public service (VR, 2:330).
WATSON, CATHERINE   SC
  She supplied provisions for the troops (SI, L-N:36).
WATSON, EDITH   VA
  Greensville. The wife of Alexander Watson, she is recognized
  for public service (VR, 3:33).
WATSON, ELIZABETH   VA
  Charlotte. The wife of William Watson, she performed a public
  service (VR, 1:307). Also an Elizabeth Watson listed in Meck-
  lenburg (VR, 4:87).
WATSON, HANNAH   CT
  In 1777 she supplied printing for the army (CAR, 7:49).
WATSON, MARGARET   SC
  She provided supplies for the army (SI, 10, pt. 2:58).

WATSON, MARY   SC
   She supplied provisions for the troops (SI, B:107; and L-N:318).
WATSON, REBECCA   VA
   Charles City. She performed a public service (VR Ctf 1). Also
   a Rebecca Watson in Henrico County (VR, 4:323).
WATTLES, SARAH SEABURY   CT
   Norwich. She married William Wattles, who commanded the privateer sloop Nancy in 1776 and later commanded the privateer Comet. In March 1782 he was captured by the British and imprisoned (CN).
WATTS, ANN   VA
   King and Queen County. The wife of John Watts, she is credited with public service (VR Lists, 4:1).
WATTS, ANN WALKER   PA
   Her husband was killed by Indians. See Biographies.
WATTS, JEAN MURRAY   PA
   She made clothing for the soldiers. See Biographies.
WATTS, RACHEL M.   SC
   She supplied provisions for the troops (SI, B:183).
WATTS, REBECCA   SC
   She furnished provisions for the army (SI, O-Q:196).
WAYLAND, MARY   VA
   Culpeper County. The widow of John Wayland, she is recognized for public service (VR, 2:129).
WAYNE (WHAYNE), TABITHA   VA
   King and Queen County. She performed a public service (VR, 3:235).
WEAVER, ANN ELIZABETH   VA
   She was born in 1708 and married Tillman Weaver. Ann died in 1783 and is listed as a patriot in the DAR Patriot Index 2.
WEAVER (WEVER), CATHERINE MARGARET   NJ
   Hillsborough, Somerville. She suffered damage in a British raid (CDB, p. 39).
WEAVER, HANNAH   SC
   She supplied provisions for the troops (SI, 1:92).
WEAVER, MRS. JACOB   VA
   Fauquier County. Credited with public service (VR, 2:250).
WEAVER, SUSANNA   RI
   She supplied beef, pork, cloth, cordwood, etc., for the militia (MP, 48:16).
WEBB, ABIGAIL CHESTER   CT
   Generals Washington and Rochambeau held a conference in her home. See Biographies.
WEBB, CATHERINE HOGEBOOM   CT
   Her husband was taken prisoner by the British. See Biographies.
WEBB, FRANCES   VA
   Richmond. She performed a public service (VR, 5:105).
WEBB, LEANNAH   VA
   Northumberland County. The wife of John S. Webb, she is recognized for public service (VR, 4:123).

III: COMPLETE LISTING 483

WEBB, MARY EDMONDSON VA
She supplied provisions for the army. See Biographies.
WEBB, MERRY NC
She furnished provisions for the troops (RA, 6:18, fol. 1).
WEBB, PHEBE NJ
Amboy. She suffered damage in a British raid (CDB, p. 99).
WEBBER, ELIZABETH STEWART MA
Boston. She married Ignatius Webber, who commanded the privateer Neptune and in December 1779 he was captured by the British vessel Dragon (CN).
WEBSTER, ABIGAIL EASTMAN NH
"Nabby" had ten children to raise while her husband was in the army. See Biographies.
WEBSTER, ABIGAIL MARSH MA
She was born in 1705 and married Thomas Webster. Abigail died in 1790 and is listed as a patriot in the DAR Patriot Index.
WEBSTER, JAMIMA NJ
Piscataway. The wife of Thomas Webster, she suffered damage in a British raid (CDB, p. 324).
WEED, MARY CT
Stamford widow. She suffered damage in the 1781 British raid (CAR, 22:96b).
WEED, SARAH CT
Stamford widow. She suffered losses in the 1781 British raid (CAR, 22:297, 298, 300).
WEEKS, ABIGAIL CT
Norwalk. She suffered damage in the British attack (CAR, 1:63j, 98a). She was a Western Lands Grantee.
WEEKS, SARAH NC
She furnished supplies for the troops (RA, K:147B).
WEIR, ANN (ANNE) NC
She provided supplies for the army (RA, 5:15, fol. 1).
WELCH, ELEANOR SC
She provided supplies for the troops (SI, Y-Z:129).
WELLES, WIDOW CT
Stratford. In 1777 she furnished a blanket for the army (CAR, 11:222a).
WELLMAN, ANN VA
Hanover County. Credited with public service (VR, 3:209, 210).
WELLS, ELIZABETH NC
She furnished supplies for the troops (RA, 6:40, fol. 1).
WELLS, MARION NC
She opposed drinking British tea. See Background.
WELLS, RACHEL NJ
She bought Continental bonds during the Revolutionary War and in 1786, as a widow, she protested to the Congress for not receiving interest on the bonds (NL).
WELLWOOD, JANE NC
She opposed drinking British tea. See Background.

WEMPLE, MARGARETTA   NY
   She was born in 1733 and married Barent Wemple. Margaretta
   died in 1819 and is listed as a patriot in the DAR Patriot Index.
WENT, LUCY   VA
   King George County. Performed a public service (VR, 2:339).
WENTZ, ROSANNA MARGARETTA   PA
   Gen. Washington had his headquarters here. See Biographies.
WENZELL, CHARLOTTE EST   PA
   She was born in 1761 and married George Wenzell. Charlotte
   is listed as a patriot in the DAR Patriot Index.
WESCOTT, MRS.   NJ
   Gloucester County. She was the wife of Col. Wescott. Mrs.
   Wescott collected funds for the army (New Jersey Gazette, July
   4, 1780).
WESCOTT, ELIZABETH   CT
   New London. In the British attack she suffered damage (CAR,
   1:63k, 95h). She was a Western Lands Grantee.
WEST, ELIZABETH DERBY   MA
   Salem. She was the first wife of Nathaniel West, who commanded
   the ship Oliver Cromwell, then the Black Prince, which was
   captured by the British in July 1779. Later he escaped, or
   was exchanged, since in December 1779 he commanded the ship
   Three Sisters (CN).
WEST, JANE   SC
   She supplied provisions for the troops (SI, 10, pt. 1:188).
WEST, MAGDALEN   GA
   She furnished beef and pork for Gen. Anthony Wayne's troops
   (WA, p. 132).
WEST, MARGARET   VA
   Fairfax. She performed a public service (VR Court Booklet,
   pp. 9, 21).
WEST, MARY   NC
   She provided supplies for the army (RA, 1:109, fol. 4).
WEST, MARY   VA
   Gloucester County. Recognized for public service (VR Court
   Booklet, 3:14).
WESTBROOKE, ELEANOR   VA
   Southampton County. The widow of Henry Westbrooke, she
   is credited with public service (VR, 5:182).
WESTERVELT, ANNE   NJ
   Saddle River. The wife of John Westervelt, she suffered damage
   caused by American troops (CDB, claim 40).
WESTERVELT, CATERINE   NJ
   Harrington. The wife of Leah Westervelt, she suffered losses
   in a British raid (CDB, claim 4).
WESTERVELT, JANE   NJ
   Hackensack. The widow of Cornelius Damarest, she suffered
   damage caused by the British (CDB, claim 65).
WESTERVELT, MARY   NJ
   Harrington. The wife of John Westervelt, she suffered losses
   in a British raid (CDB, claim 32).

III: COMPLETE LISTING

WESTFIELD, MARY   VA
In April 1779 she was captured by Tories and Indians (HP).

WESTMORELAND, ANN LENOIR   SC
She is credited with rendering aid as a patriot. See Biographies.

WESTON, BARBARA   SC
She supplied provisions for the troops (SI, O-Q:195).

WESTON, HANNAH WATTS   ME
She collected pewter, lead, and powder for the army. See Biographies.

WESTON, SARAH   SC
She furnished supplies for the army (SI, O-Q:195).

WESTRAY, LUCY   VA
Isle of Wight. The wife of Robert Westray, she performed a public service (VR, 2:330).

WETHERAL, MRS. THOMAS   NY
Gen. Washington had his headquarters here. See Biographies.

WETMORE, SALLY   CT
In 1779 she furnished clothing for the army (CAR, 35:249a).

WHEATLAND, JANE   MD
Dorchester county. In 1782 she supplied salt pork for the army (IM, 23964).

WHEATLEY, PHYLLIS   MA
She wrote a poem praising Gen. Washington. See Biographies.

WHEATLEY, SUBMITT PECK   NH
Four of her sons served in the war and two died in service. See Biographies.

WHEELER, MARY   SC
She supplied provisions for the troops (SI, L-N:70).

WHELAN, ANN   MD
Charles County. In 1782 she furnished wheat for the army (IM, 24489).

WHELPLEY, ELIZABETH   CT
Norwalk. In a British raid she suffered damage (CAR, 1:631, 98g). She was a Western Lands Grantee.

WHETTEN, MARGARET TODD   NY
She took food to the Americans on prison ships. See Biographies.

WHIGGAM, AGNES   GA
She furnished five head of cattle for the army (WA, p. 151).

WHILDEN, MRS.   NJ
Cape May County. She collected funds for the soldiers (New Jersey Gazette, July 4, 1780).

WHIPPLE, EUNICE FAIRFIELD   MA
Manchester. She married Joseph Whipple. On June 13 he was elected captain of the Cape Ann Coast Guard and died at sea in 1777 (FP1).

WHIPPLE, SARAH HOPKINS   RI
Providence. She married Abraham Whipple, who was commissioned in 1775 as a captain in the Continental Navy. He later replaced Esek Hopkins as commodore of the Continental Navy

and led the Providence and a squadron of vessels to defend
Charleston, South Carolina. But then the American forces sur-
rendered to the British on May 12, 1789, and Whipple and thou-
sands of American soldiers and sailors were imprisoned by the
enemy (CN).
WHITAKER, ELIZABETH OGDEN   NY
    She nursed wounded soldiers. See Biographies.
WHITAKER, RACHEL   VA
    James City. She performed a public service (VR Court Booklet,
    p. 36).
WHITALL, ANN COOPER   NJ
    She nursed wounded soldiers. See Biographies.
WHITCHER, HANNAH MORRILL   NH
    The fourth of eleven children, she had eleven children of her
    own. See Biographies.
WHITE, AGNESS   VA
    Accomack County. Credited with public service (VR Ctf 1).
WHITE, ANN   VA
    Culpeper County. She performed a public service (VR Court
    Booklet, 1:50).
WHITE, CATHARINE   VA
    Henrico County. Credited with public service (VR, 3:109, 111).
WHITE, MRS. EBENEZER   NJ
    Gen. Charles Lee was captured in her home. See Biographies.
WHITE, HANNAH   VA
    Northampton County. Recognized for public service (VR Lists,
    p. 1).
WHITE, JANE BROWN   SC
    She was born in 1758 and married William White, a private. Jane
    died in 1841 and is listed as a patriot in the DAR Patriot Index.
WHITE, LOVINA TOTTEN   PA
    She was born in 1761 and married Benjamin White. Lovina died
    in 1857 and is listed as a patriot in the DAR Patriot Index.
WHITE, MARGARET ELLIS   NJ
    She married Lt. Col. Anthony Walton White of the 4th Continental
    Dragoons. He was made a colonel in February 1780 and com-
    manded the 1st Continental Dragoons. Col. White was taken
    prisoner at Lanneaus Ferry, South Carolina, in May 1780 and
    was exchanged in October 1780 (FW).
WHITE, MARTHA HALL. See FORBES
WHITE, MARY   NC
    She supplied provisions for the troops (RA, 6:44, fol. 4).
WHITE, MARY   VA
    Henrico County. The widow of Elisha White, she performed
    a public service (VR, 3:110). Also King George County (VR,
    2:339).
WHITE, MERCY HATHAWAY   NH
    She cared for the sick and wounded soldiers. See Biographies.
WHITE, NANCY   VA
    Accomack County. Credited with public service (VR, 1:34).

III: COMPLETE LISTING 487

WHITE, PHEBE RI
The wife of William White. She furnished corn, rye, beef, pork, sugar, cordwood, shoes, etc., for the army (MP, 48:33).
WHITE, SARAH NC
She furnished provisions for the troops (RA, 4:57, fol. 3).
WHITEAR, ABIGAIL CT
Fairfield. In the 1779-1780 British attacks she suffered losses (CAR, 15:25ic; 19:73c).
WHITEHEAD, ELIZABETH VA
Halifax County. Recognized for public service (VR Court Booklet, p. 12).
WHITEHEAD, JANE GA
She supplied beef for the army (WA, p. 178).
WHITEHEAD, JANE. See TICHENOR
WHITEHEAD, MARTHA NJ
Burlington. She suffered damage in a British raid (CDB, claim 109).
WHITEHEAD, MARY VA
Southampton. The wife of James Whitehead, she is recognized for public service (VR Lists, p. 1).
WHITEHEAD, RAHAB CULPEPPER NC
She was born in 1724 and married Nathan Whitehead. Rahab died in 1815 and is listed as a patriot in the DAR Patriot Index 3.
WHITEHEAD, SUSANNAH TOMLINSON. See FORT
WHITEHURST, MARY VA
Princess Anne County. Credited with public service (VR, 55:229).
WHITFIELD, CHRISTY SC
She furnished provisions for the troops (SI, O-Q:100).
WHITING, AMY LATHROP CT
She was born in 1735 and married William Bradford Whiting of New York. Amy died in 1815 and is listed in the DAR Patriot Index.
WHITING, ELIZABETH JUDSON CT
She was born in 1723 and married Col. Samuel Whiting. Elizabeth died in 1793 and is listed as a patriot in the DAR Patriot Index.
WHITING, LYDIA PARTRIDGE MA
of Newton Highlands. She was born in 1728 and married Nathaniel Whiting. Lydia died in 1799 and is listed as a patriot in the DAR Patriot Index.
WHITING, MARY VA
King and Queen County. The wife of Beverly Whiting, she performed a public service (VR, 3:235).
WHITLOCK, ANN VA
Hanover County. The wife of John Whitlock, she is credited with public service (VR, 3:208, 210).
WHITLOCK, ANNA VA
Henrico County. Credited with public service (VR, 3:109, 111).
WHITLOCK, ELIZABETH VA
Halifax County. Recognized for public service (VR, 2:297, 299).

WHITLOCK, SARAH   VA
Caroline County. Credited with public service (VR, 1:271).
WHITNEY, ESTHER WEEKES   NY
Westchester County. She was the wife of Josiah Whitney, who was wounded and then taken prisoner in the skirmish of Saint John on September 17, 1775 (FP1).
WHITNEY, LOIS   CT
Norwalk. In the 1779-1780 British raids she suffered damage (CAR, 20:379g, 380g).
WHITTLESLEY, ELIZABETH WILLIAMS   CT
Saybrook. She married Azariah Whittlesley, who commanded the Fanny in 1777; then he was taken by the enemy and imprisoned. After his exchange, in December 1779, he commanded the Neptune and in April 1779, he was captured a second time and imprisoned (CN).
WHITTON, LYDIA   NJ
Burlington. She suffered damage in a British attack (CDB, claim 5).
WHORTON, MRS.   VA
Stafford County. She performed a public service (VR Lists, 1:3).
WIGGINTON, ELEANOR   VA
Loudoun County. Credited with public service (VR, 3:233).
WIGGINTON, SARAH   VA
Loudoun County. Recognized for public service (VR, 3:298, 333).
WILBOURN, ELIZABETH   NC
She supplied provisions for the troops (RA, 1:109, fol. 4).
WILBURNE, MARY   NC
She furnished provisions for the troops (RA, 9:69, fol. 2).
WILCOX, MARY   NC
She provided supplies for the army (RA, 11:82, fol. 4).
WILCOX, MARY EDDY   CT
Chatham. She was born on September 15, 1734, and married Ebenezer Wilcox of Hebron, Connecticut, on November 17, 1760. He served as a private under Col. Zebulon in the war and was killed at the Battle of Wyoming, on July 3, 1778. Ebenezer Wilcox's name is on the monument of the Battle of Wyoming as one of the defenders killed in battle (submitted by Edward L. Mix, Williamsport, PA).
WILCOXSON, SARAH BOONE   KY
Bryan's Station. The daughter of Sarah Morgan and Squire Boone, Sr., she was born in June 1724 in Berks County, Pennsylvania. She was the sister of Col. Daniel Boone. On June 29, 1742, she married John Wilcoxson (or Wilcoxsen). About 1775 they moved to western Virginia (now Kentucky). They had seven sons and five daughters. In 1782 her husband was killed by Indians close to Bryan's Station. She died in 1815 (submitted by Katherine Blaylock, Winston-Salem, NC).
WILCOXSON, SARAH FALCONER   KY
Bryan's Station. She was born in 1779, the daughter of Joice

III: COMPLETE LISTING

Craig and John Falconer (or Faulkner) and married Daniel Wilcoxson (or Wilcoxsen). In November 1780 they were living in Bryan's Station. On August 15, 1782, the Indians attacked. See Biographies: Craig, Polly Hawkins.

WILEY, SARAH VA
Gloucester County. Credited with public service (VR Court Booklet, 3:24).

WILKINS, AMY DRAPER PA
She was born in 1752 and married Caleb Wilkins. Amy died in 1839. She is listed as a patriot in the DAR Patriot Index 3.

WILKINS, ARABELLA VA
Mecklenburg. The wife of Clement Wilkins, she performed a public service (VR, 4:86).

WILKINS, LYDIA VA
Norfolk. The wife of Thomas Wilkins, she performed a public service (VR, 4:141).

WILKINS, REBECCA SC
She supplied provisions for the troops (SI, B:61).

WILKINSON, ELIZA SC
British troops plundered her home. See Biographies.

WILLETS, MARY NC
She provided supplies for the army (RA, 6:20, fol. 1).

WILLIAMS, ANNE PA
She was the wife of Maj. William Williams, who was taken prisoner on October 4, 1777. He managed to escape from the British on April 20, 1778, and became lieutenant colonel of the 3rd Pennsylvania Regiment in June 1778 (DAR; FW).

WILLIAMS, ANNE NEWTON NC
Since her husband was too old to fight, Anne made clothing for the soldiers while her husband repaired muskets.. She also cooked meals, which her husband took to the soldiers while Gen. Gates's army was in North Carolina (GP).

WILLIAMS, ELIZA CT
Wethersfield. On November 27, 1780, Samuel Stillman obtained a letter of marque to command the brigantine Jason with ten guns and twenty-five men. Witnesses to the bond were Elisha Williams and Eliza Williams (CN).

WILLIAMS, ELIZABETH SC
She supplied provisions for the troops (SI, B:163; I:93; 10, pt. 1:38).

WILLIAMS, ELIZABETH VA
Brunswick County. She performed a public service (VR Court Booklet, p. 20).

WILLIAMS, ELIZABETH VA
Norfolk. The wife of Thomas Williams, she is recognized for public service (VR, 4:137).

WILLIAMS, EUNICE CT
Groton. She was widowed by the British attack on Fort Griswold (CAR, 28:333b; 29:107a).

WILLIAMS, FRANCES MD
Calvert County. In 1778 she made a loan to the Continental Congress (IM, 7162).

WILLIAMS, HANNAH WILSON. See VAN HOOK
WILLIAMS, MRS. HENRY SC
   She furnished provisions to the army (SI, U-W:148).
WILLIAMS, JOANNA NJ
   Orange. She suffered damage in a British raid (CDB, claim 21).
WILLIAMS, LUCY VA
   Culpeper County. Recognized for public service (VR, 2:132, 135).
WILLIAMS, MARGARET VA
   Stafford County. She performed a public service (VR Court Booklet, 1:28; 2:9).
WILLIAMS, MARTHA CT
   Wethersfield. On September 22, 1780, John Bulkley, Jr., obtained a letter of marque to command the twelve-gun schooner Experiment with twenty men. Witnesses to this bond were Elisha Williams and Martha Williams (CN).
WILLIAMS, MARY SC
   She supplied provisions for the troops (SI, 1:15; 10, pt. 1:58).
WILLIAMS, MARY VA
   Brunswick County. The wife of William Williams, she performed a public service (VR, 1:132). Also Mary Williams, Monongolia County (VR Court Booklet, p. 25).
WILLIAMS, MARY TRUMBULL CT
   She fed and clothed soldiers. See Biographies.
WILLIAMS, NANCY NC
   She provided supplies for the army (RA, 5:27, fol. 4).
WILLIAMS, RACHEL VA
   Westmoreland County. Credited with public service (VR, 5:226).
WILLIAMS, SARAH VA
   Norfolk. Recognized for public service (VR, 4:137). Also Sarah Williams, Prince William County (VR, 4:207).
WILLIAMS, THEODA CT
   Groton. In the British attack she suffered damage (CAR, 1:79c).
WILLIAMSON, AGNESS NJ
   North Brunswick. The wife of William Williamson, she suffered losses in a British raid (CDB, p. 151).
WILLIAMSON, ANNE NEWTON NC
   She was born in 1738 and married Thomas Williamson. Anne died in 1820 and is listed as a patriot in the DAR Patriot Index.
WILLIAMSON, CELIA SC
   She supplied provisions for the troops (SI, L-N:37).
WILLIAMSON, MARY SC
   She provided supplies for the army (SI, O-Q:104).
WILLIAMSON, MILDRED VA
   King George County. Recognized for public service (VR Lists, pp. 7, 15).
WILLIAMSON, RACHEL CT
   She cared for a sick soldier in 1775 (CAR, 3:644b), and also entertained the Rifle Battalion (CAR, 3:637b).

III: COMPLETE LISTING 491

WILLIAMSON, SARAH GILLMAN   GA
 The wife of Lt. Col. Micajah Williamson, she is listed as a patriot in the DAR Patriot Index.
WILLIAMSON, SUSANNA   VA
 Henrico County. The wife of John Williamson, she performed a public service (VR, 3:108, 111).
WILLIFORD, ISBELL   NC
 She supplied provisions for the troops (RA, K:106).
WILLING, ANNE McCALL   PA
 Philadelphia. The eldest daughter of Samuel McCall, on June 9, 1763, she married Thomas Willing, who was a member of the firm of Willing, Morris and Company, with Robert Morris. Anne had thirteen children. On September 11, 1774, John Adams dined at the Willing home. Mrs. Willing died on September 5, 1781 (BA; BD).
WILLIS, MRS. AGERTON   NC
 She supplied provisions for the troops (RA, 11:9, fol. 3).
WILLIS, ELIZABETH   VA
 Sussex County. Credited with public service (VR, 5:209).
WILLORY, PRISCILLA   VA
 Princess Anne County. Recognized for public service (VR, 4:229).
WILLOUGHY, SARAH   VA
 Norfolk. The wife of John Willoughy, she performed a public service (VR, 4:137).
WILLSON, ANN   VA
 Amelia County. Recognized for public service (VR, I:99).
WILLSON, CATHARINE   NC
 She furnished provisions for the army (RA, A:203).
WILSON, ANN   VA
 Chesterfield County. Credited with public service (VR Ctf 1).
WILSON, ANN KENNEDY. See LINDSAY; POGUE
WILSON, CHARITY   MD
 In 1780 she furnished wheat for the army (IM, 13691).
WILSON, ELEANOR   NC
 She had seven sons who served in the war. Mrs. Wilson also sassed Lord Cornwallis. See Biographies.
WILSON, ELINOR   WV
 Botetourt County. Credited with public service (RW).
WILSON, ELIZABETH   MD
 She boarded Capt. George Cook, commander of the ship Defence, John Black of the privateer Black Yankee, in 1777 (IM, 3445, 3555).
WILSON, ELIZABETH   VA
 Charles City. She performed a public service (VR, 1:317). Also Elizabeth Wilson of Surry County (VR Court Booklet, p. 6).
WILSON, HANNAH   VA
 Brunswick County. Recognized for public service (VR Court Booklet, p. 12).

WILSON, JANE   NC
    She supplied provisions for the troops (RA, A:275).
WILSON, JANE. See ELLEN McDOWELL
WILSON, MRS. JOHN   NC
    She provided supplies for the army (RA, 11:9, fol. 2).
WILSON, MARGARET   NC
    She furnished provisions for the troops (RA, A:147).
WILSON, MARTHA   SC
    She supplied provisions for the troops (SI, Y-Z:241; 10, pt.
    1:40).
WILSON, MARY   NC
    She furnished supplies for the army (RA, 11:82, fol. 3).
WILSON, MARY   WV
    Berkeley County. She is credited with public service (VR Ctf
    1, Thomas Kennedy).
WILSON, MARY GORDON   SC
    The wife of Robert Wilson, she supplied provisions for the troops
    (SI, L-N:37).
WILSON, NANCY   NC
    She furnished supplies for the army (RA, 12:25, fol. 4).
WILSON, RACHEL   NC
    She supplied provisions for the troops (RA, 10:21, fol. 3).
WILSON, RACHEL BIRD   PA
    She was active in the ladies' association for the welfare of the
    soldiers. See Biographies.
WILSON, SARAH   NC
    She supplied provisions for the troops (RA, 5:46, fol. 1).
WILSON, WINIFRED   SC
    She supplied funds for the army (AA, 3:55-57), and also pro-
    visions (SI, 10, pt. 1:100).
WILSTED, MARGARET   NJ
    Hunterdon County. She suffered damage caused by American
    troops (CDB, claim 23).
WINCKLES, ELIZABETH   SC
    She furnished provisions for the troops (SI, 1:13).
WINDOW, JANE (JINNIE)   NJ
    Franklin Township, Bergen County. She suffered losses in
    a British raid (CDB claim 5).
WINIFIELD, SUSANNA   VA
    Sussex County. She performed a public service (VR Ctf 1).
WINFREY, JUDITH   VA
    King William County. Credited with public service (VR, 3:264).
WINKLER, MARY   SC
    She supplied provisions for the army (SI, U-W:149).
WINN, ANN   VA
    Caroline County. The wife of Benjamin Winn, she performed
    a public service (VR, 1:271).
WINN, MARGARET   VA
    Fauquier. The wife of Minor Winn, she is recognized for public
    service (VR Ctf 1).

III: COMPLETE LISTING 493

WINN, MARY VA
    Brunswick County. Credited with public service (VR Lists, p. 1).
WINN, SARAH VA
    Lunenburg County. The widow of Thomas Winn, she performed a public service (VR Ctf 1).
WINSLOW, ANNA GREEN MA
    Boston. As a girl she learned to spin, and joined the "Daughters of Liberty." Instead of buying imported British goods, she was one of the Boston girls who spun their own clothing and that of soldiers (NL).
WINSTEAD, CONSTANCE NC
    The wife of Samuel Winstead, she supplied provisions for the troops (RA, D:52).
WINSTON, ANN VA
    Hanover County. The widow of James Winston, she performed a public service (VR, 3:211).
WINTHROP, HANNAH FAYERWEATHER MA
    She corresponded with Mercy Warren. See Biographies.
WISANT, CATHARINE VA
    Frederick County. Credited with public service (VR Court Booklet, p. 13).
WISDOM, MARTHA NC
    She provided supplies for the army (RA, 11:52, fol. 2).
WISE, ALICE CT
    New Haven. In the British attack she suffered damage (CAR, 1:63d, 91g). She was a Western Lands Grantee.
WISHER, HANNAH VA
    Accomack County. Credited with public service (VR, 1:25).
WISHER, WIDOW SC
    She furnished supplies for the troops (SI, 1:38).
WITCHELL, SARAH NJ
    Burlington. She suffered damage in a British raid (CDB, claims 159, 200).
WITHERS, MARY CARTWRIGHT SC
    The wife of James Withers, she supplied provisions for the army (SI, U-W:200; DAR).
WITHERSPOON, ELIZABETH MONTGOMERY NJ
    Her home was plundered by the British. See Biographies.
WITHERSPOON, MARTHA NC
    She supplied provisions for the troops (RA, A:195).
WITT, MARY VA
    Buckingham County. The wife of Benjamin Witt, she performed a public service (VR Ctf 1).
WOLCOTT, LAURA COLLINS CT
    Her family and friends molded the lead statue of King George III into 42,088 bullets. See Biographies.
WOLFE, ELIZABETH VA
    Berkeley. The widow of a soldier, she performed a public service (VR, 1:143).

WOMACK, ELIZABETH VA
　Prince George County. The wife of Miles Womack, she is recognized for public service (VR, 4:257).
WOMACK, SARAH VA
　Chesterfield County. The widow of Joel Womack, she is recognized for public service (VR, 2:55).
WOOD, ABIGAIL CT
　Danbury. In the April 1777 British raid she suffered damage (CAR, 8:382a).
WOOD, ANN SC
　She furnished provisions for the army (SI, B:101).
WOOD, CATHERINE SC
　She provided supplies for the troops (SI, 10:pt. 1:42).
WOOD, HANNAH CT
　Danbury. She suffered damage in the British raid (CAR, 1:51b, 63v). She was a Western Lands Grantee.
WOOD, MARTHA SC
　She supplied provisions for the troops (SI, B:101).
WOOD, MARY CT
　Greenwich. In the 1783 British raid she suffered losses (CAR, 24:274k, 276d).
WOOD, MARY SC
　She furnished supplies for the army (SI, 10, pt. 1:87).
WOOD, SARAH NC
　She supplied provisions for the troops (RA, 5:40, fol. 4).
WOODARD, FANNY VA
　Norfolk. The wife of Caleb Woodard, she performed a public service (VR, 4:139).
WOODFORD, MARY VA
　Caroline County. The widow of William Woodford, she is recognized for public service (VR, 1:271; 4:300).
WOODHULL, RUTH FLOYD NY
　She provided money for American prisoners of war. See Biographies.
WOODROP, MARY VA
　Charles City. Credited with public service (VR Lists, p. 3).
WOODS, HANNAH WALLACE KY
　She was attacked by Indians. See Biographies.
WOODS, MARTHA POAGE WV
　Botetourt County. The wife of Andrew Woods, she died in 1818. Mrs. Woods performed a public service (VR, 1:185).
　She is listed in the DAR Patriot Index.
WOODS, SUSANNA WV
　Greenbrier. The wife of John Woods, she is recognized for public service (VR, 3:18).
WOODSON, RENE VA
　Fluvanna County. The wife of Benjamin Woodson, she is credited with public service (VR, 1:361, 367).
WOODWARD, ELIZABETH NJ
　Burlington. She suffered damage in a British raid (CDB, claim 12).

III: COMPLETE LISTING

WOODWARD, MARGARET MOUNT   NJ
She was born in 1756 and married George Woodward. Margaret was a spy for the Americans. She died in 1830 (DAR).

WOODY, MARY   NC
She supplied provisions for the troops (RA, 9:85, fol. 3).

WOOLARD, MARY   NC
She opposed drinking British tea. See Background.

WOOLEY, HANNAH   NJ
Springfield. She suffered damage in a British raid (CDB, claim 25).

WOOLF, ELIZABETH   WV
Berkeley County. She supplied provisions for the army (RW).

WOOLFOLK, MRS.   VA
Caroline County. She performed a public service (VR Lists, 2:22, 31).

WOOLFOLK, ELIZABETH   VA
Caroline County. Recognized for public service (VR, 1:271).

WOOSTER, MARY CLAP   CT
She paid her husband's soldiers from the family funds. See Biographies.

WOOSTER, SARAH   CT
Derby. In 1777 she supplied a blanket for the army (CAR, 11:105a).

WOOTERS, LILLY   SC
She supplied provisions for the troops (SI, O-Q:254).

WORDS, ELIZABETH   NC
She provided supplies for the army (RA, A:128).

WORKMAN, MARGARET   NJ
Bound Brook widow. She suffered damage in a British raid (CDB, p. 29).

WORSHAM, ELIZABETH   VA
Chesterfield County. The wife of Thomas Worsham, she performed a public service (VR, 2:56).

WORSHAM, JANE   VA
Dinwiddie. The wife of Thomas Worsham, she is recognized for public service (VR Court Booklet, p. 31).

WORSHAM, MARY   VA
Pittsylvania County. Recognized for public service (VR Court Booklet, p. 33).

WORSLEY, JANE   NC
The wife of John Worsley, she supplied provisions for the army (RA, D:122).

WORTHAN, MARGARET   VA
Caroline County. The wife of Charles Worthan, she performed a public service (VR Court Booklet, 2:33).

WORTHINGTON, MARGARET   WV
Berkeley. The wife of Ephraim Worthington, she is credited with public service (VR, 1:15).

WRAGG, HENRIETTA   SC
She supplied provisions for the troops (SI, 10, pt. 1:108).

WRENN, CATHARINE   VA
    Frederick County. Credited with public service (VR, 1:217).
WRIGHT, MRS.   CT
    Middletown. In 1777 she furnished a blanket for the army (CAR, 6:179).
WRIGHT, MRS.   VA
    King William County. Credited with public service (VR, 3:263).
WRIGHT, MRS. See MRS. ROBERT HIGGINS
WRIGHT, ALICE   NJ
    Burlington. The wife of Israel Wright, she suffered damage in a British raid (CDB, claim 138).
WRIGHT, ANN   NC
    She supplied provisions for the troops (RA, A:221).
WRIGHT, ANN   RI
    She nursed sick soldiers (MP, 23:29).
WRIGHT, ANN   VA
    Norfolk. Recognized for public service (VR, 4:137).
WRIGHT, ANNE   NC
    She provided supplies for the army (RA, 6:42, fol. 2).
WRIGHT, EASTER   NJ
    Woodbridge. She suffered losses in a British raid (CDB, p. 49).
WRIGHT, ELIZABETH   NC
    She supplied provisions for the troops (RA, 9:3, fol. 1).
WRIGHT, ELIZABETH   NJ
    Middlesex County. She suffered damage in a British raid (CDB, p. 186).
WRIGHT, ELIZABETH   SC
    She supplied provisions for the army (SI, 10, pt. 1:107).
WRIGHT, ESTHER   NJ
    Burlington. Widow of John Wright, she suffered losses in a British raid (CDB, p. 11).
WRIGHT, MARGARET   VA
    Princess Anne County. The wife of Jeremiah Wright, she performed a public service (VR, 4:225, 228).
WRIGHT, MARTHA   NC
    She supplied provisions for the troops (RA, 9:36, fol. 2).
WRIGHT, MARY   GA
    She provided rice for the army (WA, p. 178).
WRIGHT, MARY   NJ
    Woodbridge. She suffered damage in a British raid (CDB, p. 186).
WRIGHT, MARY   VA
    King William County. She performed a public service (VR, 3:265). Also Mary Wright of Princess County (VR, 4:228).
WRIGHT, NANCY   VA
    Hansemond. The wife of Nathaniel Wright, she is recognized for public service (VR, 4:359).
WRIGHT, PENELOPE   NJ
    Burlington. She suffered losses in a British raid (CDB, p. 53).

III: COMPLETE LISTING 497

WRIGHT, PRUDENCE CUMMINGS   MA
   She captured a Tory messenger. See Biographies.
WRIGHT, MRS. REUBEN   NY
   Gen. Washington had his headquarters there. See Biographies.
WRIGHT, SARAH   VA
   Gloucester County. The wife of Francis Wright, she is credited
   with public service (VR, 3:55, 57; 4:289).
WRIGHT, SARAH BOWMAN   SC
   She was born in 1741 and married George Wright, Jr. She pro-
   vided supplies for the army (SI, U-W:60; DAR).
WRIGHT, WINIFRED   NC
   She supplied provisions for the troops (RA, D:44).
WYATT, CATHARINE   VA
   Prince George County. Credited with public service (VR, 4:257).
WYCHE, MARY   VA
   Greensville. Recognized for public service (VR, 3:34).
WYCHE, MARY   VA
   Sussex County. The wife of James Wyche, she performed a
   public service (VR, 5:208, 209).
WYCKOFF (WICOFF), CHARITY   NJ
   Middlebush, Somerville. The wife of John Wyckoff, she suffered
   damage in a British raid (CDB, p. 147).
WYCKOFF, POLLY   NJ
   She warned her mother of approaching British troops. See
   Biographies.
WYCKOFF, SARAH HART   NJ
   She was an active member of the ladies' association for the
   welfare of the soldiers. See Biographies.
WYNKOOP, ABIGAIL   CT
   Fairfield. In the British raid she suffered damage (CAR, 1:53f,
   63r). She was a Western Lands Grantee.
WYNN, MARY   VA
   Greensville. She performed a public service (VR, 3:33).
WYTHE, ELIZABETH TALIAFERRO   VA
   Gen. Washington had his headquarters there. See Biographies.

Y

YANCEY, MARY   VA
   The wife of Richard Yancey, she died in 1796. She is listed
   as a patriot in the DAR Patriot Index.
YANCEY, MARY CRAWFORD   VA
   She was born in 1742 and married Capt. Charles Yancey. Mary
   is listed as a patriot in the DAR Patriot Index.
YANCEY, NANCY   VA
   Louisa County. Credited with public service (VR, 3:377).
YARBOROUGH, MARY   VA
   Caroline County. The wife of Henry Yarborough, she is recog-
   nized for public service (VR Court Booklet, 2:33).

YARBOROUGH, SARAH   VA
    Hanover County. Recognized for public service (VR, 3:213).
YARD, SARAH   PA
    John Adams stayed in her home. See Biographies.
YATES, SARAH   VA
    New Kent County. The wife of John Yates, she performed a
    public service (VR Court Booklet, p. 21).
YEARLING, SARAH   MD
    In 1782 she furnished wheat for the army (IM, 20034).
YERBY, JUDITH   VA
    Lancaster County. Recognized for public service (VR, 3:280).
YOAKUM, ELIZABETH   VA
    Hampshire County. The wife of John Yoakum (?), she is credited
    with public service (VR Lists, p. 17).
YOCUM, ELIZABETH   WV
    Hampshire County. She was born in 1725 and married Jacob
    Yocum (or Yoakum). Elizabeth died in 1790. She provided
    provisions for the army (RW; submitted by Ivolue Lantrip, Benicia,
    CA).
YOE, ANNA   MD
    Queen Anne County. In 1778 she supplied bacon for the army
    (IM, 6432).
YOST, MARGARET   MD
    Frederick County. In 1782 she furnished wheat for the army
    (IM, 20990).
YOUNG, ANN   VA
    Greensville. She performed a public service (VR, 3:34, 35).
YOUNG, ELIZABETH   GA
    The wife of Thomas Young, she furnished forage and provisions
    for public use (WA, p. 120).
YOUNG, ELIZABETH   SC
    She supplied provisions for the troops (SI, R-T:250).
YOUNG, MARY   PA
    At age twenty-two she was captured by Indians and sent to
    Canada. On August 22, 1782, she was sent home (MR).
YOUNG, PRUDENCE   NJ
    Orange. The wife of Jonas Young, she suffered damage in
    a British raid (CDB, claim 27).

Z

ZABRESKY, ELIZABETH   NJ
    New Barbadoes, Essex County. She suffered losses in a British
    raid (CDB, claim 47).
ZABRISKIE, ELIZABETH   NJ
    Saddle River. She suffered damage caused by American troops
    (CDB, sec. 2, claim 39).
ZABRISKY, MARGARET   NJ
    New Barbadoes, Bergen County. She suffered damage in a
    British raid (CDB, claims 66, 68).

III: COMPLETE LISTING

ZABRISKY, MARY   NJ
  Saddle River. She suffered damage caused by American troops (CDB, sec. 2, claim 13).
ZABRISKY, MARY   NJ
  New Barbadoes, Bergen County. She suffered losses in a British raid (CDB, claim 60).
ZANE, ELIZABETH McCULLOCH   VA
  She was born in 1748 and married Col. Ebenezer Zane. Elizabeth is listed as a patriot in the DAR Patriot Index.
ZANE, HESTER SCULL   DE
  She was born in 1740 and married Joel Zane. Hester died in 1818 and is listed as a patriot in the DAR Patriot Index.
ZEBRISKIE, ANNE   NJ
  Hackensack. The wife of John Zebriskie, she suffered damage caused by American troops (CDB, claim 37).
ZIMMERMAN, MARY   SC
  She furnished provisions for the troops (SI, U-W:151).
ZUBER, RACHEL   SC
  She supplied provisions for the army (SI, X, pt. 2:142).

THE EVANS LIBRARY
FULTON-MONTGOMERY COMMUNITY COLLEGE
2805 STATE HIGHWAY 67
JOHNSTOWN, NEW YORK 12095-3790